Handbook of Research on Educational Technology Integration and Active Learning

Jared Keengwe
University of North Dakota, USA

A volume in the Advances in Educational
Technologies and Instructional Design (AETID)
Book Series

KH

Managing Director:	Lindsay Johnston
Managing Editor:	Austin DeMarco
Director of Intellectual Property & Contracts:	Jan Travers
Acquisitions Editor:	Kayla Wolfe
Production Editor:	Christina Henning
Typesetter:	Tucker Knerr
Cover Design:	Jason Mull

Published in the United States of America by
Information Science Reference (an imprint of IGI Global)
701 E. Chocolate Avenue
Hershey PA, USA 17033
Tel: 717-533-8845
Fax: 717-533-8661
E-mail: cust@igi-global.com
Web site: http://www.igi-global.com

Library of Congress Cataloging-in-Publication Data

Handbook of research on educational technology integration and active learning / Jared Keengwe, editor.
     pages cm
 Includes bibliographical references and index.
  ISBN 978-1-4666-8363-1 (hardcover) -- ISBN 978-1-4666-8364-8 (ebook) 1. Educational technology. 2. Education--Effect of technological innovations on. 3. Active learning. I. Keengwe, Jared, 1973- editor of compilation.
 LB1028.3.H3554 2015
 371.33--dc23
                          2015008263

This book is published in the IGI Global book series Advances in Educational Technologies and Instructional Design (AE-TID) (ISSN: 2326-8905; eISSN: 2326-8913)

British Cataloguing in Publication Data
A Cataloguing in Publication record for this book is available from the British Library.

All work contributed to this book is new, previously-unpublished material. The views expressed in this book are those of the authors, but not necessarily of the publisher.

For electronic access to this publication, please contact: eresources@igi-global.com.

5/9/16

Advances in Educational Technologies and Instructional Design (AETID) Book Series

Lawrence A. Tomei
Robert Morris University, USA

ISSN: 2326-8905
EISSN: 2326-8913

MISSION

Education has undergone, and continues to undergo, immense changes in the way it is enacted and distributed to both child and adult learners. From distance education, Massive-Open-Online-Courses (MOOCs), and electronic tablets in the classroom, technology is now an integral part of the educational experience and is also affecting the way educators communicate information to students.

The **Advances in Educational Technologies & Instructional Design (AETID) Book Series** is a resource where researchers, students, administrators, and educators alike can find the most updated research and theories regarding technology's integration within education and its effect on teaching as a practice.

COVERAGE

- Instructional Design
- Game-Based Learning
- Educational Telecommunications
- Digital Divide in Education
- Adaptive Learning
- Curriculum Development
- Hybrid Learning
- Collaboration Tools
- Classroom Response Systems
- Bring-Your-Own-Device

IGI Global is currently accepting manuscripts for publication within this series. To submit a proposal for a volume in this series, please contact our Acquisition Editors at Acquisitions@igi-global.com or visit: http://www.igi-global.com/publish/.

Titles in this Series

For a list of additional titles in this series, please visit: www.igi-global.com

Macro-Level Learning through Massive Open Online Courses (MOOCs) Strategies and Predictions for the Future
Elspeth McKay (RMIT University, Australia) and John Lenarcic (RMIT University, Australia)
Information Science Reference • copyright 2015 • 313pp • H/C (ISBN: 9781466683242) • US $200.00 (our price)

Implementation and Critical Assessment of the Flipped Classroom Experience
Abigail G. Scheg (Elizabeth City State University, USA)
Information Science Reference • copyright 2015 • 333pp • H/C (ISBN: 9781466674646) • US $175.00 (our price)

Transforming the Future of Learning with Educational Research
Helen Askell-Williams (Flinders University, Australia)
Information Science Reference • copyright 2015 • 381pp • H/C (ISBN: 9781466674950) • US $185.00 (our price)

Intelligent Web-Based English Instruction in Middle Schools
Jiyou Jia (Peking University, China)
Information Science Reference • copyright 2015 • 354pp • H/C (ISBN: 9781466666078) • US $185.00 (our price)

Handbook of Research on Teaching Methods in Language Translation and Interpretation
Ying Cui (Shandong University, Weihai, China) and Wei Zhao (Shandong University, Weihai, China)
Information Science Reference • copyright 2015 • 458pp • H/C (ISBN: 9781466666153) • US $325.00 (our price)

Methodologies for Effective Writing Instruction in EFL and ESL Classrooms
Rahma Al-Mahrooqi (Sultan Qaboos University, Oman) Vijay Singh Thakur (Dhofar University, Oman) and Adrian Roscoe (Sultan Qaboos University, Oman)
Information Science Reference • copyright 2015 • 417pp • H/C (ISBN: 9781466666191) • US $185.00 (our price)

Student-Teacher Interaction in Online Learning Environments
Robert D. Wright (University of North Texas, USA)
Information Science Reference • copyright 2015 • 450pp • H/C (ISBN: 9781466664616) • US $185.00 (our price)

Cases on Technology Integration in Mathematics Education
Drew Polly (University of North Carolina at Charlotte, USA)
Information Science Reference • copyright 2015 • 521pp • H/C (ISBN: 9781466664975) • US $200.00 (our price)

Promoting Global Literacy Skills through Technology-Infused Teaching and Learning
Jared Keengwe (University of North Dakota, USA) Justus G. Mbae (Catholic University of Eastern Africa, Kenya) and Simon K. Ngigi (Catholic University of Eastern Africa, Kenya)

DISSEMINATOR OF KNOWLEDGE

www.igi-global.com

701 E. Chocolate Ave., Hershey, PA 17033
Order online at www.igi-global.com or call 717-533-8845 x100
To place a standing order for titles released in this series, contact: cust@igi-global.com
Mon-Fri 8:00 am - 5:00 pm (est) or fax 24 hours a day 717-533-8661

Editorial Advisory Board

List of Contributors

Table of Contents

Detailed Table of Contents

Chapter 1
Victoria M. Cardullo, Auburn University, USA
Nance S. Wilson, SUNY Cortland, USA
Vassiliki I. Zygouris-Coe, University of Central Florida, USA

This chapter examines a model for an active learning classroom and emerging technologies that support learning for the 21st century. Using vignettes, they model how the metacognitive teacher supports the use of emerging technologies for active learning using the Metacognitive Technological Pedagogical Content Knowledge Framework (M-TPACK).

Chapter 2
Amy Eguchi, Bloomfield College, USA

This chapter introduces educational robotics as a transformational tool for learning, which promotes learning of computational thinking, coding, and engineering – critical ingredients of STEM learning in K-12 education. The purpose of this chapter is to highlight the importance of integrating educational robotics as a technological learning tool into K-12 curriculum to promote Rich Environments for Active Learning (REALs) to prepare students for the technology-driven future.

Chapter 3
Jennifer L. Penland, Sul Ross State University, USA

This study examines changes that have occurred recently in the distance education arena and the impact on higher education institutions focusing on undergraduate and graduate students taking these courses. Findings suggested: (1) increased enrollment in distance education courses, (2) courses allow for flexible schedules (3) better communication with instructor and (4) more meaningful learning overall for students.

The purpose of this chapter is to create a sense of urgency for teacher preparation programs to model integrating technology into the instructional process. This chapter discusses: 1) the need for technology literate teachers, 2) the role of teacher preparation programs, 3) the need for technology literate faculty, and 4) one training model for integrating technology into instruction, enhancing Missouri'sInstructional Network Teaching Strategies (e-MINTS).

Chapter 5

This chapter offers a perspective on e-learning at Canadian Universities. This perspective includes a snapshot of the Canadian e-learning landscape as well as the results of a multi-university research study called the Meaningful E-Learning or MEL project. The authors explore four themes derived from the MEL project and represented by the acronym HIDI (human interaction, IT support, design, and institutional support) in relation to three e-learning scenarios.

This chapter contributes to the technology-enhanced pedagogical designs discourse by proposing knowledge-centred models that integrate sound pedagogical strategy, ubiquitous technologies and situated learning to address student learning priorities and challenges in a Global Citizenship course at a South African university. Findings suggest that although collective engagement and peer-based networking were salient in the course, challenges of fostering deep learning, scaling the course, enhancing sustainable course delivery and accommodating diverse learning needs of students were reported.

Chapter 7

This chapter extends a new definition and critical components of active learning in the context of technology integrated classrooms. Further, the chapter offers active learning strategies aligned with technology tools that could be used effectively in K-12 classrooms to promote active learning. Finally, the chapter opens up a discussion for potential new research that could be conducted to explore in depth some of the strategies using a large sample size stratified by grade levels, content areas, and geography.

This chapter examines one strategy for enhancing teaching history of mathematics through digital storytelling. Additionally, the chapter provides components of digital storytelling (point of view, dramatic question, emotional content, the gift of your voice, the power of the soundtrack, economy, pacing, purpose of story, choice of content, quality of images, grammar and language usage) and necessary steps (tellable story, compositing script, choosing visual and audio components, preparing digital stories, presenting digitals stories) that are to be taken into consideration while preparing digital stories.

Chapter 9

This chapter reports findings from an interdisciplinary literature review on pedagogical approaches and technological integration processes to facilitating active learning and deliberate practice toward expertise in professional education. The review covers selective domains that emphasize life-long learning, including teacher education, professional music education, athletic education, and medical education.

Chapter 10

This chapter presents findings of a study seeking to investigate if there is a relationship between active learning strategies (ALS) and skills and attributes that enhance learning (SAEL). The findings have implications for student success especially in the development of skills and attributes that enhance learning (SAEL) among college students. Additionally, SAEL help the students develop a sustained learning commitment while in college and after graduation.

This chapter examines the reliability and validity of the items used in the Student Ratings of Instruction [SRI] instrument. Three SRI factors were analyzed: efficacy, validity, and reliability. The additional application of Goodman & Kruskal's Lambda, and Principal Component Factor Analysis with Varimax Rotation also found strong construct validity within the SRI. The findings have implications for improving SRI for course evaluation purposes.

This chapter discusses an eLearning platform that is usable by persons with low vision. To start with, such a platform is achieved by incorporating technological advances such as: Use of text with the highest possible contrast; use of varying font size; among other customized Human Computer Interaction (HCI) effects. In summary, this chapter supports the fact that eLearning is possible for persons with low vision, provided that all the necessary technological advances have been considered.

This chapter seeks to examine how a teacher educator engages preservice teachers in the world of diversity using technology. The findings have far reaching implications for teaching and learning especially in the 21st century technology-rich classrooms.

This chapter attempts to conceptually generalize the findings of a recent collective case study and develop a relevant theoretical framework for online formative assessment. The theoretical framework is intended to inform successful implementation of formative assessment in online learning contexts.

This chapter examines a review of literature on the existing opportunities and challenges of adopting e-learning in education in Tanzania and the possible measures to overcome the identified challenges. Based on the findings, it is suggested that, once there are sufficient technological tools and supply of electricity, accessibility to Internet, and availability of a good model for technology use, both teachers and students will implement e-learning programs in their learning institutions.

This chapter examines the opportunities and challenges in implementing Distance Learning (DL) and e-learning in Tanzania. This chapter concludes that Mzumbe University (and other institutions in Tanzania) need an appropriate budget and resource investment to support capacity building for teaching staff and students, and formulating policies, guidelines and operational framework on DL and e-learning.

Chapter 17

This chapter seeks to find out whether the investment in buying computers, for departments, lecturers' offices, and equipping computer labs for the students while increasing bandwidth and connectivity and other infrastructure in Kenyan Universities is translating to actual faculty and student use in blended classrooms.

This chapter examines opportunities for Social Networking Sites' Complementation of Writing Centres. Findings suggest that students lacked confidence in asserting their authorial presence and familiarisation with academic conventions. Further, students and consultants' essays demonstrated a balanced appropriation of attitudinal and judgement categories and engagement resources, with implications for the potential of Facebook to mediate student expression of their voice.

Chapter 19

This chapter presents a research study on mathematics education pre-service teachers' perceptions of competencies developed in an active learning course. The results of the study showed that, according to the mathematics education pre-service teachers, their Internet search skills, content knowledge about distance education, web interface design skills, and technological knowledge increased or improved due to the web-based instruction (WBI) project.

Chapter 20

Joel S. Mtebe, University of Dar es Salaam, Tanzania
Mussa M. Kissaka, University of Dar es Salaam, Tanzania

This chapter proposes deployment and adoption strategy of cloud computing to enhance blended learning services in sub-Saharan Africa. The chapter contributes towards helping higher education stakeholders in sub-Saharan Africa understand cloud services as well as plan for successful migration of computing services into cloud.

Foreword

Over thirty years have passed since many of us embarked on the journey to integrate technology into teaching and learning. Technology innovations and possible theoretical frameworks have taken us down many paths and at times this exploration of technology integration has been to the detriment of student learning and the field of educational technology.

Looking back, the early 1980's brought us computer programming, the 'turtle' of logo and computers that could actually store programs for later use on 5.25 floppy disks. As an educator, I was ecstatic to have what the business world and scientists had long been using for my K-12 classroom. Firm was my belief that Seymour Papert was right—computers were instruments for learning and enhancing creativity—and now I had the disk to prove it.

I had visions of learners constructing knowledge and sharing it through the swapping of disks between learners. Programming could be used to help develop critical and logical thinking, one of my key goals in my 7th grade science classroom. Computer clubs appeared in schools and programming competitions abounded. Logo and Lego brought robotics within the reach of my learners. Learning the Logo language kept me on my toes as I tried to stay one step ahead of my learners. These were heady times, as everyday was a new innovation in technology equipment and software! Technology integration was but a glimmering hope as we teachers tried to obtain the desired equipment and – of course – those wonderful dot-matrix printers.

The 1990's took me on a different path in the realm of technology integration as I returned to Ohio University to work on my doctoral degree and really think about how technology integration could influence/impact learners. The many Department of Education Challenge grants and Preparing Teachers to Use Technology grants provided a research playground for examining the integration of technology into teaching and learning. As with the '80s, the focus was on the technology and software but the infancy of the Internet was coming into play as we all learned how to build a webpage. I spent hours with learners examining the ways in which a web page might provide the most efficient level of teaching and learning. Connectivity was interesting but content distribution was the goal for so many of us involved in the use of technology at this time.

The 21st Century began an explosion as Web 2.0 applications and software truly allowed for connectivity around the world with a multitude of connections to classrooms and environments for learning. Gone was the overwhelming desire to build websites with tons of content: everyone was building content and placing it on Twitter, Facebook, Vine and other web-based applications. Integration was still a concern within our traditional education frameworks but connection and participatory engagement for learning began to drive integration into our classrooms through the use of smartphones, tablets, netbooks and more. Teachers began to see that those tiny little pieces of code born in 80's were now the foundation for the ubiquitous integration of technology into teaching and learning. The wide variety of available technologies allows for a more personal engagement with learning that can actively challenge the learner. Customization of content delivered to one or many and the ability to connect to experts for advisement, discussion and collaboration is now the central focus of learning. And while not everyone has the desired access to these tools, as an educator, I have finally realized that the real technology integration problem is access to the Internet and those fantastic Web 2.0 applications and the leadership in our institutions to demand access.

We have in some ways come full circle from the use of the computer by an individual to program learning to collective learning by individuals on the Web. Beginning with computer programming as an individual activity in our classrooms to the use of Web 2.0 to connect our classrooms all as participants, each of educator seeks to find that 'magic bullet' to improve teaching practice and student achievement. This new book, *Handbook of Research on Educational Technology Integration and Active Learning*, provides a wide range of examples and research on how to actively engage both educators and learners to connect us all as we continue to examine the issues surrounding the integration of technology to improve teaching and learning.

I wish the readers of this handbook the same exciting journey that has led me down many paths and I challenge each reader to think about how we can use technology as a tool for learning and creativity. Engaged learning and creativity are foundationally the path to the ability to think critically and solve problems. Education is a noble profession and the integration of technology helps us to provide access to more content and research, more opportunities to learn, more collaboration, more participation in problem solving, and better teaching practice through the development of best practices in the use of technology.

May you never lose the joy of learning – it can change the world.

Teresa Franklin
Professor, Instructional Technology
Educational Studies

Teresa Franklin's *educational technology pursuits of 37 years include an 18-year career as a middle school and high school teacher of biology, chemistry, mathematics, and computer science and a 20-year career as an instructional technology Professor in The Patton College of Education, Ohio University, USA. Dr. Franklin teaches instructional design, online course design, research and program evaluation. Her research focuses on the integration of technology through curriculum development for f2f and online learning, the development of virtual learning environments; mobile technologies; and training in the use of technology both nationally and internationally. Dr. Franklin is the co-author of a widely used science education textbook, Science for All Children 5th edition, numerous book chapters, journal articles, video development projects, and keynote and invited speaker to numerous conferences worldwide. As a Fulbright Senior Research Scholar, Dr. Franklin has examined teacher preparation and technology integration in Turkish Higher Education and Middle East.*

Preface

Technology is rapidly changing the teaching and leaning landscape. This implies that pedagogical shifts including the teacher's roles, learner's styles, and the process of learning are inevitable especially in classrooms where technology tools and applications are incorporated in authentic and innovative ways. Additionally, as technology becomes a critical part of the 21st century classroom, a teacher's decision to integrate technology into the learning process is no longer a personal choice.

There is also a need for teachers to prepare active learners for a digital global economy that is characteristic of the 21st century. Key forms of active learning include discovery learning, problem-based learning, experiential learning, and inquiry-based instruction (Kirschner, Sweller, and Clark, 2006). Active learning is also primarily concerned with what students do with information as opposed to how much information the teacher and the learning environments can provide (Grabe & Grabe, 2008). Additionally, the ubiquitous presence of technology in schools implies the need for competent teachers who can teach effectively with these tools.

A majority of the current students are technology-savvy, consider traditional methods of teaching boring, and have short attention spans (Horne, 2010). Teachers can build on their prior knowledge bases and engage these learners through technology to be successful in the classroom. Thus, technology changes the roles of teacher and students: The traditional role of teacher as dispenser or information is challenged, and the teacher's new role is that of a guide: to challenge students' thinking and encourage reflection in the learning process. Also, just having technology tools in the classroom by itself does not translate to active and engaged student learning. However, innovative pedagogical approaches with technology leaves students with a more effective learning environment that promotes quality teaching and active student learning (Grabe & Grabe, 2008).

Educational technology may challenge the entire approach to the classroom experience, the essence of teaching, and the purpose of a school, but as tools, it presents great opportunities to support engaged and active student learning (Keengwe, Onchwari, & Wachira, 2008). Additionally, technology provides great opportunities to enhance student learning if used appropriately and selectively (Keengwe, 2007; Keengwe & Onchwari, 2009; Kim & Hannafin, 2011). However, "it seems reasonable that teachers will be more likely to help their students learn with technology if the teachers can draw on their own experiences in learning with technology" (Grabe & Grabe, 2008, p. 4).

Given that the majority of teachers are still hesitant or not prepared to incorporate technology into education (Lei, 2009; Project Tomorrow, 2010) in ways that can enhance active student learning, it is logical to argue that the synchrony of pedagogy, technology, and change knowledge can transform classrooms by deeply engaging students in ubiquitous computing, authentic learning, and student-centered instruction, which in turn will enhance meaningful student learning beyond the classroom (Fullan, 2013).

Similarly, preservice teacher programs need to provide teachers with effective strategies and techniques to help them enhance their experiences with the various instructional technologies. Such training has to take into consideration the need to promote preservice teachers' self-efficacy beliefs and intrinsic goal orientation as this will make them value instructional technology and the role it will play in their future classrooms. This would also translate to more effective use of such technology with their future students (Chen, 2010).

Pedagogical practices should also guide faculty decisions about the appropriate and relevant forms of instructional technology tools best suited for specific learning objectives and outcomes in a specific learning environment. Thus, teachers should strive to create environments in which students actively engage in a cognitive partnership with content and technology. Technology-based learning environments enhance constructive interactions between learners and teachers to share meanings and develop new powerful meanings (Novak, 1998). Further, the ultimate goal of teaching is to guide learners to think critically, to learn how to solve-problems, and to create knowledge.

Effective classroom technology integration implies the need for professional development (PD) opportunities that are tailored to the individual teachers' needs (Linton & Geddes, 2013). Given the vast differences in knowledge and experience with technology, differentiated PD allows participants the opportunity to learn at their own pace and understanding. Providing extended time to practice what was learned during a technology-based PD session would also help to improve teachers' knowledge base (Linton & Geddes, 2013).

Consequently, education planners and policy makers must think beyond technology to keep teachers trained in various pedagogical uses of appropriate technology tools. There is also need for schools to determine the goals of technology in teaching and learning, and the types of technology tools that will support efforts to meet those goals. School leaders, for instance, should assure teachers that the goal of technology tools is to improve teaching and learning, and not to replace them.

The critical role of technology in education and the noble obligation for teachers to prepare active learners for a digital global workplace imply the urgent need for educators to review appropriate and effective ways to integrate education technology into the teaching and learning process to support active and engaged student learning. Therefore, *Handbook of Research on Educational Technology Integration and Active Learning* offers best practices, challenges, and opportunities in the process of incorporating educational technologies into the teaching and learning process to enhance active student learning.

Chapter One examines a model for an active learning classroom and emerging technologies that support learning for the 21st century. Using vignettes, the authors model how the metacognitive teacher supports the use of emerging technologies for active learning using the Metacognitive Technological Pedagogical Content Knowledge Framework (M-TPACK).

Chapter Two introduces educational robotics as a transformational tool for learning, which promotes learning of computational thinking, coding, and engineering: critical ingredients of STEM learning in K-12 education. The purpose of this chapter is to highlight the importance of integrating educational robotics as a technological learning tool into K-12 curriculum to promote Rich Environments for Active Learning (REALs) to prepare students for the technology-driven future.

Chapter Three examines changes that have occurred recently in the distance education arena and the impact on higher education institutions focusing on undergraduate and graduate students taking these courses. Findings suggested: (1) increased enrollment in distance education courses, (2) courses allow for flexible schedules (3) better communication with instructor and (4) more meaningful learning overall for students.

Chapter Four discusses: 1) the need for technology literate teachers, 2) the role of teacher preparation programs, 3) the need for technology literate faculty, and 4) one training model for integrating technology into instruction, enhancing Missouri's Instructional Network Teaching Strategies (e-MINTS). The purpose of this chapter is to create a sense of urgency for teacher preparation programs to model integrating technology into the instructional process.

Chapter Five provides a perspective on e-learning at Canadian Universities. This perspective includes a snapshot of the Canadian e-learning landscape as well as the results of a multi-university research study called the Meaningful E-Learning or MEL project.

Chapter Six weighs in on the technology-enhanced pedagogical designs discourse by proposing knowledge-centred models that integrate sound pedagogical strategy, ubiquitous technologies and situated learning to address student learning priorities and challenges in a Global Citizenship course at a South African university.

Chapter Seven extends a new definition and critical components of active learning in the context of technology integrated classrooms. Also, it offers active learning strategies aligned with technology tools that could be used effectively in K-12 classrooms to promote active learning.

Chapter Eight examines one strategy for enhancing teaching history of mathematics through digital storytelling. Additionally, the chapter provides components of digital storytelling and necessary steps to be taken into consideration while preparing digital stories.

Chapter Nine reports findings from an interdisciplinary literature review on pedagogical approaches and technological integration processes to facilitating active learning and deliberate practice toward expertise in professional education. The review covers selective domains that emphasize life-long learning, including teacher education, professional music education, athletic education, and medical education.

Chapter Ten presents findings of a study seeking to investigate if there is a relationship between active learning strategies (ALS) and skills and attributes that enhance learning (SAEL). The findings have implications for student success especially in the development of skills and attributes that enhance learning (SAEL) among college students.

Chapter Eleven examines the reliability and validity of the items used in the Student Ratings of Instruction [SRI] instrument. Three SRI factors were analyzed: efficacy, validity, and reliability. The additional application of Goodman & Kruskal's Lambda, and Principal Component Factor Analysis with Varimax Rotation also found strong construct validity within the SRI. The findings have implications for improving SRI in course evaluation.

Chapter Twelve discusses an eLearning platform that is usable by persons with low vision. Specifically, this chapter supports the fact that eLearning is possible for persons with low vision, provided that all the necessary technological advances have been considered.

Chapter Thirteen examines how a teacher educator engages preservice teachers in the world of diversity using technology. The findings have implications for changing teaching and learning practice especially in the 21st century technology-rich classrooms.

Chapter Fourteen attempts to conceptually generalize the findings of a recent collective case study in order to develop a relevant theoretical framework for online formative assessment. The emerging theoretical framework is intended to inform successful implementation of formative assessment in online learning contexts.

Chapter Fifteen examines a review of literature on the opportunities and challenges in adopting e-learning programs in Tanzania as well as the possible measures to overcoming some of the identified challenges.

Chapter Sixteen examines the opportunities and challenges in implementing Distance Learning (DL) and e-learning in Tanzania. It is suggested that effective DL implementation would require an appropriate budget and resource investment to support capacity building for teaching staff and students, and formulating policies, guidelines and operational framework on DL and e-learning.

Chapter Seventeen seeks to find out whether the investment in buying computers, for departments, lecturers' offices, and equipping computer labs for the students while increasing bandwidth and connectivity and other infrastructure in Kenyan Universities is translating to actual faculty and student use in blended classrooms.

Chapter Eighteen examines opportunities for Social Networking Sites' Complementation of Writing Centres. Findings suggest that students lacked confidence in asserting their authorial presence and familiarization with academic conventions. Further, students and consultants' essays demonstrated a balanced appropriation of attitudinal and judgment categories and engagement resources, with implications for the potential of Facebook to mediate student expression of their voice.

Chapter Nineteen presents a research study on mathematics education pre-service teachers' perceptions of competencies developed in an active learning course. The results of the study showed that, according to the mathematics education pre-service teachers, their Internet search skills, content knowledge about distance education, web interface design skills, and technological knowledge increased or improved due to the web-based instruction (WBI) project.

Chapter Twenty proposes deployment and adoption strategy of cloud computing to enhance blended learning services in sub-Saharan Africa. The chapter contributes towards helping higher education stakeholders in sub-Saharan Africa understand cloud services as well as plan for successful migration of computing services into cloud.

In summary, the critical role of educational technology in education imply the need for educators to review effective ways to integrate these tools into the teaching and learning process to support active and engaged student learning. However, technologies are not ends in themselves: a focus on just technology may not help, but good pedagogical practices that focus on teaching first and technology second will possibly lead to effective classroom technology integration that can support active and engaged student learning. Therefore, the hope is that each of the scholarly works presented will help forward the agenda and discourse on the significance as well as the need to review existing pedagogical practices to enhance effective teaching and learning with technology.

Jared Keengwe
University of North Dakota, USA

REFERENCES

Chen, R. J. (2010). Investigating models for preservice teachers' use of technology to support student-centered learning. *Computers & Education*, 55(1), 32–42. doi:10.1016/j.compedu.2009.11.015

Fullan, M. (2013). *Stratosphere: Integrating technology, pedagogy, and change knowledge.* Toronto, Ontario: Pearson.

Grabe, M., & Grabe, C. (2008). *Integrating technology for meaningful learning* (5th ed.). Boston, MA: Houghton-Mifflin.

Horne, M. (2010). A new role for CTE. *Techniques: Connecting Education and Careers, 85*(4), 10–11.

Keengwe, J. (2007). Faculty integration of technology into instruction and students' perceptions of computer technology to improve student learning. *Journal of Information Technology Education, 6*, 169–180.

Keengwe, J., & Onchwari, G. (2008). Constructivism, Technology, and Meaningful Learning. In T.T. Kidd. & H. Song. (Eds.), Handbook of Research on Instructional Systems & Technology (pp. 51-64). Hershey, PA: IGI Global.

Keengwe, J., & Onchwari, G. (2009). Technology & early childhood education: A technology integration model for practicing teachers. *Early Childhood Education Journal, 37*(3), 209–218. doi:10.1007/s10643-009-0341-0

Keengwe, J., Onchwari, G., & Wachira, P. (2008). The use of computer tools to support meaningful learning. *AACE Journal, 16*(1), 77–92.

Kim, M. C., & Hannafin, M. J. (2011). Scaffolding problem solving in technology-enhanced learning environments (TELEs): Bridging research and theory with practice. *Computers & Education, 56*(2), 403–417. doi:10.1016/j.compedu.2010.08.024

Kirschner, P. A., Sweller, J., & Clark, R. E. (2006). Why minimal guidance during instruction does not work: An analysis of the failure of constructivist, discovery, problem-based, experiential, and inquiry-based teaching. *Educational Psychologist, 41*(2), 75–86. doi:10.1207/s15326985ep4102_1

Lei, J. (2009). Digital natives as preservice teachers: What technology preparation is needed? *Journal of Computing in Teacher Education, 25*(3), 87–97.

Linton, J., & Geddes, C. (2013). Growing technology leaders: Learn how a small, underserved school district built capacity through collaborative, teacher-led professional development. *Learning and Leading with Technology, 41*(1), 12–15.

Novak, J. D. (1998). *Learning, Creating, and Using Knowledge: Concept Maps as Facilitative tools in Schools and Corporations*. Mahwah, NJ: Lawrence Erlbaum and Associates.

Project Tomorrow. (2010). *Unleashing the future. Educators "speak up" about the use of emerging technologies for learning*. Retrieved from http:// www.tomorrow.org/speakup/ pdfs/ SU09UnleashingTheFuture.pdf

Acknowledgment

I am forever indebted to my loving wife and children: Grace, Gabe, and McKayla – you constantly support, encourage, and inspire me to smile, laugh, and write often. Also, I deeply appreciate that YOU ALWAYS BELIEVE IN ME!

Thanks to the wonderful staff at IGI Global who participated in the overall development and successful completion of this exciting project.

Finally, I am very grateful to the Editorial Advisory Board (EAB) team.

Jared Keengwe
University of North Dakota, USA

Chapter 1
Enhanced Student Engagement through Active Learning and Emerging Technologies

Victoria M. Cardullo
Auburn University, USA

Nance S. Wilson
SUNY Cortland, USA

Vassiliki I. Zygouris-Coe
University of Central Florida, USA

ABSTRACT

Active learning and emerging technologies are enhancing student learning though an explicit intentional educational design such as Flipping the Classroom and Project Based Learning to empower students. In this chapter, the authors describe an active learning classroom and emerging technologies that support learning for the 21st century. Using vignettes, the authors model how the metacognitive teacher supports the use of emerging technologies for active learning using the Metacognitive Technological Pedagogical Content Knowledge Framework (M-TPACK) (Wilson, Zygouris-Coe, Cardullo, & Fong, 2013). Finally, the authors describe Blooms Taxonomy (Bloom et al., 1956) for active learning and make connections to emerging technologies and the level of integration using the SAMR Model: Substitution, Augmentation, Modification, and Redefinition (Puentedura, 2006).

INTRODUCTION

Today's students differ from the students our educational system was designed to teach. American education for students was designed for agrarian and industrial eras and it does not meet the needs of the 21st century (West, 2012). Education of the 21st century must be active, engaging, and customized to fit the needs of the individual learner. According to the Framework for 21st Century Learning (see http://www.p21.org/our-work/p21-framework), the most important skills for preparing students to learn in the 21st century include communication, collaboration, and creativity. In addition, the

DOI: 10.4018/978-1-4666-8363-1.ch001

Assessment and Teaching of 21st Century Skills (ATC21S) organization (see http://atc21s.org/index.php/about/what-are-21st-century-skills/), postulated that 21st century skills are found in four categories:

1. **Ways of Thinking:** Creativity, critical thinking, problem-solving, and decision-making and learning;
2. **Ways of Working:** Communication and collaboration;
3. **Tools for Working:** Information and communication technology (ICT), and information literacy; and
4. **Skills for Living in the World:** Citizenship, life and career, and personal and social responsibility.

The ATC21S has also identified two skills that span across all of the aforementioned categories: collaborative problem-solving and Information Communication Technologies (ICT)—learning in digital networks. As a nation, we must develop students' 21st century skills to ensure that they will have a place in a global competitive economy.

Active Learning

Current research (e.g., McGlynn, 2005; Peck, Ali, Matchock, & Levine, 2006; Michel, Carter & Varela, 2009) advocates for teaching techniques that foster students to actively engage with the material presented. In active learning classrooms, the teacher or instructor sets up the context for learning (i.e., the activity, the situation, the task, the process) that engages student in active learning. Active learning is generally defined as any instructional method that engages students in the learning process. Active learning requires students to do meaningful learning activities and think about what they are doing (Bonwell & Eison, 1991). Active learning can empower students with skills and strategies for problem solving both inside and outside the walls of the classroom,

or learning space. Learning is not the same as receiving information; transfer of knowledge and information is learning. Instead, it should be the development of intellectual curiosity for students as well as teaching students to learn how to learn.

Active learning has been an explicit intention of educational design since Dewey's advocacy of experimental learning nearly a century ago. Instructional design for active learning must take into consideration learning for the next 20, 30, or 40 years. Successful planning and design will support emerging technologies and technology based pedagogies. Currently, the educational system is exploring opportunities that will redefine teaching and learning. Building and classroom designers are also exploring change; they have begun to experiment with spaces that depart from the industrial era of learning, tailoring learning spaces for their students and the 21st century. Education will never again be what it was in the industrial age of learning; the possibilities for the future are exciting and populated with questions about the ideal learning space.

Several universities are experimenting with the concept of an *incubator* classroom. Incubator classrooms are new learning spaces designed to facilitate active teaching and learning. Essentially the classroom design allows the instructor to experiment with flexible learning environments and emerging technologies to enhance faculty-student engagement. This type of environment encourages active learning and fosters increased student interaction. Incubator classrooms are often designed using state of the art equipment, including some of the latest hardware and software. Auburn University, the institution of the first author, (www.auburn.edu/easl) has developed an active learning space called the Engaged Active Student Learning (EASL) Spaces or the EASL classroom. The purpose of building this type of classroom was designed to test furniture and instructional technologies, and receive faculty and student feedback. It also gave faculty the opportunity to think about how they could use new spaces to teach their courses without major adjustments to teaching pedagogies and content delivery. The design of the room supported active learning and collaboration. Strategic placement of pods of furniture allowed for group activities, with up to nine students per "pod" as well as glass boards on all walls, which allow for collaboration and effective group work. The technology in the room allows students to bring their own devices (i.e., laptops, tablets, smart phones and other mobile devices) to connect to the projecting devices and share their work with other students across the room or within their group. Students and instructors also have access to microphones, document camera, and a virtual lab.

In an interview, with Wiebke Kuhn (personal communication, July 17, 2014), the manager of informational technologies at Auburn University, the first author asked her to share some of the issues associated with the creation of the EASL space for active learning in higher education. She proposed that student reaction to the EASL space is a major concern. Students often want to know what exactly will be on the exam, what notes should I capture. Active learning is based on students' active participation in problem–solving and critical thinking as they are constructing their own knowledge. In this new space, the roles and responsibilities between teacher and student are shifting by putting more of the learning responsibility on the student. This shift is causing some disequilibrium for students who are used to passive learning. Creating learning spaces that challenge students to become active co-constructors of learning is critical. Faculty will need to approach teaching and learning differently, helping students make the transition from passive to active learning.

Active learning spaces such as the EASL room provide learning opportunities that support emerging technologies. For example, on several occasions I (first author who teaches in the EASL space) noticed students using their device to further understand a concept, verify a statement made, or to check on the validity of a

notion posed within the course of discussion or lecture. Students were using their second screen (Masie, 2011) to continually evaluate, enhance, contextualize, or expand on a concept. The second screen is any mobile device (e.g., tablet, smart phone, laptop) with wireless connectivity that can be used by the learner in addition to using other media devices. Learners now have access to more back channels and secondary content as they engage in learning. The second screen is not a new technology, but it is an emerging one. It has been used to revolutionize how people consume media for years (Cruickshank, Tsekleves, Whitham, Hill, & Kondo, 2007). During a 2014 summer course, we were discussing culturally responsive teaching. Students were following along on their iPads as I went through several key elements in the Power Point presentation I had created. I noticed one student was on her cell phone; I made my way toward her and positioned myself behind her thinking she was texting or checking her Facebook page. I was surprised to see that she was actually using a second screen to search for additional information about culturally responsive instruction for first graders. The second screen became an extension or accelerator for her learning, and it did not replace the first screen (i.e. the instructor-created Power Point presentation).

There are various developments that reflect the importance of active learning in grades K-20. In the following section, we will describe two such developments (i.e., the flipped classroom model and project-based learning) that also carry implications for K-20 learning spaces.

FLIPPED CLASSROOM

In 2012, Bergmann and Sams published a book titled, *Flip Your Classroom: Reach Every Student in Every Class Every Day*. The flipped classroom is a pedagogical model in which lecture and homework are reversed this model is a type of blended learning that "flips" the way time is used in the classroom. As part of this instructional model, the teacher spends more time on an individualized basis with students in class explaining, guiding, challenging, and extending their knowledge and understanding of the subject matter. Rote lecture content is delivered online (through videos, podcasts, and Power Point Presentations) for students to study outside the classroom and class time is used for discussions, active learning, and applications. The advantages of this instructional model include more student responsibility over one's own learning, developing communication, and collaboration skills, approaching learning in unique ways, and keeping the student actively learning inside and outside the classroom.

The flipped classroom model is used in K-12 and higher education. Implications for higher education learning include moving content delivery outside the college classroom and using in-class time for modeling, discussions, and enrichment activities that facilitate the development of students' 21st century skills. In addition, the flipped classroom model has been found to improve better faculty-student interactions, minimize student absenteeism, make learning student-centered, and even compensate for limited classroom space (Bowen, 2012). This model is also appropriate for improving student engagement and learning in large introductory courses (Deslauriers, Schelew, & Wieman, 2011) and also for providing differentiated learning. Although there are several benefits for students and teachers, there are also challenges associated with it such as, instructors needing extra time and support to redesign courses and decide how to use technology, student buy-in, and even student evaluations as some students may find it challenging to follow this learning pace (Aronson & Arfstrom, 2013).

PROJECT-BASED LEARNING

Project-based learning (PBL) is an instructional model that is aimed at developing students' deep knowledge of subject matter through actively engaging students in exploring real-world problems and issues (Baron & Darling-Hammond, 2008). Project-based learning provides students with opportunities to develop and practice critical thinking skills, communication, collaboration, problem-solving, and creativity. In these types of learning environments, students actively work in pairs or small groups to solve authentic problems and teachers play the role of the facilitator. Teachers or students create real-world problems and engage students in questioning, creating, communicating, collaborating, and reflecting. Problem-based learning places the student on the "driver's seat" of the learning process; it improves students' attitudes toward learning, and it also develops 21st century skills. Technology is at the heart of PBL as teachers use real tools for real projects and purposes. As part of PBL, students and teachers use different technology tools not only for research and problem-solving, but also for presentation purposes. For example, teachers could use Prezi, blogs and Twitter for microblogging as vehicles for students to collaboratively work on a project and present their work to the local or the world community. Implications of PBL for K-20 teaching and learning include rethinking teacher preparation and practice across grade levels and subjects areas, reflecting on the role of technology in PBL, and preparation of students who will be able to learn, collaborate, work, problem-solve, innovate, and live in a highly networked and interconnected world.

Questions seem to be an important driver for active learning albeit a flipped classroom, project based learning or an active classroom. Bloom's Taxonomy (Bloom, Englehart, Furst, Hill & Krathwohl, 1956) presents a way of thinking about the types of questions instructors can ask to elicit the different levels of knowledge in an active learning environment. In the following sections, we describe Blooms Taxonomy for active learning and make connections to emerging technologies and the level of integration using the SAMR Model: Substitution, Augmentation, Modification, and Redefinition (Puentedura, 2006).

Active Learning and Critical Thinking in the Context of Emerging Technologies

Active learning requires students to think and learn beyond remembering and understanding. Bloom's Taxonomy has been used as a tool for helping educators to understand the types of thinking that leads to active learning, learning that requires higher order thinking (Bloom et al., 1956). Bloom's taxonomy was based on behaviors that teachers can observe and it is the most widely used taxonomy used to create learning objectives.

Bloom hoped that this classification system would support the development of a comprehensive theory by providing a framework that educators could use to identify research problems, develop hypotheses, plan learning, and identify methods and metrics, and by defining a common language to use when setting learning goals, measuring outcomes, and sharing findings (Munzenmaier & Rubin, 2013, p. 4).

In 2001, Anderson and Krathwohl revised Bloom's earlier work to add relevance for 21st century students and changes were made to three broad categories: terminology, structure, and emphasis. Terminology changes included changing the six major categories to verb form, as well as changes to the cognitive level of complexity. Bloom's Taxonomy (Bloom et al., 1956) provided educators with the first systematic classification of the process of thinking and learning. Using the verbiage aligned in the taxonomy teachers and test developers began developing assessment questions aligned to Bloom's cognitive levels. In 2007, Churches updated Bloom's Revised Taxonomy creating Bloom's Digital Taxonomy. He developed this multi-tiered model to incorporate new ways of learning facilitated by technology. He added current examples at all cognitive levels and stated that what determines cognitive levels is not the tool itself, but rather how the technological tool is used to facilitate learning and understanding.

Models of Emerging Technology Integration

Understanding that digital tools can be used to facilitate learning and understanding via the development of higher order thinking skills is only one piece of the puzzle. Another piece is how the teacher integrates that technology into the classroom. The SAMR model (Puentedura, 2006) illustrates how teachers process a task when adopting educational technology. In the substitution stage there really is no functional change in the implementation of learning and technology, it is simply substituting one for another. In the augmentation stage, technology acts as direct substitution of the task, with some functional improvement. The modification stage, technology allows for the significant redesign of the task and in the redefinition stage, technology allows for the creation of a new task, a task previously unconceivable (Puentedura, 2006).

How can emerging technologies promote active student learning and the development of critical thinking skills? The following vignette displays an active learning classroom in which students and instructor move through all levels of the SAMR model (Puentedura, 2006) aligned to Bloom's Taxonomy (Bloom et al., 1956) for learning.

Vignette #1: University Level-Using an iPad

In a summer writing course, all students had an iPad for learning. In this course, students and instructor were able to move fluently through all levels of the SAMR model. As the class began with a brief introduction on persuasive writing for children, undergraduate education students used the IOS notes App to take notes (substitution level/ remembering or understanding). This level is a direct substitution, with no functional change. The following class period students were asked to explore note-taking Apps and to choose their own App to take notes (augmented level/applying or analyzing). Some of the choices they made were Noteability, iAnnotate, TopNotes, and Note Anytime. This level is a direct substitution with some functional change. This level starts to move along the teacher/ student centric continuum. Computer technology offered students effective tools to perform a common task. In the modification level, all students used notability for note taking. Although the task was only slightly altered, it allowed for significant task redesign. Before all students left, the classroom that day the teacher asked all students' to email her a copy of their notes for the day. This allowed for instant feedback, real time evaluation, and adjustment of the next lesson (modification/ applying, analyzing or evaluating). In the final level redefinition, students were asked to use the ShowMe App (an interactive whiteboard that allows for voice recording tutorials that can be shared) to create a tutorial for persuasive writing for fourth graders. This level allowed for the complete redesign of the task, creating a new purpose for taking notes and assessing student level of understanding (redefinition/ evaluating or creating).

The selection of technology for learning purposes and the manner in which the teacher uses it in his or her classroom have the potential to transform teaching and active student learning. In the above vignette if the instructor only stayed at the substitution stage of the SAMR model (Puentedura, 2006), she would have only focused on the *remembering* level of Bloom's taxonomy (Bloom et al., 1956) without actively engaging students in the learning process. As students moved through the stages, they also moved through Bloom's taxonomy taking on a more active role in their learning. Let us take a look at how this active learning vignette used technology and is supported by the different stages of the SAMR (Puentedura, 2006) model as well as the strong alignment of Bloom's Taxonomy

Table 1. The alignment of Bloom's taxonomy and the SAMR model

SAMR Stages	Task and Application	Bloom's Taxonomy
Substitution	Note taking using the IOS Note Taking App	Remembering
Augmentation	Choose their own App to take notes	Applying & Understanding
Modification	All used Notability for note taking. All students emailed a copy of their notes for evaluation.	Applying, Analyzing & Evaluating
Redefinition	Using the ShowMe App students created a tutorial for persuasive writing for fourth graders.	Evaluating & Creating

to elicit different levels of knowledge from the students in an active learning environment (see Table 1).

One challenge with the integration of technology for learning purposes in academic settings is that the technology is constantly emerging. Emerging technologies are constantly evolving. Although they offer new opportunities for supporting learning of these skills through active learning, teachers and academic settings are not following technological advancements in a parallel pace or fashion.

Veletsiano (2010a) described emerging technologies as tools, concepts and advancements utilized in diverse educational settings to serve a variety of education related purposes. He further defines and outlines five characteristics of an emerging technology: 1) may or may not be new; 2) evolving or coming into new; 3) experience hype cycles; 4) are not fully understood or researched in a mature way; 5) are potentially disruptive (p. 3).

The five characteristics of emerging technologies help to put technology into perspective for academic learning. Take for instance the first characteristic: *may or may not be new*. Virtual worlds have been around since the 1980's or earlier. Take for instance the virtual world of *SimCity* (1989) or *Dungeons & Dragons* (1976). Massive Multiplayer online games (MMOG) such as *World of Warcraft* (Blizzard Entertainment) and *Everquest*

(Sony Online Entertainment) allow players to interact in a virtual collaborative environment to problem solve and think critically. Massive Player Online Games have all of the characteristics of critical learning, problem solving, and problem representation in the quest. These are often developed and enhanced throughout debriefing, theorizing, and the apprenticeship stage of the game using 1) conditions; 2) goals; 3) procedures; 4) strategies; and 5) mega-strategies. There is inherent cognitive and social complexity in massive multiplayer games in which players seek out challenges just beyond the current level of ability in a virtual environment. Emerging communities such as modding (the ability to change models or create new models in a program) and machinima (real-time virtual games to create animated video) are creating opportunities for users to create real-time content via video capturing and programing.

MMOGs or virtual worlds could be powerful learning environments if the content were educational (Steinkuehler, 2006).

Despite the increase of sophisticated technology outside of school, classrooms seldom leverage any of these interfaces for teaching or learning (Clarke, Dede, & Dieterle, 2008). Therefore, virtual worlds are considered emerging technologies for education. Second life and SimCityEdu are relatively new in the education realm and educators are still trying to figure out how they fit into education and where they can add these new emerging technologies to the active classroom-learning environment. Transformative learning experiences cannot be imposed or forced upon learning; deeper forms of learning cannot be just made to happen, they are invented, explored, encouraged and facilitated (Valetsiano, 2010a). In essence, they transform.

As Veletsiano (2010b) stated technology is evolving and *coming into being*. Twitter (founded 2006) is constantly in an evolutionary state and is one of the most popular social networking tools used to send and resend short 140 character text messages called tweets. Yet, new features are changing the way this technology is used in active classrooms, and new users engage in practices that differ from the intended use, thus *coming into being*. The networking and microblogging platform represents an illustrative example of how emerging technologies are *coming into being* as noted in Vignette # 2.

Vignette # 2: University Graduate Level Online Content Area Reading Course

As a wrap-up and formative assessment strategy, I often implement exit slips. After completing each module students use the quiz tab to leave an exit slips on a given topic. The purpose of this exit slip is to help them process the new concepts, reflect on information learned, and provide an avenue for them to express their thoughts or questions about the new information. Student feedback from exit slips has allowed me to make course modifications and adjustments based on student interest and understanding.

Next semester at the conclusion of the lesson instead of using the quiz tab to leave an exit slips, I plan to ask students to use a Twitter feed to type 140 characters or less summary of what they learned today, questions they still have, or muddy points they still may need clarification. Exist slips using Twitter can be viewed by all students and offer a voice to all students, even the reluctant hand raisers. As an extension to this lesson, I plan to ask students to use the microblog format to record their initial and final responses on a given topic. This will allow me to see how their perspective on the topic has changed overtime.

Emerging technologies have so much potential, yet we as educators are only beginning to see the potential and are scrambling to figure out how and where to use it effectively for active learning. Aligning emerging technologies with Bloom's taxonomy (Bloom et al., 1956) and the SAMR model (Puentedura, 2006) could help teachers see the potential of emerging technologies. A teacher is always searching for new ways to allow technology *to come into being* in an active learning environment.

Veletsiano (2010a) discusses the stages in which technology often travels through, the cycle of excitement or hype, adoption, activity, maturity, impact, and enthusiasm. Some technology will stay while others will simply fade away. Emerging technologies of today may very well be the fading technology of tomorrow, but a simple transformation from its intended purpose (i.e., Twitter) could be the key to longevity in education.

App Smashing is a new *hype;* it has developed a lot of enthusiasm because it seems to integrate both the SAMR model (Puentedura, 2006) and Blooms taxonomy (Bloom et al., 1956) creating a very active learning environment. The impact on learning could be astounding as students and educators find new ways for technology *to come into being*. App smashing is a term coined by Greg Kulowiece at EdTechTeacher.org (2014). App smashing is content created in one App, then transferred, and enhanced by a second App and sometimes a third, or fourth App and the final product is published for public consumption. This process moves learners through Bloom's Taxonomy and requires educators to have a clear vision for the use of technology and the level of integration (SAMR model) all the while supporting active learning.

Just imagine studying viral biology and using technology to create real world scenarios for students to problem solve, and think critically as Biological Warfare wreaks havoc on a small heavily populated community-using App smashing. App smashing supports and enables limitless content creation. The following vignette offers a glimpse at how an instructor could use App smashing to facilitate active learning in a university classroom.

Vignette # 3: Undergraduate Freshmen University Level

Students in a freshmen year college biology course are studying viruses as small as a parasite, the instructor begins the lesson with an App called Biological Warfare (cost .99$). This App affords the foundation for studying real world viruses and biological weapons (substitution level/ understanding). Also located within this App is a comprehensive repository of information about agencies and organizations associated with biological weapons. After using the Biological Warfare App the instructor uses Hazmat Evac App (cost $4.99) to begin setting the stage for a virtual disaster (augmentation level/ Application & analysis). Using the App students can assume the role of first responders and emergency management responders and view maps based on potential hazmat spills and review evacuation protocols (Modification level/ evaluation). After a successful evacuation, health care can be provided using HumanSim (coming soon) to develop assessment and discussion making skills and strategies without risk to real patients. These tools offer authentic, challenging, and immersive environment offers meaningful performance feedback as students actively construct knowledge about biological viruses. As students venture on this realistic journey they capture their notes, they identify evidence and details using the Explain Everything App (cost $2.99), and produce a final product using iMovie or other video-producing Apps to document the life of a virus and its potential impact on the public (redefinition level/ creating).

As you can see from the above-proposed vignette a single App can be powerful, yet many Apps working together can be transformative in an active learning classroom. The teacher could multiple

Apps in conjunction with one another to complete a final project closely aligning the SAMR model (Puentedura, 2006) and Blooms Taxonomy (Bloom et al., 1956) to support active learning. This is an example of a redefinition of teaching and learning according to the SAMR model moving students beyond the lower order thinking defined by Bloom's Taxonomy and positioning learning in the realm of higher order thinking (applying, analyzing, evaluating, and creating).

The integration of technology in the aforementioned manner requires a transformation of the context for teaching and learning through the adoption of a new pedagogy for the digital age (Beethan & Sharpe, 2013). Research continues to show that "access" to technology alone has limited impact on learning outcomes and instructional methods (Bednarz & Vander Shee, 2006; Cuban, 2001, Schrum et al., 2007). Technology in or outside of school must be aligned with the pedagogy. Recent literature on emerging technologies highlights the negotiated and symbiotic relationship between pedagogy and technology, noting that technology sculpts educational practices and educational practice molds technology use and implementation (Veletsiano, 2010a; Whitworth & Benson, 2010). Pedagogy must serve as the starting point for the optimum design for active learning and active classroom design.

Learner engagement is critical as we begin to see the possibilities of the emerging technologies. In the '60s and '70s, "instructional TV was going to revolutionize everything," the hype behind the motion picture was thought to be the demise of the book. Over one hundred years ago, Thomas Edison made a similar statement "Books will soon be obsolete in the schools... Our school system will be completely changed in 10 years" (1913). This statement shows that change in education is often not a sudden transformation; education has a history of resistance to change (Cuban, 1993).

When emerging technologies are implemented into the realm of education what does it offer education, what does it do to support teaching and learning? Emerging technologies are not fully understood or researched in a mature way. We are *not yet* able to distinguish emerging technologies from other technologies. We are *not yet* able to understand the implications of these technologies. For example, what does socialization mean for higher education distance learning? Can we add a friend, researcher, or experts in the field via add a friend button to our course canvas home page? If we could what would be the educational benefit, implication, or transformation?

Finally, because of the disruption of teaching and learning, although technologies have the potential to disrupt current teaching and learning practices, their potential is mostly unfulfilled or has yet to be realized. Disruptive teaching leads to powerful changes in pedagogy and learning; it also reflects and creates new dispositions toward 21st century teaching and learning.

When technology is implemented effectively, the classroom environment supports multiple learning styles, interests, and experiences that allow students to take responsibility for their own learning. Research shows "what students learn, is greatly influenced by how they learn, and many students learn best through active, collaborative, small group work inside and outside the classroom" (Springer, Stanne, & Donovan, 1999, p. 21). Technology supports this because metacognitive teachers have more opportunities to personalize learning, actively involve students in the learning process, enable students to collaborate, co-construct knowledge, and transfer learning in new learning situations, this is the foundation of an active learning classroom.

Designing and implementing an active learning classroom warrants strong teacher knowledge base and metacognitive thinking and learning dispositions. The M-TPACK (Metacognitive Technological Pedagogical Content Knowledge) framework best supports the active learning classroom (Wilson et al., 2013). The M-TPACK framework propositions that the teacher is knowledgeable regarding content, technology, curriculum, and students while maintaining the disposition that supports technology integration and an adaptive approach to teaching and learning. A pedagogy that places student learning at the center with a metacognitive teacher who has a metacognitive disposition towards active learning with technology could support and enhance learning in an active classroom.

The M-TPACK framework (Wilson et al., 2013) supports our understanding of what this new pedagogy should look like in an active classroom. The M-TPACK framework demonstrates that the teacher is knowledgeable regarding content, technology, curriculum, and students, while maintaining a disposition that supports technology integration and an adaptive approach to teaching and learning.

The Role of the Metacognitive Teacher in Student Active Learning

Active learning as an instructional technique requires the teacher to be aware of her knowledge and to consciously understand, control, and manipulate one's cognitive processes (Meichenbaum, 1985). A metacognitive teacher is an adaptive, self-regulated, and reflective teacher who considers what she knows regarding content, pedagogy, students, and technology when designing and implementing active learning opportunities for students. The metacognitive teacher adapts this knowledge to assure student learning through professional development, self-monitoring, and reflection.

When building an active learning classroom using emerging technologies the metacognitive teacher considers how she can use the technology using the SAMR Model (Puentedura, 2006) to have students create representations of what they are learning. She has the philosophy that knowledge and technology is forever evolving and changing and uses it to develop student knowledge and support their learning. When students and teachers build knowledge together, they are

both active learners. The metacognitive teacher guides students to create by utilizing her knowledge flexibly to help students achieve learning goals. Notice how the following seventh grade science teacher adapts her instruction using her knowledge of technology, content, pedagogy, and students to promote deep student learning about the layers of a lake.

Vignette # 4: Seventh Grade Science Teacher

The learning goal is "All students will understand the layers of a lake." The teacher has shared a diagram of the layers and is working with the students as they design their own diagram. As she walks around the room, she realizes that some of the students are just copying the image she has shared rather than actively thinking about the layers on their own. She decides to adapt her instruction and asks students to erase their original images. She uses her knowledge of Google images gained from her own search for a diagram and asks the students to find three diagrams that describe the layers of a lake. She has them compare the three Google images and she has them draw their own diagram.

When using emerging technologies this teacher considers how the use of technology can transform engagement with learning. The metacognitive teacher "requires an orchestration of learning rather than the dispensing of knowledge" (Wilson et al., 2013, p. 9).

Pedagogical Knowledge and Active Learning

Pedagogical knowledge refers to teachers' knowledge about the processes and methods of teaching and learning. Pedagogy refers to the approaches that a teacher uses to guide student active learning. An understanding of active learning techniques such as PBL, flipped classrooms, etc. is a key aspect of the teacher's pedagogical knowledge. Additionally, there is a strong understanding of the teaching techniques that build students' abilities and opportunities to use technology to create, evaluate, analyze, and apply knowledge. The metacognitive teacher uses her knowledge of these approaches to make decisions regarding everything from designing and managing the educational environment to knowing the strategies for student engagement, to developing habits of mind, and learning. In a classroom where technology is strategically and meaningfully integrated, it is critical for the metacognitive teacher to consider methods for keeping devices charged, sharing work, holding students accountable for strategic thinking, determining the applications that will guide the students' learning, and determining how and when to apply those applications.

In addition, the metacognitive teacher will also have established classroom and student roles for collecting, charging, using, and storing devices. She would have a written set of instructions for saving content to the Cloud that is visible in the classroom and also included on each student's device, along with a repertoire of tools and strategic activities in which students can act in order to solve problems while working independently with a device. The metacognitive teacher uses her pedagogical knowledge when she is planning and teaching lessons. For instance, when teaching the skill of observation to sixth graders a science teacher used her pedagogical knowledge of strategies for building observation to integrate the iPad into the classroom. The iPad allows students to take photos, but also to draw. In the vignette below notice how she utilizes her pedagogical knowledge to teach students that observation involves much more than just taking a picture and studying an image (Driver & Bell, 1986).

Vignette # 5: Sixth Grade Science

Good morning, today we will learn more about the fruit fly. Yesterday we talked about why scientists study the fruit fly. Today we are going to start observing our fruit flies so we can learn as we watch them…. The students are given a small container with a fruit fly. In the container, they put a piece of banana. They are told to take notes about what they see when they look at the fruit fly with and without a magnifying glass. Chelsea asks, "Why can't we just use the iPad to take a video or a picture of our Fruit Fly? It would be easier." The teacher, anticipating this question responds by explaining how taking pictures is just one technique for recording data; but how being active during observation in science is used as a stimulus for asking questions. The teacher then modifies her directions. She has the students record their observations using descriptive lists and drawn images for 2 minutes, then lets them pause to take two still images, and a 30 second video before observing the fruit fly for another two minutes from a different angle; i.e., looking at the fruit fly from the bottom of the container. The lesson continues in this manner for approximately ten minutes. The students recorded data, took photos, and shot videos, saving all of them in the Explain Everything App. At the end of the observation period, the students shared their observations while the teacher created a class record of the data and led a discussion on how the medium (i.e., photos, videos, handwritten notes, or illustrations) affects how we share what is observed and the questions the students ask about what they are observing. She finished the discussion on why and how observation is an important part of science and how observation requires more than taking a picture.

This metacognitive teacher used her pedagogical knowledge of how to organize the timing of a lesson, how to build off a conversation, and how to establish an active learning experience where students integrate technology effectively. According to the SAMR model (Puentedura, 2006); she has used technology to modify her teaching transforming her task to create an active learning experience where students created knowledge beyond the knowledge level of understanding (Bloom's Taxonomy, Bloom et al., 1956).

Content Knowledge and Active Learning

Content knowledge refers to knowledge about subject matter to be learned or taught. This is often described as knowledge of the facts, concepts, and strategies that make up a particular discipline. It includes knowledge of the instructional materials available and the objectives to be met. In the M-TPACK (Wilson et al., 2013) framework, this also includes a teacher's knowledge of how to teach a particular content, their Pedagogical Content Knowledge (PCK). The metacognitive teacher uses her knowledge of the discipline, the standards, and the available materials to plan active learning with technology. They will decide in advance how to implement technology to support and enhance learning to meet the needs of the learner. These considerations will include how they will guide students to think about the content and at which stages of Bloom's Taxonomy (Bloom et al., 1956), as well as whether technology would be used as an enhancement versus for transformation (SAMR). The metacognitive teacher will provide support and examples along the way with feedback to help students grasp new concepts. The vignette below illustrates how a sixth grade science teacher uses her content knowledge of the scientific method to redefine the traditional lab report in a one-to-one iPad classroom.

Vignette #6: Sixth Grade Science Teacher

Today we are going to do a lab centered on the question, Should ice be cubed? This lab connects to what we have learned about surface area. Before we begin use Notability to open, the file labeled: Should ice be cubed? and save it in your Google drive. Then use Notability to draw at least three different shapes of ice cubes you have seen and predict which one you think will melt faster based on you knowledge of surface area. While the students complete the task, the teacher removes three sets of ice cubes from the freezer. She uses the iPad camera to project images of the ice cubes and tells the students that they can us the shapes projected. After predictions are made, the teacher assigns the students to lab groups of three and gives each student in the group a role. One student videotapes the ice melting, another takes narrative observational notes, and the third is a timekeeper who is watching a clock and tells the others when 15 seconds pass. At the end of the observation period, the video and observation notes were shared with each member of the group so that all could finish their lab report integrating all the data on Notability at home.

The teacher had the students analyze and synthesize their findings by redefining (SAMR Model, Puentedura, 2006) the traditional lab report to include multiple mediums (APP Smashing) allowing the students to build their own content knowledge (Bloom's Taxonomy, Bloom et al., 1956). The teacher's content knowledge of the scientific process, surface area, and the sixth grade curriculum informed her decision-making in creating this experience for students.

Technological Knowledge and Active Learning

As with knowledge of content and pedagogy, the metacognitive teacher uses her knowledge of technology to plan, implement, and adapt her teaching to assure student learning. Knowledge of technology is not simply knowing what is available and how it works, but more importantly, it is a comprehensive understanding of how the technology can enhance content and improve student learning (Cardullo, Zygouris-Coe, & Wilson, 2014). Knowing how to use a device, an App, or a program is a not the same as knowing how to teach and truly implement content using the technology. The metacognitive teacher will not just teach with the technology; she will also seek to implement technology to transform learning, redefining, and modifying the design of learning (SAMR Model, Puentedura, 2006) to create skills and strategies needed for the 21st century learning. The metacognitive teacher is a lifelong learner of technologies and they continually look for ways to integrate new technologies effectively and strategically to enhance student learning and content knowledge as displayed in the following vignette:

Vignette # 7: Fifth Grade Science Teacher

A fifth grade science teacher was looking for a way to have each of her students present their knowledge of wave energy. She wanted to formatively assess each student, but wanted to give them a different modality for demonstrating their knowledge. After consultation, research into different Applications, and some experimentation she decided to have the students use Educreations as a tool. Educreations allows students to draw or import images, label the images, and to explain those images as if they are giving a presentation to the class. She had the students use their knowledge

of how wave energy works through the different phases of matter to record a presentation sharing that knowledge. The App allowed the teacher to see how a student could explain a concept without the constraints of lengthy written descriptions.

The metacognitive science teacher described above used her knowledge of the iPad to search and use an Application that supported student learning. She used the Application to redefine (SAMR model, Puentedura, 2006) her assessment having the students create an explanation (Bloom's Taxonomy, Bloom et al., 1956) versus answering questions or completing a traditional paper and pencil task. By having the students create explanations of the information using technology, the assessment experience has been transformed.

Student Knowledge and Active Learning

In determining to use Educreations, the metacognitive science teacher in vignette # 7 used her knowledge of students—she knew that students do not like writing long explanations and she also knew that responding to learning via writing is a useful way to promote further thinking and processing of information. She determined that a verbal explanation would also meet her goal of assessing student understanding of wave energy. Knowledge of students includes the metacognitive teacher's knowledge of learner characteristics including background knowledge, skills, and strategies as well as learning preferences. Knowledge of students includes the understanding of students' knowledge of technology, the students' role in an active learning classroom, and students' capabilities with technology. The metacognitive teacher uses her knowledge of students to determine how she will organize instruction as noted in the following vignette:

Vignette # 8: Eighth Grade Social Studies Teacher

When introducing iPads to a class of eighth graders a social studies teacher used his knowledge of the iPad to take the time to demonstrate and give the students practice in using the device for academic purposes. The teacher knew that the students were familiar with the IOS operating system and that they had used iPods, iPhones, and some iPads for various functions like gaming, social media, texting, etc., but had not used these devices to engage in active learning. Therefore, the teacher modeled a lesson on how he could use Notability in combination with Safari to document and share learning. He created a document with two websites about how a bill becomes a law. He shared the document with students with Google Drive. The students opened the file with Notability and went to the websites. They worked on their own iPads while the teacher demonstrated how to synthesize notes form the website into one document.

The teacher knew that his students needed to both see and experience the iPad as a tool for learning, thus the demonstration with the students being able to use their iPads to mirror the task. The students saw how the iPad could help them document their learning in new ways from importing images, to linking websites directly to a document, and to taking notes. Their learning was augmented as the students built an understanding of how the iPad could be used for academic purposes.

CONCLUSION

The landscape of education is rapidly changing and the focus must remain on the student to empower, engage, and enable learning in ways that will transform the learning environment from passive to active. Educators must be empowered to use technology to engage, motivate, and personal-ize learning for all students effectively moving beyond the substitution level of integration. All learners must have access to learning technologies for when everyone participates, everyone learns. Albeit Digital Natives, Millennials, or the upcoming GenZ, successful planning and design with regard to technology must have a line of sight toward the future (20-30 years) to effectively integrate and redefine the use of technology for active learning. Educators will need to address each Generation's heightened technological expectations, yet perhaps the most challenging generation will be Generation Alpha, they are the children born after 2010 to the Generation X & Y (McCrindle, 2009). Because these children have been raised with technology, they will be far more superior and well informed, and even more technology-focused expecting a deeper level of integration of technology and critical thinking. They will no longer be passive learners waiting for the dispersal of knowledge they will be co-creators in a collaborative learning environment an environment that supports active learning and the inclusion of emerging technologies.

REFERENCES

Aronson, N., & Arfstrom, K. M. (2013). *Flipped learning in higher education*. Boston, MA: Pearson.

Azevedo, R. (2005). Using hypermedia as a metacognitive tool for enhancing student learn-ing? The role of self-regulated learning. *Educational Psychologist, 40*(4), 199–209. doi:10.1207/s15326985ep4004_2

Barron, B., & Darling-Hammond, L. (2008). *Teaching for meaningful learning: A review of research on inquiry-based and cooperative learn-ing in Powerful learning: What we know about teaching for understanding*. San Francisco, CA: Jossey-Bass.

Bednarz, S. W., & Schee, J. V. D. (2006). Europe and the United States: The implementation of geographic information systems in secondary education in two contexts. *Technology, Pedagogy and Education, 15*(2), 191–205. doi:10.1080/14759390600769573

Beetham, H., & Sharpe, R. (Eds.). (2013). *Rethinking pedagogy for a digital age: Designing for 21st century learning.* New York, NY: Routledge.

Bloom, B. S., Engelhart, M. D., Furst, F. J., Hill, W. H., & Krathwohl, D. R. (1956). *Taxonomy of educational objectives: Cognitive domain.* New York: McKay.

Bloom, B. S., & Krathwohl, D. R. (1956). *Taxonomy of educational objectives: The classification of educational goals, by a committee of college and university examiners. Handbook 1: Cognitive domain.* London: Longmans.

Bonwell, C. C., & Eison, J. A. (1991). ASHEERIC Higher Education Report: Vol. 1. *Active learning: Creating excitement in the classroom.* Washington, DC: George Washington University.

Bowen, J. A. (2012). *Teaching naked: How moving technology out of your college classroom will improve student learning.* John Wiley & Sons.

Cardullo, V., Zygouris-Coe, V., & Wilson, N. S. (2014). The benefits and challenges of mobile learning and ubiquitous technologies. In S. J. Keengwe (Ed.), *Promoting Active Learning through the Integration of Mobile and Ubiquitous Technologies* (pp. 185–196).

Churches, A. (2007). *Bloom's Digital Taxonomy.* Retrieved from http://edorigami.wikispaces.com/file/view/bloom%27s+Digital+taxonomy+v3.01.pdf

Churches, A. (2008). *Bloom's Digital Taxonomy v2.12.* Retrieved from http://www.scribd.com/doc/8000050/Blooms-Digital-Taxonomy-v212

Clarke, J., Dete, C., & Dieterle, E. (2008). Emerging technologies for collaborative, mediated, immersive learning. In International Handbook of Information Technology in Primary and Secondary Education. (Vol. 20, pp. 901-909). Springer.

Cruickshank, L., Tsekleves, E., Whitham, R., Hill, A., & Kondo, K. (2007). Making interactive TV easier to use: Interface design for a second screen approach. *The Design Journal, 10*(3), 41–53. doi:10.2752/146069207789271920

Cuban, L. (1993). *How teachers taught: Constancy and change in American classrooms, 1880–1990* (2nd ed.). New York, NY: Teachers College Press.

Deed, C., & Edwards, A. (2011). Unrestricted student blogging: Implications for active learning in a virtual text-based environment. *Active Learning in Higher Education, 12*(1), 11–21. doi:10.1177/1469787410387725

Deslauriers, L., Schelew, E., & Wieman, C. (2011, May 13). Improved learning in a large enrollment Physics class. *Science, 332*(6031), 862–864. doi:10.1126/science.1201783 PMID:21566198

Driver, R., & Bell, E. (1986). Students' thinking and the learning of science: A constructivist view. *The School Science Review, 67,* 443–456.

McGlynn, A. P. (2005). Teaching millennials, our newest cultural cohort. *Education Digest,* 12–16.

Meichenbaum, D. (1985). *Stress inoculation training.* New York: Pergamon Press.

Michel, N., Cater, J. J. III, & Varela, O. (2009). Active versus passive teaching styles: An empirical study of student outcomes. *Human Resource Development Quarterly, 20*(4), 397–418. doi:10.1002/hrdq.20025

Moran, C., & Young, C. A. (2014). Active learning in the flipped English language arts classroom. *Promoting Active Learning Through the Flipped Classroom Model,* 163.

National Governors Association Center for Best Practices, Council of Chief State School Officers. (2010). Common Core State Standards. National Governors Association Center for Best Practices, Council of Chief State School Officers, Washington D.C.

Park, E. L., & Choi, B. K. (2014). Transformation of classroom spaces: Traditional versus active learning classroom in colleges. *Higher Education*, 1–23.

Peck, A. C., Ali, R. S., Matchock, R. L., & Levine, M. E. (2006). Introductory psychology topics and student performance: Where's the challenge? *Teaching of Psychology, 33*(3), 167–170. doi:10.1207/s15328023top3303_2

Powell, N. W., Cleveland, R., Thompson, S., & Forde, T. (2012). Using multi-instructional teaching and technology-supported active learning strategies to enhance student engagement. *Journal of Technological Integration in the Classroom, 4*(2), 41–50.

Puentedura, R. (2006). *Transformatiom, technology, and education*. Presentation given August 18, 2006 as part of the Strengthening Your District Through Technology workshops, Maine, US. Retrieved from http://hippasus.com/resources/tte/part1.html

Schrum, L., Thompson, A., Maddux, C., Sprague, D., Bull, G., & Bell, L. (2007). Editorial: Research on the effectiveness of technology in schools: The roles of pedagogy and content. *Contemporary Issues in Technology & Teacher Education, 7*(1), 456–460.

Settles, B. (2010). Active learning literature survey. University of Wisconsin, Madison, 52, 55-66.

Sharples, M. (2000). The design of personal mobile technologies for lifelong learning. *Computers & Education, 34*(3-4), 177–193. doi:10.1016/S0360-1315(99)00044-5

Sharples, M. (2005). *Re-thinking learning for the mobile age*. Retrieved from: http://www.noe-kaleidoscope.org/pub/lastnews/last-0-read159-display

Springer, L., Stanne, M. E., & Donovan, S. S. (1999). Effects of small-group learning on undergraduates in science, mathematics, engineering, and technology: A meta-analysis. *Review of Educational Research, 69*(1), 21–51. doi:10.3102/00346543069001021

Steinkuehler, C. A. (2006). Massively multiplayer online video gaming as participation in a discourse. *Mind, Culture, and Activity, 13*(1), 38–52. doi:10.1207/s15327884mca1301_4

Veletsianos, G. (2010a). A definition of emerging technologies for education. In G. Veletsianos (Ed.), *Emerging technologies in distance education* (pp. 3–22). Edmonton, AB: Athabasca University Press.

Veletsianos, G. (2010b). *Emerging technologies in distance education. Theory and practice*. Edmonton: AU Press. Retrieved from http://www.aupress.ca/books/120177/ebook/99Z_Veletsianos_2010-Emerging_Technologies_in_Distance_Education.pdf

West, D. (2012). *Digital schools: How technology can transform education*. Brookings Institution Press.

Whitworth, A., & Benson, A. (2010). Learning, design, and emergence: Two cases of Moodle in distance education. *Emerging technologies in distance education* (pp. 195-213).

Wilson, N., Zygouris-Coe, V., Cardullo, V., & Fong, J. (2013). Pedagogical frameworks of e-reader technologies in education. In S. Keengwe (Ed.), *Pedagogical applications and social effects of mobile technology integration*. doi:10.4018/978-1-4666-2985-1.ch001

ADDITIONAL READING

Anderson, L. W., & Krathworhl, D. R. (Eds.). (2001). *A taxonomy for learning, teaching, and assessing*. New York: Longman.

Benek-Rivera, J., & Mathews, V. E. (2004). Active learning with jeopardy: Students ask the questions. *Journal of Management Education, 28*(1), 104–118. doi:10.1177/1052562903252637

Berger, B. (2002). Applying active learning at the graduate level: Merger issues at Newco. *Public Relations Review, 28*(2), 191–200. doi:10.1016/S0363-8111(02)00126-1

Bergmann, J., & Sams, A. (2012). *Flip your classroom: Reach every student in every class every day*. Alexandria, VA: ASCD.

Bonwell, C. C., & Eison, J. A. (1991). *Active learning: Creating excitement in the classroom (ASHE-ERIC Higher Education Rep. No. 1)*. Washington, DC: The George Washington University, School of Education and Human Development.

Duffy, G. G., Miller, S. D., Parsons, S. A., & Meloth, M. (2009). Teachers as metacognitive professionals. In D. J. Hacker, J. Dunlosky, & A. C. Graesser (Eds.), *Handbook of Metacognition in Education* (pp. 240–256). New York, NY: Routledge.

Ebert-May, D., Brewer, C., & Allred, S. (1997). Innovation in large lectures—Teaching for active learning. *Bioscience, 47*(9), 601–607. doi:10.2307/1313166

Ertmer, P. A., Ottenbreit-Leftwich, A. T., Sadik, O., Sendurur, E., & Sendurur, P. (2012). Teacher beliefs and technology integration practices: A critical relationship. *Computers & Education, 59*(2), 423–435. doi:10.1016/j.compedu.2012.02.001

Fogarty, R. (1994). *How to teach for metacognition*. Palatine, IL: IRI/Skylight Publishing.

Jacobson, M. J., & Azevedo, R. (2008). Advances in scaffolding learning with hypertext and hypermedia: Theoretical, empirical, and design issues. *Educational Technology Research and Development, 56*(1), 1–3. doi:10.1007/s11423-007-9066-1

Laurillard, D. (2013). *Teaching as a design science: Building pedagogical patterns for learning and technology*. New York, NY: Routledge.

Leu, D. J. Jr. (2000). Literacy and technology: Deictic consequences for literacy education in an information age. In M. L. Kamil, P. Mosenthal, P. D. Pearson, & R. Barr (Eds.), *Handbook of reading research* (Vol. III, pp. 743–770). Mahwah, NJ: Erlbaum.

Liu, G. Z., & Hwang, G. J. (2010). A key step to understanding paradigm shifts in e-learning: Towards context-aware ubiquitous learning. *British Journal of Educational Technology, 41*(2), E1–E9. doi:10.1111/j.1467-8535.2009.00976.x

Looi, C. K., Seow, P., Zhang, B., So, H. J., Chen, W., & Wong, L. H. (2010). Leveraging mobile technology for sustainable seamless learning: A research agenda. *British Journal of Educational Technology, 41*(2), 154–169. doi:10.1111/j.1467-8535.2008.00912.x

McCridle, M. (2009). *The abc of xyz: Understanding the global generation*. Sydney, Australia: University of New South Wales Press.

Noble, T. (2004). Integrating the Revised Bloom's Taxonomy with multiple intelligences: A planning tool for curriculum differentiation. *Teachers College Record, 106*(1), 193–211. doi:10.1111/j.1467-9620.2004.00328.x

Shulman, L. (2002). Making differences: A table of learning. *Change, 34*(6), 36–44. http://www.carnegiefoundation.org/elibrary/docs/making_differences.htm doi:10.1080/00091380209605567

Van Horne, S., Murniati, C., Gaffney, J. D., & Jesse, M. (2012). Promoting active learning in technology-infused TILE classrooms at the University of Iowa. *Journal of Learning Spaces*, *1*(2). Retrieved from https://libjournal.uncg.edu/index. php/jls/article/view/344/280

Van Oostveen, R., Muirhead, W., & Goodman, W. M. (2011). Tablet PCs and reconceptualizing learning with technology: A case study in higher education. *Interactive Technology and Smart Education*, *8*(2), 78–93. doi:10.1108/17415651111141803

Weigel, V. (2002). *Deep learning for a digital age: Technology's untApped potential to enrich higher education*. New York: Jossey-Bass.

Wilson, N. S., Zygouris-Coe, V., & Cardullo, V. (2014). Teacher Development, Support, and Training with the iPad. In S. Keengwe & M. Maxfield (Eds.), *Advancing Higher Education with Mobile Learning Technology: Cases*. Trends, and Inquiry Based Methods.

Wilson, N. S., Zygouris-Coe, V., & Cardullo, V. (2014). Trying to make sense of e-readers. *Journal of Reading Education*, *39*(3), 36–42.

Yoder, J. D., & Hochevar, C. M. (2005). Encouraging active learning can improve students' performance on examinations. *Teaching of Psychology*, *32*(2), 91–95. doi:10.1207/s15328023top3202_2

KEY TERMS AND DEFINITIONS

Active Learning: Any instructional method that engages students in the learning process.

App Smashing: Content created in one App, then transferred, and enhanced by a second App and sometimes a third, or fourth App and the final product is published for public consumption.

Emerging Technology: Tools, concepts and advancements utilized in diverse educational settings to serve a variety of education related purposes.

Flipped Classroom: A pedagogical model in which lecture and homework are reversed this model.

Project-Based Learning: An instructional model used to develop students' deep knowledge of subject matter through actively engaging students in exploring real-world problems and issues.

Second Screen: Any mobile device (e.g., tablet, smart phone, laptop) with wireless connectivity that can be used by the learner in addition to using other media devices.

Chapter 2
Educational Robotics as a Learning Tool for Promoting Rich Environments for Active Learning (REALs)

Amy Eguchi
Bloomfield College, USA

ABSTRACT

In our ever-changing society where new technological tools are being introduced into daily life more rapidly than ever before, more and more innovative and creative people are needed for the work of advancing technology. However, current educational practice in schools seems to be moving away from helping to educate our future innovative and creative workforce. With the extensive focus on assessments through standardized testing, the concern is raised that more and more teachers are forced to teach to the test. In this chapter, educational robotics is introduced as a transformational tool for learning, which promotes learning of computational thinking, coding, and engineering, all increasingly being viewed as critical ingredients of STEM learning in K-12 education. The purpose of this chapter is to highlight the importance of integrating educational robotics as a technological learning tool into K-12 curriculum to promote Rich Environments for Active Learning (REALs) to prepare students for the technology-driven future.

INTRODUCTION

The rapid pace of technological advancements enhanced by the interconnectedness brought on by the power of the Internet and social media has resulted in the 'flattening' of the world (Friedman, 2005). New technological tools are being introduced into our daily life more rapidly than

ever before. The introduction of new iProducts in almost every six months is in turn accelerating the development of similar products including other smartphones and tablet technologies. Creative project crowd-funding platforms, such as Kickstarter (http://www.kickstarter.com), Indiegogo (https://www.indiegogo.com/), and Quirky (https://www.quirky.com) are contributing to

DOI: 10.4018/978-1-4666-8363-1.ch002

the accelerated birth of innovative technological tools by providing essential funding directly from potential and/or interested consumers.

Among these various technological advancements, robotics technology has been highlighted in recent media reports. News headlines from major news sources, including the New York Times, CNN, Wall Street Journal, and BBC, featuring various robotic innovations, are a strong indication of how much popular attention robotics technology has garnered in recent years. When watching the Jetsons television program in the 1960s and 1980s, very few people might have believed that a humanoid robot, like Rosie, would become a reality in their lifetime. On June 5, 2014, Softbank Mobile, a Japanese company, in collaboration with Aldebaran Robotics, a French company, unveiled *Pepper*, the world's first personal humanoid robot. Costing less than US$2,000, Pepper is able to assist humans by reading and responding to human emotions (SoftBank Mobile Corp. & Aldebaran Robotics SAS, 2014). Prior to the introduction of Pepper, Amazon announced its plans for a drone delivery system and, in July 2014, asked the Federal Aviation Administration for permission for the drone use (Amazon.com, 2014). Google revealed the drone that they are developing and announced that they would also start drone delivery in December 2014 (A. Barr, Nicas, & Bensinger, 2014). Prior to the drone delivery plan, Google announced its acquisition of eight robotics companies, including Boston Dynamics, a Boston-based robotics company that produces robotics creations supported by the Department of Defense, and Schaft Inc., a Japanese robot venture start-up company (Ackerman, 2013). The Defense Advanced Research Projects Agency (DARPA), an agency of the US Department of Defense, held DARPA Robotics Challenge trial in December 2013, followed by its final in June 2015 [1]. Aldebaran Robotics' *NAO*, an autonomous and programmable humanoid robot, has been used in various educational settings including RoboCup Soccer league for the development of

algorithms for humanoid soccer and for the research of children with Autism. Moreover, iRobot Corporation, an American advanced technology company, introduced the popular room-cleaning robot, *Roomba*, in 2002, which has been sold in the market more than a decade already.

The world and its economy are changing at such a rapid pace that it is impossible to predict what the economy will look like even at the end of next week (Robinson, 2010). Despite all the dramatic changes that have taken place in the world, public education has maintained almost the same system since its introduction in the 19th century (Robinson, 2010). The majority of schools persist in trying to prepare students for the future by continuing what was done in the past (Robinson, 2010). More than 40 years ago Paulo Freire introduced his view of education, leading to the development of the critical pedagogy approach to education. In his book, Pedagogy of Oppressed, Freire argued that existing educational practice expects teachers to be narrators of facts and requires students "to memorize mechanically the narrated content" (Freire, 1994). In essence, students are turned into containers to be filled by the teacher. When using this *banking* approach to education (Freire, 1994), students are required to receive, memorize, and repeat knowledge and/or facts that are provided by their teachers. Freire argues, "The teacher talks about reality as if it were motionless, static, compartmentalized, and predictable. Or else he expounds on a topic completely alien to the existential experience of the students" (Freire, 1994, p.52). He continues:

...it is the people themselves who are filed away through the lack of creativity, transformation, and knowledge in this (at best) misguided system. For apart from inquiry apart from the praxis, individuals cannot be truly human. Knowledge emerges only through invention and re-invention, through the restless, impatient, continuing, hopeful inquiry, human beings pursue in the world, with the world, and with each other. (p.53)

In current society where more and more innovative and creative people are needed to help advance technology, how much has occurred due to educational reform efforts? With the extensive focus on assessments through standardized testing, the concern is raised that more and more teachers are forced to teach to the test in recent years. Interestingly, the same point was made in the mid-1990s by Grabinger, Dunlap and Duffield (Grabinger & Dunlap, 1995; Grabinger, Dunlap, & Duffield, 1997). They warned that simply having knowledge in a single domain and knowing how to use tools does not help individuals to stay effective and competitive in our increasingly complex society. Rather, learning to think critically, to analyze and synthesize information to solve interdisciplinary problems, and to work collaboratively and productively with others are important skills for participating effectively in society. They argue that students are not taught to acquire skills essential for effective thinking and reasoning (Grabinger & Dunlap, 1995). In the conventional educational setting, the authors observed teachers use examples and problems that are simplified and decontextualized, leading to inadequate understanding of the acquired knowledge, and an inability to effectively apply the knowledge to real situations. Students are often presented knowledge in conjunction with problems and examples that are not relevant to them and their needs and have no connection to their real life. Grabinger et al argue, "students are asked to solve problems that cause them to wonder: 'Why do I need to know this?'" (Grabinger & Dunlap, 1995, p.7). Because there is no connection between the knowledge acquired and their life, student learning becomes an exercise of merely memorizing facts transferred from their teachers. This becomes inert knowledge, "knowledge that cannot be applied to real problems and situations"(Grabinger & Dunlap, 1995, p7).

The concept of Rich Environments for Active Learning (REALs) was introduced by Grabinger et al as an important strategy for educational reform (Grabinger & Dunlap, 1995; Grabinger et al., 1997). REALs are comprehensive instructional frameworks that help educators develop pedagogical interventions to promote skill acquisition necessary for students to be effective in current society. This chapter aims to introduce educational robotics as a technological learning tool to promote REALs as a potentially effective way to change current education practices.

RICH ENVIRONMENTS FOR ACTIVE LEARNING (REALs)

In our rapidly changing world, knowledge and skills that students learn today can easily become outdated by the time that they are ready to use them in real life. Moreover, the knowledge and skills that were learned specifically connected to one situation rather than expanded to other contexts, making it difficult for students to in turn apply their learning to real life situations. Knowledge and skills are tools necessary for students to be effective citizens in society. Students need to 'retool' (Swanson *et al*, cited in (Grabinger et al., 1997), or adjust their knowledge and skills in order to solve new and modern problems. Grabinger et al emphasize that teaching and learning should occur in an environment where the problem-solving and challenge-meeting strategies that professionals use in real life are reflected in the process of student learning. They suggest that learners need to:

- Determine for themselves what issues need to be addressed when facing a new problem;
- Identify knowledge and skills they already possess that can be applied to the situation;
- Determine which skill and knowledge areas are deficient, and create learning plans to address those deficiencies;
- Apply what they know to problems that may change substantially from one moment to another; and

- Assess their performance and make changes in personal processes for use to meet subsequent challenges. (Grabinger et al., 1997, p.6).

It is crucial for learners to take an active role in the process of knowledge construction and the problem-solving processes. The core idea of rich environments for active learning (REALs) is to hold learners accountable by putting them in the "driver's seat of the learning process – involving them in the planning, controlling, and directing of learning activities and the application and assessment of learning processes and outcomes" (p.6). REALs utilize student-centered approach to learning that focuses on the development of life-long learning skills.

REALs have its foundation in constructivist learning theories (Grabinger & Dunlap, 1995; Grabinger et al., 1997). Constructivists emphasize three core characteristics of learning; 1) knowledge cannot be transmitted from one to the other simply by depositing the knowledge; 2) knowledge is constructed by an individual in personal ways; and 3) people construct knowledge through their interaction with environment and people around them, with social interaction. Jean Piaget, the founder of constructivism, emphasizes that:

[k]nowledge is not a commodity to be transmitted. Nor is it information to be delivered from one end, encoded, stored and reapplied at the other end. Instead, knowledge is experience, in the sense that it is actively constructed and reconstructed through direct interaction with the environment. (Ackermann, 1996, p.27)

Piaget argues that children's new knowledge is actively constructed from their interaction with their world, not by the mere transfer of knowledge from others. Piaget also emphasizes that children hold onto their worldviews with very good reasons that support their views, and they rarely abandon them simply because someone else tells them that those are wrong (Ackermann,

2001). Children construct new knowledge through their *own* experience. Children construct their knowledge best by manipulating artifacts. They need an *object to think*. What adults can do to facilitate knowledge construction is to "offer opportunities for children to engage in hands-on explorations that fuel the constructive process" (Ackermann, 2001, pp.1-2). Piaget explains that learning involves constructing new knowledge out of prior knowledge by manipulating artifacts and observing their behavior (Piaget, 1929, 1954). This process is crucial for children for constructing the new knowledge even if they end up reinventing the wheel (Ackermann, 2001) because *to know is to relate* (Ackermann, 1996).

When applying Piaget's constructivist theory to modern educational practice, Ackermann (2004) suggests that teaching should never be direct. Ideally children should not take in information that is simply presented to them. Rather, they need to interpret or translate *what they hear* into *what makes sense to them*, in relation to their prior knowledge and experience. In addition, knowledge is not simply information to be delivered. Instead, knowledge is the experience that children have through their interactions with their world including people and things around them. Their experiences provide the knowledge with meaning in relation to what is significant to children. Another important point that she makes is that the learning environment should let students explore according to their own interests rather than being forced to adhere to a teacher's or adult's agenda. As previously explained, Piaget emphasizes that children rarely let go of their own view of the world. When children construct new knowledge based on their interactions with the world and social exchanges, they establish good reasons to hold onto their views even when someone points out that their view is wrong. In an effective learning environment, children should be encouraged to explore, express and exchange their views, instead of a teacher or an adult telling them what is right or what to do to prove the *right* answer (Ackermann, 2004).

REALs aim to provide learning environments and activities that engage students in the collaborative process of constructing, modifying, and reconstructing their knowledge through their experiences and interaction with their world because learning is not a simple act of acquiring new knowledge, but requires continuous reconstruction and refinement of previously acquired knowledge (Grabinger & Dunlap, 1995; Grabinger et al., 1997). REALs encourage learners to participate in the development of their own learning thereby helping them develop skills and attitudes as well as construct knowledge that contributes to effective problem solving. Since it benefits learners to have many contextual links when they construct knowledge, REALs helps teachers to contextualize their teaching by providing as many possible links with other domains as possible, rather than simply presenting an abstract set of decontextualized knowledge and skills (Grabinger & Dunlap, 1995). Grabinger et al explain that REALs are comprehensive instructional frameworks that:

- Evolve from and are consistent with constructivist philosophies;
- Promote study and investigation within authentic (i.e. realistic, meaningful, relevant, complex, and information-rich) contexts;
- Encourage the growth of student responsibility, initiative, decision-making, and intentional learning;
- Cultivate an atmosphere of knowledge-building learning communities that utilize collaborative learning among students and teachers;
- Utilize dynamic, interdisciplinary, generative learning activities that promote high-level thinking process (i.e. analysis, synthesis, problem-solving, experimentation, creativity, and examination of topics from multiple perspectives) to help students integrate new knowledge with old knowledge and thereby create rich and complex knowledge structures; and

- Assess student progress in content and learning-to-learn through realistic tasks and performances. (Grabinger & Dunlap, 1995, p.10)

There are five critical attributes held by REALs that embody the characteristics of constructivism. They are 1) student responsibility and initiative; 2) dynamic, generative learning activities; 3) authentic learning contexts, 4) authentic assessment strategies, and 5) co-operative support (Grabinger & Dunlap, 1995; Grabinger et al., 1997).

Student Responsibility and Initiative

Student-centered learning contributes to the development of intentional and life-long learning skills including higher-order thinking skills to guide learning, reflect on consequences and inferences of actions, and observe and modify personal cognitive ability (Grabinger & Dunlap, 1995). Grabinger et al consider this attribute to be crucial because students need experiences to actively engage in the construction of their knowledge structures by taking responsibility and initiative for their learning. In REALs, through student directed activities, students learn to identity their own deficiencies, inquire about their knowledge base, and select and manage their learning (Grabinger et al., 1997). Intentional learning is purposeful learning with cognitive processes that see learning as "a goal rather than an accidental outcome" (Bereiter & Scardamalia, 1989, p.363), in which students learn skills in questioning, self-reflection and metacognition.

Dynamic, Generative Learning Activities

REALs require students to engage in generative learning. Generative learning emphasizes the active construction of knowledge – one of the important characteristics of constructivist learning. Grabinger et al emphasize that "students cannot construct or evolve their own learning without generating something through active involvement" (Grabinger & Dunlap, 1995, p. 19). With generative learning, students are required to take on the role of investigators and problem solvers. Generative learning expects students to be involved "deeply and constantly with creating solutions to authentic problems via the development and completion of projects" (Grabinger & Dunlap, 1995, p. 19).

Authentic Learning Contexts

REALs focus is on student learning within an authentic context. The tasks, activities and/or goals are authentic and promote their learning experiences in realistic settings, with problems relevant to the learners (Grabinger & Dunlap, 1995). Grabinger et al highlight that successful authentic learning happens when learners are involved in contextualized and realistic activities that promote realistic thinking, movement and emotions (Grabinger et al., 1997). They point out that authenticity is important because:

- Realistic problems provide more relevance to the needs and experiences that students have because the more realistic they are, the more connection students can make between what students are learning and problems and goals that they see everyday, which encourages them to take ownership of their learning;
- What students encounter during learning is authentic and reflect real world problems, it promotes deeper and richer, indexicalized and conditioned, knowledge structure among the students, which will help them to transfer their learning and knowledge to new situations;
- A team approach is essential for tackling realistic problems successfully, which leads to encouraging learners to share,

test, and refine their ideas. It promotes collaboration among learners. (Grabinger & Dunlap, 1995)

Authentic Assessment Strategies

The use of authentic assessment strategies to evaluate student performances is an important part of REALs. Assessments for REALs need to use various assessment tools, not only relying on simple testing. Some of the assessment tools for the authentic assessment include observations, various assignments, essays, journals, reports or logbooks, documentation of the process, and student presentations of their work and solutions.

Co-Operative Support

Grabinger et al consider co-operative support the most important attribute of REALs (Grabinger & Dunlap, 1995). While working collaboratively with others, students learn to become collective problem solvers by constructing their knowledge through discussions, sharing, negotiations, planning, revisions, testing of ideas, and establishing new perspectives. In addition, when learning co-operatively, students become willing to take on risks needed to solve complex and authentic problems (Grabinger & Dunlap, 1995). By working collaboratively, students can successfully solve problems that they would struggle with if attempting them individually (Grabinger et al., 1997). Grabinger et al (1995) also point out that, with co-operative problem solving learning, providing scaffolding is important. Because collaborative work skills are one of the crucial skills that students need to obtain in order to become successful members of society, REALs can provide important learning opportunities for students.

The following section first introduces educational robotics as a learning tool and then explains how it benefits students engaged in REALs learning.

EDUCATIONAL ROBOTICS (ROBOTICS IN EDUCATION)

Educational robotics or *Robotics in Education* (RiE) is the term widely used to describe the use of robotics as a learning tool in education. In recent years, robotics technology has become popular and accessible for both graduate and undergraduate students as well as for school age children (Cruz-Martin, Fernandez-Madrigal, Galindo, Gonzalez-Jimenez, & Stockmans-Daou, 2012; Mataric, 2004). Mataric (2004) emphasizes that robotics has "the potential to significantly impact the nature of engineering and science education at all levels, from K-12 to graduate school" (para 1). For school age children, unfortunately, most robotics activities have mainly been part of informal education, such as after school programs and summer camps (Benitti, 2012; Eguchi, 2007a; Sklar & Eguchi, 2004) even though it has the potential to make learning more effective in formal education. As several studies show, educational robotics benefits student learning STEM content areas such as physics, biology, geography, mathematics, science, electronics, and mechanical engineering, and as well as critical academic skills, such as writing, reading, research, creativity, collaboration, critical thinking, decision making, problem solving, and communication skills (Alimisis & Kynigos, 2009; Atmatzidou & Demetriadis, 2012; Benitti, 2012; Carbonaro, Rex, & Chambers, 2004; Elkind, 2008; Kolberg & Orlev, 2001; Miller, Nourbakhsh, & Sigwart, 2008; Nourbakhsh, Hamner, Crowley, & Wilkinson, 2004; Oppliger, 2002; Sklar & Eguchi, 2004; Sklar, Eguchi, & Johnson, 2002, 2003).

Hardware for Educational Robotics

Robotics technology as a learning tool for K-12 students has become more accessible because of recent technological advancements. Today's educational robotics kits provide users with a graphic-based programming environment, readily accessible for beginners, as well more advanced users who wish to program complex robotic behaviors. A typical educational robotics kit includes a programmable brick or controller, which functions as a robot's *brain*, different types of sensors, such as touch sensor, light sensor, ultrasonic (distance) sensor, rotation sensor, motors, wheels, and other parts needed to construct a robot. There are various robotics construction kits available on the market for educational use, range in price from a couple of hundred dollars to about a thousand dollars. Those kits include LEGO Mindstorms – NXT or EV3, LEGO WeDo kit both by LEGO; TETRIX by TETRIX Robotics; ROBO by The fischertechnik, a German company; OLLO and BIOLOID by Robotics, a Korean company, VEX Robotics Design System and VEX IQ by VEX Robotics, to name a few. In addition, there are many third party sensors and motors that can be controlled by kit controllers, which help to expand the kit robots that students already own. Starting with a robotics kit is ideal for younger students who want to continue learning with robotics since a kit generally comes with various expansion options that allow students to continue learning more advanced robotics with the same kit after they have acquired the basic knowledge and skills of robotics.

More advanced and older students can challenge themselves to construct a robot from scratch using a controller, motors, sensors, and other individually purchased components. The introduction of Arduino, an open-source single board microcontroller, much less expensive than robotics kits and accessible for use because of many online resources and publications to support Arduino robotics, has made it much easier for school age students to engage in do-it-yourself types of robotics projects (Figures 1 & 2). RaspberryPi and BeagleBone Black are credit-card size microprocessors/computers that can be used to control robotics projects. Although a controller itself cannot be directly connected with other necessary parts to create a robot, using Arduino with breadboard and different shields to build

Figure 1. Do-it-yourself type soccer robots created by Chinese students

Figure 2. Do-it-yourself type soccer robots created by Chinese students

a robotic creation is much easier than before. Ardiuno has produced several different types of boards available to the robotics makers depending on their needs, which makes it more powerful. BeagleBone.org has also developed cape plug-in boards that allow robotics developers to use BeagleBone Black with other components. In addition, starter kits using controllers have become available in recent years. Arduino sells an Arduino Robot kit, developed in collaboration with Complubot, a Spanish educational organization, that offers a base for robotics with Arduino. Bot'n Roll, another Arduino based robotics kit, manufactured by SAR, a Portuguese company, provides all necessary parts to build a robot with soldering. BrickPi by Dexter Industries makes it possible to create robots using the RaspberryPi. BrickPi allows RaspberryPi to communicate with LEGO Mindstorms NXT motors and sensors, which opens up a door for NXT users to advance their robotics learning to the next level. The development of other affordable tools, such as 3D printers and laser cutters are now accessible to young developers for use with the do-it-yourself/ originally designed robotics projects.

Programming with Educational Robotics

Programming levels can range from very basic to advanced. Most robotics kits include a graphic-based programming software suitable for younger students and beginner programmers. Graphic-based programming environments utilize simple *drag & drop* icons to create a code. Young students who can use a mouse to move blocks on a computer screen can create a codes to control the robots created with the kit. The icons make it easy to teach programing, basic logical thinking, and computational thinking skills to young and old beginners.

Robotics kits not only provide specific graphic-based programming environments but also allow users to move onto text-coding environments. For example, LEGO Mindstorms users can progress to text-coding by transitioning to the ROBOTC, a C-based programming language developed by Carnegie Mellon Robotics Academy, or NCQ, C++, C#, JAVA etc. LabView, which is originally for developers for industries, is also available for LEGO Mindstorms users. The fischertechnik ROBO can be controlled with C languages, Visual Basic, Delphi etc. VEX uses a C-based language and can be programmed with easyC or ROBOTC. Older and/or more advanced students with do-it-yourself type robotics using controllers such as Arduino, RaspberryPi, and BeagleBone Black, use text-coding languages. For example, Arduino is controlled by a C-based programming language using Arduino IDE. RaspberryPi for robotics is usually programmed with Python. Educational robotics is an ideal learning tool not only in K-12 settings but also in higher education classrooms because it provides various programming options suitable for novices to advanced/pre-professionals.

Theoretical Background: Constructionism Theory

The concept of using robotics in education arose from the constructionism theory developed by Seymour Papert, a student of Piaget. Constructionism is a theory of learning that Papert developed from Piaget's constructivism theory of epistemology – theory of knowledge. Papert explains:

Constructionism – the N word as opposed to the V word – shares constructivism's connotation of learning as "building knowledge structures" irrespective of the circumstances of the learning. It then adds the idea that this happens especially felicitously in a context where the leaner is con-

sciously engaged in constructing a public entity, whether it's a sand castle on the beach or a theory of the universe. (Papert & Harel, 1991, p.27)

Although both Piaget and Papert highlight that knowledge is actively constructed by children through interactions with their world, there is a slight difference between the two theories. While Piaget's constructivism focuses on the construction of knowledge in one's head, Papert's constructionism has the particular focus on the knowledge constructions that happen in the real world supporting those in the head (Rogers & Portsmore, 2004). In the real world children can show what is physically constructed with their friends, teachers and families, which can then be discussed, examined, probed, and admired, thereby supporting the construction of knowledge from the experience *in their head*. The physical experience in the real world assures that the constructionist learning sticks with the children. Moreover the continuous process of constructionist learning, by building, rebuilding, and revising using physical materials, can bring more learning experiences that will be built upon, revised or reconstructed using previously constructed knowledge (Papert, 1993). In other words, Papert considers the externalization of our inner feelings and ideas as an important part of the knowledge construction (Ash & Kluger-Bell, 2000). By expressing ideas in some tangible form, as we communicate with one another, we are turning our ideas into a sharable form. This, in turn, helps us shape and sharpen our ideas.

When using the constructionism approach, the child becomes the central player of the construction of his own knowledge. It is important that the construction of knowledge happens with the child's initiative. In order for children to have the opportunity for self-exploration, an effective teacher will support their reinvention or rediscovery of the *wheel*. In the constructionist learning environment effective learning happens when there is less direct instruction or teaching involved and more student-initiated exploration is

encouraged and supported. Papert (1993) further explains:

Constructionism is one of a family of educational philosophies that denies this "obvious truth [teach better]." It does not call in question the value of instruction as such. ... Constructionist attitude to teaching is not at all dismissive because it is minimalist – the goal is to teach in such a way as to produce the most learning for the least teaching. (p.139)

In this sense, constructionism provides strategies for education as Bers points out (Rogers & Portsmore, 2004). Constructionism offers the framework for developing the learning environment that supports meaningful learning in which "children and adults are engaged in learning by making, creating, programming, discovering and designing their own *object to think with* in a playful manner" (p.15). Since the focus of the constructionist learning approach is *learning through making* or *learning by design,* constructionism directs our attention to how our ideas are transformed from *our head* into *the real world* by expressing them through different media, in particular contexts, and how they are reshaped and reconstructed by individual minds (Ash & Kluger-Bell, 2000). The learning environment supporting a constructionist approach should be organized in such a way that encourages a child's conversation with his own representations, artifacts or *object to think*. The focus is on the individual child's understanding and view of the world around her. The theory of constructionism became real through the creation of Logo, a computer programming language for children, which became the base of the development of the *Programmable Brick* for the LEGO Mindstorms (Martin, Mikhak, Resnick, Silverman, & Berg, 2000). Educational robotics provides a manipulative that a child can not only think with but also bring her abstract idea and understanding of her world in her *head* into *the real world*.

EDUCATIONAL ROBOTICS AS LEARNING TOOL IN REALS

Educational robotics is a learning tool, like computers and tablets, which enhances student learning within the REALs framework.

Student Responsibility and Initiative: Student-Centered to Learner-Centered Approach

Student-centered learning promotes students' responsibility and their taking the initiative in directing their own learning. Some consider that bringing technologies into a classroom contributes to effective student learning. Papert argues that unfortunately, computer-aided instruction in schools simply means making the computer teach or the computer is used to program children (Papert, 1993). According to Papert's constructionist approach, children come to the center of their learning. They are the agents who *program* the computer and robots, not the entity to be programmed. By taking the initiative to program an object, children acquire "a sense of mastery over a piece of the most modern and powerful technology" (p.5). Moreover, technology, specifically educational robotics, helps children acquire in-depth knowledge and ideas in science, mathematics, engineering and the art of intellectual model building. Papert, following Piaget's model, considers children to be the "builders of their own intellectual structures" (p.7). Papert describes children as naturally gifted learners who acquire a vast quantity of knowledge through a process that he calls *Piagetian learning*, or *learning without being taught*. This process begins long before children attend school. He believes that technologies can become powerful learning tools when they are used to support *Piagetian learning*. Ideally the exploration of children's ideas and curiosity are encouraged and the design and construction of projects that are personally meaningful and relevant to children's lives are supported (Papert,

1993). When children are encouraged to explore their ideas and curiosity, they are eager to work on a project that is relevant to them because they are interested. When such learning happens, the project gains personal meaning to the students. In this sense, students will take initiative and assume responsibility for their learning because their ideas are encouraged, shared, and developed.

To give students responsibility and initiative with their learning, traditional ways of *teaching* in which teachers provide information and knowledge to students following rigidly set curriculum, has to change. REALs teachers are facilitators who encourage student-driven learning. In successful educational robotics classrooms, instead of lecturing, the teacher provides *on-demand* technical and content knowledge in response to the needs of the students. It is crucial that teachers develop new types of learning communities "where peer interaction is supported and the development of different roles [of both students and the teacher] and forms of participation in the classroom culture is encouraged" (Bers, 2008, p.20).

As seen in REALs learning, students are also required to be active participants of the learning community. Over the past decade of experience with teaching educational robotics, I have witnessed a greater number of students who come to the classroom expecting a teacher to *teach* them – directly telling them what to do and what is right because of the traditional education that they experience in school. Students approach learning with a firm belief that they must have the *right* and the *only* answer. Typical questions that I am asked while teaching educational robotics are, "Is it right?", "Can you make sure this is correct?", and "You should tell me how to do it because you are the teacher." These questions are posed even before testing their program on a robot. Students are afraid of making mistakes because they are accustomed to traditional classroom settings. Their educational experiences have been designed to help them pass standardized tests. Teachers expect their students to do the work *right*. This does not help students because they do not experience the construction of knowledge with them taking the lead in their learning. The experience of learning with educational robotics forces students to change their view of teaching and learning. What makes them confused is that, with educational robotics as well as other hands-on, student-centered projects, there usually is no one *right* answer (Rogers & Portsmore, 2004). Students are, instead, encouraged to find their own learning path to arrive at their own best solution.

A student-centered approach confuses many teachers as well. When starting educational robotics lessons, teachers often feel uncomfortable with not having one *right* answer because there are in truth multiple ways of tackling and solving a problem. In general, teachers prefer to know all the answers before they start teaching. This is the conventional expectation of teaching. With the student-centered educational robotics, learning environment, teachers often face the situation where they do not know the answer to the questions that students pose. During educational robotics teacher training sessions, teachers often insist that they need to know all the answers so that they can provide the right answers to their students. This is very similar to the questions that students tend to ask. Not knowing the *right* answer makes both teachers and students feel uncomfortable, however, this can be a wonderful learning opportunity for both of them. As Rogers and Portsmore point out, effective "student learning comes from discussion and the teacher asking penetrating questions" (Rogers & Portsmore, 2004, p.23). With educational robotics, and many of new and emerging technologies, there will be many unknowns for teachers. They need to prepare themselves to be good facilitators in order to help students find solutions or answers to the situation and/or problems. We are in an era of rapid technological advancements, a time when it is impossible for teachers to know everything. Teachers should take advantage of the opportunity to learn from the educational experience together

with their students. Since children are often tech-experts, teachers should encourage students to teach to each other as well as teachers. With REALs, teachers are not the ones providing all the answers. Rather, teachers are exploring with the students in order to understand their thinking and learning processes, encouraging them to take initiative with their learning. Instead of *student-centered*, we should call the approach *learner-centered*, to include both teachers and students as learners.

With learner-centered educational robotics, not only the role of the teacher changes, but also that of students. Students are in the center of their learning. They drive the inquiry and are responsible for their own learning. Students are allowed to move around freely in the classroom, interacting with and talking to each other. There should be no students sitting quietly in their seats. Teachers and students learn together through *chaos* and excitement (Rogers, 2008). With educational robotics projects, students work in groups and they are encouraged to exchange their ideas, solve problems and come up with solutions together. Typically, over several sessions, groups progress at different rates. The needs of each group starts to vary, making it difficult for a teacher to provide necessary help to *all* students and groups simultaneously. There may be times when one group needs help with basic programming, while another is asking more complicated questions. Other students might face some difficulties with their robot construction, a robot's battery might be dead and need replacing, and any number of other problems may arise. The teacher needs to multi-task as well as encourage students to help and teach each other. Here, another paradigm shift has to occur, both for the teacher and students. The teacher needs to accept that she is not the only teacher in the class. As some students advance, they can become teacher-aids. Advanced students can help other students by providing much needed support. This helps the establishment of teacher-student trust, encouraging students to develop self-esteem. True collaboration may not spontaneously occur with the initiative of students. The teacher needs to identify those who can provide help, then ask or even require them to help others. Usually, students are very excited to help their peers. Once the expectation that students assist one another is conveyed and practiced, mutual help among students becomes a natural habit. Advanced students learn by teaching. In order to teach, they need to have established a strong foundation of knowledge. Even if the foundation has not been strongly established, the experience of teaching others helps students identify and address their weaknesses. The learner-centered educational robotics classroom environment has a tendency to appear very *chaotic* to those who are new to this kind of learning situation. However, this learning environment benefits both teachers and students, and promotes effective knowledge construction experiences among students.

Dynamic, Generative Learning Activities: Project-Based/Inquiry-Based Learning Approach

REALs require students to actively engage in generating a final project through their involvement (generative learning). Educational robotics is a hands-on learning tool that supports students as they construct knowledge and skills through the act of making. The types of pedagogical approaches for dynamic, generative learning that make learning with educational robotics most effective are project- and inquiry-based approaches. Project-based and inquiry-based learning are receiving more attention in K-12 science education. These classrooms focus on creating a student-centered learning environment and *learning by doing*. Educational robotics also emphasizes the importance of the investigation by self-directed inquiry and collaboration among peers (Hmelo-Silver, Duncan, & Chinn, 2007).

The key elements of project-based learning are inquiry, student-directed or student-driven, academic content, problem solving, and collaboration. These elements are similar to what is found in inquiry-based learning settings. With both approaches, the focus is on a project being created by student-driven inquiry. The projects require students to be directly involved in the planning of the process of investigations and then solving the problems set by their inquiry. This process makes projects personally meaningful for students – one of the essential elements for creating the constructionist learning and REALs.

Simply using educational robotics learning tools in a classroom does not ensure a meaningful learning experience. If students are only following lessons and instructions provided by a teacher, personally meaningful student-centered learning will not occur. By setting up the project-/inquiry-based learning environment with student-driven inquiry, and engaging students in their own projects with educational robotics, students' enthusiasm for learning grows.

Following the project design process can ensure students' deep and constant engagement in learning through development and revisions of solutions to the problems that they face during student-driven educational robotics projects. There are several sets of similar processes that can benefit the learning process, such as the engineering process, project-based learning process, and Learning by Design process. The project-based learning process includes the following five-steps: (1) engagement, (2) exploration, (3) investigation, (4) creation, and (5) sharing (Carbonaro et al., 2004). With Learning by Design, the focus is on authenticity, namely, 1) finding a task based in real world applications, 2) providing rich and varied feedback, 3) carrying discussions and collaboration, 4) experimenting and exploring, and 5) reflecting (Han & Bhattacharya, 2001). The engineering design process (cycle) is similar to both project-based learning and Learning by

Design processes. Bers (2000), and Rogers and Portsmore (2004) recommend the following engineering design cycles for educational robotics projects.

1. Identify problems or challenges
2. Brainstorm and decide the best possible solution
3. Create or construct a prototype
4. Test and evaluate the prototype
5. Redesign based on the feedback from the test and evaluation
6. Communicate and share the results (disseminate the solution at the end)

During the process of working on a project, the design cycle should be repeated over and over again until the result is satisfactory to the group. Step 6 should lead to the initial step of defining new problems or challenges and move naturally onto the subsequent steps to improve upon the first result. Rogers and Portsmore (2004) argue that, in general, identification of a problem for a project, redesign of the prototype and communication, and sharing of the results/dissemination of the solution are neglected and less valued steps when doing projects in traditional classroom settings. However, real scientists and roboticists use similar reiterative processes in the real world. These steps do make a difference between success and failure in the real world (Rogers & Portsmore, 2004). In other words, these are valuable steps not only for successful educational robotics projects but also for obtaining important skills needed for future success in life. By following the engineering design steps, we can ensure the success of desired knowledge construction among students through generative learning with educational robotics.

Authentic Learning Contexts

Constructionists and constructivists take the view that decontextualized learning that does not provide real-world tasks and activities will not lead students to learn future applications of their learning in the real world. Effective REALs must involve contextualized and realistic activities that are relevant to students, which promote construction of knowledge and skills that can be applied in the real world.

Educational robotics is a learning tool that involves construction and programming of robotics projects, bringing authentic learning contexts to its learners. Learning with robots is especially beneficial when dealing with abstract concepts. Educational robotics offers a concrete and tangible way to understand abstract concepts and ideas. In REALs with educational robotics, students use hands-on manipulatives that give instant feedback to the learners (Rogers & Portsmore, 2004). Bers explains using examples of students learning with educational robotics:

By adding gears to their machines, they explore the mathematical concept of ratio. By programming movement of these mechanical parts they start to explore the concepts of cause and effect, programming loops, and variables in a concrete and fun manner. By including sensors to detect input from the world, such as light or touch, they encounter the concept of feedback. (Bers, 2008, p.21-22)

Students are able to receive instant and unequivocal feedback on whether their program was successful or not when using robots. The feedback provides students with opportunities to examine, understand, and evaluate their work, thereby constructing new knowledge for the given real world context. Students have the opportunity to revise their project or strategy and try out new iterations. The students can continue polishing and improving their project as they repeat the engineering design process.

Atmatzidou, Markelis and Demitridis (2008) observed that students who encountered difficulty with comprehending basic programming concepts, such as variables, conditions, and loop structures, while programming on a computer screen, became motivated and interested in solving the same problems when using educational robotics. Learning with educational robotics led students to accomplish notably higher and better learning outcomes. Atmatzidou et al concluded that student learning was reinforced because of the immediate feedback that a robot could provide after testing a program (Atmatzidou et al., 2008). In addition, because the robotics projects are student-lead and contextualized with a real world setting, the knowledge constructed through their work on the projects is meaningful to each student and easily applicable to other real-life situations.

Authentic Assessment Strategies

REALs require the use of authentic assessment strategies to evaluate student performances, not just with simple testing, but also with various other assessment tools. It can be challenging to assess student learning in REALs especially with educational robotics projects. Educational robotics often brings an element of chaos and excitement into the classroom. While engaged in their work, students are constantly moving around and discussing with peers how to improve their robotic inventions. It may be difficult for a teacher to fully understand what is happening in all parts of the classroom. As students work on their robotics projects they encounter different problems and challenges, leading them to ask one another, "Why doesn't this program work?", "Why isn't the robot going straight?" or "How can I make the robot do what I want?" These simple questions spark students to engage in serious logical thinking processes, leading to a deeper understanding of the problem and thought-provoking discussions among students. However, the conversations also tend to be *invisible* to teachers in the chaos of the classroom.

To make the invisible *visible*, documentation of their engineering process plays an important role in robotics learning. With educational robotics, it becomes important to encourage self-reflective

practices through documentation following the Reggio Emilia approach (Rogers & Portsmore, 2004). The Reggio Emilia approach considers documentation as a collection of a broad range of artifacts, from videos, tape recordings, written notes, graphics, and drawings, which are produced and used during the process of completing a project (Rinaldi, 2001). Through documentation, both by students and teachers, the learning path becomes clear and visible (Eguchi, 2007a). Documentation makes the nature of the learning processes and strategies used by each child visible, which can be shared among the learners—students and teachers. Because it makes student learning process and strategies sharable, documentation not only helps teachers to assess students' work but also allows students to read, revisit, and revise their practice in order to better their project results.

Bers (Rogers & Portsmore, 2004) has a number of suggestions for the types of documentation to be created by students. Students are encouraged to perform self-reflection to gain a deeper understanding and awareness of how their knowledge is constructed. Since the focus of constructionism is more on student's learning than teaching, Bers emphasizes that "the tools of documentation should be put in the hands of children, who can assume responsibility for documenting their own learning process" (p.28). As Duckworth (2005) points out, sharing their own learning with others helps students make sense of their own process of constructing knowledge and makes learning *visible* to others. However, most importantly, it makes their learning *visible* to themselves.

One of the best approaches to documentation with educational robotics projects involves the use of a design journal, similar to what engineers or software developers do with their work (Rogers & Portsmore, 2004). Design journals can be created with traditional pencil and paper approach, computer, or using an online documentation tool, such as wiki, Google drive tools or Google sites, or any tools available for the K-12 learning community. Design journals should encourage the use of the steps in the engineering design cycle process when students document their learning experience. Students should take the initiative when selecting the materials to be included in their journals, from pictures of robots, drawings of the design (prototypes to final version), and screen shots of programs, as well as written reflections of their learning. The process of developing the design journal can provide many opportunities for sharing students' ideas, and discussing details of the implementation of their ideas as common practice in constructionist learning environments (Rogers & Portsmore, 2004). As part of a design journal, video recording can be useful for recording student projects. Carbonaro, *et al.* (2004) used video recording as part of their assessment and evaluation process with an educational robotics project-based learning. They reported that it appeared to be the most valuable element for both the teacher and students. The video recording provided a feedback mechanism for students, which helped them assess their own project. In addition, because students needed to publicly explain various elements of their problem solving process, it reinforced students to further and more fully understand their learning. Robotics students in my class discovered that video recordings of robot's movement helped them more carefully analyze the accuracy of their programs, leading to more efficient debugging of problems. Multiple iterations and revisions are expected and desired in the process of students' robotics projects. The design journal is a great tool for keeping all updates and changes in one place, accessible for both students and teachers to reflect on their learning during and after the process.

Co-Operative Support

REALs place an emphasis on the importance of collaborative learning. Most educational robotics project-based learning involves students working in small groups. Unlike traditional computer instruction in which typically one student works on one computer or two students share a computer but little collaboration is encouraged, educational robotics projects emphasize and value collaboration among students. When working in groups, students are excited and motivated to share their ideas, engage in collaborative decision-making, provide constructive criticism, and acquire communication skills (D. Barr, Harrison, & Conery, 2011; Berns, Braun, Hillenbrand, & Luksch, 2005; Eguchi, 2007b). In addition, when students were engaged in team-based/project-based robotics learning, there was measurable improvement among students with low-esteem in their technology capacity, teamwork skills, and communication skills (D. Barr et al., 2011). A collaborative learning environment promotes student learning in the zone of proximal development (ZPD).

The zone of proximal development (ZPD), introduced by Vygotsky, is an important concept of constructivist learning (Vygotsky, 1978). Vygotsky believes that by interacting with peers, students can develop skills and strategies up to a level that they could not develop otherwise. Vygotsky (1978) describes ZPD as:

the distance between the actual developmental level as determined by independent problem solving and the level of potential development as determined through problem solving under adult guidance, or in collaboration with more capable peers. (p.86)

He suggests that with cooperative learning, students who are less competent can develop skills and knowledge with the help of more skillful peers within ZPD.

For successful inquiry-/project-based learning to occur, especially with inexperienced students, providing scaffolding becomes very important (Han & Bhattacharya, 2001). Scaffolding can provide students opportunities to "engage in complex tasks that would otherwise be beyond their current abilities" (Hmelo-Silver et al., 2007, p.100). In the scaffolded learning environment, a teacher's role as a facilitator and mentor becomes essential. Although it is crucial to provide learning opportunities that are open and welcoming for students to create and design technological projects following their interests and ideas, students, especially young children who have big ideas, sometimes get lost in their own ideas because they might not have the ability to make their big idea happen (Rogers & Portsmore, 2004). They may not be able to plan steps necessary to successfully execute their project and become frustrated. By providing coaching, modeling, guidance, and structuring tasks, the teacher pushes the students to think more deeply. The role of the teacher should be to provide support for students as they become effective information-seekers and problem-solvers, as well as expert at finding help and necessary resources for themselves (Bers, 2008; Hmelo-Silver et al., 2007). To become a good problem-solver with robotics, you need to be a good observer and logical thinker. Good observers can observe their robot closely to identify possible causes for the robot not functioning the way it was planned or programmed. Good logical thinkers can break down their observation into logical steps in order to more easily recognize the actual cause of the malfunction through testing each possible cause one by one. These are skills that cannot be obtained from a textbook or are not something that they can come up with by themselves. These are skills that they can learn from watching someone doing it or from their experience with engaging in the activity. The scaffolded learning environment can provide these types of learning opportunities for students.

EDUCATIONAL ROBOTICS AS TRANSDISCIPLINARY APPROACH IN REALS

Educational robotics is a learning tool that enhances student learning in REALs with a project-/inquiry-based learning approach. It is an effective learning tool not only for teaching a wide range of subject knowledge but also the skills necessary for students to be successful in future technology-driven society.

Several educational movements in recent years have encouraged educational renovation and innovation, such as the introduction of K-12 coding, movements to integrate computational thinking and engineering education in K-12 education, and the maker movement. During the Computer Science Education Week in December 2013, the Hour of Code, an initiative to bring coding into classrooms around the world, was launched. Its creator, Code.org, reported that during the week of December 9th to 15th, 15 million students from 170 countries participated in coding activities. One in five U.S. students participated in the Hour of Code, and more girls in U.S. schools participated in computer science through the Hour of Code than in all of the past 70 years (Code.org, 2013). The initiative to integrate coding in primary and secondary education had begun earlier in the United Kingdom. In the United Kingdom, a new curriculum framework published in 2013 emphasized coding and engineering design (The United Kingdom Department of Education, 2013). It reported, that every primary school student should have the opportunity to explore the creative side of computing through activities such as writing computer programs (such as Scratch and Kodu - programming environment geared toward young students). At secondary school every student should have the opportunity to work with microcontrollers and simple robotics, build web-based systems, and/or similar activities. (The Royal Society - Education Section, 2012,)

Integrating computational thinking in primary and secondary education curriculum is another movement that encourages K-12 coding. Computational thinking is a problem-solving method that uses techniques typically practiced by computer scientists. Computational thinking is viewed as an important element of STEM learning in primary and secondary education (Grover, 2011). Since modern economies are profoundly influenced by technology-related industries, acquiring computational thinking is crucial for the success of the next generation of students. Engineering education has become an important focus of the proponents of K-12 STEM education. "Engineering in K-12 Education: Understanding the Status and Improving the Prospects" (published in 2009) emphasizes the importance of integrating engineering education into primary and secondary education curriculum (Katehi, Pearson, Feder, Committee on K-12 Engineering Education, & National Academy of Engineering and National Research Council, 2009). The report suggests that engineering education enhances students' learning in STEM subjects, as well as their awareness and willingness to pursue careers in the field of engineering. In addition, integration of engineering into STEM curriculum will increase the technological literacy of students.

The maker movement has contributed to bringing about innovative change and encouraging creativity in schools. K-12 coding, computational thinking, engineering and understanding of STEM fields are integral parts of *making*. Maker Faire, an annual event for *makers*, launched in 2006 by Make Magazine, has spread around the world, inspiring school-age makers to actively participate in the act of making. The White House has announced plans to host their own Maker Faire in the near future (Kalil & Miller, 2014). Maker Education Initiative (http://www.makered.org/) is a non-profit organization formed "to create more opportunities for young people to develop confidence, creativity, and spark an interest in science, technology, engineering, math, the arts, and learning as a whole through making" (Maker Education Initiative, n.a., para 1).

The focus on STEM education as critical to improving the U.S. economy has been widely discussed in the field of education as well as in industries. STEM education is commonly understood as an educational approach that integrates Science, Technology, Engineering and Mathematics (Gerlach, 2012). A successfully educated STEM workforce for the future requires a transdisciplinary approach to teaching of STEM knowledge and skills. As students integrate STEM academic concepts (not just one of four subjects in isolation) and real-world lessons, they will then learn to apply STEM knowledge in a context that links school, community, work, and the global enterprise (Tsupros, N., Kohler, R., & Hallinen, J. cited in Gerlach, 2012). Educational robotics is an effective learning tool for project-/inquiry-based learning where STEM, coding, computer thinking and engineering skills are all integrated into one project. Robotics provides opportunities for students to explore how technology works in real life, *all with one tool* through the act of making.

Educational robotics is a technological tool that provides students with opportunities for them to stop, question, and think deeply about technology. In the process of designing, constructing, programming and documenting autonomous robots, students learn how technology works. Moreover it provides them with opportunities to apply the skills and content knowledge learned in school in a meaningful and exciting way through authentic projects. Educational robotics is a robust *hands-on mind-on* learning tool for integrating not only STEM but also many other disciplines, including literacy, social studies, dance, music and art, while giving students the opportunity to find new ways to work together to foster collaboration skills, express themselves using the technological tool, problem-solve, and think critically and innovatively. Most importantly, educational robotics provides a fun and exciting REALs learning environment because of its hands-on nature and the integration of technology. The engaging learning environment created with projects of their interests motivates students to learn whatever skills and knowledge needed for them to accomplish their goals in order to complete the projects.

The following section provides some examples of the transdisciplinary integration of various subjects including STEM, coding, computational thinking and engineering skills as students work to learn how technology works through robotics projects.

WaterBotics (http://waterbotics.org/)

WaterBotics is an NSF funded underwater robotic curriculum targeting middle and high school students. The curriculum was developed by the Stevens Center for Innovation in Engineering & Science Education at Stevens Institute of Technology. The WaterBotics program provides hands-on experiences for participating students to learn engineering design and STEM concepts, while using information technology tools to increase awareness and interest in engineering and IT careers. The curriculum requires students to work collaboratively in small groups as they design, construct, test, and redesign their underwater robots using the engineering design cycle. The robotics tool for the curriculum is LEGO Mindstorms NXT kits and other LEGO and non-LEGO components for the construction of the underwater robots. The goal is to build an underwater robot that navigates underwater as it completes different missions. The curriculum provides small daily tasks of increasing complexity. Students use Mindstorms software to program a remote controller built with an NXT brick to control the robots as they maneuver under water. The WaterBotics curriculum covers various standards including the National Science Education standards, International Technology and Engineering Association (ITEEA) Technological Literacy Standards, and the International Society for Technology in Education (ISTE) National Educational Technology Standards.[2] The curriculum also emphasizes the engineering design process (1. design task; 2. brainstorm; 3. design; 4. build; 5. test; 6. redesign; and 7. share), an important element of the engineering thinking process. From the author's experience when participating in the teacher training workshop provided by the project, the WaterBotics program has the potential to enhance students' learning of computational

thinking skills defined by ISTE and CSTA (International Society for Technology in Education (ISTE) & Computer Sciene Teachers Association (CSTA), 2012), including confidence in dealing with complexity, persistence when working with difficult problems, ability to deal with open-ended problems, and ability to communicate and work with others to achieve a common goal or solution. Students also learn up-to-date underwater robotics technology by watching various videos and visiting research facilities. Since the curriculum provides problems with real-life scenarios, students have an opportunity to apply science concepts they learned in class, such as buoyancy, weight and mass, to real-life settings, which helps them construct and deepen their knowledge.

The WaterBotics program has reported positive impacts on student learning of science concepts and programming knowledge, based on a state-wide New Jersey program with more than 2,600 participating middle and high school students during the period of 2006 to 2009 (McGrath, Lowes, Sayres, & Lin, 2008, 2009).

RoboParty (http://www. roboparty.org/en/)

RoboParty is an educational robotics camp developed and organized at Universidade do Minho in Guimarães Portugal, by Professor A. Fernando Ribeiro, and his students and staff from the institution's Industrial Electronics department. It is a three-day camp held on campus for school age children, which provides student learning in electronics, mechanical engineering and programming, while participating in various cultural and sports activities. Three students with one teacher or mentor participate as a group. The teacher/mentor is expected to learn with his students side by side following the RoboParty curriculum. Each team receives one Bot'n Roll One A, an Arduino based robotics kit. The kit comes with one Arduino based controller board with all the necessary connection ports printed on the board

(Figures 3 and 4). The kit requires soldering of all necessary kit components, including motors and sensors, to complete the circuit. Students learn electronics and mechanical design through the hands-on, trial and error experience of building. Once the robot is built (Figure 4), the students learn C-based programming using Arduino IDE.

The curriculum provides three different final challenges that the students may attempt to solve: 1. pursuing competition (a line following race), 2. obstacle competition (maze with walls), and 3. dance competition (free robotics dance to music). Students can decide which challenge to attempt. The challenges provide students with a real-life setting in which they learn to program by developing algorithms to tackle the challenge. On the final day, the teams compete in each challenge and showcase their robotic creations and algorithms. According to the preliminary study conducted in 2011, participating students gave very positive feedback and showed an increased interest in engineering (Soares, Leão, Santos, Ribeiro, & Lopes, 2011). In addition, students indicated that they had positive learning experiences while working as a team, communicating their process and product, managing disagreements and engaging in productive decision-making.

Artbotics (http://artbotics. cs.uml.edu)

The Artbotics program, another NSF funded project, developed at University of Massachusetts Lowell (Martin, Kim, Silka, & Yanco, 2007; Yanco, Kim, Martin, & Silka, 2006) uses a project-based approach for introducing computing as students create interactive, kinetic sculptures. The program aims to broaden student participation in computing by reaching out to women and minorities as well as people who might not have previously expressed an interest in computer science (Yanco et al., 2006). It also aims to broaden the understanding that computing can be integrated into many different disciplines and used in a variety of ways. The program is available for various age levels, including middle school, high school, and

Figure 3. Bot'n Roll Robot Kit

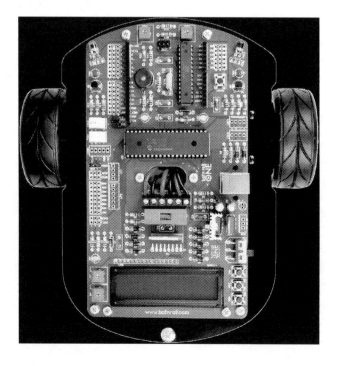

Figure 4. Bot'n Roll Robot Kit

college. Students can use a variety of technologies, including the Super Cricket, LEGO Mindstorms, and Arduino to create Artbotics projects. The program promotes STEAM (science, technology, engineering, art, and mathematics) education through the integration of art in STEM. It provides positive, realistic experiences in teamwork through the art project's design and programming process.

RoboCupJunior (http://robocupjunior.org)

RoboCupJunior (RCJ) is an educational robotics initiative that promotes STEM learning, computing, computational thinking and engineering skills, while working on teams, with hands-on, project-based and goal-oriented learning through an educational robotics competition. RCJ is open to all children up to 19 years of age. RCJ has three leagues – soccer, rescue and dance (Figures 5-7),

designed to attract and motivate students to pursue robotics. Since the challenges of each league remain relatively unchanged from year to year, student learning is scaffolded, allowing students to continuously develop and refine their solutions as they grow and expand their skills and knowledge over time. RCJ is committed to the *education* of young robotics scientists rather than a pure focus on competition. All three Junior leagues emphasize both the cooperative and collaborative nature of engineering design, programming and building in a team setting (Sklar & Eguchi, 2004). Since its launch in 2000, RCJ has grown to attract participating teams from many countries and regions from around the world (Eguchi, Hughes, Stocker, Shen, & Chikuma, 2012). Each year there are more than 40 countries participating in RCJ initiatives. The annual RoboCupJunior World Championship attracts more than 250 teams from participating countries. In a study conducted with the U.S.

Figure 5. RoboCupJunior soccer robots (Photographer Albert van Breemen)

Figure 6. RoboCupJunior dance robot (Photographer Albert van Breemen)

Figure 7. RoboCupJunior rescue robot (Photographer Albert van Breemen)

teams participating in the RoboCupJunior World Championship of 2013, participating students provided very positive feedback on their learning of STEM concepts, computational thinking and engineering skills as well as learning of soft skills including communication, collaboration, presentation skills, learning to be patient, and not giving up (persistence) (Eguchi, 2014).

CONCLUSION

There have been increasing concerns that the pressure of preparing students for standardized testing has changed teaching practices in schools. Honey and Kanter (2013) urge us:

Today, science, at the elementary level, is taught for less than three hours a week. There is a growing body of evidence indicating that grade-level, high-stake testing is heavily biasing the curriculum toward the teaching of tested subjects and away from less-frequently tested subjects such as science. Further, when science is given time during the school week, students are much more likely to be memorizing information presented in textbooks and answering questions at the end of the chapter than engaging in the kind of real-world problem-solving that is key to building young people's passion for science learning. (p.2)

They further point out that children are born with curiosity and a desire to learn (Honey & Kanter, 2013). The best way to motivate children to learn is to inspire their innate curiosity about the world around them. Once their curiosity is sparked, they will not stop learning. Rogers and Portsmore (2004) describe:

One of the more unique attributes of the [e]ngineering program is that all students are always excited about it and it holds their attention for as long as the teacher is willing or able to give. Teachers are always surprised at how long even the younger kids stay on task and complain when the time is over. Students will stay in during recess or come early to improve their projects. (p.24)

A middle school mathematics teacher, who teaches robotics after school at a charter school in an urban school district that serves an African American and Hispanic underprivileged population, excitedly shared with me a story about her students. Following a severe snowstorm, her students became very upset at the threat of losing time with their robots when their school was closed. They begged her to keep the after school robotics session open. I have witnessed similar reactions from students of robotics on numerous occasions, no matter how old they are and whether it is after school or regular class. Students look forward to robotics lessons. Learning becomes *fun* with educational robotics. Although it can be *hard* when they face difficulties such as their program not functioning the way they expected or their robots falling apart because the structure is not sturdy, students do not give up. They continue to tackle the challenges that they face and benefit greatly from the experience of working with robotics. Their accomplishment after the struggle becomes a reward and gives students a sense of pride in their efforts. Honey and Kanter (2013) emphasize *design-make-play* learning methodologies, which have the potential of fostering students' scientific imaginations. They consider that design is a powerful medium for STEM learning in an integrated and inspiring way. They explain that, through the process of design, students learn:

how to identify a problem or need, how to consider options and constraints, and how to plan, model, test, and iterate solutions, rendering higher-order thinking skills, tangible and visible. (p.3)

In addition, *making*, which Honey and Kanter (2013) consider an act of *doing* science, involves "deep engagement with content, experimentation, exploration, problem-solving, collaboration, and learning to learn" (p.4). Children's innate desire to play, invent, and explore, motivated by their inclination to investigate, joy of discovery, and, most importantly, curiosity, are all integral parts of the act of science and learning (Honey & Kanter, 2013).

Students can focus for lengthy amounts of time while engaged in making activities with educational robotics because the medium creates a *hands-on, minds-on* learning experience and provides an opportunity for students to *design-make-play*. Through the act of *design-make-play*, their robotics project gains personal meaning and value. I continuously witness that those students who do not *shine* in traditional classrooms become excited and engaged learners and makers in the robotics classroom. Rogers and Portmore also (2004) argue:

High stakes standardized testing forces a lot of teaching to focus on topics that are easily pencil and paper testable. Students with excellent memories and the ability to sit still for long periods of time succeed at these tests and are identified as 'intelligent.' While the intelligence of students who are able to quickly interpolate a graph or building and explain a complex gear system but are slow to memorize their multiplication tables is not necessarily recognized or appreciated. Designing, building and programming [with robotics technology] invoke knowledge, intelligences and learning styles not often used or valued in a traditional classroom. (p.24)

Educational robotics can provide the non-traditional learning environment that sparks interests in learning among the students who are not normally motivated to learn in traditional educational settings. It can inspire students' curiosity, enthusiasm for learning, and build self-confidence (Rogers & Portmore, 2004). By utilizing project-based/inquiry-based approach in REALs, educational robotics becomes a powerful learning tool that realizes the transdisciplinary integration of STEM, coding, computational thinking and engineering skill learning to ensure students' mastery of those critical skills they need to be successful 21st century citizens. Educational robotics is an *all-in-one* technological learning tool that can ensure the future success of our students and should be integrated more and more into school curriculum.

REFERENCES

Ackerman, E. (2013). Google Acquires Seven Robot Companies, Wants Big Role in Robotics. *IEEE Spectrum*. Retrieved December 15, 2013, from http://spectrum.ieee.org/automaton/robotics/industrial-robots/google-acquisition-seven-robotics-companies

Ackermann, E. K. (1996). Perspective-taking and object construction: Two keys to learning. In Y. Kafai & M. Resnick (Eds.), *Constructionism in Practice: Designing, Thinking, and Learning in a Digital World* (pp. 25–37). Mahwah, New Jersey: Lawrence Erlbaum Associates.

Ackermann, E. K. (2001). *Piaget's constructivism, Papert's constructionism: What's the difference?* Retrieved from http://learning.media.mit.edu/content/publications/EA.Piaget%20_%20Papert.pdf

Ackermann, E. K. (2004). Constructing Knowledge and Transforming the World. In M. Tokoro & L. Steels (Eds.), *A Learning Zone of One's Own: Sharing Representations and Flow in Collaborative Learning Environments* (pp. 15–37). Washington, DC: IOS Press.

Alimisis, D., & Kynigos, C. (2009). Constructionism and Robotics in Education. In D. Alimisis (Ed.), *Teacher Education on Robotics-Enhanced Constructivist Pedagogical Methods*. Athens, Greece: School of Pedagogical and Technological Education.

Amazon.com Inc. (2014). *Amazon Prime Air*. Retrieved July 30, 2014, from http://www.amazon.com/b?node=8037720011

Ash, D., & Kluger-Bell, B. (2000). Identifying Inquiry in the K-5 Classroom. In Division of Elementary Secondary and Informal Education (Ed.), Foundations, Volume 2: Inquiry: Thoughts, Views, and Strategies for the K-5 Classroom (pp. 79-86). Arlington, VA: National Science Foundation.

Atmatzidou, S., & Demetriadis, S. (2012). *Evaluating the role of collaboration scripts as group guiding tools in activities of eduational robotics*. Paper presented at the 2012 12th IEEE International Conference on Advanced Learning Technologies, Rome, Italy.

Atmatzidou, S., Markelis, I., & Demitridis, S. (2008). *The Use of LEGO Mindstorms in Elementary and Secondary Education: Game as a way of triggering learning*. Paper presented at the International Conference of Simulation, Modeling and Programming for Autonomous Robots (SIMPAR), Venice, Italy.

Barr, A., Nicas, J., & Bensinger, G. (2014). Google Drones Lift Industry Hopes: Internet Giant's Entry Brings Financial and Lobbying Clout to Fledging Field. *The Wall Street Journal*. http://online.wsj.com/articles/google-drones-lift-industry-hopes-1409353944

Barr, D., Harrison, J., & Conery, L. (2011). Computational Thinking: A Digital Age Skill for Everyone. *Learning and Leading with Technology*, (March/April): 20–23.

Benitti, F. B. V. (2012). Exploring the educational potential of robotics in schools: A systematic review. *Computers & Education*, 58(3), 978–988. doi:10.1016/j.compedu.2011.10.006

Bereiter, C., & Scardamalia, M. (Eds.). (1989). *Intentional learning as a goald of instruction*. Hilsdale, NJ: Lawrence Erlbaum.

Berns, K., Braun, T., Hillenbrand, C., & Luksch, T. (2005). *Developing Climbing Robots for Education*. Paper presented at the Climbing and Walking Robots: Proceedings of the 8th International Conference on Climbing and Walking Robots and the Support Technologies for Mobile Machines (CLAWAR 2005).

Bers, M. U. (2008). *Blocks to Robots: Learning with Technology in the Early Childhood Classroom*. New York, NY: Teachers College Press.

Carbonaro, M., Rex, M., & Chambers, J. (2004). Using LEGO Robotics in a Project-Based Learning Environment. *Interactive Multimedia Electronic Journal of Computer Enhanced Learning, 6*(1).

Code.org. (2013). *Anybody can learn*. Retrieved January 13, 2014, from http://codeorg.tumblr.com/post/70175643054/stats

Cruz-Martin, A., Fernandez-Madrigal, J. A., Galindo, C., Gonzalez-Jimenez, J., Stockmans-Daou, C., & Blanco-Claraco, J. L. (2012). A LEGO Mindstorms NXT approach for teaching at Data Acquisition, Control Systems Engineering and Real-Time Systems undergraduate courses. *Computers & Education, 59*(3), 974–988. doi:10.1016/j.compedu.2012.03.026

Duckworth, E. (2005). Critical Exploration in the Classroom. *New Educator, 1*(4), 257–272. doi:10.1080/15476880500276728

Eguchi, A. (2007a). *Educational Robotics for Elementary School Classroom*. Paper presented at the Society for Information Technology and Education (SITE), San Antonio, TX.

Eguchi, A. (2007b). *Educational Robotics for Undergraduate Freshmen*. Paper presented at the Proceedings of World Conference on Educational Multimedia, Hypermedia and Telecommunications, Vancouver, Canada.

Eguchi, A. (2014). *Learning Experience Through RoboCupJunior: Promoting STEM Education and 21st Century Skills with Robotics Competition*. Paper presented at the Society for Information Technology and Education (SITE), Jacksonville, FL.

Eguchi, A., Hughes, N., Stocker, M., Shen, J., & Chikuma, N. (2012). RoboCupJunior: A decade later. In T. Röfer, N. M. Mayer, J. Savage & U. Saranlı (Eds.), RoboCup 2011: Robot Soccer World Cup XV: Springer.

Elkind, D. (2008). Forward. In M. U. Bers (Ed.), *Block to Robots* (pp. xi–xiv). New York, NY: Teachers College Press.

Freire, P. (1994). *Pedagogy of the Oppressed* (30th ed.). New York, NY: Bloomsbury Academic.

Friedman, T. L. (2005). *The World is Flat: A Brief History of the Twenty-First Century*. New York, NY: Farrar, Straus & Giroux.

Gerlach, J. (2012). STEM: Defying a Simple Definition. *NSTA WebNews Digest - NSTA Reports*. Retrieved February 10, 2014, from http://www.nsta.org/publications/news/story.aspx?id=59305

Grabinger, S., & Dunlap, J. C. (1995). Rich environments for active learning: A definition. *Research in Learning Technology, 3*(2), 5–34.

Grabinger, S., Dunlap, J. C., & Duffield, J. A. (1997). Rich environment for active learing, in action: Problem-based learning. *Research in Learning Technology, 5*(2), 5–17. doi:10.1080/0968776970050202

Grover, S. (2011). *Robotics and Engineering for Middle and High School Students to Develop Computational Thinking*. Paper presented at the Annual Meeting of the American Educational Research Association, New Orleans.

Han, S., & Bhattacharya, K. (2001). Constructionism, Learning by Design, and Project Based Learning. In M. Orey (Ed.), *Emerging Perspectives on Learning*. Teaching and Technology.

Hmelo-Silver, C., Duncan, R. G., & Chinn, C. A. Hmelo-Silver. (2007). Scaffolding and Achievement in Problem-Based and Inquiry Learning: A Response to Kirschner, Sweller, and Clark. *Educational Psychologist, 42*(2), 99–107. doi:10.1080/00461520701263368

Honey, M., & Kanter, D. E. (2013). Design, Make, Play: Growing the Next Generation of Science Innocators. In M. Honey & D. E. Kanter (Eds.), *Design, Make, Play: Growing the Next Generation of STEM Innovators* (pp. 1–6). New York, NY: Routledge.

International Society for Technology in Education (ISTE), & Computer Science Teachers Association (CSTA). (2012). *Operational Definition of Computational Thinking for K-12 Education*. Retrieved February 15, 2014, from http://www.iste.org/docs/ct-documents/computational-thinking-operational-definition-flyer.pdf?sfvrsn=2

Kalil, T., & Miller, J. (2014, February 3). *Announcing the First White House Maker Faire*. Retrieved September 8, 2014, from http://www.whitehouse.gov/blog/2014/02/03/announcing-first-white-house-maker-faire

Katehi, L., Pearson, G., & Feder, M. Committee on K-12 Engineering Education, & National Academy of Engineering and National Research Council. (2009). Engineering in K–12 Education: Understanding the status and improving the prospects. Washington, DC: The National Academies Press.

Kolberg, E., & Orlev, N. (2001). *Robotics Learning as a Tool for Integrating Science-Technology Curriculum in K-12 Schools*. Paper presented at the 31st ASEE/IEEE Frontiers in Education Conference, Reno, NV. Maker Education Initiative. (n.a.). Maker Education Initiative - Mission. Retrieved January 13, 2014, from http://www.makered.org/about/

Martin, F., Kim, H. J., Silka, L., & Yanco, H. (2007). *Artbotics: Challenges and Opportunities for Multi-Disciplinary, Community-Based Learning in Computer Science, Robotics, and Art*. Paper presented at the Workshop on Research in Robotics for Education at the Robotics Science and Systems Conference, Atlanta, GA.

Martin, F., Mikhak, B., Resnick, M., Silverman, B., & Berg, R. (2000). To Mindstorms and Beyong: Evolution of a Construction Kit for Magical Machines. In A. Druin & J. Hendler (Eds.), *Robots for Kids: Exploring New Technologies for Learning* (pp. 9–33). San Diego, CA: Academic Press.

Mataric, M. J. (2004). *Robotics Education for All Ages*. Paper presented at the American Association for Artificial Intelligence Spring Symposium on Accessible, Hands-on AI and Robotics Education. http://robotics.usc.edu/~maja/publications/aaaissymp04-edu.pdf

McGrath, E., Lowes, S., Sayres, J., & Lin, P. (2008). *Underwater LEGO Robotics as the Vehicle to Engage Students in STEM: The BUILD IT Project's First Year of Classroom Implementation*. Paper presented at the American Society for Engineering Education Mid-Atlantic, Hoboken, NJ.

McGrath, E., Lowes, S., Sayres, J., & Lin, P. (2009). *Analysis of Middle- And High-School Students' Learning Of Science, Mathematics, And Engineering Concepts Through A Lego Underwater Robotics Design Challenge*. Paper presented at the American Society for Engineering Education Annual Conference, Austin, TX.

Miller, D. P., Nourbakhsh, I. R., & Sigwart, R. (2008). Robots for Education. In B. Siciliano & O. Khatib (Eds.), *Springer Handbook of Rootics* (pp. 1283–1301). New York, NY: Springer-Verlag New York, LLC. doi:10.1007/978-3-540-30301-5_56

Nourbakhsh, I. R., Hamner, E., Crowley, K., & Wilkinson, K. (2004). *Formal Measures of Learning in a Secondary School Mobile Robotics Course*. Paper presented at the 2004 IEEE International Conference on Robotics & Automation, New Orleans, LA. doi:10.1109/ROBOT.2004.1308090

Oppliger, D. (2002). *Using FIRST LEGO League to Enhance Engineering Education and to Increase the Pool of Future Engineering Students (Work in Progress).* Paper presented at the 32nd ASEE/IEEE Frontiers in Education Conference, Boston, MA. doi:10.1109/FIE.2002.1158731

Papert, S. (1993). *Mindstorms - Children, Computers, and Powreful Ideas* (2nd ed.). New York, NY: Basic Books.

Papert, S., & Harel, I. (1991). *Constructionism.* New York, NY: Ablex Publishing Corporation.

Piaget, J. (1929). *The Child's Conception of the World.* New York: Harcourt, Brace and Company.

Piaget, J. (1954). *The Construction of Reality in the Child.* New York: Basic Books. doi:10.1037/11168-000

Rinaldi, C. (2001). Making Learning Visible: Children as Individual and Group Learners. In Project Zero & Reggio Children (Ed.), Making Learning Visible: Children as Individual and Group Learners (pp. 78-89). Bloomfield, MI: Olive Press.

Robinson, K. (2010). *Changing education paradigms.* Retrieved from http://www.ted.com/talks/ken_robinson_changing_education_paradigms.html

Rogers, C. (2008). A Well-Kept Secret: Classroom Management with Robotics. In M. U. Bers (Ed.), *Blocks to Robots* (pp. 46–52). New York, NY: Teachers College Press.

Rogers, C., & Portsmore, M. (2004). Bringing Engineering to Elementary School. *Journal of STEM Education, 5*(3&4), 17–28.

Sklar, E., & Eguchi, A. (2004). RoboCupJunior - Four Years Later. *Proceedings of RoboCup-2004: Robot Soccer World Cup VIII.*

Sklar, E., Eguchi, A., & Johnson, J. (2002). *Examining the Team Robotics through RoboCupJunior.* Paper presented at the the Annual Conference of Japan Society for Educational Technology, Nagaoka, Japan.

Sklar, E., Eguchi, A., & Johnson, J. (2003). Scientific Challenge Award: RoboCupJunior - Learning with Educational Robotics. *AI Magazine, 24*(2), 43–46.

Soares, F., Leão, C. P., Santos, S., Ribeiro, F., & Lopes, G. (2011). An Early Start in Robotics - K-12 Case-Study. [iJEP]. *International Journal of Engineering Pedagogy, 1*(1), 50–56.

SoftBank Mobile Corp., & Aldebaran Robotics SAS. (2014). *SoftBank Mobile and Aldebaran Unveil "Pepper" – the World's First Personal Robot That Reads Emotions.* Retrieved June 8, 2014, from http://www.softbank.jp/en/corp/group/sbm/news/press/2014/20140605_01/

The Royal Society - Education Section. (2012). Shut down or restart? The way foeard for computing in UK schools - Executive summary. London, UK.

The United Kingdom Department of Education. (2013). *The national curriculm in England - Framework document.* United Kingdom: Crown Retrieved from https://http://www.gov.uk/government/uploads/system/uploads/attachment_data/file/210969/NC_framework_document_-_FINAL.pdf

Vygotsky, L. (1978). *Mind in society: the development of higher psychological processes.* Cambridge, MA: Harvard University Press.

Yanco, H. A., Kim, H. J., & Martin, F. G., & Silka, Linda. (2006). *Artbotics: Combining art and robotics to broaden participation in computing.* Paper presented at the AAAI Spring Symposium on Robots and Robot Venues: Resources for AI Education.

KEY TERMS AND DEFINITIONS

Constructionism: Constructionism is a learning theory developed by Seymour Papert. He was inspired by Piaget's experimental learning theory and believes that children construct their new knowledge by constructing physical and manipulative materials, like blocks, beads, and robotics kits.

Computational Thinking: Computational thinking is first used by Seymour Papert, and made widely known by Jeanette Wing at Carnegie Mellon University, in 2006. She explains it is problem-solving process and a fundamental skill for everyone in the world. Recently, there is a strong need to introduce computational thinking in the PK-12 educational environment.

Educational Robotics: Educational robotics uses robotics kits, programming software and computer as hands-on learning tools. It can create a learning environment that can enhance collaboration and communication among students, problem-solving skills, critical thinking skills, and creativity.

Engineering Design Cycle: Engineering design cycle is a iterative process of solving a problem, especially in engineering. The process is usually less linear, often going from later steps in the cycle back to earlier steps as new information is gathered. There are many variations of engineering design cycle. The basic structure is 1) identify problem, 2) explore solutions/ideas, 3) design, 4) test and evaluate, 5) re-design, and 6) presentation of solution.

Reggio Emilia: Reggio Emilia is a city in northern Italy where Reggio Emilia approach – an educational philosophy, has established. Reggio Emilia approach focuses on preschool to elementary education. The philosophy emphasized on student-centered constructivist learning environment, in which students are encouraged to have some control over their learning.

Rich Environments for Active Learning (REALs): Rich Environments for Active Learning (REALs) are comprehensive instructional system based on constructivism. REALs consider learning as a continuous collaborative process to develop, revise, and reshape knowledge through activities that authentically reflect the world around students.

Robotics Kits: Robotics kits are educational products developed as tools to teach programming, electronics, and various sensor technologies through the construction of robotics projects. A kit generally provides a controller, motors, sensors, and various building components. One of most popular robotics kits is LEGO Mindstorms NXT and EV3. LEGO Mindstorms was developed based on the Logo programming, which has its foundation in constructionist theory.

ENDNOTES

[1] http://www.theroboticschallenge.org

[2] For more information: http://waterbotics.org/curriculum/standards/

Chapter 3
Constructivist Internet–Blended Learning and Resiliency in Higher Education

Jennifer L. Penland
Sul Ross State University, USA

ABSTRACT

This chapter focuses on the changes that have occurred recently in the distance education arena and the impact on higher education institutions focusing on undergraduate and graduate students taking these courses. Data were gathered from 164 individual participants enrolled in education courses at Shepherd University during the spring 2013, fall 2013 and spring 2014 semesters from end of course surveys with ten questions focusing on the following areas: when students learn, why students learn and how students learn. Findings suggested; (1) increased enrollment in distance education courses, (2) courses allow for flexible schedules (3) better communication with instructor and (4) more meaningful learning overall for students.

INTRODUCTION

The latter part of the 20th century provided the fertile environment for change in educational institutions not particularly at the tertiary level of education, but especially in the K-12 environment. Various approaches to education were implemented, some of which included an open classroom concept, continuous education, grammar schools, schools for the gifted, alternative education, and distance education. It is this last approach to education that caught the attention of tertiary educators particularly at the undergraduate and graduate levels because of the way that economics and technology began intersecting in unforeseen ways. The cost of education all over the country along with the need to cater to a diverse population provided fertile ground for changing the traditional methods of education for the traditional students who enter college immediately

DOI: 10.4018/978-1-4666-8363-1.ch003

after leaving high school. The first decade of the 21st century has seen some dramatic changes in the way that institutions are able to reach out to diverse populations, and in the way education is delivered.

According to a national study (Allen, 2005) released by the Sloan Consortium in November, 2005, over 2.35 million students took at least one online course online; 65% percent of higher education institutions are using primarily core faculty to teach their online courses; schools identifying online education as a critical long-term strategy grew from 49% in 2003 to 56% in 2005, 63% of schools offering undergraduate face-to-face courses also offer undergraduate courses online.

Higher educational institutions find themselves no longer insulated from economic and social pressures as they might have been a quarter of a century ago. The face of the United States is changing rapidly for reasons among which include increased immigration, a social upheaval with a dwindling middle class population, and the consequences of a rapidly changing world in which technology is playing a leading role (Penland & Rice, 2005). Institutions of higher education are facing increasing demands for providing alternative scheduling, multiple course offerings, and blended technology-based programs that would more closely service the needs of changing populations.

To illustrate what has happened in the field of Distance Education in the last decade, interesting findings have emerged from the most recent report to Congress from the National Center for Education Statistics (2011). In 2007-08, 20 percent of all undergraduates (4.3 million) took at least one distance education course and of these students, about 4 percent took their entire program through distance education. The percentage of undergraduates who took any distance education courses rose from 16 percent in 2003 to 20 percent in 2007-08; over the same period, however, the percentage who took their entire program through distance educa-

tion decreased from 5 to 4 percent. By contrast, the percentage of post-baccalaureate students who took their entire program through distance education (9 percent) was higher than the percentage at the undergraduate level (NCES, 2011).

As adult learners adjust their learning role to become more active and self-directed, a careful exploration of their preferences for learning environments can help instructors to plan and design on-line courses more efficiently and effectively (Markel, 1999; Huang, 2002; Lee & Tsai, 2005). Older undergraduates enrolled in distance education classes and degree programs at higher rates than did younger students. Fifteen percent of undergraduates age 23 or younger participated in a distance education course, compared with 26 percent of those between ages 24 and 29 and 30 percent of those age 30 or older (NCES, 2011). Students who had a dependent or were married also participated in distance education classes or degree programs more often than other students. Twenty-nine percent of students with one or more dependents and 32 percent of married students took a distance education class, in contrast to 18 percent of students without these characteristics.

As for distance education degree programs, 8 percent of students who had at least one dependent or were married participated, as compared with 2 percent and 3 percent of their respective counterparts. While 18 percent of all undergraduates in 2007-2008 were married, 40 percent of all undergraduates in a distance education program were married. In addition, though 25 percent of all undergraduates had one or more dependents, 55 percent of all undergraduates in a distance education degree program had at least one dependent.

Therefore, to understand the preferences of an adult in a constructivist internet-blended learning environment means not only providing adult learners with opportunities to experience a student –centered and more controllable learning setting, but also retaining and motivating for lifelong learning (Chu, 2001; Sabry & Baldwin, 2003).

BACKGROUND

In the past decade, the focus of constructivist Internet-blended learning environments has expanded from actual classrooms to virtual settings (Tenebaum *et al.,* 2001; Chuang & Tsai, 2005). Research results have indicated that constructivist-blended learning can increase support to students and help their critical thinking skills, (Ng'ambi & Johnston, 2006; Roschelle, & Teasley, 1995), promote meaningful learning, motivation, and change attitudes towards their learning (Fok & Watkins, 2007). Blended learning arose to overcome the disadvantages of traditional learning and our ever changing society and to obviate the failure of e-learning by providing a combination of various learning strategies or models. It mixes various event-based learning activities, including face-to-face classroom instruction; live e-learning, student centered learning and self-paced learning, which increases learning quality, social contents and learners' interactivity. According to Al-Huneidi and Schreurs (2013), blended learning is an evolution of e-learning; it provides the best mix of traditional learning and e-learning.

In blended learning environments, teachers should use a variety of management tools such as synchronous and asynchronous learning technologies to facilitate and encourage collaboration, interaction, communication, knowledge construction and sharing among students.

However, research findings have also suggested that students have a lower awareness of constructivist learning, though their instructors and program designers assert that they design courses based on constructivist pedagogy (Tenebaum et al., 2001). Consequently, there is a need to develop a better understanding of constructivist Internet-blended learning environments (CILE) (Zualkernan, 2006). Therefore, the key elements to define a student-centered constructivist Internet-blended learning environment have become a concern for practitioners, designers and researchers.

Constructivist Internet-blended learning can help all types of learners overcome learning participation barriers and provide a self-paced, self-directed learning (SDL) environment. Additionally, Internet-blended learning is more cost effective and convenient than traditional educational environments (Richardson & Swan, 2003; Inoue, 2007). There is no one true reality – rather, individual interpretations of the world. These are shaped by our experience and our social interactions. Learning is a process of adapting to and organizing one's quantitative world, rather than discovering pre-existing ideas imposed by others (Clements & Battista, 1990).

MAIN FOCUS OF THE CHAPTER

In recent months, there has been an explosion of discussion surrounding the quality of instruction in fully on-line programs. Institutions should begin to think of information as an institutional asset that must be handled and developed thoughtfully and with care. At the front end, individual faculty members have usually been incorporating all the responsibilities of a technologist with competency-based functions of the curriculum without constructivist learning embedded. Increased members of students and courses are now forging a "deliberate division of labor among the faculty, creating new kinds of instructional staff" (Paulson, 2002), thus "unbundling" and shifting the traditional roles of faculty. Effectiveness of interaction of distance or Internet-blended education personnel, especially on campus, is based on whether or not an individual can understand the concerns and problems being faced by faculty or students. Because of this, faculty support and training take on new importance if an institution is to be successful in the field of Internet-blended education (Green, 2002; Crawford et al., 2003).

Social E-Learning

It is relatively easy to create a social constructivist environment in a classroom. It is more difficult to do so in the context of distance learning, whether paper based (these still exist in developing countries) or electronic. Early distance education e-learning environments tended to be simple electronic versions of old paper based ones, where lecture notes was provided for students to read on screen. Communication was more or less limited to e-mail discussion with the course tutor. The attrition rate in distance education has always been high, one of the reasons being that the systems designed to deliver e-learning has tended to leave students feeling isolated (Flood, 2002). E-learning designers have struggled to design systems which provide a social constructivist environment, largely because it is impossible with the technology available at this stage to recreate classrooms online. According to Valentine (2002), problems include "the quality of instruction, hidden costs, misuse of technology, and the attitudes of instructors, students, and administrators."

The kinds of applications used to 'deliver' online content have forced users down a narrow, highly directed path and are not particularly user friendly as a result. However, vast improvements have been made by open source developers, who are involved in ongoing work on more flexible applications like Moodle, which is more capable of supporting constructivist pedagogies (Downes, 2008). Fernandez (2009) makes the point that Moodle "isn't just a piece of software used for teaching and learning, it's also a community of educators and software developers who have incorporated the culture of the guild and apprenticeship into their work processes." The influence of educators is important when it comes to providing systems which match the needs of learners.

Attitudes toward Distance Learning

Despite problems with hardware that may or may not get worked out with new advances in technology, we must come back to instructors and their attitudes towards teaching in a distance-learning environment as a major potential roadblock to effective distance education. As in any educational situation, the instructor can set the tone for learning in the educational environment. This instructor must be properly trained and motivated to be effective, "guide on the side". An instructor must have technological skills and confidence to use all of the various electronic devices in order to be truly effective in the electronic classroom. Instructors must also change the manner in which information is delivered. While lecture does not work well, multimedia presentations are successful (Weber, 1996). Of course this means more preparation time for the instructor and the motivation must be there.

Radford (2011) states that "to effectively bridge the gaps between classroom and distance teaching, faculty need to look at the distance teaching from the students' point of view". The faculty must also be aware of getting instructional materials, handouts, tests, and other class items to both sites simultaneously. It is important for the instructors to develop a sense of community between the sites, achieve maximum participation, and get the participants to buy in to the process. The idea of learning as a collaborative process is very important when students are separated by distance. According to research by Palloff and Pratt (2000), "collaborative learning processes assists students to achieve deeper levels of knowledge generation through the creation of shared goals, shared exploration, and a shared process of meaning making" (p 6). It is up to the instructor to be aware of this in the distance learning environment and to encourage collaborative learning and a sense of community among the students.

There are also student concerns with distance learning classes. Not all students are suited to this type of learning and not all subjects are best taught via this medium. More mature students are the most likely to find success with distance learning. The successful student needs to exhibit characteristics such as tolerance for ambiguity, intrinsic motivation, and an ability to be flexible. Hardy and Boaz (1997) found that "compared to most face-to-face learning environments, distance learning requires students to be more focused, better time managers, and to be able to work independently and with group members" (p.43). Many distance learners are different from traditional undergraduates in that they are already in professions.

Being involved in a collaborative learning process is an important part of forming the foundation of a learning community. When this is not encouraged, participation is generally low and dialog is absent (Palloff & Pratt, 2000). Students also need the attention of the instructors. This may be truer in a distance situation than in a traditional classroom. In a situation where eye contact and proximity are limited, students cannot be disciplined nor affirmed by eye contact and body language (McKnight, 2000).

Students may also have a difficult time reading the reactions of the remote location class members. This lack of interaction can cause problems when there is a dissenting opinion that cannot be picked up on with non-verbal cues, and is misperceived as a verbal attack. This type of miscommunication can cause the community problems as the class progresses. It is fair to say that compressed video can magnify the strengths and weaknesses of the instructor. Students are prone to pick up on a lack of organization and direction and respond with apathy and absenteeism (West, 1994).

A Pilot Study

The Constructivist Internet-Blended study (CIB) conducted by Penland in 2013-2014, addressed attitudes and feelings of undergraduates and graduate students in campus-based blended courses in an attempt to discover ways of improving and structuring her courses and to determine if this type of instructional delivery significantly contributed to their educational resiliency and persistence in school. Though the CIB study is only a pilot, the initial findings are shown below:

- **Undergraduate Students:** Liked more hand-on approach and face to face interaction, enjoyed the flexible times on campus classes; instructor provided continuous communication; majority are traditional learners; somewhat stressed about deadlines
- **Graduate Students:** Able to work more independently; confidence building due to good communication with partner and instructor; working with a flexible schedule; enjoyed practical uses for technology in the classroom and for personal growth
- **Traditional Learners:** 60 percent of graduate students; 68 percent of undergraduate students
- **Non-Traditional Learners**: 20 percent of graduate students; 18 percent of undergraduate students
- **Both T and NT Learners**: 20 percent of graduate students; 22 percent of undergraduate students

METHODOLOGY

This study used a qualitative method approach to examine attitudes of undergraduate and graduate education majors with equal representation of both traditional and non-traditional learners. The selected sample was given as an end of course questionnaire which focused on using a blended approach with technology for communication, documents, searches and field lessons during the semester. The following questions were used for data collection:

- When have I learned and under what circumstances?
- What difference has the learning made to me intellectually, personally, and ethically?
- In what ways is what I learned valuable to learn at all?
- Why did I learn?
- Highest moments in completing my assignments?
- Lowest moments in completing my assignments?
- What was the most significant thing that happened to me as a learner this semester?
- Was there quality communication?
- Do you consider yourself a traditional or non-traditional learner?
- Graduate or undergraduate?

SOLUTIONS AND RECOMMENDATIONS

Communication and collaboration proved to be an important part of the learning process. The key to making this a success was frequent and rapid feedback to each assignment submitted, opportunity for both synchronous and asynchronous communications between students and the instructor. Communications included face-to-face instruction and collaboration, email, on-line chats, telephone, and discussion forums which were introduced early in the semester. Diversity of assignments, and flexibility along with multiple means of content delivery were designed to meet the diverse needs of students by attempting to use their strengths to support areas of weakness. Formative evaluation in the form of frequent learn-

ing assessments was developed to help students evaluate and guide their learning. It concurrently provided an opportunity for instructors to modify the courses to adjust to the needs of the learners. Summative evaluation was introduced in the form of a final comprehensive unit project using an ST-11 teaching evaluative tool.

This relates to the current trend in higher education that is shifting from course completion to competency and understanding thus being dictated by what Callahan (2003) sees as what learners need to meet employer expectations rather than what has traditionally been done. The Penland Study questionnaire also gave students the opportunity to provide valuable, contextualized information that is being used to strengthen the courses the next time they are offered. Instructors of distance/blended learning courses are often asked as to why students selected these courses. Data being collected to date indicate that these courses meet the needs of students because of conflicting work schedules, conflicts with on-campus classes, geographic isolation and increased cost of travel and child care. Most of the graduate students and a growing number of undergraduate students wanted on-line courses because it gave them greater control over their time and pace of learning.

Virtual Learning Environments (VLE) as we understand them today are unlikely to be as powerful as blended learning environments for the simple reason that it is impossible to mirror the classroom, with all its nuances, vocal and visual clues. However, e-learning providers have learned much in recent years, supported by more powerful computers, communications infrastructures, Internet technologies and applications enabled by the changing way in which we understand and use the web. What has become clear is that a high level of personalized support or "hand-holding" (Martinez, 2003) is important for distance learning students and that learning management packages need to come bundled with tools which enable students to communicate effectively with one another to make use of the potential of socially constructed learning.

Computer mediated communication plays an important part in this, providing the potential for supporting both personalized and social learning in terms of choice of tools and the means to communicate with one another to create effective learning networks. More and more communication tools are on offer – email, messaging, sms texting, discussion boards, video-conferencing, blogs, wikis, podcasts, microblogging applications like Twitter, Plurk and (until recently) Pownce. The number of choices grows almost daily. Downes (2008) has suggested that developments in conferencing applications "will make actual in-person meetings less necessary, and the 'blended' aspect of blended learning will come increasingly to reflect the in-person activities people undertake in their own workplaces or communities."

This last point elicits an important finding from the data obtained a U.S. Department of Education study (Sikora, 2000). Distance/ blended education courses offered nationally are breaking down the traditional concept of semesters and pace learning. Universities are structured by semesters, and financial aid has always fit into the concept of fall and spring semesters and maybe some courses during the summer. Financial aid is usually distributed for two semesters annually over a 4-year period. Distance/ blended courses do not lock students into this "learning metaphor". It is gradually breaking down these traditional barriers allowing students to complete work in shorter or longer periods.

There is a growing trend where even traditional, on-campus students are now selecting either the on-line and/or blended classes that fit their schedules and learning preferences, regardless of where the course emanates from, even if it is offered by the campus from which they expect to earn a degree. This new world of asynchronous, self-paced, distributed blended education calls into question the current academic accounting system and requires institutional leaders to envision new ways to measure student learning (Johnston, 2002).

FUTURE RESEARCH DIRECTIONS

Universities are struggling as they face the dilemma of reaching out to the diverse student who in former years would have fallen through the cracks in the system and were overlooked. Solutions are not easy to come by, but if institutions are to survive in the 21st century, they must be willing to think "outside the box" and come up with viable, forward looking solutions. Some correlates affecting retention identified by one of the studies from the government report show that students who receive financial aid are more likely to remain in a program than students who do not receive assistance; women are more likely to be retained, while African-Americans are retained at a lower rate; pre-registered students have a higher rate of retention than those who register in the first week of a course; students who transfer in with 60 or more credits hours have a higher retention rate, while out-of-state students have lower retention rates (US DOE, 2005).

The informational age is bringing about drastic change in the higher education landscape. It was Aslaian (2001) who said, "In the past, information doubled every ten years; now it doubles every four years." This is likely to take even less time in the near future, thus increasing pressure on institutions to come up with ways of spreading distant and blended resources. At the turn of the century Dunn (2000) predicted the "number of degree-granting institutions will continue to grow, while the number of traditional campuses will decline. By 2025, half of today's existing independent colleges will be closed, merged or significantly altered in mission".

In addition to this White (2003) observed that the line between public and private universities and non-profit and for-profit universities is blurring and will continue to do so. Universities that survive are faced with the dichotomy of instituting or maintaining a centralized versus a decentralized organizational structure (Hickman, 2003). There appears to be a shift towards decentralization, however, there are advantages and disadvantages of each structure depending on prevalent factors (Donaldson, 2003).

CONCLUSION

The paradigm shift in education in higher learning institution is inevitable and challenging. It also presents many opportunities for educators, learners, facilitators and management staffs to work closely and improve learning outcomes and quality. An outgrowth of the increase in distant/blended education is that instruction is becoming more learner-centered. It is non-linear in nature, and is seen as being more self-directed. Feedback from the (CIB) Penland Study has shown that the students like the idea of having control over when and where they learn, but at the same time they have problems shifting from the traditional teacher-controlled environment to one in which they assume responsibility for their learning. There is a shift from a transmission model to constructivist, sociocultural and metacognitive models (Miller, 2001; Rumble, 2001).

Many educational institutions around the country have been forced in recent years to pursue national accreditation. An outgrowth of this is the question as to what the status of accreditation will be by the end of this quarter century. Pond (2003) gives us his opinion when he says that there will not be one national accreditation system though the U.S. Department of Education may provide some type of safety net to maintain some level of quality.

Leaders must create conditions conducive to energy, initiative and innovation in their particular milieu, and bring others along, both above and beyond them in the organizational hierarchy. Creating on-line and blended programs is relatively easy; sustaining high quality programs is where the challenge lies. The core elements of planning both on-line and blended courses must consider academic standards, student engagement and quality assurance. Transformational leaders are recognized as change agents who are good role models, who can create and communicate a clear vision for an institution or organization, who can empower followers to achieve at higher standards, who act in ways that make others want to trust them and who give meaning and purpose to organizational life.

Educational institutions as we now know them are bound to change as we move into the next decade. We already see lectures being replaced by podcasts and a steady reduction in tutor-student face to face time as management types replace academics as leaders of universities and universities become more like businesses, trimming costs and urging faculty to 'work smarter' not 'harder'. New applications like *Second Life* are already attracting a good deal of interest in academic circles, raising the possibility of adding value to both distance education and replacing at least some part of current face to face blended learning. In the future, the brave new world of virtual reality will have an even larger impact on the way we communicate, learn and educate societies.

From a pedagogic perspective, the importance of Professional Learning Environments provide a high level of personal control as opposed to institutional control, providing a good fit with the constructivist paradigm. 'Digital natives', as Prensky (2001) calls them, are natural networkers, highly 'connected', social, collaborative, multi-taskers. They use information and communications technologies intuitively; even if they do not always understand the educational potential of all the applications they are familiar with (Trinder, et al., 2008). The idea of 'connectivism' (Drexler, 2008) ties in well with social constructivism, demonstrating how this new generation of learners will use the power of our networked world.

REFERENCES

Al-Huneidi, A., & Schreurs, J. (2013). Constructivist based blended learning in higher education. CCIS, 581-591, Springer-Verlag, Berlin and Heidelberg.

Allen, E. (2005). *Growing by degrees: online education in the United States, 2005*. The Sloan Consortium.

Aslanian, C. (2001). *Adult students today*. New York: The College Board.

Callahan, P. (2003, March 28-30). *UCEA 88th Annual conference*. Chicago, Illinois.

Chu, J. (2001). Class size effects on the adult student learning social environment. *Asia Pacific Adult Education, 1*, 161–210.

Chuang, S., & Tsai, C. (2005). Preferences toward the constructivist internet-based learning environments among high school students in Taiwan. *Computers in Human Behavior, 21*(2), 255–272. doi:10.1016/j.chb.2004.02.015

Clements, D., & Battista, M. (1990). Constructivist learning and teaching. *The Arithmetic Teacher, 38*(1), 34–35.

Crawford, G., & Rudy, J.EDUCAUSE Current Issues Committee. (2003).. . *Fourth Annual EDUCAUSE Survey, 38*(11), 12–26.

Donaldson, J. (2003). *Continuing education organizational models*. Unpublished email correspondence.

Downes, S. (2008). *The Future of Online Learning: Ten Years On*. Retrieved August, 2014: http://halfanhour.blogspot.com/2008/11/future-of-online-learning-ten-years-on_16.html

Drexler, W. (2008). *Finally! A video that explains what I'm aiming for as a teacher*. Dougbelshaw.com Retrieved August 2014: http://dougbelshaw.com/blog/2008/11/28/finally-a-video-that-explains-what-im-aiming-for-as-a-teacher/

Dunn, S. (2000). The futurist. *Virtual World*, Mar/Apr, 34-38.

Fernandez, A. (2009). The role of new technologies in the learning process: Moodle as a teaching tool in Physics. *Computers & Education, 52*(10), 35–44.

Flood, J. (2002). Read all about it: Online learning facing 80% attrition rates. *TOJDE 3*(2).

Fok, A., & Watkins, D. (2007). Does a critical constructivist learning environment encourage a deeper approach to learning? *Asia-Pacific Education Researcher, 12*(1), 1–10.

Green, K. (2002). *Campus Computing 2002: The 13th National Survey of Computing and Information Technology in American Higher Education*. Encino, CA: Campus Computing.

Hardy, D., & Boaz, M. (1997). Learner development: Beyond the technology. *New Directions for Teaching and Learning, 71*(71), 41–48. doi:10.1002/tl.7106

Hickman, C. (2003). Results of survey regarding distance education offerings. University Continuing Education Association (UCEA). *Distance Learning Community of Practice, Research Committee Report*.

Huang, H. (2002). Toward constructivism for adult learners in online learning environments. *British Journal of Educational Technology, 33*(1), 27–37. doi:10.1111/1467-8535.00236

Inoue, Y. (2007). *Online education for lifelong learning*. Hershey, PA: Information Science Publication. doi:10.4018/978-1-59904-319-7.ch001

Johnston, S. (2002). Student learning as academic currency. *ACE Center for Policy Analysis*. Retrieved January 2006:http://www.acenet.edu/bookstore/pdf/distributed-learning/distributed-learning-04.pdf

Lee, M., & Tsai, C. (2005). Exploring high school students' and teachers' preferences toward the constructivist internet-based learning environments in Taiwan. *Educational Studies, 31*(2), 149–167. doi:10.1080/03055690500095522

Markel, M. (1999). Distance education and the myth of the new pedagogy. *Journal of Business and Technical Communication, 13*(2), 208–223. doi:10.1177/1050651999013002005

Martinez, M. (2003). High attrition rates in e-learning: Challenges, predictors and solutions. *The e-learning Developers' Journal,* Retrieved August 2014: http://www.elearningguild.com/pdf/2/071403MGT-L.pdf

McKnight, M. (2000). *Distance education: Expressing emotions in video-based classes.* Paper presented at the Annual meeting of the Conference on College Composition and Communication, Minneapolis, Minnesota. (Eric Document Reproduction Service No. ED 441 270).

Miller, G. (2001). General education and distance education: Two channels in the new mainstream. *The Journal of General Education, 50*(4), 314–322. doi:10.1353/jge.2001.0028

Ng'ambi, D., & Johnston, K. (2006). An ICT-mediated constructivist approach for increasing academic support and teaching critical thinking skills. *Journal of Educational Technology & Society, 9,* 244–253.

Office of Postsecondary Education, Office of Policy, Planning and Innovation. (2005). Third report to congress on the distance education demonstration program. *U.S. Department of Education.* Washington, DC, Retrieved January 2006: http://www.ed.gov/programs/disted

Palloff, R., & Pratt, K. (2000). "Making the transition: Helping teachers to teach online". Paper presented at *EDUCAUSE: Thinking it through.* Nashville, Tennessee. (ERIC Document Reproduction Service No. ED 452 806).

Paulson, K. (2002). Reconfiguring faculty roles for virtual settings. *The Journal of Higher Education, 73*(1), 123–140. doi:10.1353/jhe.2002.0010

Penland, J., & Rice, D. (2005).Emerging changes under the education canopy. *Teaching in Higher Education Forum.* April 17-19, 2005. Louisiana State University, Baton Rouge.

Pond, W. (2003). *Lifelong learning: The changing face of higher education. E-Learning Summit, 2003.* California: La Quinta Resort.

Prensky, M. (2001). Digital natives, digital immigrants. On the Horizon (MCB University Press, Vol. 9 No. 5, October 2001).

Radford, A. (2011). Learning at a distance: Undergraduate enrollment in distance education courses and degree programs. *U.S. Department of Education, National Center for Education Statistics,* Retrieved July 2014: http://nces.ed.gov/pubsearch/pubsinfo.asp?pubid=2012154

Richardson, J., & Swan, K. (2003). Examining social presence in online courses in relation to students' perceived learning and satisfaction.*Journal of Asynchronous Learning Networks, 7,* 78–82.

Roschelle, J., & Teasley, S. (1995). The construction of shared knowledge in collaborative problem-solving in computer communication and cognition Vygotskian perspectives, 67-197. Cambridge: Cambridge University Press.

Rumble, G. (2001). Re-inventing distance education, 1971-2001. *International Journal of Lifelong Education, 20*(1/2), 31–43.

Sabry, K., & Baldwin, L. (2003). Web-based learning interaction and learning styles. *British Journal of Educational Technology, 34*(4), 443–454. doi:10.1111/1467-8535.00341

Sikora, A. (2000). A profile of participation in distance education: 1999-2000. *U.S. Department of Education, National Center for Education Statistics,* Retrieved July 2014: http://www.nces.ed.gov/pubs2006/2006187.pdf

Tenebaum, G., Naidu, S., Jegede, O., & Austin, J. (2001). Constructivist pedagogy in conventional on-campus and distance learning practice: An exploratory investigation. *Learning and Instruction, 11*(2), 87–111. doi:10.1016/S0959-4752(00)00017-7

Trinder, K., Guiller, J., Margaryan, A., Littlejohn, A., & Nicol, D. (2008). *Learning from digital natives: bridging formal and informal learning.* The Higher Education Academy.

Valentine, D. (2002). Distance learning: Promises, problems, possibilities, Retrieved August 2014: http://www.westga.edu/~distance/ojdla/fall53/valentine53.html

Weber, J. (1996). "The compressed video experience". Paper presented at *Summer Conference of the Association of Small Computer Users.* North Myrtle Beach, South Carolina. (ERIC Document Reproduction Service No. ED 405 838).

West, G. (1994). Teaching and learning adaptations in the use of interactive compressed video. *T.H.E. Journal, 21*(9), 71–74.

White, L. (2003). Deconstructing the public-private dichotomy in higher education. *Change, 35*(3), 48–54. doi:10.1080/00091380309604102

Zualkernan, I. (2006). A framework and a methodology for developing authentic constructivist e-learning environments. *Journal of Educational Technology & Society, 9*, 198–212.

ADDITIONAL READING

Al-Khalidi, S. (2014). New paradigm of effective e-Learning through system development life cycle structure. *International Journal of Information and Education Technology, 2*(4), 185–188http://www.ijiet.org/papers/395-IT156.pdf. RetrievedAugust2014. doi:10.7763/IJIET.2014.V4.395

Alvermann, D. E., Hutchins, R. J., & McDevitt, R. (2012). Adolescents' Engagement with web 2.0 and Social media: Research, theory, and practice. *Research in the Schools, 19*(1), 33–44.

Ausburn, L. (2002). The freedom versus focus dilemma in a customized self-directed learning environment: A comparison of the perceptions of adult and younger students. *Community College Journal of Research and Practice, 26*(3), 225–235. doi:10.1080/106689202317245428

Bandura, A. (1997). *Self-efficacy: The exercise of control.* New York: Freeman.

Bonk, C., & Graham, C. (2012). *The Handbook of Blended, Learning Global Perspectives and Local Designs.* John Wiley & Sons.

Bronack, S., & Tashner, J. (2006). Learning in the zone: A social constructivist framework for distance education in a 3-dimensional virtual world. *Interactive Learning Environments, 14*(3), 265–286. doi:10.1080/10494820600909157

Bruce, B. (1997). Literacy technologies: What stance should we take? *Journal of Literacy Research, 29*(2), 289–309. doi:10.1080/10862969709547959

Carrington, V., & Robinson, M. (Eds.). (2009). *Digital Literacies: Social Learning and Classroom Practices.* London, United Kingdom: Sage. doi:10.4135/9781446288238

Coiro, J. (2011). Talking about reading as thinking: Modeling the hidden complexities of online reading comprehension. *Theory into Practice, 50*(2), 107–115. doi:10.1080/00405841.2011.558435

Compton-Lilly, C. (2007). What can video games teach us about reading? James Gee's work on learning principles and video games is extended to learning to read. *The Reading Teacher, 60*(8), 718–727. doi:10.1598/RT.60.8.2

de Castell, S., & Luke, A. (1988). Defining "literacy" in North American schools: Social and historical conditions and consequences. In E. R. Kingten, B. M. Kroll, & M. Rose (Eds.), *Perspectives on literacy* (pp. 159–174). Carbondale, IL: Southern Illinois University Press. (Original work published 1983)

Dede, C. (2007). Reinventing the role of information and communication technologies in education. In L. Smolin, K. Lawless, & N. C. Burbules (Eds.), Information and communication technologies: Considerations of current practices for teachers and teacher educators. 106th Yearbook of the National Society for the Study of Education (Part 2, pp. 11–38). Malden, MA: Blackwell. doi:10.1111/j.1744-7984.2007.00113.x

Farmer, J. (2008). Social constructivists and e-learning. *Michael Feldstein's e-Litrate* blog, Retrieved August 2014: http://mfeldstein.com/social-constructivists-and-elearning/

Friedman, T. L. (2006). *The world is flat.* New York, NY: Farrar, Straus and Giroux.

Garrison, D., & Vaughan, N. (2008). *Blended learning in higher education: Framework, principles and guidelines.* John Wiley & Sons.

Gee, J. (2010). A situated-sociocultural approach to literacy and technology. In E. A. Baker (Ed.), *The new literacies: Multiple perspectives on research and practice* (pp. 165–193). New York, NY: Guilford.

Greenhow, C., Robelia, B., & Hughes, J. (2009). Web 2.0 and classroom research: What path should we take *now? Educational Researcher, 38*(4), 246–259. doi:10.3102/0013189X09336671

Gunasekaran, A., McNeil, R. & Shaul, D. (2002). *"E-learning: research and applications," industrial and commercial training,* 34(2), 44-53.

Hawkins, B. (2006). Twelve habits of successful IT professionals. *EDUCAUSE Review, 41*(1), 57–66. http://www.educause.edu/ir/library/pdf/erm0613.pdf Retrieved July, 2014

Hebel, S. (2010). Lumina describes how far states have to go to meet college completion goals. *Chronicle of Higher Education.* Retrieved August, 2011: http://chronicle.com/article/Lumina

Helton, C. (2005). Mentoring distance learning faculty from a distance. In C. Crawford, (Eds.), Proceedings of Society for Information Technology & Teacher Education International Conference 2005 (pp. 412–413). Chesapeake, VA: AACE; http://www.editlib.org/p/19024, Retrieved August 18, 2014.

Indiana Higher Education Telecommunication System. (2005). Guiding Principles for Faculty in Distance Learning, Retrieved July, 2014: http://www.ihets.org/progserv/education/distance/guiding_principles/index.html#intro

Jaschik, S. (2009). The Obama plan. *Inside Higher Ed.,* Retrieved September, 2011: http://www.insidehighered.com/news/2009/07/15/obama

Kist, W. (2009). *The socially networked classroom: Teaching in the new media age.* Thousand Oaks, CA: Corwin Press.

Kolowich, S. (2010). Buying local, online. *Inside Higher Ed.,* Retrieved September, 2011: http://www.insidehighered.com/news/2010

Kuiper, E., & Volman, M. (2008). The Web as a source of information for students in K–12 education. In J. Coiro, M. Knobel, C. Lankshear, & D. Leu (Eds.), *Handbook of research on new literacies* (pp. 241–246). Mahwah, NJ: Lawrence Erlbaum.

Leander, K. M. (2008). Toward a connective ethnography of online/ offline literacy networks. In J. Coiro, M. Knobel, C. Lankshear, & D. Leu (Eds.), *Handbook of research on new literacies* (pp. 33–66). Mahwah, NJ: Lawrence Erlbaum.

McGinnis, T. A. (2007). Khmer rap boys, X-Men, Asia's fruits, and Dragonball Z: Creating multilingual and multimodal classroom contexts. *Journal of Adolescent & Adult Literacy, 50*(7), 570–579. doi:10.1598/JAAL.50.7.6

Mezirow, J. (1991). *Transformative dimensions of Adult Learning*. San Francisco, CA: Jossey-Bass.

Mills, K. A. (2010). Shrek meets Vygotsky: Rethinking adolescents' multimodal literacy practices in schools. *Journal of Adolescent & Adult Literacy, 54*(1), 35–45. doi:10.1598/JAAL.54.1.4

Moore, J. (2004). Synthesis of sloan-c effective practices. *The Sloan Consortium*. Retrieved July, 2014: http://www.sloanc.org/publications/books/epsyn1104.pdf

Moorman, G., & Horton, J. (2007). Millenials and how to teach them. In J. Lewis & G. Moorman (Eds.), *Adolescent literacy instruction: Policies and promising practices* (pp. 263–285). Newark, DE: International Reading Association.

Patrick, S. (2013). Education domain: Blended and online learning. *INACOL*, Retrieved July, 2014: http://susanpatrick.inacol.org/tag/blended-learning/

Pear, J., & Crone-Todd, E. (2001). A social constructivist approach to computer-mediated instruction. *Computers & Education, 38*(1-3), 221–231. doi:10.1016/S0360-1315(01)00070-7

Roach, A., & Beck, J. (2012). Before coffee, Facebook: New literacy learning for 21st century teachers. *Language Arts, 89*(4), 244–255.

Rowsell, J., & Lapp, D. (2011). New literacies in literacy instruction. In L. M. Morrow & L. B. Gambrell (Eds.), *Best practices in literacy instruction* (4th ed., pp. 395–411). New York, NY: Guilford.

Shoffner, M., De Oliviera, L., & Angus, R. (2010). Multiliteracies in the secondary English classroom: Becoming literate in the 21st century. *English Teaching, 9*(3), 75–89.

Sotillo, S. (2002). Constructivist and collaborative learning in a wireless environment. *TESOL Journal, 11*(3), 16–20.

Sweeny, S. (2010). Writing for the instant messaging and text messaging generation: Using new literacies to support writing instruction. *Journal of Adolescent & Adult Literacy, 54*(2), 121–130. doi:10.1598/JAAL.54.2.4

Tarnopolsky, 0. (2011). Experiential B.E. teaching/learning: A happy combination of intercultural and communicative approaches. *Business Issues, 78*, 7-8.

Walton, A. (2011). Learning at a distance: Undergraduate enrollment in distance education courses and degree programs. *U.S. Department of Education, National Center for Education Statistics,* Retrieved July 2014: http://nces.ed.gov/pubsearch/pubsinfo.asp?pubid=2012154

Wan, A. (2014). How can learners learn from experience? A case study in blended learning at higher education. *International Journal of Information and Education Technology, 5*(8), 615–619http://www.ijiet.org/papers/578-X0014.pdf. RetrievedAugust2014. doi:10.7763/IJIET.2015.V5.578

Wolcott, L. (1995). The distance teacher as reflective practitioner. *Educational Technology*, January/February Issue, 39-43.

KEY TERMS AND DEFINTIONS

Adult Learning: Andragogy (adult learning) is a theory that holds a set of assumptions about how adults learn. Andragogy emphasizes the value of the process of learning.

CIB: represents the constructivist internet-blended approach used by Penland in her study.

Constructivism: Is a type of learning theory that explains human learning as an active attempt to construct *meaning* in the world; learners ultimately construct their own knowledge for meaning.

Internet-Blended Education: Formal education program in which a student learns at least in part through online delivery of content and instruction with some element of student control over time, place, path or pace.

Professional Learning Environment/ Community: Social groupings of people who come together over time for the purpose of gaining new information, reconsidering previous knowledge and beliefs, and building on their own and others' ideas and experiences in order to work on a specific agenda intended to improve practice and enhance learning.

Resiliency: The ability to absorb disturbances and still retain basic function and structure and has the capacity to change in order to maintain the same identity.

Self-Directed Learning (SDL): Is learning that is related to but different from informal learning; "learning on your own" or "by yourself; auto didacticism or self-education.

Chapter 4

A Call for Teacher Preparation Programs to Model Technology Integration into the Instructional Process

Judi Simmons Estes
Park University, USA

ABSTRACT

The purpose of this chapter is to create a sense of urgency for teacher preparation programs to integrate technology into the instructional process. School administrators expect that first-year teachers will know how to integrate technology with instruction to enhance the teaching-learning process (Webb, 2011). Yet, teacher preparation program faculty, do not consistently model the use or pedagogy of technology-infused coursework. The intentional embedding of technology in teacher preparation courses and assignments is critical in developing teacher candidates with requisite technology knowledge and skills for P-12 teaching in the 21st century. This chapter discusses: (a) the need for technology literate teachers, (b) the role of teacher preparation programs, (c) the need for technology literate faculty, (d) one training model for integrating technology into instruction, enhancing Missouri's Instructional Network Teaching Strategies (e-MINTS).

INTRODUCTION

Today's educational technology discussions focus on teachers using strategies for integrating technology into instruction in meaningful ways that enhance the learning experience of a diversified group of students. Attention has shifted from providing teacher training upon employment to an expectation that first-year teachers will arrive

at their jobs with needed technology knowledge and skills. Twenty years ago, a report concluded that teacher preparation programs were not preparing graduates to use technology as a teaching tool (Office of Technology Assessment [OTA], 1995). About the same time, Cooper and Bull (1997) discussed how teacher educators were faced with increasing pressure to "…integrate technology in their programs and to graduate new

DOI: 10.4018/978-1-4666-8363-1.ch004

teachers who are knowledgeable about and skilled in use of technology" (p. 97). Today, Cooper and Bull's call for action remains applicable; while there has been progress, many teacher educators still do not focus on instruction that integrates technology tools. Furthermore, technology has not universally been integrated into the curriculum of teacher preparation programs. This chapter will discuss: (a) the need for technology literate P-12 teacher candidates and teachers; (b) the role of teacher preparation programs in providing technology literate teacher candidates; (c) the need for technology-literate teacher preparation faculty; (d) a professional development training model for integrating technology into instruction that is being used in P-12 schools.

BACKGROUND

While accessibility to and use of technology in the classroom has increased, most teachers and students tend to only use technology for basic tasks such as communication, record keeping, and Internet research (National Center for Statistics [NCES], 2000). In a national survey of P-12 classroom teachers, only 40% indicated that they or their students frequently use technology for instructional activities (NCES, 2010). It is clear that effectiveness and efficiency in meeting today's high demand for technology in the P-12 classroom goes beyond availability and use and must include delivering curriculum content and instruction to meet the diverse learning needs of students (King-Sears & Emenova, 2007).

"Administrators generally expect new teachers entering the classroom for the first time to be fully prepared to integrate technology into the curriculum and their classrooms" (Webb, 2011, p. 4). Hiring a competent, capable, and technology literate teacher benefits an administrator because this individual will potentially need less technology guidance the first year of employment and the focus of support can be on instructional delivery

and orientation to the school community. Many P-12 teachers struggle to keep current with the use of emerging and rapidly advancing tools of instructional technology; this lack can be attributed, in part, to a paucity of training opportunities (Teclehaimanot, Mentzer, & Hickman, 2011; U.S. Department of Education, 2005). The reality is that daily life as an educator is time intensive and schools often do not have the ability to provide release time, nor the dollars to pay for professional development. School administrators want to hire first-year teachers who are technology literate; technology-literate graduates who successfully complete teacher preparation programs are the first to be hired.

THE NEED FOR TECHNOLOGY LITERATE TEACHERS

There is a need for today's P-12 teachers to be technologically literate which includes: (a) knowing how to use technology tools; (b) demonstrating pedagogy for technology-integrated instruction, (c) having the self-efficacy for implementing pedagogy through integration of technology with instruction.

Knowing How to Use Technology Tools

The National Council for the Accreditation of Teacher Education (n.d.) Glossary defines the use of technology as: "What candidates must know and understand about information technology in order to use it in working effectively with students and professional colleagues in (a) the delivery, development, prescription, and assessment of instruction; (b) problem solving; (c) school and classroom administration; (d) educational research; (e) electronic information access and exchange; and (f) personal and professional productivity."

Teachers tend to be comfortable using word processing applications in front of students, but they aren't as comfortable with presentation programs, databases, spreadsheets, and other content application programs or cloud-based technology. Additionally, being expected to use technological tools for communicating with parents, tracking student progress, and preparing reports can be a sense of unnecessary pressure for a first-year teacher. Pressure can intensify when a teacher doesn't have or isn't comfortable with the needed technology skills. Given that teachers can be overwhelmed the first year they teach, these teachers shouldn't have to spend the first year learning technology in addition to their other duties.

As important as the administrative functions that technology serves, technology has the potential to provide new strategies for teaching and learning in our P-12 schools (Rakes, Flowers, Case, & Santana, 2006; Siemens & Matheos, 2010); the increase in availability of electronic resources in schools results in a critical need for teachers to be prepared to effectively integrate technology into the instructional and assessment processes. Unfortunately, studies have demonstrated that teachers do not feel adequately trained to integrate technology into instruction; in fact, teachers are poor at integrating technology with other activities in support of student-centered learning (Flemming, Motamiti, & May, 2007; Lawless & Pellegrino, 2007).

When classroom teachers arrive at their teaching assignment as a technology-literate professional, they can be a change agent, within their schools for infusing technology into instruction and the learning process (Rudnesky, 2003). Yet, in a study of teacher candidates self-reported perceptions of their own technology competencies, researchers found that toward the end of their program, teacher candidates self-reported needing further instruction and experience in pedagogical application of technology (Milman, Kortecamp, & Peters, 2007). The expectations for the 21st century P-12 teacher are high. A deficit in any

needed area of knowledge becomes handicapping and a potential source of stress. When a teacher does have knowledge, skills, confidence, a well-grounded pedagogy of technology integration with instruction and assessment, as well as ideas of strategies for implementation, efficiency increases, instruction is enriched, and contributions to the overall school environment are noticeable.

Developing a Pedagogy for Technology Integrated Instruction

Teacher candidates need to be trained not only in the use of technology, but also in the pedagogy of technology use including integration of technology into the instructional process. Pedagogical approaches, how teachers orchestrate classroom learning, do matter, especially today as changes are occurring in traditional methods of teaching in order to meet the needs of students (McKenzie, 2003). Rather than technology creating educational improvement, educational improvement results from technology integration with effective instruction and assessment collectively supporting high-quality student learning (Goldman, Lawless, Pellegrino, & Plants, 2006). Therefore, one way to further integrate technology with teaching is to link the critical features of instructional practices with an appropriate aspect of technology (Smith & Okolo, 2010). King-Sears and Emenova (2007) posit three premises for integrating technology into teacher preparation program instruction: technology must be part of teacher candidates' instructional programs because they will be called upon as teachers to have these skills, integration is ensuring that the technology itself does not become the point of instruction, and knowing about the newest advances in technology is a responsibility shared among educators and not the responsibility of any single faculty member.

Technology training alone does not lead to teacher candidates' high levels of technology use in the classroom. The access to instructional technology in the school environment and the availability of ongoing support and mentoring related to technology use are necessary to help teacher candidates' implement what they learn from the initial technology training. Technology mentoring can provide relevant and practical support for teacher candidates to improve the ways they integrate technology in their teaching. (Oigara & Wallace, 2012).

Copley and Zivani (2003) distinguish the notion that technology is perceived by teachers and students as a separate activity used to train isolated skills from the notion of teachers and students routinely and naturally accessing technology as part of students' daily activities. Dias (1999) contends that "...technology is integrated when it is used in a seamless manner to support and extend curriculum objectives and to engage students in meaningful learning" (p. 10). Technology should be used in the context of specific curriculum and learning activities rather than becoming an isolated focus of instruction (Gardner, Wissick, Schweder, & Canter 2003). "Decisions about when to use technology, what technology to use, and for what purposes cannot be made in isolation of theories and research on learning, instruction, and assessment" (Lawless & Pellegrino, 2007, p. 581).

Constructivism as Active Learning:. The idea of constructivism as active learning is steeped in the theories of Dewey (1859-1952), Piaget (1896-1980), and Vygotsky (1896-1934); collectively these theorists are responsible for the emergence of the pedagogy of constructivism. Constructivism promotes social interaction among students, engagement, and processes that stimulate critical thinking, inquiry, and problem-based learning. Teachers play an integral role in promoting and sustaining critical discourse and constructive social dynamics, managing both learning (e.g., promoting higher-level thinking) and social connections between students. The pedagogy of constructivism provides more of a risk-taking mindset. For example, typically, technology available in the classroom is not likely to be used if the teacher has not had at least some minimal

training. In the business of a school day, teachers will use tools and strategies with which they are most comfortable. However, a teacher who has had training in constructivism and the value of active community learning is more apt to experiment with unknown technology tools and the teacher's necessity to know everything diminishes. It becomes acceptable for students to help the teacher as they collaborate and learn together in a spirt of community, rather than the teacher feeling a need to be the sole source of information.

There are differences of opinion among educators regarding the effectiveness of a constructivist approach to teaching (Kirchner, Sweller, & Clark, 2006; Schmidt, Loyens, van Gog, & Paas, 2007). These differences in opinion can result from a misunderstanding; the constructivist approach to instruction does not translate to minimal guidance, nor does it preclude the use of direct instruction. The position that constructivism and integrating technology with instruction couple naturally will be discussed at length in the section of this chapter pertaining to pedagogy of teacher preparation faculty.

Self-Efficacy in Implementing Pedagogy

Knowing how to use technology tools and developing pedagogy for using those tools in an intentional and meaningful way to enhance instruction are first steps, but having self-efficacy related to implementation of knowledge, skills, and pedagogy is critical. When a teacher has positive attitudes about the role of technology as an integrated aspect of instruction, the more likely he or she will be to integrate technology into the curriculum (Wang, Ertneme, & Newby, 2004) and to offer peer support, which in turn assists colleagues in taking more risks to integrate technology themselves (Murphy, Richards, Lewis, Carmen, 2005). Having a positive attitude is typically related to having confidence in one's abilities, one's sense of self-efficacy.

Self-efficacy refers to an individual's judgment about being able to perform an activity (Murphy & Alexander, 2001); self-efficacy is influenced by an individual's judgment about their own past performances (e.g., "I have/haven't been successful in using technology in the past."), impressions of performance of others (e.g., "Others are better at technology use than I am."), verbal persuasion (e.g., "I can do this."), and physiological states (e.g., a sense of calmness or upset stomach, jitters, etc.).

There are several reasons for preparing teacher candidates to be first-year teachers who enter the classroom with a strong sense of technology-related self-efficacy. First, a new teacher can be overwhelmed with the plethora of duties and responsibilities; while a teacher candidate gets exposure to the "real life of a teacher" during directed teaching, having full responsibility is quite a different experience. Secondly, due to the time commitment of the many duties and responsibilities, having confidence in using technology for efficiency and effectiveness of instruction can be a significant benefit. Thirdly, as much as principals want to be readily available to provide assistance to new teachers, many teachers find themselves "on their own" and needing to find answers to dilemmas. Teachers with high degrees of efficacy persist longer in situations that are seen as difficult; students who are innately capable sometimes do not learn because they lack a belief in their abilities to accomplish the actions necessary to learn; they lack self-efficacy (Bandura, 1977; Bandura, 1986).

Increasingly, teacher preparation programs are being called upon to provide candidates instruction on how to use technology tools, a pedagogy of integrating technology into instruction using active learning, and providing opportunities to do both through coursework assignments that provide ample practice and thus contribute to a sense of self-efficacy in one's technology knowledge and skills.

THE ROLE OF TEACHER PREPARATION PROGRAMS

The International Society for Technology in Education (2000) has argued that technology must become integrated into the teaching and learning processes supporting the preparation of teachers for P-12 classrooms; teacher preparation programs are critical in providing modeling, training, and subsequent implementation of technology use for integration with instruction in P-12 schools (Zhao, 2007). Furthermore, NCATE (2008) accreditation standards emphasize the need for teacher preparation programs to use educational technology to help candidates' master skills in meeting the needs of diverse learners. Nevertheless, in a teacher survey from the NCES (2010), only 25% of respondents reported that their undergraduate teacher education programs had a moderate or major impact on their ability to effectively integrate technology into instruction. Sutton (2011) surveyed teacher candidates regarding the technology training that they received in their teacher preparation program; three themes emerged: (a) a disconnect between technology training and other aspects of teacher training; (b) a lack of content area training in relation to technology; (c) inadequate attention and transfer opportunities. There is a need for teacher training programs to intentionally include technology, as an instructional tool, into course learning outcomes.

Curriculum Planning to Infuse Technology into Coursework

Teacher preparation programs need to consider programmatic changes to address the growing need for preparing teachers to become effective users of emerging educational technology. A single technology course is not sufficient to prepare teacher candidates for integrating technology into instruction and assessment; technology training needs to be infused throughout teacher preparation programs, covered in all classes, modeled in all instruction received and utilized in all field experiences (Sutton, 2011).

To best prepare teacher candidates to be effective users of instructional technology students should be trained to understand the benefits of technology and be provided with specific assignments designed to help them acquire the knowledge, confidence, and skills during their coursework. For teacher candidates to make instructional technology part of their practice, with confidence, they must also have easy access to the technology, be in a supportive environment, and have opportunities to reflect on its role in their own practice. For example, integrating technology into methods courses provides teacher candidates an opportunity to learn about the technology applications available for their particular content area (Bolick, Berson, Coutis, & Heineke, 2003).

The Importance of Support from Administration

Kotrlik, Harrison, and Remann (2000) posited that instructional leaders directly and indirectly determine the success or failure of teacher knowledge and skills in technology and are instrumental in the success or failure of technology being integrated into curriculum. In general, academic leaders are critical in creating an environment in higher education which encourages and supports effective teaching. It is the role of university leaders such as deans, to set the priorities for the academic unit they supervise. Lessen and Sorenson (2006) identified four key actions for a dean to demonstrate in support of technology integration: (a) setting technology integration as a priority, through personal use and expectations of faculty; (b) creating an environment and departmental infrastructure where technology integration is possible, including providing access to technology tools and locating funding for needed and sustainable resources, and alignment with university departments; (c)

building a resource base which may tap outside resources or involve fund-raising; (d) ensure that faculty, staff, and students have access to training and support. In short, administration can set the course for technology integration. Mandating faculty use of technology is not an effective strategy. However, once curriculum integration has begun and the majority of faculty are modeling the integration of technology into coursework, setting training and expectations, for all new faculty, is appropriate.

Implementing the aforementioned action steps for technology integration is an organic process. It takes time to create a culture of technology integration. It takes planning and allowing time for change and adaptions. For example, location of a room that will gradually become a technologically-rich environment can take time. Also, purchasing technology is not a one-time expense; maintenance is also an expense and having a plan for on-going purchases of new technologies is important given the rapid pace of technological innovations. Thus, sustainability of commitment to technology integration is critical. Purchasing technology hardware and software without a long-term plan for implementation of technology integration does little toward integrating technology into coursework and instruction as a permanent part of the curriculum.

Partnering with P-12 Schools

Every academic year, teacher candidates go into P-12 schools to observe, complete field experiences or practicums, or perhaps complete their directed teaching and these students find technology in use that they have never seen or had experience with in their teacher education program. This fact alone is reason enough for teacher preparation programs to be meeting regularly with their school partners to learn what technology knowledge and skills are needed by entry level teachers. This authentic information is as meaningful as NCATE or ISTE guidelines and standards and perhaps informs at a more meaningful level. Because P-12 schools often have better technology facilities and more experienced technology teachers and staff than do the colleges and universities with whom they are partnering, they can be a resource for teacher preparation programs as students have observation and field experiences. However, assuring technology exposure for teacher candidates is not always a factor considered in field experiences and clinical placements.

Because technology changes progress so quickly, P-12 principals can be challenged to keep teachers updated on the newest trends and applications. What if a first-year teacher entered his or her classroom already confident in technology use and instructional pedagogy? How would this benefit both the teacher and the employing school? When a School for Education does not properly train teacher candidates in the pedagogy and use of technology to enhance instruction, employing school districts become responsible for providing initial knowledge and skill development. Colleges and Schools of Education must collaborate with and provide support to partnership schools through the preparation of teacher candidates and ensure that teacher candidates are placed with mentor teachers proficient in the use of technology for instruction with the ultimate and mutual goal of improving student learning in our P-12 schools.

THE NEED FOR TECHNOLOGY LITERATE HIGHER EDUCATION FACULTY

Just as there is a need for today's P-12 teachers to be technologically literate, there is a need for faculty in teacher preparation programs to have similar skills, including use of technology tools, as well as development of pedagogy for technology-integrated instruction and self-efficacy for implementing this pedagogy.

Knowing How to Use Technology Tools

Telling students about the possible uses of technology tools is not enough. If teacher candidates are to learn to integrate technology effectively into the classroom, they must see the use of technologically integrated instruction modeled effectively by faculty; education faculty must integrate a wide range of technology tools in their courses to help teacher candidates develop an understanding of how technology might be used and differentiated to facilitate learning for a population of diverse students. If teacher candidates are to learn to integrate technology effectively into the classroom they must be given specific training in current instructional technology use, and the multiple applications for instruction. If teacher candidates are to learn to integrate technology effectively into the classroom instruction, they must be provided with ongoing mentoring support for their emerging skills in the use of technology in the field. However, there is often limited faculty modeling of appropriate use of technology in teacher education courses (NCES, 2000; Teclehaimanot, Mentzer, & Hickman, 2011). Modeling effective classroom technology practices by teacher education faculty and cooperating teachers in field placements is critical to successful mastery of instructional technology integration by teacher candidates.

In some institutions of higher education, technology is a catalyst for discussions about learning, teaching, web-based approaches, and rethinking best teaching practices (de la Harpe & Peterson, 2009; Huber & Hutchings, 2005). Technology has the potential to provide new opportunities for creating exciting learning and teaching environments, offering as yet undiscovered and unimagined ways of creating, integrating and disseminating knowledge (Gregorian 2005). There are faculty who are optimistic about the use of technology and its potential beyond personal productivity, such as enhancing teaching, providing greater access and flexibility to learning, and facilitating collaboration. Some faculty believe that technology has been a magnet for transforming the way faculty think about learning and teaching and discussing these ideas with one another.

There is reluctance from some faculty to use technology and integrate it with instruction because use of technology challenges traditional notions of teaching and lacks a theoretical framework for sound practice (Swan, 2007). Others believe that the use of technology may not provide better learning and achievement for students (Steimberg, Ram, Nahmia, & Esheel, 2006). There are a few faculty who fear technology may reduce personal interaction and isolate students from teachers (Roblyer, 2003). While some reluctant faculty will agree that student exposure to technology is important, some see use of technology as a responsibility for others and not to be integrated into their own teaching. Other faculty may simply have limited experience in technology use or lack an understanding of meaningful integration with instruction.

Developing a Pedagogy for Technology Integrated Instruction

Previously, there was a discussion of pedagogy as related to teacher candidates. Perhaps a discussion of pedagogy for technology integrated instruction is more important in relation to faculty in teacher preparation programs. These are the teachers who are serving as role models for students. If a faculty member does not model and believe in the student benefits of experiencing technology integrated instruction, then teacher candidates will not see the value either. Introducing a culture of technology integration into the culture of a teacher preparation program can raise fundamental and difficult questions about the role of faculty. Technology adds another layer of complexity to teaching; it can require a shift in viewing oneself as the "sage on the stage" to a facilitator of the learning process.

Chickering and Gamson (1987) introduced seven principles for good practice in undergraduate education. The seven practices include: (a) encourage contact between students and faculty; (b) develop reciprocity and cooperation among students; (c) encourage active learning; (d) give prompt feedback; (e) emphasize time on task; (f) communicate high expectation; (g) respect diverse talents and ways of learning. Collectively, these principles are consistent with a constructivist pedagogy that views teachers as facilitators of the learning process and active learning as a way to support critical thinking and problem solving which was also discussed when describing teacher candidates' development of a pedagogy supporting technology integration.

Constructivism and Active Learning: There is a substantial amount of research citing the benefits of collaborative learning (Johnson & Johnson, 1989, 2004). Studies have demonstrated that when individual students engage in collaborative learning, they demonstrate higher academic achievement, social connections, self-efficacy (Johnson & Johnson, 1989; Johnson, Johnson, & Smith, 1991) and critical thinking (Schultz, 2003). The goal of providing a collaborative learning environment goes beyond "knowledge acquisition" and "participation" to building new knowledge (Paavola, Lippnen, & Hakkarainen, 2004) and social connection. Activities that require student interaction and encourage sharing of ideas promote critical thinking (Conrad & Donaldson, 2004). These examples are also benefits of integrating technology with instruction to expand the learning process. As students work together to solve a problem, to investigate a topic, to create a graphic organizer, they can experience the benefits of collaborative learning while also engaging in the use of technology.

Faculty in teacher education programs transmit the technological pedagogy that is conveyed to the students in the program. In order for faculty to be effective in guiding students in use of technology to enhance instruction, faculty must have knowledge and confidence; in turn students are then more likely to integrate technology into their own teaching practices.

Self-Efficacy in Implementing Pedagogy

Earlier, the importance of technology self-efficacy for teacher candidates was discussed. Technology self-efficacy is also important for teacher preparation faculty because it is difficult to model the use of technology and integration of technology into instruction if you don't believe in your own skill set. There has been little research related to the self-efficacy, particularly technology self-efficacy, but Kagima and Hausafu (2000) conducted a study of university faculty and integration of electronic communication in teaching; results demonstrated a statistically significant relationship between technology integration and the technology self-efficacy. Faculty who demonstrated a high level of integrating electronic communication in teaching also had a high sense of self-efficacy.

It is important to note that self-efficacy differs from self-concept in that self-concept is a general self-perception of one's overall abilities; self-efficacy is belief specific to a certain area of learning. This is important to note in a discussion of technology self-efficacy among teacher preparation faculty. These individuals tend to have doctoral degrees and high degrees of success professionally. However, they may lack self-efficacy as related to technology. One of the challenges for all teachers and perhaps particularly for faculty in higher education is that technology changes are constantly occurring and it takes an intentional commitment to stay abreast of these changes. Similar to P-12 teachers, faculty in teacher preparation programs find their days filled, not only with teaching, but also with scholarship and service requirements that involve committee meetings, action research, and writing for publication. It has been reported that students' self-efficacy can increase from self-modeling, or watching videos

of their own successful performance (Schunk, 2008). Presumably, the same may be true with teacher preparation faculty also, but access to these opportunities can be limited unless there is a college or university culture of support for technology integration with instruction.

ONE TRAINING MODEL FOR TECHNOLOGY-INTEGRATED INSTRUCTION

A model has been developed to support teachers in the acquisition of skills so that they will, in turn, provide students with assignments requiring the use of technology. This model is called enhancing Missouri's Instructional Networked Teaching Strategies (eMINTS); it is a model of learner-centered instruction powered by technology for P-20 classrooms. The eMINTS National Center at the University of Missouri is a non-profit organization that has provided comprehensive research-based professional development services to educators since 1999. eMINTS professional development uses interactive group sessions and in-classroom coaching/mentoring to help teachers integrate technology into their teaching using an instructional model that (a) supports high-quality lesson design; (b) promotes authentic learning; (c) creates technology-rich learning environments; (d) builds community among students and teachers. To date, there have been sixteen empirical studies of e-MINTS and the impact of how teachers teach and how students learn. For example, in a summary of ten annual external evaluations conducted between 1999 and 2009, evidence was compiled documenting the effects of eMINTS professional development on teacher and student outcomes. Consistently, elementary students in classrooms where eMINTS has been implemented significantly outperformed students (math, science, social studies, and communication arts) who had not been exposed to eMINTS. Teachers trained in e-MINTS self-report improvement in their inquiry-based teaching activities, their computer use, and their perception of their own computer skills (Office of Social and Economic Data Analysis, 2001). The comprehensive eMINTS Professional Development program received a Seal of Alignment from ISTE in 2005 and 2008. The Seal of Alignment for Mastery is more rigorous and is awarded to resources or programs that include the ISTE standard learning objectives, specified implementation plans, and embedded tools that measure performance skills; the Seal of Alignment for Mastery was awarded to eMINTS in 2013.

Currently, institutions of higher education faculty have not universally accepted and employed the practice of a learner-centered approach to teaching (Weimer, 2010), nor are they consistently integrating technology into their own teacher practices. Teacher preparation programs must begin to offer a learner-centered instruction practice of technology integration in support of preparing teacher candidates to meet the demands required of twenty-first century P-12 teachers. Integrating the eMINTS model into teacher preparation curriculum is inclusive of elements of professional development that have been found to be most effective: training occurs over a two- year period, using a cohort model, and with mentoring to meet the needs of the individual attendees, as well as an annual national conference to keep abreast of emerging technology and applications.

Applying eMINTS in a Teacher Preparation Program: The School for Education at Park University began working with e-MINTS trainers in 2013 to integrate the two-year training modules into the teacher preparation curriculum so that teacher candidates will graduate as eMINTS certified teachers. This multi-step process began with securing funds for four university personnel to attend the two-year eMINTS training program (two SFE faculty member, a SFE data analyst and technical specialist, and the assistant director of the Center for Teaching and Learning Excellence). Each training year requires participants

to complete topical modules that pertain to high quality lesson planning, authentic learning, and critical thinking.

The second step has been a combined effort to provide faculty access to (a) technology tools (e.g., move Smart boards out of a closet and mount in classrooms); (b) technology training (e.g., how to use Smart boards); (c) a computer lab in which an introductory technology course can be taught. Step three has been to work with interested faculty to begin the process of integrating technology into the delivery of coursework including an integration of e-MINTS modules. For example, the School for Education data analyst and technical specialist is working with a faculty member who is teaching educational psychology supporting students in using technology for course assignments (e.g., development of a course blog, use of Google docs for student peer assignments, use of Webquests, developing presentations using Animato and Powtoon, as well as creation of You Tube videos). While none of these tools are currently innovative to the field of technology, the use of these tools are innovative for faculty who are integrating them into coursework for the first time.

Step four emerged as individual faculty have made requests to have access to eMINTS modules for use in their courses. For example, an introductory technology course is in process of being redeveloped for both face-to-face and online delivery including eMINTS modules on the topics of constructivism, building community, and cooperative learning groups and a faculty member who teaches an assessment course is integrating the two eMINTS assessment modules. A curriculum map is being created to identify eMINTS modules being integrated into SFE courses. An intentional decision was made at the onset of this journey, not to initially focus on securing funds to secure new technology hardware and software, but rather to capitalize on technology that was already available within the university system and to build faculty skills in technology use and pedagogy for integration in instruction.

Step 5 will entail completing the curriculum map of integration of eMINTS modules and building a sustainable plan with the university's Instructional Technology department for purchasing technology tools that our teacher candidates will encounter in P-12 schools (e.g., Chromebooks, IPADS, etc.). A future goal includes inviting faculty to observe in P-12 classrooms that are led by eMINTS certified teachers and where the pedagogy of eMINTS is visible. While these SFE efforts are in their infancy, steps that have been taken thus far, have forged new partnerships among faculty within the School for Education and with other University departments.

CHALLENGES

Integration of technology into coursework offered in teacher education programs is a complex process. In Godard's (2002) discussion of technology integration into higher education, a caution was given regarding focusing on the purchase of hardware without the needed discussions around pedagogy and value of thoughtful integration technology into the teaching learning process: "All across America blank computer screens stare out at teachers, and the teachers stare back" (p. 19).

In this chapter, a call has been given for teacher preparation programs to model integrating technology into instruction. Many programs are graduating candidates who are not technology literate and this is putting pressure on P-12 school districts to provide basic training which takes the focus away from instruction and keeping up with emerging technologies. The solution that has been offered is for teacher education programs to integrate the use of technology throughout coursework, modeling integration through faculty instruction and through coursework assignments. Integration of technology into the coursework of teacher preparation programs is not new; this action was initially proposed by Cooper and Bull (1997). Eighteen years later, integration of tech-

nology into teacher preparation programs is still not a common practice. There can be challenges to teacher preparation programs including:

- A lack of administrative leadership and support;
- The need for the time-consuming process of long-term planning and curriculum planning;
- The need for faculty to develop self-efficacy in the use of technology and the pedagogy of active learning inherent in the modeling of technology integration;
- Development of a sustainable culture of technology integration;
- Funding for needed resources.

To prepare our teacher candidates for 21st century teaching, individual teacher preparation programs must begin to take steps toward leading the cause of modeling technology integration for our teacher candidates.

FUTURE RESEARCH DIRECTIONS

As teacher preparation programs engage in the process of integrating technology into instruction, processes and practices for integration will continue to be an important area for inquiry.

1. It is important that faculty, within teacher education programs, share with one another strategies to implement technology into coursework. This discussion may include taking an inventory of available technology, accessibility, faculty training needs, and ongoing discussions of challenges.
2. Follow-up is needed with teacher candidate graduates, identifying how they are transferring their knowledge of technology tools, use, pedagogy, and instructional strategies to diverse populations of students.

3. Teacher preparation programs must partner with K-12 stakeholders, including school administration and teachers with whom candidates are placed for clinical experiences (practicums and directed teaching). Partnering could include providing professional development that offers candidates and practicing teachers opportunities to co-construct knowledge and skills, as well as providing access to shared resources and support.

REFERENCES

Bandura, A. (1977). Self-efficacy: Toward a unifying theory of behaviors change. *Psychological Review*, *84*(2), 191–215. doi:10.1037/0033-295X.84.2.191 PMID:847061

Bandura, A. (1986). *Social foundations of thought and action: A social cognition theory*. Englewood Cliffs, NJ: Prentice-Hall.

Bolick, C., Berson, M., Coutts, C., & Heinecke, W. (2003). Technology applications in social studies teacher education: A survey of social studies methods faculty. *Contemporary Issues in Technology & Teacher Education*, *3*(3), 300–309. Retrieved July 27, 2014 from http://www.citejournal.org/vol3/iss3/socialstudies/article1.cfm

Chickering, A., & Gamson, Z. (1987). Seven principles for good practice in undergraduate education. *AAHE Bulletin*, *39*(7), 3–6.

Conrad, R. M., & Donaldson, A. (2004). *Engaging the online learner: Activities and resources for creative instruction*. San Francisco: Jossey-Bass.

Cooper, J. M., & Bull, G. (1997). Technology and teacher education: Past practice and recommended directions. *Action in Teacher Education*, *19*(2), 97–106. doi:10.1080/01626620.1997.10462871

Copley, J., & Ziviani, J. (2004). Barriers to the use of assistive technology for children with multiple disabilities. *Occupational Therapy International*, *11*(4), 229–243. doi:10.1002/oti.213 PMID:15771212

Dias, L. B. (1999). Integration technology: Some things you should know. *Learning and Leading with Technology*, *27*(3), 10–13.

Digenti, D. (1998). Toward an understanding of the learning community. *Organization Development Journal*, *16*(2), 91–96.

Fleming, L., Motomedi, V., & May, L. (2007). Predicting preservice teacher competence in computer technology: Modeling and application in training environments. *Journal of Technology and Teacher Education*, *15*(2), 207–231.

Gardner, J. E., Wissick, C. A., Schweder, W., & Canter, L. S. (2003). Enhancing interdisciplinary instruction in general and special education: Thematic units and technology. *Remedial and Special Education*, *24*(3), 161–172. doi:10.1177/07419325030240030501

Goddard, M. (2002). What do we do with these computers? Reflections on technology in the classroom. *Journal of Research on Technology in Education*, *35*(1), 19–26. doi:10.1080/15391523.2002.10782367

Goldman, S. R., Lawless, K., Pellegrino, J. W., & Plants, R. (2005). Technology for teaching and learning with understanding. In J. M. Cooper (Ed.), *Classroom Teaching Skills* (8th ed., pp. 185–234). Boston: Houghton Mifflin.

Huber, M. T., & Hutchings, P. (2005). *The advancement of learning: Building the teaching commons*. San Francisco, CA: Jossey-Bass.

International Society for Technology in Education. (2000). *National education technology standards for teachers*. Eugene, OR: Author.

Johnson, D., & Johnson, R. (1989). *Cooperation and competition: Theory and research*. Edina, MN: Interaction Book Company.

Johnson, D., & Johnson, R. (2004). Cooperation and the use of technology. In D. H. Johanssen Handbook of research on educational communications and technology (2nd ed.) (pp. 785-811). Mahwah, NJ: Lawrence Erlbaum Associates.

Johnson, D., Johnson, R., & Smith, K. (1991). *Active learning: Cooperation in the college classroom*. Edina, MN: Interaction Book Company.

Kagima, L. K., & Hausafus, C. O. (2000). Integration of electronic communication in higher education: Contributions of faculty computer self-efficacy. *The Internet and Higher Education, 2*(4), 221–235. doi:10.1016/S1096-7516(00)00027-0

King-Sears, M., & Evmenova, A. S. (2007). Premises, principles, and processes for integrating technology into instruction. *Teaching Exceptional Children, 40,* 6–14.

Kirchner, P. A., Sweller, J., & Clark, R. E. (2006). Why minimal guidance during instruction does not work: An analysis of the failure of constructivist, discover, problem-based experiential, and inquiry-based teaching. *Educational Psychologist, 41*(2), 75–86. doi:10.1207/s15326985ep4102_1

Kotrlik, J. W., Harrison, B. C., & Redmann, D. H. (2000). A comparison of information technology training sources, value, knowledge, and skills for Louisiana's secondary vocational teachers. *Journal of Vocational Education Research, 35*(4), 396–444. doi:10.5328/JVER25.4.396

Lawless, K. A., & Pellegrino, J. W. (2007). Professional development in integrating technology into teaching and learning: Knowns, unknowns, and ways to pursue better questions and answers. *Review of Educational Research, 77*(4), 575–614. Retrieved June 6 2014 from http://www.jstor.org/stable/4624911. doi:10.3102/0034654307309921

Lessen, E., & Sorensen, C. (2006). Integrating technology in schools, colleges, and departments of education: A primer for deans. *Change, 38*(2), 44–49. doi:10.3200/CHNG.38.2.44-49

McCannon, M., & Crews, T. (2000). Assessing the technology training needs of elementary school teachers. *Journal of Technology and Teacher Education, 8*(2), 111–121.

McKenzie, J. (2003). Pedagogy does matter. *The Educational Technology Journal, 13*(1).

Milman, N. B., Kortecamp, K., & Peters, M. (2007). Assessing teacher candidates' perceptions and attributions of their technology competencies. *International Journal of Technology in Teaching and Learning, 3*(3), 15–35.

Murphy, K. L., Richards, J., Lewis, C., & Carman, E. (2005). Strengthening educational technology in K-8 urban schools and in preservice education: A practioner-faculty collaborative process. *Journal of Technology and Teacher Education, 13*(1), 125–139.

Murphy, P. K., & Alexander, P. A. (2001). A motivated exploration of motivation terminology. *Contemporary Educational Psychology, 25*(1), 3–53. doi:10.1006/ceps.1999.1019 PMID:10620380

Myers, C., & Brandt, W. C. (2010). *A summary of external program evaluation findings for the e-MINTS (enhancing Missouri's Instructional Networked Teaching Strategies) program from 1999-2009*. Naperville, ILL. Learning Points Associates, Retrieved July 30, 2014 from http://www.emints.org/wp-content/uploads/2013/09/summary_emints_research.pdf

National Center for Education Statistics. (2000). *Teachers' tools for the 21st century: A report on teacher's use of technology* (Report No. NCES 2000-102). Washington, DC: U.S. Department of Education. Retrieved June 15, 2015, from http://nces.ed.gov/pubsearch/pubsinfo.asp?pubid=2000102

National Center for Education Statistics. (2010). *Teacher' use of educational technology in U.S. public schools: 2009*. Washington, DC: U.S. Department of Education.

National Council for the Accreditation of Teacher Education. (2008). Professional standards for the accreditation of schools, colleges, and departments of education: NCATE Glossary. Washington, DC: Author. Retrieved July 31, 2014, from http://ncate.org/Standards/NCATEUnitStandards/NCATEGlossary/tabid/477/Default.aspx

Office of Social and Economic Data Analysis. (2001). *Final results from the e-MINTS teacher survey*. Columbia, MO: Author.

Office of Technology Assessment. (1995). *Teachers and technology: Making the connection*. Washington, DC: U.S. Government Printing Office.

Oigara, J. N., & Wallace, N. (2012). Modeling, training, and mentoring teacher candidates to use SMART Board technology. *Issues in Informing Science and Information Technology*, *9*, 297–315.

Palloff, R. M., & Pratt, K. (2007). *Building online learning communities*. San Franciso, CA: Jossey-Bass.

Rakes, G. C., Flowers, B. F., Casey, H. C., & Santana, R. (2006). Analysis of instructional technology use and constructivist behaviors in K-12 teachers. *International Journal of Educational Technology*, *1*(12).

Robler, M. D. (2003). *Integrating educational technology into teaching* (3rd ed.). Upper Saddle River, NJ: Merrill Prentice Hall.

Rudnesky, F. (2003). From vision to classroom. *Principal Leadership*, *3*(6), 44–47.

Schmidt, H. G., Loyens, S. M. M., van Gog, T., & Paas, F. (2007). Problem-based learning is compatible with human cognitive architecture: Commentary on Kirschner, Sweller, and Clark (2006). *Educational Psychologist*, *42*(2), 91–97. doi:10.1080/00461520701263350

Schultz, B. (2003). Collaborative learning in an online environment: Will it work for teacher training? In *Proceedings of the 14th annual Society for Information Technology and Teacher Education International Conference* (pp. 503-504). Charlottesville, VA: Association for the Advancement of Computers in Education.

Schunk, D. (2008). *Learning theories: An educational perspective* (5th ed.). Upper Saddle River, NJ: Pearson.

Siemens, G., & Matheos, K. (2010). Systemic changes in higher education. *Education: Technology & Social Media, 16*(1). Retrieved June 20, 2014, from http://www.ineducation.ca/

Smith, S. J., & Okolo, C. (2010). Response to intervention and evidence-based practices: Where does technology fit? *Learning Disability Quarterly*, *33*(4), 252–272. http://www.jstor.org/stable/23053229 Retrieved June 6, 2014

Steimbert, Y., Ram, J., Nachmia, R., & Eshel, A. (2006). An online discussion for supporting students in preparation for a test. *Journal of Asynchronous Learning Networks*, *10*(4). Retrieved June 20, 2014http://www.soan-c.org/publications/jaln/index.asp Retrieved June 20, 2014

Sutton, S. R. (2011). The preservice technology training experiences of preservice teachers. *Journal of Digital Learning in Teacher Education.*, *28*(1), 39–47. doi:10.1080/21532974.2011.10784678

Swan, K. (2007). Research on online learning. *Journal of Asynchronous Learning Networks*, *11*(1). http://www.sloan-c.org/publications/jaln/index.asp Retrieved May 15, 2014

Teclehaimanot, B., Mentzer, G., & Hickman, T. (2011). A mixed methods comparison of teacher education faculty perceptions of the integration of technology into their courses and student feedback of technology proficiency. *Journal of Technology and Teacher Education*, *19*(1), 5–21.

Wang, L., Ertner, P. A., & Newby, T. J. (2004). Increasing preservice teacher's self-efficacy beliefs for technology integration. *Journal of Research in Education*, *3*(3), 231–250.

Webb, L. (2011). Supporting technology integration: The school administrator's role. *National Forum of Educational administration & Supervison Journal*, *28*(4), 1-6.

Zhao, Y. (2007). Social studies teachers' perspectives of technology integration. *Journal of Technology and Teacher Education*, *15*(3), 311–333.

ADDITIONAL READINGS

Adelman, N., Donnelly, M. B., Dove, T., Tiffany-Morales, J., Wayne, A., & Zucker, A. (2002). *The integrated studies of educational technology: Professional development and teacher's use of technology*. Arlington, VA: SRI International.

Albion, P. R. (2001). Some factors in the development of self-efficacy beliefs for computer use among teacher education students. *Journal of Technology and Teacher Education*, *9*(3), 321–347.

Doering, A., Hughes, J., & Huffman, D. (2003). Preservice teachers: Are we thinking with technology? *Journal of Research on Technology in Education*, *35*(3), 342–362. doi:10.1080/15391 523.2003.10782390

Fulton, K., Glenn, A. D., & Valdez, G. (2004). *Teacher education and technology planning guide*. Naperville, ILL: Learning Point Associates.

Hoy, A. W., & Spero, R. B. (2005). Changes in teacher efficacy during the early years of teaching: A comparison of four measures. *Teaching and Teacher Education*, *21*(4), 343–356. doi:10.1016/j.tate.2005.01.007

Schuldman, M. (2004). Superintendents conceptions of institutional conditions that impact teacher technology integration. *Journal of Research on Technology in Education*, *36*(4), 319–343. doi:1 0.1080/15391523.2004.10782418

Technology in Schools Task Force. (2003). *Suggestions, tools, and guidelines for assessing technology in elementary and secondary education*. Retrieved May 20, 2014, from http://nces.ed.gov/pubs2003/tech_school/chapter7.asp

KEY TERMS AND DEFINITIONS

Constructivism: A pedagogy that underlies an approach to teaching and learning based on the belief that students learn in a social environment with and from one another and that the role of the teacher is to facilitate the learning process while embracing the roles of both teacher as facilitator and as a fellow member of the learning community.

e-MINTS: Enhancing Missouri's Instructional Network Teaching Strategies; a professional development model that that supports high quality lesson design, promotes authentic learning, creates a technology-rich learning environment and builds community among students and teachers.

ISTE: The International Society for Technology in Education is a not-for-profit organization that provides standards and criteria for what teachers need to teach and what students need to learn, as well as what content needs to be provided by a professional development program in relation to educational technology.

P-12: P-12 represents preschool through twelfth grades, terminology typically used in public schools.

P-20: P-20 represents the education systems inclusive of preschool through higher education.

NCATE: The National Council for the Accreditation of Teacher Education was founded as an accrediting body for teacher certification programs colleges and universities which joined with the Teacher Education Accreditation Council (TEAC) to form the Council for the Accreditation of Educator Preparation (CAEP).

Office of Technology Assessment: The Office of Technology Assessment opened as an office of the U.S. Congress from 1972 to 1995 and responsible for providing Congress with authoritative and bipartisan reports on a wide range of issues in science and technology, including issues related to education. Princeton University now hosts the OTA legacy website https://www.princeton.edu/~ota/.

Pedagogy: Beliefs that guide the actual function of teaching; what teachers believe that in turn guides what they do when implementing their craft to assist student learning.

Self-Efficacy: Self-efficacy refers to an individual's judgment about being able to perform an activity; in this chapter self-efficacy refers specifically to the confidence that a teacher has in their own ability to use technology tools to enhance instruction.

Technology Literacy: Technology literacy is the ability to effectively use technology to access, evaluate, integrate, create and communicate information to enhance the learning process through problem-solving and critical thinking.

Technology Tools: Chalk, posters, and overhead projectors were once "technology;" today we think of technology only as computer-related tools, yet technology includes all teaching tools that enhance the delivery of instruction and these tools have changed and will change over time.

Chapter 5
A Model for Meaningful E-Learning at Canadian Universities

Lorraine Carter
McMaster University, Canada

Vince Salyers
Mount Royal University, Canada

ABSTRACT

There is no questioning the growth of e-learning in universities around the world. Whether or not we are doing it effectively and meaningfully is where the uncertainty lies. In this chapter, two e-learning researchers from Canada offer their perspective on e-learning in that country. This perspective includes a snapshot of the Canadian e-learning landscape as well as the results of a multi-university research study called the Meaningful E-Learning or MEL project. The authors explore four themes derived from the MEL project and represented by the acronym HIDI (human interaction, IT support, design, and institutional support) in relation to three e-learning scenarios. While each element of HIDI is recognized as important, the criticality of institutional support and design cannot be overemphasized in the pursuit of excellence in e-learning.

INTRODUCTION

There is no dispute about it: e-learning has exploded in popularity (Allen & Seaman, 2013; Cramer, Collins, Snider & Fawcett, 2007; Kerns, McDonough, Kolynch & Hogan, 2006; McCord & McCord, 2010; Muirhead, 2007). Still, there is uncertainty about whether or not we are doing it effectively and whether or not it holds meaning for us.

In this chapter, we explore contemporary e-learning literature from student and faculty perspectives and share the findings of a multi-institutional mixed methods study called the Meaningful E-Learning project—the MEL project. In our discussion of the findings of the MEL project, we pay particular attention to four concepts represented by the acronym HIDI: human interaction (H), IT support (I), design support (D), and institutional support (I). HIDI

DOI: 10.4018/978-1-4666-8363-1.ch005

was a model that emerged from the MEL study. Given the extensiveness of the MEL project and the largeness of the dataset, there are a number of papers associated with it. The first paper was published in the Fall 2014 issue of the Canadian Journal of the Scholarship of Teaching and Learning; the second paper was published the Fall 2014 issue of the International Review of Research in Open and Distance Learning. Each manuscript provides recommendations for further research and possible directions for e-learning initiatives. By comparison, this chapter applies the HIDI model to specific e-learning scenarios in Canadian university settings.

As suggested above, in the latter part of the chapter, we provide an up-close look at e-learning practice in three contexts: an RPN to BScN blended learning program offered to nurses by Nipissing University in North Bay, Ontario; two pre-licensure nursing programs (a program offered at three campuses in northern British Columbia, Canada and a second program offered at a private university in San Diego, California); and the use of iPads as a teaching and learning tool in an undergraduate business program also offered by Nipissing University. Each e-learning scenario is discussed in relation to the HIDI model. The chapter closes with our views on the potential of meaningful e-learning in Canadian universities.

A REVIEW OF THE LITERATURE

A Definition of E-Learning

The definitions of e-learning in the literature are numerous and, at times, confusing. In this chapter, e-learning is understood as learning that may occur outside of the face to face setting and typically involves a variety of learning technologies and teaching approaches (Moore, Dickson-Deane & Galyen, 2011). It is not to be confused with distance learning which, historically, has been defined as geographically distributed learning and, presently,

involves online or internet-supported educational strategies. Instead, e-learning has adopted some of the characteristics of both distance learning and online learning and refers to the integration of pedagogy, instructional technology, and the Internet in teaching and learning environments. Based on this definition, e-learning environments may include face-to-face (f2f) classrooms in which instructional technologies (e.g. learning management systems, video- and web-conferencing, mobile applications, etc.) are used; blended and web-enhanced learning environments; and fully online learning environments (Salyers, Carter, & Barrett, 2010a; Salyers, Carter, Barrett & Williams, 2010b).

The Landscape of E-Learning in Canadian Universities

In Canada, like elsewhere in the Western world, e-learning in universities has reached participation levels that necessitate the attention of faculty, teaching and learning staff including instructional designers, and academic and senior administrators. As evidence, in a 2012 report called *Online Learning in Canada: At the Tipping Point. A Cross-Country Check-Up*, online learning—a specific kind of e-learning—has been described as "thriving across the country at the post-secondary level" while "new investments are being made to support its continued growth and development, particularly in Ontario and in British Columbia" (Contact North | Contact Nord, p. 2). Six Canadian universities focus specifically on online and distance learning. These institutions are Royal Roads University (British Columbia), Thompson Rivers University (British Columbia), Athabasca University (Alberta), Memorial University (Newfoundland and Labrador), TÉLUQ (Québec), and Centre collégial de formation à distance (Québec). By comparison, all Canadian universities participate in different forms of blended learning and some universities offer dual delivery—usually online and face to face—versions of courses.

Significantly, the greatest uptake in e-learning appears to be in programs in which professional designations or requirements are offered. Two of the e-learning scenarios considered later in this chapter fall into this category.

Based on data used in the Contact North | Contact Nord (2012) report, between 875,000 and 950,000 students in Canadian post-secondary institutions take a fully online course at any one time (p. 14). In Ontario—one of the two provinces noted earlier as particularly active in online learning—approximately 500,000 online course registrations have been reported. This level of activity is two times greater than that of any other Canadian province or territory (p. 14). The Contact North | Contact Nord data include students enrolled at both universities and community colleges. Online enrolment data specific to universities alone is not available at this time.

Despite the evidence of growth in e-learning on Canadian campuses, there have been challenges with its evolution. For instance, Canadian universities, like universities in the United States, continue to struggle with funding systems that do not always align with twenty-first century realities. In particular, most Canadian universities continue to build programs based on what is called the Carnegie unit (Contact North | Contact Nord, 2012, p. 28). This measure, developed in the 1920s, links time on task and time in class to the funds made available to support student learning. So long as this funding model persists, new and different educational experiences will not reach full potential (The Glossary of Education Reform, 2013). Additionally, there are inadequate data gathering systems to ensure the validity and reliability in the reported numbers of Canadian university students enrolled in courses that use e-learning strategies. Other e-learning challenges include considerable variability in the quality of e-learning courses due, in part, to mixed support for instructional design and spotty commitment to standards and benchmarks. Finally, as noted above, work is still required to increase e-learning

beyond its use in professional programs. Although there are one off situations of faculty embracing e-learning, in smaller liberal arts universities as well as those where the brand is face to face interaction (Carter & Graham, 2012), some perceptions continue to exist that education facilitated through e-learning cannot be as good as more traditional teaching and learning experiences. Similarly, more work needs to be done to ensure the uptake of e-strategies in support of lifelong and continuing education (Carter, Salyers, Myers, Hipfner, Hoffart, MacLean, White, Matus, Forssman, & Barrett, in 2014; McLean & Carter, 2012).

More about E-Learning in Canada

Although e-learning has had its challenges, in the overall, e-learning as it includes an integration of technology and pedagogy has captured the imaginations of hundreds of instructors and researchers across the country. A quick review of the manuscripts by two journals supported by the Canadian Network for Innovation in Education—namely, the *International Journal of E-learning and Distance Education* (formerly *Journal of Distance Education*) and the *Canadian Journal of Learning Technology*—provides a snapshot of the e-learning activity happening in Canadian universities. In 2013, the two journals reflected activity in the following e-learning domains: mobile learning, social and academic presence in graduate courses through the use of educational technology, gaming and virtual reality in learning, teaching and learning philosophies held by educational technologists, screen capture technology, digital technologies and assessment strategies, electronic portfolios, and web-based learning analytics. Other peer reviewed journals such as the *Canadian Journal of the Scholarship of Teaching and Learning* and the *Canadian Journal of University Continuing Education* are now publishing manuscripts on a variety of e-learning initiatives. Regarding the increased number of e-learning papers in the *Canadian Journal of University*

Continuing Education, the takeaway here is that e-learning is a means of serving not only direct entry students but also adult learners seeking opportunities to continue their professional and personal learning (McLean & Carter, 2013).

Other areas in which Canadian advocates of e-learning continue to find their way include but are not limited to the following: issues of duplication of effort and of scale; insufficient focus on rethinking pedagogy, especially for First Nations learners and immigrant learners; the digital divide; national and international credit transferability; the costs of greening technology and maintaining currency; policy issues such as who should supply the technology; designing learning for engagement (Murgatroyd, 2012). Canadian educators are also grappling with the strengths, weaknesses, and opportunities of MOOCs; flipped classrooms and blended learning; on-demand competency-based online courses and modules; the use of technology for adaptive curriculum and assessment; the arrival of the private sector in university education; learning badges; and open source content and resources (Murgatroyd).

Two further observations: up until now, much of the research in e-learning in Canada has involved graduate education. There is, however, increasing research into e-learning at the undergraduate level. In the MEL project which will be discussed later in the chapter, the experiences of faculty and undergraduate students at three universities in Ontario, Saskatchewan, and Alberta were explored. In these three settings, there is significant interest in e-learning as it affects undergraduates and their teachers. Like elsewhere in the world, Canada's university landscape is changing and a major influence on this transformation is e-learning.

Secondly, there is no question that the 'e-factor' is enabling learning and research partnerships with fewer borders than ever before. As a variable with significant potential, e-learning has been the impetus for the coming together of domains which hitherto were discrete in their identities (Carter, Graham, & Nowrouzi, 2013) and for a

re-thinking of the idea of a national scholarship. Examples of the former are the 2015 and 2016 joint conferences of the Canadian Association of University Continuing Education and the Canadian Network for Innovation in Education. While there are various points of shared vision held by these two organizations, e-learning is the major factor bringing them together.

Regarding the phenomena of Canadian e-learning and research, the recent name change of the *Journal of Distance Education* to the *International Journal of E-learning and Distance Education* is important. As a journal, the *Journal of Distance Education* has been a well-recognized peer reviewed journal since 1986. In Spring 2014, however, it underwent a name change. Previously, distance education practice in Canada was a means of teaching students who were not physically present in traditional classroom settings. In other words, students studied from locations that were "at a distance" or remote from the source of instruction. Today, distance education in Canada remains an important field of practice (Killam & Carter, 2010). However, distance is conceptualized more broadly and can include factors such as busy lives and time constraints that can prohibit learners from attending classes on campus; at the same time, these learners can continue to study if an instructional setting can be enabled through distance education thinking and infrastructure. While there may always be a need for distance education in its more historical forms including correspondence-based learning, e-learning is today's primary conduit of a distance learning experience. Thinking conceptually, language such as "the other side of the globe" is redundant when students and their teachers can connect quickly and inexpensively through synchronous and asynchronous means and experience e-based teaching and learning ranging in scope, size, and level.

In Canada, there is a new kind of distance if we reflect on those post-secondary students who choose to study online rather than attend the university campus. It would seem that, for these learners, the affordances of e-learning may outweigh those of the face to face classrooms. There is little question that time and cost are major barriers in the lives of university students. Mitigating these challenges through flexible educational responses is a deeply powerful reality with many personal, professional, and societal benefits.

E-Learning: The Student Perspective

Many of today's university students have grown up with technology and use it for socializing, personal banking, gaming, and accessing 'apps' for managing their lives (Buzducea, 2010; Carter, Salyers, Page, Williams, Hofsink, & Albl, 2011). Based on this new lifestyle approach called e-living (Brocade, 2011), it follows that some students may expect to use e-learning strategies in their studies, while others may choose to keep their social and educational lives separate. With a plethora of mobile devices to choose from to support their learning, students may also want to be free to engage with resources and ideas in ways that fall outside of the strategies of traditional classrooms. According to Fisher (2009), the flexibility of e-learning requires understanding of how institutions think about time, place, instructional pace, delivery methods, and learner entry.

University faculty may choose to leverage the social aspect of e-learning and balancing it with pedagogical strategies that foster student satisfaction. Social presence and pedagogy grounded in the practices of interactivity and engagement have been repeatedly identified as tied to student satisfaction and learning success in e-learning contexts (Brocade, 2011; Cobb, 2011; McCord & McCord, 2010). In short, e-learning experiences that include occasions for social engagement and interaction may influence both satisfaction and achievement positively. Other concepts that dominate the e-learning literature and demonstrate relationship with student satisfaction are collaboration, community, and connectedness (Bolliger

& Inan, 2012; Wenger, McDermott, & Snyder, 2002; Wenger, 2004; Yukawa, Kawano, Suzuki, Suriyon & Fukumura, 2008).

In contrast with students who appreciate e-learning environments, there are also students who may struggle with it for reasons including learning style differences and limited technical skills (Dorian & Wache, 2009; Perry & Edwards, 2010). Working from the idea that 'one size [never] fits all,' universities that embrace e-learning must be prepared to respond to the needs and preferences of individual learners as well as learner groups (Guri-Rosenblit, 2005).

E-Learning: The Faculty Perspective

There has been increasing interest in faculty perceptions of e-learning including its adoption and utilization. Although the early e-learning literature profiles keeners and early adopters, it also describes faculty reticence and resistance to e-learning implementation (Bower, 2001; McKenzie, Mims, Bennett, & Waugh, 2000; Naidu, 2004; Newton, 2003). In more recent literature, many of the same themes appear. Reasons cited for resistance include issues of workload, experience, accessibility, connectivity, and institutional infrastructure to support e-learning (Allen & Seaman, 2006; Bolliger & Wasilik, 2009; Cook, Ley, Crawford & Warner, 2009; Georgina & Olson, 2008; Kennedy, Jones, Chambers & Peacock, 2011; Panda & Mishra, 2007; Ward, Peters & Shelley, 2010).

Inadequate technology skills among faculty have been associated with resistance to e-learning. Technology changes quickly, and many faculty are unable to keep up with the knowledge and skills they require to deal with the moving target of technology (Childs, Blenkinsopp, Hall & Walton, 2005). According to some researchers, faculty interested in innovative teaching approaches must develop competencies in order to integrate technologies successfully into their teaching practices (Childs et al.; Jones & Wolf, 2010). In some instances, faculty are not interested in developing these competencies and are quite comfortable using more traditional teaching strategies. Additionally, faculty involved in e-learning must integrate web-based and online delivery techniques, engagement strategies, and other activities as grounded in evidence-based pedagogical principles into their e-teaching repertoires. In the case of online learning, Reeves and Reeves (2008) have suggested that success is based on pedagogical dimensions that work well in e-learning environments. Institutional strategic plans that support faculty adoption of e-learning and provide for e-learning resources and infrastructure are equally critical (AACTE, 2008; Darling-Hammond, 2006; Miller, 2009; Carter, Salyers, 2014).

E-Learning: Designing for Engaged Learning

Two terms prevalent in e-learning design literature are scaffolding and engagement, with the first enabling the second. Effective e-learning experiences require scaffolding rooted in learning theory and instructional design practices that enable diverse occasions for interaction (Salyers, Carter, Cairns, & Durrer, 2014). When e-learning occurs this way, the engagement and skill challenges experienced by some e-learners may be resolved (Winter, Cotton, Gavin & Yorke, 2010). Stated another way, scaffolding is a framework that enables the learner to pace learning and internalize knowledge as manageable chunks of learning (Baker, 2010; Kim & Hannafin, 2011; Lipscomb, Swanson, & West, 2004; Verenikina, 2008). Scaffolding can increase motivation and accommodate the student's ability to self-regulate, self-assess, and engage in experiences with peers while the instructor provides guidance and benchmarking opportunities (Murtagh & Webster, 2010).

Because design considerations are part of the scaffolding process, instructors should seek early and active engagement with an instructional designer and a learning technologist (Salyers, Carter, Cairns, & Durrer, 2014). Generally, scaffolding will unfold as follows: i) identification of what the student can do, ii) establishment of shared goals, iii) provision of ongoing assessment of learning needs, iv) provision of individualized assistance, v) reflection on activities and identification of what works well, and vi) inclusion of opportunities for internalization and generalization of the learning (Ginat, 2009).

Interaction in the e-learning environment comes in many forms. Most common are activity-based and collaborative initiatives. E-learning likewise offers potential for tasks, projects, simulations, and scenarios that require the student to do something including thinking critically and acting authentically (Lam, Yeung, Cheung, & McNaught, 2009; Parker, Maor, & Herrington, 2013; Schank, 2002). As new technologies emerge and others are finessed, the opportunities for collaborative e-learning will only increase and become less cumbersome than in the past. Given this phenomenon, guidelines that govern collaborative assignments and the behaviours of group members are highly recommended (Carter & Rukholm, 2008).

Some Special Considerations

Some scholars have argued that technology changes how people learn (Tapscott, 2008). Others suggest that learning is the same as it was in years past—that learning is a situation that involves dedicated time on task and access to expert knowledge transferred from the teacher to the student (Bullen, Morgan, Belfer, & Qayyum, 2008; Bullen, Morgan, & Qayyum, 2011). Research evidence based on work by Margaryan, Littlejohn, and Vojt (2011) does not "support popular claims that young people adopt radically different learning styles [in technology-supporting learning settings]" (p. 429). Those involved in the design of e-learning in Canadian institutions, including subject matter experts and instructional designers, must, therefore, make decisions based on the kind of content they are working with, the general character of the learner group, and the constantly evolving understanding of how students learn in technology-mediated environments (Herrington, Reeves & Oliver, 2010; Kanuka, 2006).

Controversy exists about whether those who use technology in other aspects of their lives wish to use it for learning when the engagement is complex and the role of learner is significantly different than in other technology-supported situations (Cleveland-Innes, Garrison, & Kilsen, 2008).While university students may prefer to use technology to connect, communicate, and manage their lives, they may or may not have the skills they need for success in technology-mediated learning environments (Bolinger & Inan, 2012; Dahlstrom, Walker & Dziuban, 2013; Johnson, Adams-Becker, Cummins, Estrada, Freeman & Ludgate, 2013; Means, Toyama, Murphy, Bakia & Jones, 2010; Yukawa, Kawano, Suzuki, Suriyon, & Fukumura, 2008). Recent evidence suggests that there are no differences between net generation and non-net generation students' use of technology, their preferences for it, and their behavioral characteristics (Bullen, Morgan, & Qayyum, 2011; Margaryan, Littlejon, & Vojt, 2011; Palfrey, Gasser, Simun, & Barnes, 2009; Selway, 2009).

Because many e-learning courses and programs in Canada serve adult learners including professionals, a quick mention of adult learning rounds out these remarks on theory and practice. Without question, Knowles' (1978) theory of andragogy is as important today in this discussion of e-learning as it was more than 35 years ago. Designing e-learning for adults requires commitment to the principles that adults need to know why they need to learn something. Additionally, as much as possible, they need to learn experientially and be provided opportunities for problem solving. Finally, based on the busy lives of adults and their differing levels of technical competence, those involved in e-learning design and teaching must make sure that adult learners studying online are adequately supported from a technical point of view and that all learning and assessment activities are based on a need to know basis (Carter & Rukholm, 2008; Salyers, Carter, Cairns & Durrer, 2014).

THE MEANINGFUL E-LEARNING (MEL) PROJECT: INTRODUCTION AND CONTEXT

Introduction to the Project

As suggested already this chapter, most universities now use e-learning strategies to offer courses and programs in a variety of ways including fully online and blended learning experiences. E-learning strategies are likewise used in face to face courses delivered on main campuses and at geographically distributed satellite campuses. Among the many reasons that increasing numbers of first degree university students and returning adult learners are turning to e-learning, two stand out. The first is student demand for flexibility in where and how they learn (Ali, 2012; Burge, Campbell Gibson, & Gibson, 2011; Carter, Salyers, Page, Williams, Hofsink, & Albl, 2012; Salyers, Carter, Barrett, &Williams, 2010b; Elliott, 2011; Hammersley, Tallantyre & Le Cornu, 2013; Hanover, 2011; Higher Education Academy, 2013; Johnson, Smith, Willis, Levine & Haywood, 2011; McLinden, 2013; Oye, Salleh & Iahad, 2011). The second is that, since many university students are technologically sophisticated, there is increasing demand by students for ways to integrate technology with their learning lives (Dahlstrom, Walker & Dziuban, 2013; Johnson, Smith, Willis, Levine & Haywood, 2011; Tapscott, 2008).

Just as advantages related to access and flexibility are clear, the challenges of e-learning are equally real. These challenges include but are not limited to geographic and technological barriers, lack of instructional design support, inadequate or unreliable infrastructure support, and varying degrees of faculty and student experience with e-learning environments (Carter, Salyers et al., 2014; Salyers, Carter, Barrett, & Williams, 2010b).

Reflecting on all of these ideas at a national conference in 2011, a group of colleagues from Mount Royal University in Alberta, Saskatchewan Institute of Applied Science & Technology in Saskatchewan, and Nipissing University in Ontario met to discuss the possibility of conducting a national e-learning study. Based on the work of these individuals two of whom are the authors of this chapter, the three institutions committed to undertake the MEL project.

Mount Royal University, the lead university, has an enrollment of nearly 13,000 students who take a variety of programs and courses leading to bachelor's degrees, applied degrees, diplomas, and certificates. SIAST provides post-secondary technical education and skills training, and is recognized nationally and internationally for its commitment to educational innovation; SIAST serves 26,000 students and offer a wide variety of courses and programs through distance education. Nipissing University enrolls approximately 6,500 full and part-time students. The majority of programs are at the undergraduate level although graduate programs in areas of particular strength for the University are offered. Nipissing has experienced substantive growth over the last five years in a number of professional programs offered through e-learning (Carter, Salyers et al., 2014).

The specific impetus for the study was that students and faculty seem to continue to lack the knowledge, skills, desire, and/or time they require to experience e-learning in effective and meaningful ways (Carter, Salyers et al., 2014; Salyers, Carter, Barrett & Williams, 2010b). Based on

this observation, the purpose of the MEL study was to evaluate a number of key components of e-learning courses and their impact on the student and faculty experience: the components were ease of navigation, course design, resource availability, technical ability, adequacy of e-learning supports. Four questions were used to frame the study: (i) What challenges do students and faculty experience when they use e-learning strategies?, (ii) What technological knowledge and skills do students and faculty require in order to use e-learning strategies effectively for learning and teaching?, (iii) What are the characteristics of excellent e-learning courses?, and (iv) To what extent do specific e-learning components predict enhanced learning, active participation, user comfort with technologies, user competence in relation to e-learning skills, enjoyment of e-learning, preference for e-learning over face to face classes, and development of enhanced e-learning skills for students and faculty?

MEL Theoretical Orientation

The theoretical orientation that guided the MEL research was based on Khan's (2010) Global E-Learning Framework as summarized by Aguti, Walters, and Wills (2013). Table 1 summarizes eight dimensions associated with the design, development, and evaluation of e-learning.

The research team for the MEL project was particularly interested in the pedagogical, technological, interface design, evaluation, and resource support dimensions and their impact on student e-learning perceptions. Based on the Global E-learning Framework (Khan, 2010) as presented by Aguti, Walters and Wills (2013), an e-learning skills inventory (ESI) was developed as a survey and administered to students and faculty at the three institutions. Not insignificantly, the findings of the MEL study closely aligned with the pedagogical, technological, design, and resource dimensions described by Aguti et al.

Table 1. Khan's (2010) global e-learning framework as summarized by Aguti, Walters and Wills (2013)

Dimension	Focus on E-learning Environment	Specific components
Pedagogical	Teaching and learning	• Analysis of content, audiences, goals, media • Organization and layout of e-learning systems • Design strategies, methods and approaches
Technological	Technology infrastructure	• Infrastructure planning • Hardware and software
Interface Design	Aesthetics and design	• Page, site, and content design • Navigation, accessibility • Usability testing
Evaluation	Assessment of learning and environment	• Assessment of learners • Evaluation of instruction • Evaluation of learning environment • Evaluation of content development processes • Evaluation of individuals involved in content development • Evaluation of institutional e-learning program
Management	Maintenance of learning environment	• Managing information distribution • Managing e-learning content development • Managing e-learning environment
Resource Support	Technical and human resource support	• Online support • Teaching and learning support • Technical support • Online and offline resources
Ethical	Social, cultural, digital	• Social and political influences • Cultural diversity • Learner diversity, digital divide • Legal issues
Institutional	Administration, academic affairs and student services	• Admissions, finances, payments • Information technology services, policies • Graduation and grades

Study Design

Grounded in a descriptive mixed-methods design, the MEL study occurred over two years. Ethics approval was received from all three institutions. Data collection and analysis occurred from December 15, 2012 to April 30, 2013. A concurrent triangulation strategy was used to guide and facilitate data collection. In this approach, both quantitative and qualitative data are collected at designated points and triangulated (Creswell, 2009; Creswell, Plano Clark, Gutmann, & Hanson, 2003). Data are then compared to identify similarities, differences, gaps, and unanswered questions.

Quantitative and Qualitative Data Gathering

Quantitative data were generated through two online surveys, one for students and one for faculty. Significantly, the content of the surveys was highly similar but some tailoring was necessary given the two target groups. Each institutional lead sought permission to invite participation from students and faculty in all faculties to complete the surveys made available through an online link distributed through the university's email system. The surveys which functioned as an e-learning skills inventory (ESI) included 34 items;

a 5-point Likert scale was used in each item (1 = strongly disagree; 2 = disagree; 3 = agree; 4 = strongly agree; and 5 = not applicable). Areas assessed in the ESI included level of e-learning knowledge, prior e-learning experience, access to e-learning and other resources, and general technology skills and usage. Scale reliability for the ESI was calculated based on rank transformations. The internal consistency for each scale was as follows: student ESI (α=.71) and faculty ESI (α=.73). These alpha coefficients are satisfactory based on using Nunnally's (1978) criterion of .70 as a cut-off point. Basic demographic information was also collected for each group. At the end of each survey, participants were invited to provide narrative comments. These narrative comments were triangulated with the qualitative data derived from focus groups.

Students and faculty were recruited to participate in semi-structured focus groups through a campaign of print flyers and emailed invitations. The semi-structured questions for the focus groups were developed collaboratively by the four lead researchers with input from other research team members. All sessions were audiotaped and transcribed verbatim. Sessions were approximately one hour in length. Questions such as "What recommendations do you have so that e-learning technologies are meaningfully and effectively integrated into educational experiences/practices?" were explored in the focus group sessions.

Data Analysis

All data were aggregated. SPSS 19.0 was used to generate descriptive and inferential statistics based on responses to the ESI. Analysis of focus group data was based on a process outlined by Miles and Huberman (1994) that included three concurrent flows of activity: data reduction whereby participant responses were coded and sorted into individual clusters of varying main themes; data display whereby participant responses were organized, compressed, and assembled into various tables and figures which permitted conclusions to be readily visible and easily drawn; and conclusion drawing/verification whereby conclusions were verified and validated through repeated readings, discussion, and debate (Carter, Salyers et al., 2014; Salyers, Carter, Barrett, & Williams, 2010b).

QUANTITATIVE FINDINGS

Demographic Profiles

Student respondents included 1, 377 students across the three universities, of which 76.7% were female. The majority of students were between the ages of 17 and 25 (66.1%). Asked about levels of experience with e-learning, 85.4% reported up to 5 years of experience taking courses that use e-learning strategies; 10.6% reported 6-10 years of experience with courses that use e-learning strategies and 4% indicated more than 10 years of experience with e-learning courses (Salyers, Carter, Carter, Myers, & Barrett, 2014).

Faculty respondents included 187 faculty across the three post-secondary institutions; 65.6% were female. With respect to age, 87.0% of faculty reported age as between 35-64. Most faculty, 48.6%, reported 0-5 years of experience teaching courses that use e-learning strategies; 29.4% of faculty had 6-10 years of experience while 22% had greater than 10 years of experience teaching using e-learning strategies. Table 2 summarizes student and faculty characteristics across the three post-secondary institutions.

General Perceptions of E-Learning

Student and faculty responses demonstrated consistent to strong agreement with a cross-section of ESI items. In general, the student findings were positive with respect to e-learning: 80% of students strongly agreed or agreed with the statement that "e-learning technologies enhance my learning" while 84% strongly agreed or agreed

Table 2. Demographic profile of students and faculty who completed the online survey

Total Sample Size	STUDENTS (n =1346)	FACULTY (n=187)
Gender *		
Male	310 (22.9%)	120 (65.6%)
Female	1039 (76.7%)	64 (34.4%)
Other	6 (0.4%)	N/A
Age *		
17 – 19	316 (23.2%)	N/A
20 – 22	369 (27.1%)	N/A
23 – 25	215 (15.8%)	N/A
26 – 28	118 (8.7%)	4 (2.2%)
29 – 35	133 (9.8%)	14 (7.6%)
35 – 64	208 (15.3%)	161 (87%)
> 64	2 (0.1%)	6 (2.2%)
Years Taking/Teaching Courses using E-Learning Strategies *		
0 – 5	1103 (85.4%)	86 (48.6%)
6-10	137 (10.6%)	52 (29.4%)
> 10	52 (4%)	39 (22%)
Current Institution		
Post-Secondary A	816 (59.3%)	61 (32.6%)
Post-Secondary B	456 (33.1%)	64 (34.2%)
Post-Secondary C	104 (7.6%)	62 (33.2%)

*Category had missing data. Percentages were calculated based on responses received.

with the statement that "overall, I have adequate e-learning skills to take courses using e-learning technologies." Of the student-participants, 85% indicated that they were comfortable using computers and software applications before they took an e-learning course. Just over half (51%) of students indicated agreement to strong agreement with the statement that "e-learning encourages me to participate more actively (in my learning)." Less than half (43%) of students agreed or strongly agreed with the statement that "I prefer courses using e-learning technologies more than traditional courses" (Salyers, Carter, Carter, Myers & Barrett, 2014).

Faculty strongly agreed or agreed that "e-learning technologies enhance student learning" (88%). Faculty (76%) strongly agreed or agreed

with the statement that "I am comfortable teaching courses using e-learning technologies"; 73% strongly agreed or agreed with the statement that "overall, I have adequate e-learning skills to teach courses using e-learning technologies." Like the students, 49% of faculty indicated that they agreed or strongly agreed with this statement, "E-learning encourages students to participate more actively in their learning." Only 36% of faculty agreed or strongly agreed with the statement that "I prefer teaching courses using e-learning technologies more than traditional courses" (Salyers, Carter, Carter, Myers & Barrett, 2014).

Students (97%) and faculty (98%) indicated that students in post-secondary institutions need to be able to navigate well in e-learning course environments. Students and faculty (84% for each group) strongly agreed or agreed that "students attending post-secondary institutions should have moderate to high e-learning skills." Students (84%) strongly agreed or agreed that "students attending post-secondary institutions should have moderate to high e-learning skills." Moreover, students (85%) agreed or strongly agreed that "the design of courses using e-learning strategies is important" (Salyers, Carter, Carter, Myers & Barrett, 2014).

E-Learning Components and Predictive Capacities

Ease of navigation, course design, adequacy of e-learning supports, and previous experience with e-learning consistently demonstrated statistically significant ($p \leq .05; p \leq .001$) capacity to predict enhanced student learning, active student participation, comfort with e-learning, adequacy of technical and e-learning skills, enjoyment with e-learning, preference for e-learning over traditional formats, and the development of e-learning skills among students and faculty. Statistically significant results and cumulative student r-square values for each regression analysis are provided in Tables 3-9.

QUALITATIVE FINDINGS

The findings shared here are discussed in greater detail in a paper called Qualitative insights from a Canadian multi-institutional research study (Carter, et. al., 2014). Some key ideas related to the qualitative findings from the MEL study are offered here, however, in order for the reader to understand the full nature of the study. These highlights also contextualize the HIDI model which will be applied to specific learning scenarios later in the chapter.

Four major themes emerged based on faculty and student responses during the focus group discussions and in narrative comments shared in the online surveys. Participants' insights into the research questions about the challenges of e-learning and characteristics of exceptional e-learning experiences are reflected within these themes.

To assist with organizing the themes, the acronym HIDI was developed to designate the following: human interaction (H), IT support (I), design (D), and institutional infrastructure (I) (Carter, et. al., 2014). Data were further organized into sub-themes. Table 10 displays the themes and sub-themes.

Table 3. Regression analysis - dependent variable: Enhanced student learning

Independent Variable	Parameter Estimate	Standard Error	Standardized Coefficients Beta	T for Ho: Parameter=0	Prob>|T|
Faculty Design of e-learning courses	.004	.001	.282	3.160	.002**
Ease of navigation in e-learning courses	.240	.085	.248	2.826	.006**
Students Ease of navigation In e-learning courses	.392	.036	.365	10.922	.000***
Design of e-learning Courses	.173	.033	.161	5.211	.000***
Adequacy of e-learning supports	.112	.036	.108	3.070	.002**

R^2 (Students) = .31; R^2 (Faculty) = .23

Note. *p < .05, **p < .01, ***p < .001

Table 4. Regression analysis - dependent variable: Active student participation

Independent Variable	Parameter Estimate	Standard Error	Standardized Coefficients Beta	T for Ho: Parameter=0	Prob>|T|
Faculty Ease of navigation in e-learning courses	.496	.119	.362	4.167	.000***
Students Ease of navigation in e-learning courses	.389	.051	.278	7.593	.000***
Previous experience with e-learning	.098	.044	.077	2.215	.027*
Adequacy of e-learning supports	.140	.052	.103	2.685	.007**

R^2 (Students) = .18; R^2 (Faculty) = .24
Note. *p < .05, **p < .01, ***p < .001

Table 5. Regression analysis – dependent variable: Comfort with e-learning technologies

Independent Variable	Parameter Estimate	Standard Error	Standardized Coefficients Beta	T for Ho: Parameter=0	Prob>|T|
Faculty Previous experience with e-learning	.292	.069	.329	4.216	.000**
Design of e-learning courses	.003	.001	.162	2.050	.043*
Adequacy of e-learning supports	.210	.082	.224	2.563	.012**
Students Ease of navigation in e-learning courses	.461	.036	.392	12.690	.000***
Previous experience with e-learning	.153	.031	.143	4.855	.000***
Design of e-learning Courses	.206	.034	.174	6.058	.000***
Adequacy of e-learning supports	.138	.038	.120	3.665	.000***

R^2 (Students) = .18; R^2 (Faculty) = .39
Note. *p < .05, **p < .01, ***p < .001

Table 6. Regression analysis – dependent variable: Adequacy of technical and e-learning skills

Independent Variable	Parameter Estimate	Standard Error	Standardized Coefficients Beta	T for Ho: Parameter=0	Prob>|T|
Faculty Ease of navigation in e-learning courses	.159	.068	.161	2.320	.022*
Previous experience with e-learning courses	.470	.059	.555	7.922	.000***
Adequacy of e-learning supports	.185	.070	.207	2.654	.009**
Students Ease of navigation in e-learning courses	.206	.025	.215	8.117	.000***
Previous experience with e-learning	.422	.022	.487	19.255	.000***
Adequacy of e-learning supports	.061	.026	.066	2.354	.019*
Design of e-learning Courses	.196	.024	.203	8.256	.000***

R^2 (Students) – .39; R^2 (Faculty) = .51
Note. *p < .05, **p < .01, ***p < .001

Table 7. Regression analysis – dependent variable: Enjoyment with using e-learning

Independent Variable	Parameter Estimate	Standard Error	Standardized Coefficients Beta	T for Ho: Parameter=0	Prob>|T|
Faculty Ease of navigation	.184	.078	.182	2.361	.020*
Design of e-learning courses	.005	.001	.290	3.707	.000**
Adequacy of e-learning supports	.201	.080	.219	2.517	.013*
Students Ease of navigation in e-learning courses	.399	.038	.330	10.642	.000***
Previous experience with e-learning	.099	.033	.090	3.052	.002**
Adequacy of e-learning supports	.244	.038	.207	6.382	.000***
Design of e-learning Courses	.186	.035	.153	5.335	.000***
Availability of e-learning and technology resource	.000	.000	.101	3.212	.001**

R^2 (Students) = .55; R^2 (Faculty) = .40; Note. *p < .05, **p < .01, ***p < .001

Table 8. Regression analysis – dependent variable: Preference for e-learning over traditional formats

Independent Variable	Parameter Estimate	Standard Error	Standardized Coefficients Beta	T for Ho: Parameter=0	Prob>|T|
Faculty Ease of navigation in e-learning courses	.302	.116	.228	2.603	.010*
Design of e-learning courses	.005	.002	.228	2.558	.012*
Students Ease of navigation in e-learning courses	.461	.053	.316	8.772	.000***
Previous experience with e-learning	.102	.045	.077	2.266	.024**
Adequacy of e-learning supports	.185	.053	.131	3.468	.001**

R² (Students) = .41; R² (Faculty) = .25
Note. *p < .05, **p < .01, ***p < .001

Table 9. Regression analysis – dependent variable: Development of greater e-learning skills

Independent Variable	Parameter Estimate	Standard Error	Standardized Coefficients Beta	T for Ho: Parameter=0	Prob>|T|
Faculty Previous experience with e-learning courses	14.403	4.745	.261	3.035	.003**
Design of e-learning courses	.367	.091	.346	4.034	.000***
Students Ease of navigation in e-learning courses	.136	.031	.157	4.393	.000***
Previous experience with e-learning	.056	.027	.072	2.079	.038*
Availability of e-learning support and technology resources	.000	.000	.106	2.879	.004**
Design of e-learning Courses	.179	.029	.208	6.236	.000***

R² (Students) = .21; R² (Faculty) = .29
Note. *p < .05, **p < .01, ***p < .001

Table 10. HIDI themes and sub-themes

Themes	Sub-Themes
H = Human Connection	Social Presence Timely Feedback Engagement Strategies
I = Institutional Infrastructure	Technology Skills Support and Capacity Faculty Development
D = Design	Pedagogy Academic and IT Support Educational Technology Resources
I = Institutional Infrastructure	Funding and Resources Standards and Processes Buy-in and Support

H: Human Connection

The theme of human connection emerged as important to both learners and instructors. Sub-themes included social presence, timely feedback, and engagement strategies that promote positive student-faculty and student-student interactions. One participant stated the following:

When I am seeing the professor I get the feedback and I get it right away. Even from his body language I know if where I am going is the right direction or the wrong direction. By the time I send an email and organize my thought to the professor, it is two, three days later, and then it takes twenty-four, to thirty-six hours later [for the instructor] to return [to me with a response], if [the instructor] understood my query completely.

Other participants described engagement strategies as critical to the establishment and maintenance of human connection.

I: IT Support

The theme of IT support was a dominant one and seemed to emerge from the fact that university students and faculty have varying levels of skill with technology. Based on the variance in e-learning skill among both groups, e-learning can be a major source of discomfort and frustration if sufficient supports are not in place. Sub-themes that presented included the need for adequate technology skills, IT support, capacity to address issues as they occur, and faculty development activities to enhance technical skills. One faculty participant emphasized the importance of technical proficiency among students:

Students should be taught how to install programs, plug-ins, and applets on their computers. They appear to be simple tasks but they could become major stumbling blocks for some students. …I do not feel adequate enough in my computer skills to use them efficiently as I can, so [I do] not feel as successful. Also, using computer resources seems like another step in the process…with no training, I have to figure out the e-learning tools.

Because some students may want to participate in e-learning "anywhere, anytime," respondents commented that it would be ideal if IT support was available 24 hours each day 7 days per week. Participants also spoke about infrastructure needs including library resources, reliable Internet access, user-friendly learning management systems, and technology-equipped classrooms.

Faculty participants mentioned the need for IT support and training to enhance their e-teaching efforts:

A dedicated ed tech or IT professional to assist us as we plan new curriculum and learning strategies would be so beneficial because we would use these things more. We cannot be experts at nursing practice and at all things IT, so the e-education features that would make the environment more learner-centered are often sacrificed, I believe.

Finally, some students commented that faculty must understand the technologies they ask students to use and be able to explain them to students, "When [an] instructor does not know how to use e-learning, that is when the course becomes more difficult to follow through with [and] finish."

D: Design

The importance of design in e-learning initiatives was repeatedly emphasized. Design was described as adherence to pedagogical principles, IT and academic support to design meaningful e-learning courses, and curriculum and pedagogical choices specifically designed for e-learning.

Commitment to pre-determined learning objectives was recognized as a major contributor to effective e-learning contexts and maintenance of high academic standards. To ensure that e-learning materials meet requisite standards, faculty indicated that they require time to develop their resources and courses as well as time to collaborate with peers and receive support from IT professionals.

The idea that curriculum must be specifically designed for e-learning emerged as critically important. Contrarily, a lack of congruence between the content and the delivery experience was noted as problematic and not conducive to learning. One participant remarked on this idea in the following passage: "It's appropriate to use e-learning when the content and the medium of the e-learning has been structured appropriately for the e-learning environment."

I: Institutional Infrastructure

The final theme was institutional infrastructure. Its subthemes included funding and resources, standards and processes to support e-learning, institutional buy-in, and overall support. Faculty participants were strongly vocal about the need for dedicated funding and resources at the institutional level. Technical requirements including adequate bandwidth, up-to-date hardware, and innovative software were likewise reported as necessities in e-learning contexts. Research funds for investigating technological infrastructure and e-learning techniques were recommended, "[T]he more resources and money you put into a faculty or staff... is going to pay big dividends in the end because you're planting seeds."

Technical expertise, support, and maintenance were noted by both groups as essential in e-learning. In addition to facilitating development and delivery of e-learning opportunities, technical experts are required when faculty and students use new software applications and equipment upgrades happen. One faculty participant concluded that technical support for e-teaching should include a variety of items, big and small, with support starting at the top of the institution:

And I think checking the links—or whatever we're using in there—that they work, if the embedded software or whatever the people need to work with; whatever link is expected, that those are checked and they're working. ...Support's at the top of your pyramid and then any other things that will help with learning after that.

DISCUSSION OF THE MEL FINDINGS

Through the MEL project, meaningful e-learning, as based on the responses by faculty and students at three Canadian universities, emerged as a system composed of four distinct components represented by the HIDI model: human connection, IT support, design, and institutional infrastructure. Notably, the experience of the whole is a function of the subsystems. Subsystems are interdependent and, when they work well in their interdependence, the result is a positive e-learning experience for students and faculty.

In order to make e-learning effective and thus meaningful, it is clear that faculty and students require greater support than their institutions currently offer. Participants also spoke of a trickle-down effect in the provision of support; one study participant summarized this idea as follows, "It is vital that instructors (faculty) be supported by their institutions if they are to be successful in their use of e-learning strategies." If faculty experience adequate support, it is likely that their students will be supported and reap rewards.

Deriving from the requirement for excellence in support are questions about who manages e-learning services and the nature of these services. These questions tie to the larger question of institutional support for e-learning and models ranging from centralized to de-centralized approaches. The role of educational development centres through which instructional design expertise is typically available is part of this discussion. Complicating the discussion are massive open online courses (MOOCs), personal mobile devices, and sophisticated classroom designs. All of these phenomena present opportunities and challenges with potential to disrupt university structures. Support of technology-enabled teaching and learning is not just about technology; it is about infrastructures and processes designed, in most cases, before the advent of e-learning on university campuses.

While some university administrators suggest that technology is everywhere and does not need to be embedded in academic plans (Allen & Seaman, 2013), others argue that not to do so is shortsighted: unless the role of technology in 21st century universities is acknowledged, managed, and supported in planned ways, the potential for

mishap is just too great. How we adopt, diffuse, and integrate technology into how we teach, learn, and undertake research is not an even playing field.

The politics and language of technical support as well as its history are clearly components in the e-learning discussion. For instance, IT departments tend to manage different client needs than e-learning departments do. IT departments typically provide support for the administrative functions of the university including enrolment management and tracking; student information systems and alumni, community, and fund-raising systems; HR functions, payroll systems, and records management.

In order to meet the e-learning needs of faculty and students, a different support model is required; this model should be grounded in a specific mandate and carefully articulated roles. While the participants in the study were asked to share their experiences and challenges with e-learning, they were not explicitly asked about the capacity of post-secondary institutions to address the gap between and among the promise, the expectation, and the reality of e-learning. This discussion is one we need to initiate on our campuses as soon as possible.

How is e-learning supported so that the outcome is meaningful and sustaining for students and faculty? According to Dahlstrom, Walker and Dziuban (2013), e-learning units must include instructional designers, professional development staff, educational developers, videographers, graphic designers, apps developers, and learning management system experts. Such centres should also maintain responsibility for supports in e-based classrooms, audio-visual systems, lecture podiums with computers, document cameras, and embedded room control systems. High functioning classroom technologies are important to the adoption and diffusion of technologies within post-secondary organizations. A learner-centered framework that honours human connection is, according to MEL study participants, at the heart of a meaningful e-learning community. Through

Table 11. Challenges and characteristics of e-learning

Challenges of e-learning: Faculty	Insufficient technical support and training Insufficient instructional design support Insufficient institutional support
Challenges of e-learning: Students	Insufficient technical support Inadequate technical proficiency Instructors who are not timely in their responses
Characteristics of exceptional e-learning: Faculty	Human connection including easy interactions with students Instructional design support to ensure that curriculum is appropriate for e-delivery and to facilitate ease in navigation Adequate technical support Adequate institutional support
Characteristics of exceptional e-learning: Students	Human connection including timely feedback, social presence, easy interactions with the instructor and other students, interactive learning strategies Adequate technical support

this connection, the students experience the safety and support required for learning. Indeed, one of the biggest challenges for those involved with e-learning is the design of educational experiences where technology is used to support students and their learning experiences in contrast with technology being the 'main event.' Furthermore, the learning design must value and support diverse learners in highly accessible contexts (McCombs, 2004; Rennie & Morrison, 2013).

E-learning design, development, and adoption are closely associated with the thorny issue of managing the metrics of faculty workload. The development of an online course typically requires more time than the development of a face-to-face course. The bottom line is that e-learning requires an investment in faculty and staff that extends well beyond technical considerations. E-learning when done well exists in an ecosystem of organizational design and support. Within this ecosystem, resources are required that range from educational development to expertise in e-learning design to 24-7 support for anytime, anywhere service for faculty and students (Carter & Graham, 2012).

The MEL study revealed four components of the e-learning system which if, acted upon, take us much closer to effective and meaningful learning than otherwise. At the same time, human connection, IT support, design, and institutional infrastructure comprise only the "tip of

the e-learning iceberg." As suggested in the MEL study, universities need to reflect thoughtfully on the organizational and cultural shifts occurring around and within them rather than on more investments in technology. Effective e-learning is far more than technology: institutions may need to reallocate resources and assess their e-learning infrastructures. Additionally, the needs of learners are changing, thus challenging educational institutions to continue to change. Refusal to change is a risk that most universities cannot afford to take based on the needs and interests of today's students.

While the previous discussion has focused on the resulting themes of the study, we would remiss not to return to the questions around which discussion occurred in the focus groups: questions about the challenges of e-learning and the characteristics of exceptional e-learning experiences. Based on the above themes and sub-themes, the ideas presented in Table 11 are offered as partial answers to these questions.

E-LEARNING IN PRACTICE: HIDI APPLIED

In this section of the chapter, three different e-learning scenarios presently occurring in Canadian universities are considered through the HIDI lens. The first involves e-learning in one of its newer forms; that is, as a blended learning program which, in this case, enables Registered Practical Nurses in Ontario to become baccalaureate prepared nurses. In the second scenario, the HIDI lens is brought to e-learning in the context of pre-licensure nursing programs that use face to face, blended and fully online formats and research findings based on the use of a learning design framework called ICARE. In the third scenario, mobile learning as experienced by students in an undergraduate business program at an Ontario university are considered.

Case 1: RPN to BSCN Blended Learning Program, Nipissing University

A responsive and timely program. Nipissing University's blended learning program is one of kind among Ontario's nursing education programs. This uniqueness stems from the fact that the program enables Registered Practical Nurses (RPNs) to acquire their Baccalaureate of Science in Nursing (BScN) through distance-based part-time study. In keeping with Nipissing University's identity as a small institution in northern Ontario, this program began small but has grown substantively: in three years, it has grown from an initial intake of 60 students to an enrollment of over 600 students (Fitzgerald, Beattie, Carter & Caswell, 2014).

The program is the only BScN program in Ontario for RPNs that combines the following three elements: a "bridge" from the nurse's college diploma; a part-time curriculum that enables students to continue to practice nursing as they study; and a blended delivery model. Structured as online theory-based courses complemented by face to face clinical practice courses and supports provided by the nurses' employers and the University, this program is evidence of what partnership-based, technology-supported programs can be.

Applying the HIDI lens to the program today. The program offers significant opportunity for human interaction and has benefitted from dedicated instructional design. As noted, while the program is e-based (it would not exist without e-learning), it includes face to face learning in the clinical context; hence, it is called a blended learning program with courses occurring either as online or face to face courses. The instructors who teach in the program are individuals who are vigilant about the need to stay close to their students as they balance busy professional and family lives. Students and faculty are likewise supported by a highly competent program manager and clinical placement team.

Regarding the underpinning design process, courses in the program undergo a development process of approximately nine months. The course development team includes the subject matter expert, two peer reviewers (one internal and one external), an instructional designer, and the program manager. The build-out of a course involves an educational technologist who constructs the course in the environment of the learning management system and possibly a multimedia expert. Various administrative supports are provided across the university and include the School of Nursing office, the Dean's office, the Registrar, Student Support Services, and so forth.

The areas in which the program experiences some possibility of risk are IT support and institutional infrastructure. Within the six months prior to the writing of this chapter, a re-structuring at the University led to the dismantlement of the teaching and learning centre in which supports for online course development and delivery were undertaken. Positively, the School of Nursing has acquired the instructional designer who, in the previous centre, worked on courses for the program. While this is fortuitous for the program, there is a separation between those who are invested in the pedagogy of courses and those who provide technical assistance and now reside with the university's IT department. Still, the program at the developmental level will sustain because key players in the School of Nursing are still in place, and the designer has strong collegial relationships within nursing.

The greater risks for the program involve instructors and students who now need to go various places for IT and administrative supports during the delivery of a course. While all universities involve different areas working together, when learners are at a physical distance from the campus, a centralized 'one stop shop' is desirable, especially when there are technical issues involved. The further risk given the dismantlement of the centre is that no single person knows or is responsible for the university's full e-learning picture. Hence, it is possible that senior administrators may make decisions based on misinformation and /or complete information. In simplest terms, e-learning at this university is now without a champion at the level of senior management. As the literature reveals, e-learning requires championship because of its complexity and relative newness. Finally, if there is a genuine commitment at a university to online programming, it follows that centralized approaches to infrastructure and support are best practices.

In the case of this program in particular, substantive work related to pedagogical and administrative supports as well as processes had occurred before the re-structuring. As well, the invested faculty and staff in the School of Nursing

are competent and conscientious professionals. Still, according to HIDI, the risks to the program are greater today than one year ago while enrolments continue to grow.

Case 2: BSCN Programming and the ICARE Model, University of Northern British Columbia

An introduction to ICARE. The Introduction, Connect, Apply, Reflect, and Extend (ICARE) system is a scaffolding framework developed by staff and faculty at San Diego State University in 1997 to structure and organize course modules, modules being natural sub-sections of courses (Carter & Salyers, 2013; Salyers, 2005; Salyers, Carter, Barrett & Williams, 2010b). Table 12 provides a summary of each component of ICARE and potential scaffolding activities. While the ICARE model was created for use in different delivery contexts, it holds specific value in online and blended learning and with adult learners. The five steps of ICARE are repeated in each module of a course, and the structure can be used in different subject areas. More information regarding ICARE is presented by Hoffman and Ritchie (1998; 2005). Here, it is worth noting here that this scaffolding model as

Table 12. Components of the ICARE framework and scaffolding activities

Phase	Description
Introduction (I)	This phase consists of the introduction to the unit of instruction including: ■ Context ■ Objectives ■ Prerequisites ■ Required study time ■ Equipment required ■ Essential reading materials
Connect *or* Content (C)	Almost all content will reside in this section
Apply All activities (A)	Exercise, thinking questions, etc. are implemented in this phase
Reflect (R)	This phase provides an opportunity for learners to reflect on their acquired knowledge and articulate their experience. This section may include: topics for discussion, a learning journal/log, a self-test, formative and summative assessment
Extend (E)	An amalgamation of all the previous phases which offers materials and learning opportunities which can be remedial, supplemental, or advanced, depending on learner performance

Retrieved from: http://elearningcurve.edublogs.org/2009/06/11/discovering-instructional-design-12-the-icare-model/

suggested by its name—ICARE—provides an appropriate acronym for health science programs.

In the Introduction section of any ICARE module, context is provided. For example, an overview of the module, learning objectives, and reading assignments are presented. The Connect (or Content) section provides conceptual material and information to be discussed in other ICARE sections of the module. In the Apply section, students might be required to write a short paper or complete a self-assessment requiring synthesis and application of ideas; examples of this might include a pre-test or short quiz. In the Reflect section, students might be asked to reflect on newly developed skills and knowledge (e.g., lessons learned, etc.). The Extend section might be structured around evidence-based research and "real world" applications (Salyers, 2005; Salyers, Carter, Barrett & Williams, 2010b).

ICARE evaluated. The following paragraphs describe why and how ICARE was implemented in nursing programs at two universities—one in Canada and one in the United States—that offer course work in face to face, blended, and fully online formats. High level findings based on the implementation of ICARE are also reported. One of the authors of this chapter was employed at both universities when the ICARE model was evaluated.

At each university, the nursing faculty and instructional designers made a conscious decision to utilize the ICARE framework whenever possible because of the scaffolding and consistency it provided (Carter, Salyers, Cairns, & Durrer, 2014; Salyers, 2005; Salyers, Carter, Barrett & Williams, 2010b). Significantly, ICARE can be used in any learning environment including face to face, web-enhanced, and fully online contexts. It is, however, especially valuable in contexts where students require a consistent means for easily navigating e-learning environments.

Based on student surveys and anecdotal feedback provided by faculty at the two institutions, challenges in course delivery had been identified and, hence, the institutions were open to new approaches such as ICARE. The first challenge related to faculty experience with e-learning formats and how e-learning was utilized. Also, some faculty were avid users of Blackboard, Moodle, and/or Desire2Learn and, thus, provided students with learning experiences including discussion board activities, online quizzes and exams, links to online resources, and so forth. Others were not as enthusiastic and/or skilled with e-learning and, thus, used the learning management system strictly to host course syllabi (Carter, Salyers, Cairns, & Durrer, 2014; Salyers, Carter, Barrett & Williams, 2010b).

A second challenge was the variation among students' skill in navigating their courses prior to implementation of the ICARE scaffolding framework. Students cited difficulties in finding course materials and general navigational issues. Ease in finding resources and navigation in general are integral to student success in online and blended learning.

A third challenge was the limited availability of instructional design support for faculty. While instructional design was recognized at both institutions as important to effective e-learning, it was not available to the extent that faculty required. As the literature suggests, adequate instructional design is integral to e-learning (Christensen, 2008; Tennyson, 2010; Winter, Cotton, Gavin & Yorke, 2010). At the American university, design support was provided by one full-time individual who supported approximately 30 full-time faculty. At the Canadian university, one full-time and two part-time individuals provided design support for approximately 15 full-time faculty.

While other technological and geographic variables affected student and faculty satisfaction, the previously discussed challenges were identified as highest priority for improvement or change. In order to address these issues, the ICARE framework was implemented in both institutions.

In 2010, research on the ICARE framework within the Canadian university provided evidence to support the use of the ICARE framework to structure e-learning courses (Salyers, Carter, Barrett, & Williams, 2010b). Based on the study, the researchers also made instructional design recommendations for the implementation of ICARE in all programs at this School of Nursing.

Previous research based on the ICARE model at the American university revealed no differences in technical ability, learning styles, learning outcomes, and course satisfaction for graduate nursing students enrolled in face-to-face and web-enhanced sections of a course that used the ICARE framework (Salyers, 2005). However, students in the web-enhanced section of the graduate course were more satisfied with their overall course experience, and reported advantages such as greater flexibility in scheduling, less travel, and greater independence and self-pacing in relation to content (Dimitrova, Mimirini & Murphy, 2004; Salyers, 2005; Salyers, Carter, Barrett, & Williams, 2010b).

In both educational settings, comments and data provided by students and faculty were highly aligned with the HIDI model. Across both institutions, students and faculty highlighted the importance of quality human interactions in all courses including face to face, blended, and fully online courses. This finding underscores the need for faculty to dedicate sufficient time, energy, and willingness to engage learners in satisfying interactions that may transcend traditional classroom walls.

Technology support was also an important aspect that required special consideration for the Canadian university with a number of satellite campuses across northern British Columbia. Frequently, when faculty and students tried to access course materials, there was limited Internet access or the learning management system was experiencing technical difficulties. This kind of occurrence was not a problem at the American university. Students at both institutions, however, had full expectation that they would be able to access technical support 24-7, and this was not available at either university. Generally, IT support was available less frequently than what students wanted.

Prior to ICARE, ability to navigate in e-learning environments was negatively affected due to the inconsistent design of courses. This circumstance was partly due to the need to develop faculty teaching expertise in general as well as the need to develop faculty's technical skills and abilities. Neither of the universities, at that time, had academic development centres where faculty could seek out professional development supports to improve their pedagogical practices. Many of these centres now exist in the United States and Canada and emphasize the need for faculty, instructional designers, and staff to have full knowledge of e-learning best practices and course design principles in e-learning.

Applying the HIDI lens to ICARE today. Perhaps the greatest alignment between the ICARE research at the two universities and HIDI relates to institutional capacity. Competition for campus resources is increasing, and, all too frequently when budgets are constrained, infrastructure to support e-learning, IT, instructional design, and so forth may not be allocated for these purposes. There are great benefits to e-learning but also great risks and costs associated with its development and delivery. Significantly, institutional support for e-learning is paramount to its success. Moreover, it is imperative that key stakeholders including faculty, staff, administrators, IT, academic development support staff, and instructional designers be at the table with clear plans for how e-learning will be supported institutionally.

The scaffolding provided by the ICARE framework has been shown to support both teaching and learning in e-based courses. Adhering to the principles for effective scaffolding, ICARE provides a means for faculty to develop and deliver effective e-learning experiences for students. It also affords students the opportunity to self-pace through course material in bite-sized chunks that are consistent, easy to navigate, and stimulating (Salyers, Carter, Barrett, & Williams, 2010). In short, ICARE is an excellent means for addressing the challenges associated with e-learning that HIDI illustrates.

Case 3: The iLearn-iPad Program, Nipissing University

Mobile learning as e-learning. Another example of e-learning at Nipissing University is the iLearn program. The program is a direct response to the increasingly powerful multimedia, social networking, communication and geo-location competences of portable handheld devices and the phenomenon of mobile learning which offers numerous opportunities and challenges in education (Kearney, Schuck, Burden, & Aubusson, 2012). According to some experts, higher education is moving from teacher-centered to learner-centered environments as well as more customized learning approaches such as mobile learning offers (Alyahya & Gall, 2012). Other experts, by considerable contrast, point to the implementation and integration challenges of instructional technology in higher education. Among others, these challenges include technology infrastructure, faculty effort, technology satisfaction, and graduate competency (Park, 2009; Surry, Ensminger, & Haab, 2005).

In the iLearn program at Nipissing University, first year students in the undergraduate business program are provided iPads to use in their four years of study. The students are expected to bring their iPads to class and use them for course work inside and outside of the classroom. Students in other programs as well as upper year business students taking first-year business courses do not receive their own iPads. However, through a portable cart system, they are provided iPads to use during class time. The expectations for participating instructors are to develop teaching and assessment strategies where iPads can, as much as possible, be used to facilitate learning.

While all of this may sound straightforward enough, considerable effort and infrastructure are required given unique design elements and human interaction considerations: for instance, why would an instructor want to use a tablet for teaching a new concept when the students are attending face to face classes? Why not capitalize on the ease of a classroom not distinguished by technology? What if the teacher is simply not adept with using an iPad or does not understand how to use it for teaching and assessment? Where does the instructor go for instructional and technical support? What about support for students? What if the cart with the iPads is not brought to the classroom? How do we know that learning is enhanced through iPad use? These questions and others were all part of the development and delivery of the rollout of the program in 2012.

On the occasion of the first offering of iLearn in September 2012, the bulk of supports existed within the Centre for Flexible Teaching and Learning, discussed earlier in the first scenario. Prior to the term targeted for deployment of the iPads to faculty and students, personal and group sessions with faculty were held by instructional designers and technologists from the teaching and learning centre. While not all faculty took advantage of these professional development sessions—in general, the literature on faculty turnout for professional development sessions reports mediocre turnout in most cases (Carter & Brockerhoff, 2011)—these same sessions as well as individualized coaching opportunities were nonetheless available. Similar supports were available once the term began in the forms of just in time supports (Carter, Salyers, Page, Williams, Hofsink, & Albl, 2012) and face to face classroom visits. Training and support for students were also available through the Centre. While responsibility for the transport for the iPad carts to classrooms fell to the IT department, at that time, there was a strong working relationship between IT and Centre staff. In the overall, the success of the rollout was solid. The following insights offered by students based on their experiences in Fall 2012 are testimony to the strengths, weaknesses, and opportunities of the program.

Some student insights about the program. One of the authors of this chapter had the opportunity to participate in a research project involving the iLearn project (Carter, Nowrouzi, & Fitzgerald, in review). In the study, the students' perspectives during the rollout semester were captured. Conducted as a qualitative study involving focus groups, the study revealed four distinct themes which are outlined below. In two instances, a student statement is included as evidence that teachers, in general, require guidance to learn how to use the iPad for teaching and learning:

1. Students vary in their preferences for mobile devices. The laptop continues to be the device of choice for many students.
2. Students, for the most part, see the iPad as an organizing tool rather than a learning tool. This point noted, some students may see organization via the iPad to be as a first step in their personal learning experiences. This perception is in contrast with viewing the iPad to be an integral part of the teaching and learning experience in the face to face classroom:

In all honesty, I would have to say, it hasn't really, it probably has enhanced my learning experience in an indirect way. Not necessarily, like I feel like, I've got more of an education because of the iPad directly. But, I feel that because I'm able to, you know, have basically, the hard drive of my computer on my iPad, at times, I connected with some files. I can transport files on my iPad like, if I'm in class and something comes up and I really want to look at, I google search it quickly.

3. Teachers tend to use the iPad for purposes of participation (polls, surveys, e-clicker functions) and assessment (quizzes) in contrast with other kinds of learning activities.

4. Teachers need time to learn about using iPads for teaching and learning. Although the students were appreciative of the efforts made by their teachers, they also perceived gaps in their teachers' competence in using the iPad to support learning. The following passage captures this idea well:

I would just add to that, that all of the efforts that I have seen by professors, to integrate technology; sometimes, they didn't go perfectly at first but, after a couple of tries, they normally integrated it in the classroom and into the learning environment and it's worked fairly well. I think it's just a matter of developing it over time.

Applying the HIDI model to the program today. As explained earlier in the chapter, the university where the program is offered has recently transitioned from pedagogical and technical support through a teaching and learning centre to a system of decentralized supports provided across the university. This structural change is considered in relation to the HIDI model.

The expertise of an instructional designer is critical if, in fact, the goal is interactive and, ideally, scaffolded learning experiences. Instructors need to be supported pedagogically since, in likelihood, the iPad is a new technology as well as a new teaching medium for them. Activities and assessments must be re-cast and, for some faculty, this transition is not an easy one.

In the case of iLearn, there is, at the time of writing this chapter, access to design support. However, this support now comes from an individual designer assigned to a faculty rather than a team of designers working together to re-design more traditional teaching methods and to create new methods created with the tablet in mind. Professional development opportunities for faculty as well as students now fall to single persons rather than to a team.

Similarly, while there is still IT support for the program, there is more work for the instructor who must now track down IT assistance which exists in a physically different part of the university than the instructional designer. It follows that the interactions between the designer and the technologist have changed and not always to a positive end. New devices need to be well understood by the designer so that he or she can facilitate teaching and learning; in the case of the iPad, it was not originally conceived to be a learning tool. Hence, dedicated time and conversation between the instructional designer and the IT expert is especially important. When they do not belong to the same team, they may, to some measure, have varying allegiances: the designer to the learning process and the IT expert to the device or technology.

Institutional support does seem evident for iLearn since the program is continuing at a time of fiscal restraint. New business students still receive iPads when they enter the program. Technology without appropriate pedagogical underpinnings, however, is what gives e-learning a bad name. In this case, the money spent by the University on the purchase of the tablets could lead to situations of decreased teaching and learning success and increased frustration by other university stakeholders. These stakeholders could include those who care about fiscal responsibility and view the iPad expenditure as frivolous; those who want to use the technology well but who are confronted with inadequate supports; and those who did not receive funding for their projects while the iLearn project was funded. Countering these gloomy possibilities, the business faculty may now be sufficiently competent in using the devices for teaching and learning purposes. Moreover, there are still supports, simply not the same supports as were available a year ago.

FINAL THOUGHTS

The scenarios just discussed represent different kinds of and approaches to e-learning: e-learning at the programmatic level; within individual courses and modules; and as mobile learning. Respecting that there will always be variation in how much universities value e-learning, in virtually all cases, institutional support is foundational to the success of e-learning initiatives. If there is genuine support for e-learning, there will be technical and pedagogical infrastructure and resources that, taken together, will enable learning characterized by human interaction and appropriately designed learning experiences. Additionally, it is the authors' opinion that the functioning of the interprofessional team that supports e-learning functions best when the team is situated together in shared spaces rather than dispersed throughout an institution. Centralized models of support such as those offered by academic development centres or centres for teaching and learning offer greater assurance of e-learning effectiveness than other models.

There is no university that does not want to offer its students anything less than a first-rate experience. Given the prevalence of e-learning in our universities and its many complexities, conversations about meaningful e-learning are essential. Specifically, these conversations need to involve stakeholders at many levels. In short, conversations about meaningful e-learning are not a 'nice to pursue' goal; they are, as instructional designers would tell us, a 'need to pursue' goal. Pandora is out of the so-called box, and she is not going back in.

Having declared an imperative, how achievable is meaningful e-learning? And what is the cost? Through the HIDI model, we know what the essential ingredients are: human interaction, IT, design, and, of course, institutional support. Extrapolating, HIDI provides educational institutions four areas in which to focus time and energy. By adhering to HIDI while conducting e-learning research and implementing quality assurance strategies, universities will make important headway in their development, implementation, and evaluation of e-learning now and in the future. Additionally, if Canadian universities are committed to excellence in e-learning, financial investments that extend beyond the short-term are vital. At the same time, with e-learning occurring from coast to coast in Canada and at all levels, there may be opportunities for sharing of best practices. For example, in the province of Newfoundland and Labrador situated in Canada's North Atlantic, one learning management system (LMS) is used for all educational institutions from elementary school to college and university. The cost savings and sharing made possible through such an approach are worth very serious consideration. Equally important is the impact that this single LMS experience will have on students. As students move through their primary, secondary, and post-secondary experiences, they will be able to navigate comfortably through their online and blended learning courses and experience confidence in various e-learning environments.

As for the human elements of teaching and learning, are they possible in an e-learning setting? Of course, they are. Think about the many Canadian nurses and other health care professionals who interact with their colleagues and teachers to achieve new credentials through e-based courses and programs. Imagine how many lives are made richer through learning brought to a remote or rural community through e-learning infrastructure. The list could go on. The point is that, in all learning settings—face to face, blended, and fully online—it is design, pedagogy, and engagement that drive student-instructor and student-student interactions and, ultimately, influence the teaching experiences of faculty and learning experiences of students.

Today, Canadian universities are facing pressures of fiscal restraint, accountability mandates, patterns of internationalization, calls for program priorization, and changing demographics. While there are no easy answers to any of these challenges, e-learning has a role to play in each: as examples, e-learning may be a means of recruiting new students and supporting students who need to work while they study. As this chapter has set out, e-learning has real challenges associated with it but it can also lead to real solutions. In short, the authors of this chapter believe that HIDI will be a useful compass for faculty, administrators, instructional designers, and other staff involved in e-learning on Canadian campuses. As a last thought, the authors trust that the MEL study, its findings, and the application of the HIDI model to different e-learning situations as presented in this chapter have provided important insights into the e-learning landscape of Canadian universities where, without question, e-learning is here to stay and where meaningful e-learning experiences are well within reach.

REFERENCES

AACTE. (2008). *Handbook of technological pedagogical content knowledge for educators (TPCK)*. New York, NY: Routledge.

Aguti, B., Walters, R., & Wills, G. (2013). A framework for evaluating the effectiveness of blended e-learning within universities. In R. McBride & M. Searson (Eds.), *Proceedings of Society for Information Technology & Teacher Education International Conference 2013* (pp. 1982-1987). Chesapeake, VA: AACE.

Ali, W. (2012). Factors affecting nursing students' satisfaction with e-learning experience in King Khalid University, Saudi Arabia. *International Journal of Learning and Development*, 2(2), 201–215. doi:10.5296/ijld.v2i2.1666

Allen, E., & Seaman, J. (2006). *Making the grade: Online education in the United States, 2006.* US: Sloan Consortium. Available at: http://sloanconsortium.org/publications/survey/making_the_grade_southern06

Allen, E., & Seaman, J. (2013). Changing course: Ten years of tracking online in the United States. Babson Park, MA: Babson Survey Research Group and Quahog Research Group; Retrieved from http://faculty.washington.edu/rvanderp/DLData/AllenSeaman2013.pdf

Alyahya, S., & Gall, J. E. (2012). *iPads in education: A qualitative study of students' attitudes and experiences.* Paper presented at the World Conference on Educational Multimedia, Hypermedia and Telecommunications.

Baker, R. (2010). *Examples of scaffolding and chunking in online and blended learning environments.* Available at http://ssrn.com/abstract=1608133 or10.2139/ssrn.1608133

Bolliger, D., & Inan, F. (2012). Development and validation of the online student connectedness survey (OSCS). *International Review of Research in Open and Distance Learning, 13*(3), 41–65.

Bower, B. L. (2001). Distance education: Facing the faculty challenge. *Online Journal of Distance Learning Administration, 4*(2), 1–6. Available at http://www.westga.edu/~distance/ojdla/summer42/bower42.html

Brocade. (2011). *Enterprise and mobility: What e-living is teaching about e-learning?* San Jose, CA: Brocade Communication System. Available at: http://www.brocade.com/downloads/documents/technical_briefs/mobility-e- living-teaching-e-learning-tb.pdf

Bullen, M., Morgan, T., Belfer, K., & Qayyum, A. (2008, October). *The digital learner at BCIT and implications for an e-strategy.* Paper presented to the EDEN Research Workshop, Paris.

Bullen, M., Morgan, T., & Qayyum, A. (2011). Digital learners in higher education: Generation is not the issue. *Canadian Journal of Learning and Technology/La revue canadienne de l'apprentissage et de la technogie, 37*(1). Retrieved from http://www.cjlt.ca/index.php/cjlt/issue/view/71

Burge, E., Campbell Gibson, C., & Gibson, T. (2011). *Flexible pedagogy, flexible practice: Notes from the trenches of distance education.* Athabasca, AB: AU Press.

Buzducea, D. (2010). Social work in the new millennium: A global perspective. *Social Work Research, 1*, 31–42.

Carter, L., & Graham, R. (2012). The evolution of online education at a small northern university: Theory and practice. *Journal of Distance Education, 26*(2).

Carter, L., Graham, R., & Nowrouzi, B. (2013). The coming down of fences: What Continuing educators are doing and saying about online and other forms of technology-supported learning. *Canadian Network for Innovation in Education Conference.* Ottawa, ON.

Carter, L., Nowrouzi, B., & Fitzgerald, S. *What undergraduate business students have to say about the iPad as a teaching and learning tool.* (in review)

Carter, L., & Rukholm, E. (2008). A study of critical thinking, teacher-student interaction, and discipline-specific writing in an online educational setting for registered nurses. *Journal of Continuing Education in Nursing, 39*(3), 133–138. doi:10.3928/00220124-20080301-03 PMID:18386701

Carter, L., & Salyers, V. (2013). E-learning as educational innovation in Canada: Two case studies. In L. Shavinina (Ed.), *International handbook of innovation education.* New York: Taylor & Francis/Routledge.

Carter, L., Salyers, V., Page, A., Williams, L., Hofsink, C., & Albl, L. (2012). Highly relevant mentoring (HRM) as a faculty development model for web-based instruction. *Canadian Journal of Learning Technology*, *38*(1).

Carter, L. M., & Brockerhoff-Macdonald, B. (2011). The continuing education of faculty as teachers at a mid-sized Ontario university. *The Canadian Journal for the Scholarship of Teaching and Learning*, *2*(1). http://ir.lib.uwo.ca/cjsotl_rcacea/vol2/iss1/4 doi:10.5206/cjsotl-rcacea.2011.1.4

Carter, L. M., Salyers, V., Myers, S., Hipfner, C., Hoffart, C., MacLean, C., & Barrett, P. et al. (2014). Qualitative insights from a Canadian multi-institutional research study: In search of meaningful e-learning. *Canadian Journal of Scholarship of Teaching and Learning*, *5*(1), 1–17. doi:10.5206/cjsotl-rcacea.2014.1.10

Childs, S., Blenkinsopp, E., Hall, A., & Walton, G. (2005). Effective e-learning for health professionals and students: Barriers and their solutions. A systematic review of the literature: Findings from the HeXL project. *Health Information and Libraries Journal*, *22*(2), 20–32. doi:10.1111/j.1470-3327.2005.00614.x PMID:16279973

Christenson, T. K. (2008). The role of theory in instructional design: Some views of an ID practitioner. *Performance Improvement*, *47*(4), 25–32. doi:10.1002/pfi.199

Cleveland-Innes, M., Garrison, R., & Kinsel, E. (2008). The role of learner in an online community of inquiry: Responding to the challenges of first-time online learners. In N. Karacapilidis (Ed.), *Solutions and innovations in web-based technologies for augmented learning: Improved platforms, tools and applications*. Hersey, Penn.: IGI Global Publishing.

Cobb, S. C. (2011). Social presence, satisfaction, and perceived learning of RN-to-BSN students in web-based nursing courses. *Nursing Education Perspectives*, *32*(2), 115–119. doi:10.5480/1536-5026-32.2.115 PMID:21667794

Contact North. (2012). *Online Learning in Canada: At the Tipping Point. A Cross-Country Check-up*. Retrieved from http://contactnorth.ca/online-learning-canada

Cook, R. G., Ley, K., Crawford, C., & Warner, A. (2009). Motivators and inhibitors for university faculty in distance and e-learning. *British Journal of Educational Technology*, *1*(1), 149–163. doi:10.1111/j.1467-8535.2008.00845.x

Cramer, K. M., Collins, K. R., Snider, D., & Fawcett, G. (2007). The virtual lecture hall: Utilization, effectiveness and student perceptions. *British Journal of Educational Technology*, *38*(1), 106–115. doi:10.1111/j.1467-8535.2006.00598.x

Creswell, J. W. (2009). *Research design: Qualitative, quantitative, and mixed methods approaches*. Los Angeles, CA: Sage.

Creswell, J. W., & Plano Clark, V. L. (2007). *Designing and conducting mixed methods research*. Thousand Oaks, CA: Sage.

Creswell, J. W., Plano Clark, V. L., Gutmann, M., & Hanson, W. (2003). Advanced mixed methods research designs. In A. Tashakkori & C. Teddlie (Eds.), *Handbook of mixed methods in social and behavioral research* (pp. 209–240). Thousand Oaks, CA: Sage.

Dahlstrom, E., Walker, J., & Dziuban, C. (2013). ECAR study of undergraduate students and information technology, 2013 (Research Report). Louisville, CO: EDUCAUSE Center for Analysis and Research; Available at http://www.educause.edu/ecar

Darling-Hammond, L. (2006). *Powerful teacher education: Lessons from exemplary programs.* San Francisco: John Wiley & Sons.

Dimitrova, M., Mimirinis, M., & Murphy, A. (2004, Aug/Sept.). Evaluating the flexibility of a pedagogical framework for e-learning. *Proceedings of the IEEE International Conference on Advance Learning Technologies, Joensuu, Finland.* doi:10.1109/ICALT.2004.1357422

Dorrian, J., & Wache, D. (2009). Introduction of an online approach to flexible learning for on-campus and distance education students: Lessons learned and ways forward. *Nurse Education Today, 29*(2), 157-167. doi:10/jnedt.2008.08.010

Downes, S. (2012, February 11). *Half an hour: E-learning generations.* Retrieved from: http://halfanhour.blogspot.ca/2012/02/e-learning-generations.html

Elliott, A. (2011). Increasing higher education access and pathways through normalization of flexible pedagogies and course structures. *Proceedings of the 2011 Barcelona European Academic Conference, Barcelona, Spain.* Retrieved from: http://conferences.cluteonline.com/index.php/IAC/2011SP/paper/viewFile/538/55

Fisher, R. (2009). Should we be allowing technology to remove the "distance" from "distance education"? *New Zealand Annual Review of Education, 18,* 31–46.

Fitzgerald, S., Beattie, B., Carter, L., & Caswell, W. (2014). Responsive BScN programming at Nipissing University: The continuing education of Ontario nurses. *Canadian Journal of University Continuing Education, 40*(1).

Georgina, D. A., & Olson, M. R. (2008). Integration of technology in higher education: A review of faculty self-perceptions. *The Internet and Higher Education, 11*(1), 1–8. doi:10.1016/j.iheduc.2007.11.002

Ginat, D. (2009). Interleaved pattern composition and scaffolded learning. *Proceedings of the Annual Conference on Innovation and Technology in Computer Science Education (ITiCSE).* Paris, France.

Guri-Rosenblit, S. (2005). 'Distance education' and 'e-learning': Not the same thing. *Higher Education, 49*(4), 467–493. doi:10.1007/s10734-004-0040-0

Hammersley, A., Tallantyre, F., & Le Cornu, A. (2013). Flexible learning: A practical guide for academic staff. York: Higher Education Academy; Retrieved from http://www.heacademy.ac.uk/resources/detail/flexible- learning/fl_guides/staff_guide

Hanover Research. (2011). *Trends in global distance learning.* Washington, DC. Retrieved from: http://www.hanoverresearch.com/wp-content/uploads/2011/12/Trends-in- Global-Distance-Learning-Membership.pdf

Herrington, J., Reeves, T. C., & Oliver, R. (2010). *A guide to authentic e-learning.* New York: Routledge.

Higher Education Academy. (2013). *Flexible pedagogies: Technology-enhanced learning.* Retrieved from: http://www.heacademy.ac.uk/assets/documents/flexiblelearning/Flexiblepedagogi es/tech _enhanced_learning/TEL_report.pdf

Hoffman, B., & Ritchie, D. C. (1998). Teaching and learning online: Tools, templates, and training. In WillisJ.WillisD.PriceJ. (Eds.), *Technology and Teacher Education Annual Conference,*1998. Charlottesville, VA: Association for Advancement of Computing in Education.

Johnson, L., Adams-Becker, S., Cummins, M., Estrada, V., Freeman, A., & Ludgate, H. (2013). NMC Horizon Report: 2013 Higher Education Edition. Austin, TX: The New Medium Consortium; Retrieved from http://www.nmc.org/pdf/2013-horizon-report-HE.pdf

Johnson, L., Smith, R., Willis, H., Levine, A., & Haywood, K. (2011). The 2011 Horizon Report. Austin, TX: The New Media Consortium; Retrieved from http://wp.nmc.org/horizon2011/

Jones, D. P., & Wolf, D. M. (2010). Shaping the future of nursing education today using distant education and technology. *The Association of Black Nursing Faculty Journal, 21*(2), 44–47. PMID:20533754

Kanuka, M. (2006, Sept.). Instructional design and e-learning: A discussion of pedagogical content knowledge as a missing construct. *e-Journal of Instructional Science and Technology, 9*(2). Retrieved from: http://www.ascilite.org.au/ajet/ejist/docs/vol9_no2/papers/full_papers/kanuka.htm

Kearney, M., Schuck, S., Burden, K., & Aubusson, P. (2012). Viewing mobile learning from a pedagogical perspective. *Research in Learning Technology, 20*(1).

Kennedy, G., Jones, D., Chambers, C., & Peacock, J. (2011, Dec.). Understanding the reasons academics use–and don`t use–endorsed and unendorsed learning technologies. *Proceedings of the Ascilite 2011 Changing Demands, Changing Directions Conference.* Hobart Tasmania, Australia. Available at: http://www.ascilite.org.au/conferences/hobart11/downloads/papers/Kennedy- full.pdf

Kerns, A., McDonongh, J. P., Groom, J. A., Kalynych, N. M., & Hogan, G. T. (2006)... *American Association of Nurse Anesthetists, 74*(1), 19–21.

Killam, L., & Carter, L. (2010). The challenge of the student nurse on clinical placement in the rural setting: A review of the literature. *Rural and Remote Health, 10*(1523). Retrieved from http://www.rrh.org.au PMID:20715883

Killam, L., Carter, L., & Graham, R. (2013). Facebook and issues of professionalism in undergraduate nursing education: Risky business or risk worth taking? *Journal of Distance Education, 13*(2).

Kim, M., & Hannafin, M. (2011). Scaffolding problem solving in technology-enhanced learning environments (TELEs): Bridging research and theory with practice. *Computers & Education, 56*(2), 403–417. doi:10.1016/j.compedu.2010.08.024

Knowles, M. S. (1978). *The adult learner: The neglected species* (2nd ed.). Houston: Club Publication Company.

Lam, P., Au Yeung, M., Cheung, E., & McNaught, C. (2009). Using the development of elearning material as challenging and authentic learning experiences for students. In same places, different spaces. In *Proceedings Ascilite Auckland 2009.* Retrieved from: http://www.ascilite.org.au/conferences/auckland09/procs/lam.pdf

Lipscomb, L., Swanson, J., & West, A. (2004). Scaffolding. In M. Orey (Ed.), *Emerging perspectives on learning, teaching, and technology.* Retrieved from: http://projects.coe.uga.edu/epltt/

Margaryan, A., Littlejohn, A., & Vojt, G. (2011). Are digital natives a myth or reality? University students' use of digital technologies. *Computers & Education, 56*(2), 429–440. doi:10.1016/j.compedu.2010.09.004

McCombs, B. L. (2004). The learner-centered psychological principles: A framework for balancing a focus on academic achievement with a focus on social and emotional learning needs. In J. E. Zins, R. P. Weissberg, M. C. Wang, & H. J. Walberg (Eds.), *Building academic success on social and emotional learning: What does the research say?* New York: Teachers College Press.

McCord, L., & McCord, W. (2010). Online learning: Getting comfortable in cyber class. *Teaching and Learning in Nursing, 5*(1), 27–32. doi:10.1016/j.teln.2009.05.003

McKenzie, B. K., Mims, N., Bennett, E., & Waugh, M. W. (2000). Needs, concerns and practices of online instructors. *Online Journal of Distance Learning Administration, 3*(3), 1–9. Available at http://www.westga.edu/~distance/ojdla/summer42/bower42.html

McLean, S., & Carter, L. (2013). University continuing education for adult learners: History and key trends. In T. Nesbit, S. M. Brigham, N. Taber, & T. Gibb (Eds.), *Building on critical traditions. Adult education and learning in Canada.* Toronto: Thompson Educational Publishing.

McLinden, M. (2013). Flexible pedagogies: Part-time learners and learning in higher education. York, UK: The Higher Education Academy, University of Birmingham; Retrieved from http://www.heacademy.ac.uk/assets/documents/flexiblelearning/Flexiblepedagogi es/ptlearners/fp_ptl_report.pdf

Means, B., Toyama, Y., Murphy, R., Bakia, M., & Jones, K. (2009). *Evaluation of evidence-based online learning: A meta-analysis and review of online learning studies.* U.S. Department of Education Report, Office of Planning Evaluation and Policy Development, Policy and Program Studies Service, 1-66. Retrieved from: http://www2.ed.gov/rschstat/eval/tech/evidence-based-practices/finalreport.pdf

Miles, M. B., & Huberman, A. M. (1994). *Qualitative data analysis: An expanded sourcebook.* London: Sage.

Miller, M. (2009). *Teaching for a new world: Preparing high school educators to deliver college- and career-ready instruction. Policy Brief, Washington.* D.C.: Alliance for Excellent Education.

Moore, J., Dickson-Deane, C., & Galyen, K. (2011). E-learning, online learning and distance learning environments: Are they the same? *The Internet and Higher Education, 14*(2), 129–135. doi:10.1016/j.iheduc.2010.10.001

Muirhead, R. J. (2007). E-Learning: Is this teaching at students or teaching with students? *Nursing Forum, 42*(4), 178–185. doi:10.1111/j.1744-6198.2007.00085.x PMID:17944698

Murgatroyd, S. (2012, November). *Online learning: MOOC's, iPads and other things that can support or get in the way of engaged learning.* Presentation to Nipissing University Board of Directors. Huntsville, ON.

Murtagh, L., & Webster, M. (2010). Scaffolding teaching, learning and assessment. *Teacher Education Advancement Network, 1*(2). Retrieved from http://bit.ly/tyfJ5M

Naidu, S. (2004). Trends in faculty use and perceptions of e-learning. *Asian Journal of Distance Education, 2*(2). Retrieved from http://www.asianjde.org/2004v2.2.Naidu.Abstract.htm

Newton, R. (2003). Staff attitudes to the development and delivery of e-learning. *New Library World, 104*(10), 412–425. doi:10.1108/03074800310504357

Oye, N. D., Salleh, M., & Iahad, N. A. (2011). Challenges of e-learning in Nigerian university education based on the experience of developed countries. *International Journal of Managing Information Technology, 3*(2), 39–48. doi:10.5121/ijmit.2011.3204

Palfrey, J., Gasser, U., Simun, M., & Barnes, R. F. (2009). Youth, creativity and copyright in the digital age. *International Journal of Learning and Media, 1*(2), 79–97. doi:10.1162/ijlm.2009.0022

Panda, S., & Mishra, S. (2007). E-learning in Mega Open University: Faculty attitudes, barriers and motivators. *Educational Media International, 44*(4), 328–338. http://cohortresearch.wiki.west-ga.edu/file/view/faculty+attitude+barriers+and+motivators.pdf doi:10.1080/09523980701680854

Park, S. Y. (2009). An analysis of the technology acceptance model in understanding university students' behavioral intention to use e-learning. *Journal of Educational Technology & Society, 12*(3).

Parker, J., Maor, D., & Herrington, J. (2013). Authentic online learning: Aligning learner needs, pedagogy and technology. *Issues in Educational Research, 23*(2), 227–241. Retrieved from http://www.iier.org.au/iier23/parker.html

Perry, B., & Edwards, M. (2010). Creating a culture of community in the online classroom using artistic pedagogical technologies. In G. Veletsianos (Ed.), Using emerging technologies in distance education. Edmonton, AB: AU Press; Retrieved from http://www.veletsianos.com/2010/11/14/data-on-our-open- access-book/

Reeves, P. M., & Reeves, T. C. (2008). Design considerations for online learning in health and social work. *Learning in Health and Social Care, 7*(1), 46–58. doi:10.1111/j.1473-6861.2008.00170.x

Rennie, F., & Morrison, T. (2013). *E-learning and social networking handbook: Resources for higher education*. New York: Taylor & Francis.

Salyers, V. (2005). Web-enhanced and face-to-face classroom instructional methods: Effects on course outcomes and student satisfaction. *International Journal of Nursing Education Scholarship, 2*(1). *Article, 29*, 1–13.

Salyers, V., Carter, L., & Barrett, P. (2010a). *Evaluating student and faculty satisfaction with a pedagogical framework*. Presentation at the Centennial Symposium on Scholarship of Teaching and Learning Conference. Banff, AB.

Salyers, V., Carter, L., Barrett, P., & Williams, L. (2010b). Evaluating student and faculty satisfaction with a pedagogical framework. *Journal of Distance Education/Revue de l'Éducation à Distance, 24*(3). Available at: http://www.jofde.ca/index.php/jde/article/view/695/1145

Salyers, V., Carter, L., Cairns, S., & Durrer, L. (2014). Strategies in online courses for working nurses: Implications for adult and online education. *Canadian Journal of University Continuing Education, 40*(1).

Salyers, V., Carter, L., Carter, A., Myers, S., & Barrett, P. (2014). The search for meaningful e-learning at Canadian universities: A multi-institutional research study. *International Review of Research in Open and Distributed Learning, 15*(6), 313–337. Available at http://www.irrodl.org/index.php/irrodl/article/view/1713

Schank, R. C. (2002). *Designing world class e-learning: How IBM, GE, Harvard Business School, and Columbia University are succeeding at e-learning*. New York: McGraw-Hill.

Selwyn, N. (2009). The digital native: Myth and reality. *Aslib Proceedings: New Information Perspectives, 61*(4), 364–379. doi:10.1108/00012530910973776

Siemens, G. (2010). *Connectivism*. Retrieved from: http://connectivism.ca/?p=220

Siemens, G., & Conole, G. (2011). Connectivism: Design and delivery of social networked learning. *International Review of Research in Open and Distance Learning, 12*(3), i–iv.

Tapscott, D. (2008). *Grown up digital: How the net generation is changing your world*. McGraw-Hill.

Tennyson, R. D. (2010). Historical reflection on learning theories and instructional design. *Contemporary Educational Technology, 1*(1), 1–16.

The Glossary of Education Reform. (2013). Retrieved from http://edglossary.org/carnegie-unit/

Verenikina, I. (2008). Scaffolding and learning: Its role in nurturing new learners. In Kell, P., Vialle, W., Konza, D., & Vogl, G. (Eds.), Learning and the learner: Exploring learning for new times (pp. 161-80). Wollogong, AU: University of Wollongong.

Ward, M., Peters, G., & Shelley, K. (2010). Student and faculty perceptions of the quality of online learning experiences. *International Review of Research in Open and Distance Learning*, *11*(3), 57–77.

Wenger, E. (2004). Communities of practice: A brief introduction. Retrieved from: http://onlinelibrary.wiley.com/store/10.1002/9781405198431/asset/homepages/7_ Online_Communities_of_Practice.pdf?v=1&s=cfd3645273384e59ea802 c0d8cb2a b87e98054c4

Wenger, E., McDermott, R., & Snyder, W. M. (2002). *Cultivating communities of practice*. Boston, MA: Harvard Business School Press.

Winter, J., Cotton, D., Gavin, J., & Yorke, J. (2010). Effective e-learning? Multitasking, distractions and boundary management by graduate students in an online environment. *Research in Learning Technology*, *18*(1), 71–83. doi:10.1080/09687761003657598

Yukawa, T., Kawano, K., Suzuki, Y., Suriyon, T., & Fukumura, Y. (2008). Implementing a sense of connectedness in e-learning. In LucaJ. WeipplE. (Eds.), *Proceedings of World Conference on Educational Multimedia, Hypermedia and Telecommunications 2008* (pp. 1198-1207). Chesapeake, VA: AAC.

ADDITIONAL READING

Akyol, Z., & Garrison, D. R. (2011). Assessing metacognition in an online community of inquiry. *The Internet and Higher Education*, *14*(3), 183–190. doi:10.1016/j.iheduc.2011.01.005

Baker, R. (2010). *Examples of scaffolding and chunking in online and blended learning environments.* Retrieved from http://papers.ssrn.com/sol3/papers.cfm?abstract_id=1608133

Bates, T. (2005). *Technology, e-learning and distance education*. London: Routledge. doi:10.4324/9780203463772

Bates, T. (2008). What is distance education? Retrieved from: http://www.tonybates.ca/2008/07/07/what-is-distance-education/

Bullen, M., Morgan, T., & Qayyum, A. (2011). Digital learners in higher education: Generation is not the issue. *Canadian Journal of Learning Technology*, *37*(1), 1–24. Retrieved from http://www.cjlt.ca/index.php/cjlt

Carter, L., & Rukholm, E. (2008). A study of critical thinking, teacher-student interaction, and discipline-specific writing in an online educational setting for registered nurses. *Journal of Continuing Education in Nursing*, *39*(3), 133–138. doi:10.3928/00220124-20080301-03 PMID:18386701

Christenson, T. K. (2008). The role of theory in instructional design: Some views of an ID practitioner. *Performance Improvement*, *47*(4), 25–32. doi:10.1002/pfi.199

Cismaru, R., & Cismaru, M. (2011). Laptop use during class: A review of Canadian universities. *Journal of College Teaching & Learning*, *10*(11), 21–28.

Drexler, W. (2010). The networked student model for construction of personal learning environments: Balancing teacher control and student autonomy. *Australasian Journal of Educational Technology*, *26*(3), 369–385.

Fisher, R. (2009). Should we be allowing technology to remove the "distance" from "distance education"? *New Zealand Annual Review of Education*, *18*, 31–46.

Gabriel, M. A., Campbell, B., Weibe, S., Mac-Donald, R. J., & McAuley, A. (2012). The role of digital technologies in learning: Expectations of first year university students. *Canadian Journal of Learning and Technology, 38*(1), 1–18. Retrieved from http://www.cjlt.ca/index.php/cjlt

Garrison, D. R., & Kanuka, H. (2004). Blended learning: Uncovering its transformative potential in higher education. *The Internet and Higher Education, 7*(2), 95–105. doi:10.1016/j.iheduc.2004.02.001

Guri-Rosenblit, S., & Gros, B. (2011). E-learning: Confusing terminology, research gaps and inherent challenges. *Journal of Distance Education, 25*(1). Retrieved from www.jofde.ca/index.php/jde/article/view/729/1206

Kanuka, H. (2008). Understanding e-learning technologies-in-practice through philosophies-in-practice. In T. Anderson (Ed.), *The theory and practice of online learning* (pp. 91–119). Athabasca, CA: Athabasca University Press.

Kruger, M. (2010). Students' changing perceptions on the impact of the online learning environment: What about good teaching practice? *Proceedings of the European Conference on e-Learning*, 188-196.

Laurillard, D. (2003). *Rethinking university teaching: A conversational framework for the effective use of learning technologies*. New York, NY/London, UK: Routledge/Flamer.

Legg, T. J., Adelman, D., Mueller, D., & Levitt, C. (2009). Constructivist strategies in online distance education in nursing. *The Journal of Nursing Education, 48*(2), 64–69. doi:10.3928/01484834-20090201-08 PMID:19260397

Merrill, M. D. (2007). The future of instructional design: The proper study of instructional design. In R. A. Reiser & J. V. Dempsey (Eds.), *Trends and issues in instructional design and technology* (2nd ed., pp. 336–341). Upper Saddle River, NJ: Pearson Education.

Njenga, J. K., & Fourie, L. C. H. (2008). *The myths about e-learning in higher education. British Journal of Educational Technology*. Retrieved from Wiley Interscience; doi:10.1111/j.1467-8535.2008.00910.x

Parchoma, G. (2011). Toward diversity in researching teaching and technology philosophies-in-practice in e-learning communities. In B. Daniel (Ed.), *Handbook of research on methods and techniques for studying virtual communities: Paradigms and phenomena* (Vol. 1, pp. 61–86). Hershey, PA: IGI Global. doi:10.4018/978-1-60960-040-2.ch004

Parker, K., Lenhart, A., & Moore, K. (2011, August 28). The digital revolution and higher education: College presidents, public differ on value of online learning. Retrieved from: www.pewsocialtrends.org/files/2011/08/online-learning.pdf

Rossing, J. P., Miller, W. M., Cecil, A. K., & Stamper, S. E. (2012). iLearning: The future of higher education? Student perceptions on learning with mobile tablets. *Journal of the Scholarship of Teaching and Learning, 12*(2), 1–26.

Staffordshire University. (2013). *Best practice models for e-learning: Principles*. Retrieved from https://bestpracticemodels.wiki.staffs.ac.uk/Best_Practice_Models_for_e-Learning%3a_Principles</eref>

Turkle, S. (2011). *Alone together: Why we expect more from technology and less from each other*. New York: Basic Books.

Walsh, P. (2009). *Global trends in higher education, adult and distance learning.* International Council for Open and Distance Education (ICDE). Retrieved from www.icde.org/en/resources/reports/reports_2009/Global+Trends+in+Higher+Education%2C+Adult+and+Distance+Learning.9UFRvY0L.ips

White, D. S., & Le Cornu, A. (2011). Visitors and residents: A new typology for online engagement. *First Monday, 16*(9). http://firstmonday.org/htbin/cgiwrap/bin/ojs/index.php/fm/index doi:10.5210/fm.v16i9.3171

KEY TERMS AND DEFINITIONS

Carnegie Unit: This measure, developed in the 1920s, links time on task and time in the classroom to the funds made available to support student learning. So long as this funding model persists, new and different educational experiences will not reach full potential.

Distance Learning: Distance learning is a form of learning historically defined as geographically distributed learning. Today, many distance learning situations involve online or Internet-supported educational strategies.

E-Learning: E-learning is learning that may occur outside of the face to face setting and typically involves a variety of learning technologies and teaching approaches. It should not be confused with distance learning and online or internet-supported learning although it has, in many cases, adopted some of the characteristics of both. Simply put, e-learning refers to an integration of pedagogy, instructional technology, and the Internet in teaching and learning environments.

E-Living: This term has been used to described the phenomenon of using Internet applications for a wide spectrum of life tasks including but not limited to socializing, networking, banking, planning vacations, and studying.

HIDI: HIDI is an acronym for human interaction (H), IT support (I), design support (D), and institutional support (I). Based on a study called the Meaningful E-Learning project, HIDI is recommended as model for e-learning excellence.

ICARE: ICARE is an acronym representing a form of scaffolding for learning. While ICARE can be used in various learning settings, it is particularly useful in e-learning settings and health education contexts. ICARE means Introduction, Connect, Apply, Reflect, and Extend.

Mobile Learning: Mobile learning refers to learning facilitated through handheld devices such as tablets. The iPad has recently caught attention as a tool of mobile learning or m-learning.

Scaffolding: In learning situations involving scaffolding, the learner is guided progressively from simpler to more complex ideas and applications. In e-learning, scaffolding is particularly important to a successful experience.

Chapter 6
Technology-Enhanced Pedagogical Models to Learn Critical Citizenship at a South African University

Patient Rambe
Central University of Technology, South Africa

Edem Agbobli
Central University of Technology, South Africa

ABSTRACT

Although knowledge-centred approaches anchored in students' knowledge production abilities, heterogeneous learning styles and diverse learning needs are widely celebrated, perplexing questions persist on how these learning capabilities and enablements can be sufficiently harnessed to support technology-enhanced pedagogical designs. This chapter contributes to this discourse by proposing knowledge-centred models that integrate sound pedagogical strategy, ubiquitous technologies and situated learning to address student learning priorities and challenges in a Global Citizenship course at a South African university. Laurillard's (2001) Conversational Framework rendered a theoretical lens for interpreting the learning priorities, challenges experienced and the appropriateness of the proposed technology-mediated pedagogical interventions. Findings suggest that although collective engagement and peer-based networking were salient in the course, challenges of fostering deep learning, scaling the course, enhancing sustainable course delivery and accommodating diverse learning needs of students were reported. Technology-mediated pedagogical models that drew on emerging Web based technologies were designed to resolve these challenges.

INTRODUCTION

Technology integration (TI) is a heavily contested term in higher education. Its operational definition ranges from: the adoption of computers and net-works as integral components of diverse curriculum aspects (Panel on Educational Technology, 1997), the appropriation of technology in ways that shift pedagogical styles and learning experiences (Sheingold & Hadley, 1990), to supporting teach-

DOI: 10.4018/978-1-4666-8363-1.ch006

ing effectiveness and learning outcomes through the use of technology (Dexter, 2002; Redmann, Kotrlik & Douglas, 2003). However, contemporary literature on technology integration has focused more on how the inclusion of learning technologies in academic settings has affected learning environments and classroom cultures (Orlando, 2005), and the effects of technology adoption on qualitative changes of the curriculum like the accomplishment of more authentic and complex goals (Ertmer, 2005). Other TI studies have emphasised using technology to support active learning and participation in classrooms (Weathersbee, 2008) and to target higher level thinking, procedural and technical skills in the curricula (Dexter, 2002). Therefore, an overarching theme in TI definitions is the deployment of specific combinations of information and communication technologies (ICTs) and learning platforms to ensure effective delivery of pedagogical goals.

TI into the course enhances student on-task behaviors, allows their deep engagement with content, supports knowledge application and analysis of information and trains them to sift authentic information in an information driven world (Dockstader, 1999). Despite the good intentions of TI into curricula components, many technology-enhanced pedagogical approaches are still predominantly transmission-based because technology is merely harnessed as a supplement rather than an integral component of the learning process. As such, the availability of technology equipment does not in itself guarantee its effective and successful adoption in the classroom (Vrasidas & Kyriakou, 2008). Unsurprisingly, students continue to find technology-enhanced lectures less captivating and uninspiring. To further compound the challenge of insufficiently transformed pedagogical designs, the increasing cultural diversity and cosmopolitan nature of South African universities coupled with students' varying access to emerging technologies in-class and out of classrooms means that the pedagogical challenge at these universities lies in designing technology-enhanced pedagogical designs that

harness the learning capabilities of heterogeneous students with diverse learning needs, complex learning priorities, and learning styles.

This paper argues that effective pedagogical design of knowledge-centred learning environments necessitates a pragmatic, strategic integration of traditional learning designs with knowledge generating environments of the cloud (which the new generation of students have traditionally grown up in but educators have sub-optimally exploited) to capitalise on the educational benefits of both environments. This blend is critical because traditional learning environments like Learning Management Systems (LMSs) have "largely failed to empower the strong and effective imaginations that students need for creative citizenship" (Campbell, 2009, p. 58-59) in the Social Web. On the other hand, over reliance on flexible, cloud-based environments like Personal Learning Environments (PLE) can be costly as institutions and students have little leverage with application providers when performance degrades, applications crash, or data is exposed or lost (Mott, 2010). A comparison of traditional environments' educational benefits to those of PLEs triggers a Gordian Knot, where choosing one learning environment over the other creates tradeoffs where the value of one environment is relinquished while simultaneously taking on its weaknesses (Mott, 2010). Practically, the study unravels the pedagogical challenges which the Global Citizenship programme team encountered during the pilot phase (pre-design) of a citizenship programme implemented at an English speaking South African university and the constitution of the pedagogical models implemented in the programme (post design).

LITERATURE REVIEW

Critical Citizenship

Critical citizenship (CC) is an inexorably complex concept that defies a precise definition. Bickmore (2005, p. 2) conceives it as "difficult citizenship" due to the competing requirements it imposes on academics to balance intellectual engagement with social responsibility for citizens in their locales. It embraces informed, analytical interventions aimed at understanding the cultural dynamics of inclusion and exclusion (O'Shea, 2004). CC also foregrounds the development of active, critically conscious citizens who are aware of the socio-political contexts within which they live and building commitment to ideals of democratic citizenship (James & Iverson, 2009). Yet developing technology-enhanced pedagogical designs that foster equality of civic participation and a just society is an intractably complex endeavor. This is due to the perplexing conundrums about the different combinations of technologies that can ideally support a citizenship-inclined pedagogy coupled with the competing interpretations of ideal types of critical citizenship.

The Value of Critical Citizenship

The Crick Report (1998) summarises the value of citizenship education (/ CC) as:

1. **Social and Moral Responsibility:** Learning self-confidence and socially and morally responsible behaviour in and beyond the classroom, both towards those in authority and each other.
2. **Community Involvement:** Learning about and becoming helpfully involved in the concerns of learners' communities, learning through community involvement and service.
3. **Political Literacy:** Learning about institutions, problems and practices of democracy and being effective in the life of the nation, through the development of knowledge, skills and values (Cited in Smith et al., 2007).

In summary, CC revolves around student moral commitment and passion to invest in marginalised communities to eradicate social deprivation, in-

equalities and exclusion from mainstream policies and interventions. It finds its expression in student critical inquiry and political activism.

Technology Integration

Pro Integration Arguments

Chandler & An (2007) contend that TI adds significant value to the content taught and shifts the manner in which tasks are accomplished. It leverages students' personal independence and access to the general education curriculum and environment while it also fosters a "sense of control over decision-making processes and expands student life experiences" (Gold & Lowe, 2010, p. 5). TI also engenders meaningful learning in situated contexts by foregrounding learning processes and outcomes rather than technology. When offered in tandem with educator professional development, TI may positively impact on educators' professional understandings of their discipline, professional identity and their practice (Kervin & Mantei, 2010). As such, TI contributes directly to improvements in teaching and learning and generates a model for confronting the demands of educator training (Guzman & Nussbaum, 2009). TI demands that teachers not only demonstrate their knowledge of how to integrate content or concepts into a particular discipline but rather provide evidence of positive effects on student learning the strategy brings (Bucci, Copenhaver, Lehman, & O'Brien, 2003).

Challenges of TI

Naidu (2009) highlights TI challenges as: failure of educators to focus on teaching and learning questions, a lack of attention to careful design of suitable learning experiences and inappropriate selection of tools and technology. An inference from Naidu (2009) is that the pedagogical emphasis should not necessarily be on technology but rather on creating powerful, meaningful learning environments that gainfully leverage the quality of instruction and foster deep learning. Becta (2003) classifies TI challenges according to their level of operation: individuals (teacher level barriers) or institutions (school-level barriers). The former involves lack of time, lack of confidence and resistance to change while the latter relates to limited training in solving technical problems or limited access to resources. Groff & Mouza (2008) articulate the challenges of TI as: a lack of concrete research and consensus among experts on the objectives and outcomes of TI into the curriculum; lack of teacher input on the development of innovations for instructional use; pressure and insufficient support from the administration, community, and policy-makers to use the technology, inappropriate teacher beliefs and attitudes about classroom technology use.

THEORETICAL FRAMEWORK

From a theoretical viewpoint, Laurillard's (2002) Conversational Framework was put into conversation with Community of Inquiry Theory (CoI) (Garrison, Anderson & Archer, 2000) and Mott's (2010) Open Learning Framework, which emphases self-publishing, social networking and multiple collaboration in Web 2.0 environments.

Laurillard's (2002) Conversational Framework

Given our concern with developing knowledge-centred models that integrate robust pedagogical strategies, appropriate technology, situated learning priorities, Laurillard's (2002) Conversational framework rendered a useful theoretical lens for conceptualising the ideal pedagogical designs for the Critical citizenship course. Laurillard's (2002) framework aligns specific media forms with teaching and learning events in support of particular teaching and learning strategies. It documents: 1. The complex roles of interactants in the

learning process, 2. The different technological and educational media to use and 3. The diverse knowledge constructions enabled or hindered by these interactions (see Figure 1).

Figure 1 illustrates the educator-student conversations in light of educator assigned tasks and goals, which unfold with(out) with mediation of technology. Laurillard's (2002) model, provides five main processes of pedagogical delivery: *acquisition, discovery, dialogue, practice* and *creation* (see Table 1). These processes are enabled by complex, non-linear intersections of interactants' roles, the mediating technology and specific teaching strategies.

As Czerniewicz & Brown (2005) rightly observe, the way the teacher and learner roles intersect is through specific engagements and activities, which form teaching and learning "events". Since the current study's intervention was to identify specific media forms and functionalities that were ideal for executing specific teaching and learning activities, Laurillard's (2002) framework provided a useful foundation for conceptualising pedagogical activities, interactants' roles linked to feedback loops and specific technologies.

The framework is then connected to particular forms of media and different pedagogical activities. Meeting the goals of critical citizenship demands technology combinations that afford dialogic interactions, in-depth critical inquiry leveraged by pedagogical content and individualised creation of content in personal learning environments.

Community of Inquiry

For Garrison and Cleveland-Innes (2005) a Community of Inquiry (CoI) supports a discursive environment where interaction and reflection are sustained, ideas are explored and critiqued; and processes of critical inquiry are scaffolded. It comprises three interdependent structural elements: *social presence, cognitive presence* and *teaching presence* (Akyol, Garrison & Ozden, 2009). For

Figure 1. Adapted from Laurillard's conversational framework (2002)

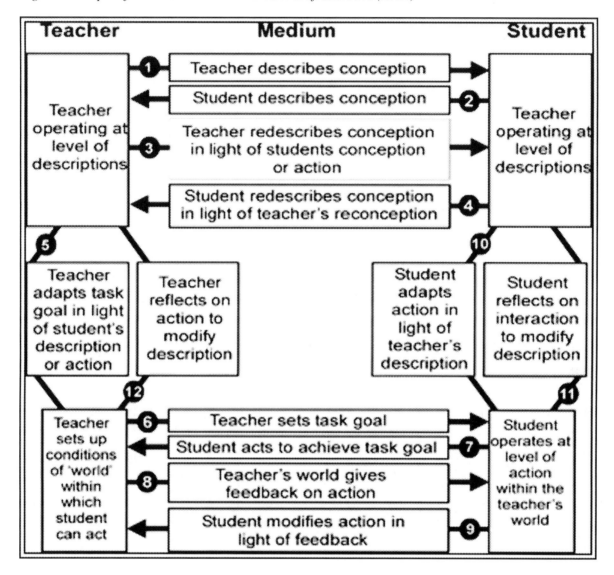

Garrison (2009) social presence is "the ability of participants to identify with the community (e.g., course of study), communicate purposefully in a trusting environment, and develop inter-personal relationships by way of projecting their individual personalities" (p. 352). Cognitive presence is the "the extent to which the participants in any particular configuration of a community of inquiry are able to construct meaning through sustained communication" (Garrison, Anderson, & Archer, 2001, p. 11). It is critical to the generation and sustainability of a CoI focused on the exploration, integration and testing of concepts and solutions (Garrison & Cleveland-Innes, 2005). Teaching presence underscores the design of the pedagogical environment, facilitation of learning and definition of participants' roles. Akyol, Garrison and Ozden (2009) foreground the regulatory and mediating role of teaching presence that entails three areas of responsibility: design and organization, facilitating discourse, and direct instruction.

Table 1. Teaching and learning events and associated media forms

Teaching & Learning Event	Teaching action or strategy	Learning action or experience	Related media form	Examples of non-computer based activity	Example of computer based activity
Acquisition	Show, demonstrate, describe, explain	Attending, apprehending, listening	**Narrative** Linear presentational. Usually same "text" acquired simultaneously by many people	TV, video, film, lectures, books, other print publications	Lecture notes online, streaming videos of lectures, DVD, Multimedia including digital video, audio clips and animations
Discovery	Create or set up or find or guide through discovery spaces and resources	Investigating, exploring, browsing, searching	**Interactive** Non-linear presentational. Searchable, filterable etc but no feedback	Libraries, galleries, museums	CD based, DVD, or Web resources including hypertext, enhanced hypermedia, multimedia resources. Also information gateways.
Dialogue	Set up, frame, moderate, lead, facilitate discussions	Discussing, collaborating, reflecting, arguing, analysing, sharing	**Communicative** Conversation with other students, lecturer or self	Seminar, tutorials, conferences	Email, discussion forums, blogs
Practice	Model	Experimenting, practising, repeating, feedback	**Adaptive** Feedback, learner control	Laboratory, field trip, simulation, role play	Drill and practice, tutorial programmes, simulations, virtual environments
Creation	Facilitating	Articulating, experimenting, making, synthesising	**Productive** Learner control	Essay, object, animation, model	Simple existing tools, as well as especially created programmable software

Adapted from Laurillard's Rethinking University Teaching (2002)

Open Learning Network (OLN)

Mott's (2010) Open Learning Network (OLN) draws on the strengths of LMSs and personal learning environments (PLE). The PLE is a flexible Web-based learning environment that allows for self-generation of content and self-paced learning. It is a looser, non-institutional collection of tools aggregated by individuals to support their own learning activities (Mott, 2010). The OLN has three profound qualities: (1). It is *malleable*. (2). It *leverages technologies that did not exist when the LMS was born* in the late 1990s, (3). It strikes a manageable balance between *imperatives of institutional networks* and the *promise of the cloud*. Unlike a traditional LMS, the OLN is *modular*, consisting of stand-alone, best-of-breed applications that perform core teaching and learning functions. Educators and students can use additional modular tools or replace the default tools with the ones more appropriate for their learning needs (Mott, 2010). The framework is designed to support *flexibility, interoperability*, open *community engagement* and *networking* in a cloud (the OLN).

The unified theoretical framework therefore, draws on pedagogical affordances of the Conversational Framework, various forms of presence necessary for these pedagogical processes to unfold (CoI) and OLN.

RESEARCH QUESTIONS

1. What are the *pedagogical challenges* of the Global Citizenship course?
2. How can the *salient features* of students enrolled on this course be epitomised?
3. How can technology-enhanced pedagogical models be *conceptualised and constituted* to effectively address the challenges of this course?

METHODOLOGY

Since this research combined the exploration of student challenges with technology-enhanced interventions, a case study approach ideally suited this investigation. Cohen, Manion & Morrison (2007) observe that case studies investigate and report the complex dynamic and unfolding interactions of events, human relationships and other factors in a unique sequence. The study investigated challenges that emerged from the complex human-technology interaction and how these dynamic relations could inform the pedagogical designs of rich technology-mediated environments. Case studies also strive to portray 'what it is like' to be in a particular situation, to catch up the close reality and 'thick descriptions' (Geertz, 1973) of participants' lived experiences of, thoughts about and feeling for a situation (Cohen, Manion & Morrison, 2007).

The Case Study

Case Description

The case described in this study is pre and post design of the Global Citizenship programme. The South African university at which this case study was conducted is currently undergoing transformation. One such mandate of its transformation agenda is to promote social responsibility through the expansion of community service programmes. To realise this mandate, the Global Citizenship: Leading for Social Justice (Global-CLSJ) programme was formulated in the Office of Deputy Vice Chancellor in 2009. Subsequently, the Department of Extramural Studies (DES) in liaison with Centre for Educational Technology (CET) staff was tasked with implementing the programme. The DES subsequently formed a Global-CLSJ programme team, which comprised the Programme coordinator, Programme head and two tutors in this department. The CET staff rendered advisory expertise on technology-enhanced pedagogical conception of the programme. The Global-CLSJ is an extra-curricular programme that renders students an opportunity to engage critically with contemporary global debates and reflect on issues of citizenship and social justice. Its rationale is anchored in two main themes, which are *global citizenship* and the *quest for social justice*.

The G-CLSJ comprised two modules namely: *Global Debates, Local voices* (Module 1) and *Thinking about volunteering: service, boundaries and power* (Module 2). Module 1 was constructed around four themes namely: *Debating Development; War and Peace; Climate Change* and *Africa in the Globalised world*, with compulsory, recommended and optional activities (see activities in Table 2).

Module 1 Activities

The module encapsulated face-to-face lectures and online learning that bridged the perceived "disconnect" between the following: the local and global, theory and practice, the elite institutional practices and realities of (marginalised) neighbourhoods and communities. Students also participated in group forums and chats, executed written tasks, participated in learning events and contributed to opening and closing discussion sessions.

Table 2. Module 1 imperatives and activities of the G-CLSJ

Imperative	Description of activities	Application of Laurillard (2001), Garrison, Anderson and Archer (2000) frameworks to Module 1 activities
Student building on prior knowledge	Student reflection on prior personal knowledge and diverse experience	**Dialogue**-Use of LMS tools (chat rooms, discussion forums) and personal reflections to build knowledge on critical citizenship (*Cognitive presence*). Reflective seminars for engaging with students (*Teaching presence*)
Need identification and problem solving	Identification of needs / challenges in local communities and formulation of pragmatic interventions to address them	**Practice**-Student participation in field trips and volunteer organisations to experience service learning (Social presence) Virtual simulations and films on contemporary global issues (war, famine, poverty) to instil social responsibility in students (*Cognitive presence*)
Collaborative learning	Participating in enriching collaborative learning activities (learning events, lectures, watching brief films and animations)	**Acquisition**-Representational forms of delivery / acquisition involving lectures, digital video and audio clips (*Teaching presence*)
Critical inquiry	Critical questioning practices (posting, responding to, and interpreting questions) that prompt students interpret and construct knowledge drawing on learned content.	**Discovery**-Use of digital media (blogs, chats, discussion forums) and information gateways to engage in critical literacy practices (*Cognitive presence*)

Module 2 Activities

Module 2 comprised *five themes* based on student participation in service work namely: *self and service, contexts of inequality, the ethics and paradigms of service, development and sustaining new insights*. Students were required to volunteer 15 hours of community service and use their experiences as reflective "scripts" for engaging with the academic content taught. As volunteers, they employed their prior and present experience of volunteering, partnered with local organisations to acquire experience, seek guidance and develop intellectual capital required for effective service. Module 2 learning activities included: 15 hours of community service, 12 hours of reflective face-to-face sessions, 2 short reflective papers and self-reflection and peer commenting on blogs.

Data Collection Procedures

Online Academic Socialisation and Virtual Ethnography

Tutors used Facebook forums and discussion forums to discuss citizenship and social justice concepts, questions and problems learnt in seminars and to provide additional information to students. Students also employed blogs for journaling their personal reflections on community service and critical citizenship after their service learning assignments in local communities. Educators used chat rooms mainly for making announcements to students while students reciprocally communicated academic-related information. The co-author was also given full access to all the aforementioned four interactional spaces through which lecturers, tutors and students engaged on academic matters. This academic immersion was meant to ensure: 1) This researcher's academic immersion into the existing course-related activities and interactions, 2). Determine the appropriateness of technologies-in-use for the pedagogical goals intended at this programme's pilot phase, 3) Ascertain the consistency of student activities with the educator's pedagogical intentions.

In-Depth Personal Reflections

Although the G-CLSJ team discouraged the researcher from directly citing student postings for privacy considerations, they however, allowed him to make his personal reflections of these educator-student and peer-based interactions. Therefore, researcher used his reflective diary to document his observations of online interactions. The journal reflections were made over two months. The diarised reflections of each consultative environment were corroborated and merged to create a consolidated reflective report.

In-Depth Semi Structured Interviews

The G-CLSJ team were also interviewed as a group to solicit their diverse experiences of teaching on the programme. The interviews targeted the programme' rationale, pedagogical intentions, learning activities, expected learning outcomes and the team's pedagogical challenges. The group interview lasted one and half hours. An educational technologist from the CET whom G-CLSJ team consulted with during the piloting phase of the programme was also interviewed on his personal experiences of the programme and its associated challenges. This interview lasted about an hour. All interviews were audio recorded using a digital audio recorder to capture the original reflections, transcribed in Microsoft Word and analysed using content analysis.

Data Analysis

For all personal reflections on educator-student and peer-based interactions on all discursive spaces, the researcher (the co-author) relied on *interpretive analysis,* and the *epoche* (or bracketing process). In interpretive analysis, the researcher attempts to "get closer to the participant's personal world" by putting her own conceptions in dialectical engagement with participants' "to make sense of that other personal world" (Smith & Osborn, 2008, p. 53). It constitutes a two-stage inter-subjective interpretive activity. For Veletsianos and Kimmons (2012) the epoche refers to the researchers' conscious and systematic attempt to contain their own experiences to allow the phenomenon to be understood without their preexisting beliefs, biases, and understandings of the phenomenon. Epoche was applied during personal reflections on all observed online data, during interviewing, data analysis, and the write up of the manuscript.

Content analysis was used for analysing of CET expert and GC team group interviews to develop a holistic view of the problems encountered and their implications for pedagogical design. Content analysis is an inductive analysis which involves "generating units of meaning, classifying, categorising and ordering these units of meaning, structuring the narratives to describe the interview contents and then interpretation of these contents (Cohen, Manion & Morrison, 2007, p. 368). Therefore, results emerge from the manual coding of *central categories* of the pedagogical challenges experienced by different research subjects. Strauss and Corbin (1998) define central categories as those that "appear frequently in the data." Words, phrases and meanings which were frequently extracted from interviews and students reflections online constituted our central categories.

Since the researcher (co-author) was tasked with developing detailed technology-enhanced pedagogical designs that would contribute to

Table 3. Issues and challenges identified in use of technology in the pilot phase of the GCLSJ Programme

Technology tool in use	Teaching and learning event (Laurillard, 2001)	Researcher's reflections on interesting issues identified on collaborative spaces (drawing on Garrison, Anderson & Archer, 2000; Mott 2010)	Challenges identified
Student blogs	Discovery	**Teaching presence:** *Flexibility and openness* Synergy of learning spaces-Some students drew on resources provided in class (videos watched, URLs, seminars attended) to make propositions about introducing volunteering to the first years classes.	*Limited technological confidence*-In the initial phases of blogging, students with limited technological confidence tended to be cautious and apologetic in their reflections for fear of being misinterpreted.
	Acquisition	**Teaching presence** *Flexible web-based services* Synergy-Tutors drew on constructs covered in class to engage with students' blog postings. Their moderation included clarifying concepts, exhorting students to contribute to peers' blogs and summarising themes in the students' postings.	*Discrepancies in academic support*-Senior academics were marginally involved (social presence) in blog postings.
	Dialogue	**Cognitive presence** *Community engagement and academic networking* Critical engagement-Many interesting reflections, puzzles and contradictions emerged from a few prolific bloggers: For instance, in *"Does it count as service"* post, a female student expressed the contradictions between voluntarism and medical students' assistance of women in labour. She emphasised that in an obstetrics course where students were expected to assist 15 mothers in labour to deliver, they were tempted to assist mothers undergoing normal delivery while neglecting those in early labour or with complications.	*Challenge of deep learning*-While many blog posts were experiential in nature, few bloggers drew on concepts learnt in class or were enthusiastic about commenting on peers' blog posts. *Inadequacy:* Due to the time lag between service learning and online reflections, some students confessed to having forgotten their experience of volunteering and struggled make logical posts.
Discussion forums	Acquisition	**Teaching presence** *Open Community Engagement and networking* Diagnostic purpose-Discussion forums provided diagnostic tools for tracking student understanding of global citizenship, practical knowledge of problem solving and argumentation. For example, in "lets play the balloon game" discussion thread, one student professed ignorance by suggesting that former President Julius Nyerere was on retirement.	*Opinion reinforcement*- the argument that fame with limited regard for marginalised communities is less helpful was universal but was not sufficiently questioned.
	Dialogue	**Social presence** *Simple course content creation* Playful learning-Tutors' use of icebreakers enticed student reflection on learned content. Tutors were also critical in moderation of discussions and establishing netiquette .	*Moderation*-Although tutors' summarisation of student points was commendable, it was done less often.
	Practice	**Cognitive presence** *Open communication and networking* Evidence- Some students exhibited some valid justifications for their arguments. For instance, the association of multiple births with lack of knowledge of family planning. One student justified his choice of a personality in a problem solving task this way: Bono's nomination for Nobel Peace Prize, being named TIME's 'Person of the Year' and earning a knighthood as a sign of achievement.	*Emotive discourses*- some debates were emotional and lend themselves to misunderstandings of peers' views.
	Dialogue	**Cognitive presence** *Academic networking* Theory informed-Few students were cogniscent of how their discussions impacted on theoretical constructs /issues and hence drew on such theoretical concepts in argument building. As such, one student conceived volunteerism as some form of "martyrdom" to serve his community.	*Peer-critique*-Limited peer-based critique of peers' postings, which compromised student ownership of debates.

addressing these challenges, all data from analysed interview transcripts, online data and the researcher's reflections were put in conversation with learning design theories. From a theoretical viewpoint, this data was integrated with Conversational Framework, CoI concepts and OLN to provide an integrated interpretive framework (see Table 3).

FINDINGS

Researcher's Reflections

The reflections can be grouped into educators' pedagogical challenges and students' learning challenges. These are discussed in subsequent sections.

Educators' Pedagogical Challenges

Based on his reflections on the interactions, the researcher (co-author) identified the following pedagogical constraints faced by educators: 1) Choosing the most effective combination of technologies among a myriad of Web based technologies that facilitate the realisation of their pedagogical goals (dilemma of choice), 2). Fulfilling the "balancing act" between their choice of technologies guided by their pedagogical intentions and student choice of available networking technology already in their use, 3). Establishing the format and sequence of academic interactions and activities within and across different technology platforms, mindful of the compressed nature of the programme (7 months) and limited contact time, 4). The complexity of anchoring and sequencing interactions and activities in the face of multiple citizenship goals sought, 5. Building and sustaining the momentum of productive interactions and participation among students over an extended duration.

Student Learning Challenges

The following table summarises some of the interesting issues and challenges the researcher discerned from student use of collaborative tools (Facebook discussion forums, discussion forums, chat rooms and blogs). The analysis is informed by Laurillard's (2001) Conversational Framework, Garrison, Anderson and Archer's (2000) CoI Concepts and Mott's (2010) OLN concepts (see Table 3). This is followed by a presentation of interview data.

Table 3 illustrates researchers' reflections on the findings from educator-student and student-peer interactions. Dialogic interactions and open engagement were often compromised by student opinion reinforcement, emotive discourses and lack of substantiations of positions taken.

Interview transcriptions: Challenges of the G-CLSJ Programme

The following section reports on the findings on G-CLSJ team and the CET staff's challenges in programme implementation. These challenges include: enhancing learners' meaningful participation, promoting high calibre graduates, coordination of the programme, scaling the programme and developing a cohesive learning community. These issues are discussed in subsequent sections.

1. Enhancing Meaningful Learning Experience of Learners

The programme team's daunting challenge was how to foster student meaningful learning experiences and sustain their active participation in an extra-curriculum course. Although the course would appear on student transcripts as a short university course, there were no credits for participation in the course. The pedagogical dilemma was identifying and adopting the right combinations of learning activities and complementary technologies that would support an ideal technology-enhanced pedagogical environment. In the absence of direct inducements for student involvement, online participation depended on the goodwill, passion and civic duty of students, educators and communities. As the CET educational technologist observed:

[…] deeper interaction and rigorous engagement which involve more application of concepts are difficult to impose because there are no marks and credits. Partly, student excitement with the course is its difference from other courses that have strict curricula, many readings and highly conceptualised interactions […] (CET Expert Interview).

The challenge, therefore, was to generate high student interactivity and meaningful participation in a non credit bearing course through different pedagogical activities without diluting the intellectual rigor demanded of any typical university course. Learning designs had to activate student interest and enable them to discern the intrinsic value of active engagement and reflexive inquiry.

2. Promoting a High Calibre Graduate

Given the course's accommodation of diverse learning types (adult learning, lifelong learning and traditional learning), the challenge was conceptualising learning environments that generate "high calibre graduates." This term implies self-motivated graduates who possess knowledge, skills, and competencies on global issues and who shoulder the civic responsibility to serve their community. Such "graduateness" necessitated not only student critical inquiry but their grasp of real-world problems and their contribution to their eradication. Students had to balance intellectual demands (critical inquiry and reflection) with the emotional elements of both courses (reflexive practice in service learning).

Notwithstanding nascent critical engagement noticeable among the learners, the GC team was concerned about the emotional tone of student sentiments.

Many blog posts were emotional, about civic action and not necessarily reflection-based intellectual exchanges, or and application of concepts in real world situations. Students often reinforced peers' postings as they posted just to comply with course requirements. The question is how to get students transcend reinforcement and compliance to engage and share their thinking [GC Team coordinator-Group interview].

While emotions are inevitable in any social justice project, such feeling need to be balanced with objective intellectual traits like substantiation of

arguments and provision of factual evidence to ensure that high quality debates are sustained. Students' varying levels of intellectual maturity also compounded this problem:

The course brings a different character to social networking as some interesting tensions exist: Level of maturity of students, and academic interactions vs social interaction. [...] There are some first years, many second years, third and post graduates. How you bring meaningful conversations amongst such a diverse group is painstaking. If you introduce technologies students are readily familiar with like social media, there might be significant buy-in, but won't academic engagements be sacrificed? [GC Programme head-Group Interview]

The dilemma, therefore, was the academic value of appropriating familiar ubiquitous technologies for a heterogeneous cohort without compromising academic engagements particularly among university entrants.

3. Challenges of Well-Coordinated Action

Developing a well-coordinated strategy for cohesive team work in programme delivery requires integrating members' diverse experiences with technology and sharing of their academic knowledge. The programme head and coordinator were mature academics who were less anchored in emerging technologies than their tutors. As such, team members' varying technological skills potentially constrained the smooth rollout of a well-coordinated strategy. As the CET expert professed:

The disjuncture between tutors approaches and senior team members is another limitation. Tutors often review their facilitation processes to improve them and are good at integrating face-to-face interactions and online interactions. Senior staff members are either struggling or reluctant digital immigrants who do not use online environments much for deep conversations. They don't use social media much nor adequately understand its use for online communication. It's not just about tutor development but also facilitating cognitive shifts in the whole team (CET Expert Interview).

Given the different technological orientation of the team, deliberate interventions that leverage team members' exposure and confidence with technology were critical to the advancement of a shared overall strategy of the programme. Leveling the technological field required tutors to master technological-pedagogical content knowledge and senior academics to familarise with and appropriate emerging technologies sufficiently.

4. Scaling the Programme

The dilemma was ascertaining the long-term scalability of a programme in light of uncertainties about the size of enrolment for the following year. Since the programme was in its pilot phase, its prospective rollout depended on the size of the future enrolment, which was unknown. In light of this uncertainty, radical approaches to technology-enhanced pedagogical designs were conceivably uneconomical:

I don't think we need to go radical – like drop Vula [University's Sakai based learning management system], and adopt a cloud of Facebook ecosystem and Twitter. That would be useful for students and not for staff. It's a course and not a social network /voluntary activity where we don't mind if students drop out. Moreover, the course is supplementary to the curriculum (CET Expert).

The rollout size and ICT investment projections needed to be commensurate with the size of demand and respond to prospective students' techno-savvy nature to avoid inefficient expenditure.

5. Sustainability and Flexibility

Critical questions revolved around the extent of sustainability of the programme. In the absence of an ideal pedagogical framework to inform the learning design processes, several learning theories would be drawn upon to support the theoretical design of the programme. Mindful of this uncertainty, the challenge was whether any proposed design model adopted would adequately flex to the multiple demands of the academic ecological environment. As the CET Expert observed:

There are contradictions between peer-to-peer learning and structured learning within a course. Teachers are conceived as intruder in online spaces, which students conceive as theirs. Do we need different spaces for different interactions or need spaces which are particularly for peer-to-peer interaction, where we let tutors go and lecturers stay out? Tutors are in terms of status, academic levels and attitude closer to the students than lecturers. They are likely to trust lecturers for the intellectual stuff but find tutors more approachable than lecturers (CET Expert).

Therefore, the uncertainty about the appropriate combinations of technologies to adopt for effective student learning challenged programme sustainability. This design complexity left the GC Team ruminating on whether exclusive technologies with restrictive access for particular academics were conceivable. Student enactment of their voice through conversational technologies was another issue:

Face-to-face conversations can be spontaneous but for online interactions you need some commitment to your words as they will be read by peers. So how do students learn to take voice in an online environment and recognise the provisional nature of online communication-where you change our mind about previous utterances? Partly, its about facilitation, technical and social design.

You need some ease with the interface and safety (GC Programme coordinator).

Long-term sustainability of interactions necessitated the creation of "safe," secure technology-mediated learning environments where students grasped the provisional and contested nature of knowledge. These environments needed to empower them to enact their agency by presenting multiple and competing ideas without the fear of ridicule or exclusion from their online audiences.

More so, developing a high-calibre graduate constituted a short-term mutual commitment of academics and students, which would culminate in an academic transcript. On the contrary, developing a responsible, global citizen demanded continuous lifelong learning and long-term investment of both students and academics. In terms of programme design, the former normally cohered with the duration of student enrolment in the course while the latter raised questions about the long-term sustainability of the learning strategies and technological platforms to embrace the contributions of alumni.

6. Developing a Cohesive Learning Community

The pilot phase of the G-CLSJ programme comprised undergraduates (from first year to fourth year) and postgraduate learners who came from different disciplines and with varied prior experiences and exposure to service. The project team comprised senior academics, young tutors and instructional designers who were expected to develop a shared vision of a networked learning community. The challenge of the team was to become a dedicated cohesive group with unified goals, learning strategies, learning activities and technologies that contributed to student critical scholarship, social responsibility in service and volunteering. The senior management was responsible for the production of course materials and learning activities and overseeing the operation

of the online environment. Tutors assumed the administrative and support responsibilities of coordinating learning events and moderation of online interactions. Developing a shared "game plan" for such a diverse group of academics, tutors and support staff was a daunting challenge for all those concerned.

SOLUTIONS AND RECOMMENDATIONS

Towards a Technology-Enhanced Pedagogical Model of Technology Integration

The detailed discussion above informed the development of two technology-mediated pedagogical models that served as interventions (for Modules 1 and 2) to address these aforementioned challenges. Consistent with Laurillard's (2002) framework, the models were designed with the research context, different academic and experiential learning activities, technologies which students and academics were familiar with, and the sequence of learning events in mind. This understanding was put in conversation with Garrison, Anderson and Archer's (2001) CoI, which requires a discursive environment to support meaningful interaction, critical reflection and the provision of educator support through social presence, cognitive presence and teaching presence. The OLN was then imputed into the resultant composite typology to ensure flexibility, openness, academic and social networking capabilities of the resultant framework. This was critical mindful of the short course duration, lack of assessments for participation, limited contact time for educators and uncertainty about the scalability of the programme (see Table 4, Table 5, and Figures 2-4).

This middle of the road approach was first presented to educators, discussed in groups in two seminars (a seminar and follow-up seminar) to familiarise and train educators in the operations

Table 4. Profile of activities and tools for the pedagogical design of Module 1

Lecture [lecturer welcomes students, clarifies course goals and student and staff roles]
Podcasts-[podcasts help provide additional materials]
Socialisation into the institutional Learning Management System (Vula) - [lecturer introduces students to the online course tools on Vula, course content is uploaded on Vula, students are taught the netiquette]
Live journals- [for updating students on latest events, general course management and links to latest readings].
Podcasts –[clarifying the netiquette, different uses of applications used in the Module]
Discussion forums and Chats, - [students are encouraged to sign onto the discussion forums, and to raise their personal concerns and queries regarding the Module][student chats enhance the general management of the Module]
DFAQ mobile interface and/Mixit- [allows students to consult anonymously with the tutor. Shy students use this space to engender communication, question-based engagement and access group resources].
E-portfolios-[students keep e-portfolios to plan and track their progress on learning tasks, and to assess their development trajectory]
Seminar –[A seminar is conducted to cover specific content issues]
Podcasts-[podcasts help provide additional materials and lecture resources to students from geographically distributed students][RSS aggregators keep students updated on the latest audio files/vodcasts].
Live journals-[for updating students on current events]
Learning event/ seminar-[learning events in which students actively engage are organised][lectures provide support and guidance in executing these activities]
Blogs-[students actively reflect on learning events using blogs] [RSS aggregators provide useful contact points for students to share their latest postings with peers and tutors].
Closing Lecture-[the final lecture is conducted]

Table 5. Profile of activities and tools for the pedagogical design of Module 2

Lecture-[lecturer welcomes students, clarify the course goals, clarify students and staff roles]
Socialisation into the Learning Management System (Vula)-[lecturers introduce students to the online course tools on Vula, course content is uploaded on Vula, students interact with content and are assigned small group projects]
Blogs- [blogs are used for student personal reflections and brain storming on collaborative tasks][lecturers and students critique the collaborative projects, provide suggestions or useful resources or links][students also document their experiences of service][RSS feeds provide updates on students individual blogs]
Collaborative wiki-[students groups collaboratively work on collaborative service projects on a Wiki, they document their experiences in learning communities via a wiki][To ensure the development of a cohesive engaging community, students are expected to interact and construct knowledge within and across groups. Students can contribute 450 words for each of the activities, however the distribution of these words across activities is not stipulated-The words could be spent on different issues like developing a sketch for a detailed report on Rural Youth Skills Development programme, or developing an executive summary of the programme, or developing proper referencing on the programme]
Discussion board and MXit-[topical issues/questions and queries on student experiences and constructs developed in wikis are posted on the discussion forum][tutors are assigned the role of online administrators to give feedback on student projects][MXit allows anonymous consultations with peers and with the entire group-via MXit Groups]
Collaborative wiki-Students are required to work in groups of five in a collaborative wiki to brainstorm ideas on digital story telling][they can also collaborate via document sharing applications like Google docs][students audio-record the stories of elders of a particular community using cameras, or handhelds]
Digital story telling on YouTube-[The stories may be posted on YouTube, flexible learning is promoted as students use MP3 players/mobile phones or iPods to play the videos] ***Blogs*** –[personal blogs are used for student reflections on this process and to provide tutors' comments][student poll is conducted and students whose video wins the most votes is screened in class]
Celebration- [the video of the most interesting story is watched in class, a seminar in which students with the most innovative ideas are deliberated is held and they are congratulated on their expertise].

Figure 2. Diagrammatic sequence of activities and tools for the pedagogical design of Module 1

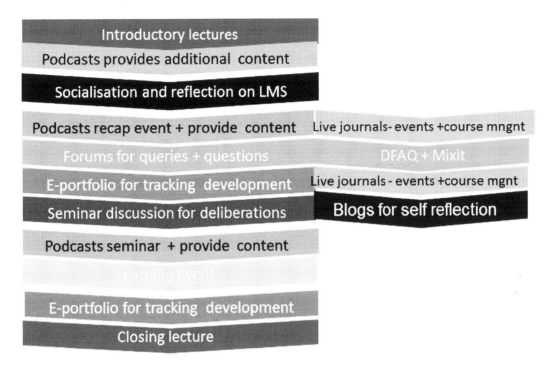

of the new environment. Although, the researcher (co-author) advised educators about the value and tradeoffs of adopting this model, no additional training was offered to the educators. However, the CET educational technologist who had contributed to the conception stages of these redesigns pledged to liaison constantly with G-CLSJ staff to support their adoption of this redesign. Table 4 and Figures 2 and 3 summarise the proposed profile of activities, diagrammatic sequence of technology tools and activities of the actual proposed design of Module 1 respectively.

DFAQ mobile is a special purpose mobile instant messaging service (MIM) developed at the CET to support anonymous academic consultations between educators and academically-challenged students. MXit is a popular South African MIM service, which supports socialisation among young adults. The profile of activities and tools in Table 4 are summarised diagrammatically in Figure 2 and Figure 3 respectively.

There is strong lecturer cognitive and social presence in face-to-face contact but less presence in LMS and social media environment because they serve as mentors, coaches and conversationalists. In contrast, tutors have a stronger cognitive and social presence online but are less involved in class activities. The resources /knowledge driven nature of the model is evidenced by the centrality of podcasts as knowledge dissemination tools.

Pedagogical Implication of Module 1 Design

The value of the proposed model lies in the following issues discussed below:

Balancing Learning Community Roles

The balancing of senior experts and tutors' roles in the online learning environment is critical to the advancement of a networked learning com-

Figure 3. Module 1 Design-An Emporium Model

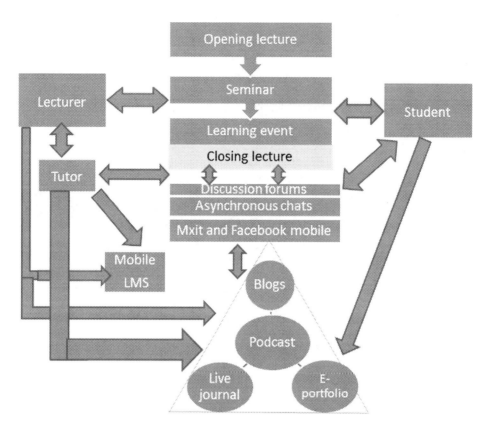

Figure 4. Sequence of Activities and tools for the design of Module 2

munity. While lecturers' moderate involvement in online activities (see the size of the arrow linking academics to online environments) affords the growth of the critical mass of a CoI, it sufficiently sustains this community over time. The strategic alignment of existing technologies with the participants' roles and their collective contributions is consistent with Laurillard (2002) conversational framework's focus on talk-back processes between educators and students at the level of conception, reflection, goal setting and pedagogical delivery.

Podcast-Driven PLE

A podcast-driven PLE affords a portable learning space for student learning across different spaces. When podcasts are integrated with blogs (for self-reflection) and e-portfolios (for self-regulated learning) through RSS aggregators, they offer self-paced learning for student intellectual growth. The integration of different media at the level of engagement and reflection approximates Laurillard's (2002) emphasis on aligning media forms, learning actions / experiences with the actual teaching strategy to ensure optimal delivery of outcomes. Mindful of this course's emphasis on reflexive practice, student academic development would be "most effective when grounded in reflection, inquiry, and action, with work directly related to [...] students' learning" (Lemke & Lesley, 2009, p. 9). More so, students would have broader options for voicing their emotions and diverse perspectives on different issues through public dialogue (discussion board and chats) or through private peer-based consultation (Mixit and DFAQ mobile).

Proposed Design for Module 2

Module 2 design's activities are summarised in Table 5, while the sequence of these activities

and tools constituting the model are illustrated in Figures 4 and 5 respectively.

In Figure 5, the lecturer has less influence in the online learning environment where students and tutors have a proportionately higher level of involvement. Synchronous communication enhances the smooth integration of learning activities. RSS aggregators allow the aggregation of content from different learning environments for flexible access while MXit communication enhances anonymous consultations.

Pedagogical Implications for Model 2 Design

These are summarised in subsequent sections.

Cultural artifact production

Critical citizenship would be fostered when students develop artifacts that "speak" to their role as "participative citizens" of a learning community. Student production of videos in context affords them direct experience in applying concepts and constructs learned. Laurillard's (2002) pedagogical events of *practice* and *creation* find expression in practical, experiential practices like digital story telling using YouTube videos. Students practically create cultural artifacts (videos, audio recordings, or animations) drawn from real contexts and experiences of communities to which they constitute critical stakeholders in their redress. The transmission approach is put in conversation with meaningful constructionist approaches in which students engage with resources they develop themselves and have a sense of ownership.

Critical Questioning

Critical questioning emerges from service learning projects that require collaboratively group work, and when modalities and strategies for implementing group work are complex, uncertain and

Figure 5. Design for Module 2

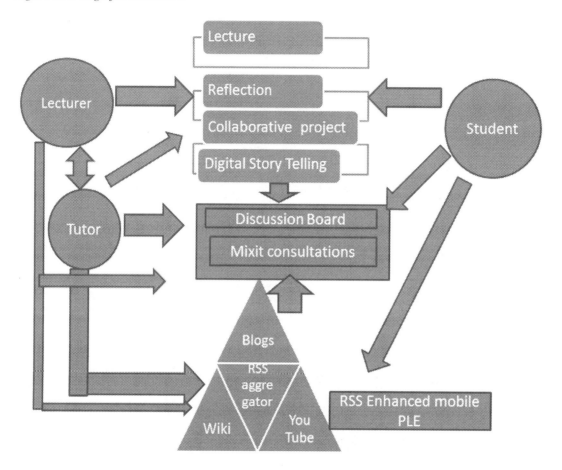

messy. Students are forced to critically question their roles in community development and rethink how the enactment of their social identities would contribute or hinder the execution of their social responsibilities. Laurillard (2002) emphasises a dynamic, evolving and recursive relationship between academics and students in the realisation of pedagogical goals. Similarly student-community relationships, roles and identities need continuous reconfiguration to support effective service learning and reflexive engagement.

DISCUSSION

Complexity of Nurturing Meaningful Interactions

The GC-LSJ team professed the complexity of engaging students in a non-credit bearing course. The disciplinary diversity of students coupled with the complexity of sustaining meaningful theory-based conversations were notable challenges. Some students came from disciplines with a limited culture of strong argumentation like Engineering and Architecture. Literature attributes suboptimal online interactions to superficial student engagements (Rambe, 2010), lack of confidence in expressing personal opinions (Ponnusawmy, & Santally, 2008), low levels of participation (Mazzolini &Maddison, 2003), students' low intrinsic motivation and their perceptions about the value of online interaction (Xie, Durrington & Yen, 2011). Although online participation was high in the two courses, the depth of intellectual engagement was a cause for concern. Laurillard's (2002) university teaching model provided some insights into how pedagogical intentions embodied in teaching strategies can be strategically connected to teaching practice (teaching / learning events/ activities). Her model's prioritisation of teaching strategy and learning events over technology is ideally suited for the Global Citizenship course, which was plagued by suboptimal participation amid media forms, face-to-face and computer based activities being conceptualised in light of educators' pedagogical questions and intentions.

Mindful of the complexity of generating highly informed, critical conversations that drew on concepts learnt in class, training students to assert their voices and assume ownership of knowledge production would positively contribute to meaningful engagements insulated from academic hegemony. Realising these goals laid in harnessing conversational technologies to scaffold student deep engagement with content and support intellectual reflexivity drawing on student subjective experiences. These processes ensured that students marshaled the digital technologies to "create cultural texts portraying their experiences, emotions and opinions" (Munar, 2010).

Contradictions in Perspectives

Some notable disjuncture existed between short term imperatives of nurturing all-ground graduates and the long term goal of producing global citizens who were socially responsible and demonstrated profound civility to the world (upon graduation). The former intellectual investment necessitated an immediate, intensive provision of content, critical engagement with learning resources and devotion to study. The latter was tied to continual, life time commitment to social responsibility to communities, collective identification of social needs and perpetual engagement in social activism. This long term perspective is captured in Bickmore's (2005) conception of critical citizenship as engaged citizen participation for social change, more comfort with openness and uncertainty than teaching for unquestioned dominant 'common sense' (p. 3). Reference to sustained uncertainty and open projections alludes to the far reaching consequences of critical citizenship for students and affected communities. These goals were hard to realise in a short academic calendar as cohorts often disintegrated after the completion of the course and personal ties with their communities would be severed. The perceived incompatibility of long term goals with immediate imperatives of citizenship often complicated pedagogical design and academic planning. Therefore, learning and teaching is optimised when media have been carefully selected and applied with sound instructional strategies to serve specific learning needs in different domains of learning (Naidu, 2006).

Fostering Future Global Leaders

Creating pragmatic, problem-oriented future leaders was the other challenge of the Global Citizenship course. Realising this called into question the constructive alignment of deep, experiential learning, problem-based learning and critical inquiry premised on theoretical concepts learnt in class. Challenges of limited contact time and of immersing students in practically oriented collaborative activities in class and online often militated against the following: marrying theory to practice, transferring experiential learning to classroom contexts and vice versa. Given the multidisciplinary nature of students, the challenge of "disjoint disciplines" (Youniss, 2006) became self-evident. Disjoint disciplines constitute "discipline[s] that are splintered into niches of expertise without unifying theoretical stances" (Youniss, 2006). Therefore, drawing on the knowledge amongst disciplines to support the central theme of critical citizenship was inexorably complex as some disciplinary practices do not necessarily cohere with each other and their experiences are not transferable across other disciplines. As such, the pedagogical challenge laid in making sense of and integrating knowledge from different domains, and building knowledge models that drew on powerful tools that allow deep reflection, collaborative engagement and self-generation of content.

Community of Inquiry-Based Pedagogical Models

Pedagogical models for advancing critical citizenship among heterogeneous with different levels of confidence with technology should be situated in Community of Inquiry (CoI). CoI documents how deep, reflective learning can be practically fostered within a complex formal educational context (Garrison, Anderson & Archer, 2000) of situated learning that unfolds in online asynchronous communication (McDonald & Loch, 2008). The learning communities had to be built into the Programme and different conversational technologies to allow the cognitive scaffolding of learners (cognitive presence), provision of learning material and appropriate pedagogical strategies (teaching presence) and opportunities for open communication and dialogue (social presence).

However, the interactions between student and peers, and students and tutors on the different conversational spaces (chat rooms, discussion forums, blogs) provided demonstrated some semblance of emerging critical discourses on critical citizenship. Intellectually engaging practices on student reflective blogs and discussion forums came from prolific bloggers who drew on

classroom concepts in their personal reflections and collaborative discourses on service learning, volunteerism and social responsibility. This collaborative networking coheres with popular claims that 'knowledge building' draws on the collective intelligence of a group engaged in researching, theorizing, critiquing, doing, and synthesizing in order to progressively evolve some body of theory and practice (Murray, 2006, p. 212).

Nurture Secure, Sustained Interactions

A pedagogical model that provides students with a safe, secure induction process into critical citizenship, and that accommodates different interaction processes (reflection, collaboration, knowledge sharing, social construction of knowledge) was necessary. The platform also needed to provide meaningful individual, cluster and whole group interaction to allow transactional exchanges between personal reflections and group collaborations. It also needed to extend the conversations already present in classroom activities (seminars, learning events) to online interactions, as well as allow for their cross fertilization. For example, some knowledgeable students employed puzzles, contradictions and personal reflections experienced in their service learning to engage in theoretical problem solving and co-production of knowledge in discussion forums. This needed to be extended to all students.

Academic Leveraging

Academics' facilitative and mentoring roles needed extension to cover student conversations and provide instant, meaningful feedback to students where necessary. The scaffolding of students when they encountered complex problems and puzzles would gradually give learners more ownership of face-to-face and online learning spaces and allow their progressive maturity into self-regulated academics. These processes would advance "civic education as the concerted effort to prepare students to assume responsibility for moving society forward in a more just direction […]" (James &Iverson, 2009, p. 34). Lecturers could build on students' deeply rooted passion to engage with their communities as empathetic partners and potential future global leaders to deepen their intellectual engagement.

Foreground Multiple Perspectives

A pedagogical model that discourages opinion reinforcement and engenders multiple perspectives on issues, problems and concepts was necessary. Students training in providing justification of their arguments, rendering substantive evidence for propositions made and their embrace of the propositional and contested nature of knowledge would make them more accomplished scholars on critical citizenship. Therefore, technology platforms that allowed for dialogue and conversations (e.g., blogs, discussion forums) and provided continual streams of updated information on topical issues (like RSS feeds) would be needed. The seamless integration of these technologies with personal learning environments like podcasts would provide information rich, converged environments that broadened student domain of knowledge.

CONCLUSION

This research explored the pedagogical challenges of Global-CLSJ Programme, an extracurricular programme introduced at a South African university, during its pilot phase. It provided a context-driven, knowledge-centred approach/designe to address the challenges of meaningful engagement, developing high calibre graduates, course scalability and sustainability and developing a cohesive learning community. Data from the researchers' reflections on student generated artifacts (chats, discussion forums, blog postings), group interviews with G-CLSJ team and a detailed interview with CET technology expert provided

rich evidence on the diverse problems encountered in the programme. These dilemmas included contradictions between short-term imperatives of nurturing all-round graduates (based on a time-bound curriculum) and long-term requirements of social responsibility and service.

The fundamental challenge was generating and sustaining deep critical engagement at three highly interwoven levels namely, academic-student, student-peer, student-content levels. Engagement challenge was further compounded by students' varied levels of experience with conversational technologies and service learning as well and variations in engagement culture across disciplines. The programme enrolled students at different academic levels who brought different levels of academic maturity, learning needs and priorities to it. The often emotional discourses that lacked intellectual depth resonated with the complexities of sustaining deep learning among heterogeneous learners with varying levels of academic maturity. The last challenge was the wide scale rollout of a programme given the uncertainty on the size of future enrollments.

Two knowledge-centred, technology-enhanced models that brought appropriate, conversational technologies, invaluable learning content, and meaningful pedagogical strategy at the centre of the implementation process were proposed. The models considered students' varied technological skills base, accommodated ubiquitous technologies they were already familiar with and leveraged the support from academics.

ACKNOWLEDGMENT

This research was made possible through the generous funding from the Andrew W. Mellon Foundation, the academic support from the Global Citizenship Learning for Social Justice Team and two experts from the Centre for Educational Technology.

REFERENCES

Akyol, Z., Garrison, D., & Ozden, M. Y. (2009). Online and Blended Communities of Inquiry: Exploring the developmental and perceptional differences. *International Review of Research in Open and Distance Learning, 10*(6), 65–83.

British Educational Communications and Technology Agency (BECTA). (2003) Primary Schools-ICT and Standards. Retrieved from http://www.becta.org.uk

Bucci, T. T., Copenhaver, L. J., Lehman, B., & O'Brien, T. (2003). Technology integration: Connections to educational theories. *Contemporary Issues in Technology & Teacher Education, 3*(1), 26–42.

Bickmore, K. (2005). Teacher Development for Conflict Participation: Facilitating Learning for 'Difficult Citizenship.'. *Education International Journal of Citizenship and Teacher Education, 1*(2), 2–16.

Campbell, G. (2009). A Personal Cyberinfrastructure. *EDUCAUSE Review, 44*(5), 58–59.

Chandler, T., & An, H. (2007) Using Digital Mapping Programs to Augment Student Learning in Social Studies http://innovateonline.info/pdf/vol4_issue1/Using_Digital_Mapping_Programs_to_Augment_Student_Learning_in_Social_Studies.pdf

Cohen, L., Manion, L., & Morrrison, K. (2007). *Research Methods in Education* (6th ed.). New York, NY: Routledge.

Report, C. (1998). *Education for Citizenship and the teaching of Democracy in Schools*. http://www.qca.org.uk/downloads/6123_crick_report_1998.pdf

Czerniewicz, L., & Brown, C. (2005). Information and Communication Technology (ICT) use in teaching and learning practices in Western Cape higher education institutions. In L. Czerniewicz, & C. Hodgkinson-Williams (Eds.), (In press). Education in South Africa: what have Information and Communication Technologies (ICTs) got to do with it? Special Issue of Perspectives in Education.

Dexter, S. (2002). eTips – educational technology integration and implementation principles: Why a set of principles to guide teachers about integrating and implementing educational technology into the K12 classroom? Hershey, PA: IGI Global.

Dockstader, J. (1999). Teachers of the 21st Century Know the What, Why, and How of Technology Integration. Technological Horizons in Education, 26(6).

Ertmer, P. A. (2005). Teacher pedagogical beliefs: The final frontier in our quest for technology integration? *Educational Technology Research and Development, 53*(4), 25–39.

Garrison, D. R. (2009). Communities of inquiry in online learning: Social, teaching and cognitive presence. In C. Howard, ... (Eds.), *Encyclopedia of distance and online learning* (2nd ed., pp. 352–355). Hershey, PA: IGI Global.

Garrison, D., & Cleveland-Innes, M. (2005). Facilitating cognitive presence in online learning: Interaction is not enough. *American Journal of Distance Education, 19*(3), 133–148. doi:10.1207/s15389286ajde1903_2

Garrison, D. R., Anderson, T., & Archer, W. (2001). Critical thinking and computer conferencing: A model and tool to assess cognitive presence. *American Journal of Distance Education, 15*(1), 7–23. doi:10.1080/08923640109527071

Garrison, D., Anderson, T., & Archer, W. (2000). Critical inquiry in a text-based environment: Computer conferencing in higher education. *The Internet and Higher Education, 2*(2-3), 87–105. doi:10.1016/S1096-7516(00)00016-6

Geertz, C. (1973). Thick description: Towards an interpretive theory of culture. In C. Geertz (Ed.), *The Interpretation of cultures*. New York, NY: Basic Books.

Gold, M., & Lowe, C. (2010). The Integration of Assistive Technology into Standard Classroom Practices: Practical Recommendations for K-12 General Educators. *The Journal of Multiculturalism in Education, 6*(1), 1–16.

Guzman, A., & Nussbaum, M. (2009). Teaching competencies for technology integration in the classroom. *Journal of Computer Assisted Learning, 25*(5), 453–469. doi:10.1111/j.1365-2729.2009.00322.x

Groff, J., & Mouza, C. (2008). A framework for addressing challenges to classroom technology use. *Association for the Advancement of Computing In Education Journal, 16*(1), 21–46.

James, J., & Iverson, S. (2009). Striving for Critical Citizenship in a Teacher Education Program: Problems and Possibilities. *Michigan Journal of Community Service Learning*, 33–46.

Kervin, L., & Mantei, J. (2010). Supporting educators with the inclusion of technology within literacy classrooms: A framework for "action". *Journal of Technology Integration in the Classroom, 2*(3), 43–54.

Laurillard, D. (2002). *Rethinking university teaching: A conversational framework for the effective use of learning technologies* (2nd ed.). London: Routledge/Falmer. doi:10.4324/9780203304846

Lemke, C., & Lesley, B. (2009). Advance 21st century innovation in schools through smart, informed state policy. In E. Coughlin & S. Kajder (Eds.), *The Impact of Online Collaborative Learning on Educators and Classroom Practices*. The Metiri Group in Collaboration with Cisco.

Mazzolini, M., & Maddison, S. (2003). Sage, guide or ghost? The effect of instructor intervention on student participation in online discussion forums. *Computers & Education, 40*(3), 237–253. doi:10.1016/S0360-1315(02)00129-X

McDonald, C., & Loch, B. (2008). Adjusting the community of inquiry approach to a synchronous mathematical context (pp. 603-606). In *ASCILITE 2008: 25th Annual Conference of the Australasian Society for Computers in Learning in Tertiary Education: Hello! Where Are You in the Landscape of Educational Technology?* 30 Nov - 03 Dec 2008, Melbourne, Australia.

Mott, J. (2010). *Envisioning the Post-LMS Era: The Open Learning Network*. Educational Review online. Retrieved from http://www.educause.edu/ero/article/envisioning-post-lms-era-open-learning-network

Munar, A. (2010). Digital Exhibitionism: The Age of Exposure. *Culture Unbound, 2*, 401–422. http://www.cultureunbound.ep.liu.se

Murray, T. (2006). Collaborative knowledge building and integral theory: On perspectives, uncertainty, and mutual regard. *Integral Review, 2*, 210–268.

Naidu, S. (2006). Pedagogical designs for e-learning. In S. Naidu (Ed.), E-learning: A Guidebook of Principles, Procedures and Practices (pp. 11-28). Commonwealth Educational Media Center for Asia (CEMCA) University of Melbourne, Australia.

Naidu, S. (2009). Pedagogical affordances of technology. In S. Mishra (Ed), E-learning (STRIDE Handbook 8). New Delhi, IGNOU.

Orlando, A. (2005). *The Integration of Learning Technologies in the Elementary Classroom: Identifying Teacher Pedagogy and Classroom Culture.* PhD Thesis, Drexel University.

O'Shea, A. (2004). Teaching 'critical citizenship' in an age of hedonistic vocationalism. *Learning and Teaching in the Social Sciences, 1*(2). doi:10.1386/ltss.1.2.95/0

Panel on Educational Technology. (1997). *Report to the President on the use of technology to strengthen K-12 education in the United States.* Washington, DC: President's Committee of Advisors on Science and Technology.

Ponnusawmy, H., & Santally, M. (2008). Promoting (quality) participation in online forums: A study of the use of forums in two online modules at the University of Mauritius http://www.itdl.org/Journal/Apr_08/article04.htm

Rambe, P. (2010). Using Contradictions to Ravel Teaching and Learning Challenges in a Blended IS Course in an African University. *Journal of Information, Information Technology, and Organizations, 5*, 101–124.

Redmann, D., Kotrlik, J., & Douglas, B. (2003). Factors related to technology integration in instruction by marketing education teachers. *Journal of Career and Technical Education, 19*(2), 29–46.

Shiengold, K., & Hadley, M. (1990). *Accomplished teachers: integrating computers into classroom practice.* New York: Centre for Technology in Education, Bank Street College of Education.

Smith, G., Ottewill, R., Jubb, E., Sperling, E., & Wyman, M. (2007). Teaching citizenship in higher education, PSA 2007. Retrieved from www.psa.ac.uk/2007/pps/Smith2.pdf

Smith, J. A., & Osborn, M. (2008). Interpretative phenomenological analysis. In J. A. Smith (Ed.), *Qualitative Psychology* (2nd ed., pp. 53–80). London: Sage.

Strauss, A., & Corbin, J. (1998). *Basics of qualitative research: Techniques and procedures for developing grounded theory.* Thousand Oaks, CA: SAGE Publications.

Vrasidas, C., & Kyriakou, E. (2008). Integrating Technology in the classroom. *Pliroforiki, 18-20.* www.pliroforiki.org/joomla/index.php?option=com...gid

Veletsianos, G., & Kimmons, R. (2012). Scholars and faculty members' lived experiences in online social networks. *The Internet and Higher Education, xxx-xxx.* doi:10.1016/j.iheduc.2012.01.004

Weathersbee, J. (2008). Impact of Technology Integration in Public Schools on Academic Performancc of Tcxas School Children. Masters Thesis, Texas State University, Spring 2008.

Xie, K., Durrington, V., & Yen, L. (2011). Relationship between Students' Motivation and their Participation in Asynchronous Online Discussions. *MERLOT Journal of Online Learning and Teaching, 7*(1), 17–29.

Youniss, J. (2006). Situating ourselves and our inquiry: A first-person account. In C. Conrad & R. Serlin (Eds.), *The SAGE handbook for research in education: Engaging ideas and enriching inquiry* (pp. 303–314). Thousand Oaks, CA: SAGE. doi:10.4135/9781412976039.n17

KEY TERMS AND DEFINITIONS

Collective Engagement: Participatory learning processes that allow multiple interactions among participants, mutual exchange of ideas and knowledge.

Conversational Framework: A pedagogical approach that draws on multiple media forms, teaching activities and events and stakeholders (educators, tutors, students) to support various learning processes (practice, reflection, dialogue, acquisition, discovery) by stakeholders.

Deep Learning: knowledge generation processes that trigger deep reflection, critical inquiry and collaborative generation of information by students and for students.

Emerging Technologies: Technologies that may, depending on context, be new or not so new but whose application leads to qualitatively different educational results for the stakeholders concerned. Depending on context of application and regions, these may include social media technologies, cloud based technologies, virtual worlds and mobile technologies.

Global Citizenship Course: Extracurricular University programme that bridged critical citizenship, academic inquiry and service learning by diverse cohorts of learners, and was mediated by various experiential learning events, seminars and activities and emerging technologies.

Peer-Based Networking: Affinity based connections often mediated by emerging technologies that render possible collaborative knowledge generation and social exchange of ideas, social artifacts and social practices.

Student Centred Approaches: Perspectives on learning that emphasise student learning styles, learning priorities and learning needs and goals including their prior learning experiences and prior knowledge to ensure their meaningful, productive construction of knowledge.

Technology Integration: When curricula design, pedagogical processes and activities are seamlessly aligned with, informed by and draw on technology as a (cognitive, transactive, informative) lever and mediator of these processes.

Chapter 7
Active Learning Strategies in Technology Integrated K–12 Classrooms

Esther Ntuli
Idaho State University, USA

ABSTRACT

Active learning is central to student retention and application of learned information. Research indicates that technology has reshaped the classroom environment and some of the teaching methods that traditionally supported active learning are no longer compatible with the emerging technologies. The question is; how best can teachers promote active learning through the use of technology? With technology flooding the school learning environments, teachers need effective strategies that promote active learning. Using research-based theories and literature review; this chapter extends a new definition and critical components of active learning in the context of technology integrated classrooms. Further, the chapter offers active learning strategies aligned with technology tools that could be used effectively in K-12 classrooms to promote active learning. Finally, the chapter opens up a discussion for potential new research that could be conducted to explore in depth some of the strategies using a large sample size stratified by grade levels, content areas, and geography.

INTRODUCTION

Computer technology has become a prevalent feature in K-12 classrooms, and has altered the surface of the educational terrain in the U.S. (Aldrich, 2002; Collis, et. al., 1996; Jenkinson, 2009; Wood, Specht & Willoughby, 2008). Research indicates that billions of dollars are invested in the schools to buy the most current technology on the market (Amiel & Reeves, 2008; Bohlin,

2002; Chen, 2004; Shieber, 2014). The questions are: Are teachers integrating these technologies effectively for teaching and learning processes? How best can teachers promote active learning through the use of technology? Does technology increase student performance? There are so many questions that educational researchers are working hard to answer. In this chapter only one question would be addressed: How best can teachers promote active learning through the use

DOI: 10.4018/978-1-4666-8363-1.ch007

of technology? This question is fundamental to effective and meaningful technology integration in the classroom. The question that needs to be addressed first is: What is active learning?

Without appropriate definitions of terms, concepts, and strategies related to computer technology integration into teaching and learning processes, technology will not promote active learning; neither will technology increase student performance. Research indicates that when teachers are not able to define terms or concepts, in most cases, they are not able to integrate effectively that specific concept(s) into teaching and learning (Ntuli & Kyei-Blankson, 2010). Therefore, being able to define a concept is one of the major indicators that one has the knowledge about the concept and is able to apply it. Before extending the active learning working definition, this chapter begins with a brief background of the study.

BACKGROUND

Research indicates that even though teachers are aware of the benefits that technology offers in teaching and learning processes, most teachers are hesitant to integrate technology due to reasons including; lack of relevant technological knowledge (TK), and technological pedagogical knowledge (TPK) (Lawless & Pellegrino, 2007; Ertmer & Ottebbreit-Leftwich, 2009). Ntuli (2010)'s K-3rd grade study reveals that most teachers are aware of cognitive developmental gains that technology may bring in young children; however, what stopped teachers from integrating technology frequently was the lack of developmentally appropriate technology knowledge and recommended strategies. In a more recent study, Pamuk (2012) found that despite well-grounded technology backgrounds, the pre-service teachers understudy lacked technology pedagogical experiences and

that leads to very limited use of technology during practicum. Based on this study and literature review that offer similar findings (e.g., Bingimlas, 2009; Ertmer, 1999; Hew & Brush, 2007), it can be concluded that teachers lack technology integration strategies that promote active learning. In addition, teachers need strategies on how to differentiate pedagogies depending on different technology tools, content, and grade level.

Current research also indicates that the problem of technology integration in K-12 classrooms is still far from resolved (Bauer & Kenton, 2005; Ertmer, 2009; Mueller, Wood, Willoughby, Ross, & Specht, 2008). One of the reasons may be that teachers learn about instructional technology tools in isolation of teaching strategies, content, and the authentic classroom experience (Chan & Lee, 2007; Friedman & Kajder, 2006; Ntuli, 2010). Ntuli (2010) found that more than three quarters of the teachers surveyed indicated that their experiences with instructional technology courses during teacher preparation and professional development were divorced from the classroom experience. For instance, teachers learned about the technology tools (how they work), how to create web pages, PowerPoints, etc., however, little was taught on how best to integrate the technology tools in the classroom, and how to differentiate technology strategies depending on the learners. Related literature also indicates that teachers are not using technology to support *student-centered* learning which is believed to be central to active learning and high student achievement (Ertmer, 2009; International Society for Technology in Education (ISTE), 2008). This chapter seeks to offer student-centered active learning strategies that could be used successfully in K-12 technology integrated classrooms. However, before the strategies could be discussed, this chapter provides a working definition of active learning in technology integrated learning environments.

DEFINING ACTIVE LEARNING: A CONSTRUCTIVIST APPROACH

A constructivist approach to learning is derived from theorists who believed that knowledge (and meaning) is constructed by the learner(s) as a result of the learning process (Dewey, 1938; Piaget 1936; Vygotsky, 1978). The slight difference in Piaget and Vygotsky theories is that Piaget believed that active learning involves the learner constructing meaning or knowledge alone by interacting with the environment. Whereas, Vygotsky believed that learning is a social process in which the learner constructs knowledge collaboratively/socially with the help of expert adults (Wadsworth, 2004). The word "construct" is central to constructivism, and it implies active involvement of the learner in the learning process. The learner is not an empty vessel that waits for the teacher to "bank" knowledge (Freire, 1970; Cooper, 2010); however, the learner participates actively in the process of creating and understanding new knowledge, with the teacher acting as a facilitator. Piaget (1977) asserts that learning occurs by an active construction of meaning, rather than by passive recipience. The constructivists' perspective to active learning requires students to learn through observations and modeling (Bandura, 1992), and through experience and discovery (Brunner, 1973; Dewey, 1938). The following discussion highlights how active learning through a constructivist approach has been perceived from the 1930s until present.

According to Dewey (1938), active learning entails that students learn by doing not through the transfer of information from knowledgeable sources, such as textbooks, teachers, elders or "from one who is more informed, to the passive recipient, where it is stored along with other information, until drawn upon for a particular purpose" (Farell, 2009, p. 2). In the same vein, Holzer (1994) argued that through active learning, knowledge is directly experienced, constructed, acted upon, tested, or revised by the learner. Currently, the University of Michigan, Center for Research on Learning and Teaching defined active learning as a process "whereby students engage in activities, such as reading, writing, discussion, or problem-solving that promote analysis, synthesis, and evaluation of class content" (CRLT, 2014, ¶ 1). A close analysis of the aforementioned definitions portrays active learning as "doing something" meaningful while learning. According to Bobbi DiPorter of *Quantum Learning,* people learn more when they are actively doing something, they retain; 10% of what they read, 20% of what they hear, 30% of what they see, 50% of what they see and hear, 70% of what they say, and 90% of what they say and do (Changing Minds, 2013). The definitions also revealed that active learning is not only characterized by physical movements while learning; e.g., raising hands or writing notes, however, it also involves cognitive processes that may not be observable by physical movements during class time but through acting upon learned materials in different ways.

In technology integrated classrooms, active learning may take a different form, therefore, there is need to define active learning in such classrooms. For instance, Tong, Marlin and Frost (1995) note that if students explore the environment by peddling a stationary bike while they travel through a virtual environment that would be considered an active activity. On the other hand, Chi (2009) note that "if students were merely watching a video recording of what the active participants saw but without being able to explore or manipulate the environment that would be considered to be passive…" (p. 75). The latter may not be correct if students have a project or a product to complete based on what they watched. The following section discusses the critical elements that characterize active learning in technology integrated classrooms.

ACTIVE LEARNING'S CRITICAL COMPONENTS IN TECHNOLOGY INTEGRATED CLASSROOMS

In this chapter, critical components of active learning include; use of multiple senses (e.g., hearing, seeing, and feeling) (Sirinterlikci et.al, 2009), doing (hands-on) (Dewey, 1938), interacting (and collaboration) (Chi, 2009; Vygotsky 1978), and constructing (Holzer, 1994). Below is a detailed description of each component in light of technology integrated activities.

Use of multiple senses is one of the critical components in active learning. When students are able to see, hear, and feel, they retain more information and in most cases they are likely to "act upon" the information they receive (Holzer, 1994). Acting upon the information (or knowledge) leads to "*doing*" or "*hands-on*" where information is tested either individually or collaboratively. The process of testing the information requires the students to *record* what they hear, see, or feel. Depending on the level of testing required, hypotheses are formed and students may *interact collaboratively* to prove or disprove hypotheses. Finally students should be able to *construct knowledge* (e.g. new information, tangible materials, and non-tangible materials such as change in attitude, etc.) based on what they learned.

In the selection of technology (or software) to integrate in the classroom, teachers need to be aware of active learning critical components. Technology should be selected that allow for multiple senses, hands-on, collaboration, and construction (including problem solving). Figure 1 illustrates the complex inter-relationship between critical components and the sample technology tools and strategies that could be used to promote active learning.

Teachers may integrate any critical component of active learning (including technology tools/ strategies) at any time depending on the goals and objectives of the unit. For instance, Figure 1 illustrates that one teacher may choose to have students collaborate (or interact with peers) in the lesson while (watching) on a virtual field trip. Another teacher may choose to have students engage in hands-on learning while collaboratively creating a virtual field trip. Figure 1 also reveals the complex relationship among the critical components necessary to support active learning in technology integrated classrooms. The illustrated complex relationship calls for a teacher who has comprehensive knowledge of the content to be taught, the level of students, current technologies available, and technological pedagogical knowledge. Mishra and Koehler called such comprehensive type of knowledge "technological pedagogical content knowledge" (Mishra & Koehler, 2006).

The following active learning strategies and technology options provide teachers with comprehensive knowledge, and could be used by K-12 teachers in technology integrated classrooms. These strategies are based on extensive literature review and online reviews of effective software used in K-12 classrooms.

STRATEGIES TO SUPPORT ACTIVE LEARNING AND TECHNOLOGY OPTIONS

It is important to note that all technology tools (including web-based software) are created with a theoretical orientation to support different learning styles (Buckleitner, 2006; Miller & Miller, 2000); this chapter will only focus on technology tools with a (constructivist) theoretical orientation that support active learning. The strategies discussed in this section are aligned with technology tools, and these tools may be integrated effectively in K-12 learning environments (see Table 1). Each strategy is discussed in depth.

Figure 1. Complex inter-relationship between critical components and technology tools /strategies

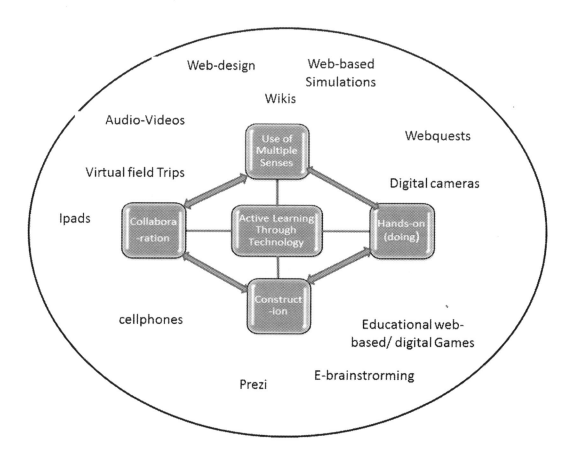

Strategy One: Electronic Brainstorming

Research indicates that people only learn 20 percent of what they hear, 70 percent of what they say as they talk, and 90 percent of what they say as they are engaged in doing something (Ekwall & Shanker, 1998). This makes brainstorming an effective strategy in active learning that helps with comprehension and retention of information as it allows students to think, say, and do something simultaneously (Tate, 2014). Brainstorming of ideas in the classroom may be conducted at any time (e.g. at the beginning, middle, etc.) during the lesson to generate new ideas. The teacher introduces a topic or problem and then asks for

students' input. In the traditional way of oral brainstorming, the teacher gives students about a minute to think and write down ideas individually before all the ideas are recorded on the board. Brainstorming is a vital component in problem based learning (PBL) which has been found to increase student's active involvement in learning (Goodnough, 2005; Massa, 2008). However, there is literature that reveals that traditional ways of brainstorming can affect negatively students who are introverts or shy to talk in group settings (Jablin, 1981). Electronic brainstorming has been found to work effectively when discussing or generating ideas for socially sensitive issues or topics (McLeod, 2011). In addition, if students are not sure, they feel intimidated to contribute during

Table 1. Active learning strategies and technology tools aligned

Strategies	Technology Tools
Electronic Brainstorming	Scribblar- http://www.scribblar.com/dmucs16 Padlet -http://padlet.com/ Mind42- http://mind42.com/ *Lucidcharts*https-://www.lucidchart.com/
Self and Peer-Assessment	QuizStar- http://quizstar.4teachers.org/ Quizlet- http://quizlet.com/ Kubbu- http://www.kubbu.com Engrade- https://www.engrade.com/ Socrative- http://www.socrative.com/
Collaboration and Peer review	Wikispaces- https://www.wikispaces.com/ PbWorks- https://my.pbworks.com/ Kubbu- http://www.kubbu.com Edmodo- https://www.edmodo.com/ Google groups-www.google.com
Simulations	PhET Interactive Simulations- http://phet.colorado.edu/ SimCalc- http://math.sri.com/ National Library of Virtual Manipulatives -http://nlvm.usu.edu/ Lesson planet -http://www.lessonplanet.com
Infographics	Visulize.me- http://vizualize.me/ Piktochart- http://piktochart.com/ Visual.ly- http://create.visual.ly/ iCharts- http://www.icharts.net/ Microsoft Powerpont- http://www.microsoftstore.com
Inquiry learning	Webquests –examples: Living in an Alkaline Environment-http://serc.carleton.edu/microbelife/k12/alkaline/WQintro.html Zunal-http://zunal.com/webquest.php?w=17520 Science webquests-http://www.techtrekers.com/webquests/science.html Virtual Field Trips-examples: Tramline-http://tramline.com/trips.htm Smithsonian Museums (http://www.si.edu) Active volcano-http://imina.soest.hawaii.edu/mauna_loa/ Agriculture in the classroom-http://utah.agclassroom.org/ America in 1831 - http://xroads.virginia.edu/~HYPER/DETOC/home.html Museum lesson: http://www.clta.net/lessons Science, Art, and Technology course from Art Institute of Chicago for science teachers -http://www.artic.edu/aic/student/sciarttech National Gallery of Art-http://www.nga.gov InterLingo Spanish-http://www.interlingospanish.com Exploratorium- http://www.exploratorium.org/ Nasa- http://www.nasa.gov/ USGS- http://www.usgs.gov/ Boston Museum of Science- http://www.mos.org/ Globe- http://www.globe.gov/ Live Virtual Field Trips-examples: Smithsonian National Zoological Park-http://nationalzoo.si.edu/Animals/WebCams/ Old Faithful Geyser -http://www.nps.gov/features/yell/webcam/oldFaithfulStreaming.html National Park Service-http://www.nps.gov/yell/photosmultimedia/webcams.htm

large group oral brainstorming activities (Jone, 2007). Use of electronic brainstorming supports active learning and minimizes anxiety as students contribute privately without their identity being revealed (Coskun, 2011). Studies have shown that electronic brainstorming groups are more productive than oral brainstorming groups (Gallupe et al., 1992). Given the fact that electronic brainstorming increases active engagement in learning, teachers need to be aware of some electronic brainstorming tools they could use in the classroom. Table 1 illustrates some of the electronic brainstorming tools that have been used by teachers effectively. The list of tools was created based on the online teacher software reviews. Below is a brief description of each electronic brainstorming tool:

Scribblar (https://www.scribblar.com/) is an online, web-based whiteboard collaboration tool used for real life lesson or tutoring sessions. This tool could be used from K-12 grade successfully. With Scribblar students are able to make contributions at the same time while sitting at their own computers. Student contributions may be projected on the smartboard or any classroom projected interactive white board. One teacher who uses the Scribbler program indicated how effective Scribblar is for electronic brainstorming with young children. Below are the teacher's comments:

A great resource is Scribblar.com, an online whiteboard that is good for young students who are able to draw to explain their ideas. It also is great for brainstorming in groups using drawing tools as well as text. (K-12 Teachers Alliance, 2014)

The Scribblar program has an advantage that teachers can connect two classrooms in a school, or district, or the world. It can also connect homebound students (for instance, weather-bound, sick students, etc.) to a class activity. The only concern is that schools or districts have to pay a fee for a more private and secure site that is safe to use with students.

Padlet (http://padlet.com) is a free online collaborative tool, which allow for not more than 160 characters. This tool is effective for electronic brainstorming with middle and high school students. The teacher can post a question or a topic on an electronic Padlet wall and invite students to contribute. As students would be contributing their answers, the results may be projected on the interactive whiteboard or on individual student computers. Figure 2 shows an example of how the wall looks after brainstorming.

On the Padlet electronic brainstorming wall, students have a choice to write their names or use pseudonyms. Padlet allow for audio files, images, and text. The Padlet platform is aligned with the universal design framework (UDL) which requires teachers to allow students to express themselves in multiple ways (CAST, 2008). Students may contribute using audio, text, or images depending on the goals and rules of the brainstorming session.

There are also electronic web-based platforms that allow for collaborative or individual electronic brainstorming. Students may use individual electronic platforms for concept mapping or drawing connections between ideas and concepts. With such platforms, individual students have a choice to share their ideas with the whole class or with the teacher depending on the requirements of the activity. The following software could be used for individual or group brainstorming and concept connection:

Lucidcharts (https://www.lucidchart.com/) is a free, web-based flow chart maker and online diagram software that could be used (collaboratively or) by individual students for brainstorming or concept mapping and connections. This could be used by middle school and high school students as it is too complex for young children.

Mind42 (http://mind42.com/) is a free mind mapping software that could be used in individual or collaborative brainstorming. Like Lucid charts, this could be used effectively with middle school and high school students.

Figure 2. Sample padlet brainstorming wall

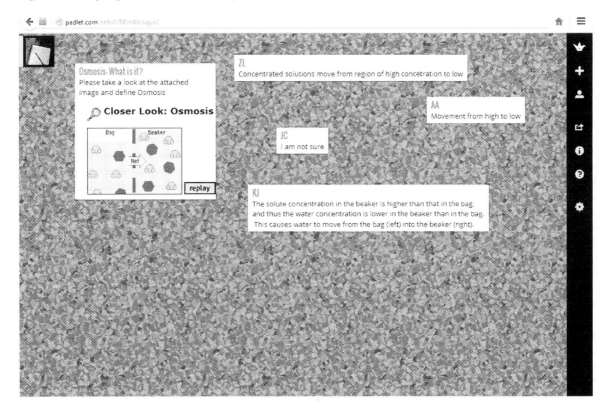

Conditions for Effective Electronic Brainstorming

For effective electronic brainstorming, teachers need to engage in comprehensive lesson planning before students could be invited for brainstorming. Below are the steps that will ensure effective electronic brainstorming:

Step I: Know Why You Want to Integrate an Electronic Brainstorming Strategy in Your Lesson

It is important to plan ahead, and decide why it is necessary to begin the lesson or a new topic with brainstorming. This first step is crucial because some lessons do not require brainstorming, and some topics may not need the use of technology but oral brainstorming. Brainstorming should be used for generating lots of new ideas and solutions not for analysis of ideas or for decision making in the classroom.

Step II: Decide How You Will Run the Brainstorming Session

Making decisions in step II requires the teacher to know the different technology tools that allow for electronic brainstorming. Some tools are compatible with collaborative large and small group brainstorming, and some are for individual brainstorming as discussed earlier in this chapter. Teachers need to decide early if students will engage in small groups or individual brainstorming. Decisions are also made on whether students will brainstorm during class time or after class.

Electronic brainstorming may be conducted at any time before, during, or after the class as long as the students are connected to the internet.

Step III: Prepare the Room and Materials

After steps I & II, the teacher needs to prepare the classroom (that is if the brainstorming would be conducted during class time). Preparing requires the teacher to download (if necessary) the software or programs that students will be using for brainstorming. The programs should be tested before the lesson begins to avoid frustration that happens in the event that the technology fails to work, and to minimize loss of time. Research reports that teachers complain that technology failures in the classroom result in loss of lesson time (Porter, 2013; Wang & Reeves, 2003). This is one of the causes many teachers resist technology.

Step IV: Prepare the Students and Issue Invites

The last step is to prepare students and to invite them to brainstorm. Preparation of students requires the teacher to explicitly teach the students how to use the program for brainstorming. Rules for electronic brainstorming (see sample in Figure 3) need to be spelled out before students could begin brainstorming. Literature indicates that one of the major causes of ineffective brainstorming is fear of classmates' judgments and criticisms (Tate, 2014). Most electronic brainstorming programs offer options to hide the students' identity. Teachers may choose to have student hide their identity as they make contributions in addition to the following rules in Figure 3.

The rules in Figure 3 will help to maintain order and focus during electronic brainstorming sessions. Teachers may add or adapt the rules in figure 3 depending on the grade level, age of students, topic, lesson goals, and objectives.

Strategy Two: Self and Peer -Assessment

Self and peer-assessment have been used successfully in teaching and learning as active learning methods (Amo & ve Jareño, 2011; Gaytan & McEwen, 2007; van Hattum-Janssen & Lourenço, 2008). Usually, self and peer-assessment are discussed in most literature concurrently, and some teachers use the two methods jointly even though they pursue different outcomes. Amo and veJareño (2011) made the following distinction between the two methods;

Self-assessment develops skills of critical awareness and enables students to become reflective and self-managing, to identify the next steps in learning and to move forward 'under their own steam' while peer assessment offers feedback between students and also allows students to make comparisons with each other. (p. 42)

In this chapter, the two methods are discussed concurrently due to the fact they complement each other, and the technologies offered as examples support both self and peer assessment. Self and peer-assessment may come in form of multiple choice quiz, checklist, true/false questions, etc., and it is not graded by the teacher. Students are given the assessment to check for individual (or group progress), or check for understanding pertaining to the concepts learned or to be learned in the course. With self and peer assessment, students are actively involved in their own learning, they do not depend on the teacher to check for understanding. Technology makes it easy for the teacher to create and deliver the self-assessment quizzes. One advantage is that most programs that allow for self and peer-assessment offer a platform for quick feedback to students; as the quiz is being created, the teachers has an option to write explanations on why certain answers are correct or wrong. When the student misses

Figure 3. Sample electronic brainstorming rules

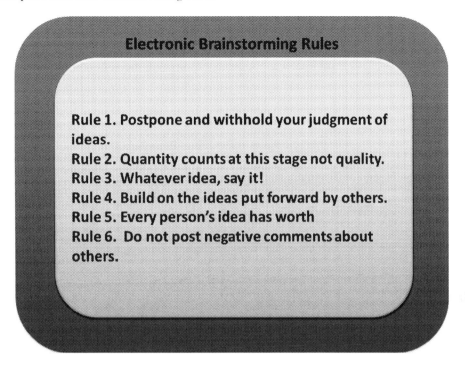

the answer, automatically the program offers the correct answer and the explanation created by the teacher. Below are some of the technology programs that teachers may use for student self and peer-assessment:

QuizStar (http://quizstar.4teachers.org/) is a free online quiz maker software that allows teachers to create online quizzes for course evaluation (or final grades), and for formative assessments which includes student self-assessment online. The advantages of using QuizStar are that the software allows the teacher and students to do the following; attach multimedia files to questions, create the quiz in different languages, the quiz could be accessed from any internet –connected computer, and students can complete and review their own work anywhere in the world.

Quizlet (http://quizlet.com/) is a free online learning tool which allows teachers to create quizzes. Through Quizlet teachers can create flash cards, games, speller, or a multiple choice quiz that allow for student self-assessment of

new concepts, and checks for understanding of the whole unit as they progress in the course. Quizlet is designed also for multi-languages. It is important to note that this software meets the universal design for learning (UDL) framework requirements. Students may choose to self-assess in different ways. They can self-assess using flash cards, games, speller, or games such as scatter or race, etc. The software is also responsive to English language learners as it has a feature that reads back and spell words for students who are still learning the language. Literature reveal that instructional materials that allow for learners to be engaged in a variety of ways increase active learning and student performance (Eison, 2010).

Kubbu (http://www.kubbu.com/) is an e-learning tool designed to facilitate teachers' work and enhance the learning process. Kubbu allows students to self-assess through games, quizzes, or crossword puzzles. Advantages are that, the platform is free for teachers and students, assessment results (either self-assessment or teacher assessments) are calculated automatically and stored in a database. Students can keep a record of individual progress, and increase effort in the areas that show that they require more work to succeed in the course.

Engrade (https://www.engrade.com/) is a platform with a set of web-based tools for educators that allow them to connect online with parents and students. Engrade offer apps for assessment such as apps for quizzes and flashcards which could be used effectively for student self-assessment.

There are more technology assessment tools online that teachers could use to create student self and peer-assessments after every unit is completed. Teachers are encouraged to search for technology assessment tools that are developmentally appropriate, and that meet the needs of diverse students. Students become actively involved in their learning when they are able to monitor their progress through self-assessment quizzes, checklists, flash cards, educational games, etc. Tools that offer quick feedback (such as those discussed above) during self and peer-assessment increase active involvement in learning and student achievement (Gaytan & McEwen, 2007; McMillan & Hearn, 2008).

Strategy Three: Collaboration and Peer Review

Collaboration strategies involve students working together as a team. Students engaged in successful active learning tasks within team environments develop good communication skills, higher-level thinking skills, an emphasis on teamwork, a positive attitude toward the subject, and motivation to learn (Sirinterlikci, Zane & Sirinterlikci, 2009). A team that includes fellow students also generates an environment with less pressure and fear of failure (Grabinger & Dunlap, 2000). Technology makes collaboration less intimidating, easy, and effective as students are able to continue collaborating beyond the classroom. Students who are shy and have anxiety during face to face discussions may

have a relief during online discussions. Teachers are encouraged to use technology platforms or software that allow for collaboration to continue beyond the traditional face to face collaborative methods. To maximize online collaboration, teachers need to embed the concept of peer review. Collaboration should not only mean working as a team to achieve a desired goal, however, peer review could be included as a subset of collaboration where individual students review their peers' work and give guidance (Curtis et. al., 2002; ITS Training Services at Penn State, 2013; Tseng & Tsai, 2007). Below are some of the online platforms (or software) that teachers could use to promote collaboration and peer-review beyond the classroom.

Wikispaces (https://www.wikispaces.com/) is a free wiki that provides community wikispaces, visual page editing, and discussion areas. A teacher may use the discussion area for students to continue discussions online beyond the face to face classroom discussion. Students may create their own wikis and invite peers to give peer feedback on any concept, or class assignments they are working on.

PbWorks (https://my.pbworks.com/) offers a free online platform and a commercial platform that allow users to create workspaces that could be shared. Users may collaborate in real time (synchronously) on the workspaces. Teachers may create a workspace and invite students to join and engage in discussions. Similar to Wikispaces, students may create their own workspaces and invite peers to give peer feedback.

Kubbu (http://www.kubbu.com) allows students to collaborate as they play games, or use flash cards. For more on Kubbu, please see discussion under self and peer-assessment.

Edmodo (https://www.edmodo.com/) is a free web-based platform that may be used for social networking by teachers and students. Edmodo allow teachers to create collaborative groups for students in which they can participate synchronously and asynchronously.

Google groups (https://groups.google.com), just like Edmodo, Google groups is a free web-based tool that allows the teachers and students to create and participate in group discussion synchronously and asynchronously. Google groups are mobile friendly, they can be accessed on mobile phones and mobile computer tablets from anywhere in the world as long as the mobile devices are connected to the internet.

Conditions for Effective Online Collaboration

For online collaboration to be effective, teachers need to explicitly teach students online acceptable behavior which includes digital citizenship. Research reveals that some individuals change their character (become negative or rude) when they are communicating online (Salmivalli, Sainio & Hodges, 2013; Suler, 2004). Such behavior hinders team spirit in learning environments, and if not addressed at the beginning of the class, team work online will not increase students' achievement as research purports. Questioning and discussion techniques need to be taught before students could collaborate online. Lipponen, Rahikainen, Lallimo and Hakkarainen (2003) studied patterns of participation and discourse in elementary students' computer-supported collaborative learning and found that much is needed to improve the quality of their discussions. Students lack "questioning and discussion techniques" that are central to the quality of online discussions (Toledo, 2006). Teachers should be encouraged to use probing questions during discussions and collaborative work with students. Sample probing questions that promote active collaborative learning are categorized and aligned with Blooms Taxonomy in

In addition to learning probing questions, students need to learn the use of invitational stems in online discussions. Invitational stems not only encourage peers to move to higher-level thinking, but they open up discussions. Where students would feel uneasy to comment on their peers' work, such invitational stems create a good online-discussion climate and make students feel welcome to give their opinion (see Table 3).

Strategy Four: Web-Based Simulations

Simulations can be used to represent real or imaginary situations, when used effectively they provide a fertile active learning environment for students (Hertel& Mills, 2002). Web-based simulations allow users to try things that would be difficult or impossible to accomplish in real life (see Figure 4). The use of web-based simulated activities in education is widely acknowledged as an important tool in K-12 learning (Hertel& Mills, 2002; Coffman, 2006). Table 1 offers examples of web-based educational simulation websites (including simulated activities and sample lesson plans) that could be used from elementary and beyond. Web-based simulations offer several benefits including the following:

1. Simulations are often cheaper and easier to create than real life processes.
2. Simulations are useful when real life processes take too long.
3. Simulations remove the element of danger from the situation.
4. Simulations can be paused, whereas real life activities cannot. Pausing allows more time for students to assess and record what is going on.

Real life experiences promote active learning as they involve using multiple senses (e.g., hearing, seeing, and feeling), interacting with other people and materials, and responding to or solving a problem (Sirinterlikci, et al, 2009). Educational simulations need to involve some of these elements stipulated by Sirinterlikci, et al. (2009). Literature indicates that effective web-based simulated activities that promote active learning need to meet the following criteria (Kincaid, Hamilton, Tarr & Sangani, 2004; SIIA, 2009):

Table 2. Probing questions

Questions that probe for:	Sample Questions	Blooms Taxonomy Level of Questioning
Clarification and Understanding	State in your own words. Which are facts? What does this mean? Is this the same as. . .? Give an example. Select the best definition. Am I right to say_? Would this be an example? How does this relate to_? What would you say more about that?	Knowledge
Assumptions and Suppositions	What are you assuming? What is Jenny assuming? What could we assume instead? You seem to be assuming __. Do I understand you correctly? All of your reasoning depends on the idea that __. Could you have based your reasoning on __ instead of __? Is that always the case? Why do you think the assumption holds here? Why would someone make that assumption	Comprehension
Reasoning and thinking process	Could this have happened in...? What are some comparisons between... In what ways night you apply this... How might you compare/contrast... Based on this activity, what are some generalizations... Given your experience, what might be causing this.... What would be an example? What led you to that belief? How does that apply to this case? What would change your mind?	Application
Evidence	Is there a reason to doubt that evidence? Who is in a position to know that is true? What would you say to someone who said that __? What other evidence can support that view? Do you have any evidence for that? Describe... What other information do you need? Did the character remind you of yourself? Describe five ways you are similar..	Analysis
Viewpoints or perspectives	How many ways can you...? When you say __, are you implying __? But, if that happened, what else would happen as a result? Why? What effect would that have? Can you see a possible solution to...? Would that necessarily happen or only possibly/probably happen? What is an alternative? If __ and __ are the case, then what might also be true?	Synthesis
Implications and consequences	How can we find out? Can we break this question down at all? Is this question clear? Do we understand it? To answer this question, what other questions must we answer first? Why is this issue important? Is this the most important question, or is there an underlying question that is really the issue? What changes to...would you recommend?	Evaluation

Adapted from Stepien, n.d., ¶ 3

Table 3. Invitational stems in online discussions

Sample Invitational Stems
What are some…
In what ways…
How might you…
What seems to be…
Given your…
Based on...
In your own words explain…

Strategy Five: Infographics

An infographic is a visual image such as a chart or a diagram used to represent information or data. Literature indicates that traditional K-12 curriculum supports reading and writing to interpret events, self-express, and meaning making (Krauss, 2012). However, literature on active learning and student engagement encourages diverse ways of showing understanding and meaning making (CAST, 2008), and one such way is through the use of infographics. Infographics "represent data and ideas visually, in pictures, engaging more parts of the brains to look at a problem from more than one angle" (Krauss, 2012, p. 10). It is important to note that during elementary years, students are not able to express themselves effectively in words, and using pictures help them to visually express ideas. Early childhood/elementary literature

reveal that young children learn more visually. Eighty-percent of what children learn in their first 12 years is processed visually (Midwestern University, 2012; United Health Care, 2012), therefore, it is encouraged for elementary teachers to use more infographics in teaching. Krauss (2012) argues that infographics ask for an active response from the viewer, raising the questions, "What I am I seeing?" and "What does it mean?" (p. 10). Infographics, therefore, provide cues to elementary students as they try to make meaning of what they read. In addition, young children may also express meaning through pictures. In the older grades, infographics may help with data presentation, creating connections between concepts, summarizing concepts (see Figure 5), for instance, a summary of the life cycle of a butterfly, etc.

Today, the Internet provides open source infographic templates that could be used at K-12 grade levels. Table 1 offers websites that students and teachers could access for infographic templates, some of the templates are interactive; they allow instant sharing, and peer editing.

Strategy Six: Inquiry Learning

Inquiry learning promotes active learning as it requires students to use investigative processes to discover evidence or concepts for themselves (Grabinger, 1996; O'Neal & Pinder-Grover, n.d.;

Table 4. Criteria for effective web-based simulations

1. They should simulate an activity that is real, and so it can be said that they are virtually real.
2. They should simulate the activity so well that students need to use some of the senses, for instance, seeing, hearing, and feeling.
3. There is little difference between the simulated environment and the real one, and the same kind of learning experience can take place.
4. They are interactive, allow for hands-on, *involving* students so they become participants solving problems in the environment, not mere listeners or observers.
5. Simulations typically incorporate free-play environments that provide the learner with experience in understanding how a set of conditions interact with each other.
6. They are developmentally adaptable, they could be adjusted to meet the needs, age level, and of all students.
7. They are user friendly. Student input is welcome and activities are designed to encourage students to enrich the activity by contributing their own ideas and thoughts.

Figure 4. Natural selection (Concord Consortium, 2014)

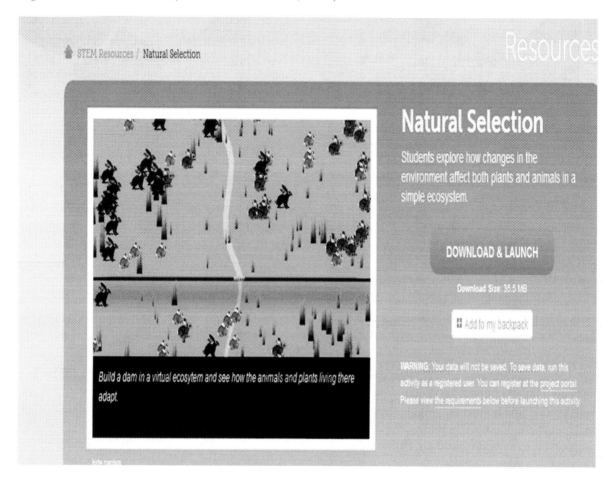

Torp & Sage, 1998). Investigative processes require students to hypothesize, experiment, search for information, observe, record, evaluate, etc. Use of technology tools such as those listed in Table 1 under inquiry learning maximizes student participation in learning. For inquiry learning methods, teachers are encouraged to create and use webquests, virtual field trips, and data recording tools such as those that come with mobile devices (e.g., cellphones and tablet computers). The following discussion is about each inquiry strategy and how it promotes active learning.

Webquests

A webquest is an inquiry-oriented lesson format in which most of the information that learners work with come from the web (Dodge, 1995). Webquests are student centered; they allow students to take charge of their own learning as they challenge students to explore the web in the search of information on a particular topic. A webquest typically has an introduction, a process, a task, a list of resources, a conclusion, and an evaluation. Effective webquets are created on a website (see Figure 6 for a sample webquest), this makes the webquest more interactive to students as they move from one activity to another. This example follows the recommended model for an effective

Figure 5. Sample infographic summary of the life of a butterfly

Life Cycle of a Monarch Butterfly

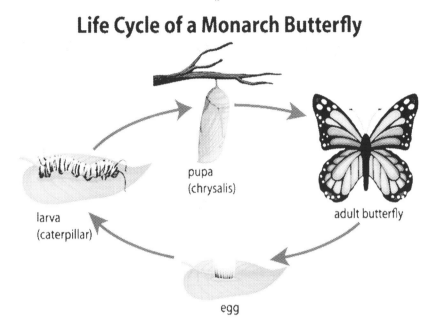

webquest (Robyler & Doering, 2013; Webquest. org, 2007).

The sample wequest was developed using Google sites. In the event that teachers are not able to create Google sites, a PowerPoint could be used, or any other software that allows for website development. When using Powerpoint, the challenge is to know how to make the webquest interactive through the use of hyperlinks. Examples of K-12 webquests are found in Table 1.

Virtual Field Trips

The 3rd-grade students bounced up and down with excitement as they looked over the shoulders of ocean explorers using sonar technology to map the deep sea nearly 20,000 feet below the water's surface near Indonesia. The students were on a virtual field trip called "Voyages of Discovery: NOAA's Okeanos Explorer" on the website of the Exploratorium museum. (Cox, 2014)

The above quote reveals how a virtual field trip could make young students active participants in learning; full of life and excitement. A virtual field trip is a digital tour (e.g: a tour of websites, video tour, etc.) that allows the students to experience being somewhere through their computers (Roblyer & Doering, 2013). Stoddard (2009) provided a conceptual model for successful virtual field trips. In addition, Stoddard noted that virtual field trips allow student learning to be more authentic. Depending on the goals and objectives of the lesson, teachers may decide to use a live virtual field trip. A live virtual field trip allows users to practically visit a site in real time, and usually there is interaction between site workers (or experts) and students. There are live virtual field trips offered by museums, national park, national geographic centers, and government agencies. Examples of live tours are listed in Table 1. For an interactive live virtual tour, teachers need to make arrangements with the site workers ahead of

Figure 6. Sample interactive webquest

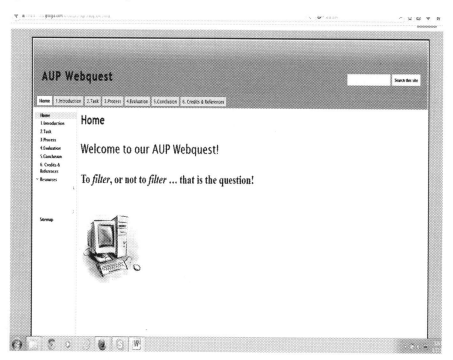

time, and prepare the classroom using face to face interactive technology (e.g. Skype, Google +, or any other web-based audio-video communication tools). To maximize learning, teachers need to prepare students before the live virtual field trip; preparation may come in form of writing down questions or items ahead of time related to what they would need to observe, and what questions should be asked of the experts in addition to those questions that would arise during the live tour.

For a virtual tour (not live) of websites and videos, teachers need to ensure that students are aware of what they should look for, record what they see and hear, discuss with peers, etc. This type of preparation ensures that students participate actively during the virtual field trip and they have meaningful engagement. It is important to note that virtual field trips are highly recommended for English language learners (ELL), and foreign language students (FL). Roblyer and Doering (2013) note that for ELL and FL students, virtual field

trips offer extended opportunities for language acquisition since they allow students to "visit" and participate in locations and have experiences not available to them in person.

Literature indicates that effective virtual field trips that allow active engagement and participation meet some of the following criteria (Cox, 2014; Roblyer & Doering, 2013; Sage, 1999):

Teachers may create virtual field trips by taking videos and delivering them on a web-based platform such as Youtube, Google website, Wiki, etc., however, it is advised that the virtual trips should offer an authentic experience (Shaffer & Resnick, 1999). As noted by Shaffer and Resnick (1999), authentic experiences include the following characteristics: "(a) learning that is personally meaningful for the learner, (b) learning that relates to the real-world outside of school, and (c) learning that provides an opportunity to think in the modes of a particular discipline" (p. 195). It is important to note that active participation in learning is usu-

Table 5. Criteria for effective virtual field trips

1. The virtual field trip takes the students somewhere to give them the virtual experience of what it would be like to actually visit that place, time, etc.
2. The site visited should offer 360 degree views of the real location.
3. The virtual trip allows the use of multiple senses; students see, hear, feel, etc.
4. The virtual trip allows students to travel through space and time.
5. Emotions are invoked by the events in the field trip.
6. Students participate in the environment; there are discussions with experts, classmates, etc.
7. Students are allowed to pause, rewind, or fast forward; for instance, students can re-live the interesting experiences by watching over and over, or they can fast forward when the experiences are not conducive to their mental state.
8. The trip is developmentally appropriate, adaptions (e.g. use of caption, enlarging pictures, etc.) for those with needs could be made without altering the experience.

ally invoked by authentic learning experiences (Hung, Chee & Seng, 2006; Lombardi, 2007).

CONCLUSION AND RECOMMENDATIONS

This chapter defined active learning in technology integrated classrooms, and highlighted the active learning critical components that are central to technology integrated K-12 learning environments. Effective active learning strategies and technology options were aligned and discussed so as to provide teachers with technology knowledge and technological pedagogical knowledge. There is need for empirical research that documents effective strategies and technology options using a large sample size stratified by grade levels, content areas, type of school (urban/rural), etc. This will help in offering a broad and generalizable picture of effective strategies that could work with certain types of technologies, content area, and different age levels. There is need for studies that review the current teacher preparation and professional development programs to ensure that they offer meaningful instructional technology experiences that are not divorced from the classroom practice. Meaningful technology courses provide solid technological pedagogical content knowledge

fundamental to student-centered active learning strategies.

REFERENCES

Aldrich, J. (2002). Early childhood teacher candidates evaluate computer software for young children. *Information Technology in Childhood Education Annual*, (1): 295–300.

Amiel, T., & Reeves, T. C. (2008). Design-based research and educational technology: Rethinking technology and the research agenda. *Journal of Educational Technology & Society*, *11*(4), 29–40.

Amo, E. ve Jareño, F. (2011). Self, peer and teacher assessment as active learning methods. *Research Journal of International Studies*, *18*, 41–47.

Bingimlas, K. A. (2009). Barriers to successful integration of ICT in Teaching and learning environments: A review of the literature. *Eurasia Journal of Mathematics. Science & Technology Education*, *5*(3), 235–245.

Bohlin, R. (2002). *Avoiding computer avoidance*. Retrieved from http://it.coe.uga.edu/itforum/paper35/paper35.html

Brunner, J. (1973). *The relevance of education.* New York: W.W. Norton & Company.

Buckleitner, W. (2006). The relationship between software design and children's engagement. *Early Education and Development, 17*(3), 489–505. doi:10.1207/s15566935eed1703_8

CAST. (2008). *Universal design for learning guidelines version 1.0.* Wakefield, MA: Author.

Center for Research on Learning and Teaching. (2014). *Active learning.* Retrieved from, http://www.crlt.umich.edu/tstrategies/tsal

Chan, A., & Lee, M. J. W. (2007).We want to be teachers, not programmers: In pursuit of relevance and authenticity for initial teacher education students studying an information technology subject at an Australian University. *Electronic Journal for the Integration of Technology,* Retrieved from http://ejite.isu.edu

Changing Minds. (2013). *Active learning.* Retrieved from http://changingminds.org/explanations/learning/active_learning.htm

Chen, L.-L. (2004). Pedagogical strategies to increase pre-service teachers' confidence in computer learning. *Journal of Educational Technology & Society, 7*(3), 50–60.

Coffman, T. (2006). Using simulations to enhance teaching and learning: Encouraging the creative process. *The VSTE Journal, 21*(2), 1–7.

Cooper, R. (2010). *Those who can teach.* Boston, MA: Wadsworth Cengage Learning.

Coskun, H. (2011). The effects of group size, memory instruction, and session length on the creative performance in electronic brainstorming groups. *Educational Sciences: Theory and Practice, 11*(1), 91–95.

Cox, C. (2014). *Virtual field trips.* Retrieved from, http://www.readingrockets.org/article/42383

Curtis, M., Luchini, K., Bobrowsky, B., Quintana, C., & Soloway, E. (2002). Handheld Use in K-12: a descriptive account. *Proceedings of the IEEE International Workshop on Wireless and Mobile Technologies in Education,* Los Alamitos, CA: IEEE Computer Society. doi:10.1109/WMTE.2002.1039217

Dewey, J. (1938). *Experience and education.* New York: Touchstone.

Eison, J. (2010). *Using active learning instructional strategies to create excitement and enhance learning.* Retrieved from, http://www.cte.cornell.edu/documents

Ekwall, E. E., & Shanker, J. L. (1998). *Diagnosis and remediation of the disabled reader.* Needham Heights, USA: Allyn and Bacon.

Ertmer, P. (1999). Addressing first-and second-order barriers to change: Strategies for technology integration. *Educational Technology Research and Development, 47*(4), 47–61.

Ertmer, P., & Ottebbreit-Leftwich, A. (2009). Teacher technology change: How knowledge, beliefs, and culture intersect. AERA. Retrieved from, http://www.edci.purdue.edu/ertmer/docs/aera09_ertmer_leftwich.pdf

Farell, J. B. (2009). *Active learning: theories and research.* Retrieved from, http://www.lookstein.org/online_journal.php?id=260

Freire, P. (1970). *Pedagogy of the oppressed.* New York: Herder and Herder.

Friedman, A., & Kajder, S. (2006). Perceptions of beginning teacher education students regarding educational technology. *Journal of Computing in Teacher Education, 22*(4), 147–151.

Gallupe, R. B., Dennis, A. R., Cooper, W. H., Valacich, J. S., Bastianutti, L., & Nunamaker, J. F. (1992). Electronic brainstorming and group size. *Academy of Management Journal, 35*(2), 350–369. doi:10.2307/256377

Gaytan, J., & McEwen, B. C. (2007). Effective online instructional and assessment strategies. *American Journal of Distance Education, 21*(3), 117–132. doi:10.1080/08923640701341653

Goodnough, K. (2005). Fostering teacher learning through collaborative inquiry. *The Clearing House: A Journal of Educational Strategies, Issues and Ideas, 79*(2), 88–92. doi:10.3200/TCHS.79.2.88-93

Grabinger, R. S. (1996). Rich environments for active learning. In D. H. Jonassen (Ed.), *Handbook of Research for Educational Communications and Technology*. New York: Simon Schuster McMillan.

Hew, K. F., & Brush, T. (2007). Integrating technology into K-12 teaching and learning: Current knowledge gaps and recommendations for future research. *Educational Technology Research and Development, 55*(3), 223–252. doi:10.1007/s11423-006-9022-5

Holzer, S. M. (1994). From constructivism to active learning. *The Innovator, 2*. Retrieved from http://www.succeednow.org/innovators/innovator_2/innovator002.html

Hung, D., Chee, T. S., & Seng, K. T. (2006). Engaged learning: making learning an authentic experience. In D. Hung & M. S. Khine (Eds.), *Engaged learning with emerging technologies* (pp. 29–48). Dordrecht, The Netherlands: Springer. doi:10.1007/1-4020-3669-8_2

ITS Training Services at Penn State. (2013). *ANGEL: Using teams and peer reviews for collaborative learning*. Retrieved from, http://ittraining.psu.edu/wp-content/uploads/sites/7689/2013/12/ANGEL_Using-Teams-and-Peer-Reviews-for-Collaborative-Learning_HO_02142014.pdf

Jablin, F. M. (1981). Cultivating imagination: Factors that enhance and inhibit creativity in brainstorming groups. *Human Communication Research, 7*(3), 245–258. doi:10.1111/j.1468-2958.1981.tb00572.x

Jenkinson, J. (2009). Measuring the effectiveness of educational technology: What are we attempting to measure? *Electronic Journal of e-Learning, 7* (3), 273-280.

Jones, L. (2007). *The student-centered classroom*. New York, NY: Cambridge University Press.

K-12 Teachers Alliance. (2014). Online collaboration tools for 21st century learning. Retrieved from, http://www.teachhub.com/online-collaboration-tools-21st-century-learning

Krauss, J. (2012). Infographics: More than words can say. *Learning and Leading with Technology, 39*(5), 10–14.

Lawless, K. A., & Pellegrino, J. W. (2007). Professional development in integrating technology into teaching and learning: Knowns, unknowns, and ways to pursue better questions and answers. *Review of Educational Research, 77*(4), 575–614. doi:10.3102/0034654307309921

Lipponen, L., Rahikainen, M., Lallimo, J., & Hakkarainen, K. (2003). Patterns of participation and discourse in elementary students' computer-supported collaborative learning. *Learning and Instruction, 13*(5), 487–509. doi:10.1016/S0959-4752(02)00042-7

Lombardi, M. M. (2007). Authentic learning for the 21st century: An overview. *EDUCAUSE*. Retrieved from, http://net.educause.edu/ir/library/pdf/ELI3009.pdf

Massa, N. M. (2008). Problem based learning (PBL). *New England Journal of Higher Education, 22*(4), 19–20.

McLeod, P. L. (2011). Effects of anonymity and social comparison of rewards on computer-mediated group brainstorming. *Small Group Research, 42*(4), 475–503. doi:10.1177/1046496410397381

McMillan, J. H., & Hearn, J. (2008). *Student self-assessment: The key to stronger student motivation and higher achievement*. Retrieved from, http://files.eric.ed.gov/fulltext/EJ815370.pdf

Midwestern University. (2012). *Uncorrected vision issues misdiagnosed as learning disabilities in children.* Retrieved from, https://www.midwestern.edu/news-and-events/university-news/uncorrected-vision-issues-misdiagnosed-as-learning-disabilities-in-children.html

Miller, S. M., & Miller, K. L. (2000). Theoretical and practical considerations in the design of Web-based instruction. In B. Abbey (Ed.), *Instructional and cognitive impacts of Web-based instruction* (pp. 156–177). Hershey, PA: IGI Global. doi:10.4018/978-1-878289-59-9.ch010

Mishra, P., & Koehler, M. J. (2006). Technological Pedagogical Content Knowledge: A new framework for teacher knowledge. *Teachers College Record, 108*(6), 1017–1054. doi:10.1111/j.1467-9620.2006.00684.x

November, A. (2008). *Web literacy for educators.* Thousand Oaks, CA: Corwin Press.

Ntuli, E. (2010). *A study of K-3 inservice teachers' understanding, selection, and use of developmentally appropriate technology.* (Doctoral Dissertation). Illinois State University, ProQuest Dissertation & Thesis A& I. 3485926.

Ntuli, E., & Kyei-Blannkson, L. (2010). Teachers' understanding and use of developmentally appropriate computer technology in early childhood education. *Journal of Technology Integration in the Classroom, 2*(3), 23–35.

Pamuk, S. (2012). Understanding preservice teacher's technology use through TPACK framework. *Journal of Computer Assisted Learning, 28*(5), 425–439. doi:10.1111/j.1365-2729.2011.00447.x

Piaget, J. (1936). *Origins of intelligence in the child.* London: Routledge & Kegan Paul.

Piaget, J. (1977). *The development of thought: Equilibration of cognitive structures.* New York: The Viking Press.

Pinsonneault, A., Barki, H., Gallupe, R. B., & Hoppen, N. (1999). Electronic brainstorming. Retrieved from http://pubsonline.informs.org/doi/pdf/10.1287/isre.10.2.110

Porter, A. (2013). *The problem with technology in schools.* Retrieved from, http://www.washingtonpost.com

Roblyer, M. D., & Doering, A. H. (2013). *Integrating educational technology into teaching* (6th ed.). Boston, MA: Pearson Education, Inc.

Sage, K. (1999). Science activities using the World Wide Web: Grade 4–6+. Monterey, CA: Evan-Moor Educational Publishers.

Salmivalli, C., Sainio, M., & Hodges, E. V. E. (2013). Electronic victimization: Correlates, antecedents, consequences among elementary and middle school students. *Journal of Clinical Child and Adolescent Psychology, 42*(4), 442–453. doi:10.1080/15374416.2012.759228 PMID:23384048

Shaffer, D., & Resnick, M. (1999). "Thick" authenticity: New media and authentic learning. *Journal of Interactive Learning Research, 10*(2), 195–215.

SIIA. (2009). *Best practices for using games & simulations in the classroom: Guidelines for K–12 Educators,* Retrieved from, http://siia.net/index.php?option=com_docman&task=doc_view&gid=610&tmpl=component&format=raw&Itemid=59

Sirinterlikci, A., Zane, L., & Sirinterlikci, A. L. (2009). Active learning through toy design and development. *Journal of Technology Studies, 35*(2), 14–22.

Stepien, B. (n.d.). Tutorial on problem-based learning: Taxonomy of Socratic questioning. In C. A. Toledo "Does your dog bite?" creating good questions for online discussions. *International Journal of Teaching and Learning in Higher Education, 18*(2). Retrieved from: http://www.isetl.org/ijtlhe/pdf/IJTLHE85.pdf

Stoddard, J. (2009). Toward a virtual field trip model for the social studies. *Contemporary Issues in Technology & Teacher Education*, *9*(4). Retrieved from http://www.citejournal.org/vol9/iss4/socialstudies/article1.cfm

Suler, J. (2004). The online disinhibition effect. *Cyberpsychology & Behavior*, *7*(3), 321–326. doi:10.1089/1094931041291295 PMID:15257832

Tate, M. L. (2014). *Brainstorming and discussion*. Retrieved from, http://www.corwin.com/upm-data/58810_Tate_RLA_Worksheets_Don%27t_Grow_Dendrites_ch_1.pdf

Toledo, C. A. (2006). "Does your dog bite?" Creating good questions for online discussions. *International Journal of Teaching and Learning in Higher Education*, *18*(2), 150–154.

Torp, L., & Sage, S. (1998). *Problems as possibilities: Problem-based learning for K-12 education*. Alexandria, VA: Association for Supervision and Curriculum Development.

United Health Care. (2012). *Did you know that 80% of what kids learn in school is learned visually?* Retrieved from, http://www.indstate.edu/humres/staff-benefits/docs/100-10982%20VI%20Children%20Eye%20Health.pdf

van Hattum-Janssen, N., & Lourenço, J. M. (2008). Peer and self-assessment for first-year students as a tool to improve learning. *Journal of Professional Issues in Engineering Education and Practice*, *134*(4), 346–352. doi:10.1061/(ASCE)1052-3928(2008)134:4(346)

Wadsworth, B. J. (2004). *Piaget's theory of cognitive and affective development: Foundations of constructivism*. Longman Publishing.

Wang, F., & Reeves, T. C. (2003). Why do teachers need to use technology in their classroom? Issues, problems, and solutions. *Computers in the Schools*, *20*(4), 49–65. doi:10.1300/J025v20n04_05

Wood, E., Specht, J., Willoughby, T., & Mueller, J. (2008). Integrating computer technology in early childhood education environments: Issues raised by early childhood educators. *The Alberta Journal of Educational Research*, *54*(2), 210–226.

KEY TERMS AND DEFINITIONS

Active Learning: Being able to search for new information, organize, analyze and create new meaning through the use of technology.

Electronic Brainstorming: A computer aided-approach for generating ideas individually or collaboratively.

Infographics: Use of visual images such as charts, graphic organizers, diagrams, photos, etc. in teaching and learning.

Inquiry Learning: is a form of active learning, where students participate in searching for information, developing experiments, analyzing data, and constructing new knowledge and skills.

Live Virtual Field Trip: virtual tour in real time.

Peer-Assessment: A process where students review their peer's work for accuracy or growth using the assessment rubrics aligned with the goals and objectives of the learned materials.

Self-Assessment: A process whereby students review (individually) their own work for accuracy or growth using the assessment rubrics aligned with the goals and objectives of the learned materials.

Virtual Field Trip: a tour of websites and videos.

Webquest: An inquiry-oriented lesson format in which most or all the information that learners work with comes from the Internet (or the web).

Chapter 8
Teaching History of Mathematics through Digital Stories:
A Technology Integration Model

Lutfi Incikabi
Kastamonu University, Turkey

ABSTRACT

This chapter introduces a way for enhancing teaching history of mathematics through digital storytelling. Adapting digitals stories in the form of historical documentaries, this chapter also provides components of digital storytelling (point of view, dramatic question, emotional content, the gift of your voice, the power of the soundtrack, economy, pacing, purpose of story, choice of content, quality of images, grammar and language usage) and necessary steps (tellable story, compositing script, choosing visual and audio components, preparing digital stories, presenting digitals stories) that are to be taken into consideration while preparing digital stories.

INTRODUCTION

Nowadays, technology has surrounded our lives such a way that we become overly dependent on it because of its priceless benefits. This close relationship between (modern) technology and humanity also affected the way of learning and teaching. In turn, the term "technology enhanced learning" becomes evident in recent literature in education. Technology enhanced learning covers all those circumstances where technology plays a significant role in making learning more effec-

tive, efficient or enjoyable (Goodyear, & Retalis, 2010). Moreover, literature provides several models of technology integration of educational environments that include accessing and studying learning material, learning through inquiry, learning through construction, learning through communication and collaboration, assessing learning, and developing digital and multimedia literacy (Bruce, &Levin 1997; Chickering, & Ehrmann, 1996; Conole, Dyke, Oliver, & Seale, 2004; Jonassen, 2008).

DOI: 10.4018/978-1-4666-8363-1.ch008

Instructional Technology: Advantageous or Not?

In educational settings, learning and technology interacts in two ways: Learning from technology, and learning with technology. The former adopts technologies as teachers by using them to teach concepts to students in the same ways that teachers had always taught. Learning from technology process requires two steps. The first step is embedding the information in the technology, and technology, in the next step, transmits that information to the learners. Learning with technology, on the other hand, necessitates uses of technologies for engaging and facilitating thinking that produces learning. Successful integration of technology urges efficient adaptation of learning theories and content-specific approaches to curriculum development. In order to robust students' learning with technology, teachers are required to guide their students to construct their knowledge. Teachers' guidance for knowledge construction will also help students for learning with understanding (meaningful learning) that requires interacting in a way that allows discussion, communication, collaboration, and reflection (Jonassen, Howland, Moore, & Marra, 2003).

Sociological framework of technology introduces the terms of "educational technology" and "instructional technology." Most of the time, we face similar definitions for these terms that states " both share a common interest in the processes of human learning and teaching, with some variations in definitions and levels of complexity, depending upon one's personal viewpoint" (Earle, 2002, p. 6). The term of educational technology, regarded as a fundamental factor for improving students' achievement, generally refers to the introduction of computers and related pieces of equipment to the classroom (Wenglinsky, 2005). Different definitions of the instructional technologies are evident in literature. By relating instructional technology with the strategies that adapted for impediment of the problems encountered during

teaching, Gentry (2002) defines instructional technology as "the systemic and systematic application of strategies and techniques derived from behavioral and physical sciences concepts and other knowledge to the solution of instructional problems" (p. 7). As a subdivision of educational technologies, instructional technology are usually in charge of improving the effectiveness and efficiency of learning in educational contexts, regardless of the nature or substance of that learning (Cassidy, 1982). A broader definition comes from Commission on Instructional Technology (1970), instructional technology is

...the media born of the communications revolution which can be used for instructional purposes alongside the teacher, textbook, and blackboard... [as well as]...a systematic way of designing, carrying out, and evaluating the total process of learning and teaching in terms of specific objectives, based on research in human learning and communications, and employing a combination of human and nonhuman resources to bring about more effective instructions (p. 19).

Despite these more comprehensive viewpoints from the literature that instructional technology encompasses the broader processes of teaching and learning, most people nominates computer technology as a synonym for instructional technology (Earle, 2002). No one argue the impact of technology in the educational settings. Surveys (e.g. Commission on Instructional Technology, 1970), conducted at the beginning of educational technology era, indicated that computer technology, most of the time, were utilized as a tool to access information outside the classroom and improved student motivation, not as a facilitator for teaching of a specific content.

According to Wager (1992), considering educational technology as a "hardware" does not possess a huge contribution to the quality of education. Impact of technology depends on the process of designing effective instruction that integrates computer technology and other media appropriately to meet instructional/learning needs (Robey, 1992). However, literature (e.g. Bosch, 1993; Niess, 1991; Trotter, 1997) indicates teachers' eagerness to use of educational technologies but their weaknesses integrating technologies with curriculum. Difficulty is more evident in determining appropriate technologies for teaching of a specific content.

Attributions of teachers' efficacy of integrating technology inside the classroom can be gathered under three headings. External factors, the first heading, cover access to hardware and software as well as funding (Hope, 1997; Lan, 2000; Leggett, & Persichitte, 1998; Lumley, & Bailey, 1993), technical and administrative support and resources (Leggett, & Persichitte, 1998; Schrum, 1995). The second one is pedagogical/professional factors that include time for planning, personal exploration, and skill development (Duffield, 1997; Hope 1997; Lan, 2000; Leggett, & Persichitte, 1998; Sheingold, & Hadley, 1990), training and expertise (Hope, 1997; Knee, 1995; Shelton, & Jones, 1996), support for integration of technologies into instruction and the curriculum (Cuban, 1986; Hancock, & Betts, 1994), and vision and leadership (Ely, 1995; Hope, 1997; Knee, 1995; Lan, 2000; Lumley & Bailey,1993). Cultural factors, the third heading, consist of resistance, passivity, school cultures, and traditions of teaching (Beacham, 1994; Cohen, 1987; Cuban, 1986; Ertmer, 1999; Hope, 1997; Knee, 1995; Lumley & Bailey, 1993).

Educational Technologies in Mathematics

Nowadays, research relating educational technology takes significant attention. Within last century, major literature reviews have been conducted in this area (e.g. Christmann, & Badgett, 2003; Hartley, 1977; Ouyang, 1993; Rakes, Valentine, McGatha, & Ronau, 2010; Slavin, Lake, & Groff, 2009). These reviews included a wide range of subjects, from reading to mathematics, and sub-

jects from kindergarten to college. Most of the educational technology literature review studies in the subject of mathematics indicated positive effects of educational technology on mathematics achievement with the widely ranged effect sizes (Hartley, 1977; Lee, 1990; Li, & Ma, 2010; Rakes, et al., 2010; Slavin & Lake, 2008; Slavin, et al., 2009).

Educational technology is generally regarded as an effective way of engaging students in complex mathematical processes (Zbiek, Heid, Blume, & Dick, 2007). In mathematics teaching and learning process, however, students' engagement in complex mathematical processes usually do not go beyond of the use of graphic calculators rather than engaging students in higher order thinking (Cohen, 1987; Cuban, 1986; U.S. Department of Education, 2008; Wenglinsky, 2005).

The extant literature offers a number of explanations for limited technology use in schools such as maladjustment between technology and curricular goals, lack of time to integrate technology into already tightly scheduled class periods, teachers' skill of technology use, and institutional factors including lack of resources and lack of support systems (Baylor, & Ritchie, 2002; Hawkins, Spielvogel, & Panush, 1996; Windschitl, & Sahl, 2002; Zbiek, & Hollebrands, 2008). Moreover, the prevailing teaching theories of mathematics, such as social constructivism and realistic mathematics education, may cause for teachers to struggle with their "forced" roles in technology-rich, learner-centered classrooms.

A Different Way of Technology Integration: Digital Storytelling

Many different types of technology can be used to support and enhance learning. In a general sense, technology is comprised of both hardware such as smart boards and software such as educational games and web 2.0 social applications. Among the recent educational technologies that can be applied to educational settings is digital storytelling, a technique that combines pictures with a soundtrack including both voice and music (Bull, & Kajder 2004; Sadik 2008). Robin (2008) defines digital storytelling as "a technology application that is well-positioned to take advantage of user-contributed content and to help teachers overcome some of the obstacles to productively using technology in their classrooms" (p. 222).

Educational uses of stories can carry different means including enriching students' learning, improving quality of teaching, and conducting academic research (McEwan, & Egan, 1995). According to Balacheff et al. (2009) story preparation process improves creative and logical thinking, while storytelling stimulates recognition of main elements and memory. Digital storytelling differs from conventional storytelling by having computers as mediums and requiring technological competency (Dorner, Grimm, & Abawi, 2002). According to many sources, digital storytelling was first introduced to the literature in 1993 through the work of Joe Lambert and Dana Atchley from the center for digital storytelling at the University of California, Berkeley (Bull, & Kajder 2004; Chung 2007; Robin 2008).

Digital storytelling combines today's technologies with the conventional storytelling, the most effective communication tool of the past (Nguyen, 2011). Moreover, digital storytelling also improves conventional stories by adding visual and musical elements and provides opportunities for educational uses in teaching and learning environments. Students' adaptation of technology such as digital storytelling helps them learn to "convert data into information and transform information into knowledge" (Cradler, McNabb, Freeman, & Burchett, 2002, p. 3). Hence, teacher education programs are expected to prepare future teachers who are able to create digital stories and integrate them to their teaching environment.

Components of Digital Story Telling

Within last decade, digital stories have come into sight as a powerful teaching and learning tool that engages both teachers and their students (Robin,

2008). Literature provides 11 components that are to be considered in the creation process of effective digital stories (See Figure 1). First seven of these components were introduced by Lambert (2003) while the rest has been defined by Robin (2008) as follows.

1. Point of view: This component includes the main point of the story and reflects the perspective of the author.
2. Dramatic question: This component includes an attentive question to be asked and answered within the context of the story.
3. Emotional content: Story grasps the audience's attention and engages.
4. The gift of your voice: The narration provides greater meaning to and better understanding of the story.
5. The power of the soundtrack: This component considers sounds and music that add further emotional response to the story line.
6. Economy: The story should effectively employ a small number of images or shortened text.
7. Pacing: This components deals with rhythm of a story.
8. Purpose of story: The author should establish a purpose early on the story and maintain a clear focus throughout.
9. Choice of content: Contents needs to create a distinct atmosphere or tone that matches different parts of the story.
10. Quality of images: Images are expected to support story line and to create a distinct atmosphere or tone that matches different parts of the story.
11. Grammar and language usage: Grammar and language usage are to be correct and provide contribution to clarity, style and character development.

Educational Uses of Digital Stories

Robin (2008) categorizes digital stories in three major groups: The first one is personal narratives

Figure 1. Components of digital storytelling

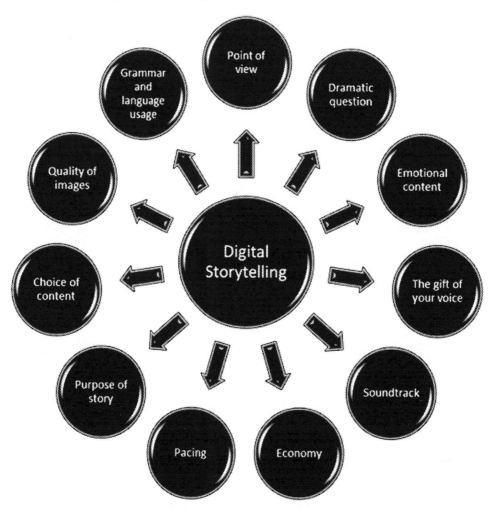

that contain accounts of significant incidents in one's life. In these stories, author narrates their personal experiences or memories to the audience. Second category contains the stories that inform or instruct the viewer on a particular concept or practice, and the third category is historical documentaries. Stories in this category analyze events that help audience understand the past so as to foster students' understanding of history of mathematics. This book chapter will adapt digital stories in the category historical documentaries.

Literature provides some beneficiary ways of using digital stories in education to support student learning (Dogan, & Robin, 2008; Incikabi, &

Kildan, 2013, Jenkins, & Lonsdale, 2007; Jonassen, & Hernandez-Serrano, 2002; Yuksel, 2011). The research studies investigated educational uses of them mostly focus on benefits of digital storytelling in the activities making children compose their own stories (e.g. Bran, 2010; Liu, Chen, Shih, Huang, & Liu, 2011). Yuksel, Robin and McNeil (2010) conducted a study to evaluate educational uses of digital stories in 26 countries. According to the results, digital stories were found supportive to robust students' understanding of concepts; digital stories improved such skills as researching, writing, and presenting. In addition, some studies also stated that digital story telling had also have a positive effect on students' academic performance (Combs, & Beach, 1994; Tsou, Wang, & Tzeng, 2006; Yang, & Wu, 2012). Moreover, preparing digital stories also enhances students' skill of creativity (Liu et al., 2011).

Uses of Digital Stories in Mathematics Education

While digital storytelling is most often associated with the arts and humanities (Combs, & Beach 1994), and language learning (Tsou et al., 2006; Yang, & Wu 2012), research indicates that it can also be an effective strategy for teaching and learning mathematics. According to Schiro (2004), digital storytelling enriches mathematics teaching and learning by providing in a context that is interesting, engaging and relevant.

While students' reading and writing abilities remain among the chief concerns of educators, the ability to solve problems has also gained much attention in recent years. Problem solving activities in mathematics education mostly rely on story problems (Jonassen, 2003). Digital storytelling offers many opportunities to practice problem-solving and decision-making skills. Researchers who have implemented or observed students working with digital storytelling report high engagement in various types of problem-solving and decision-making (Chung, 2007). According to Robin (2008), digital storytelling is a technique that forces students to decide the (impressive and tell able) stories, and to solve the problem of processing a digital story that combine visuals, linguistics, music, and narration to achieve desired outcomes. Hence, digital storytelling requires and improves the skills of synthesis, creativity, conducting research, and critical thinking (Hull, & Katz, 2006; Ohler, 2008; Ware, 2006).

The literature also provides applications of digital storytelling for teaching mathematics in early childhood education (Casey, 2004; Casey,

Erkut, Ceder, & Young, 2008; Casey, Kersh, & Young 2004). Casey et al. (2008) investigated the benefits of using storytelling to teach geometry to kindergarten students and indicated its usefulness for improving mathematics learning in children from culturally diverse backgrounds. Some studies also investigated early childhood teacher candidates' experiences of using digital storytelling to teach mathematics. Kildan and Incikabi (2013) indicated that teacher candidates' evaluations of digital storytelling were affected by their preparation experiences. Moreover, results showed a shift from dual intersections of technology, pedagogy, and content knowledge to the triple intersection of TPACK. In another study, Incikabi and Kildan (2013) also indicated that most of the digital stories aimed to be used during teaching of the subject while few of them applied as warm-up activities or reinforcement at the end of the lesson. Moreover, majority of the digital stories had presented a weak compatibility with the related early childhood curriculum since they did not cover the stated behavior completely and/or include a scientific mistake.

History of Mathematics: Why and How to Teach

History of humanity possesses an endless collection of mathematical knowledge that covers methods and techniques for solving problems, tools for surveying and measurement, logical problems and proofs. However, teaching environments usually suffers from lack of integrating historical moments or methods of calculations. Providing excerpts from history of mathematics encourages appreciation of mathematics (Panasuk, & Horton, 2013). Moreover, integrating history of mathematics into classroom teaching also enriches and robust students mathematical content knowledge by demonstrating how history of mathematics provides "conditions for gaining a rich experience and understanding of the development of mathematical concepts and their connections and interrelation" (Panasuk, & Horton, 2013, p. 37).

Literature provides insufficient amount of researches (Siu, 2004; Swetz, 1994; Swetz, Fauvel, Bekken, Johansson, & Katz, 1995; Weng Kin, 2008) that "enthusiastically argue that the history of mathematics supplies endless opportunities to trace the roots and development of humanity, development of civilizations, and is likely to make an effect on students' perception of the power of mathematics" (Panasuk, & Horton, 2013, p.37). Some researchers in the field of mathematics education give confidence in emphasizing history of mathematics and integrating it into the curriculum so as to develop positive attitudes towards mathematics (Monk, & Osborne, 1997). Radford (1997) defines two ways of using history of mathematics in mathematics education. The first way is to relate historical anecdotes to students, while the second way is to view the history of mathematics "as a huge arsenal of chronologically ordered problems to be "imported" into the classroom and to have students solve them" (p.26).

Empirical studies focused on teachers' perceptions of history of mathematics (e.g., Philippou, & Christou, 1998; Schram, Wilcox, Lapan & Lanier, 1988; Siu, 2004; Smestad, 2009; Stander, 1989) indicated that introducing teachers to the history of mathematics activated their interests in the significance of mathematics and its history for learning the discipline. Fauvel and van Maanen (1997) and Ponza (1998) investigated the influence of including topics from the development of mathematics on students' attitudes, and found a positive change, with significant improvement in their attitude towards mathematics.

The National Council of Teachers of Mathematics (NCTM) in the USA recommends integrating the history of mathematics and emphasizes its importance (NCTM, 2000, p. 4): "Mathematics represents one of mankind's greatest cultural and intellectual achievements and it is important that the country's citizens will value and understand the strength of this achievement, including the

aesthetic and enjoyable aspects." According to NCTM, teaching of history of mathematics motivates students and develops positive approach to mathematics; it helps teachers to overcome current learning issues by using obstacles to the development of mathematics in the past; it provides a clear picture of interaction between human and mathematics; it develops students' skills of mathematical thinking.

According to Baki (2008), mathematics programs that are enriched through history of mathematics help students to realize that mathematics is a science that renovate itself, to figure out the interaction between culture and mathematics, to introduce theories and works of mathematicians in chronological order, understand the relationship among mathematics and other fields, to improve their interest in mathematics topics placed in the teaching programs, to learn about how mathematicians work, and to follow that intuition, prediction, refutation and justification are indispensable activities of mathematicians. An extensive study conducted by the International Commission of Mathematics Instruction between 1997 and 2000 examined the place of the history of mathematics in the national curricula of different countries throughout the world (Fauvel, Maanen, & van Maanen, 2000). Their study emphasizes the belief of mathematicians, researchers and educators in the need to incorporate topics relating to the history of mathematics in lessons at all levels of study in the schools, colleges and universities.

PROCEDURES FOR PREPARING DIGITAL STORIES

According to Robin (2008), the following sequence of steps is necessary to be useful when working with whole classes of students:

1. Determining a story with 'tellability': In this step, the author decides the main theme of the story in order to fulfill the targeted goal and to answer "dramatic" question

2. Writing an initial story script. This step will help to clarify the main ideas that the story aims to convey.

3. Discussing the script with peers and revising: Conferring the script with colleagues helps to keep the story focused and clarify some of the ideas and word choices. In turn, this contributes on conveying the message and emotion intended.

4. Devising a storyboard to accompany the script: This step contains visualizing all components of the story. Author decides the images and the parts of the script that are narrated under each images.

5. Importing and queuing images: This step includes creating a new folder containing all the images for the story in the sequence that was designed in the storyboard.

6. Narrating the story: A main advantage of digital story is narrating the digital story by using your own voice. In this step, it is crucial to determine what sort of pacing, rhythm, and inflection would best convey the intended message (Robin, 2008).

7. Adding special effects and transitions. Special effects can add punch to the right type of story.

8. Adding a musical soundtrack: This step contains selecting a soundtrack that is appropriate to the story and will add much to the emotion to be conveyed.

Lesson Design for Teaching History of Mathematics through Digital Storytelling

This section of the chapter provides a lesson design that can be adapted to grade 8 through college level and to teach or enhance students' knowledge on history of mathematics through preparing digital stories. Figure 1 provides steps to be taken while creating digital stories within this context.

Tellable story: The very first step of the creating digital story is to decide a story with tellability.

Within this step students are expected to conduct a research regarding history of mathematics and chose a mathematician from the past who they think to be interesting from one aspect to introduce to their peers. This step also requires from students to make a decision about the message that will be accompanied by dramatic "question." The starting point of digital stories requires creativity since the author needs to begin to the story with an incident or memory that is related to the message conveyed through.

Compositing script: After deciding, mathematician, the goal of the story, and the beginning point of the story, authors are to be expected to compose the story. If this course designated for teacher candidates, then they could chose two different paths for compositing the story. The first one is to make their own story without interacting with the students. The second path requires from teacher candidates to have students participate to the composition process actively. Compositing of the story also requires from students to discuss their stories with their peers and revise it accordingly.

Choosing visual and audio components: Digital stories differ from conventional stories due to its audibility. This step includes choosing visual and audio components. Coordinated with the music, images should create a distinct atmosphere or tone that matches different parts of the story. Music needs to stir a rich emotional response that matches the story line well. Composing of the storyboard is the next step that clearly distinct the images and the part of the script narrated for each of them and followed by choosing soundtrack.

Preparing Digital Stories: MS Photo Story 3 software is utilized to prepare digital stories. This step requires importing and queuing images and followed by narrating stories based on the storyboard. Later, effects and transitions are set, and a soundtrack is inserted to escort to the story line.

Presenting digitals stories: The whole process of digital storytelling is completed by presenting digital story to students or peers and reflecting on the stories. Reflection parts should consider

Figure 2. Flowchart for creating digital story (Adapted from Yuksel Arslan, 2013)

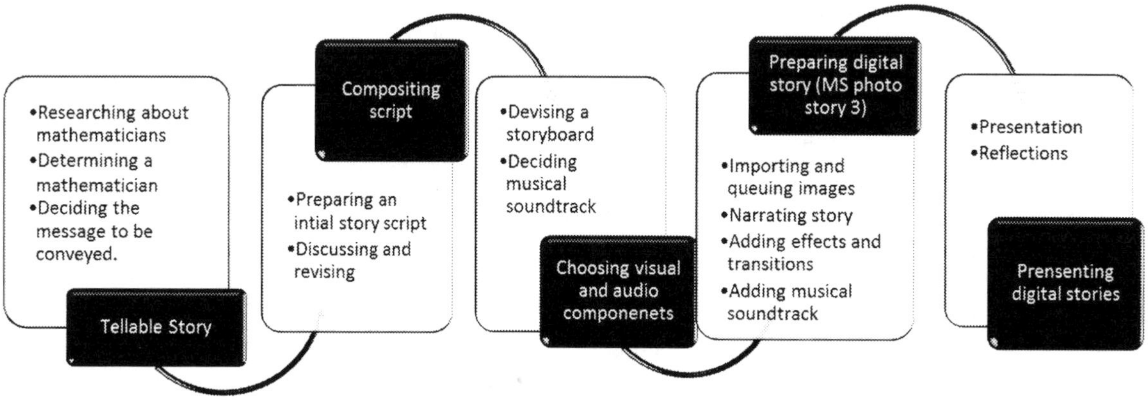

whether the story achieves the intended goal and what are the impressions of the students (as users or as receivers) and the about the digital storytelling technique.

CONCLUSION

This book chapter aims to introduce a way of teaching history of mathematics by means of digital storytelling. Storytelling is a form of thought which is inherent in human beings (Bruner, 1990). Dettori and Paiva (2009) highlights that story telling "can support learning and skill formation with regard to cognition, motivation and emotion in the most diverse fields" (p. 67). Being an improvement from the conventional storytelling of the past, digital storytelling combines today's technologies with the conventional storytelling by adding visual and musical elements.

Educational uses of digital stories include personal narratives, informative/instructive stories, and historical documentaries (Robin, 2008). This book chapter adapts digital stories in the category historical documentaries so as to foster students' understanding of history of mathematics. Literature provides such advantages of integrating digitals stories inside the teaching environments as digital storytelling enriches mathematics teaching and learning by providing in a context that is interesting, engaging and relevant; digital storytelling offers many opportunities to practice problem-solving and decision-making skills; digital storytelling improves the skills of synthesis, creativity, conducting research, and critical thinking.

Literature provides uses of digital stories from early childhood education (frequently) to teacher education in the field of mathematics. Most of the digital story applications include teaching of mathematical learning areas (such as geometry). However, literature suffers from lack of integrating digital stories to inform on or instruct about history of mathematics.

Integrating history of mathematics into classroom teaching also enriches and robust students mathematical content knowledge by demonstrating how history of mathematics provides conditions for gaining a rich experience and understanding of the development of mathematical concepts and their connections and interrelation (Panasuk, & Horton, 2013; Philippou, & Christou, 1998; Schram, Wilcox, Lapan & Lanier, 1988; Siu, 2004; Smestad, 2009; Stander, 1989). Moreover, mathematics programs that are enriched through history of mathematics help students to realize that how mathematics as a science has been improved, how it has been shaped, how mathematics interacts within its sub-domains and with other fields of study (Baki, 2008).

REFERENCES

Baki, A. (2008). *Kuramdan uygulamay matematik eğitimi* [Mathematics education from theory to practice]. Ankara, Turkey: Harf Education Publishing.

Balacheff, N., Ludvigsen, S., De Jong, T., Lazonder, A., Barnes, S., & Montandon, L. (2009). *Technology-Enhanced Learning*. Berlin, Germany: Springer. doi:10.1007/978-1-4020-9827-7

Baylor, A. L., & Ritchie, D. (2002). What factors facilitate teacher skill, teacher morale, and perceived student learning in technology-using classrooms? *Computers & Education, 29*(4), 395–414. doi:10.1016/S0360-1315(02)00075-1

Beacham, B. (1994). Making connections: Transforming ivory towers and little red school houses. In J. Willis, B. Robin, & D. A. Willis (Eds.), *Technology and teacher education annual 1994* (pp. 742–744). Charlottesville, VA: Association for Advancement of Computing in Education.

Bosch, K. A. (1993). Is there a computer crisis in the classroom? *Schools in the Middle, 2*(4), 7–9.

Bruce, B. C., & Levin, J. A. (1997). Educational technology: Media for inquiry, communication, construction, and expression. *Journal of Educational Computing Research, 17*(1), 79–102. doi:10.2190/7HPQ-4F3X-8M8Y-TVCA

Bruner, J. (1990). *Acts of meaning*. Cambridge, MA: Harvard University Press.

Bull, G., & Kajder, S. (2004). Digital storytelling in the language arts classroom. *Learning and Leading with Technology, 32*(4), 46–49.

Casey, B. (2004). Mathematics problem-solving adventures: A Language-arts-based supplementary series for early childhood that focuses on spatial sense. In D. H. Clements, J. Sarama, & A. M. DiBiase (Eds.), *Engaging young children in mathematics: Standards for early childhood mathematics education* (pp. 377–389). Mahwah, NJ: Erlbaum.

Casey, B., Erkut, S., Ceder, I., & Young, J. M. (2008). Use of a Storytelling Context to Improve Girls' and Boys' Geometry Skills in Kindergarten. *Journal of Applied Developmental Psychology, 29*(1), 29–48. doi:10.1016/j.appdev.2007.10.005

Casey, B., Kersh, J. E., & Young, J. M. (2004). Storytelling Sagas: An effective medium for teaching early childhood mathematics. *Early Childhood Research Quarterly, 19*(1), 167–172. doi:10.1016/j.ecresq.2004.01.011

Cassidy, M. F. (1982). Toward integration: Education, instructional technology, and semiotics. *Educational Communications and Technology Journal, 20*(2), 75–89.

Chickering, A. W., & Ehrmann, S. C. (1996). Implementing the seven principles: Technology as lever. *AAHE Bulletin, 49*(2), 3–6.

Christmann, E. P., & Badgett, J. L. (2003). A meta-analytic comparison of the effects of computer-assisted instruction on elementary students' academic achievement. *Information Technology in Childhood Education Annual*, 91–104.

Chung, S. K. (2007). Art education technology: Digital storytelling. *Art Education, 60*(2), 17–22.

Cohen, D. (1987). Educational technology, policy, and practice. *Educational Evaluation and Policy Analysis, 9*(2), 153–170. doi:10.3102/01623737009002153

Combs, M., & Beach, J. D. (1994). Stories and storytelling: Personalizing the social studies. *The Reading Teacher, 47*(6), 464–471.

Commission on Instructional Technology. (1970). *To improve learning: A report to the President and the Congress of the United States.* Washington, DC: Commission on Instructional Technology.

Conole, G., Dyke, M., Oliver, M., & Seale, J. (2004). Mapping pedagogy and tools for effective learning design. *Computers & Education, 43*(1), 17–33. doi:10.1016/j.compedu.2003.12.018

Cradler, J., McNabb, M., Freeman, M., & Burchett, R. (2002). How does technology influence student learning? *Learning and Leading, 29*(8), 46–49.

Cuban, L. (1986). *Teachers and machines: The classroom use of technology since 1920.* New York, NY: Teachers College Press.

Dettori, G., & Paiva, A. (2009). Narrative learning in technology-enhanced environments. In N. Balacheff, S. Ludvigsen, T. De Jong, A. Lazonder, S. Barnes, & L. Montandon (Eds.), *Technology-Enhanced Learning* (pp. 55–69). Berlin: Springer. doi:10.1007/978-1-4020-9827-7_4

Dogan, B., & Robin, B. (2008). Implementation of digital storytelling in the classroom by teachers trained in a digital storytelling workshop. In *Society for Information Technology & Teacher Education International Conference.* Las Vegas, NV: USA.

Dorner, R., Grimm, P., & Abawi, D. F. (2002). Synergies between interactive training simulations and digital storytelling: A component-based framework. *Computers & Graphics, 26*(1), 45–55. doi:10.1016/S0097-8493(01)00177-7

Duffield, J. A. (1997). Trials, tribulations, and minor successes: Integrating technology into a preservice preparation program. *TechTrends, 42*(4), 22–26. doi:10.1007/BF02818596

Earle, R. S. (2002). The integration of instructional technology into public education: Promises and challenges. *Educational Technology, 42*(1), 5–13.

Ely, D. P. (1995). *Technology is the answer! But what was the question?* Capstone College of Education Society, University of Alabama (ERIC Document Reproduction Service No. ED 381 152).

Ertmer, P. (1999). Addressing first- and second-order barriers to change: Strategies for technology implementation. *Educational Technology Research and Development, 47*(4), 47–61. doi:10.1007/BF02299597

Fauvel, J., Maanen, J., & van Maanen, J. A. (Eds.). (2000). *History in mathematics education: An ICMI study* (Vol. 6). Springer Science & Business Media.

Fauvel, J., & Van Maanen, J. (1997). The role of the history of mathematics in the teaching and learning of mathematics: Discussion document for an ICMI study (1997-2000). *Educational Studies in Mathematics, 34*(3), 255–259. doi:10.1023/A:1003038421040

Gentry, C. G. (1995). Educational technology: A question of meaning. In G. Anglin (Ed.), *Instructional technology: Past, present, and future.* Englewood, CO: Libraries Unlimited.

Goodyear, P., & Retalis, S. (2010). *Technology-enhanced learning.* Rotterdam: Sense Publishers.

Hancock, V., & Betts, J. (1994). From the lagging to the leading edge. *Educational Leadership, 51*(7), 24–29.

Hartley, S. S. (1977). *Meta-analysis of the effects of individually paced instruction in Mathematics.* Unpublished Doctoral dissertation, University of Colorado at Boulder.

Hawkins, J., Spielvogel, B., & Panush, E. M. (1996). *National study tour of district technology integration* (Summary report). Retrieved from http://cct.edc.org/admin/publications/report/natstudy_dti96.pdf

Hope, W. C. (1997). Why technology has not realized its potential in schools. *American Secondary Education, 25*(4), 2–9.

Hull, G. A., & Katz, M. L. (2006). Crafting an agentive self: Case studies of digital storytelling. *Research in the Teaching of English, 41*(1), 43–81.

Incikabi, L., & Kildan, A. O. (2013). An analysis of early childhood teacher candidates' digital stories for mathematics teaching. *International Journal of Academic Research Part B, 5*(2), 77–81. doi:10.7813/2075-4124.2013/5-2/B.10

Jenkins, M., & Lonsdale, J. (2007). Evaluating the effectiveness of digital storytelling for student reflection. In *ICT: Providing choices for learners and learning. Proceedings ASCILITE*. Singapore.

Jonassen, D. H. (2003). Designing research-based instruction for story problems. *Educational Psychology Review, 15*(3), 267–296. doi:10.1023/A:1024648217919

Jonassen, D. H. (2008). Instructional design as a design problem solving: An iterative process. *Educational Technology, 48*(3), 21–26.

Jonassen, D. H., & Hernandez-Serrano, J. (2002). Case-based reasoning and instructional design using stories to support problem solving. *Educational Technology Research and Development, 50*(2), 65–77. doi:10.1007/BF02504994

Jonassen, D. H., Howland, J. L., Moore, J., & Marra, R. M. (Eds.). (2003). *Learning to solve problems with technology: A constructivist perspective*. Pearson Education.

Kildan, A. O., & Incikabi, L. (2013). Effects on the technological pedagogical content knowledge of early childhood teacher candidates using digital storytelling to teach mathematics. *Education 3-13: International Journal of Primary. Elementary and Early Years Education, 41*(3). doi:10.1080/03004279.2013.804852

Knee, R. (1995). Factors limiting technology integration in education: The leadership gap. In *Society for Information Technology & Teacher Education International Conference* (pp. 556-560). Charlottesville, VA: Association for Advancement of Computing in Education.

Lambert, J. (2003). *Digital storytelling cookbook and traveling companion*. Berkeley, CA: Digital Diner Retrieved May 10, 2010, from http://www.storycenter.org/cookbook.pdf

Lan, J. (2000). Leading teacher educators to a new paradigm: Observations on technology integration. *AACTE Briefs, 21*(10), 4–6.

Lee, W. C. (1990). *The effectiveness of computer assisted instruction and computer programming in elementary and secondary mathematics: A meta-analysis*. Amherst: University of Massachusetts-Amherst.

Leggett, W. P., & Persichitte, K. A. (1998). Blood, sweat, and TEARS: 50 years of technology implementation obstacles. *TechTrends, 43*(3), 33–36. doi:10.1007/BF02824053

Li, Q., & Ma, X. (2010). A meta-analysis of the effects of computer technology on school students' mathematics learning. *Educational Psychology Review, 22*(3), 215–243. doi:10.1007/s10648-010-9125-8

Liu, C. C., Chen, H. S., Shih, J. L., Huang, G. T., & Liu, B. J. (2011). An enhanced concept map approach to improving children's storytelling ability. *Computers & Education, 56*(3), 873–884. doi:10.1016/j.compedu.2010.10.029

Lumley, D., & Bailey, G. D. (1993). *Planning for technology: A guidebook for school administrators*. New York, NY: Scholastic.

McEwan, H., & Egan, K. (Eds.). (1995). *Narrative in teaching, learning, and research*. New York: Teachers College Press.

Monk, M., & Osborne, J. (1997). Placing the history and philosophy of science on the curriculum: A model for the development of pedagogy. *Science education, 81*(4), 405–424. doi:10.1002/(SICI)1098-237X(199707)81:4<405::AID-SCE3>3.0.CO;2-G

NCTM (National Council of Teachers of Mathematics). (2000). *Principles and Standards for School Mathematics*. Reston, VA: Commission on Standards for School Mathematics.

Nguyen, A. (2011). *Negotiations and challenges: An investigation into the experience of creating a digital story*. Doctoral Dissertation, University of Houston, TX, USA.

Niess, N. L. (1991). Computer-using teachers in a new decade. *Education and Computing, 7*(3), 151–156. doi:10.1016/S0167-9287(09)90002-4

Ohler, J. (2008). *Digital storytelling in the classroom: New media pathways to literacy, learning, and creativity*. Thousand Oaks, CA: Corwin Press.

Ouyang, R. (1993). *A meta-analysis: Effectiveness of computer-assisted instruction at the level of elementary education*. Unpublished Dissertation, Indiana University of Pennsylvania, Indiana.

Panasuk, R. M., & Horton, L. B. (2013). Integrating History of Mathematics into the Classroom: Was Aristotle Wrong? *Journal of Curriculum & Teaching, 2*(2), 37–46. doi:10.5430/jct.v2n2p37

Philippou, G. N., & Christou, C. (1998). The effects of a preparatory mathematics program in changing prospective teachers' attitudes towards mathematics. *Educational Studies in Mathematics, 35*(1), 189–206. doi:10.1023/A:1003030211453

Ponza, M. V. (1998). A Role for the History of Mathematics in the Teaching and Learning of Mathematics: An Argentinian Experience. *Mathematics in school, 27*(4), 10-13.

Radford, L. (1997). On psychology, historical epistemology and the teaching of mathematics: Towards a socio-cultural history of mathematics. *For the Learning of Mathematics, 17*, 26–33.

Rakes, C. R., Valentine, J. C., McGatha, M. B., & Ronau, R. N. (2010). Methods of instructional improvement in Algebra: A systematic review and meta-analysis. *Review of Educational Research, 80*(3), 372–400. doi:10.3102/0034654310374880

Robey, E. (Ed.). (1992). *Opening the doors: Using technology to improve education for students with disabilities*. Silver Spring, MD: Macro International Inc.

Robin, B. (2008). *Handbook of research on teaching literacy through the communicative and visual arts* (Vol. 2). New York: Lawrence Erlbaum Associates.

Robin, B. R. (2008). Digital storytelling: A powerful technology tool for the 21st century classroom. *Theory into Practice, 47*(3), 220–228. doi:10.1080/00405840802153916

Sadik, A. (2008). Digital storytelling: A meaningful technology-integrated approach for engaged student learning. *Educational Technology Research and Development, 56*(4), 487–506. doi:10.1007/s11423-008-9091-8

Schiro, M. (2004). *Oral storytelling and teaching mathematics*. Thousand Oaks, CA: SAGE Publications.

Schram, P., Wilcox, S. K., Lapan, G., & Lanier, P. (1988). Changing preservice teachers' beliefs about mathematics education. In C. A. Mahers, G. A. Goldin, & R. B. Davis (Eds.), *Proceedings of PME-NA 11* (Vol. 1, pp. 296-302). New Brunswick, NJ: Rutgers University.

Schrum, L. (1995, April). *Telecommunications for personal and professional uses: A case study.* Paper presented at the annual meeting of the American Educational Research: Association, San Francisco.

Sheingold, K., & Hadley, M. (1990). *Accomplished teachers: Integrating computers into classroom practice.* New York: Bank Street College of Education, Center for Technology in Education.

Shelton, M., & Jones, M. (1996). Staff development that works! A tale of four T's. *NAASP Bulletin, 80*(582), 99–105. doi:10.1177/019263659608058214

Siu, M.-K. (2004). No, I do not use history of mathematics in my class. Why? In S. Kaijser (Ed.), *History and pedagogy of mathematics: Proceedings of HPM 2004* (pp. 375-376). Uppsala, Sweden: HPM.

Slavin, R. E., & Lake, C. (2008). Effective programs in elementary mathematics: A best evidence synthesis. *Review of Educational Research, 78*(3), 427–455. doi:10.3102/0034654308317473

Slavin, R. E., Lake, C., & Groff, C. (2009). Effective programs in middle and high school mathematics: A best evidence synthesis. *Review of Educational Research, 79*(2), 839–911. doi:10.3102/0034654308330968

Smestad, B. (2009). *Teachers' conceptions of history of mathematics.* Retrieved from http://home.hio.no/~bjorsme/HPM2008paper.pdf

Stander, D. (1989). The use of the history of mathematics in teaching. In P. Ernest (Ed.), *Mathematics teaching: The state of the art* (pp. 241–246). Philadelphia, PA: The Falmer Press.

Swetz, F., Fauvel, J., Bekken, O., Johansson, B., & Katz, V. (Eds.). (1995). *Learn from the masters.* Washington, DC: The Mathematical Association of America.

Swetz, F. J. (1994). *Learning activities from the history of mathematics.* Portland, ME: J. Weston Walch.

Trotter, A. (1997). Taking technology's measure. *Education Week, 17*(11), 6–11.

Tsou, W., Wang, W., & Tzeng, Y. (2006). Applying a multimedia storytelling website in foreign language learning. *Computers & Education, 47*(1), 17–28. doi:10.1016/j.compedu.2004.08.013

U.S. Department of Education. (2008). *National educational technology trends study: Local-level data summary.* Washington, DC: Office of Planning, Evaluation and Policy Development, Policy and Program Studies Service.

Wager, W. (1992). Educational technology: A broader vision. *Education and Urban Society, 24*(4), 454–465. doi:10.1177/0013124592024004003

Ware, P. D. (2006). From sharing time to showtime! Valuing diverse venues for storytelling in technology-rich classrooms. *Language Arts, 84*(1), 45–54.

Weng Kin, H. (2008). Using history of mathematics in the teaching and learning of mathematics in Singapore. In *Proceedings of 1st RICE*, Singapore.

Wenglinsky, H. (2005). *Using technology wisely: The keys to success in schools.* New York, NY: Teachers College Press.

Windschitl, M., & Sahl, K. (2002). Tracing teachers' use of technology in a laptop computer school: The interplay of teacher beliefs, social dynamics, and institutional culture. *American Educational Research Journal, 39*(1), 165–205. doi:10.3102/00028312039001165

Yang, Y. T. C., & Wu, W. C. I. (2012). Digital storytelling for enhancing student academic achievement, critical thinking, and learning motivation: A year-long experimental study. *Computers & Education, 59*(2), 339–352. doi:10.1016/j.compedu.2011.12.012

Yuksel, P. (2011). *Using digital storytelling in early childhood education: A phenomenological study of teachers' experiences* (Upublished doctoral dissertation), Middle East Technical University, Ankara.

Yuksel, P., Robin, B., & McNeil, S. (2010). Educational uses of digital storytelling around the world. In *Proceedings of Society for Information Technology & Teacher Education International Conference* (pp. 1264-1271). Chesapeake, VA: AACE. 2011.

Yuksel Arslan, P. (2013). Eğitim amaçlı dijital öykünün hazırlanması ve kullanılması: TPAB temelli örnek bir Fen Bilgisi eğitimi uygulaması. In Tuğba Yanpar Yelken, Hatice Sancar Tokmak, Sinan Özgelen ve Lutfi İncikabı (eds.), Fen ve matematik eğitiminde teknolojik, pedagojik alan bilgisi (TPAB) temelli öğretim tasarımları (pp.106-128). Ankara: Anı Publishing.

Zbiek, R. M., Heid, M. K., Blume, G. W., & Dick, T. P. (2007). Research on technology in mathematics education: A perspective of constructs. In F. Lester (Ed.), *Second handbook of research on mathematics teaching and learning* (pp. 1169–1208). Reston, VA: National Council of Teachers on Mathematics.

Zbiek, R. M., & Hollebrands, K. (2008). A research-informed view of the process of incorporating mathematics technology into classroom practice by inservice and prospective teachers. In M. K. Heid & G. W. Blume (Eds.), *Research on technology and the teaching and learning of mathematics* (Vol. 1, pp. 287–344). Charlotte, NC: Information Age.

KEY TERMS AND DEFINITIONS

Digital Storytelling: Technique that stories are narrated and enhanced through multimedia devices and passed on to audiences.

Educational Technology: The term of educational technology generally refers to the introduction of computers and related pieces of equipment to the classroom.

History of Mathematics: The area of study is primarily an investigation into the origin of discoveries in mathematics and, to a lesser extent, an investigation into the mathematical methods and notation of the past (http://en.wikipedia.org/wiki/History_of_mathematics).

Instructional Technology: The systemic and systematic application of strategies and techniques derived from behavioral and physical sciences concepts and other knowledge to the solution of instructional problems (Gentry, 2002, p.7).

Chapter 9
Active Learning, Deliberate Practice, and Educational Technology in Professional Education:
Practices and Implications

Heeyoung Han
Southern Illinois University School of Medicine, USA

Seung Hyun Han
University of Illinois, USA

Doo Hun Lim
University of Oklahoma, USA

Seung Won Yoon
Western Illinois University, USA

ABSTRACT

This chapter is an interdisciplinary literature review on pedagogical approaches and technological integration processes to facilitating active learning and deliberate practice toward expertise in professional education. The review covers selective domains that emphasize life-long learning, including teacher education, professional music education, athletic education, and medical education. The authors' review finds that concepts and principles of active learning are recognized in all of them and technology is frequently implemented to facilitate the process of active learning, but systematic and system-wide processes for incorporating active learning with deliberate practice are lacking, especially at the institution or curriculum level. To fill the gap, the authors discuss how the selected instructional design or established performance improvement processes in the educational technology literature can be applied.

DOI: 10.4018/978-1-4666-8363-1.ch009

INTRODUCTION

Active learning has been recognized as a foundational pedagogical concept in the last several decades. Despite the widespread use of the concept in various educational fields, its core elements and desired implementation in relation to educational technology in professional educational areas are not clear yet. Active learning is generally understood as a type of instructional strategy or method involving learners' active engagement in the learning process. Beyond passively receiving information from the instructor, active learners identify their own learning needs, seek learning resources, process and interpret information, and metacognitively manage their learning processes through reflections on what they are learning and doing (Bonwell, Eison, & Association for the Study of Higher Education, 1991). This learner-centered concept of active learning has been widely adopted and supported in professional education fields such as medical education. It is argued that instructor-centered curricula, such as lecture-based credit courses, insufficiently prepare students to transfer their school learning to clinical settings (Barrows, 2000). Particularly, problem-based learning (PBL), a contemporary instructional development method branched out of active learning, has grown in this context to promote students' active and deep learning experiences.

In PBL, lectures are not the central activities in the curriculum. Instead, PBL in medical education mainly focuses on students' learning in small groups and uses an authentic patient problem as an anchor to build up and measure students' knowledge. Thus, PBL typically involves a considerable amount of self-directed learning on the part of learners (Barrows, 1988, 2000; Barrows & Wee, 2007). In some schools, lectures are viewed as one of many available resources that students can access instead of required activities to attend. At others, lectures are still a foundation in curriculum to build upon clinical experiences.

Most importantly, there is little consensus on what active learning is in professional education and how it should be practiced.

Recent growing interest and exploration of flipped classrooms in medical education shows the imperative need for leveraging the concept of active learning in technology-rich environments (Han, Resch, & Kovach, 2013; Prober & Khan, 2013). Instructional strategies that emphasized student-centered learning have long existed (e.g., simulation, inquiry-based learning, inductive learning, and cognitive apprenticeship), but flipped classrooms provide additional innovative benefits in the curriculum in that the traditional primacy of information acquisition in classroom and subsequent problem solving outside the classroom are replaced by the students' authentic problem solving in class guided by teachers (Berrett, 2012). We believe that technology holds a key to advancing the notion and practice of active learning as well as curriculum innovation in professional education. The central tenet of active learning is for the learner to discover their knowledge deficiency and improve on it in the deep process and struggle of achieving their desired learning and performance goals. Effective learning environments tend to allow learners to safely struggle to fill their knowledge and skill gaps (Coyle, 2009).

Current discussion of educational technologies in professional education is largely limited to affordances and potentials that selective tools provide. Technology integration for active learning should address this need for students to struggle in the sense of identifying and constructing meaning and gain knowledge in a safe and authentic environment. Additionally, students require deliberate practice during deep learning to be professionally competent. Therefore, it is important to understand how the notion of active learning through technology integration should be extended to a discussion of deliberate practice in professional education. Given the value of outcome-based and competence-based education, deliberate learner thought-action practices and processes must be promoted in technology integration. For that goal, this paper will report the result of an interdisciplinary literature review on technological integration processes and the pedagogical opportunities for facilitating active learning and deliberate practice toward expertise in professional education. The review will cover selective domains that emphasize life-long learning, including teacher education, professional music education, athletic training and education, and medical education. The paper will also discuss technological and pedagogical implications for professional education.

Professional Education and Deliberate Practice

Professional education is an educational process or program that develops individuals for professional practice. Professionals are highly educated and intensively trained individuals who serve the community through their professions (Hoberman & Mailick, 1994). They become professionals generally through professional education, which qualifies them to be part of a professional community with similar education, training, and practices. Therefore, "professional education is directed toward helping students acquire special competencies for diagnosing specific needs and for determining, recommending, and taking appropriate action"(Hoberman & Mailick, 1994, p. 3). Once individuals become professionals, they have a great deal of autonomy in their jobs and make decisions based on their own professional competence with minimum supervision. Examples include medical education, teacher education, athletic training, music, and law.

Professional education is practice-centered; therefore, practice sites become the ultimate places for learning and inquiry. Book learning or classroom learning can be part of the educational process yet should ultimately be transferred to workplace practice. Given this emphasis on practice, professional education has its own pedagogical characteristics. Davidoff (2011) elicited ten

aspects of professional education by comparing the professionalization of medicine with professional musician development.

1. One of the main characteristics is the emphasis of performance. In professional education, performance is an essential learning goal and should be appreciated in authentic professional contexts.

2. Coaching that provides meaningful and timely feedback in performance development is another essential part of professional education. "Great teachers… are coaches, not lecturers" (p. 426).

3. Teachers have to move back and forth in their roles between master teachers and performers in a workplace. Students also do so by moving between actor and observer roles.

4. Professional performance is not formed by biological gifts but developed only through practice, training, and experience.

5. Professional expertise requires a lot of time to be developed. Longitudinal efforts and seamless curriculum plans are essential in professional education.

6. Expertise is demonstrated for brief moments, yet a massive amount of deliberate practice exists behind the exceptional performance.

7. Acquiring technical skills are essential but not sufficient. Professional practice often goes beyond technical skills and requires nontechnical aspect of practice, such as caring of patients and professionalism.

8. Teamwork is a crucial element in developing professional expertise. Developing learners to perform in a teamwork environment dealing with various kinds of realities is one of the areas that professional education should consider.

9. Standardized practice is important for basic needs and performance, yet it is also essential to develop abilities to deviate from standardized practice for necessary adjustment for performance.

10. Professionals choose a specialty for their career within the profession and are required to develop a deeper understanding and practice in the area.

Given the characteristics of professional education that Davidoff (2011) identified, pedagogy to develop professionals is centered in practice and performance in real environments. Proposing future directions for teacher education, Ball and Cohen (1999) also recognized the value of authentic practice in professional education. Professional education should make real artifacts of practice available for learners' inquiry because it is critical to develop practical knowledge to perform in a profession. Practical knowledge does not simply indicate skills but holistic and integrated sets of abilities to function as a professional. Therefore, professional education should ground its curriculum in the critical activities, authentic tasks, questions, and problems of practice (Ball & Cohen, 1999).

Investigating how professional talents are developed, Coyle (2009) identified a central process of developing talent: Learners overcome knowledge and performance gaps through struggles in connecting learning with practice. Struggling and working hard on problems and skill gaps helps learners retain knowledge and skills more effectively for their practice. Ball and Cohen (1999) also recognized the importance of deep learning and deep practice focusing on problems that allow learners to have opportunities for inquiry. Working on disequilibrium is required for deep learning in professional education. Deliberate practice is widely recognized as another critical technique in pedagogy in professional education (Ball & Cohen, 1999; Coyle, 2009; Ericsson, 2004). Developed professional skills are not unchanged but decay without deliberate practice. Repeated deep practice is required to maintain and constantly refine expertise and professional performance. While it has been recognized that professional education has specific aspects of teaching and learning and different pedagogical demands, implementing the ideas of deep learning and deliberate practice in professional education has also been challenging.

Active Learning

In education, active learning is known to boost learner control and self-regulation. It allows learners to actively identify learning goals, solve problems, and constantly evaluate their learning and performance (Weimer, 2002). In that environment, the critical role of instructor is to guide learners towards discovery and knowledge construction. The foundational concept of active learning is drawn from constructive orientation of learning, in which knowledge must be built through internal cognitive processes utilizing learners' own mental representations of the real world, often called *schemata*. In this process, the learner should construct the accumulation of new knowledge and is responsible for his or her own knowledge building (Bransford, Brown, & Cocking, 1999). In this sense, one primary notion of active learning can be claimed as "the iterative process of building mental models from existing and new information and testing these models" within the professional community (Michael & Modell, 2003, p. 6). This constructive approach of active learning has several implications for meaningful learning:

1. Learning processes for declarative and procedural knowledge are differentiated, as each requires different knowledge accumulation patterns;
2. Appropriate feedback and practice opportunities for procedural learning are critical for active learning to occur; and
3. Collaborative and cooperative activities are central to active learning (Michael & Modell, 2003).

As a result of active learning, learners will possess the capabilities to solve problems and apply knowledge to both foreign and familiar contexts.

In practical educational settings, such as K-12 classrooms and professional education, teachers and instructors view active learning as a process in which students are intensely engaged and both mentally and physically involved. The following are key characteristics of instructional situations in which active learning is applied:

1. Learners are energetic and intense;
2. Learners are excited and emotionally involved;
3. Instructors tend to relate learning to learners' career or life goals;
4. Instructors utilize various strategies for active learning using art, movement, and senses; and
5. They vary the pace and type of learning activities to keep learners mentally aroused and challenged (Hollingsworth & Lewis, 2006).

One unique state of active learning is that instructors intentionally control the flow of the learners' state of consciousness so that they can be intensely immersed in learning activities while enjoying the learning process itself (Csikszentmihalyi, 1990). Rea (2003) conceptualized this immersive learning state as *serious-fun*. More specifically, for active learning to happen in instructional settings, the following instructional strategies and techniques may be used:

1. Strategies for active start to learning (e.g., team building, active learning analysis, start-up collaborative learning techniques);
2. Strategies for the active process of learning (e.g., techniques for active lecture, active discussions, active questioning, active team learning, active peer tutoring); and
3. Strategies for sustaining active learning (e.g., active review session, self-evaluation, action planning) (Silberman, 1996).

In contemporary learning theories, some variations of active learning can be found. For example, collaborative learning resembles active learning in that it emphasizes the collaborative and interactive nature of learning process among learners toward a common learning goal within group learning settings (Cuseo, 1992). Cooperative learning shares characteristics similar to active learning in that it is structured to facilitate learning in group settings where each individual learner cooperates together to achieve common goals. In problem-based learning (PBL), real-life problems are introduced to initiate instruction followed by intense self-directed learning conducted by the learner and active engagement in learning process to solve problems (Barrows, 1988, 2000; Barrows & Wee, 2007). Another important aspect of active learning is that, originally, the concept emphasized the process of active individual learning, and over the years, collaborative processes within a community that shares the same goal or interest have been recognized as another key element. In answering a question about whether active learning and these variations of active learning work improve learning, Prince (2004) conducted a number of meta-analyses and found that active learning, collaborative learning, cooperative learning, and problem-based learning promote learners' perception of learning progress, learning outcomes, and satisfaction from learning.

Role of Educational Technology in Active Learning and Deliberate Practice

Traditionally, in the field of school and corporate education, technology was implemented to enhance various aspects of direct instruction and learning (e.g., presenting multimedia information, managing files, completing diagnostic tests, and automating learner feedback). Nowadays, technology is conceptualized as a strategic force and the primary source of obtaining and sharing knowledge. Numerous related terms exist, particularly instructional technology, learning technology, educational technology, and performance technology. Understanding similarities and distinctions among these terms and adopting a clear picture of what technology is and must do for active learning and deliberate practice are important.

Reiser and Dempsey (2012) explained that instruction is a systematic approach to structuring learning; therefore, both instructional and learning technology focus on creating desirable conditions and behaviors to facilitate learning, largely at the micro-level (i.e., individual, small group, or classroom). They stated that educational technology is commonly used in K-12 and postsecondary education settings to investigate macro-level curriculum or systemwide use of technology, but educational and instructional technology are frequently used interchangeably, and the former is probably more familiar to professionals in other fields. Performance technology was born out of the recognition that the effectiveness of instructional approaches is limited to solving knowledge-, skills-, or attitude-related (KSA) problems only. Many problems at work require using both instructional (e.g., training and structured self-paced learning) and non-instructional solutions (e.g., culture, incentives, and work processes improvement). For the discussion of using technology for active learning of professionals at individual, institutional, and community levels, we adopted the term *educational technology* here.

Yoon (2008) stated that technology is a systematic treatment of art and craft that finds contextualized meaning from the application of knowledge in a particular domain to accomplish targeted tasks using technical processes, methods, knowledge, or tools. As seen in labels such as *educational* or *medical technology* the effectiveness and efficiency of solutions greatly matter. Frameworks for strategically selecting, designing, implementing, and evaluating technology (e.g., instructional design, learning activities, or collaboration software) for active learning and deliberate practice at both the micro- (individuals, group, or classroom) and the macro- (curriculum,

institution, or discipline) levels for professional education are necessary. Depending on the goal of an individual professional, an institution that trains future professionals, or a discipline that certifies them (one form of community), to promote, coordinate, and systematize active learning and deliberate practice, educational technology should be conceptualized as systematic technological processes to improve learning experience and performance toward professional competence (Han et al., 2013).

The literature of instructional technology, learning technology, educational technology, and performance technology present numerous useful frameworks for integrating tools with instructional or learning processes. For example, at the individual or course level, David Merrill's First Principles of Instruction framework (2002) highlighted that establishing an authentic problem first, and then anchoring and sequencing the components of:

1. Learning activation (e.g., prior knowledge and advance organizers),
2. Demonstration (e.g., worked examples and learner guidance),
3. Application (e.g., practice, feedback, and coaching), and
4. Integration (e.g., performance, creation, and reflection)

This helps trigger learner otivation, analysis, new content acquisition, thought processes, practice, and internalization. In presenting this framework, Merrill (2002) extracted learning principles reported from empirical studies of behaviorism, cognitive learning, and constructivism. There are other widely practiced frameworks, including Gagné's Nine Events of Instruction (Gagné, Briggs, & Wager, 1992), the ADDIE (Analysis, Design, Development, Implementation, and Evaluation) model (Dick, Carey, & Carey, 2000), and the 4C/ID model (van Merriënboer, Clark, & de Croock, 2002). The Nine Events of Instruction (triggering attention, informing objectives, relating to prior knowledge, presenting content, providing learner guidance, eliciting performance, giving feedback, assessing performance, and enhancing retention and transfer) is grounded on the cognitive learning theories of attention, perception, working memory, and long-term memory. The ADDIE model and its variations are popular in corporate training and manifest a strong root in behaviorism by working with observable and measurable behaviors and reinforcing desirable behaviors. In comparison, grounded on the cognitive load theory (knowledge about how working memory works and is limited), the 4C/ID model emphasizes the proper mix of a whole task and part tasks for complex problem-solving by utilizing integrative objectives, coordinating problem-solving challenges, and utilizing job aids for non-recurrent tasks and procedural information. Although each framework is slightly different in terms of core theoretical grounds, all existing design frameworks aim to systematically improve motivation, cognition, and learning environments.

Macro-level frameworks that guide the use of technology system-wide are relatively few in number because core skills, processes, and learning needs differ across professions and organizations). Nevertheless, discussion of technology at this level, especially in organizations or communities, is important because active learning and deliberate practice are no longer domains of individual or structured group-level learning activities. Active learning and deliberate practice prosper when a larger system, particularly an institution or professional community, actively defines and attracts the process of learning and practice. When members' learning is closely aligned with the larger system's strategic initiatives, particularly work practices and talent management, impactful active learning and deliberate practice can be sustained. One example at the organizational level is the Learning and Performance Architecture, which incorporates onsite and e-learning, knowledge management (information repository, virtual communities,

and expertise network), electronic performance support systems, and coaching and mentoring with change management (Rosenberg, 2005). In such an environment, individuals have access to various formal and informal learning channels as well as human and impersonal resources to connect learning with work.

Study Purpose

Given the roles of educational technology and the pedagogical importance of active learning and deliberate practice in professional education, in this paper, we have two research questions:

- How are concepts or principles of active learning, deliberate practices, and educational technology practiced in major professional education fields?
- What are the pedagogical integration processes and effects of technologies on active learning or deliberate practice in professional education?

To answer each question, we conducted an interdisciplinary literature review on technological integration processes and their pedagogical effect on facilitating active learning and deliberate practice toward expertise in professional education. The review covers selective domains that emphasize lifelong learning, including teacher education, professional music education, athletic training and education, and medical education.

METHODS

This study mainly focuses on active learning, deliberate practice, and educational technology in professional education. A literature search was conducted to identify studies related to the topics of technological integration process for active learning and deliberate practice in professional education. As such, the literature review first identified key search words for accessing relevant research. Particular keywords included "active learning," "deliberate learning," and "educational technology," and these terms were applied to electronic library searches via Searching the Web of Science and EBSCO for full peer-reviewed papers from 1994 to 2014, and using those keywords, we retrieved 266 articles. After reviewing the titles, we chose 86 articles for the abstract review. Since the selected articles were mostly from health care, we searched the same database using different keywords, including "sports; athletics" and "music". The expanded search provided an additional 90 results. After two scholars set a priority for journal articles and reviewed the titles of the papers, 29 articles were selected for the abstract review. From the abstract review of 115 articles in total, we selected 21 articles for the full paper review. After reading the full papers and independently reviewing the articles, 16 papers were selected to be included. In addition to this selection process, we included related papers through snowball methods by reviewing sources in the selected literature. In doing so, the researchers reviewed how the source would enhance the contribution of this study to the literature in general.

FINDINGS

Technology Integration Process for Active Learning in Professional Education

Findings from the literature review will be reported, synthesized, and discussed in this section. In order to answer the research questions, the summary will focus on current issues and solutions, applications of active learning and deliberate practice, and technological integration processes and impacts.

Teacher Education. In this section, we review the practice of teacher education (particularly in the United States and Finland), the nature and

extent of active learning in teacher education, and what is discussed and should receive more attention in the future. The preparation and continuous development of teachers are addressed in the literature review of pre-service teacher education and professional development. Pre-service teacher education is the education and training provided to student teachers before they are certified to teach officially. Although student teachers are certified after passing a test, teacher certification reciprocity across countries and states in the United States is a very complicated matter.

In the U.S., requirements to become a teacher vary by state. One who plans to teach in another state must be reviewed by that state for meeting the qualifications even between states under a reciprocity agreement. To overcome the teacher shortage and promote certification reciprocity, there are interstate and regional agreements as well as a national certificate, but teachers are still required to earn their state's teaching credentials to teach in a public education system. Pre-service teacher education programs are not designed the same across institutions in the U.S., but most programs offer courses in areas of classroom management, creating instruction, technology integration, and a practicum in addition to subject-domain content. In Finland, a country known to excel in students' academic performance and teacher preparation, the teacher education curriculum include studies in academic disciplines, research studies consisting of methodology courses and theses, pedagogical studies and teaching practice (starting very early in the program), communication and technology, and a personal study plan (Niemi, 2012).

After reviewing studies on teaching trends as well as teachers' education reforms, Hans and Akhter (2013) stated that teacher education programs fall into one of the following four traditions:

1. Academic tradition (emphasizing disciplinary knowledge),
2. Social efficiency tradition (competency- and performance-driven),

3. Developmental tradition (personal growth through involvement and commitment), and
4. Social reconstruction tradition (active agent of social changes and student development).

They also pointed out that many who enter the workforce are underprepared to deal with emerging trends of digital literacy and technology usage, which are essential for preparing students for increasingly technological futures.

Niemi (2012) reported that in Europe, teachers' competencies have been shaped by a broad view of teachers' role as a researcher and a reflective practitioner whose responsibilities entail

1. Working with others;
2. Working with knowledge, technology, and information; and
3. Working with and in society.

As such, teachers' core competencies include designing their own instruction, cooperation, ethical commitment to teaching, diversity of pupils and preparing them for the future, and commitment to their own professional learning. According to Niemi (2012), Finland's teacher education curriculum is an exemplary manifestation of active learning in that student teachers actively engage in both individual and collaborative processes of designing and improving solutions in response to variations in students' and communal needs. Experiences gained from working on community problems with others in the community; working closely with the learners to resolve individual learning needs; and displaying collegial, ethical, and lifelong learning orientations reflect the heavy emphasis placed on deliberate practice as part of Finland's teacher education. In the U.S., other than a teaching practicum, service learning has been implemented to connect meaningful community service with academic learning and civic responsibilities. However, one national survey found that although about two thirds of all teacher education programs use service learning in one

way or another, it is far from standardized, and its role in the entire curriculum is peripheral (Anderson & Erickson, 1999). When samples of teachers were interviewed, lack of time, overcrowded curriculum, lack of alignment with faculty roles, and institutional priorities were identified as major barriers to the successful use of service learning (Anderson & Pickeral, 1999). When teachers' competencies and their active learning experiences were correlated, highly positive correlations were found between active learning and professional competencies, notably in areas of the teachers' own professional learning and responding to diverse student needs (Niemi, 2012).

Technology for teacher education is a complex matter that involves numerous topics, including adoption, integration into teaching, pedagogical effectiveness, skills development, and management, to name a few. Although the concepts of active learning and deliberate practice are not new, strategic and explicit alignment between active learning, deliberate practice and technology is. For the purpose of this study, we focus our review on what roles or impacts technology has on teachers' active learning or deliberate practice. Numerous studies have reported positive effects of new technology on various aspects of active learning and deep practice, such as instructional gaming on experiential learning and flow (Kiili, 2005), virtual worlds on problem authenticity and diverse perspectives (Jarmon, Traphagan, Mayrath, & Trevidi, 2009) and social networks on engagement (van Puijenbroek, Poell, Kroon, & Timmerman, 2014). Originally intending to study how leaders used technology effectively to improve student achievement and school improvements, Schrum and Levin (2013) found that behind all eight award-winning schools, teachers who took leadership roles by strengthening classroom practice, taking ownership of change, taking up expert teacher roles, and engaging in collegiality for mutual learning were key for school success.

Although the concept and principles of active learning expected of students are clear to most teachers, technology education for teachers focuses exclusively on how to use hardware or software tools. Koehler and Mishra (2005) found that when teachers work collaboratively in small groups to develop technological solutions to solve authentic pedagogical problems, teachers' technology learning – engagement, mastery, and transfer – was most effective. They called this approach *learning-by-design*. Our experiences also support their findings. One of the authors has taught in an instructional technology department at a Midwestern state university, and the program offers one undergraduate-level course in technology integration for pre-service teachers. In that course, about several years ago, the content was basic computer skills, Microsoft Office programs, and instructional management software, but over the years, demands for interactive and free web tools increased. Topics on learning about software and hardware were replaced with problem-solving tasks utilizing interactive processes and tools such as the SMART Board, mobile platforms, and easy-to-publish-share-tools, including blogging, wikis, social bookmarking, and social networks (Richardson, 2010). Course revision also included changes in assignments and projects that strengthened individual experimentation, original work creation, and peer collaboration and critique. Such changes led to a significant increase in student satisfaction and willingness to transfer content learned in that course. The same person's experience from teaching in-service teachers at the master's level is not much different. Some districts partner with a local university or provide financial assistance to teachers who complete a post-baccalaureate degree or certificate after they are hired, but professional development at work seems largely limited to learning new tools (e.g., blogging, Google suites, or virtual conferencing) and rarely goes deeper to address pedagogy or foster a community of learning or practice. Apparently, how technology education connects between the pre-service and the in-service level and how teachers' post-baccalaureate learning

of educational technology is used to bring about active learning and school improvements are fertile grounds for further research. Moreover, their learned technology skills will decay over time, yet there is little scholarly endeavor to formalize instructional design and technology in the teacher education curriculum.

Medical Education. Changes to the healthcare environment have triggered major shifts in medical education (Irby & Wilkerson, 2003; Szulewski & Davidson, 2008). The environmental changes include more ambulatory patient visits, shorter hospitalization, reduced resident work hours, increased clinical duties for faculty, and an increased number of students. In this situation, learners have less opportunity to follow patients for comprehensive assessment and diagnosis, treatment, management, and care. Moreover, there is less time for attending physicians or residents to spend for teaching novice learners because patient care is their top priority given the limited resources. However, it is critical for students to develop appropriate clinical competencies as they begin their careers in the healthcare industry. Despite the fact that medical education should help students achieve learning objectives most effectively and ultimately their professional competence for their medical practice through more active engagement in learning and practice, most medical schools heavily rely on a lecture-based curriculum even during clerkship rotations. Some forms of traditional education (such as lectures and dyadic presentations) focus on only how they deliver the learning content to students in an effective way; little attention is paid to how learners actively learn through deep practice.

Despite the challenges, active learning and deliberate practice have received considerable attention in medical education. The main premise for applying active learning and deliberate practice to medical education is the recognition that learning should be student-centered, practice-oriented, and ultimately aligned with the learning outcomes of improved medical competence and patient care in practice. Active learning activities promote thoughtful engagement, encourage analytical thinking and reasoning, foster the integration and application of knowledge, and are designed around well-defined learning objectives (Graffam, 2007). This deep learning process through active learning such as PBL can help learners transfer learning to real healthcare practice much better than traditional passive learning (Vernon & Blake, 1993). Students no longer learn entirely from didactic lecture and multiple-choice exams. Instead, based on an assumption that learning is a constructive process, students experience patient cases and learn how to solve patient problems through action and collaboration (Chi, Bassok, Lewis, Reimann, & Glaser, 1989). Students actively engage in a learning process by identifying problems and their knowledge gaps, seeking related learning resources, solving problems, sharing ideas, giving feedback, and teaching one another. Moreover, active learning incorporates evaluation and feedback as part of the learning process for self-reflections and self-directed learning in order to ensure coherence and consistency for lifelong learning capability (Dori & Belcher, 2005; Dornan, Brown, Powley, & Hopkins, 2004). Formal clinical clerkship teaching that involves didactic seminars presented by faculty shifted recently from the traditional, lecture-based model of teaching towards new instructional methods designed to encourage student-centered learning (Dornan et al., 2004; Gill, Kitney, Kozan, & Lewis, 2010).

In addition, scholarly research in clinical medicine about the acquisition of expertise consistently shows the importance of deliberate practice in achieving desired educational outcomes. Learners should develop skills and knowledge through deliberate practice to become competent physicians (Ericsson, 2004). Deliberate practice does not simply imply repeated practice but constant development of skills and knowledge through repeated deep practice. Issenberg, McGaghie, Petrusa, Gordon, and Scalese (2005) explained that deliberate practice has four main categories:

1. Repetitive performance of intended cognitive psychomotor skills, coupled with
2. Rigorous skills assessment that provides learners with
3. Specific, informative feedback that results in increasingly
4. Better skills performance in a controlled setting.

Empirical research shows that deliberate practice, not just time and experience in clinical settings, is the key to the development of medical clinical competence. For example, a series of research studies conducted by Issenberg and his colleagues showed that the intervention group engaged in deliberate practice acquired nearly twice the core skills (80% performance level) in half the time as the comparison group (two weeks) with little faculty involvement (Issenberg et al., 1999). A replicated study found nearly identical results (Issenberg et al., 2005).

Given the external environmental changes and internal demands for better quality of curriculum, medical school reform has become a hot issue throughout the world (Irby, Cooke, & O'Brien, 2010; Irby & Wilkerson, 2003; Pugsley & McCrorie, 2007). There have been many efforts to innovate curriculum toward active learning and deliberate practice in medical education. Moreover, technological integration processes to facilitate active learning and deliberate practice have been discussed for the last several decades, which includes flipped classrooms, online learning including e-PBL and virtual patients, and simulation (Cook, Levinson, & Garside, 2010; Issenberg et al., 2005; Kim & Kee, 2013; McLaughlin et al., 2014; Prober & Khan, 2013; Rosen, McBride, & Drake, 2009; Scalese, Obeso, & Issenberg, 2008).

Redefining value-added instructional activities, Han et al. (2013) discussed the future direction of educational technology in medical education. Connecting the concept of flipped classroom to "lean medical education", they argued that the technological integration process should focus on providing individualized instruction targeted to learners' study needs. Non interactive lectures on foundational knowledge, which do not add much value, can be standardized and available online as resources to students anytime, anywhere, whereas small-group learning or personalized instruction with teachers' individual feedback on areas that learners struggle should be centered for value-added instructional practices (Han et al., 2013; Prober & Khan, 2013).

Web courseware, e-learning, computer-aided tutorials, library resources, and blogs as knowledge management have been discussed as technological processes for student-centered deep learning in medical education. They are developed to provide student-led access to curricular and instructional information and feedback (Gill et al., 2010; Irby & Wilkerson, 2003). Hudson (2004) indicated that computer-aided learning designed with active interaction with learning resources and interactive feedback would result in a statistically significant improvement in students' ability to apply and retain knowledge in the field of medical education. The average test score of a treatment group is 4 times higher than the groups using traditional passive learning methods. Blended e-learning has been discussed as a way to maximize the quality of learning in clerkship. With the blended e-learning system "Acute Hand Injuries" for clerkship students, Szulewski and Davidson (2008) were able to revise a 60-minute didactic lecture-based seminar into a 30-minute interactive case-based seminar. Even though they did not find a statistically significant difference in quiz performance between an experimental group and a control group due to the small number of participants, they found that the students in the experimental group were more engaged and confident in their knowledge through studying cases.

Simulations have become another powerful technological process that promotes active learning and deliberate practice. Advances in technology have also made advancements in medical education possible by applying an increased

amount of high-fidelity simulations to sustain learning. Student can practice field applications through technological simulations (of hospital settings or trauma situations, for example) with unlimited practice opportunities, increased access to individual feedback, and reflection with neither risking patient safety nor cost. For example, Issenberg et al. (1999) argued that procedural skills, perceptual interpretation, and clinical knowledge are enhanced through interaction with technologically enriched simulators, from full-body mannequins to virtual reality programs. A meta-analysis showed that high-fidelity simulators led to effective learning by providing feedback on learning experiences and engaging learners in deliberate practice (Issenberg et al., 2005; McGaghie, Issenberg, Petrusa, & Scalese, 2010).

While many efforts have been made to develop technological process to facilitate active learning and deliberate practice in medical education as discussed above, there are several areas to be considered for future directions. First, pedagogical change in curriculum and faculty development still remains challenging (Graffam, 2007; White et al., 2014). Even if innovation is part of the medical education landscape, it has been largely confined to new medical schools and to small activities applied to a single course (Gibson, 2000). Second, few technological efforts have been made to facilitate active learning and deliberate practice in students' workplace learning contexts, such as clerkships. Clerkship experience itself can be viewed as an active learning process, as students go to clinics and hospitals, engage in patient care, and learn through immersive experiences. Students expect to learn experts' clinical reasoning and decision making through participating in patient care during clerkships, yet they have limited access to experts' thought processes in real situations (Han, Roberts, & Korte, in press). Therefore, the clerkship curriculum is ironically didactic and lecture-based. Third, appropriate assessments to measure outcomes of active learning and deliberate practice should also be discussed. Active learning and deliberate practice aim for long-term knowledge retention, application, problem solving, and continuous competence development, which cannot be comparable with students' performance assessments in multiple-choice quizzes. In a usage of technology application, Fehr, Honkanen, and Murray (2012) argued that simulation is not only the most effective method for trainees to develop skills and experience, but it also satisfies the needs of education reform and offers the potential to guide efforts toward evaluating competence for continuous development. More in-depth discussion for assessments of active learning and deliberate practice is necessary.

Athletic Education. Like the medical education field, athletic education has been one of the primary fields undergoing reform in educational structure and competency standards in recent years. For example, the National Athletic Trainers' Association (NATA) has revised the Athletic Training Educational Competencies and requirements for certification indicating a shift away from quantity-oriented training and education toward quality-oriented educational practices (Laurent & Weidner, 2001). As this kind of change has emerged, efforts to utilize active learning strategies and practices have been ardently pursued among athletic trainers and educators. As a typical example, many athletic and sports-related training and education programs strongly advocate the use of the clinical education approach with an attempt to provide optimal education to learners entering athletic and sports education degree programs. The rationale to move toward this approach is that faculty in the athletic training and education programs believe it allows increased opportunities for learners in the athletic field with more diverse learning options for the purpose of professional development. In addition, a clinically oriented approach for athletic training and education is believed to improve professional development for athletic trainers and educators, as learners can learn modeling professional behaviors during clinical settings (Laurent & Weidner, 2001).

Clinical internships allow good opportunities for learners to observe how instructors and trainers in athletic training function as a team.

An interesting phenomenon in athletic and sports training and education is the calculation of time while learners are engaged in active learning. For example, learning time can be classified into different categories, including instructional time, managerial time (preparation time), transition time, waiting time, and active learning time (Berry, Miller, & Berry, 2004). To promote active learning within athletic and sports training and educational settings, one critical consideration for effective instruction is how to efficiently manage these different types of time and enhance quality learning by reducing unnecessary time spent on unimportant activities during the learning process. When appropriately managed, learners' critical thinking, learning engagement, and deep learning will be significantly increased.

In athletic education and training, one key debate is on what aspect of learning outcomes athletic educators should achieve between clinical proficiency and technical ability. Heinrichs (2002) asserted that clinical proficiency is a more important target for learning because it involves understanding the knowledge, skills, and attitudes aspects of athletic training, whereas mastering athletic competencies is related to analyzing factors influencing clinical situations and making correct decisions through critical thinking. In particular, Brookfield (1987) emphasized the importance of critical thinking to improve the current practices in athletic and sports training and education. Typically, critical thinking involves four phases: identifying assumptions, questioning the importance of context, exploring options and alternatives, and reflecting the selected alternatives for making appropriate decisions in athletic training and education.

The use of educational technology is growing exponentially due to the increased availability of information and communication technologies and tools such as fast Internet, computers, laptops, tablets, and smartphones, and it is no exception within athletic and sports training and education. Other impetuses to actively adopt new technologies for athletic and sports training and education are the increased opportunities for educational access, learners' flexible time management for learning, overcoming time and space barriers for quality education programs, and improved work-life balance for fulltime workers who are seeking for continuing and lifelong learning for their career and life development (Rouse, 2000; Vichitvejpaisal et al., 2001). Compared to traditional approaches for teaching and learning in athletic and sports education, several debates on the effectiveness and efficiency of utilizing educational technology for teaching and learning have persisted. In many studies, there was no significant difference found in the learning outcomes between the traditional and technology-mediated instructional approaches (Mangione, Nieman, & Gracely, 1992; Santer et al., 1995; Toth-Cohen, 1995; Vichitvejpaisal et al., 2001). However, many other studies exemplified the usefulness and effectiveness of adopting technology-enhanced instruction for athletic and sports training and education. For example, traditional teaching and learning approaches have been criticized for the high cost factors caused by staff and fixed expenses such as consumable and administrative materials. When the number of students is largely increased, in many cases, the cost of educational delivery cannot be justified, and the quality of instruction is degraded significantly. Some studies have focused on this issue and identified that the use of a CD-ROM version of a basic course in a blended format in athletic training sessions was effective in enhancing learners' learning and satisfaction (Somekh, 1998). It is also known from other studies in athletic education that multimedia-based instruction provides several advantages over traditional, lecture-based instruction, resulting in active engagement in learning, self-paced learning, and allowing critical thinking for reflective learning (Farrow & Sims, 1987; Khoiny, 1995).

Professional Music Education. Professional musicians are generally educated in either an academic program at a university or a performance-based program at a conservatory. Successfully going through these programs, individuals can build their careers as performers, singers, composers, instrumental tutors, or primary/secondary teachers in music. Becoming a professional musician often starts at an early age and involves lifetime training and education. In this section, we will discuss how active learning and deliberate practice are implemented in professional music education and how technological integration process supports active learning pedagogy.

Active learning and deliberate practice are important elements in professional music education (Davidoff, 2011; Ericsson, 2004). Describing several myths of musical talent, Lamont (2011) argued that musicians are not born with talent but develop talent through active and deep learning and deliberate practice. Learners take ownership in their mastery of learning and performance and become professional musicians through lifelong learning. For this reason, the most essential subjects of the professional music education are how learners engage in deep learning and deliberate practice, continue the lifelong journey of learning, and ultimately become independent musicians.

Learning and teaching in professional music education are practice-focused (Davidoff, 2011). Consequently, instruction often involves one-to-one tutoring for an extended period because expert-level musical performance cannot be developed without an expert's specific and continuous feedback (Welch, Howard, Himonides, & Brereton, 2005). Extensive individualization of teaching and apprenticeship between a learner and an expert performer are central parts of professional music education. While teaching practices are also regulated through institutional norms and traditions in the professional community of music, individualized instruction is pivotal in professional music education (Nerland, 2007). Even if it is true that learners are subject to expert instruction, they also need to be empowered to be self-regulated active learners and accountable for their own development (Nerland, 2007). They may have one hour of one-to-one instruction per week, and the remaining time is expected to be spent on learning and practicing on their own. In this setting, learners are required to challenge their limits constantly with high aspirations and self-driven deliberate practices to achieve a master-level musical competency. It is important that learners find their own way into music through self-determination and personal growth (Nerland, 2007). A teacher's role is to serve as a personal supporter and mediator of knowledge, whereas learners are expected to be active learners to build their knowledge in their own way.

There have been limited efforts to integrate technological processes to facilitate active learning and deliberate practice in professional music education. Discussing a new pedagogical approach for music appreciation, Levin, Pargas, and Austin (2005) described how active learning and deliberate practice could improve a learner's experience in a music appreciation course. According to the authors, music appreciation, which is one of the key areas in professional music education, is traditionally taught in a classroom setting with lecture-based courses. Before playing a musical piece, an instructor explains to students what the music contains in terms of melody, harmony, and background information, including music history, political and social history, geography, and so on. This approach may work if students engage in the active listening of music. However, they argued that this traditional instruction can be limited in providing students with active learning opportunities to develop actual music listening skills themselves. Most of the time is spent lecturing about music appreciation, not for students' listening to music per se. Therefore, when instructors assess students' music appreciation, they ironically focus on students' knowledge of the music rather than the music itself.

The main problem in this situation is that inappropriate instructional approaches can lead to passive listeners and limited practicing, thereby resulting in superficial listening skills. Levin and his colleagues (2005) argued that active listening practice and guided deliberate practice opportunities should be provided to learners. They identified several components for designing active listening: repeated listening, continued dialogue with an expert on major and specific concepts, group activity, and modeling. The instructor briefly introduced the selected music and guided the students to focused, deep listening. The students were assigned into small groups where they discussed and shared what they had heard in terms of the music appreciation elements. Students used laptops for listening to the music and an online course management system for group discussion and sharing. Moreover, they developed an online application that allowed the students and the instructor a more sophisticated active listening and feedback activity. In this new system, the instructor provided a matrix presenting all elements of music on the top and the various sections of the music on a horizontal axis. With this matrix system, learners were able to engage in deep listening for each single section of the music, and the instructor was able to provide targeted coaching and feedback to reinforce or correct the students' listening performance. They found that the students who participated in this active listening activity demonstrated better ability to identify sections of a piece and to distinguish different sections than those who did not participate.

Welch et al. (2005) developed real-time visual feedback technology in a singing studio. According to their observations, novice singers pay more attention to the lyrics rather than the musical features of the song, including pitch, rhythm, melodic structure, phrasing, implied harmony, and even musical in-depth interpretation. In this situation, the teacher's role is to unpack the complexity of singing and guide the learner to master the targeted learning goals through feedback and coaching. Identifying the limitation of teachers' post-hoc verbal feedback in singing performance, Welch et al. (2005) developed a technological process providing more robust, less ambiguous, easily understandable, and real-time visual feedback to both teachers and learners. Teaching for more advanced learners often involved using visual imagery, sensation, and aural awareness in teaching vocal technique. Learners' reflection and self-monitoring also played into aligning intended singing with actual vocal performance. While deliberate practice is an essential element for singing development, Welch et al. (2005) argued that without explicit qualitative feedback, learners can end up developing inappropriate, subjective, and idiosyncratic singing behaviors. In the visual feedback system, singers can see their vocal performance input waveform, vocal pitch and melody, the quality and consistency of vocal timbre, the power of the voice, the relative size of inner resonating cavities, and their visual posture through real-time information. In an action research study, Welch et al. (2005) found that the participants found the real-time visual feedback system useful for their learning and teaching process without being a distraction.

Professional musicians spend numerous hours in a studio for deliberate practice, yet their actual musical performance practice is executed on stage within a limited time with a public audience. Performers are under intense pressure and anxiety because of all complexities of social, emotional, psychological, and physical factors that occur simultaneously. Therefore, professional musicians are expected to develop stage performance skills to handle such intense stress, anxiety, and complexities. However, musical students' repeated exposures to realistic performance situations are limited due to the high costs of arranging a performance and limited opportunities. Williamon, Aufegger, and Eiholzer (2014) investigated simulation approaches utilizing video and audio components to provide an authentic experience

with the audience and the audition judges. Comparing the simulation participants' survey responses and performance anxiety levels measured by electrocardiogram with participants with real audiences, they found that the participants felt a similar level of pressure and anxiety during the performance simulation compared to real-world situations. They discussed that virtual simulation environments can be an effective learning process in professional music education since it is low cost yet provides repeated and consistent access to real-world practice.

The three studies (Levin et al., 2005; Welch et al., 2005; Williamon et al., 2014) discussed above depict several characteristics of technology-supported active learning and deliberate practice in professional music education. First, the technological integration processes allowed learners to take control over their learning process and have ownership in their practice and performance. The teachers' role changed to being facilitators and coaches. Learners were able to be located in the center of the practice. Second, learning and instruction went into a deeper level because learners could practice with concrete and specific guidance and teachers could observe and monitor learners' performance at a detailed level. The technological processes allowed them to deconstruct their practice as learnable and teachable objects. Last, technology allowed learners to practice in real-world performance situations as musicians on a stage with relatively small cost. Providing authentic practice environments through immersive technology is beneficial because professional musicians spend most time in a studio for practice, yet their real performance is on a stage.

DISCUSSION

This study has outlined how technological processes facilitate active learning and deliberate practice and what pedagogical effects have been applied to professional education, such as teacher, healthcare, athletic, and music education. In this section, we will highlight and discuss major findings and implications for connecting active learning, deliberate practice, and educational technology in professional education. We will also discuss implications for future research.

To begin, we recommend revisiting the concepts of active learning and deliberate practice for professional education. In the beginning of this paper, we identified the notion of active learning as "the iterative process of building mental models from existing and new information and testing these models" (Michael & Modell, 2003, p. 6). However, active learning in professional education cannot be justified without explicit integration of professional practices that reflect major competencies and problem solving skills. Deliberate practice does not only indicate time and experience in practice but also involves deep learning and practice that are pivotal to developing professional competencies (Issenberg et al., 2005). Building cognitive mental models is necessary but not sufficient in professional education because the cognitive models must be transferred to real-world performance that broadly involves psychomotor, social, emotional, and attitudinal competencies. Including clinical and field experiences as part of the curricula in all four fields that we reviewed supports this emphasis on deliberate practices. Moreover, it takes a relatively long time to reach the highest levels of expert performance in a profession. In addition, learned skills, mental models, and subject expertise tend to decay over time. Feedback and assessment systems that closely monitor and track learners' performance, progress, and mastery of desired competencies should be a key component of professional education. Therefore we propose a conceptual integration of active learning and deliberate practice to advance technological processes in order to facilitate professional competency development in professional education.

Considering the conceptual integration of active learning and deliberate practice, the pedagogical focus of educational technology in professional education should be shifted or extended to facilitate sound principles of active learning and deliberate practice, such as promoting learner motivation, engagement, active participation, sharing insights or perspectives, longitudinal competence monitoring, performance assessment, feedback, and coaching. In active learning, learner-centeredness is the most fundamental concept and emphasizes learners' control and power over their learning process. Although learner-centeredness is an essential element, experts' timely, noninvasive, and constructive feedback should be given significant attention when utilizing educational technology for professional education. Similarly, technologies can be used for leveraging deliberate practice, as in arrangements of virtual communities for peer feedback or expert coaching through computer-mediated communications.

The review of educational technology in professional education shows that benefits of using technologies are substantial for increasing learner motivation, cognition, application, but strategic and systematic approaches can be applied across different disciplines.

First, educational technology processes can allow novice learners to practice, in a sense, with real-world objects. In active learning, the focus of pedagogical approaches is on providing authentic tasks or real-world problems for students as part of their learning process. Educational technology can be used to create authentic learning challenges as well as practice environments through case studies and simulation, and when combined with feedback and assessment systems, it can provide learners with mechanisms to interact with meaningful content, expertise, and professionals in the field. In workplace learning, novice learners can acquire expert-level knowledge through legitimate peripheral participation (Lave &

Wenger, 1991). Learners start with trivial tasks in the beginning and gradually participate in the central tasks of the profession by answering and helping others. This is a central phenomenon of workplace learning and teaching. However, there are also barriers for learner participation and deliberate practice, including time constraints, lack of resources, safety, and political dynamics. Through appropriate technological processes such as simulations, novice learners can participate in mediated practice for their active learning. Learners can see patients, treat trauma patients in an emergency room, perform a complicated surgical procedure in an operating room, listen to classical music for appreciation, play a violin on a stage, perform for an audition, teach students in a guided learning environment, or fly an airplane. The meta-analytic comparative review on simulation-based medical education with deliberate practice shows the efficacy of simulation in enhancing the performance of students in terms of higher test scores (McGaghie, Issenberg, Cohen, Barsuk, & Wayne, 2011).

Second, educational technology can facilitate making experts' intelligence and performance in practice visible and accessible to learners repeatedly. Teachable moments can be missed in practice. Expert performance and thought processes tend to be not easily visible to novice learners in practice (Han et al., in press). Similarly, a novice's performance that needs correction or reinforcement can easily slip by in real-world practice (Welch et al., 2005). It is important for learners to have experts' coaching and feedback during deep learning practice. However, it is expensive to have expert professionals all the time for learners' practice. Technology such as artificial intelligence, CAL, simulation, and performance monitoring systems can be utilized to provide experts' explanations of their thought processes and detailed feedback during practice (Hudson, 2004; Issenberg et al., 2005; Welch et al., 2005).

Third, learners' meaningful struggles for deep learning and deliberate practice can be facilitated through active, individual, and collaborative learning processes arranged through technology. In active learning, the pedagogical focus shifts from instructor-centered and quantity-oriented to learner-centered and quality-oriented educational practice. Efficiency and effectiveness should be centered on students' struggles. As discussed above in the section on professional athletic education, instructional time spent for non-meaningful activities should be reduced. Flipped classroom is one example of facilitating instructional time to be spent to address students' struggles (Han et al., 2013). In flipped classrooms, students watch lectures online at their own pace, self-assess their progress, and come to a classroom to get remedial help from teachers. Educational technology plays a pivotal role in facilitating students' individualized learning and formative assessment so that instructional time can be utilized for value-added deep learning around difficult situations during learner-teacher interactions. In many cases, through context-sensitive prompts and feedback, technologies can create more frequent teachable moments where students are ready to interact with expertise expected from professional practice.

CONCLUSION AND IMPLICATIONS

Active learning and deliberate practice are essential elements of professional education. The ultimate outcomes are students' knowledge, skills, and commitment to lifelong learning in their professions. Students' learning in professional education must span a broad stroke of competence that is expected of successful and competent professionals. Our review of active learning and deliberate practices in four major fields showed that concepts and principles of active learning are recognized in all of them, but systematic processes for incorporating principles of active learning and deliberate practice, especially at the institution or in the curriculum, need to be further developed.

Professional education as seen in the four fields reviewed in this study focuses on helping students acquire competencies for their practice, which are commonly managed through practicum, clinical, or service-learning experiences. Future research will be fruitful if success factors and barriers are examined at the curriculum, individual, and workplace levels. Hoberman and Mailick (1994) pointed out that one important part of professional education is to become immersed in the profession's norms, ethics, professionalism, and lifelong learning. According to our review, the extent of learning and practicing these elements varies across disciplines. Active learning and deliberate practice can be instrumental to facilitate those values, behaviors, and professional attitudes. Current literature focuses mainly on the development of cognitive skills and knowledge but not much on social and professional attitudes and values. Future research could investigate how professionalism, ethics, and non-cognitive competencies are practiced and developed through active learning and deliberate practice in the field and how they can be incorporated into professional education programs. The teacher education curriculum in Finland, which includes student teachers' teaching performance early and collaborative problem solving for communal needs, is one good example (Niemi, 2012).

Several educational technologies are implemented to facilitate active learning and to mediate practice experiences. However, less attention has been paid to establish sound instructional or learning processes in the selection and use of technology to promote deliberate practice in professional education. Processes claimed as useful are largely based on exploratory case studies, and more emphasis seems to lie on learning and instruction than practice. Most courses we reviewed followed the order of absorbing or presenting content followed by insufficient amount

of practice and performance. There is insufficient dialogue on both connecting active learning and deliberate practice and selecting and evaluating technological processes to promote deliberate practice as well as active learning in professional education. The misalignment between theory and practice is a major reason for unsuccessful skills transfer in many professional education programs (Hoberman & Mailick, 1994). Thus, it is important to document how educational technology can improve the design and delivery of active learning and deliberate practice and continuously improve the process across the curriculum. Future research and practice should focus particularly on establishing technological processes to facilitate deliberate practice through active learning in professional education.

Assessment is another area to improve in professional education. Current educational technology practice for active learning and deliberate practice focuses on activities that create meaningful experiences for learning and practice. However, individual and meaningful learning and teaching experiences can be created only when accurate learner performance information is systematically and longitudinally assessed within practice. Multiple-choice exams should not be the major measurement for active learning and deliberate practice. Longitudinal, cross-sectional, performance-oriented assessments of learners' competencies and continuous monitoring systems to identify areas in which learners need assistance should become an essential design element in educational technology for active learning and deliberate practice.

Our final note is that most educational technology processes to facilitate active learning and deliberate practice have been at the micro-level and focused on an individual course. Given the importance of professional competencies in practice, macro-level educational technology systems, including longitudinal performance development systems such as dashboards, analytics, and e-portfolios, that are used to improve or account for institutional performance should be further incorporated into the use of active learning and deliberate practice in professional education. System-level educational technology can provide pedagogical opportunities to monitor professionals' competencies longitudinally and continuously and provide time- and context-sensitive performance feedback. This remains an under-investigated area, yet it can provide powerful instrumental processes for deep learning and deliberate practice in professional education.

REFERENCES

Anderson, J. B., & Erickson, J. A. (1999). Service learning in pre-service teacher education. *Academic Exchange Quarterly, 7*(2), 111–115.

Anderson, J. B., & Pickeral, T. (1999). *Challenges and strategies for success with service learning in pre-service teacher education*. Washington, DC: Corporation for National Service.

Ball, D. L., & Cohen, D. K. (1999). Developing practice, developing practitioners: Toward a practice-based theory of professional education. In G. Sykes & L. Darling-Hammond (Eds.), *Teaching as the learning profession: Handbook of policy and practice* (pp. 3–32). San Francisco, CA: Jossey Bass.

Barrows, H. S. (1988). *The tutorial process*. Springfield, IL: Southern Illinois University School of Medicine.

Barrows, H. S. (2000). *Problem-based learning applied to medical education*. Springfield, IL: Southern Illinois University School of Medicine.

Barrows, H. S., & Wee, K. N. L. (2007). *Principles and practice of a PBL*. Singapore: Pearson Prentice Hall.

Berrett, D. (2012, February 19). How 'flipping' the classroom can improve the traditional lecture. *The Chronicle of Higher Education*. Retrieved from http://chronicle.com/article/How-Flipping-the-Classroom/130857/

Berry, D. C., Miller, M. G., & Berry, L. M. (2004). Effects of clinical field-experience setting on athletic training students' perceived percentage of time spent on active learning. *Journal of Athletic Training, 39*(2), 176–184. PMID:15173870

Bonwell, C. C., Eison, J. A., & Association for the Study of Higher Education. (1991). Active learning: Creating excitement in the classroom. *1991 ASHE-ERIC Higher Education Reports* (pp. 121): ERIC Clearinghouse on Higher Education, Washington, DC.

Bransford, J. D., Brown, A. L., & Cocking, R. R. (1999). *How people learn: Brain, mind, experience, and school*. Washington, DC: National Academy Press.

Brookfield, S. D. (1987). *Developing critical thinkers: Challenging adults to explore alternative ways of thinking and acting*. San Francisco, CA: Jossey-Bass.

Chi, M. T. H., Bassok, M., Lewis, M. W., Reimann, P., & Glaser, R. (1989). Self-explanations: How students study and use examples in learning to solve problems. *Cognitive Science, 13*(2), 145–182. doi:10.1207/s15516709cog1302_1

Cook, D. A., Levinson, A. J., & Garside, S. (2010). Time and learning efficiency in Internet-based learning: A systematic review and meta-analysis. *Advances in Health Sciences Education: Theory and Practice, 15*(5), 755–770. doi:10.1007/s10459-010-9231-x PMID:20467807

Coyle, D. (2009). *The talent code*. New York, NY: Random House.

Csikszentmihalyi, M. (1990). *Flow: The psychology of optimal experience.* New York, NY: Harper and Row.

Cuseo, J. (1992). Collaborative & cooperative learning in higher education: A proposed taxonomy. *Cooperative Learning and College Teaching, 2*(2), 2–4.

Davidoff, F. (2011). Music lessons: What musicians can teach doctors (and other health professionals). *Annals of Internal Medicine, 154*(6), 426–429. doi:10.7326/0003-4819-154-6-201103150-00009 PMID:21403078

Dick, W., Carey, L., & Carey, O. (2000). *The systematic design of instruction.* Glenview, IL: Addison Wesley.

Dori, Y. J., & Belcher, J. (2005). How does technology-enabled active learning affect undergraduate students' understanding of electromagnetism concepts? *Journal of the Learning Sciences, 14*(2), 243–279. doi:10.1207/s15327809jls1402_3

Dornan, T., Brown, M., Powley, D., & Hopkins, M. (2004). A technology using feedback to manage experience based learning. *Medical Teacher, 26*(8), 736–738. doi:10.1080/01421590400016340 PMID:15763881

Ericsson, K. A. (2004). Deliberate practice and the acquisition and maintenance of expert performance in medicine and related domains. *Academic Medicine, 79*(10Supplement), S70–S81. doi:10.1097/00001888-200410001-00022 PMID:15383395

Farrow, M., & Sims, R. (1987). Computer-assisted learning in occupational therapy. *Australian Occupational Therapy Journal, 34*(2), 53–58. doi:10.1111/j.1440-1630.1987.tb01569.x

Fehr, J. J., Honkanen, A., & Murray, D. J. (2012). Simulation in pediatric anesthesiology. *Paediatric Anaesthesia, 22*(10), 988–994. doi:10.1111/pan.12001 PMID:22967157

Gagné, R. M., Briggs, L. J., & Wager, W. W. (1992). *Principles of instructional design* (4th ed.). Fort Worth, TX: Harcourt Brace Jovanovich.

Gibson, C. C. (2000). When disruptive approaches meet disruptive technologies: Learning at a distance. *The Journal of Continuing Education in the Health Professions, 20*(2), 69–75. doi:10.1002/chp.1340200202 PMID:11232222

Gill, P., Kitney, L., Kozan, D., & Lewis, M. (2010). Online learning in paediatrics: A student-led web-based learning modality. *The Clinical Teacher, 7*(1), 53–57. doi:10.1111/j.1743-498X.2009.00337.x PMID:21134144

Graffam, B. (2007). Active learning in medical education: Strategies for beginning implementation. *Medical Teacher, 29*(1), 38–42. doi:10.1080/01421590601176398 PMID:17538832

Han, H., Resch, D. S., & Kovach, R. A. (2013). Educational technology in medical education. *Teaching and Learning in Medicine, 25*(sup1), S39–S43. doi:10.1080/10401334.2013.842914 PMID:24246105

Han, H., Roberts, N., & Korte, R. (in press). Learning in the real place: Medical students' learning and socialization in clerkships. *Academic Medicine.* PMID:25354072

Hans, A., & Akhter, S. (2013). Emerging trends in teacher's education. *The Macrotheme Review, 2*(2), 23-31. Retrieved from http://macrotheme.com/

Heinrichs, K. I. (2002). Problem-based learning in entry-level athletic training professional-education programs: A model for developing critical-thinking and decision-making skills. *Journal of Athletic Training, 37*(4suppl.), S-189–S-198. PMID:12937544

Hoberman, S., & Mailick, S. (1994). Frame of reference. In S. Hoberman & S. Mailick (Eds.), *Professional education in the United States* (pp. 3–37). Westport, CT: Praeger.

Hollingsworth, P., & Lewis, G. (2006). *Active learning: Increasing flow in the classroom*. Norwalk, CT: Crown House.

Hudson, J. N. (2004). Computer-aided learning in the real world of medical education: Does the quality of interaction with the computer affect student learning? *Medical Education, 38*(8), 887–895. doi:10.1111/j.1365-2929.2004.01892.x PMID:15271050

Irby, D. M., Cooke, M., & O'Brien, B. C. (2010). Calls for reform of medical education by the Carnegie Foundation for the Advancement of Teaching: 1910 and 2010. *Academic Medicine, 85*(2), 220–227. doi:10.1097/ACM.0b013e3181c88449 PMID:20107346

Irby, D. M., & Wilkerson, L. (2003). Educational innovations in academic medicine and environmental trends. *Journal of General Internal Medicine, 18*(5), 370–376. doi:10.1046/j.1525-1497.2003.21049.x PMID:12795736

Issenberg, S. B., McGaghie, W. C., Hart, I. R., Mayer, J. W., Felner, J. M., Petrusa, E. R., & Ewy, G. A. (1999). Simulation technology for health care professional skills training and assessment. *Journal of the American Medical Association, 282*(9), 861–866. doi:10.1001/jama.282.9.861 PMID:10478693

Issenberg, S. B., McGaghie, W. C., Petrusa, E. R., Gordon, D. L., & Scalese, R. J. (2005). Features and uses of high-fidelity medical simulations that lead to effective learning: A BEME systematic review. *Medical Teacher, 27*(1), 10–28. doi:10.1080/01421590500046924 PMID:16147767

Jarmon, L., Traphagan, T., Mayrath, M., & Trevidi, A. (2009). Virtual world teaching, experiential learning, and assessment: An interdisciplinary communication course in Second Life. *Computers & Education, 53*(1), 169–182. doi:10.1016/j.compedu.2009.01.010

Khoiny, F. E. (1995). Factors that contribute to computer-assisted instruction effectiveness. *Computers in Nursing, 13*, 165–168. PMID:7641135

Kiili, K. (2005). Digital game-based learning: Towards an experiential gaming model. *The Internet and Higher Education, 8*(1), 13–24. doi:10.1016/j.iheduc.2004.12.001

Kim, K. J., & Kee, C. (2013). Evaluation of an e-PBL model to promote individual reasoning. *Medical Teacher, 35*(3), E978–E983. doi:10.3109/0142159X.2012.717185 PMID:22938685

Koehler, M. J., & Mishra, P. (2005). What happens when teachers design educational technology? The development of technological pedagogical content knowledge. *Journal of Educational Computing Research, 32*(2), 131–152. doi:10.2190/0EW7-01WB-BKHL-QDYV

Lamont, A. (2011). The beat goes on: Music education, identity and lifelong learning. *Music Education Research, 13*(4), 369–388. doi:10.1080/14613808.2011.638505

Laurent, T., & Weidner, T. G. (2001). Clinical instructors' and student athletic trainers' perceptions of helpful clinical instructor characteristics. *Journal of Athletic Training, 36*(1), 58–61. PMID:12937516

Lave, J., & Wenger, E. (1991). *Situated learning: Legitimate peripheral participation*. Cambridge, United Kingdom: Cambridge University Press. doi:10.1017/CBO9780511815355

Levin, A. R., Pargas, R. P., & Austin, J. (2005). Appreciating music: An active approach. *New Directions for Teaching and Learning, 2005*(101), 27–35. doi:10.1002/tl.183

Mangione, S., Nieman, L. Z., & Gracely, E. J. (1992). Comparison of computer-based learning and seminar teaching of pulmonary auscultation to first-year medical-students. *Academic Medicine, 67*(10), S63–S65. doi:10.1097/00001888-199210000-00041 PMID:1382428

McGaghie, W. C., Issenberg, S. B., Cohen, E. R., Barsuk, J. H., & Wayne, D. B. (2011). Does simulation-based medical education with deliberate practice yield better results than traditional clinical education? A meta-analytic comparative review of the evidence. *Academic Medicine, 86*(6), 706–711. doi:10.1097/ACM.0b013e318217e119 PMID:21512370

McGaghie, W. C., Issenberg, S. B., Petrusa, E. R., & Scalese, R. J. (2010). A critical review of simulation-based medical education research: 2003-2009. *Medical Education, 44*(1), 50–63. doi:10.1111/j.1365-2923.2009.03547.x PMID:20078756

McLaughlin, J. E., Roth, M. T., Glatt, D. M., Gharkholonarehe, N., Davidson, C. A., Griffin, L. M., & Mumper, R. J. (2014). The flipped classroom: A course redesign to foster learning and engagement in a health professions school. *Academic Medicine, 89*(2), 236–243. doi:10.1097/ACM.0000000000000086 PMID:24270916

Merrill, M. D. (2002). First principles of instruction. *Educational Technology Research and Development, 50*(3), 43–59. doi:10.1007/BF02505024

Michael, J. A., & Modell, H. I. (2003). *Active learning in secondary and college science classrooms: A working model for helping the learner to learn.* Mahwah, NJ: Erlbaum.

Nerland, M. (2007). One-to-one teaching as cultural practice: Two case studies from an academy of music. *Music Education Research, 9*(3), 399–416. doi:10.1080/14613800701587761

Niemi, H. (2012). Relationships of teachers' professional competencies, active learning and research studies in teacher education in Finland. *Reflecting Education, 8*(2), 23-44. Retrieved from http://www.reflectingeducation.net/

Prince, M. (2004). Does active learning work? A review of the research. *The Journal of Engineering Education, 93*(3), 223–231. doi:10.1002/j.2168-9830.2004.tb00809.x

Prober, C. G., & Khan, S. (2013). Medical education reimagined: A call to action. *Academic Medicine, 88*(10), 1407–1410. doi:10.1097/ACM.0b013e3182a368bd PMID:23969367

Pugsley, L., & McCrorie, P. (2007). Improving medical education: Improving patient care. *Teaching and Teacher Education, 23*(3), 314–322. doi:10.1016/j.tate.2006.12.023

Rea, D. (2003). Optimal motivation for creative intelligence. In D. Ambrose, L. M. Cohen, & A. Tannenbaum (Eds.), *Creative intelligence: Toward theoretic integration* (pp. 211–225). Cresskill, NJ: Hampton Press.

Reiser, R. A., & Dempsey, J. V. (2012). *Trends and issues in Instructional Design and Technology* (3rd ed.). Saddle River, NJ: Pearson Education.

Richardson, W. (2010). *Blogs, wikis, podcasts, and other powerful web tools for classrooms.* Thousand Oaks, CA: Corwin.

Rosen, K. R., McBride, J. M., & Drake, R. L. (2009). The use of simulation in medical education to enhance students' understanding of basic sciences. *Medical Teacher, 31*(9), 842–846. doi:10.1080/01421590903049822 PMID:19811190

Rosenberg, M. J. (2005). *Beyond e-learning: Approaches and technologies to enhance organizational knowledge, learning, and performance.* San Francisco, CA: Wiley.

Rouse, D. P. (2000). The effectiveness of computer-assisted instruction in teaching nursing students about congenital heart disease. *Computers in Nursing, 18,* 282–287. PMID:11105402

Santer, D. M., Michaelsen, V. E., Erkonen, W. E., Winter, R. J., Woodhead, J. C., Gilmer, J. S., & Galvin, J. R. (1995). A comparison of educational interventions: Multimedia textbook, standard lecture, and printed textbook. *Archives of Pediatrics & Adolescent Medicine, 149*(3), 297–302. doi:10.1001/archpedi.1995.02170150077014 PMID:7532074

Scalese, R. J., Obeso, V. T., & Issenberg, S. B. (2008). Simulation technology for skills training and competency assessment in medical education. *Journal of General Internal Medicine, 23*(S1), 46–49. doi:10.1007/s11606-007-0283-4 PMID:18095044

Schrum, L., & Levin, B. B. (2013). Preparing future teacher leaders: Lessons from exemplary school systems. *Journal of Digital Learning in Teacher Education, 29*(3), 97–103. doi:10.1080/21532974.2013.10784711

Silberman, M. (1996). *Active learning: 101 strategies to teach any subject.* Boston, MA: Allyn and Bacon.

Somekh, B. (1998). Supporting information and communication technology innovations in higher education. *Journal of Information Technology for Teacher Education, 7*(1), 11–32. doi:10.1080/14759399800200028

Szulewski, A., & Davidson, L. K. (2008). Enriching the clerkship curriculum with blended e-learning. *Medical Education, 42*(11), 1114. doi:10.1111/j.1365-2923.2008.03184.x PMID:18826396

Toth-Cohen, S. (1995). Computer-assisted-instruction as a learning-resource for applied anatomy and kinesiology in the occupational-therapy curriculum. *The American Journal of Occupational Therapy, 49*(8), 821–827. doi:10.5014/ajot.49.8.821 PMID:8526228

van Merriënboer, J. J. G., Clark, R. E., & de Croock, M. B. M. (2002). Blueprints for complex learning: The 4C/ID-model. *Educational Technology Research and Development, 50*(2), 39–64. doi:10.1007/BF02504993

van Puijenbroek, T., Poell, R. F., Kroon, B., & Timmerman, V. (2014). The effect of social media use on work-related learning. *Journal of Computer Assisted Learning, 30*(2), 159–172. doi:10.1111/jcal.12037

Vernon, D. T. A., & Blake, R. L. (1993). Does problem-based learning work? A meta-analysis of evaluative research. *Academic Medicine, 68*(7), 550–563. doi:10.1097/00001888-199307000-00015 PMID:8323649

Vichitvejpaisal, P., Sitthikongsak, S., Preechakoon, B., Kraiprasit, K., Parakkamodom, S., Manon, C., & Petcharatana, S. (2001). Does computer-assisted instruction really help to improve the learning process? *Medical Education, 35*(10), 983–989. doi:10.1046/j.1365-2923.2001.01020.x PMID:11564203

Weimer, M. (2002). *Learner-centered teaching: Five key changes to practice.* San Francisco, CA: Jossey-Bass.

Welch, G. F., Howard, D. M., Himonides, E., & Brereton, J. (2005). Real-time feedback in the singing studio: An innovatory action-research project using new voice technology. *Music Education Research, 7*(2), 225–249. doi:10.1080/14613800500169779

White, C., Bradley, E., Martindale, J., Roy, P., Patel, K., Yoon, M., & Worden, M. K. (2014). Why are medical students 'checking out' of active learning in a new curriculum? *Medical Education*, *48*(3), 315–324. doi:10.1111/medu.12356 PMID:24528466

Williamon, A., Aufegger, L., & Eiholzer, H. (2014). Simulating and stimulating performance: Introducing distributed simulation to enhance musical learning and performance. *Frontiers in Psychology*, *5*. doi:10.3389/fpsyg.2014.00025 PMID:24550856

Yoon, S. W. (2008). Technologies for learning and performance. In A. Rozanski, K. P. Kuchinke, & E. Boyar (Eds.), *Human resource development theory and practice* (pp. 245–262). Lublin, Poland: Lublin Technical University.

KEY TERMS AND DEFINITIONS

Active Learning: A type of instructional strategy or method to facilitate learner-centered active engagement in problem solving and knowledge construction throughout the learning process.

Deliberate Practice: A pedagogical approach for constant development of skills and knowledge through repeated deep practice, rigorous assessment and formative feedback.

Educational Technology: Systematic technological processes to improve learning experience and performance toward professional competence.

Professional Education: An educational process or program that develops individuals to acquire special competencies for professional practice.

Chapter 10
Active Learning Strategies in Enhancing Learning among College Students

Caroline C. Chemosit
University of Kabianga, Kericho, Kenya

John K. Rugutt
Illinois State University, USA

Viviline Ngeno
University of Kabianga, Kericho, Kenya

Dorothy Soi
University of Kabianga, Kericho, Kenya

ABSTRACT

This chapter explores the relationship between active learning strategies and skills and attributes that enhance learning (SAEL) among college students. Developing skills and attributes that enhance learning (SAEL) among college students is critical to student success and persistence in college. Additionally, SAEL help the students develop a sustained learning commitment while in college and after graduation. However, little evidence is there to show how higher education institutions are equipping students with SAEL. This study seeks to investigate if there is a relationship between active learning strategies (ALS) and SAEL. Secondary data from the 2007 National Survey of Student Engagement (NSSE) at a Midwestern state university in the USA were employed to examine the relationship between ALS and SAEL. The results of the analysis showed positive significant correlations between ALS and SAEL components, (p < 0.001). Multiple regression model showed that ALS predictor variables significantly predict SAEL, $R^2 = .196$, $R^2_{adj} = .188$, $F (7, 731) = 25.38$, $p < .001$. The regression model accounts for 19.6% of variance in SAEL.

DOI: 10.4018/978-1-4666-8363-1.ch010

INTRODUCTION

Facilitating the development of skills and attributes that enhance learning is critical to rewarding student learning experiences and success in college. As much as higher education institutions admit students to their institutions, ensuring student success in these institutions is crucial. As such, helping students learn and develop skills and attributes that enhance learning (SAEL) is important. Higher education institutions have a task of ensuring that students have what it takes to fully and meaningfully participate in higher education learning experiences. Some of the college experiences that can nurture and develop SAEL include student involvement in active learning strategies (ALS) like class discussion, group work, asking questions in class, and student-teacher interactions. Cropley (1981) and Knapper and Cropley (2000) have identified skills and attributes crucial to student learning to include: computing and information technology skills; critical thinking, quantitative and analytical skills; learning effectively on your own; and working effectively with others. It is important to ensure that students acquire these skills so as to have a productive learning experience in college and in their careers.

Learning today requires an effective use of computing and information technology. As such, learners should be techno-literate in order to effectively and successfully participate in the learning process (Bryce, Frigo, McKenzie & Withers, 2002; Bryce & Wither, 2003). In addition critical thinking and analytical skills are important to meaningful student learning. Students should be taught how to utilize reason, evidence, problem solve, and make logical decisions. Teaching thinking skills to students is paramount in helping them be actively engaged in learning as well as in the acquisition of lifelong learning skills. Thinking skills can also improve students' achievement,

help students develop positive self-concept, and develop habits necessary for productive citizenship (Beyer, 1988; Bryce & Wither, 2003; Knox, Lindsay, & Kolb, 1993).

Framework

Self-determined learning theory focuses on interaction between engagement, adjustment and learning. The theory predicts that "learning will maximize when engagement produces optimal adjustments to new challenges" (Mithaug, Mithaug, Agran, Martin & Wehmeyer, 2003, p. 3). The theory as noted is supported when the learners believe that their "opportunities for gaining something from a situation are valuable and manageable and when they know how to regulate their expectations, choice, and action to produce results they expect from circumstance" (Mithaug, et.al., 2003, p. 3). Students become self-determined as they acquire knowledge and skills necessary to deal with a situation, gain control over the situation, and develop a belief that "gain from the situation will give them more of what they need and want to know" (Mithaug, et.al., 2003, p. 3). Self-determined learning theory help students engage in situation they believe is valuable to them by regulating their expectations, choices, and actions in order to produce satisfactory results. Students' perceptions and beliefs will influence those students' engagement, adjustments, and learning. It is therefore important to help students embrace sustained learning commitment by conveying to them importance of this disposition and teaching them how to regulate their expectations, choices, and actions for meaningful learning.

Statement of the Problem

Even though we expect students to learn and succeed in college, little attention has been given to understanding factors that promote development of SAEL among students. More often, higher education institutions are concerned with student enrollment, fee and tuition payments, lecture attendance, student grades, and student persistence in college. Institutions should first and foremost ensure that students have what it takes to meaningfully engage in the learning process. That is, teaching students how to learn before engaging them in the learning process. However, little research has been conducted to find out college experiences that enhance the development of SAEL.

Purpose of the Study and Research Questions

The primary purpose of this study was to investigate a combination of factors that promote SAEL among college students. Specifically, this study explored the relationship between active learning strategies (ALS) and skills and attributes that enhance learning (SAEL) and was guided by the following research questions: 1) Is there a relationship between active learning strategies (ALS) and skills and attributes that enhance learning (SAEL) among college students? And 2) which of the active learning strategies (ALS) are most influential in predicting skills and attributes that enhance learning (SAEL) among college students?

Limitations of the Study

1. The type of institution and characteristics of students from which data were obtained limit the generalizability of this study's results.
2. Responses elicited from students were/ are voluntary and as such, students who completed the NSSE survey or participated in the interviews might be viewed as more conscientious or interested in the study than those who did not return the surveys or were unwilling to be interviewed.
3. Secondary data were also utilized for the study and the variables used are therefore bound by the survey used and data collection

method. Items found in the NSSE questionnaire may not capture all the key issues the study seeks to explore.

METHODOLOGY

Research Design

This study utilized a cross-section survey research design. This is because it focused on the major variables of a specific higher education teaching and learning environment at a specific period. Also, the students were surveyed on key variables about the college teaching and learning environment. The study also used a post hoc correlation design as relationships among variables were explored in a bid to understand the relationship between ALS and SAEL. The survey research design was chosen because it is an efficient way to gather a large mass of data of the higher education teaching and learning experiences quickly and effectively.

Sample and Sampling Procedures

The accessible population of the study consisted of all senior students who had completed at least 108 credit hours by the end of fall 2006 (UAO, 2009). That is, all senior students who met the selection criterion were asked to participate in the NSSE portion of the study. According to Planning and Institutional Research at a Midwestern state university, senior students totaled 5,766 in fall 2006. However, a total of 2,405 senior students met the criterion for the study (UAO, 2009). A total of 760 students completed NSSE in spring 2007 for a response rate of 32%.

Measures

Instrumentation and measurements for this study consisted of the National Survey of Student Engagement (NSSE) questionnaire. Survey items on The National Survey of Student Engagement as noted "represent empirically confirmed 'good practices' in undergraduate education. That is, they reflect behaviors by students and institutions that are associated with desired outcomes of college" (NSSE, 2009, http://nsse.iub.edu/html/about.cfm).

Validity. Validity is "the extent to which the concepts one wishes to measure is actually being measured by a particular scale or index" (Sirkin, 2006). The design team that developed the NSSE instrument devoted considerable time to make certain that the items on the survey were clearly worded, well defined, and had high content validity (NSSE, 2009). Further, logical relationships between items in ways that are consistent with the results of objective measures and other research were observed by NSSE team (Kuh, 2003). The items used in the NSSE have been used by other researchers such as the Cooperative Institutional Research Programs (CIRP) and Indiana University's College Student Experiences Questionnaire (Kuh, 2003). Further, " a good deal of evidence show that students are accurate, credible reporters of their activities and how much they have benefited from their college experience, provided the items are clearly worded and students have information required to accurately answer the questions" (Kuh, 2003, p. 4).

Reliability. Reliability analysis can be used to understand how consistent the study measures are. Reliability coefficient can be used to measure reliability of study measures and it ranges from zero (not reliable) to one (perfectly reliable). Internal consistency reliability as Vogt (2007) pointed out "is the degree to which different parts of a test or items in a test intended to measure the same thing in fact do so" (p. 114). Cronbach Alpha was used to measure internal consistency or accuracy of the study measures. An Alpha of 0.70 as Vogt (2007) pointed out is often considered satisfactory.

Unreliable measures may lead to underestimation of association between variables (Vogt, 2007).

Computation of Cronbach Alpha internal consistency reliability coefficients was performed for the study variables. The reliability coefficients reported was based upon aggregated items resulting from the factor analysis completed. The analysis was performed to determine whether the items were a reliable measure of their respective subscale.

NSSE survey benchmarks and norms accurately and consistently measure the student behaviors and perceptions represented on the survey (NSSE, 2009). Further, the results from the NSSE report are relatively stable from year to year, indicating that the instrument produces reliable measurements from one year to the next. That is, students with similar characteristics are responding approximately the same way from year to year. Factor analysis and Cronbach's alpha reliability coefficients for the survey subscale were completed by the NSSE Research office to further bolster the psychometric properties of the survey instrument (NSSE, 2009).

Data Collection Procedures

The data collection process for the study consisted of the primary collection of quantitative data by NSSE using a web-based survey. The other phase included the secondary collection of the NSSE data by the research team from the University Assessment Office (UAO). The NSSE was administered by NSSE coordinators with the University Assessment Office (UAO) coordinating the retrieval of student data that included e-mail addresses and number of hours earned. Study participants consisted of all senior students who had completed at least 108 credit hours by the end of fall 2006 (UAO, 2009). Instructions on the request-to-participate email that accompanied the survey described purpose of the survey and assurance that all responses would be confidential and respondents could refuse to participate or choose not to answer any question without penalty (UAO, 2009).

Data Analysis

Once data collection procedures and the construction of various data files had been completed a variety of data analyses were computed. Descriptive statistical analyses of all demographic and related instrument items as well as composite variables including active learning strategies and skills and attributes that enhance learning were conducted. The conducted a series of factor and reliability analyses of the instrument used in the study. Further, bivariate correlations among all study variables were completed. Multiple regression and correlational analyses were also conducted to describe associate between variables and to examine the relative contribution and combination of variables explaining variance in SAEL (Gravetter & Wallnau, 2007; Hinkle, Wiersma, & Jurs, 2003; Vogt, 2007). Correlation analysis was employed to respond to the research question "Is there a relationship between active learning strategies and skills and attributes that enhance learning among college students?

Regression analysis was used to answer the research question "Which of the active learning strategies are most influential in predicting skills and attributes that enhance learning among college students? Multiple regression analysis provided information about the total and individual contribution of the independent variables in the prediction of the dependent variable. In other words, this technique was used to investigate the amount of variance in the dependent variable that could be attributed to the set of the independent variables. The unique contribution of each independent variable in predicting the dependent variable is

presented by the regression standardized (Beta) and unstandardized (b) regression coefficients (Hinkle et al., 2003).

RESULTS

This chapter describes the results of the study that includes descriptive statistical analyses of demographic and study variables, factor and reliability analyses, the bivariate correlations and multiple regression analyses. These analyses were employed to address the study's research questions.

Demographic Descriptive Statistics

The National Survey of Student Engagement (NSSE) was sent to 2,405 senior students at a Midwestern state university who had completed at least 108 credit hours by the end of fall, 2006. Seven hundred and sixty (n = 760), that is, 32% of the students returned the survey. Of those who returned the survey, 64% were female (n = 489), and the rest, 36% were male (n = 271). Caucasian/ White students made up the largest student representation and comprised 91% (n = 694) of study participants. The remaining participants were distributed across other racial/ethnic groups and included: Blacks (2.6%), Asian (1.1%), Hispanic (1.7%), foreign (0.7%), American Indian/Alaskan native (0.1%), and unknown (2.5%).

Descriptive Statistics for Active Learning Strategies Items. Active learning strategies (ALS) comprised seven items that asked students how often they had participated in different sorts of academic experiences (on a scale of 1 to 4). Means for ALS items ranged from 2.63 to 3.50 and standard deviation ranged from .649 to .949 (see Table 1). The item with the highest mean was how often the students used e-mail to communicate with their instructors (3.50). All students indicated that they had used e-mail to communicate with an instructor at least sometimes.

Table 1. Summary Descriptive Statistics for Active Learning Items

Item: In your experience at your institution during the current school year, about how often have you done each of the following?	Percent who Responded				Mean	STD
	Very Often (4)	Often (3)	Some times (2)	Never (1)		
Worked with other students on projects during class (759)	17.9 (136)	33.6 (255)	42.0 (319)	6.5 (49)	2.63	.849
Made a class presentation (759)	23.3 (177)	38.1 (289)	35.3 (268)	3.3 (25)	2.81	.827
Worked with classmates outside of class to prepare class assignments (759)	28.5 (216)	37.9 (288)	29.8 (226)	3.8 (29)	2.91	.853
Put together ideas or concepts from different courses when completing assignments or during class discussions (741)	24.7 (183)	44.9 (333)	28.5 (211)	1.9 (14)	2.92	.776
Used an electronic medium (listserv, chat group, Internet, instant messaging, etc.) to discuss or complete an assignment (741)	37.8 (280)	31.8 (236)	23.1 (171)	7.3 (54)	3.00	.949
Asked questions in class or contributed to class discussions (759)	32.1 (244)	39.4 (299)	27.1 (206)	1.3 (10)	3.02	.804
Used e-mail to communicate with an instructor (740)	58.9 (436)	32.6 (241)	8.5 (63)	0	3.50	.649
(n): Number of Midwestern state university seniors who responded to the questions STD: Standard deviation						

Descriptive Statistics for Skills and Attributes Subscale: The skills and attributes that enhance learning variable were comprised of eight items that asked the students the extent their experiences at their institution contributed to their knowledge, skills, and personal development in a variety of areas. Thinking critically and analytically was the item with the highest mean (3.35) while analyzing quantitative problems had the lowest mean (2.94). Standard deviation of the items ranged from .689 to .870 (see Table 2). At least 30% of the students indicated that their experience at the institution contributed very much to their knowledge, skills, and personal development in the areas listed (see Table 2). The students (47%) reported that their experiences had contributed very much to acquiring job or work-related knowledge and skills.

Factor Analysis. Prior to conducting analysis pertinent to the research questions in this study, a series of factor analysis procedures were completed for the instrument. Factor analysis is performed in order to identify the factors that explain the variation among measures (Vogt, 2007). In addition, factor analysis defines the dimensions underlying the existing measurement instrument. The principal component analysis was conducted utilizing Varimax Rotation. Item loadings for the factors identified were guided by the following set of decision rules (Chemosit, C. C. 2012): (a) the minimum value for retaining an item on a factor was 0.33; (b) an item was retained if it loaded primarily on one factor; (c) an item was retained on the factor on which its loading was greatest; and (d) if an item loaded on more than one factor, the item was retained if the difference of the squared loadings was 0.20 or greater.

Factor Analysis Results of Student-faculty Interaction and Active Learning. The initial factor analysis of the first set of questions in the 2007 NSSE instrument that asked students how often they participated in college activities yielded a solution of six factors. The extraction method of the initial analysis was based on Eigen value greater than 1. After a close study of the factors

Table 2. Summary Descriptive Statistics for Skills and Attributes Items

Item: To what extent has your experience at this institution contributed to your knowledge, skills, and personal development in the following areas?	Percent who Responded				Mean	STD
	Very Much (4)	Quite a Bit (3)	Some (2)	Very Little (1)		
Analyzing quantitative problems (702)	30.3 (213)	37.3 (262)	27.9 (196)	4.4 (31)	2.94	.870
Speak clearly and effectively (703)	29.3 (206)	42.0 (295)	24.8 (174)	4.0 (28)	2.97	.836
Write clearly and effectively (703)	31.6 (222)	41.1 (289)	24.3 (171)	3.0 (21)	3.01	.824
Using computing and information technology (703)	45.0 (316)	35.8 (252)	16.4 (115)	2.8 (20)	3.23	.822
Acquiring Job or work-related knowledge and skills (703)	47.4 (333)	33.1 (233)	16.8 (118)	2.7 (19)	3.25	.829
Acquiring broad general education (703)	42.8 (301)	43.2 (304)	12.8 (90)	1.1 (8)	3.28	.725
Working effectively with other (702)	45.6 (320)	39.0 (274)	14.0 (98)	1.4 (10)	3.29	.755
Thinking critically and analytically (702)	46.9 (213)	41.9 (262)	10.4 (196)	.9 (31)	3.35	.698

(n): Number of Midwestern state university seniors who responded to the questions
STD: Standard deviation

extracted in the initial analysis, a decision was made to extract only four factors since two of the factors extracted had three items each while one factor had two items. A second factor analysis was then performed with specification to extract four factors. The question that asked the students how often they came to class without completing readings or assignments had a negative factor loading and the item was reverse coded. Of the twenty two items subjected to factor analysis, seventeen items were retained. The college activities factors identified were Student-Faculty Interaction (SFI), Active Learning (ALS), Diversity, and Class Projects/Assignments. The college activities items contained two study variables: Student-Faculty Interaction (SFI) and Active Learning Strategies (ALS). The four factors accounted for 46.03% of the total variance with factor 1, factor 2, factor 3, and factor 4 contributing 26.53%, 7.26%, 6.54%, and 5.71% respectively. The first factor, Student-Faculty Interaction had six items with

factor loadings ranging from a low of 0.35 to a high of 0.71. Items loaded on this factor are related to interactions students have with the faculty. The second factor, active learning had seven items with factor loadings ranging from 0.33 to 0.71.

Factor Loadings of Student Outcomes. Factor analysis was also performed on the NSSE question that asked students the extent their college experiences had contributed to their knowledge, skills, and personal development in a variety of areas. The two factors identified accounted for a total variance of 51.8% with factor 1 and factor 2 contributing 41.2% and 10.6% of the variance respectively. Eight items loaded on each of the factors and factor 1; skills and attributes that enhance learning were explored in the study.

Reliability Analysis. Computation of Cronbach Alpha internal consistency reliability coefficients was performed for Student-Faculty Interaction (SFI), Active Learning Strategies (ALS), Student Values (STUVAL), and Skills and Attributes that

Enhance Learning (SAEL). The reliability coefficients reported are based upon aggregated items resulting from the factor analysis completed. The alpha coefficients ranged from a low of 0.722 for ALS to a high of 0.854 for SAEL (see Table 4). The Cronbach alpha reliability coefficients for SFI and STUVAL were 0.730 and 0.761 respectively. All the items identified during the factor analysis stage were retained. Though the study generated several factors from the instrument, only two (ALS and SAEL) were the focus of the study as guided by the purpose of the study and the research questions.

Research Question 1: Correlation analysis was performed to explore the relationships between active learning strategies (ALS) and skills and attributes that enhance learning (SAEL). The bivariate correlation coefficients were computed for ALS and SAEL to try to understand relationships between the study variables and to address the study research question; "Is there a relationship between active learning strategies and skills and attributes that enhance learning among college students? The correlation analysis results showed a statistically significant direct intercorrelation at the 0.01 level of significance among all the study variables (see Table 4). The magnitude of the correlation coefficients was not strong but positive in direction.

The highest correlation coefficient, 0.433 was between active learning strategies items classgrp (worked with other students on projects during class) and occgrp (worked with classmates outside of class to prepare class assignments). Active learning strategies item email (used e-mail to communicate with an instructor) had the highest correlation coefficient (.319) with skills and attributes that enhance learning. The direct relationship between the study variables indicates that a positive change in a variable will lead to a positive change in another variable and vice versa. Thus, it is important to employ active learning strategies since that certainly promote

Table 3. Summary of standardized Cronbach alpha reliability coefficients for the instrument subscales (n = 760)

Subscale	Number of items	Cronbach Alpha Coefficient
Active Learning Strategies (ALS)*	7	0.722
Student-Faculty Interaction (SFI)	6	0.730
Skills and Attributes that Enhance Learning (SAEL)	8	0.854
Student Values (STUVAL)	8	0.761

* This study utilized ALS and SAEL as per the research questions and purpose of the study

development of skills and attributes that enhance learning (see Table 3 for details).

Research Question 2: Multiple regression analysis was performed in order to identify the best combination of active learning strategies items that promote skills and attributes that enhance learning. The analysis was performed to answer the study research question that stated: "Which of the active learning strategies are most influential in predicting skills and attributes that enhance learning among college students?" ALS accounted for 19.6% of variance in SAEL,

$$R^2 = .196, R^2_{adj} = .188, F(7,731) = 25.38, p < .001.$$

ALS items that were significant predictors of SAEL included Occgrp (worked with classmates outside of class to prepare class assignments), Intideas (put together ideas or concepts from different courses when completing assignments or during class discussions, itacadem (used an electronic medium to discuss or complete an assignment), clquest (asked questions in class or contributed to class discussions) and email (used email to communicate with an instructor). See Table 5 for details.

Table 4. Summary of correlation coefficients between active learning strategies and skills and attributes that enhance learning (n = 760)

	Classgrp	Clpresen	Occgrp	Intideas	Itacadem	Clquest	Email	SAEL
Classgrp	1	.355**	.433**	.249**	.141**	.207**	.216**	.223**
Clpresen		1	427**	.311**	.136**	.308**	.318**	.261**
Occgrp			1	.283**	.231**	.247**	.324**	.311**
Intideas				1	.218**	.330**	.293**	.289**
Itacadem					1	.149**	.393**	.231**
Clquest						1	.256**	.235**
Email							1	.319**
SAEL[a]								1

** $p < 0.01$ (2-tailed)
[a]*SAEL:* Skills and Attributes that Enhance Learning

DISCUSION

The results of the analysis indicate that ALS positively predicts SAEL. As such, it is important to encourage student involvement in the learning process. To pave the way for student involvement in the learning process, faculty and other college personnel should design activities and experi- ences that allow and encourage students to be involved in the learning process. Active learning "invites students to bring their life experiences into the learning process, reflect on their own and others' perspectives as they expand their viewpoints, and apply new understandings to their own lives" (ACPA & NASPA, 1997, p. 3) is important components of enhancing learning.

Table 5. Summary of regression analysis with skills and attributes that enhance learning (SAEL) as the dependent variable

Model	Unstandardized Coefficients (B)	Standardized Coefficients ($Beta$)	Significance (p)
(Constant)	13.483		.000
Classgrp: Worked with other students on projects DURING CLASS	.239	.047	.220
Clpresen: Made a class presentation	.347	.066	.092
Occgrp: Worked with classmates OUTSIDE OF CLASS to prepare class assignments	.704	.138	.001
Intideas: Put together ideas or concepts from different courses when completing assignments or during class discussions	.736	.131	.000
Itacadem: Used an electronic medium (listserv, chat group, Internet, instant messaging, etc.) to discuss or complete an assignment	.364	.079	.031
Clquest: Asked questions in class or contributed to class discussions	.435	.080	.028
Email: Used e-mail to communicate with an instructor	1.034	.154	.000

It is therefore important to purposefully design experiences and opportunities that allow students to actively participate in the learning process.

Active Learning Strategies Influence Development of SAEL

Active learning strategies were statistically and significantly related to skills and attributes that enhance learning and accounted for 19.6% of variance in SAEL. This indicates that active learning strategies play a significant role in the development of skills and attributes that enhanced learning among college students. It is therefore important for higher education institutions to employ active learning strategies to support the development of skills and attributes that enhance learning among students. Moreover, institutions should know the ALS components that promote skills and attributes that enhance learning so as to direct faculty and students to appropriate activities as well as provide opportunities for students to participate in those experiences.

Encourage Student Involvement in the Learning Process

To pave the way for student involvement in the learning process, faculty and other college personnel should design activities and experiences that allow and encourage students to be involved in the learning process. College leaders and administrators should inculcate among their stakeholders the need to create avenues that promote student active participation in the learning process. Participation in active learning activities such as group discussions and class presentations promote communication skills, critical thinking skills, working effectively with others, job or work-related knowledge, and effective independent learning.

According to Kolb (1984), "learners, if they are to be effective need four different kinds of abilities- concrete experience abilities (CE), reflective observation abilities (RO), abstract conceptualization abilities (AC), and active experimentation (AE) abilities" (p. 40). Exposing students to the four dimensions of learning in the teaching and learning process is important to their understanding of the complex nature of learning and the need for their active involvement in the learning process. The theory of student involvement that evolved from a longitudinal study of college dropouts (Astin, 1984, 1985, 1993) tried to identify factors that significantly affected student persistence in college. These factors that contributed to student persistence in college included involvement (participating in educationally purposeful activities) while factors that contributed to students dropping out of college implied a lack of involvement (Astin, 1993).

Employing strategies that promote effective teaching and student learning should be a priority among college professors and administrators. The teaching and learning strategies employed should be based on lesson/course objectives, cognition level, student development level, and availability of resources and technologies. Giving consideration to teaching methods, technology, teaching and learning strategies, assessment techniques, and level of content mastery is important in designing strategies that promote effective teaching and student learning.

Create a Positive and Welcoming Learning Environment

Creating a learning environment that is inviting for all students and encouraging their active participation in the learning process should be a priority since students who feel welcome are likely to actively engage in learning and attend class on a regular basis. Student safety and respect should be given due consideration since a lack of these elements can hinder effective teaching and learning (Hirst & Bailey, 1983). An inviting learning environment can be promoted by creating a class ethos that embraces a diverse student population and in effect makes students feel welcomed and accepted in the classroom. It is important to note that student learning extends beyond the classroom walls and it is a good idea to promote learning communities for meaningful interaction of the students inside and outside of the classrooms.

Design Programs That Teach Students Skills and Attributes That Enhance Learning

Regression model indicated that only 19.6% of variance in SAEL can be attributed to ALS. This shows that there are other factors that may influence development of SAEL. Thus, institutions should develop programs that teach and help students acquire SAEL. Students can be taught these skills since they can be learned. Furthermore, teaching students skills and attributes that enhance learning ensures that all students have a knowledge base of college experiences that support development of skills and attributes important to their success in college and in their careers and work places. Courses designed to teach these skills should have theoretical and practical components in order for students to connect theory to practice. Additionally, talent development that "emphasizes intellectual and personal development of individual students as fundamental institution purpose" (Astin, 1985, p. 77) should be a priority. Simply put, the role of the institution should be to develop skills and attributes important to productive living (AACU, 2002; 2007; SCANS, 1991). Institutions should promote and nurture the development of critical thinking skills, problem solving skills, basic skills in reading, writing, and arithmetic, oral, listening, and interpersonal skills (AACU, 2002, 2007; Mentkowski & Associates, 2000; Pascarella & Terenzini, 2005; SCANS, 1991).

CONCLUSION

The study involved an exploration of the relationship between active learning strategies and skills and attributes that enhance learning among college students. The study noted the important role of active learning strategies in the development of skills and attributes that enhance learning, and as such, institutions should foster enriching college experiences for their students. The perspectives observed in this study will help inform educational leaders and administrators in higher education as they plan college activities, policies, services, and programs to help students remain focused and persistent in learning. Kuh, Kinzie, Buckley, Bridges, and Hayek (2007) noted that "powerful learning environments and significant learning outcomes can be achieved no matter what the institution's resources or student's preparation" (p. 89). Therefore, institutions should make use of the available resources and provide their students with an enriching learning environment. Having a knowledge base of factors that enhance learning is important in addressing issues that may derail the learning process. Further, the constantly changing learning environment requires individuals who are equipped with what it takes to continuously learn.

Derrick (2003) pointed out that "the real purpose of education is to facilitate the learning journey and become fully autonomous in your ability to learn and endure regardless of the medium, the location, the need" (p. 10). Derrick further adds, "enduring learners continue to learn throughout life and view learning as the never-ending journey of self-fulfillment and self-satisfactions" (Derrick, 2003, p. 15). Educational institutions have a responsibility to foster this virtue among their students.

REFERENCES

American College Personnel Association (ACPA) & Nation Association of Student Personnel Administrators (NASPA). (1997). Principles of good practice for student affairs. Washington DC: Author.

Association of American Colleges and Universities (AACU). (2002). *Greater expectations: A new vision for learning as a nation goes to college.* Retrieved April 13th from http://www.greaterexpectations.org/

Association of American Colleges and Universities (AACU). (2007). *College learning for the New global century.* Retrieved January 26th from http://www.aacu.org/advocacy/leap/documents/GlobalCentury_final.pdf

Astin, A. W. (1984). Student Involvement: A developmental theory for higher education. *Journal of College Student Personnel, 25,* 297–308.

Astin, A. W. (1985). *Achieving education excellence: A critical assessment of priorities and practices in higher education.* San Francisco, CA: Jossey Bass.

Astin, A. W. (1993). *What matters in college? Four critical years revisited.* San Francisco, CA: Jossey Bass.

Beyer, K. B. (1988). *Developing a thinking skills program.* Boston, MA: Allyson & Bacon.

Bryce, J., Frigo, T., McKenzie, P., & Withers, G. (2002). *The era of lifelong learning: Implications for secondary schools.* Australian Council for Education Research. Retrieved November. 15th 2008 from http://www.acer.edu.au/documents/LifelongLearning.pdf

Bryce, J., & Wither, G. (2003). Engaging secondary school students in lifelong learning. *Australian Council for Educational Research.* Retrieved November 23, 2008 from http://www.acer.edu.au/documents/LifeLongLearning_Engaging.pdf

Cropley, J. A. (1981). Lifelong learning: A rationale for teacher training. *Journal of Education for Teaching, 7*(1), 57–69. doi:10.1080/0260747810070107

Derrick, G. M. (2003). Creating environments conducive for lifelong learning. *New Directions for Adult and Continuing Education, 100*(100), 5–18. doi:10.1002/ace.115

Gravetter, F. J., & Wallnau, L. B. (2007). *Statistics for the behavioral sciences* (7th ed.). Belmont, CA: Thomson Wadsworth.

Hinkle, D. E., Wiersma, W., & Jurs, S. G. (2003). *Applied statistics for the behavioral sciences* (5th ed.). Boston, MA: Haughton Mifflin.

Hirst, A. W. & Bailey, D. G. (1983). *A study to identify effective classroom teaching competencies for community college faculty.* ED227890.

Knapper, K. C., & Cropley, A. (2000). *Lifelong learning in higher education.* London: Kogan Page.

Knox, E. W., Lindsay, P., & Kolb, N. M. (1993). *Does college make a difference? Long-term changes in activities and attitudes.* Westport, CT: Greenwood Press.

Kolb, A. D. (1984). *Experiential learning: Experience as the source of learning and development.* Upper Saddle River, NJ: Prentice Hall.

Kuh, G. D. (2003). *The National Survey of Student Engagement: Conceptual framework and overview of psychometric properties.* Indiana University Center for Postsecondary Research & Planning. Retrieved June 10th 2009 from http://nsse.iub.edu/pdf/conceptual_framework_2003.pdf

Kuh, G. D., Kinzie, J., Buckley, A. J., Bridges, K. B., & Hayek, C. J. (2007). Piecing together the student success puzzle: Research, propositions, and recommendations. *ASHE Higher Education Report, 32*(5).

Mentkowski, M. et al. (2000). *Learning that last.* San Francisco, CA: Jossey Bass.

Mithaug, E. D., Mithaug, K. D., Agran, M., Martin, E. J., & Wehmeyer, L. M. (Eds.). (2003). *Self-determined learning theory: Construction, verification, and Evaluation.* Mahwah, NJ: Lawrence Erlbaum.

National Survey of Student Engagement (NSSE). (2009). *About the National Survey of Student Engagement.* Retrieved July 27th 2009 from http://nsse.iub.edu/html/about.cfm

Pascarella, T. E., & Terenzini, T. P. (2005). *How college affects students: A third decade of research.* San Francisco, CA: Jossey Bass.

Secretary's Commission on Achieving Necessary Skills (SCANS). (1991). *What work requires of schools: A SCANS report for America 2000.* Washington, DC: U.S. Department of Labor. Retrieved January 28th 2009 from http://wdr.doleta.gov/SCANS/whatwork/whatwork.pdf

Sirkin, M. R. (2006). *Statistics for the social sciences* (3rd ed.). Thousand Oaks, CA: Sage.

University Assessment Office (UAO). (2009). *NSSE 2007 data collection procedures.* Midwestern State University.

Vogt, W. P. (2007). *Quantitative Research Methods for Professionals.* Boston, MA: Allyn & Bacon.

KEY TERMS AND DEFINITIONS

Active Learning Strategies: Activities students engage in to enhance their own learning. Active learning strategies include, but are not limited to, how often the student made a class presentation, worked with other students on group projects, asked questions in class.

Skills and Attributes that Enhance learning: Proficiency and competence in aspects that boost knowledge acquisition, understanding, and creativity. These skills and attributes include analysis of quantitative problems, broad general education, computing and information technology, critical thinking and analytical skills, effective independent learning, job or work related knowledge and skills, speaking clearly and effectively, working effectively with others, and writing clearly and effectively.

Chapter 11
Educational Technology Assessment:
A Model for Analyzing Online Psychometric Tests for Course Evaluations

James Edward Osler II
North Carolina Central University, USA

Mahmud A. Mansaray
North Carolina Central University, USA

ABSTRACT

In this chapter a digital assessment and an associated novel mathematical statistical model are provided as online psychometrics designed to evaluate College and University courses. The psychometric evaluation tool is a Student Ratings of Instruction [SRI] instrument used at a Historically Black College and University [HBCU] for course evaluation purposes. The research methodology is an a posteriori post hoc investigation that examines the reliability and validity of the items used in the SRI instrument. The sample under analysis consisted of the responses to 56,451 total items extracted from 7,919 distributed Student Ratings Instruments delivered online during the 2012 academic year. The post hoc application of the novel Tri–Squared Test analysis methodology is used to intricately analyze the results of an earlier study on SRIs that yielded strong construct validity from Cronbach's Alpha Reliability Model, Goodman & Kruskal's Lambda, and Principal Component Factor Analysis with Varimax Rotation.

INTRODUCTION

Throughout the academy there has always been concern about improving the skills and knowledge of students. Many colleges and universities have promoted a multitude of strategies to enhance student success, and are constantly exploring ways that would further improve teaching excellence and student success. In attempting to acquire data regarding teaching efficacy, many universities have, over the years, utilized independent student survey designs to evaluate teaching and determine if student learning outcomes are met. Internationally, educational researcher Richard-

DOI: 10.4018/978-1-4666-8363-1.ch011

son noted several significant student evaluations of teaching ["Student Ratings" referred to as "Student Evaluations of Instruction" or "SEI"] in use in research projects in the US, England, and Australia, including the use of the British Noel–Levitz "Student Satisfaction Inventory"; the "Course Perceptions Questionnaire"; the "Student Evaluations of Educational Quality"; and the "Course Experience Questionnaire" (as cited in Skowronek, Friesen, & Masonjones, 2011).

Certainly, of the various assessment designs available to evaluate teaching effectiveness and student success, the student ratings are the most widely used in many universities worldwide because they offer an organized, methodical, and effective means of obtaining feedback on students' responses to instructors and courses (Agbetsiafa, 2010), and have been around since the mid–1920s (Cohen as cited in Donnon et al., 2010; d'Apollonia & Abrami as cited in Safavi, Bakar, Tarmizi, & Alwi, 2012; Wright, as cited in Gravestock & Gregor–Greenleaf, 2008). In general, there have been some agreements that, students' ratings seem sufficient to evaluate what they seek to determine: teaching effectiveness, student satisfaction, educational experience, and program curriculum (Abrami as cited in Gravestock et al., 2008; Agbetsiafa, 2010; Beran, Violoto, & Kline, 2007; Skowronek, et al., 2011; Zhao et al., 2012). Gravestock et al. (2008) also noted "the quantifiability and comparability of most course evaluations makes the imprecise art of evaluating teaching seem more objective and manageable" (pp. 10). In addition, Titus (2008) noted that, apart from securing teaching efforts to preferred outcomes, probing students about their knowledge underpins the commitment of classroom efforts and events. Additionally, other academics also agreed that student ratings can be an integral part of the evaluation of an instructor's performance (El Hassan, 2009; McKeachie & Hofer as cited in Skowronek et al., 2011).

Though most academics may reach a conclusion that student ratings are consistent tools,

there is fewer unison regarding their universal validity and reliability with respect to the level at which the design correctly evaluates concrete terms (e.g. "Teaching Effectiveness"), or present a comprehensive rating of the course or instructor (Agbetsiafa, 2010; Beran & Rokosh, 2009; Beran et al., 2007; Clayson, 2009; Gravestock et al., 2008; Marsh, 2007; McKeachie, 2007; Perry & Smart, 2007; Spooren, Mortelmans, & Denekens, 2007). Certainly, while some researchers have argued there is little evidence of a correlation between student ratings and teaching effectiveness (Madden, Dillon, & Leak, 2010; Pounder, 2007), others have considered the ratings to be a worthwhile evaluation of teaching effectiveness and student success (Abrami as cited in Gravestock et al., 2008; Frick, Chadna, Watson, Wing, & Green, 2009; Schrodt et al., 2008; Zhao et al., 2012). Student ratings can also be imperfect and answerable to manifold exterior influences independent of the teacher's capacity to teach and to foster and sustain an effectual course (Marsh, 2007; McKeachie, 2007; Perry et al., 2007). Also, some research studies have proposed student ratings may be vulnerable to elements unconnected with teaching effectiveness (Kozub, 2010). Some academics have established that, the student and the instructor's gender may affect student ratings (Emery as cited in Kozub, 2010). Donnon et al. (2010) also noted that, student ratings may vary according to the students' characteristics. Theall (2010) also said a somber difficulty was the prevalent hapless exercise in the expansion and utility of rating instruments, the assessment and reportage of data, and the explanation and usage of results.

There is an inconsistency within academia by academics in reaching an agreement on the validity and reliability of student ratings. The authors have found this is most often due to the inherent "highly contextual" method of teaching employed by institutions specifically dependent upon the particular institutions mission and vision that most often leads faculty in their development of their "varied instructional modalities". This has prompted others to promote the development of the model to include other measurements of evaluating teaching effectiveness (e.g. "peer reviews", "self–rating techniques", "student interviews", etc.) (Berk, 2005; El Hassan, 2012; Kulik as cited in Donnon et al., 2010; Marsh, Ginns, Morin, Nagengast, & Martin, 2011). Blackburn and Clark (as cited in Zhao et al., 2012) also noted a correlation between student ratings and peer ratings. Indeed, it is in this milieu of inconsistency within the academic world with regards to the validity and reliability of student ratings that this research study is conducted.

BACKGROUND

Establishing "Instructional Efficacy" or "Teaching Effectiveness" is the major emphasis in higher education. Determining teacher effectiveness may not be uncommon to academics since various studies on teaching excellence and student learning outcomes have already been completed (Hunsaker, Nielsen, & Bartlett, 2010; Perry as cited in Keeley, Furr, & Buskist, 2010; Schrodt, Witt, Myers, Turman., Barton, & Jernberg, 2008). After all, a practice that is prevalent in many universities and colleges in the United States and elsewhere is the use of student ratings to evaluate teaching effectiveness and student success (Cohen as cited in Donnon, Delver, & Beran, 2010; Kneipp, Kelly, Biscoe, & Richard, 2010; Stowell, Addison, & Smith, 2012). Marsh and Roche (as cited in Zhao & Gallant, 2012) noted that, the use of student ratings of faculty in colleges and universities is the provision of a constructive comment to faculty for teaching enhancement, as well as a cursory evaluation of teaching effectiveness for personnel or administrative decisions. Thus, this study continues to further investigate the efficacy of the SRI instrument in determining teaching

(instructional) effectiveness through an in–depth investigation of item analysis. In addition, the study will examine whether ratings completed by student ratings guarantee the validity and reliability of the instrument, in measuring what it is designed to measure: teaching effectiveness. In addition, the study will also assess for internal consistency as a means of establishing the validity and reliability of the instrument used for rating the effectiveness of the courses and programs. The study made use of existing student data from research previously conducted during the 2012 academic year at a HBCU (including the use of a quantitative approach to determine the impact of the evaluation model on teaching excellence and student success).

RATIONALE

This research is a continuation of an investigation into the practical importance of determining teaching effectiveness in terms of student learning outcomes in colleges and universities (particularly in the United States [US]). The determination of teaching excellence still appears to be exigent for researchers (Roche & Marsh, 2000; Young & Shaw, 1999). There is hardly any measurement, attribute, conduct, or classroom strategies, which completely grasps the meaning of an effective teacher. Barry (2010), for example, noted teaching effectiveness "involves a deep understanding of subject matter, learning theory and student differences, planning, classroom instructional strategies, knowing individual students, and assessment of student understanding and proficiency with learning outcomes" (pp. 4). Hassel (2009) also said the underlying specification of teacher effectiveness must be the student learning outcomes; that is, the extent to which students learn, and more valued effects. Vogt (1984), on the other hand, associated effective teaching to the potential to provide tutoring to diverse students of disparate talents while integrating teaching goals and evaluating the existing knowledge aspect of the students.

RESEARCH THAT SUPPORTS THE VALIDITY AND RELIABILITY OF SRIS

There is a growing list of literature on the uses, validity and reliability of the student ratings of faculty. Several journals on the evaluation of university faculty on teaching effectiveness and student success make use of the student ratings of instruction survey (Clayson, 2009; Jones, 2010; Zhao et al., 2012). The faculty uses student ratings to obtain a student response about their courses and register growth in their instruction parts and accountabilities (Donnon et al., 2010), which may have a significant effect on their professions (Sprinkle, 2008). Aleamoni (as cited in Zhao et al., 2012) had suggested the use of student ratings because students can offer information on the attainment of critical educational goals; affinity with the instructor; and, fundamentals of a classroom, such as instructional supplies, assignment, and instructional procedures. The Student ratings are also used to express knowledge to the students and to establish administrative resolutions, such as giving life–term tenure and advancement (Marsh, 2007; McKeachie, 2007). In addition, studies have revealed that students incline to consider teaching evaluations earnestly, and are enthusiastic to contribute and offer expressive response when they consider and can realize that their contributions are being reflected and assimilated by their teachers and the university (Agbetsiafa, 2010).

Notwithstanding, the growing list of journal articles on the usage of student ratings does not preclude the controversy surrounding their reliability, validity, generalizability, and their assessment of university teaching (Marsh, 2007). In general, the reliability of student ratings is concerned with the consistency [internal], stability and dependability of the assessment over time

(Chen & Watkins, 2010; Zhao et al., 2012). McMillan (as cited in Zhao et al., 2012) also noted a dependable resolution is one that has comparable performance at diverse times. Despite the controversy surrounding the reliability and validity of student ratings of instructors, several studies have found that student ratings of instructor are reliable, steady across items, raters, and session (Beran, Violato, Kline, & Frideres, 2009; Beran et al., 2009; Kneipp et al., 2010; Zerbini & Abbad, 2009; Spooren et al., 2007).

Several research studies have applied different statistical models to determine the reliability of the rating tools used to evaluate faculty. Most of these tests centered on the internal consistency [stability] of the ratings. The more prevalent is the Cronbach's Alpha statistics, with the alpha varying from 0 to 1; the 1 being the highest reliability score. Beran et al. (2009), for example, conducted a study to determine what students find useful about student ratings. With the application of survey responses from ($N = 1229$) students at a leading Canadian university, the authors developed a psychometrically substantial measure of the usefulness of student ratings. Using the Cronbach's Alpha model, the results established the internal consistency reliability of the 16 items on the rating scale at .93, thus indicating a high level of internal consistence for the student ratings. Kneipp et al. (2010) also reported an inter–rater reliability estimation of above .91 in the Cronbach's Alpha model, in their study, to determine the effect of the instructor's characteristics on the quality of instruction. In addition, Zuberi, Bordage, and Norman (2007) also noted the internal consistency [reliability] for student ratings obtained in their analysis of student evaluation of teaching in outpatient clinics was .98. Donnon et al. (2010) similarly realized a high internal consistency with a Cronbach's Alpha coefficient of .93 in their research on student ratings of instructors in medical sciences graduate programs. This only serves to highlight the high internal consistency of the student ratings in evaluating instructors.

Apart from the dispute surrounding their reliability, the student ratings are also faced with the problem of validity. In all–purpose, validity of student ratings denotes the degree to which student assessments of faculty instruction essentially evaluate what they are planned to evaluate (Zhao et al., 2012). Agbetsiafa (2010) also noted if student ratings are to be used to evaluate teaching effectiveness and student learning outcomes, the tools must be exposed to challenging validity trials and exploration.

Agbetsiafa's argument is preceded by Cronbach and Meehl (as cited in Zhao et al., 2012) who had noted construct validity was the level at which a perceived measurement mirrored the fundamental hypothetical construct that the researcher had planned to evaluate. Skowronek et al. (2011) also said it was essential to address issues that were related to construct validity, including answering whether the nature of the student rating procedure was reasonable for the construct that was being evaluated. Feldman (as cited in Chen et al., 2010) noted student ratings were revealed to display the correlation average with exterior catalogs of teaching quality: .29 in instructor ratings; .39 in administrator ratings; .55 in college ratings; and, .40 in student achievement. Chen et al. (2010) also surmised the correlations provided support for the construct validity of student ratings. Still, some academics recognized the problem connected with assessing the validity of the student ratings is due in part to the absence of a solitary standard for effective teaching (Abrami, d'Apollonia, & Cohen as cited in Zhao, 2012; Marsh, 2007; McKeachie, 2007; Pounder, 2007). As a result, some academics inclined to emulate student ratings with other assessments of teacher quality that were presumed to be effective (e.g. instructor self–evaluation of teacher effectiveness, peer/college evaluations etc.) (Hobson & Talbot as cited in Zhao et al., 2012). Other academics engaged statistical methods, such as factorial analysis, stepwise linear regression, multivariate analysis of variance, structural equation models, Pearson correlation, hierarchical regression, analysis of variance, and the paired sample *t*–test to validate the student–rating tool (Agbetsiafa, 2010; Héfer, 2009; Beran et al., 2009; Donnon et al., 2010; Kneipp et al., 2010; Schrodt et al., 2008; Stowell et al., 2012).

Agbetsiafa (2010), for example, employed the factorial analysis to establish the validity of the rating tool in determining the relationship between effective teaching and student ratings in a college level course, in Economics at the University of Indiana. Using ($N = 1300$) sampled students, the result of the Kaiser–Meyer–Olkin (KMO) statistics on the rating scale was .912, indicating the appositeness of the application of factor analysis to the data. In addition, the Bartlett's for the existence of interaction among the variables was significant at $p < .0001$. In all, the results found positive relationships between student awareness of teaching effectiveness, education assistance, effective communication, and lucidity of course components, and course evaluation and feedback, thus affirming the construct validity of the rating tool. Similarly, Sprinkle (2008) applied factorial analysis to assess the relationship between student biases and their perceptions of teaching effectiveness, using student ratings. Using ($N = 202$) sampled students, the KMO test for data adequacy (.79) was acceptable, and so was the Bartlett's test of sphericity, which was significant ($p = .000$). The results confirmed the validity of the test.

El Hassan (2009) was concerned about substantive and consequential validity of the student ratings. His research addressed concerns of substantive and consequential validity, and maintained they could be fully addressed where the evaluation procedures were totally strategized and implemented, including effective communication to students and faculty about the tenacity of the assessment procedures. However, Skowronek et al. (2011) were more concerned about content validity. The authors said comparatively miniature consideration had been given to the subject of content validity; the degree to which a device essentially catches a specified social construct. Héfer (2009) alternatively applied Pearson correlation and hierarchical regression statistics to verify the validity of student ratings design in determining the relationship of teaching effectiveness, course evaluation, and academic performance. The sampled students ($N = 113$) were undergraduates enrolled in six introductory courses. Using the Pearson correlation statistic, the result found associations between deferral of pleasure, motivational elements of deferral of pleasure, predicted and actual final course grade, and ratings of the course and the instructor. The result also found the students' ratings of the course and teaching effectiveness to be significantly correlated ($r = .68$). Also, the result of the hierarchical suggested students' inclination to defer pleasure was positively related to earning the final course grade.

So much has been said about the various validity studies of the student ratings of faculty. However, an often overlooked, but significant theoretical framework, applied in the validity analysis of student ratings of teaching excellence is the generalizability theory. Shavelson and Webb (as cited in Bo, Johnson, & Kilic, 2008) noted generalizability theory (G theory) describes the defect in conventional test theory in which the error term is an indistinct combination of different error bases. Bo et al, (2008) also said the analysis of variance (ANOVA) methods can be used to obtain estimates in the generalizability theory. Zuberi et al. (2007), for example, employed a repeated measure generalizability device to determine the validation of the student rating instrument in the evaluation of teaching in an outpatient clinic. Using the analysis of variance (ANOVA) and variance components, the results established a reliability score of .98 and a validity score of about 57%, indicating high reliability and validity of the student rating instrument used to evaluate teaching in outpatient clinics.

RESEARCH QUESTIONS ADDRESSED IN THE INITIAL STUDY

The research questions listed below were developed to examine the validity and reliability of the Student Ratings of Instruction [SRI] instrument used in the study to evaluate teaching quality.

Q_1: Do ratings completed by students engender internal reliability [consistency] in their measurement of teaching effectiveness?

This question calls for a quantitative research design. The ratings from the survey data at HBCU were used to determine the reliability of the question. This is specified in hypothesis H_{10} and H_{1a}. The statistical tool that will be realistic is the Cronbach's Alpha to verify the reliability [consistency] of the instrument used to evaluate teaching effectiveness.

Q_2: Do ratings completed by student ratings produce augmented validity in measuring teaching effectiveness?

The question aforementioned question calls for a quantitative research design. Again, the research made use of existing data at HBCU to determine this question. This is again outlined in hypothesis H_{20} and H_{2a}. The study will apply the factor analysis to determine the validity [construct validity] of the instrument used to determine teaching effectiveness.

RESEARCH HYPOTHESES

The below hypotheses were used to assess the research questions one and two. Each research question addresses a null hypothesis with anticipation of a non–significant association, and an alternative hypothesis that suggests that a significant association does occur between the variables.

H$_{1_0}$ **:** The student ratings do not increase the reliability of the instrument used to assess teaching effectiveness.

H$_{1_a}$ **:** The student ratings significantly increase the reliability of the instrument used to assess teaching effectiveness.

H$_{2_0}$ **:** The ratings completed by students do not create any validity of the rating instrument used in evaluating teaching effectiveness.

H$_{2_a}$ **:** The ratings completed by students generate increased validity of the rating instrument used in evaluating teaching effectiveness.

TRI–SQUARED TEST MATHEMATICAL HYPOTHESES

The first sets of Mathematical Hypotheses used in the study in terms of Tri–Squared to determine SRI item efficacy, validity, and reliability were as follows:

$$\mathbf{H}_0 : Tri^2 = 0$$

$$\mathbf{H}_1 : Tri^2 \neq 0$$

CRONBACH'S ALPHA [α] MATHEMATICAL HYPOTHESES

The second sets of Mathematical Hypotheses used in the study in terms of Cronbach's Alpha to determine reliability were as follows:

$$\mathbf{H}_{1_0} : \alpha \leq 0$$

$$\mathbf{H}_{1_a} : \alpha > 0$$

The second sets of Mathematical Hypotheses used in the study in terms of Cronbach's Alpha to determine validity were as follows:

$$\mathbf{H}_{2_0} : \alpha \leq 0$$

$$\mathbf{H}_{2_a} : \alpha > 0$$

STATISTICAL MATHEMATICAL MODELS

1. TRI–SQUARED TEST [Tri ^{2}]

Tri–Squared comprehensively stands for "The Total Transformative Trichotomous–Squared Test" (or "Trichotomy–Squared"). The Total Transformative Trichotomous–Squared Test provides a methodology for the transformation of the outcomes from qualitative research into measurable quantitative values that are used to test the validity of hypotheses. It is based on the mathematical "Law of Trichotomy". The Total Transformative Trichotomous–Squared Test provides a methodology for the transformation of the outcomes from qualitative research into measurable quantitative values that are used to test the validity of hypotheses. The advantage of this research procedure is that it is a comprehensive holistic testing methodology that is designed to be static way of holistically measuring categorical variables directly applicable to educational and social behavioral environments where the established methods of pure experimental designs are easily violated. The unchanging base of the Tri–Squared Test is the 3×3 Table based on Trichotomous Categorical Variables and Trichotomous Outcome Variables. The emphasis the three distinctive variables provide a thorough rigorous robustness to the test that yields enough outcomes to determine if differences truly exist in the environment in which the research takes place (Osler, 2013).

Tri–Squared is grounded in the combination of the application of the research two mathematical pioneers and the author's research in the basic two dimensional foundational approaches that ground further explorations into a three dimensional Instructional Design. The aforementioned research includes the original dissertation of optical pioneer Ernst Abbe who derived the distribution that would later become known as the chi square distribution and the original research of mathematician Auguste Bravais who pioneered the initial mathematical formula for correlation in his research on observational errors. The Tri–Squared research procedure uses an innovative series of mathematical formulae that do the following as a comprehensive whole: (1) Convert qualitative data into quantitative data; (2) Analyze inputted trichotomous qualitative outcomes; (3) Transform inputted trichotomous qualitative outcomes into outputted quantitative outcomes; and (4) Create a standalone distribution for the analysis possible outcomes and to establish an effective—research effect size and sample size with an associated alpha level to test the validity of an established research hypothesis. Osler (2012) defined Tri–Squared as:

$$Tri^2 = T_{Sum}[(Tri_x - Tri_y)^2 : Tri_y].$$

2. Cronbach's Alpha [α]

One of the significant statistical models in this research is the Cronbach's Alpha [α]. It is a valuable coefficient for examining the internal consistency and has been named after Lee Cronbach who first developed it in 1951. Bland and Altam (1997) defined Cronbach's Alpha as:

$$\alpha = \frac{k}{k-1}\left(1 - \frac{\sum_{i=1}^{k} s_i^2}{s_T^2}\right)$$

Where, k is the amount of objects, s_i^2 is the variance of the ith object and s_T^2, is the variance of the final total created by adding all the objects. In addition, they also said if the objects were not simply added to make the total, but were initially multiplied by weighting coefficients, then the object must be multiplied by its coefficient ahead of the analysis of the variance s_i^2. Certainly, the formula must contain at least two objects, that is, $k > 1$ or ± cannot be distinct. Field (2009) also defined the Cronbach's Alpha somewhat differently from that stated by Bland et al. (1997), even when the ideas are similar. Field defined the Cronbach's Alpha as:

$$\frac{N^2 Cov}{\sum s_{item}^2 + \sum Cov_{item}}$$

The author noted that, for every object on the scale, two things can be computed: the variance contained in the object, and the covariance amongst an explicit object and any additional object on the scale. Thus, a variance–covariance matrix of the whole objects can be computed. In addition, the author also said, in the matrix, the diagonal rudiments establish the variance contained in an exact object, and the off–diagonal rudiments comprise covariances amid sets of objects. The upper half of the formula is the quantity of objects (N) squared multiplied by the mean covariance amongst objects. The lower half is only the total of all the object variances and object covariances. The arrays of the alpha statistic are between zero and one. The greater the coefficient, the better the select items organized together in evaluating the instrument construct, and thus the better the statistical reliability of the assessment tool. An alpha of 1.00 would imply a seamlessly consistent instrument, while a coefficient of zero would imply an untrustworthy tool.

3. Factorial Analysis

The factorial model used in this study is derived from Agbetsiafa (2010), and Field (2009). Concisely, factor analysis allows the delineation of an essential or hidden configuration in a data set. It accelerates the analysis of the configuration of the associations (correlation) among an outsized number of variables by describing a set of shared essential measurements, commonly termed factors (Agbetsiafa, 2010). Field (2009) noted that, factorial is a mathematical model, resembling a linear equation but without the intercept because the lines intersect at zero and, therefore, the intercept is also zero. Field (2009) defined factorial as:

$$Y_i = b_1 X_{1i} + b_2 X_{2i} + \ldots + b_n X_{ni} + \varepsilon_i$$

The values of b are the loading factors.

Agbetsiafa's (2010) was more detailed in his description of the factorial model in his research than Field (2009). According to Agbetsiafa, it is conceivable to reorient the data to allow the first small number of measurements to explain for much of the existing data. Assuming there is any idling in the data set; it is also conceivable to explain for most of the evidence in the original data with a significantly condensed amount of measurements. Adapting his template, this study also assumes that the 15 items on the student evaluation survey instrument bears relationships with a series of functions working linearly, and they may be represented by the following mathematical formulas:

$$Y_1 = \alpha_{10+} \alpha_{11} X_1 + \ldots + \alpha_{1n} X_n + \varepsilon_i$$

$$Y_2 = \alpha_{20+} \alpha_{21} X_1 + \ldots + \alpha_{2n} X_n + \varepsilon_i$$

$$Y_3 = \alpha_{30+} \alpha_{31} X_1 + \ldots + \alpha_{3n} X_n + \varepsilon_i$$

$$Y_{15} = \alpha_{150+} \alpha_{151} X_1 + \ldots + \alpha_{15n} X_n + \varepsilon_i$$

Where: Y = a variable with recognized data; α = constant; X_i = the fundamental factors; and, ε_i = the error terms, which help to point out the conjectured associations, are not exhaustive. Thus, applying the technique to the recognized 15 items on the student rating survey instrument, factor analysis describes the unidentified X utilities. The developing loadings from the analysis are the constants, and the factors are the X utilities. The scope of the individual loading for every utility assesses the degree to which the definite utility is associated with the explicit variable (Y). Thus, for any of the 15 variables in equation one of the proposed study, the model may be written as: $Y_1 = \alpha_1 X_1 + \alpha_2 X_2 + \alpha_3 X_3 + \ldots + \alpha_n X_n + \varepsilon_i$, where X_i, denote factors, and α_is signify the loadings

CONDUCTING SRI RESEARCH AT AN HBCU

The backdrop for this research study is the Research, Evaluation, and Planning Department (REP) of Historic Black College and University. The study will make use of the student rating responses conducted during the spring semester of 2012 by REP. This is a cross–sectional data set. Arguably, REP has the responsibility to coordinate all student, faculty and administrative surveys on behalf of the university. 7,919 students responded to the spring semester survey. The students were graduates and undergraduates and were from the various departments, schools and colleges within the university, with the exclusion of the HBCU Law School. The ratings from the Law School have different components, which are incompatible with the ratings of the rest of the schools and colleges in the university.

THE SRI MEASUREMENT SCALE

The student ratings of instruction survey is employed to evaluate course instructors and is administered online during the spring and fall semesters of each academic year, with the *CourEval* assessment tool in a 5–point Likert scale, to all registered students of the university. The rating survey requires students to assess their instructors on 15 items in the assessment tool. The instrument has two subscales. Items 1 to 3 measure the student's efforts in the course, where the scale comprises the following: 1 = never, 2 = not much of the time, 3 = about half of the time, 4 = most of the time and, 5 = all of the time. Items 4 to 15 evaluate the instructor, where the scale comprises the following: 1 = strongly disagree, 2 = disagree, 3 = no opinion, 4 = agree and, 5 = strongly agree. This research considers the evaluation of the instructor as an assessment of teaching effectiveness or teaching quality. A sample of the assessment tool is presented in Appendix C of page 49. Also, the instrument has a section where students can make open–ended statements about the instructors, when these are requested by the individual colleges or departments within the university. For the 2012 spring semester ratings survey, the 7,919 responders evaluated instructors on 18,817 courses and course sections offered at HBCU. In addition, the only variables included in this study are the 15 items on the survey instrument with their respective ratings.

HOC TRI–SQUARED TEST RESULTS:

The Application of the Cronbach's Alpha Reliability Model on Three Factors as Qualitative Outcomes to Determine SRI Efficacy Using the Tri–Squared Test

Data Analyzed Using the Trichotomous–Squared Three by Three Table designed to analyze the research questions and data extracted from an Inventive Investigative Instrument designed with the following Trichotomous Categorical Variables: a_1 = Is the Student Rating of Instruction Instrument effective?; a_2 = Is the Student Rating of Instruction Instrument valid?; and a_3 = Is the Student Rating of Instruction Instrument consistent? The 3×3 Table has the following Trichotomous Outcome Variables: b_1 = Yes; b_2 = No; and b_3 = No Opinion. The Inputted Qualitative Outcomes are reported as follows in Table 1 (for $56451_{[Total Items]} \in 7919_{[Grand Total SRI]}$).

The Tri–Square Test Formula for the Transformation of Trichotomous Qualitative Outcomes into Trichotomous Quantitative Outcomes to Determine the Validity of the Research Hypothesis:

Table 1. Tri–squared test table

$n_{Tri} = 56451_{[Total Items]}$ $\alpha = 0.001$	TRICHOTOMOUS TEST: [INPUT VARIABLES]				
TRICHOTOMOUS RESULTS: [OUTPUT VARIABLES]		a_1	a_2	a_3	
	b_1	15629	15751	15125	
	b_2	1222	1058	1406	
	b_3	1966	2008	2286	
	Tri ^{2} *d.f.* = $[C-1][R-1] = [3-1][3-1] = 4 = $ ***Tri*** $^2\left[\overline{x}\right]$				

$Tri^2 = T_{Sum}[(Tri_x - Tri_y)^2 : Tri_y]$.

Tri^2 Critical Value Table = 18.467 (with $d.f.$ = 4 at α = 0.001). For $d.f.$ = 4, the Critical Value for p > 0.001 is 18.467. The Calculated Tri–Square value is 92.531, thus, the null hypothesis (H_0) is rejected by virtue of the hypothesis test which yields the following: Tri–Squared Critical Value of 18.467 < 92.531 Calculated Tri–Squared Value.

Post Hoc Tri–Squared Test Results:

1. Tri–Squared Calculated Value = 92.531
2. Tri–Squared Degrees of Freedom = 4
3. Tri–Squared Probability = 0.0096
4. Tri–Squared Alpha Level = 0.001 [for n_{Tri} = 56451 [Total Items] Maximized Test Critical Value]

Post Hoc Tri–Squared Percentage Deviations:
Percentage deviation and standardized residual are both measures of the degree to which an observed Tri–Squared cell frequency differs from the value that would be expected on the basis of the null hypothesis. The total summation of the post hoc Tri–Squared Percentage Deviations should equal zero across Trichotomous Outcome Variables as illustrated in Table 2. Table 3 immediately follows and interprets the results of Table on a level of Association Table. The Level of Association Table displays the minute variations between Trichotomous x and y Categorical and Outcome Variables as a "Reliability Index". The results of this study indicate that there are extreme variations in association between variables based upon associative measures of efficacy, validity,

Table 2. Post hoc tri–squared test percentage deviations

	a_1	a_2	a_3
b_1	+0.8%	+1.6%	–2.4%
b_2	–0.5%	–13.8%	+14.4%
b_3	–5.8%	–3.8%	+9.6%

and reliability. Table 2 shows that in terms of Post Hoc Tri–Squared Test Percentage Deviations the highest positive association between variables was +14.4% and highest negative association was –5.8%.

Table 4 displays the Post Hoc Tri–Squared Test Standardized Residuals for the application of the Cronbach's Alpha Reliability Model on the three factors of efficacy, validity, and reliability as qualitative outcomes to determine Student Ratings of Instruction efficacy using the Tri–Squared Test. The standardized residual for a cell in a Tri–Squared table is a version of the standard normal deviate, "z_{Tri}", and was calculated using the following Tri–Squared Test transformation mathematical calculation:

$$z_{Tri} = \frac{Tri_x - Tri_y}{\sqrt{Tri_y}}$$

The mathematical calculation above is defined as follows:

z_{Tri} = The Tri–Squared Calculated Standard Normal Deviate;

Tri_x = Trichotomous Qualitative Outcomes; and

Tri_y = Trichotomous Quantitative Outcomes.

Assuming the Tri–Squared Test null hypothesis to be true, values of the standardized residual belong to a normally distributed sampling distribution with a mean of zero and a standard deviation of ± 1.0. As in Table 2 the Table 3 Reliability Index can be used to interpret the Table 4 data. Table 4 shows that in terms of Post Hoc Standardized Residuals the highest positive association between variables was +5.06 and highest negative association was –4.85.

Table 3. Interpreting the value of the level of association between trichotomous x and y variables for the tri–squared test reliability index for the student ratings of instruction [sris] based upon the tri–squared standardized residuals determined from post hoc analysis:

Level Of Association	Verbal Description	Comments
−1.00+	Perfect Negative Relationship.	The independent variable cannot perfectly predict the dependent variable. They are complete opposites.
−.50 to −.99	Redundantly Negative	The two variables are obviously are not measuring the same concept.
−.40 to −.50	Extremely Strong	Either an extremely negative relationship or the two variables are not measuring the same concept equally.
−.35 to −.40	Very Strong	Extremely negative.
−.30 to −.35	Strong	Strongly negative.
−.25 to −.30	Moderately Strong Negatively	Generally negative.
−.20 to −.25	Moderately Negatively	Moderately negative.
−.15 to −.20	Weak Negative	Minimally negative.
.00 to −.15	Very Weak Negative	Weakly negative.
0.00	No Relationship	Knowing the independent variable does not help in predicting the dependent variable.
.00 to .15	Very Weak	Not generally acceptable.
.15 to .20	Weak	Minimally acceptable.
.20 to .25	Moderate	Acceptable.
.25 to .30	Moderately Strong	Desirable.
.30 to .35	Strong	Very Desirable.
.35 to .40	Very Strong	Extremely Desirable.
.40 to .50	Worrisomely Strong	Either an extremely good relationship or the two variables are measuring the same concept.
.50 to .99	Redundant	The two variables are probably measuring the same concept.
1.00+	Perfect Positive Relationship.	The independent variable can perfectly predict the dependent variable.

GOODMAN AND KRUSKAL'S LAMBDA (λ) TRI–SQUARED RESULTS

Goodman & Kruskal's Lambda (λ) is a cross tabulation analysis measure of proportional reduction in error. Lambda indicates the extent to which the modal categories and frequencies for each value of the independent variable differ from the overall modal category and frequency. The Goodman–Kruskal Values for Lambda range from zero (indicating that there is "no association"

between independent and dependent variables) to one (indicating a "perfect association" between

Table 4. Tri–squared post hoc standardized residuals

	a_1	a_2	a_3
b_1	+1.02	+2.00	−3.03
b_2	−0.18	−4.85	+5.06
b_3	−2.64	−1.72	+4.36

Table 5. Goodman & Kruskal's lambda (λ) tri–squared table

Cross Tabulation of Variables		Independent Variables			Results:
		Categorical Variable 1 = a_1	Categorical Variable 2 = a_2	Categorical Variable 3 = a_3	=
Dependent Variables	Outcome Variable 1 = b_1	15629	15751	15125	*46505*
	Outcome Variable 2 = b_2	1222	1058	1406	*3686*
	Outcome Variable 3 = b_3	1966	2008	2286	*6260*
Results:	=	*18817*	*18817*	*18817*	*56451*

independent and dependent variables). It is calculated with the following equation:

$$\lambda = \frac{\varepsilon_1 - \varepsilon_2}{\varepsilon_1}$$

Where,

ε_1 = Is the overall non–modal frequency; and

ε_2 = Is the sum of the non–modal frequencies for each value of the independent variable.

Table 5 illustrates the results of the Post Hoc Tri–Squared Goodman & Kruskal's Lambda (λ) the results of which are summarized after Table 7 to provide a holistic perspective of the Cross Tabulation of Variables.

Table 6 displays the results of the Post Hoc Tri–Squared Goodman & Kruskal's Lambda (λ):

Index of Predictive Association the results of which are summarized after Table 7 to provide a holistic perspective of all of the results of the Cross Tabulation of Variables.

The Post Hoc results of the Tri–Squared Test in this study as reported in Tables 5 through 7 provided the following results:

1. The sample size was enormous [n_{Tri} = $56451_{[Total\ Items]} \in 7919_{[Grand\ Total\ SRI]}$] which yielded large numbers of data on the efficacy of Student Ratings of Instruction;

2. The Trichotomous Categorical Variables under investigation were: Student Rating of Instruction Instrument effectiveness; Student Rating of Instruction Instrument validity; and Student Rating of Instruction Instrument consistency that were indicated as having existence based upon respondents indicating one of following three Trichotomous Outcome Variables: Yes; No; or No Opinion;

Table 6. Goodman & Kruskal's lambda (λ) tri–squared results: index of predictive association

Lambda (λ) for Predicting	Standard Error	.95 Confidence Interval Limits	
		Upper	Lower
a from *b*:	0	—	—	—
b from *a*:	0.0166	0.0052	0.0065	0.0267

Table 7. Estimated probability of correct prediction when predicting

a without knowledge of *b*:	0.8238
a from *b*:	0.8238
b without knowledge of *a*:	0.3333
b from *a*:	0.3444

3. The initial Tri–Squared statistical analysis rejected the null hypothesis via the Tri–Squared hypothesis test based upon the following results (with *d.f.* = 4 at α = 0.001): [The Tri–Squared Test Critical Value] = 18.467 < 92.531 = [The Calculated Tri–Squared Test Value]. Thus, there was enough evidence to reject H_0 at p > 0.001 (with a value of 0.001). These results illustrate that there is a significant difference in the perceptions of the research participants regarding SRI efficacy as determined by the extremely large Tri–Squared Test battery of instruments in terms of:
   a. "Efficacy",
   b. "Validity", and
   c. "Consistency" (i.e., "Reliability");
4. The Goodman & Kruskal's Lambda (λ) Tri–Squared Results yielded the following results— Due to the massive size of the data the Lambda (λ) for Predicting = 0.0166 (with a Standard Error = 0.0052); and
5. The Estimated Probability of Correct Prediction when Predicting had the following results—Predicting *a* without knowledge of *b* and conversely *a* from *b* both = 0.8238 (the highest percentage value = 82.38% indicating a high probability of predicting the Independent Categorical [Independent] Variable *a* from the Dependent [Outcome] Variable *b*) and the lowest percentage of prediction was *b* without knowledge of *a* = 0.3333 (indicating a 33.33% chance of predicting Dependent Variable *b* from Independent Variable *a*).

Tables 8 and 9 correspond to one another. Table 8 reports the results of the Cronbach's Alpha statistical test results for research Hypothesis 1. Table 9 reports the Item–Total Statistics for the Cronbach's Alpha results. The Cronbach's Alpha was computed to test hypothesis one on whether the ratings completed by the students, to evaluate faculty on the 15 items, significantly increase the reliability of the rating scale. The results of the study are revealed in the Appendix Tables A1–A4. Table A1 is the *Reliability Statistics* for the test of internal consistency. In general, the unstandardized alpha is usually used to interpret the internal consistency of the rating scale. In this regard, the Cronbach's Alpha of .954 was close to unity, and was significantly higher for the 15 items on the rating scale. Table A2 in Appendix A of page 39 is a table of descriptive statistics for each item on the rating scale. Item one [A1] (*M* = 4.57, *SD* = .670) on the rating scale, for example, required to state the level of effort a student had exerted on the course. Also, Table A3 in Appendix A of page 41 is a matrix unveiling the inter–item correlations of each item on the scale with every other item. According to the table, B2 (*The subject matter of this course is well organized*), for example, is positively correlated with B3 (*The instructor clearly presents his/her subject matter*) (*r* = .841).

Table 9 is the *Item Total Statistics* table. This is, perhaps, the most significant table of the Cronbach's Alpha statistical model. The table provides five pieces of information for each item on the scale. The two most significant portions of the table are the *Corrected –Item Total Correction* and the *Alpha if Item Deleted*. The earlier is the correlation of each detailed item with the complete total of the remaining items on the scale. If it is assumed the correlation of this to be discreetly high of say .40 or greater, then it can be surmised the precise item to be, at least temperately correlated with most of the remaining items and will generate a worthy module of this conjectured rating scale. In the case of Table 9,

Table 8. Initial research study: Cronbach's alpha hypothesis 1 results

Reliability Statistics		
Cronbach's Alpha	Cronbach's Alpha Based on Standardized Items	N of Items
.954	.949	15

Table 9. Item–total statistics

	Scale Mean if Item Deleted	Scale Variance if Item Deleted	Corrected Item–Total Correlation	Squared Multiple Correlation	Cronbach's Alpha if Item Deleted
A1	60.28	111.566	.369	.513	.957
A2	60.27	113.559	.256	.279	.959
A3	60.34	111.653	.328	.476	.958
B1	60.48	101.518	.839	.748	.949
B2	60.62	99.358	.837	.768	.949
B3	60.58	99.131	.862	.807	.948
B4	60.57	99.921	.812	.713	.949
B5	60.65	99.419	.835	.719	.949
B6	60.66	99.117	.847	.757	.948
B7	60.59	100.295	.819	.697	.949
B8	60.58	100.850	.823	.743	.949
B9	60.64	100.397	.791	.677	.950
B10	60.56	100.073	.828	.785	.949
B11	60.56	100.672	.811	.762	.949
B12	60.55	99.423	.875	.835	.948

Labels for Table 9 and Appendices Tables A4 and Table B1.

A1: I have put a great deal of effort into this course.

A2: I have attended classes regularly.

A3: I have completed the required readings for this course.

B1: The stated goals and objectives for this course are consistent with what was actually taught.

B2: The subject matter of this course is well organized.

B3: The instructor clearly presents his/her subject matter.

B4: The instructor is enthusiastic and arouses interest in his course.

B5: My power to think, criticize, and/or create have been improved as a result this course.

B6: The texts and other readings assigned for this course have been helpful.

B7: The instructor uses instructional approaches (for example, discussions, lectures, audio–visuals, field work, demonstrations, computer programs, etc.) which effectively enhance learning in this course.

B8: The examinations are consistent with the course objectives and the instruction.

B9: Quizzes, examinations and/or written assignments are provided frequently enough to help me evaluate my progress.

B10: The instructor is genuinely concerned with students' progress.

B11: I am able to get help from the instructor when I need it.

B12: This instructor is effective in promoting learning.

almost all of the items on the scale had significant inter–correlations with each other. The scale mean for Table item B4, for example, was 60.57, and a significant positive correlation ($r = .81$, supported by the results of the earlier Goodman & Kruskal's Lambda statistical results) with other items on the scale. Its coefficient alpha—the extent to which the item is consistent or inter–correlated for the scale was 0.95.

According to the results for all 15 items in Table 9, students offered optimistic assessments of the course teachings they received. Notwithstanding, the standard deviations for the 15 items were also less than unity, indicating that the scale means thoroughly mirrored the responses of most students, and there was not an extensive disparity of responses to the rating items. Therefore, the excessive coefficient alpha for the individual items on the scale revealed that, the items were consistent and highly inter–correlated and together, they indicated good internal consistency reliability. This is, in addition to Table A1, where the alpha for all 15 items was .95, thus indicating that, all 15 items produced a scale that had realistic internal consistency reliability. Therefore, the null hypothesis that student ratings do not increase the reliability of the instrument used to assess teaching quality is rejected. The instrument does show strong internal reliability.

INITIAL RESEARCH STUDY: HYPOTHESIS 2 RESULTS

The study also conducted the principal component factor analysis (PCA) with varimax rotation, to determine the underlying structure for the 15 items on the rating scale. It is also to check the validity of the rating instrument. The initial step in this analysis is the establishment of a correlation matrix for the 15 items on the scale. Non–significant correlations between the items would suggest they are distinct and will, therefore, not be expected to create one or more factors. If this is realized, it would not be realistic to forge ahead with the construction of a factor analysis. Table B1 below shows the estimated correlation and the level of significance of the 15 items on the rating scale. All of the items were significant ($p = .000$) and in correlations with one another, thus suggesting they may establish one or more factors.

Next, is the Kaiser–Meyer–Olkin (KMO) statistic, a measurement of "sampling suitability". Meaning that it tells whether there are enough items predicted by each factor. A zero value shows that the summation of fractional correlations is greater than the totality of the correlations, representing dispersal in the configuration of correlations; and; therefore, factor analysis is probably unsuitable. A value near one point to a configuration of correlations that is reasonably condensed and, therefore, factor analysis ought to produce

unique and dependable factor (Agbetsiafa, 2010). Field (2009) suggested that, the KMO evaluation must be $> .70$, and is lacking if $< .50$. Leech, Barrett, and Morgan (2011) also said KMO must be $> .70$, to justify adequate items for every factor. Thus, in the below Table B2, the KMO statistic for the 15 items on the scale was .960 ('superb', as stated by Field, 2009), confirming the sampling adequacy for the analysis. In addition, the entire KMO values (See Table B2) for individual items were $> .77$, which is beyond the tolerable margin of .50 (Field, 2009). The Barlett's test of sphericity followed the KMO measurement. This is a measure of the *null hypothesis* that, the preliminary correlation matrix is an identity matrix. Thus, for factor analysis to function, it requires certain associations between variables, and if the R–matrix is an identity matrix, it follows that the entire correlation coefficients would be zero (Field, 2009). The Barlett's assessment must, therefore, be significant to be considered worthy. Leech et al. (2011) also noted the Barlett's test of sphericity must be significant ($p < .05$) to establish that, the correlation matrix is significantly dissimilar to an identity matrix, where correlations between variables are entirely zero. Therefore, according to the above Table B2, the Bartlett's test of sphericity $\chi^2 (105) = 271591.204$, $p < .001$ was significant, demonstrating that correlations between items were adequately strong for PCA. In addition, a preliminary examination was prompted to acquire eigenvalues for each element [component] in the data. This is revealed in the below Table B4. Two elements had eigenvalues above Kaiser's condition of 1 (61.98%; 12.30%) and together, explained 74.28% of the variance. The scree plot (See Figure B1 on page 24) showed that, following the first two components, variances amongst the eigenvalues declined (the curve flattened), and were < 1.0. The graph again supported a two–component resolution.

Arguably, with the outsized sample size, and the merging of the scree plot and Kaiser's standard on two components, these were the quantities of components that were engaged in the final analysis. Table B5 displays the items and factor loadings after rotation. The first factor, which appeared to index the promotion of learning and teaching effectiveness, had strong loadings on the first twelve items. Even when quizzes and examinations also had strong loadings ($> = .82$), they had the least value of the twelve items in the first factor. In addition, the second factor, which appeared to index students' efforts also had high loadings on the remaining three items in the table. The item "*I have put a great deal of effort into this course*", had the highest loading from the students' efforts perspective. Notwithstanding, the first factor which had information on effective learning advancement, goals and objectives, student–teacher relationship, among others, were found to be significantly related to teaching effectiveness, thus affirming the construct validity of the instrument used to evaluate teaching quality. Therefore, the null hypothesis that the assessment instrument has no validity is rejected (for further supporting results see Appendices Tables B1 through B5 and Figure B1).

FINDINGS FROM EARLIER RESEARCH

The Cronbach's Alpha Test statistic of .95 (See Table A1, page 17) illustrates an extraordinarily high internal consistency of the student rejoinders to the items on the rating scale. It thus confirms the reliability of the instrument used in evaluating teaching effectiveness. The result is in consonance with similar studies on the reliability of student ratings with the application of the Cronbach's Alpha statistic (Agbetsiafa, 2010; Anastasiadou, 2011; Beran et al., 2009; Donnon et al., 2010; Kneipp et al., 2010; Zerbini et al., 2009; Zuberi et al., 2007). Additionally, it is also realized that, the 15 questions on the rating scale considered as variables, entirely disintegrated into two modules or factors: Teaching Effectiveness consisting of

12 questions with factor loads ranging between .82 and .90; and, Students' Efforts consisting of three questions with factor loads ranging between .76 and .86 (See the above Table B5). The results also confirm that, the scale offered evidence of construct validity. Indeed, the factor loads of teaching effectiveness are significantly high, thus endorsing the construct validity of teaching excellence at HBCU, even with the exclusion of end–of–course grades. Again, the results of the study are consistent with similar results on the validity of student assessment using PCA (Agbetsiafa, 2010; Zerbini et al., 2009; Sofia, 2011; Beran et al., 2009; Skowronek et al., 2011; Donnon et al., 2010; Safavi et al., 2012; Spooren et al., 2007; Beran et al., 2007).

Arguably, student ratings are crucially necessary for summative purposes at HBCU. The ratings have been extensively applied in administrative decisions in connection with faculty retention, promotion, salary increase, and tenure approval. There are studies which have suggested the unease of faculty to use the ratings by the administration for summative [personnel] purposes (Abrami as cited in Beran et al., 2007; Nasser & Fresko as cited in Beran et al., 2009). However, this study cannot confirm the perception of the faculty on the use of student ratings for summative purposes since no personal interview with the faculty was conducted. That the ratings continued to be applied by the administration at HBCU for summative purposes, is aptly justified by the results of the research, even when this is not a trend study. Again, even when this is inconclusive, still, there are indications that some instructors carry a negative view of the student ratings out of unease that the ratings may be subjective by individualities of the instructors and courses as, for example, assignment grades, among others. These indications are consistent with the findings of Eiszlet, who said the instructors were concerned that student ratings may be prejudiced by the distinctiveness of the instructors (as cited in Beran et al., 2007). Even so, there is hardly any doubt about the internal consistency and construct validity of the rating instrument used to assess teaching quality, at least with respect to the findings of this study. There are also indications that HBCU faculty has found the ratings useful for formative purposes like, for example, instructional improvement, even when some have questioned their validity.

Even with the validation of the rating instrument used in assessing teaching quality, the research is not without its limitations. There were 7,919 students who responded to the survey. However, the research made no attempt to distinguish between undergraduate and graduate students; and, between online and distance learning and class-based [traditional] students. It is conceivable; assessing online and classroom-based students independently may have resulted in different outcomes from the existing outputs. However, a similar study found no significant difference in the mean ratings between online and class-based student evaluations of instruction (Stowell et al., 2012). The only significant difference between online and class-based student evaluations of instruction was the low response rate of online students (Anderson, Brown, & Spaeth, 2006; Stowell et al., 2012). Against this backdrop, it is likely distinguishing between online and class-based students' ratings would not have had any significant effect on the findings of this research.

In addition, the study confirms a strong association between student ratings and teaching effectiveness. The inter-correlations between the 12 items on teaching effectiveness are significantly positive, and ranges between .64 and .84 on both the Cronbach's Alpha scale (See Table A3 of Appendices), and the correlation matrix result of the factorial analysis model (see also Table B1 of Appendices). It is likely the sound inter-correlations between the 12 items may have been influenced by the size of the classes. This is so because a single class at HBCU must have at least three enrolled students before the students are allowed to evaluate the instructor. White, for example, noted a positive association between class size and

comprehensive analysis of teaching (as cited in Ibrahim, 2011). Ibrahim also surmised class size had a positive influence on the dependability of student ratings of instruction. However, this cannot be independently confirmed since class–size was never a factor in this study. Class size may be considered in future research studies. It is also likely that, the strong inter–correlation between the 12 items is because each has a relationship with teaching excellence.

Now, the research also did not consider the study of generalizability. That is; how confident are we that the student ratings perfectly mimic the instructor's comprehensive teaching ability, not just how efficiently he or she was in the 2012 spring semester only. Generalizability could have been resolved if the study had compared the same instructors teaching the same courses but in different semesters; or, the same instructors teaching various courses; or, different instructors teaching the same course. Though the investigations confirmed construct validity of the rating instrument for the 2012 spring semester, it is doubtful if a similar result would have dominion for the same instructors across semesters, for example. Studies, however, have shown a higher correlation between different courses taught by the same instructor, thus concluding it was the instructor, not the course, who was the leading cause of the student rating objects (Gillmore, Kane, & Naccaranto, 1978; Hogan, 1973; Marsh, 1982).

Even when the assessment indicator has shown strong reliability and validity in the completed study, there is the unease that the psychometric properties of the student evaluation of instruction may be antiquated and would need to be updated for significant formative purposes. Arguably, while there are studies that have had three or more factor loadings produced after factorial analysis (Agbetsiafa, 2010; Anastasiadou, 2011), this study only had two psychometric properties after factorial analysis, as already realized: student efforts and teaching effectiveness. The two together formed the 15 items on the rating scale. It would have been worthwhile to ensure the student ratings of instruction evaluate the following areas as well: course composition, organization, objectives, and the attributes, complexity, and significance of a course; instructor's readiness, passion, and course understanding; and, the instructor's purpose of arranging classroom exercises and alluring students in scholastic quests. Still, the earlier properties qualify for the application of factorial analysis.

Additionally, the inter–item correlation matrixes [correlation matrix] between the three items on student efforts are significantly positive and ranges between .46 and .67 (one–tailed greater than 0). At the same time, the inter–item correlations between the three items on student efforts and the 12 items on teaching effective even though significant at $p = 0.001$ (one–tailed greater than 0) are, however, weak (See Table A3; and Table B1 in the Appendices). The low correlation is an indication the items on student efforts would require remodeling to establish a stronger association when compared with the items on teaching excellence.

In spite of the limitations of the study, the validity and reliability of the rating instrument is conclusive. Still, the study may not meet the skeptics on the validity and reliability of student ratings, even with the growing statement about their reliability. In any event, with regards to HBCU, administrators and faculty should consider reviewing or build upon the current survey instrument to include the following, to give the student ratings more useful basis for teaching quality and student learning achievement:

1. **Student Section:** (1.) Comparative effort in the course; (2.) The comparative effort to do well in the course; (3.) Comparative participation in class activities; (4.) Comparative academic challenge of the course; (5.) Hours per week spent in class; (6.) Average hours per week utilized in studying; (7.) Seeking instructor's assistance; and (8.) Significant course–work–hours available per week.

2. **Course Section:** (1.) The course in its entirety; (2.) Course material and structure; (3.) Course objectives; (4.) Attributes, complexity and significance of the course; (5.) Instructor's participation in the course; (6.) Instructor's delivery model; (7.) Expected course grade; (8.) Instructor's course understanding; (9.) Assignments in relation to course objectives; and (10.) Exams and group discussions.

3. **Instructor's Section:** (1.) Instructor's readiness and passion; (2.) Instructor's personality and idiosyncrasy; (3.) Motivating interest; (4.) Interaction with students; (5.) Instructor's role in understanding the subject matter; (6.) Challenging students, and the use of reading assignments; (7.) Instructor's support during the learning epoch; (8.) Learning presentation skills; and (9.) Feedback provided.

The above are only limited recommendations which could be strengthened or unconditionally overhauled by the administration and faculty. At the same time, it must be realized the unease of some faculty members to use the student ratings for summative purposes is complete, and cannot be easily dissuaded against such risk even with the strength of the findings of this research. If anything, the unpredictability of scholars to reach a settlement on the validity and reliability of student ratings to assess faculty, has encouraged some to endorse the improvement of the model to encompass other measurements of assessing teaching quality (e.g. peer reviews, self–rating, student interviews, etc.) (Berk, 2005; El Hassan, 2012; Kulik as cited in Donnon et al., 2010; Marsh, Ginns, Morin, Nagengast, & Martin, 2011). Thus, it would be beneficial to include student ratings with other measurements of assessing teaching effectiveness (e.g. peer reviews, self–rating, instructor's portfolio, student reviews, sophomore and graduating senior surveys, etc.) when considering instructors for tenure and salary increase.

SOLUTIONS, RECOMMENDATIONS, AND FUTURE IMPLICATIONS

The results of this study are consistent with other research in the field (see Conclusion). Future research in the area should focus on larger institutions with more diverse populations to provide a broader spectrum of data pertaining to the use of Student Ratings of Instruction. Investigations in this area can lead institutions of higher education to create better SRI instruments that truly reflect their intrinsic populations (and thereby provide a girth of information regarding overall student perceptions of institutional instructional effectiveness). Such data could provide educators and administrators the grounds for meeting the needs of their learners in a rapidly changing educational environment.

CONCLUSION

The specific item analysis conducted by the authors using the Tri–Squared Test resulted in the analysis of a massive amount of items first validated through the use of Cronbach's Alpha Test statistic of .95 (See Table A1, page 17). As previously mentioned, the Cronbach's Alpha Test yielded an extraordinarily high internal consistency of the student rejoinders to the items on the rating scale. It thus confirms the reliability of the instrument used in evaluating teaching effectiveness. The result is in consonance with similar studies on the reliability of student ratings with the application of the Cronbach's Alpha statistic as stated by the following educational researchers: Agbetsiafa, 2010; Anastasiadou, 2011; Beran et al., 2009; Donnon et al., 2010; Kneipp et al., 2010; Zerbini et al., 2009; and Zuberi et al., 2007. The Tri–Squared Test yielded the following results: *Tri*^{2} Critical Value Table = 18.467 (with *d.f.* = 4 at α = 0.001). For *d.f.* = 4, the Critical Value for p > 0.001 is 18.467. The Calculated Tri–Square value is 92.531, thus, the null hypothesis (H$_0$) is rejected by virtue of the hypothesis test which yields the following: Tri–Squared Critical Value of 18.467 < 92.531 Calculated Tri–Squared Value. This further supported the research findings attributed to the initial research Cronbach's Alpha Test results. Additionally, Tri–Squared Residuals supported SRI validity with some negative outcomes by respondents to items regarding efficacy and consistency. However, the overwhelming majority of responses supported all three factors pertaining to validity, efficacy and reliability of the SRI. As result, the initial research finds have additional support through this study. It is was again determined that 15 questions on the rating scale considered as "variables", entirely disintegrated into two modules or factors: "Teaching Effectiveness" consisting of 12 questions with factor loads ranging between .82 and .90; and, "Students' Efforts" consisting of three questions with factor loads ranging between .76 and .86 (See the above Table B5). The results also confirm that, the scale offered evidence of overall SRI construct validity. Indeed, the factor loads of teaching effectiveness are significantly high, thus endorsing the construct validity of teaching excellence at this particular HBCU [Note: This data was acquired during the 2012 Academic Spring Semester at the HBCU with the exclusion of end–of–course grades]. Again, the results of the study are consistent with similar results on the validity of student assessment using PCA (Agbetsiafa, 2010; Zerbini et al., 2009; Sofia, 2011; Beran et al., 2009; Skowronek et al., 2011; Donnon et al., 2010; Safavi et al., 2012; Spooren et al., 2007; Beran et al., 2007).

REFERENCES

Agbetsiafa, D. (2010). Evaluating effective teaching in college level Economics using student ratings of instruction: A factor analytic approach. *Journal of College Teaching & Learning*, 7(5), 57–66.

Anastasiadou, S. D. (2011). Reliability and validity testing of a new scale for measuring attitudes toward learning statistics with technology. *Acta Didactica Napocensia*, *4*(1), 1–10.

Anderson, J., Brown, G., & Spaeth, S. (2006). Online student evaluations and response rates reconsidered. *Innovate: Journal of Online Education, 2*(6). Retrieved from https://rugby.ou.edu/content/dam/provost/documents/evaluations/evaluate–Online–Student–Evaluations–and–Response–Rates.pdf

Barry, R. A. (2010). Teaching effectiveness and why it matters. *Marylhurst University and the Chalkboard Project*, Retrieved from http://chalkboardproject.org/wp– content/uploads/2010/12/teacher–effectiveness–and–why–it–matters.pdf

Beran, T., & Rokosh, J. (2009). Instructors' perspectives on the utility of student ratings of instruction. *Instructional Science, 37*(2), 171–184. doi:10.1007/s11251-007-9045-2

Beran, T., Violato, C., & Kline, D. (2007). What's the "Use" of student ratings of instruction for administrators? One university's experience. *Canadian Journal of Higher Education, 37*(1), 27–43.

Beran, T., Violato, C., Kline, D., & Frideres, J. (2009). What do students consider useful about student ratings? *Assessment & Evaluation in Higher Education, 34*(5), 519–527. doi:10.1080/02602930802082228

Berk, R. A. (2005). Survey of 12 strategies to measure teaching effectiveness. *International Journal of Teaching and Learning in Higher Education, 17*(1), 48–62.

Bland, J., & Altman, D. G. (1997). Cronbach's Alpha. BMJ: British Medical Journal (International Edition), 314(7080), 572.

Bo, Z., Johnston, L., & Kilic, G. (2008). Assessing the reliability of self– and peer rating in student group work. *Assessment & Evaluation in Higher Education, 33*(3), 329–340. doi:10.1080/02602930701293181

Chen, G., & Watkins, D. (2010). Stability and correlates of student evaluations of teaching at a Chinese university. *Assessment & Evaluation in Higher Education, 35*(6), 675–685. doi:10.1080/02602930902977715

Clayson, D. E. (2009). Student evaluations of teaching: Are they related to what students learn? *Journal of Marketing Education, 31*(1), 16–30. doi:10.1177/0273475308324086

Cronbach, L. J. (1951). Coefficient alpha and the internal structure of tests. *Psychometrika, 16*(3), 297–334. doi:10.1007/BF02310555

Donnon, T., Delver, H., & Beran, T. (2010). Student and teaching characteristics related to ratings of instruction in medical sciences graduate programs. *Medical Teacher, 32*(4), 327–332. doi:10.3109/01421590903480097 PMID:20353330

El Hassan, K. (2009). Investigating substantive and consequential validity of student ratings of instruction. *Higher Education Research & Development, 28*(3), 319–333. doi:10.1080/07294360902839917

Field, A. (2009). *Discovering statistics using spss* (3rd ed.). Thousand Oaks, CA: SAGE Publications Inc.

Frick, T., Chadha, R., Watson, C., Wang, Y., & Green, P. (2009). College student perceptions of teaching and learning quality. *Educational Technology Research and Development, 57*(5), 705–720. doi:10.1007/s11423-007-9079-9

Gillmore, G. M., Kane, M. T., & Naccarato, R. W. (1978). The generalizability of student ratings of Instruction: Estimation of the teacher and course components. *Journal of Educational Measurement*, *15*(1), 1–13. doi:10.1111/j.1745-3984.1978.tb00051.x

Goe, L., Bell, C., & Little, O. (2008). Approaches to evaluating teacher effectiveness: A research synthesis. *National Comprehensive Center for Teacher Quality*, Retrieved from http://www.tqsource.org/publications/EvaluatingTeachEffectiveness.pdf

Goodman, L. A., & Kruskal, W. H. (1954). Measures of association for Part I. *Journal of the American Statistical Association*, *49*, 732–764.

Gravestock, P., & Gregor–Greenleaf, E. (2008). Student course evaluations: Research, models and trends. Toronto, ON: Higher Education Quality Council of Ontario; Retrieved from http://www.heqco.ca/SiteCollectionDocuments/Student%20Course%20Evaluations.pdf

Hassel, B. C. (2009). How should state define teacher effectiveness? *Center for American Progress,* Retrieved from http://publicimpact.com/publications/PublicImpact–How_Should_States_Define_Teacher_Effectiveness.pdf

Héfer, B. (2009). Teaching effectiveness, course evaluation, and academic performance: The role of academic delay of gratification. *Journal of Advanced Academics*, *20*(2), 326–355. doi:10.1177/1932202X0902000206

Hogan, T. P. (1973). Similarity of student ratings across instructors, courses, and time. *Research in Higher Education*, *1*(2), 149–154. doi:10.1007/BF00991336

Hunsaker, S. L., Nielsen, A., & Bartlett, B. (2010). Correlates of teacher practices influencing student outcomes in reading instruction for advanced readers. *Gifted Child Quarterly*, *54*(4), 273–282. doi:10.1177/0016986210374506

Ibrahim, A. (2011). Using generalizability theory to estimate the relative effect of class size and number of items on the dependability of student ratings of instruction. *Psychological Reports*, *109*(1), 252–258. doi:10.2466/03.07.11.PR0.109.4.252-258 PMID:22049666

Jones, B. (2010). An examination of motivation model components in face–to–face and online instruction. *Electronic Journal of Research in Educational Psychology*, *8*(3), 915–944.

Keeley, J., Furr, R., & Buskist, W. (2010). Differentiating psychology students' perceptions of teachers using the teacher behavior checklist. *Teaching of Psychology*, *37*(1), 16–20. doi:10.1080/00986280903426282

Kneipp, L. B., Kelly, K. E., Biscoe, J. D., & Richard, B. (2010). The impact of instructor's personality characteristics on quality of instruction. *College Student Journal*, *44*(4), 901–905.

Kozub, R. M. (2010). Relationship of course, instructor, and student characteristics to dimensions of student ratings of teaching effectiveness in business schools. *American Journal of Business Education*, *3*(1), 33–40.

Leech, N. A., Barrett, K. C., & Morgan, G. A. (2011). *IBM: SPSS for intermediate statistics use and interpretation* (4th ed.). New York, NY: Taylor & Francis Group.

Lüdtke, O., Trautwein, U., Kunter, M., & Baumert, J. (2006). Reliability and agreement of student ratings of the classroom environment: A reanalysis of TIMSS data. *Learning Environments Research*, *9*(3), 215–230. doi:10.1007/s10984-006-9014-8

Madden, T. J., Dillon, W. R., & Leak, R. L. (2010). Students' evaluation of teaching: Concerns of item diagnosticity. *Journal of Marketing Education*, *32*(3), 264–274. doi:10.1177/0273475310377759

Marsh, H. W. (1982). The use of path analysis to estimate teacher and course effects in student rating's of instructional effectiveness. *Applied Psychological Measurement*, 6(1), 47–59. doi:10.1177/014662168200600106

Marsh, H. W. (2007). Students' evaluations of university teaching: Dimensionality, reliability, validity, potential biases, and usefulness. In R. Perry & J. C. Smart (Eds.), *The scholarship of teaching and learning in higher education: An evidence–based perspective* (pp. 319–383). Netherlands: Springer. doi:10.1007/1-4020-5742-3_9

Marsh, H. W., Ginns, P., Morin, A. S., Nagengast, B., & Martin, A. J. (2011). Use of student ratings to benchmark universities: Multilevel modeling of responses to the Australian Course Experience Questionnaire (CEQ). *Journal of Educational Psychology*, 103(3), 733–748. doi:10.1037/a0024221

McKeachie, W. J. (2007). Good teaching makes a difference—And we know what it is. In R. Perry & J. C. Smart (Eds.), *The scholarship of teaching and learning in higher education: An evidence–based perspective* (pp. 457–474). Netherlands: Springer. doi:10.1007/1-4020-5742-3_11

Osler, J. E. (2012). Trichotomy–Squared – A novel mixed methods test and research procedure designed to analyze, transform, and compare qualitative and quantitative data for education scientists who are administrators, practitioners, teachers, and technologists. iManager's Journal on Mathematics, 1(3).

Osler, J. E. (2013a). The Psychometrics of Educational Science: Designing Trichotomous Inventive Investigative Instruments for Qualitative and Quantitative for Inquiry. December 2012 – February 2013 *iManager's. Journal of Educational Psychology*, 8(3).

Osler, J. E. (2013b). The Psychological Efficacy of Education as a Science through Personal, Professional, and Contextual Inquiry of the Affective Learning Domain. February – April *iManager's. Journal of Educational Psychology*, 6(4).

Perry, R., & Smart, J. C. (2007). *The scholarship of teaching and learning in higher education: An evidence–based perspective*. Netherlands: Springer. doi:10.1007/1-4020-5742-3

Pounder, J. (2007). Is student evaluation of teaching worthwhile? An analytical framework for answering the question. *Quality Assurance in Education*, 18(1), 47–63.

Roche, L. A., & Marsh, H. W. (2000). Multiple dimensions of university teacher self concept. *Instructional Science*, 28(5), 439–468. doi:10.1023/A:1026576404113

Safavi, S., Bakar, K., Tarmizi, R., & Alwi, N. (2012). The role of student ratings of instruction from perspectives of the higher education administrators. *International Journal of Business and Social Science*, 3(9), 233–239.

Schrodt, P., Witt, P. L., Myers, S. A., Turman, P. D., Barton, M. H., & Jernberg, K. A. (2008). Learner Empowerment and Teacher Evaluations as Functions of Teacher Power Use in the College Classroom. *Communication Education*, 57(2), 180–200. doi:10.1080/03634520701840303

Skowronek, J., Friesen, B., & Masonjones, H. (2011). Developing a statistically valid and practically useful student evaluation instrument. *International Journal for the Scholarship of Teaching and Learning*, 5(1), 1–19.

Spooren, P. P., Mortelmans, D. D., & Denekens, J. J. (2007). Student evaluation of teaching quality in higher education: Development of an instrument based on 10 Likert–scales. *Assessment & Evaluation in Higher Education*, 32(6), 667–679. doi:10.1080/02602930601117191

Sprinkle, J. E. (2008). Student perceptions of effectiveness: An examination of the influence of student biases. *College Student Journal, 42*(2), 276–293.

Stowell, J. R., Addison, W. E., & Smith, J. L. (2012). Comparison of online and classroom–based student evaluations of instruction. *Assessment & Evaluation in Higher Education, 37*(4), 465–473. doi:10.1080/02602938.2010.545869

Theall, M. (2010). Evaluating teaching: From reliability to accountability. *New Directions for Teaching and Learning, 2010*(123), 85–95. doi:10.1002/tl.412

Titus, J. (2008). Student ratings in a consumerist academy: Leveraging pedagogical control and authority. *Sociological Perspectives, 51*(2), 397–422. doi:10.1525/sop.2008.51.2.397

U.S. Department of Education. (2008). *HBCUs: A National Resource*. White House Initiative on Historically Black Colleges and Universities.

Vogt, W. (1984). Developing a teacher evaluation system. *Spectrum (Lexington, Ky.), 2*(1), 41–46.

Young, S., & Shaw, D. G. (1999). Profiles of effective college and university teachers. *Journal of Higher Education, 70*(6), 670–686.

Zerbini, T., & Abbad, G. (2009). Reação aos procedimentos instrucionais de um curso via internet: Validação de uma escala. *Estudos de Psicologia, 26*(3), 363–371. doi:10.1590/S0103-166X2009000300009

Zhao, J., & Gallant, D. J. (2012). Student evaluation of instruction in higher education: Exploring issues of validity and reliability. *Assessment & Evaluation in Higher Education, 37*(2), 227–235. doi:10.1080/02602938.2010.523819

Zuberi, R. W., Bordage, G., & Norman, G. R. (2007). Validation of the SETOC instrument – student evaluation of teaching in outpatient clinics. *Advances in Health Sciences Education: Theory and Practice, 12*(1), 55–69. doi:10.1007/s10459-005-2328-y PMID:17160501

KEY TERMS AND DEFINITIONS

Cronbach's Alpha: In advanced statistical metrics, Cronbach's Alpha (Cronbach, 1951) is a mathematical coefficient designed to measure internal consistency. In psychometrics it is the most practically used statistic that provides (upon precise calculation) an estimate of the overall reliability of a test designed to measure a specified researchable criterion on a sample of examinees.

Factor Analysis: A statistical factorial model used in this study is derived from Agbetsiafa (2010), and Field (2009). Concisely, factor analysis allows the delineation of an essential or hidden configuration in a data set. It accelerates the analysis of the configuration of the associations (correlation) among an outsized number of variables by describing a set of shared essential measurements, commonly termed factors (Agbetsiafa, 2010).

Goodman & Kruskal's Lambda (λ): An advanced statistical cross tabulation analysis measure of proportional reduction in error (Goodman & Kruskal, 1954).

HBCU: An acronym for "Historically Black College & Universities" (U.S. Department of Education, 2008).

SRI: An acronym for "Student Ratings of Instruction" or "Student Ratings" referred to as "Student Evaluations of Instruction" or "SEI" in use in research projects in the US, England, and Australia, including the use of the British Noel–Levitz "Student Satisfaction Inventory"; the "Course Perceptions Questionnaire"; the "Student Evaluations of Educational Quality"; and, the "Course Experience Questionnaire" (as cited in Skowronek, Friesen, & Masonjones, 2011).

Teaching Effectiveness: Involves the effectiveness teaching and the transfer of knowledge. Determining teacher effectiveness may not be uncommon to academics since various studies on teaching excellence and student learning outcomes have already been completed (Hunsaker, Nielsen, & Bartlett, 2010; Perry as cited in Keeley, Furr, & Buskist, 2010; Schrodt, Witt, Myers, Turman., Barton, & Jernberg, 2008).

Tri–Squared Test: Tri–Squared comprehensively stands for "The Total Transformative Trichotomous–Squared Test" (or "Trichotomy–Squared"). The Total Transformative Trichotomous–Squared Test provides a methodology for the transformation of the outcomes from qualitative research into measurable quantitative values that are used to test the validity of hypotheses. The advantage of this research procedure is that it is a comprehensive holistic testing methodology that is designed to be static way of holistically measuring categorical variables directly applicable to educational and social behavioral environments where the established methods of pure experimental designs are easily violated. The unchanging base of the Tri–Squared Test is the 3×3 Table based on Trichotomous Categorical Variables and Trichotomous Outcome Variables. The emphasis the three distinctive variables provide a thorough rigorous robustness to the test that yields enough outcomes to determine if differences truly exist in the environment in which the research takes place (Osler, 2012).

APPENDIX A: TABLES FOR RESULTS OF HYPOTHESIS 1

Table 10. The item reliability statistics according to levels of statistical association using cronbach's alpha.

Reliability Statistics		
Cronbach's Alpha	Cronbach's Alpha Based on Standardized Items	N of Items
.954	.949	15

Table 11. The item inferential statistics according to mean, standard deviation, and total item number (for each variable).

Item Statistics			
	Mean	Std. Deviation	N
A1	4.57	.670	18817
A2	4.58	.606	18817
A3	4.51	.729	18817
B1	4.37	.884	18817
B2	4.23	1.011	18817
B3	4.27	.997	18817
B4	4.28	1.005	18817
B5	4.20	1.009	18817
B6	4.19	1.013	18817
B7	4.26	.975	18817
B8	4.27	.938	18817
B9	4.21	1.000	18817
B10	4.29	.979	18817
B11	4.29	.962	18817
B12	4.30	.967	18817

Table 12. The inter–item correlation matrix indicating levels of statistical relationship plotting the relationships diagonally.

							Inter–Item Correlation Matrix								
	A1	A2	A3	B1	B2	B3	B4	B5	B6	B7	B8	B9	B10	B11	B12
A1	–	.496	.670	.295	.258	.264	.247	.332	.290	.257	.239	.262	.238	.235	.260
A2	.496	–	.458	.209	.170	.176	.169	.204	.184	.175	.168	.173	.163	.158	.165
A3	.670	.458	–	.260	.234	.235	.211	.277	.269	.217	.219	.242	.206	.213	.219
B1	.295	.209	.260	–	.799	.817	.687	.718	.744	.705	.752	.699	.693	.683	.743
B2	.258	.170	.234	.799	–	.841	.702	.721	.746	.711	.742	.699	.695	.694	.748
B3	.264	.176	.235	.817	.841	–	.750	.745	.756	.743	.742	.689	.728	.717	.794
B4	.247	.169	.211	.687	.702	.750	–	.741	.698	.730	.665	.637	.758	.714	.799
B5	.332	.204	.277	.718	.721	.745	.741	–	.771	.722	.696	.676	.717	.694	.770
B6	.290	.184	.269	.744	.746	.756	.698	.771	–	.736	.792	.752	.708	.689	.745
B7	.257	.175	.217	.705	.711	.743	.730	.722	.736	–	.731	.699	.707	.689	.762
B8	.239	.168	.219	.752	.742	.742	.665	.696	.792	.731	–	.772	.690	.681	.726
B9	.262	.173	.242	.699	.699	.689	.637	.676	.752	.699	.772	–	.671	.654	.699
B10	.238	.163	.206	.693	.695	.728	.758	.717	.708	.707	.690	.671	–	.836	.844
B11	.235	.158	.213	.683	.694	.717	.714	.694	.689	.689	.681	.654	.836	–	.835
B12	.260	.165	.219	.743	.748	.794	.799	.770	.745	.762	.726	.699	.844	.835	–

Table 13. The Item-Total Inferential Statistics and Levels of Statistical Association Table plotting the highest elements as associative relationships using Corrected Item–Total Correlation, Squared Multiple Correlation, and lastly Cronbach's Alpha in the final column (for the individual statistics for each variable).

	Scale Mean if Item Deleted	Scale Variance if Item Deleted	Corrected Item–Total Correlation	Squared Multiple Correlation	Cronbach's Alpha if Item Deleted
A1	60.28	111.566	.369	.513	.957
A2	60.27	113.559	.256	.279	.959
A3	60.34	111.653	.328	.476	.958
B1	60.48	101.518	.839	.748	.949
B2	60.62	99.358	.837	.768	.949
B3	60.58	99.131	.862	.807	.948
B4	60.57	99.921	.812	.713	.949
B5	60.65	99.419	.835	.719	.949
B6	60.66	99.117	.847	.757	.948
B7	60.59	100.295	.819	.697	.949
B8	60.58	100.850	.823	.743	.949
B9	60.64	100.397	.791	.677	.950
B10	60.56	100.073	.828	.785	.949
B11	60.56	100.672	.811	.762	.949
B12	60.55	99.423	.875	.835	.948

APPENDIX B: TABLES FOR RESULTS OF HYPOTHESIS 2

Figure 1. The Correlation Matrices Table plotting the highest diagonal elements relationships on the complete correlation matrix (for the individual statistics for each variable).

Correlation Matrix[a]

		A1	A2	A3	B1	B2	B3	B4	B5	B6	B7	B8	B9	B10	B11	B12
Correlation	A1	1.000	.496	.670	.295	.253	.264	.247	.332	.290	.257	.239	.262	.238	.235	.260
	A2	.496	1.000	.458	.209	.170	.176	.169	.204	.184	.175	.168	.173	.163	.158	.165
	A3	.670	.458	1.000	.260	.234	.235	.211	.277	.269	.217	.219	.242	.206	.213	.219
	B1	.295	.209	.260	1.000	.799	.817	.687	.718	.744	.705	.752	.699	.693	.683	.743
	B2	.253	.170	.234	.799	1.000	.841	.702	.721	.746	.711	.742	.699	.695	.694	.745
	B3	.264	.176	.235	.817	.841	1.000	.750	.745	.756	.743	.742	.689	.728	.717	.794
	B4	.247	.169	.211	.687	.702	.750	1.000	.741	.698	.730	.665	.637	.755	.714	.799
	B5	.332	.204	.277	.718	.721	.745	.741	1.000	.771	.722	.696	.676	.717	.694	.770
	B6	.290	.184	.269	.744	.746	.756	.698	.771	1.000	.736	.792	.752	.708	.689	.745
	B7	.257	.175	.217	.705	.711	.743	.730	.722	.736	1.000	.731	.699	.707	.689	.762
	B8	.239	.168	.219	.752	.742	.742	.665	.696	.792	.731	1.000	.772	.690	.681	.726
	B9	.262	.173	.242	.699	.699	.689	.637	.676	.752	.699	.772	1.000	.671	.654	.699
	B10	.238	.163	.206	.693	.695	.728	.755	.717	.708	.707	.690	.671	1.000	.556	.544
	B11	.235	.158	.213	.683	.694	.717	.714	.694	.689	.689	.681	.654	.556	1.000	.535
	B12	.260	.165	.219	.743	.745	.794	.799	.770	.745	.762	.726	.699	.544	.535	1.000
Sig. (1-tailed)	A1		.000	.000	.000	.000	.000	.000	.000	.000	.000	.000	.000	.000	.000	.000
	A2	.000		.000	.000	.000	.000	.000	.000	.000	.000	.000	.000	.000	.000	.000
	A3	.000	.000		.000	.000	.000	.000	.000	.000	.000	.000	.000	.000	.000	.000
	B1	.000	.000	.000		.000	.000	.000	.000	.000	.000	.000	.000	.000	.000	.000
	B2	.000	.000	.000	.000		.000	.000	.000	.000	.000	.000	.000	.000	.000	.000
	B3	.000	.000	.000	.000	.000		.000	.000	.000	.000	.000	.000	.000	.000	.000
	B4	.000	.000	.000	.000	.000	.000		.000	.000	.000	.000	.000	.000	.000	.000
	B5	.000	.000	.000	.000	.000	.000	.000		.000	.000	.000	.000	.000	.000	.000
	B6	.000	.000	.000	.000	.000	.000	.000	.000		.000	.000	.000	.000	.000	.000
	B7	.000	.000	.000	.000	.000	.000	.000	.000	.000		.000	.000	.000	.000	.000
	B8	.000	.000	.000	.000	.000	.000	.000	.000	.000	.000		.000	.000	.000	.000
	B9	.000	.000	.000	.000	.000	.000	.000	.000	.000	.000	.000		.000	.000	.000
	B10	.000	.000	.000	.000	.000	.000	.000	.000	.000	.000	.000	.000		.000	.000
	B11	.000	.000	.000	.000	.000	.000	.000	.000	.000	.000	.000	.000	.000		.000
	B12	.000	.000	.000	.000	.000	.000	.000	.000	.000	.000	.000	.000	.000	.000	

a. Determinant = .001

2g

Educational Technology Assessment

Table 14. The Kaiser–Meyer–Olkin Measure of Sampling and Bartlett's Test of Sphericity for the HBCU SRI.

KMO and Bartlett's Test		
Kaiser–Meyer–Olkin Measure of Sampling Adequacy.		.960
Bartlett's Test of Sphericity	Approx. χ^2	271591.204
	df	105
	Sig.	.000

Figure 2. The Anti Image Matrices Table plotting the highest diagonal elements (highlighted in yellow) on the complete anti-image correlation matrix (which are the KMO (Kaiser–Meyer–Olkin Measure of Sampling) individual statistics for each variable).

Anti-image Matrices

	A1	A2	A3	B1	B2	B3	B4	B5	B6	B7	B8	B9	B10	B11	B12
A1	.487	-.162	-.275	-.015	.003	.004	.004	-.040	-.002	-.006	.012	-.005	.003	.006	-.006
A2	-.162	.721	-.118	-.019	.005	.002	-.008	.001	.009	-.008	-.006	.002	-.007	.001	.008
A3	-.275	-.118	.524	-.002	-.003	-.002	.002	-.002	-.019	.009	.005	-.012	.005	-.011	.008
B1	-.015	-.019	-.002	.252	-.053	-.060	.003	-.016	-.014	-.004	-.039	-.018	-.004	-.003	-.008
B2	.003	.005	-.003	-.053	.232	-.080	-.007	-.014	-.015	-.006	-.021	-.020	.003	-.013	-.002
B3	.004	.002	-.002	-.060	-.080	.193	-.031	-.011	-.013	-.021	-.007	.009	.000	-.001	-.024
B4	.004	-.008	.002	.003	-.007	-.031	.287	-.050	-.004	-.047	.005	.006	-.040	.002	-.044
B5	-.040	.001	-.002	-.016	-.014	-.011	-.050	.281	-.065	-.025	.005	-.009	-.009	-.002	-.027
B6	-.002	.009	-.019	-.014	-.015	-.013	-.004	-.065	.243	-.024	-.066	-.051	-.009	-.002	-.001
B7	-.006	-.008	.009	-.004	-.006	-.021	-.047	-.025	-.024	.303	-.038	-.034	-.004	-.004	-.027
B8	.012	-.006	.005	-.039	-.021	-.007	.005	.005	-.066	-.038	.257	-.085	-.004	-.010	-.003
B9	-.005	.002	-.012	-.018	-.020	.009	.006	-.009	-.051	-.034	-.085	.323	-.015	-.005	-.007
B10	.003	-.007	.005	-.004	.003	.000	-.040	-.009	-.009	-.004	-.004	-.015	.215	-.090	-.051
B11	.006	.001	-.011	-.003	-.013	-.001	.002	-.002	-.002	-.004	-.010	-.005	-.090	.238	-.061
B12	-.006	.008	.008	-.008	-.002	-.024	-.044	-.027	-.001	-.027	-.003	-.007	-.051	-.061	.165
A1	.799*	-.273	-.545	-.043	.010	.013	.012	-.108	-.006	-.014	.035	-.012	.010	.019	-.020
A2	-.273	.878*	-.192	-.046	.013	.006	-.017	.002	.022	-.016	-.013	.003	-.017	.001	.023
A3	-.545	-.192	.795*	-.006	-.009	-.007	.005	-.006	-.054	.023	.013	-.029	.014	-.030	.027
B1	-.043	-.046	-.006	.974*	-.220	-.273	.009	-.059	-.055	-.015	-.154	-.063	-.018	-.013	-.037
B2	.010	.013	-.009	-.220	.966*	-.379	-.028	-.055	-.063	-.021	-.086	-.073	.015	-.054	-.010
B3	.013	.006	-.007	-.273	-.379	.960*	-.130	-.046	-.060	-.087	-.031	.035	-.001	-.004	-.136
B4	.012	-.017	.005	.009	-.028	-.130	.976*	-.176	-.015	-.160	.020	.019	-.163	.009	-.204
B5	-.108	.002	-.006	-.059	-.055	-.046	-.176	.977*	-.250	-.087	.018	-.029	-.035	-.006	-.127
B6	-.006	.022	-.054	-.055	-.063	-.060	-.015	-.250	.971*	-.089	-.264	-.180	-.041	-.008	-.005
B7	-.014	-.016	.023	-.015	-.021	-.087	-.160	-.087	-.089	.984*	-.135	-.109	-.015	-.013	-.119
B8	.035	-.013	.013	-.154	-.086	-.031	.020	.018	-.264	-.135	.966*	-.294	-.018	-.042	-.014
B9	-.012	.003	-.029	-.063	-.073	.035	.019	-.029	-.180	-.109	-.294	.974*	-.057	-.019	-.032
B10	.010	-.017	.014	-.018	.015	-.001	-.163	-.035	-.041	-.015	-.018	-.057	.958*	-.400	-.270
B11	.019	.001	-.030	-.013	-.054	-.004	.009	-.006	-.008	-.013	-.042	-.019	-.400	.957*	-.310
B12	-.020	.023	.027	-.037	-.010	-.136	-.204	-.127	-.005	-.119	-.014	-.032	-.270	-.310	.962*

pling Adequacy(MSA)

243

Figure 3. An Eigenvalue Scree Plot highlighting Sample HBCU SRI (Student Ratings of Instruction Instrument) Component Numbers plotted to explore and verify Factor Analysis patterns by importance in a set of correlation coefficients.

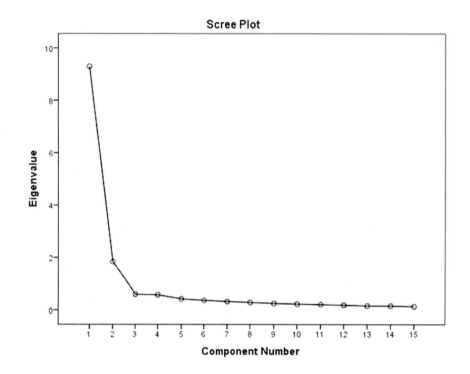

Table 15. Extraction method: principal component analysis

Total Variance Explained						
Component	**Initial Eigenvalues**			**Extraction Sums of Squared Loadings**			**Rotation Sums of Squared Loadings[a]**
	Total	**% of Variance**	**Cumulative %**	**Total**	**% of Variance**	**Cumulative %**	**Total**
1	9.298	61.984	61.984	9.298	61.984	61.984	9.245
2	1.844	12.291	74.276	1.844	12.291	74.276	2.985
3	.595	3.966	78.242				
4	.574	3.828	82.070				
5	.420	2.798	84.868				
6	.364	2.427	87.295				
7	.322	2.148	89.442				
8	.284	1.893	91.335				
9	.247	1.648	92.984				
10	.223	1.487	94.471				
11	.203	1.354	95.825				
12	.183	1.223	97.048				
13	.157	1.048	98.096				
14	.153	1.022	99.118				
15	.132	.882	100.000				

a. When components are correlated, sums of squared loadings cannot be added to obtain a total variance.

Table 16. Factor loadings for the varimax statistical rotation procedure conducted on the HBCU SRI (Student Ratings of Instruction Instrument) instrument.

Item	Factor Loading		
	1	**2**	**Communality**
This instructor is efficient in promoting learning.	.904		.83
The instructor clearly presents his/her subject matter.	.886		.80
The instructor is genuinely concerned with students' progress.	.865		.76
The subject matter of this course is well organized.	.864		.76
The texts and other readings assigned for this course have been helpful.	.860		.77
The examinations are consistent with the course objectives and the instruction.	.854		.74
The stated goals and objectives for the course are consistent with what was actually taught.	.850		.76
I am able to get help from the instructor when I need it.	.849		.73
The instructor uses instructional approaches (e.g. discussions, lectures, audio–visuals field work, demonstrations, computer programs, etc.) which effectively enhance learning in this course.	.849		.74
The instructor is enthusiastic and arouses interest in this course.	.846		.73
My power to think, criticize, and/or create have been improved as a result of this course.	.839		.75
Quizzes, examinations and/or written assignments are provided frequently enough to help evaluate my progress.	.815		.69
I have put a great deal of effort into this course.		.857	.77
I have completed the required readings for this course.		.847	.74
I have attended class regularly.		.762	.59

APPENDIX C: STUDENT RATINGS OF INSTRUCTION SURVEY INSTRUMENT

Figure 4. A sample HBCU SRI (Student Ratings of Instruction Instrument) used to collect data from the study.(Source: REP).

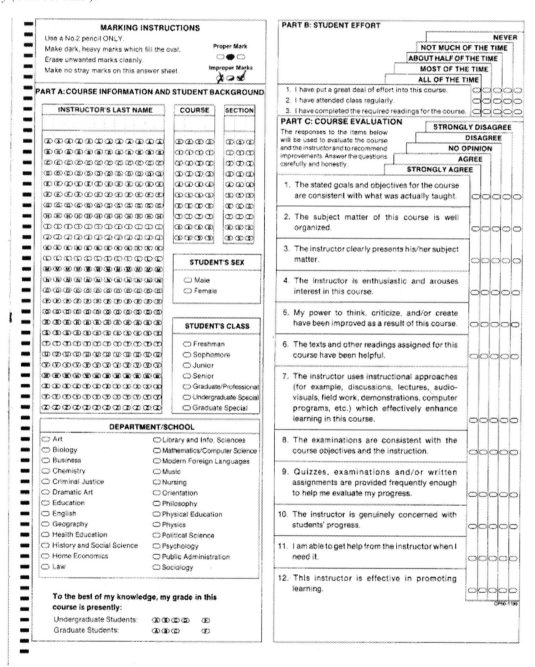

Chapter 12
ELearning for Persons with Visual Disabilities:
Case of Low Vision

Ruth N. Wambua
The University of Nairobi, Kenya

Robert Oboko
The University of Nairobi, Kenya

ABSTRACT

This chapter discusses an eLearning platform that is usable by persons with low vision. To start with, such a platform is achieved by incorporating technological advances such as: use of text with the highest possible contrast; use of varying font size; among other customized Human Computer Interaction (HCI) effects. Moreover, use of complicated, decorative or cursive fonts should be avoided, as well as italic text and capital letters, which can be difficult for users with reading impairments. In summary, this chapter supports the fact that eLearning is possible for persons with low vision, provided that all the necessary technological advances have been considered.

INTRODUCTION

Persons of low vision refer to people who have sight problems, in that they have partial sight. Consequently such individuals experience difficulties in reading/studying either from a book print or computer screen. For some individuals, the standard size of letters on a computer screen or printed in documents are too small to read, whereas others may not distinguish one color from another. The reason for low vision according to Bjork, Ottosson & Thorsteinsdottir (2008) could be because of clouding of the lens of the eye, which causes light that passes through the lens to the retina to be scattered. The scattered light causes images to be blurred and visual acuity to be reduced. Moreover, as one continues to age, the lens of the eye also yellows and becomes fixed and is thus unable to focus. In this case, the pupil does not dilate very well to changes in illumination, and the retina and cortex become less able to process visual information. Consequently, contrast sensitivity decreases, visual acuity drops somewhat, and vision in low light levels suffers.

DOI: 10.4018/978-1-4666-8363-1.ch012

Table 1. Level of visual impairment and blindness according to the World Health Organization

Level of Blindness		Definition	Implications
0	**Mild or no Visual Impairment**	Vision better than: 6/18, 3/10, 20/70	May be glasses
1	**Moderate Visual Impairment**	Vision better than: 6/60, 1/10, 20/200 Vision worse than: 6/18, 3/10, 20/70	Glasses and possible need for magnifiers on computer interface
2	**Severe Visual Impairment**	Vision better than: 3/60, 1/20, 20/400 Vision worse than: 6/60, 1/10, 20/200	Magnifiers and color contrasters for computer interfaces
3	**Blindness**	Vision better than: Can count fingers @ at 1 meter distance Vision worse than: 3/60, 1/20, 20/400	Strong magnifiers for some but mainly screen readers for computer interfaces
4	**Blindness**	Vision better than: Light perception Vision worse than: 1/60, 1/50, 5/300	Screen readers for computer interfaces
5	**Blindness**	No light perception	Screen readers for computer interfaces

On the contrary, low vision is also suffered by the young in schools and colleges.

Following the remarkable advances in technology, there is dire need for support technology which goes a long way to ensure that individuals with partial sight impairment also benefit from technological advances such as eLearning. Considering that people with low vision are still capable of using the normal standard computer keyboards and screen, improved technological advancements would ensure that they are also able to type using those keyboards and read from those screens. For example, according to Burgstahler (2012), computer-generated symbols, both text and graphics, can be enlarged on the monitor or printer, thereby allowing individuals with low vision to use standard word processing, spreadsheet, electronic mail, and other software applications. Moreover, the ability to adjust the color of the monitor or change the foreground and background colors is also of value.

This chapter discusses a technological eLearning platform for people with low vision. The level of visual impairment and blindness in this case is based on the World Health Organization document: International Statistical Classification of Diseases and Related Health Problems (World Health Organization, 2010). The details are as tabulated in Table 1: Level of visual impairment and blindness according to the world health organization

Background Research

ELearning basically refers to learning electronically. In this case, it refers to being able to acquire knowledge through reading and studying from materials that have been made accessible through a machine/computer. An education research paper by Klopfer, Osterweil, Groff & Haas (2009) discussed the need to conceptualize and experiment with new methods in education so as to be able to appreciate the dynamics of our changing world.

Naturally, persons who are medically and physically fit, in this case, they have normal eyesight, are able to access such online material with less or no struggle at all. Moreover, such individuals are in a position to add to their pool of knowledge through surfing the net for further relevant materials, in addition to accessing volumes of books and literature from the library.

On the other hand, persons with low vision have a significant vision loss that cannot be corrected medically or surgically (World Health Organization, 2012). These vision problems impact work, school, recreation and other activities of daily living. Moreover, majority of institutions of higher learning have not yet incorporated adaptive technologies to aid learning for people with low vision.

Problem Statement

An eLearning portal enables teacher – student interaction through the student's period of study. However, majority eLearning portals have not incorporated adaptive technologies to aid persons with low vision. Considering the ideal situation where the majority of any population has normal eyesight, dedicated research continues to dominate technological innovations to the advantage of the majority.

According to World Health Organization (2012), 285 million people are visually impaired worldwide: 39 million are blind and 246 million have low vision. Moreover, About 90% of the worlds visually impaired live in developing countries! Hence the dire need to incorporate such individuals in the ever growing world of technology, as a way to foster interaction and enhance online learning!

Purpose of the Chapter

A visually impaired adult or child can be trained, with the help of vision enhancement, vision rehabilitation and assistive technology and low vision aids to learn. This chapter discusses an eLearning

portal for persons with low vision. Thus providing a platform through which such persons can train and learn.

The platform allows for varied accessibility options of background color, text color, font size and style. In addition to use of large monitors and anti-glare screens, the portal allows for speech output. Consequently, online learning is provided to persons with low vision, thus fostering interaction to enhance learning in online learning environments.

Research Outcomes and their Significance to Key Audiences

The discussed eLearning portal incorporates adaptive technologies for the benefit of people with low vision. For instance, having large prints enhances visibility. Moreover, color adjustments ensure better and motivated learning. In addition, having speech output perfects the whole implementation since the individual reading through the portal gets a clear understanding of what she is reading.

Assumptions and Limitations of the Research

The discussion in this chapter assumes that the person using the portal, despite having low vision, is able to hear and understand.

This chapter is limited in the fact that it may not be usable by 100% of the population of people with low vision, since it only assumes a case whereby low vision is the only and only disability, and that the disability is to a particular level (level 2 and above only) as shown in Table 1 of this chapter.

LITERATURE REVIEW AND THEORY

The world today has all kinds of people. Each and every person has a desire to grow both physically and emotionally. Moreover, with increased technological advances, majority of people desire to grow and enhance both their educational and technological knowledge by day. Despite such desires, there happens to be forces beyond human control, such as visual disability among others. According to the Kenyan census statistics of 2009, 3.5 percent of the total population, people with disabilities in Kenya is about 1.3 million. Of those with disabilities, 51 percent are female, while 49 percent are male. The largest proportion is physical and self care disabilities, which is 31 percent, followed by visual disabilities at 25 percent and hearing disabilities at 14 percent. This discussion focuses on a case scenario of a person with a visual disability, in this case, a person with low vision.

Education for people with low vision becomes a real challenge in cases where their learning is not well facilitated. For instance, such people may suffer challenges when studying together with people of normal vision. For example, unlike normal people who would be comfortable in any well set computer laboratory, the case of a person with low vision would be different. For instance, a computer laboratory will only be comfortable and usable by a person of low vision if it's appropriately lit as desired, probably computers with magnifiers among other requirements which may not be necessary for normal sighted people. Consequently, there is need to consider all genres of people in all technological advancements.

Current Situation in Africa: Case of Kenya

In Kenya, majority learning institutions are not in a position to adopt inclusive education whereby people with special needs can be accommodated in mainstream classrooms with other students/ pupils. The reason for this is because they either lack the supporting environment for such students or lack trained personnel who would be able to handle such cases. As a result, special cases call for people to be confined in special schools with specialized curriculums and mode of study. When it comes to institutions of higher learning and specialized careers, people with disabilities are most of the time left out since the facilities to accommodate their training is either inadequate or lacking completely. According to Flores (2003), inclusive education is not easy, but it benefits kids with and without disabilities. Moreover, teachers in special needs inclusive classrooms encounter several challenges such as having to deal with individualized lesson plans, lack of teaching aides, among other challenges, as discussed by Ramos (2003).

According to the International Labor Organization (ILO) fact sheet of 2009, many disabled people in Kenya, as in most developing countries in the world, live in poverty, have limited opportunities for accessing education, health, and suitable housing and employment opportunities. Hence the dire need to look into ways of having special needs "mainstreamed" into classrooms and other modes of learning and acquisition of skills and knowledge by taking advantage of technological advancements as is the case with eLearning. As a result, there will be a positive move in ensuring a disability perspective in all aspects of policy and labour legislation, effective implementation and enforcement of existing disability laws and policies and providing for equal employment opportunities and training, among other factors that contribute to the reduction of poverty and to the social and economic inclusion of people with disabilities in Kenya.

According to the Kenya National Survey for Persons with Disabilities main report, which was compiled in November, 2008, it showed that, 67% of Persons With Disabilities attained a primary level of education, with only a small proportion of 19% attaining secondary level education. Moreover, it was reported that approximately 2% reached university level. To add on this, only 2% of those with primary level education and 0.4% with secondary level education, attended special schools. Such an analysis goes a long way in explaining the need for more focus to such persons in the society we live in.

The current Kenyan constitution is also not silent on this matter. According to Chapter four, part 3, section 54, sub section (1), part **a** and **e**, the constitution states that a person with disability is entitled to be treated with dignity and respect and to be addressed and referred to in a manner that is not demeaning; and that she is entitled to access materials and devices to overcome constraints arising from her disability (Kenyan Constitution, 2013).

Other Works that Accommodate People with Low Vision

According to the Royal National Institute for the Blind (2004), the internet is one of the most significant communication developments since the invention of Braille. For the first time ever, many blind and partially sighted people have access to the same wealth of information as sighted people and on the same terms".

The digitalization of many public services such as education and government, may allow people with disabilities to live in much the same way as those who are not disabled.

On the other hand, if the information and services provided by governments, institutions and public enterprises are not fully accessible, there is a serious risk that they erect new barriers, increasing the information gap and creating a "digital divide" between those who can benefit from opportunities provided by ICT and those who cannot. Another disadvantage of the Internet for students with disabilities is that they have to purchase special adaptive technology to make the computer accessible.

The most frequently used network technologies in eLearning are email and the Web. Moreover, the Computer Mediated Communication (CMC), such as asynchronous communication (e-mail) and synchronous communication (chat) would give the learner the chance to participate actively in cooperative learning activities and to communicate easily with other learners, without having the other participant's preconceived notions of disability. All that is required is to ensure that vocal ability is incorporated in to the implementation.

To add on to the available case studies of implementations to cater for persons who are visually impaired is Voice for Information Society Universal Access and Learning (VISUAL). This is an international project with financial support of the Information Society Technologies Programme of the European Commission to develop voice based technology in order to improve the access of visually impaired, as discussed by Torres, Trapero, Martos, Vazquez & Soluziona (2002). One of the main results of the VISUAL Project was suggested to be the creation of an eLearning portal accessible by visually impaired people.

This proposed implementation informed this study in that there is still dire need for more system implementations that are usable by persons with visual disability. Consequently, the discussed system in this chapter includes technological advances that ensure that the eventual system is adequately usable by persons of visual disability: case of low vision.

The last and not the least is the American Foundation for the Blind (AFB), whose main objective is to expand the possibilities for people with vision loss. The foundation has implemented an eLearning platform for use by persons of Low Vision. In this platform, technological enhancements have been implemented to ensure that all content availed in that site is readable by people of low vision. For instance, they have options to amend background and text colors, as well as amend text sizes.

This implementation has equally informed this chapter design and discussion in that the technological advancements applied, are still applicable. In this case, the discussed portal allows for change of background color, text color, text size, in addition to sound output.

Table 2. Sample font families

Generic family	Font family	Description
Serif	Times New Roman	Serif fonts have small lines at the ends on some characters
	Georgia	
Sans-serif	Arial	"Sans" means without - these fonts do not have the lines at the ends of characters
	Verdana	
Monospace	Courier New	All monospace characters have the same width
	Lucida Console	

Summary of Adopted Implementation

To ensure effective implementation of an eLearning portal that is usable by people of low vision, the following basic guidelines for making effective legibility choices that work for nearly everyone, as discussed by Arditi (2013), should be considered:

1. **Contrast:** Text should be printed with the highest possible contrast. For example, white letters on a black background.
2. **Type Color:** Appropriate color combinations should be used. Printed material, generally, is most readable in black and white. Different colors if at all necessary are used for larger or highlighted text, such as headlines and titles. Therefore, to ensure a usable eLearning portal, the following color combinations should be considered:
   a. Black on a light grey or white background
   b. Dark blue on a light grey or white background
   c. Dark blue on a light yellow background
   d. Black text on beige-light brown background
3. **Point Size:** Large type should be ensured, bearing in mind that the relationship between readability and point size differs somewhat among typefaces. In this case, varied letter sizes.

4. **Leading:** Leading, or spacing between lines of text, should be at least 25 to 30 percent of the point size. This should be ensured since many people with partial sight have difficulty finding the beginning of the next line while reading.
5. **Font Family:** Complicated, decorative and cursive fonts should be avoided, and ensure that if used, they are reserved for emphasis only. Standard serif or sans-serif fonts, with familiar, easily recognizable characters are the best. Sans-serif fonts are more legible when character size is small relative to the reader's visual acuity. This majorly applies to Arial and Verdana fonts. Table 2 shows the preferred fonts for this discussion as informed by research and literature review (W3Schools, 2013).
6. **Font Style:** While there is little reliable information on the comparative legibility of typefaces, there is some evidence that a roman typeface, using upper and lower cases, is more readable than italics, oblique or condensed. Hence the consideration of roman type faces in the solution implementation.

On the other hand, the following should be avoided during the implementation of the solution model:

1. Italic text and capital letters, which can be difficult for users with reading impairments.
2. Bold text and underlined text.

3. Pop-ups and other automatic appearing windows that make orientation difficult.
4. Unusual words and long sentences, which are normally problematic.
5. Blinking graphics that may cause serious problems for some people, such as people with epilepsy, whereby a frequency from 4 to 59 Hz can start an epileptic attack!
6. Red light which is more provocative than blue light for example.

The above discussed variables and technological features were decided on after the review of other related works as discussed in this chapter.

METHODOLOGY

This section discusses the implementation in detail. In this case the guiding considerations, processes and eventual implementation and evaluation. The variables identified for this discussion include:

1. Background color: whereby the appropriate background color options suitable for persons with low vision are provided.
2. Text color: whereby text color options are provided to ensure maximum contrast to the selected background color.
3. Font style: whereby font styles that work for people with low vision are provided.
4. Font size: such that varied size options are allowed as opposed to fixed font sizes.
5. Sound output: whereby sound output provided is clear and appropriate.

The Structured Systems Analysis and Development Methodology (SSADM) was adopted for this discussion. The methodology adopts a sequential design process, which is often used in software de-

velopment processes. Progress in this model flows steadily downwards (like a waterfall) through the phases of Requirements Identification, Planning, Analysis, Design, Implementation, and Testing.

Requirement identification process basically involves identifying all that is required to design and implement an eLearning portal that is usable by persons of low vision. This leads to appreciating the fact that impaired vision affects reading. This is because impaired vision often makes reading difficult by: reducing the amount of light that enters the eye; blurring the retinal image; and damaging the central portion of the retina best suited to reading. Consequently, light reduction and blurring reduces the effective contrast of the text, while central retinal damage impairs the ability to see small print and to make eye movements that are crucial to reading.

This chapter discusses Moodle as the eLearning platform of choice for a portal for use by people with low vision. Moodle (abbreviation for Modular Object-Oriented Dynamic Learning Environment) is a free source eLearning software platform, also known as a Course Management System, Learning Management System, or Virtual Learning Environment (VLE).

The adopted plan in developing the eLearning system is two-fold: First, to download the free eLearning open source software from the Internet, and secondly, to expand and adapt the FOSS to satisfy local environment. The system uses tools such as: PHP as Front-end, Apache as Middle-ware and MySQL Database as Back-end as shown in Figure 1.

Specifically, this *Moodle Windows Installer* includes the applications to create an environment in which *Moodle* will operate, namely:

1. Apache 2.2.17
2. PHP 5.3.5 (VC6 X86 32bit) + PEAR
3. MySQL 5.5.8 (Community Server)

Figure 1. Moodle architecture

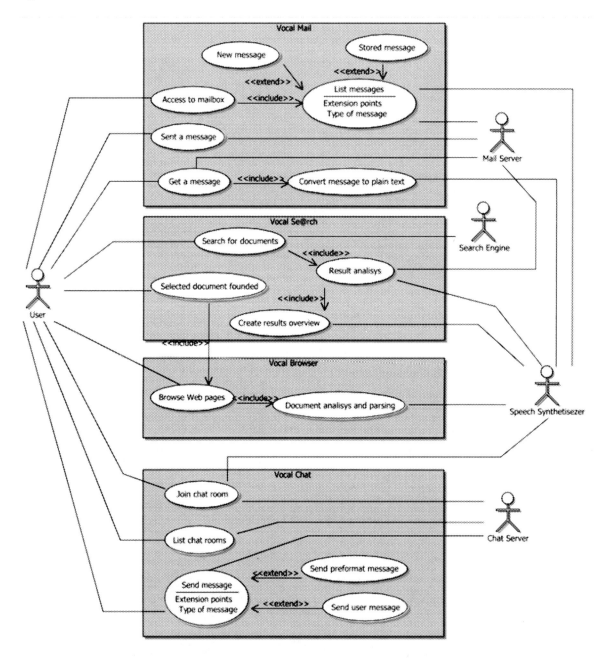

Why Moodle?

The following are the reasons as to why Moodle is preferred to other Learning Management Systems, for this discussion:

With Moodle, teachers can set up courses, create discussions, assign homework, and assign grades. They can also integrate with external content such as photos or videos, or with applications such as Google Docs. Moodle's features also include assignment submission, discussion forums, file downloading, instant messaging, an online calendar, news and announcements (college and course level), online quizzes, and a Wiki.

Moodle can scale to handle hundreds of thousands of students given enough server capacity and bandwidth and a variation called Poodle installs software to a local machine so the app can be used offline. Poodle can even boot off a thumb drive Booker (2013).

After planning, design process follows. The eLearning platform (Moodle) adopted is open source. However, all the suggested technological advancements have been incorporated in to the implementation to achieve the main objective of this chapter: an eLearning portal for people with low vision.

Moodle allows for student-based cooperative learning where feedback can be given regularly and immediately on a 'need to know' basis, as well as offer great opportunities for enquiry-based learning Ferreira-Meyers & Nkosi (2010).

Therefore, after successful installation of Moodle, keen observation of Section 508 Standards, as discussed by the United States Patent and Trademark Office (Office of the Chief Information Officer, 2012) should be considered to ensure appropriateness of implementation.

To make on-screen information easier to see, the following should be adopted:

1. The contrast between text and the background increased.
2. Placing text over a solid-color background observed. A patterned background can make text harder to discern.
3. Consistent layouts for all screens and dialogs within the portal ensured.
4. Accessing tools via a menu bar provided.
5. Line width guidelines when drawing lines on the screen followed. Using the line width information provided by operating system settings used, since that ensures that the learning application increases all lines proportionally should a user choose to enlarge the view (e.g., for horizontal separation in HTML, use HR tags instead of graphics).
6. Allowing the user to zoom into or magnify images and text.
7. A volume control option ensured.

To make software more compatible with other applications that offer low-vision access features, the following should be considered:

1. Using system pointers whenever possible.
2. Including a highlight or focus indicator when dragging the mouse cursor, even at those times when the cursor is invisible. This adjustment helps screen enlargement software using "pan and zoom" features to track the user's movements more accurately.
3. Adding support for a high-contrast setting.
4. Protecting users from the need to monitor two or more events simultaneously, especially those that occur far apart from each other on the screen.

Moreover, the implementation should allow for text enlargement, color and contrast adjustments and speech output.

The implementation phase involves putting in to place all the proposed design processes, so as to achieve the desired system. In this case, an eLearning portal that is usable by persons of low vision. According to a research conducted at Center for Assistive Technology and Environmental Access (2006), individuals with partial or low vision may use magnification software to enlarge screen images, which causes only a small portion of a page to be visible at a time. Poor contrast with text color, inconsistent layout, and cluttered pages can create confusion. Even with enlarged text, individuals with low vision may experience eyestrain, headache, nausea and/or other undesirable effects if required to read a large quantity of material within a constricted period of time. Small to medium-size text, decorative fonts, italics, and single-spaced lines of text are problematic as are formats that have less than 1 inch margins, distracting background, or text overlaying graphic content.

Testing ensures that the implemented system is usable as proposed and intended. This process involves engaging the targeted users, in this case, people with low vision, to work on the system as the end users. As a result, gaps that need to be worked on are identified.

Once the system has been fully tested, it is then ready for the intended users. During the period that the system is in use, the system will require constant maintenance to ensure that it remains relevant. Hence the need of the maintenance phase.

System Evaluation

System evaluation entails periodic evaluation of the system to assess its status in terms of original or current expectations and to chart its future direction. In this case of an eLearning portal, it will be of paramount importance to always ensure that learning is actually taking place. To do this, this discussion adopts the enquiry-based learning process model.

Inquiry-based learning is a learning process through which questions are generated from the interests, curiosities, and perspectives/experiences of the learner (Paula, 2003). It covers a range of approaches to learning and training, including case studies, investigations and research work. Moreover, it is perhaps more open to divergent ways of thinking about problems, more open to exploring and understanding different ways of perceiving the world and less concerned with providing firm solutions to problems that do not have simple or unique solutions. The process is illustrated in Figure 2.

Expected

A Challenge: After becoming aware of the issue that ought to be addressed, participants reach a state of puzzlement, curiosity and/or concern and feel challenged to enquire further. The next step is to clarify, define and redefine the particular question, issue or problem to investigate.

Active Participant Investigation: Participants gather resources and work out what they need to know and do. They consider the problem, cast around, imagine, try to predict, work out what they already know, and/or assess their ability to succeed. This is the stage when participants analyze and interpret the data before them. In this case, they check on all the provisions available on the computer screen that may be adjusted for clarity, at the same time monitoring the effects of any adjustments made.

Making Generalizations: Eventually participants synthesize what they have found into generalizations or principles which are used to decide on possible solutions.

Reflection: Participants consider how they achieved what they set out to do. They reflect, confirm, see where to improve, plan new things, evaluate, and consider possible action.

Eventually, if the participants are positively engaged and are able to follow the learning process through and through and with less strain, and at the same time achieving the intended purposes of the engagement, then it may be concluded that the participants are actually leaning. As a result, it's evident that learning is actually taking place.

Aspects of Evaluation

To ensure proper evaluation, the following aspects of evaluation should be considered:

Population: the population used should be of the intended users. In this case, this is the

Figure 2. Inquiry-based process of learning

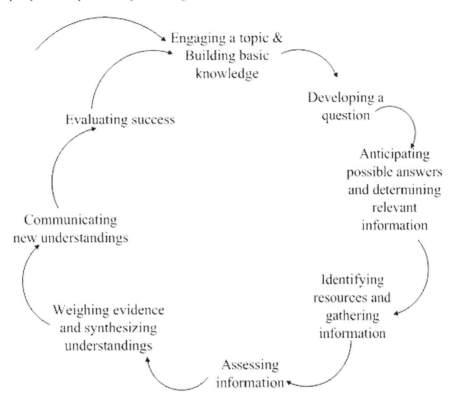

population of users with low vision. *Sampling:* this involves identifying the participants who should be involved in evaluating the system to ascertain its authenticity and relevance to goal and objectives. *Variables:* the sampling variables should be advised by the design process and the eventual implementation of the system. In this case: background color, text color, text size, font style and sound output.

Sources of Data and Information

The following are some sources of data in implementing the project:

1. The internet: for obtaining and searching for any relevant information that has been published in relation to visual disabilities, low vision and any other related data/information.

2. Previous research and publications: for exploring and understanding the scope of study that has been done in relation to the subject discussion.

3. Journals: reviewed for any relevant information on visual disabilities and low vision cases.

4. Any other relevant educational materials: exploring for any relevant data/information in relation to the subject discussion.

Instrument Development and Pre-Testing

This stage involves developing a data collection and testing instrument, in this case, a researcher administered questionnaire. The proposed data collection and testing questions should then be presented to a sample target group. This group of participants is then supposed to inform whether

Table 3. Sample data collection and testing template

Participant				
Part 1				
Preferred Accessibility Options:		**Variables**	**Response**	**Comments**
	1	Preferred Background color		
	2	preferred Text color		
	3	Preferred Size		
	4	Comment on Sound Output		
	5	General Comment		
Part 2				
Your comments on the following:			**Preferred**	**Not Preferred**
	6	Complicated, decorative or cursive fonts		
	7	Large font size		
	8	Italic text		
	9	Capital letters		

or not the proposed method of data collection and testing is acceptable.

A sample instrument for data collection and testing is shown in Table 3.

The sample population in this case comprises of people with low vision, from which a sample size of five is selected. These participants are supposed to assist in determining whether the proposed eLearning portal is acceptable and appropriate for Persons with Low Vision.

Interview method which is well interactive and allows for clarity of issues is used. Questions are posed to the selected target group and responses collected. Sample interview questions are shown in Table 4.

Table 5 shows a summary of the responses recorded from the interview questions.

Data Collection Methods, Tools, and Procedures

The methods used for data collection included a researcher administered questionnaire, and general observation. Reading of publications, journals, research papers and any other relevant material was

helpful in collecting all the required information, that informed the developed questionnaire and the general issues observed during data collection. Moreover, surfing the internet worked to expose other relevant materials which would otherwise be neglected, such as the fact that not all color combinations work for Persons with low Vision.

Participants: Fifteen (15) participants (8 females and 7 males) volunteered for this study. The mean age of the participants was 27 years with an age range from 19 to 63 years. All participants were familiar with reading from a computer screen, and suffered low vision.

Task Design: each participant was allowed to interact with the portal for at least 5 minutes. A word document had been uploaded on the system. This document was to be used to test the effects of varying the provided accessibility options and also to test the sound output.

Procedure: the participants were supposed to choose the accessibility options that worked for them among the ones provided on the portal. These options included background color, text color, font style, and font size. Lastly, the participants were expected to comment on the sound output

Table 4. Sample interview questions

		Interview Questions
	1	What are some of the challenges experienced by PWLV?
	2	What are some of the things that may be incorporated to an eLearning portal to make it usable by PWLV?
	3	Is sound output already available in your computers?
	4	Are there any challenges/difficulties experienced with using the available sound output?
	5	Would you consider the implemented eLearning portal that incorporates accessibility options and sound output as its key features helpful?

provided on the portal, in addition to giving a general comment about the eLearning portal. All these details were to be recorded by the researcher.

System Requirements

The basic requirements for Moodle are as follows:

Hardware

- **Disk Space:** 160MB plus as much as needed to store necessary materials. 5GB is probably a realistic minimum.
- **Backups:** at least 160MB (preferably at a remote location) so as to keep backups.
- **Memory:** at least 256MB. 1GB or more is strongly recommended. The general rule of thumb is that Moodle can support 10 to 20 concurrent users for every 1GB of RAM, but this will vary depending on specific

hardware and software combination and the type of use. In this case, concurrency is web server processes in memory at the same time.

Software

- **An Operating System:** Anything that runs the following software; although the choice will most likely depend on the performance needed and the skills available. Linux and Windows are the most common choices. Linux is generally regarded to be the optimal platform. Moodle is also regularly tested with Windows XP/2000/2003, Solaris 10 (Sparc and x64), Mac OS X and Netware 6 operating systems.

Table 5. Interview questions and responses

		Interview Questions	Recorded Responses
	1	What are some of the challenges experienced by PWLV?	Difficulties reading content.
	2	What are some of the things that may be incorporated to an eLearning portal to make it usable by PWLV?	Adjustable color options for background and text, adjustable text sizes, and sound output.
	3	Is sound output already available in your computers?	Yes.
	4	Are there any challenges/difficulties experienced with using the available sound output?	Yes, the speech generator just keeps talking for as the window remains open. One has to keep putting it on and off.
	5	Would you consider the implemented eLearning portal that incorporates accessibility options and sound output as its key features helpful?	YES

- **Web Server:** Primarily Apache or IIS. The following though not fully tested (or supported) should work: lightttpd, nginx, Cherokee, zeus and LiteSpeed. Moodle will refuse to install on any other web server. The web server needs to be correctly configured to serve PHP files.
- **PHP:** The minimum version is currently 5.3.2 with a number of extensions required.
- **A Database:** MySQL and PostgreSQL are the primary development databases. Oracle and MSSQL are also fully supported.
  1. MySQL - minimum version 5.1.33
  2. PostgreSQL - minimum version 8.3
  3. MSSQL - minimum version 9.0
  4. Oracle - minimum version 10.2
  5. SQLite - minimum version 2.0
- **Minimum Browser for Accessing Moodle:** Firefox 4, Internet Explorer 8, Safari 5, Google Chrome 11, Opera 9.

IMPLEMENTATION OVERVIEW AND TESTING

Implementation Overview

The discussed system incorporates the following technological advancements that are aimed at providing accessibility options to the users. The following are the accessibility options as availed in the system:

- **Background Color:** The background basically refers to the area on the screen upon which everything else on the computer screen appears. In this case, its color should be set such that any details on display are visible. In this case, various options have been provided to allow for variation of the background color as shown in Figure 3.

Figure 3. Background color options.

- **Font Color:** Font color in this case is the preferred color to the style of type within the type family being used. This color ought to be favorable to the user. Figure 4 shows various options that are available for selection in this discussion.

Figure 4. Font color options

Figure 5. Font style options

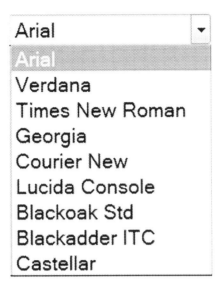

- **Font Style:** The font-style property is mostly used to specify italic text. However in this discussion only normal typeface has been adopted so as to fit the study. Figure 5 shows the font styles provided in the system.

- **Font Size:** This refers to the specific size of the font selected. Figure 6 shows options available to either increase or decrease font size.

Figure 6. Font size options

Figure 7. Sound output option

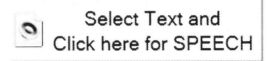

- **Sound Output:** This allows for the user to be able to listen to any portion of text on display that has been selected. Figure 7 shows the implementation as provided in the portal.

Figure 8 shows part of the system solution as implemented in the eLearning Portal:

Testing

The testing process in this discussion involves fifteen participants, who undertook the study and were required to indicate their preferences of the various variables that were provided in the portal. In this case, the following was expected:

1. Each participant was supposed to indicate the best three preferred options on background color, text color, and font style.
2. Each participant was expected to comment on whether they preferred varied or fixed font size.
3. Each participant was supposed to comment on the clarity of the sound output provided.

Figure 9 shows a tabulation of the test data as was collected for the fifteen participants. Numbers 1, 2, 3 have been used to indicate preference of background color, test color and font style, with 1 indicating the most preferred, whereas 3 indicated the least preferred of the three allowed options. For the font size, affirmative 'Yes' indicated the option chosen whereas a dash (-) was used to show

Figure 8. Part of implemented solution

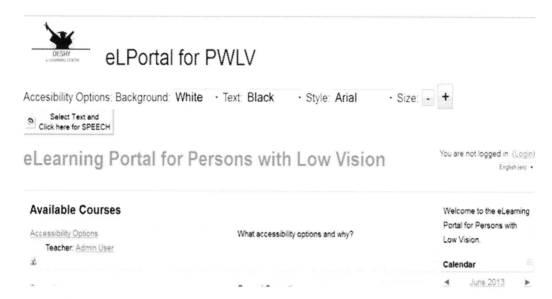

non-preference. Finally, number 1 was marked against the option chosen by each participant concerning the sound output.

SYSTEM EVALUATION, RESULTS AND CONCLUSION

System Evaluation

The discussed eLearning Portal was evaluated to ascertain that it met the proposed objectives. It was also checked for efficiency, appropriateness and its level of usability by persons with low vision.

The general objective of this chapter was to discuss an eLearning portal that was usable by persons with low vision. To begin with, persons with low vision are not comfortable with all background colors and text colors. They are also not comfortable with small font sizes since their vision is usually problematic and somehow limited. In this case, the discussed portal included variables of background color, text color, font style and size, which allowed for flexibility in terms of choices and preferences. Eventually, all the participants (people with low vision) who were

involved were able to interact with the discussed portal as desired. Consequently, it was concluded that the implemented portal was usable by people with low vision.

On the other hand, this chapter sought to discuss an eLearning portal with technological advances such as sound output. Moreover, the discussed portal was supposed to be testable with the target group, in this case, people with low vision. These two specific objectives were well met in that, other than the Human Computer Interface (HCI) effects that enhanced accessibility, sound output was also achieved. This was evident in the fact that the participants only needed to highlight the part of text that they needed to read, and it would be read out on clicking the provided sound button.

The following section discusses the results of the evaluation as was recorded, during the testing exercise.

Results

After testing the participant's preferences on Background color as compared to Text color, the results realized are shown in Table 6:

Figure 9. Recorded participants preferences

Variables	Options	1	2	3	4	5	6	7	8	9	10	11	12	13	14	15	Preference Level
Background Color	White	1	1,3	3	1	1,3		2	1,3	3	2		2	1		2	1	15
	Grey	2	2	2	3	2	3		2	3	1	3	2	1,3		2		14
	Yellow			1	2		1	2		1	3		3	2		3		9
	Brown								1			1			3			3
	Black														1			1
	Orange	-	-	-	-	-	-	-	-	-	-	-	-	-	-	-	-	
	Purple	3									2							2
	Red	-	-	-	-	-	-	-	-	-	-	-	-	-	-	-	-	
Text Color	Black	1,2	3	3	1,3	1,2,3	2,3	3	3	2	1	2	1,3	1	1,2,3	1		23
	Dark blue		1,2	1,2	2		1	1,2	1,2	1,3	3	1,3	2	2,3		2,3		20
	White	3									2							2
Font Style	Arial	1,3	2	1,2,3	2,3		2	1,2,3	2	1	2	3	1	1,2,3		1	1	22
	Verdana	2	1		1	3		3	2	3	1	2		1	2	2		12
	Times New Roman							1	3					3		3		4
	Georgia		3			1				1	2	3		2	3			7
	Courier New	-	-	-	-	-	-	-	-	-	-	-	-	-	-	-	-	
	Lucida Console	-	-	-	-	-	-	-	-	-	-	-	-	-	-	-	-	
	Blackoak Std	-	-	-	-	-	-	-	-	-	-	-	-	-	-	-	-	
	Blackadder ITC	-	-	-	-	-	-	-	-	-	-	-	-	-	-	-	-	
	Castellar	-	-	-	-	-	-	-	-	-	-	-	-	-	-	-	-	
Font Size	Fixed	-	-	-	-	-	-	-	-	-	-	-	-	-	-	-	-	0
	Variable	Yes	Yes	Yes	Yes	Yes	Yes	Yes	Yes	Yes	Yes	Yes	Yes	Yes	Yes	Yes		15
Sound	Clear	1	1			1	1	1		1		1		1		1		9
	Not Clear			1											1			2
	Not Sure				1				1		1		1					4

Results, Interpretation, Discussion, and Conclusion

According to the testing carried out and the analysis thereof, it is concluded that people of low vision prefer text with the highest possible contrast. For example, majority preferred white letters printed on a black background. Moreover, appropriate color combinations are preferred, such as black on a light grey or white background, dark blue on a light grey or white background, dark blue on a light yellow background, and black text on beige-light brown background.

To add on this, majority prefer to work on the large font size. The fact that font size is easily varied is preferred by all. This results from the fact that, with the enlarged fonts, vision is enhanced, thus making reading easier. On the other hand, the enlarged fonts mean that spacing between words is more clear, making it easier to distinguish between a start and end of a sentence or paragraph.

On the other hand, it is noticeable that almost all participants avoided the use of complicated, decorative or cursive fonts. Standard serif or

Table 6. Background to text color preferences

Background Color	Text Color	Preference Level	% of Preference
White	Black	13	39.4
Grey	Black	6	18.18
White	Dark Blue	2	6.06
Yellow	Dark Blue	9	27.27
Brown	Black	1	3.03
Purple	White	2	6.06
		33	100

The above results are graphically represented as shown in Figure 10:

Figure 10. Background color to Text color Preference shown in percentage (%)

Background/Text	Preference (%)
White/Black	39.4
Grey/Black	18.18
White/Dark blue	6.06
Yellow/Dark blue	27.27
Brown/Black	3.03
Purple/White	6.06
	Total = 100%

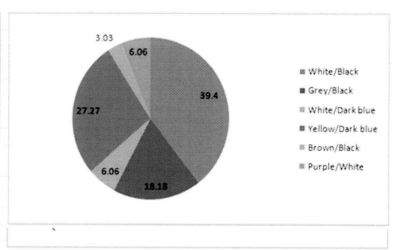

Table 7. Font style preferences

Font Style	Preference Level	Preference in %
Arial	22	48.88
Verdana	12	26.67
Times New Roman	4	8.89
Georgia	7	15.56
Courier New	0	0
Lucida Console	0	0
Blackoak Std	0	0
Blackadder ITC	0	0
Castellar	0	0
Total	45	100

The level of preference of font style varied as tabulated in Table 7:

Table 8. Font size preferences

Font Size	Level of Preference	Preference in %
Fixed	0	0
Variable	15	100

Out of the possible 15 participants, all of them preferred varied font size as opposed to a case whereby the font size is fixed. The results of the analysis are as shown in Table 8:

The above results expressed graphically are as shown in Figure 12:

Table 9. Sound preferences

Sound	Level of Preference	Preference in %
Clear	9	60
Not Clear	2	13.33
Not Sure	4	26.67
Total	15	100

Sound was analyzed as shown in Table 9:

The sound preferences expressed graphically are as shown in Figure 13:

sans-serif fonts, with familiar, easily recognizable characters are best preferred. The reason for the preference is concluded to be the fact that sans-serif fonts are more legible when character size is small relative to the reader's visual acuity. In addition to this, normal typeface is considered to font style in italics, oblique or condensed.

On further investigation and observation, it is concluded that, italic text and capital letters, which can be difficult for users with reading impairments is avoided. Moreover, bold text, underlined text, pop-ups and other automatic appearing windows that make orientation difficult is never preferred. Unusual words and long sentences, which are

Figure 11. Font style preference in percentage (%)
The analysis in Figure 11 shows how many times a style is preferred to another, expressed as percentages.

Font Style	Preference in %
Arial	48.88
Verdana	26.67
Times New Roman	8.89
Georgia	15.56
Courier New	0
Lucida Console	0
Blackoak Std	0
Blackadder ITC	0
Castellar	0
Total	100

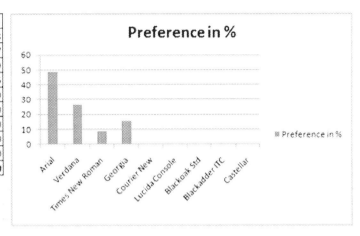

Figure 12. Font size preference expressed in percentage (%)

Font Size	Preference in %
Fixed	0
Variable	100

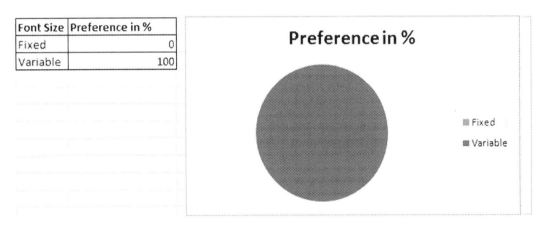

Figure 13. Sound preference expressed in percentage (%)

Sound	Level of Preference	Preference in %
Clear	9	60
Not Clear	2	13.33
Not Sure	4	26.67
Total	15	100

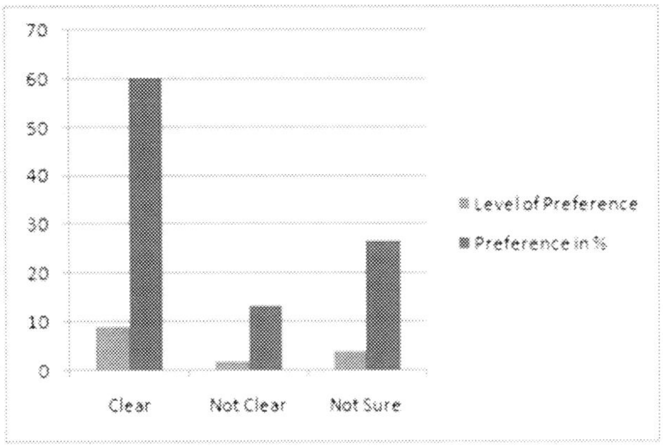

normally problematic and blinking graphics that may cause serious problems for some people, are seriously not preferred.

Gauging from the results of the test, and again by general observation of the current society where we live in, it is noticeable that there is need of usable eLearning portals to cater for persons with visual disability. Majority of the users today have been forced to struggle with eLearning, since no conducive environment has been provided to ensure their comfort. Therefore, the discussed portal works as an enhancement to the existing implementations that cater for persons with visual disabilities.

FUTURE RESEARCH AND RECOMMENDATIONS

Public Policy and assistive technology for low vision are stalled. With few exceptions, typographic flexibility of web language has been ignored in research, assistive technology and policy regarding low vision. Research is needed to determine efficacy of typographic intervention. Typometrics provides an engineering approach that uses basic findings of psychophysics and the flexibility of web technology. Formal clinical trials are needed to verify the efficacy of emerging assistive technologies. This should protect consumers with low vision and enable informed policy (Dick, 2012).

In this regard, there will be need to check on Public Policy and assistive technology for persons with low vision. It is recommended that eLearning portal usable by all categories of people considering their visual capability be adopted by all learning institutions. Consequently, some of the population, in this case, persons with visual disabilities will not left out by the advancing technology.

REFERENCES

Arditi, A. (2013). *Designing for People with Partial Sight.*

Bjork, E., Ottosson, S., & Thorsteinsdottir, S. (2008). e-Learning for All. In A. R. Lipshitz and S. P. Parsons (Eds.), E-Learning: 21st Century Issues and Challenges. Nova Science Publishers, Inc.

Booker, E. (2013). *Why Moodle Matters To Teachers.* Retrieved from http://www.informationweek. com/education/instructional-it/why-moodle-matters-to- teachers/240145508

Burgstahler, S. (2012). *Working Together: People with Disabilities and Computer Technology.* Retrieved from https://www.washington.edu/doit/ Brochures/PDF/wtcomp.pdf

Center for Assistive Technology and Environmental Access. (2006). *Individuals who are Blind or have Low Vision.* Retrieved from http://www. accesselearning.net/mod1/1_04.php

Dick, W. E. (2012). Typometric Rx: New for Low Vision Readers. *CSUN Conference on Technology and People with Disabilities.*

Ferreira-Meyers, K., & Nkosi, J. (2010). *Incorporating the Enquiry-Based Approach into Moodle? Academic Literacy Development.* Swaziland: University of Swaziland.

Flores, K. (2003). *Special needs, "Mainstream" classroom Inclusive education isn't easy, but it benefits kids with-and without-disabilities.*

Government of Kenya. (2013). *Kenyan Constitution*, 2013.

ILO-International Labour Organization. (2009). Inclusion of people with Disabilities in Kenya.

Inquiry-Based Learning. (n.d.). Retrieved from http://teorije- ucenja.zesoi.fer.hr/doku. php?id=instructional_design:inquiry-based_ learning

Klopfer, E., Osterweil, S., Groff, J., & Haas, J. (2009). *Using the technology of today, in the classroom today*. Retrieved from http://education.mit.edu/papers/GamesSimsSocNets_EdArcade.pdf

Moodle. (2012). *Installation Quickstart*. Retrieved from http://docs.moodle.org/23/en/Installation_Quickstart

Office of the Chief Information Officer. (2012). *Section 508 Reference Guide Appendix B: Tips for Creating Accessible Products*. The United States Patent and Trademark Office. Retrieved from http://www.uspto.gov/about/offices/cio/section508/11b.jsp

Paula, S. (2006). *What is inquiry-based learning?* Retrieved from http://www.inquirylearn.com/Inquirydef.htm

Ramos, T. (2003). *Top Challenges Teachers Face in Special Needs Inclusive Classrooms*.

Royal National Institute for the Blind. (2004). *Communicating with blind and partially sighted people*. Peterborough, England.

Torres, J. L., Trapero, J., Martos, F., Vazquez, G., & Soluziona, A. F. (2002). *Voice for Information Society Universal Access and Learning* (VISUAL). Retrieved from http://www.afb.org

World Health Organization (2010). *International Statistical Classification of Diseases and Related Health Problems*.

World Health Organization Media Centre. (2012). *Visual impairment and blindness*. Retrieved from http://www.who.int/mediacentre/factsheets/fs282/en/

W3Schools. (2013). *CSS Font*. Retrieved from http://www.w3schools.com/css/css_font.asp

KEY TERMS AND DEFINITIONS

Apache: Is the most popular of all the web servers available because it supplies basic web server functionalities.

eLearning: Refers to leaning electronically. In this case, being able to acquire knowledge through reading and studying from materials that have been made accessible through a machine/computer.

FOSS: Free and open source software.

HCI: Human Computer Interface.

MySQL (Pronounced My SEE Q EL): Is one of the standard query languages for interacting with databases. MySQL is an open source database server that is free and extremely fast. MySQL is also cross platform and it has a high customer base for its flexible licensing terms, ease of use and high performance.

PHP: Is the web development language written by and for web developers. PHP stands for Hypertext Preprocessor. It is a robust, server-side, open source scripting language that is extremely flexible and very easy to learn.

PWLV: Persons with Low Vision refer to people who have sight problems, in that they have partial sight.

PWLV: Persons With Low Vision.

Chapter 13
iPad:
Integrating Positive, Active, Digital Tools and Behaviors in Preservice Teacher Education Courses

Ursula Thomas
Georgia Perimeter College, USA

ABSTRACT

It is the unavoidable and it is not going away. The gravity of technology has firmly planted itself in our daily existence and yes, this includes teacher education. As technology has because our normative environment in daily life it has also become normative in educator preparation; our new oxygen. This commonplace element is hailed as a tool of equity for learners, preschool through college. Our current populations of learners are digital natives, but many educational leaders are digital tourists. As we look to challenge the traditional notions of distance learning, program offerings, and educator preparation models we must rapidly embrace the persona of the digital native to increase relationships with those we prepare as teachers while at the same time valuing and increasing diversity and voice. This chapter seeks to examine how a teacher educator engages preservice teachers in the world of diversity using technology.

INTRODUCTION

The phenomenon of education is dynamic. We must engage students in multiple domains to include the physical, psychosocial, and the intellectual. It is also the goal of the teacher to engage students keeping in mind the stages of human development; hence developmentally appropriate practice. Along with traditional pedagogical approaches, we must consider current technologies and multiple formats to compliment student's opportunities to build and navigate their knowledge bases. These knowledge bases are culturally and linguistically mediated. This process is delicate, complicated and robust.

Educators are a part of this and must utilize every opportunity to reinforce the "content and process" approach to learning. It is the objective of this chapter to examine the challenges of engaging technology in teacher education classrooms;

DOI: 10.4018/978-1-4666-8363-1.ch013

cognizant of diversity. This chapter will also identify tools that are appropriate for such a task. Finally, this chapter will provide case scenarios in which the technological tools were successfully implemented with diversity and student-centered learning at its crux.

BACKGROUND

Technology is received by its' critics as "the next new thing" with each application, product or latest version. More importantly, technology has its own unique challenges, perspectives and characteristics. Technology education has progressed through many cycles for the past 100 years and continues to develop as the principal channel for preparing children and youth in technological literacy.

Technology in Teacher Education

In order to begin examining the landscape of teacher education and technology, we must start with a national picture. Facts indicate that many programs in technology education in the past five years escalated at all levels to include elementary, middle, and high school. Among thirty-nine states, there are just 10 states that report a decline in the quantity of programs. An added national curricula trend was the integration of technology education into disciplines to include math and science. The primary impetus for technology education teachers has enlarged yet roughly; all states reported a deficiency in the preparation of new technology education teachers.

Whom are we including in the landscape? Just as with the recruitment of women, twenty-nine out of thirty-nine reporting state administrators describe that their state did not have guidelines, recruitment procedures or incentive plans for inviting minorities into technology teacher preparation programs. Ninety-seven percent of respondents corroborate that students with special needs participated in technology education in their states. All states report having their students participating

through inclusion models. Three states supplement these programs with separate technology education classes for exceptional learners. This funnels into funding structures as well.

A distinct difference subsists amid those states that continue to financially supplicate technology education and those states that did not. The very levels of funding technology education programs across states clarified what happen when the resources available are limited and problems must compete four dollars. The same funding trials influence technology teacher preparation institutions as well. Consequently, political, programmatic, state and budgetary constraints are eliminating university teacher preparation programs and creating an increased demand for new technology education teachers. The integration of technology education into other disciplines was cited as a growing curricular trend (Akmal, Oaks & Barker, 2008).

Teacher education and technology can be used to connect meaning making and learning in the electronic classroom reflections on facilitating distance-learning. The rising use of technology to meet the immense educational needs of our increasing world has led to heightened apprehension about learning experiences with educational environments that are removed from the immediate contact of instructors. Underscored are the trials linked with creating the suitable conditions for learning when transferring from the face-to-face exchanges of the regular classroom to the venue of compressed video. The implications of the professorial role as facilitator, the establishment of learning community techniques of questioning and inquiry and group collaborations are of concern.

The initial tentativeness, dissatisfaction, and perplexity concerning a constructivist approach and its expectations were coming at a distance-learning as a face-to-face course; with each succeeding class meeting, their instructor learned more about the significance of the sense of community. This was essential for the class in terms of student interaction and involvement; which are fundamental to the effectiveness of the pedagogical methods and student assignments. The experience of distance education students with library resources is characteristic of the logistical problems and the hidden curriculum embedded within distance education that has elicited inadequate attention in the literature. To ensure that the experiences of distance education students; especially those in less developed areas are equitable with the students on campus, access arrangements must be made for technological linkages (Johnson & Brescia, Jr, 2006).

Technology education is also a part of the broader conversation about students at risk. This leads us to the examination of social adjustment of at risk of technology education students (Ernst & Moye, 2013). The rationale of this study was to ascertain the degree of social aptitude for technology education students identified at risk. This study reveals several items of interest. Firstly, it supports the declaration made by Cardon (2000) that "technology education programs have historically attracted at risk students in that technology education programs have received little attention regarding their influence on at risk students." In the milieu of this study, large percentages of students believed to be at risk in the six participating technology education course sections for the evidences Cardon's statements. Given the disposition of the scale items and analysis of the results, it can be assumed that at risk technology education students in this sample had significantly lower social proficiency for school modification application than the normative portion of adolescent students provided by the instrument, employed. Another study looked at influencing technology education teachers to accept teaching positions. The purpose of this study was to address the technology education teacher shortage by probing the issues that influence technology education teachers to accept teaching positions. The results of the study exposed that the factors most influencing a technology education teacher to accept a teaching position included having resources available for the classrooms and labs

having resources for professional development and a collaborative environment (Steinke & Putnam, 2008).

This leads us to competencies and engagement in technology education. The current level of the-learning technology development imparts chances for collaborative engagement across information interface with content and individual empowerment. Now, swift changes in communication technologies allow teachers to move from traditional face-to-face classroom activities to online activity or online activities in the regular classrooms. Current teaching that is a socially interactive process is based on the constructivist and social constructivist concepts too.

There are three dimensions of information-technology competencies (ICT). One is the teacher knows what learning activities can be used in teaching. Two, the teacher has the compulsory skills for using the hardware and software for ICT. Three, the teacher knows the pedagogical didactical elements of ICT competencies. Teacher education is becoming an important part of the education system. In conclusion e-teaching requires a wide gamut of the roles compulsory for teachers in the education environment to acquire sufficient knowledge about learning and teaching differences in e-learning master programs are implemented in the preservice and inservice teacher education provided by post secondary institutions (Bjekic, Krneta & Milosevic, 2010). In what ways are these competencies delivered and employed purposefully? How do we further integrate this conversation into teacher education explicitly? This leads us into how pedagogical decisions are constructed and what that looks like in teacher education.

An additional part of this research conversation is teacher knowledge about technology integration and examination of inservice and preservice teacher's instructional decision-making.

This study relates the capacity of inservice and preservice teachers to give an appreciation of technology integration into such knowledge to instructional decision-making. Overall, inservice teachers demonstrated consideration of an expansive breadth of classroom and school level aspects in making a technology integration decision. Comprehending, capturing, and measuring these differences is essential to advance theory on dimensions of technological pedagogical content knowledge and how it matures in different teacher subgroups to press forward the work teacher educators enact with designing courses about technology integration to learners needs (Greenhow, Dexter & Hughes, 2008).

It would be unwise to ignore the influence or impact of teacher educators on technology education. In scrutinizing one-to-one computing in teacher education faculty apprehension and implications for teacher educators, Donovan and Green (2010) found that data pointed to the three major implications regarding technology-rich teacher education and faculty. This includes topics to be addressed for program accomplishments that incorporate faculty readiness, faculty preparation, and faculty disparity. Miranda and Russell (2011) explored predictors of teacher-directed student use (TDS) of technology and elementary classrooms a multilevel approach using data from the USEIT study. This study is a secondary data analysis of the USEIT data to inform school administration and policymakers about the factors impinging on instructional technology use in elementary classrooms. The strongest predictors of TDS teacher directed student use of technology were a teacher's experience with technology deem that technology is valuable to meet instructional goals and supposed pressure to use technology core beliefs, employ technology, technology learning objectives, teacher and student accountability to standards, and principles of technology discretion.

Heafner, Petty and Hartshorne (2011) focused on evaluating types of teacher preparation; comparing a face-to-face and remote observation of graduate interns. In comparing the two observational processes of face-to-face and e-learning, the researchers found that genres of observation are not equivalent methods for evaluating graduate students; however data intimates that these processes are comparable and each type of observation has both benefits and limitations. Neither process was overall a more effective method of evaluating the quality of teaching.

Teacher's use of technology lessons learned from teacher education program to the classroom was investigated by Wright and Wilson (2011). This paper describes 10 teachers' awareness of technology integration and technology use in their classrooms five years after their graduation from a teacher education program, which promote technology use in teaching and learning. These researchers use Hooper and Rieber's five phases of technology: familiarization, utilization, integration, reorientation, and evolution to categorize the teachers' effort. The researchers found that five teachers were at orientation evolution phase where teachers with continued professional development had engage students in using technology and had encouragement from their school community. Outcomes indicated that the participants continued to be accustomed to ways in which to use technology and continue to utilize primary technology proficiency and practices learned in their teacher preparation program. As a whole, the participants became contented with the technologies learned and used during their teacher preparation program. For those teachers who moved beyond using technology for specific tasks and teacher-centered objectives, three things emerged; participants continued to seek professional development, participants used technology to engage students and felt compelled to do so for the students, and the school community supported their use of technology through accessibility of sources and professional learning opportunities.

Technology in Methods Courses

This further narrows the focus onto the relationship of technology and methods courses. A research study investigated the concept of preservice secondary English teacher's use of technology in the field following the completion of an instructional technology methods course. The qualitative study scrutinizes the ways in which graduate preservice secondary English teachers incorporate technology into their practice during the semester immediately following a content specific course and methods of teaching with technology. Findings specify that the requisite of connections between introductory course work and subsequent methods courses is essential.

Three unexpected and fundamental ideas covered the results of the study many of which reverberate the current literature based on educational technology coursework. First, preservice teachers require a connection between their introductory teaching with technology coursework and subsequent methods and field placement courses. Similarly, if preservice teachers are expected to amalgamate technology into their preliminary fieldwork they must be placed with supportive cooperating instructors who will afford instructional autonomy needed to investigate new uses of tools. Lastly, technology integrated coursework across courses needs to implement and expand pedagogical content knowledge in conjunction with technical skills. Researchers are learning results from a sequence of reflection and reconception added research is in progress that follows the study participants into semester long teaching placements. This is to inspect how they maintain pedagogical processing and how they combine technology into their instruction (Kajder, 2005).

One such study is the promise of technology to confront dilemmas in teacher education the use of WebQuest and problem-based methods courses. This research found that WebQuest by design supported a problem-based approach to instruction introducing students to multiple perspectives related to science with literacy teaching and learning to increase pedagogical content knowledge and skills and impart learning experiences that assimilate technology inside the framework of science and literacy instruction. Even though these deliberations generally take place in preservice technology courses, it is compulsory for those conversations

to occur within the context of particular content area instruction. Eventually the research found WebQuest to be a productive instructional tool. The researchers feel that the experience improved and lengthened students understanding, skills and dispositions related to teaching literacy and science (Smith, Draper & Sabev, 2005).

Herron (2010) focused on implementation of technology in an elementary mathematics lesson experience of preservice teachers at one university. The study observed preservice teacher's reaction to implementing technology into elementary mathematics lessons. The instructional designer was the web-based technology used by the preservice teachers. Four themes emerged from the data; insights into technology, struggles with technology, access to the mathematics and learning communities. Preservice teachers describe equally positive and negative experiences with technology in the classroom. The implementation of technology into a mathematics lesson can be a daunting task for many teachers. The preservice teachers in the study had an extensive range of experiences with the assignment.

The key themes the preservice teachers conversed about in the reflection were self-awareness into technology, struggles with technology, and access to mathematics learning communities. The expansion of mathematics learning communities via technology as a vehicle for discussion was a revelation of the data. Teacher education programs need to investigate methods that allow elementary preservice teachers to acquire the knowledge compulsory for employing technology into the mathematics classroom.

Horzum, Gungoren and Ceit (2012) considered a model for beliefs and tools where pedagogical content knowledge of science and technology preservice teachers has towards web-based instruction. The point of this study was to learn the relationship between pedagogical content knowledge of science and technology with preservice teachers. The study was comprised of 363 preservice teachers. As a result of the research, behavioral and contextual beliefs in web-based instruction were at a medium level of perceived usefulness, ease of use perceived attitudes, and intention positively affected web based instructional tools accept its levels of preservice teachers.

Kalemoglu (2014) studied the relationship between the attitudes of perspective physical education teachers towards education technology and computer self-efficacy beliefs. According to findings obtained by the research, the attitudes of respect the physical education teachers have about education technology reached high levels. This finding has shown parallelism with some studies in which attitudes towards education technology was determined. On the other hand, another finding obtains from the research of computer self-efficacy beliefs revealed the perspective physical education teachers again at high levels. When considering the factor of self-efficacy, beliefs directly created a positive effect on the intention to use computers technology, it could be said that the qualities of perspective to encourage teachers to use computer knowledge and technologies on their lessons in future and various educational qualities could be higher.

Keeler (2008) found that technology integration arose in two primary set-ups: administrative productivity and instructional delivery. In terms of administrative productivity, course resources were made available online and the instructor developed technology-rich record keeping strategies. Technology-infused instructional methods, then, were intermingled throughout the course with anticipation that students would universally make use of technologies to complete course tasks. Through this study, it became apparent that even though teacher candidates knew how to use explicit technological tools, they infrequently knew how to utilize those tools in educational contexts. Even fewer students had knowledge of how to use technological tools to augment and fortify content learning.

Habre and Grundmeier (2007) explored teachers' views of the function of technology in mathematics education before, during, and after their experience in a mathematics class that focused on technology in mathematics education. These results disclose a chief concern among participants, specifically that mathematics and not technology should remain the focal point of instruction in mathematics classrooms. Most participants showed concern that technology should not be the core but rather a tool; and although the majority agreed with the statement that technology should be used in a mathematics classroom, only one participant gave a legitimate pedagogical argument, namely that students have different learning styles. The majority of participants in the class had strong mathematical backgrounds and for this reason was able to articulate creative ways to explore mathematics using technology.

Their lack of experience teaching mathematics may have caused participants not to recognize the pedagogical possibility of the dynamic nature of the software. This insufficiency almost certainly held up participants from being able to illustrate the teacher's role in a classroom where technology is utilized. Based on these results, it seems feasible that a course of this nature has the potential to begin the prospective teachers' compulsory reflection on the role of technology in mathematics education. The results also recommend that such a course should be combined with authentic activities that allow prospective teachers to relate what they are-learning to mathematics classrooms. These realistic activities could include watching videos of classroom situations, becoming comfortable with adopted curricula in local schools, talking to local teachers, adapting school curricula to include technology, and developing and implementing prospective activities that make use of technology to teach mathematics in a local school.

Matthew, Felvegi and Callaway (2009) explored a wiki as a collaborative-learning tool in a language arts methods class. The purpose of this study was to determine how contributing to a class wiki influenced the learning of preservice teachers enrolled in a language arts methods class. Students' reflections indicate that contributing to the class wiki led to a deeper processing of the course content and was personally constructive to the students in spite of continual technology trials. As students contributed to the wiki pages, their reflections on the progression and their interview comments exposed that they spent time reading and rereading the pages. As they researched content to add to the pages, they made links to their prior knowledge and experiences, to the content they were learning in other classes, to their tutoring meetings with elementary students, and to an assortment of internet resources.

In 2009, Duran, Brunvand and Fossum studied the impression of a professional development program where a K-16 networked learning community method was implemented to afford training and provision for technology integration in science education. Findings indicate that over the course of the program the project participants drastically increased their self-assurance and proficiency to integrate technology into the teaching and learning process. Technology integrated lessons developed by the project participants included the use of a variety of advanced technology tools to make possible learning in science. Using mutual partnerships helped many teachers to use technology with their students and increased their drive and interest towards technology based training.

Crowe (2004) looked at integrating technology into social studies education courses. This study principally concentrates on how one social studies teacher education faculty member integrated technology into a succession of social studies education courses. Most students reported that the instructor's exemplar of methods and resources encouraged them to use technology in their teaching.

Meagher, Özgün-Koca, and Edwards (2011) explored the emergent Technological Pedagogical and Content Knowledge (TPACK) of a group of secondary mathematics preservice teachers in a methods course as they designed and implemented technology-rich teaching resources in field settings. The results specify that the participants' comprehension of technology transferal from viewing technology as a tool for support into view-

ing technology as a tool for developing student understanding. Collected data supports the notion that preservice teacher TPACK development is closely related to a shift in identity from "learners of mathematics to teachers of mathematics."

Goodson-Espy, Davis, Schram and Quikenton (2010) investigated using 3D computer graphics multimedia to motivate preservice teachers' learning of geometry and pedagogy.

This study describes the origin and rationale of a geometry methods course, focusing on a geometry-teaching technology created using NVIDIA® Chameleon demonstration. End-of-course survey results point toward moderate increases in student teachers' knowledge of basic geometry and its applications. Their utilization of geometric terminology improved and was more visible than in the pre-survey. They also describe believing they are more prepared to teach the subject matter to young learners. After screening the Nvidia presentation, preservice teachers were better able to detail nontraditional occupations that make use of geometry.

Diversity and education process have a unique and dynamic relationship. It is imperative that we examine the way it influences and shapes the education process.

Diversity in Teacher Education

Gaudelli (2007) found that web based courses, which represent a revamping of venerable efforts, and distance education are a robust trend amongst post secondary institutions. Teacher preparation and development has also taken part in this endeavor as web based distance-learning courses are utilized as a instrument for the integration of knowledge, skills, and attitudes about teaching with technology and content area specialty. Institutions of teacher preparation and organizations like CAEP see this as a compulsory feature of teacher candidate preparation, progressively viewing the blending of technology and diversity. It is inadequate to think of knowledge in separate ways but rather as an incorporated foundation that teachers draw on according to classroom situations that surface. Some of this mixture occurs obviously in coursework like distance learning, multicultural education course work whereby beginning teachers had to become proficient with learning technology, and learning about global diversity yet the remnant of this integration continues to be a daunting challenge even for veteran teachers not to mention novice teachers.

A national study of teacher preparation for diverse student populations was conducted in 2002 and published by the Center for Research on Education Diversity and Excellence (CREDE). One of the profound tenants of the study was that all teachers should be prepared to address sociocultural linguistic and economic backgrounds of the entire spectrum of the American student. This particular study found the least knowledge and use was reported in the area of technology and the most knowledge and use in the area of preparing candidates to work with culturally and linguistically diverse populations (Akmal, Oaks & Barker, 2001).

This is just as true with international, special needs populations. Starcic (2010) investigated the introduction of the SEVERI, an e-learning environment in Slovenian schools. Students were able to examine the development and implementation of the applications for special needs pupils in Slovenian schools and plan teaching and learning experiences within their project. In preservice teacher education in educational technology, the spotlight is on inquiry-based learning and on planning and incorporating the innovative use of ICT into teaching. The importance is also on improving the student's standards for his or her own professional learning. Accordingly, researchers found the preservice educational technology course has late theory and practice. The work in an instructional technology laboratory was linked with teaching behaviors in the school setting. The students who participated in the assessment had a distinctive opportunity to transfer a new

knowledge to their day today teaching practices of their normal professional work. The focal point of planning, listening, performance, and on learning the material design was essential. In the process of assessment student learning was measured as a grouping of learning objectives, activities, and learning outcomes. Student teachers developed and implemented ICT for their pedagogical work.

Both planning and teaching were provided with the opportunity to contribute to and to increase the quality of diversity in inclusive education. Inquiry-based learning with the work of the project facilitated the use of ICT tools with a follow up effect within a pedagogical context. The learning environment and inclusive classroom versus the classroom management facilitated the individual and collaborative engagement of activities. In the process of development of abilities, the interest of every individual student was found to be the focus of the study outcomes.

Diversity and Its Relationship with Technology

Technology has been a bridge for addressing the needs of diverse learners. Mulrine (2007) researched creating a virtual learning environment for gifted and talented learners. In recent years, information technology has become a universal instructional method used with gifted and talented learners. Information technology can also be used to draft a virtual learning setting that makes available enriching learning experiences and more sophisticated study for these high ability learners. Constructing a virtual learning environment is a way to differentiate instruction unifying the field of gifted and talented education and information technology. The content for the virtual learning unit used in this article focuses on multicultural awareness that integrates technology with curricula. It incorporated hyperlinks to lessons, assistive technology, virtual museum tours, online-learning games and assessment rubrics. Concisely, gifted and talented students can be educationally augmented through a virtual learning setting. Virtual learning environments can be used as a way to combine curriculum with information technology. Technology is also a voice for learners of diverse backgrounds and families served. And in this study, the researchers developed inventive model for using digital storytelling as a process to present students to significant topics facing people with disabilities and their families to foster interaction and discourse with them (Skouge & Rao, 2009). They worked together with persons with disabilities and their families to produce video stories prearranged with thematic scenes, each attending to a fundamental concern that contends with issues of inclusion and autonomy. There were two interconnected goals; the first was to provide voice to the individual and their family in recounting the reality of their lived experiences and situations.

The second was to generate a genuine and informative discussion among individuals their families and the students registered in the program. As a result, researchers established that this project could be difficult to teach multimedia skills to novice learners; especially when they are concurrently employing themselves in an innovative endeavor. In addition, this could be demanding work with menial outcomes instead of valuing experiential learning outcomes.

Technology and diversity not only includes learners but higher education faculty and researchers as well. A narrative analysis on how teachers who were enrolled in a master's program from two university campuses of the same predominately white university participated in an in-depth look at their different cultural experiences through thought and discussion. Two researchers, one African-American female employs a critical race theory perspective the other; a Caucasian female using socio constructivism interact with one another and the teachers narratives through a number of individual exchanges. The resulting teacher researcher dialogue on culture and adversity exposed how when the restriction of different

theoretical frameworks and earlier interactions with culture in harsh conditions exposed a window for dialogue on culture diverse city characterized by growth, opens up. This study demonstrates how pinpointing culture and diversity in education and research care provider for open discourse for individuals to have individual reflections about upbringing using cultural elements to lead them (Hairston & Strickland, 2011).

Technology can be used to facilitate difficult conversations. Teacher educators are deliberate and conscientious in terms of seeking approaches to best operate and buttress culturally responsive practices of preservice teachers nonetheless; there are a number of trials in front of those educators in their mission to serve and support preservice teachers and considering issues of equity and social justice. In a recent study examine the data from 142 institutions and surmise that the major challenges to inclusion of diversity within courses was faculty this interest faculty discomfort faculty lack of knowledge time constraints and students this interest and discomfort.

In this study, the researcher shared the objectives of structures, expectations, and outcomes for six various professional development forums intended over a two-year period. To develop culturally responsive dispositions and preservice teachers, numerous teachers' education programs put into action multicultural education courses however; many preservice teachers are deficient in the skill of disposition compulsory to make them successful in the classroom. In facing these conflicts, key questions surfaced on how faculty members are going to make possible a more dynamic approach to features of diversity and how can they deal with world concerns that engage preservice teachers in a social justice stance. This research included a number of professional forums that were comprised of brownbag lunches, annual faculty diversity showcases, professional reading response groups, evening video night, faculty and staff retreat, and finally a diversity portal (Potts & Schlichting, 2011).

It is of the essence that all preservice teachers understand the distinctive role in the development of equity in a global society in their schools, communities and society at large. Researchers discovered that by developing professional forums that supported faculty in tackling issues of equity social justice and culturally responsive practices along with presenting and sharing materials and resources that support of these goals the faculty began to create more connections within and across programs. These links allow faculty to grow in their commitment to meeting the multidimensional needs of preservice teachers and supporting their knowledge of diversity and social justice. The faculty begins connecting in authentic multicultural dialogue that appreciably influences their teaching, research, and exchanges with preservice teachers, schools and communities.

A dual case study examined the 21st-century teacher education imperatives that blend technology and critical multicultural reading instructional practices. The researchers investigated the incorporation of a blog as a tool to endorse technology used in a graduate course on reading and technology within a thematic focal point on the Holocaust. Findings propose that blogging has the promise to augment knowledge of the techniques technology can be channeled to promote critical multicultural reading instruction (Stevens & Brown, 2011). All of these issues, challenges and pathways lead the conversation to a formulaic context and tailored situation.

EDUCATOR PREPARATION, TECHNOLOGY, AND DIVERSITY; HOW DOES IT ALL UNFOLD

It is imperative that these case studies are situated in a certain transparency. The tenets of Bloom's Taxonomy and Rosenblatt's Reader Response Theory are central to the case studies presented. The cases are situated in these tandem frameworks.

What is Situated Learning?

Situated learning is a universal theory of knowledge that was first propositioned by Jean Lave. The manner of learning is through the employ of social interaction with others (Conkling, 2007). This learning model is based on knowledge that is within milieu of the conversation (Arnseth, 2008). This permits people to be involved in a "community of practice". Community of Practice is when a faction of people work together with each other to acquire information. As they network, the more operational and occupied they are on an activity. Situated learning makes people learn unintentionally rather than deliberately, this is a process called "legitimate peripheral participation". "The pedagogy of the lifelong-learning era is evolving in the direction of dependence on interaction. Sometimes this involves interacting with a rich technological environment such as a computer tutor or a game on the web and sometimes with other people by means of a computer network.

The pedagogy of computer tutors echoes the apprenticeship model in setting individualized tasks for learners and offering guidance and feedback as they work."_Situated learning is developing into more concerned with technology and ways to help individuals learn information in a different way than they have previously." The type of learning skill through technology imitates how individuals learned in the past from an expert in that skill. In the past when individuals learned about a particular topic, it was done in person, in a hands-on environment. Technology causes it possible to do these similar things using a computer or any other similar device (Huang, Lubin, & Ge, 2011).

Theoretical Framework

Dr. Benjamin Bloom identified six levels within the cognitive domain, from the minimal recall or recollection of facts, as the lowest level, through increasingly more complex and abstract mental levels, to the highest order, which is classified as evaluation. Action examples that represent intellectual activity on each level are listed here. 1. Knowledge: arrange, define, duplicate, label, list, memorize, name, order, recognize, relate, recall, repeat, and reproduce state. 2. Understanding (or Comprehension): classify, describe, discuss, explain, express, identify, indicate, locate, recognize report, restate, review, select, and translate. 3. Application: apply, choose, demonstrate, dramatize, employ, illustrate, interpret, operate, practice, schedule, sketch, solve, use, write. 4. Analysis: analyze, appraise, calculate, categorize, compare, contrast, criticize, differentiate, discriminate, distinguish, examine, experiment, question, and test. 5. Synthesis: arrange, assemble, collect, compose, construct, create, design, develop, formulate, manage, organize, plan, prepare, propose, set up, and write. 6. Evaluation: appraise, argue, assess, attach, choose compare, defend estimate, judge, predict, rate, core, select, support, value, evaluate (Bloom, 1956; Lautenbach, 2008).

Rosenblatt's Theory Reader Response criticism includes various approaches to literature that delve into and search to explain the diversity (and often deviation) of readers' responses to literary works. Louise Rosenblatt is commonly credited with officially introducing the idea that the reader's experience and interface with the text creates the true meaning. This thought developed into what came to be recognized as Transactional Reader Response Criticism. Rosenblatt argued that, while the reader is directed by the ideas and words that the author put out, it is in due course each individual reader's *experience in reading the work* that essentially gives it meaning. Given that every person brings inimitable knowledge and beliefs to the reading transaction, the text will mean various things to various people. It is that connotation — the reader's meaning — that should be gauged, as opposed to exclusively looking at the author's text in a void (Broad & Labercane, 2001).

Case Studies

The Case of Technology and Reading Methods Courses

In an undergraduate reading methods course the instructor conceptualized methods to be intentionally inclusive of technology from the courses beginning. The instructor design each assignment to include developmentally appropriate reading strategies a web-based application and differentiation for learners and their families. There are three assignments highlighted in this case: the national reading panel resource books the chapter content presentation, Glogster, and the visual thinking representation blog. The national reading panel resource booklet was an assignment designed to identify and analyze the recommendations of the national reading panel. The national reading panel highlighted five major areas that should be explicitly addressed and literacy: comprehension phonics phonemic awareness vocabulary and fluency.

The students were directed to create or identify five web-based activities for each of the five dimensions for a total of 25 activities. Undergraduate teacher education students could make this a PDF with hyperlinks in bed or make it a website. For each activity they work required to identify an objective purpose and directions for the activity as well as several extensions from the original activity for additional use or practice. As students construct of these assignments they were required to think about the audiences that would use these tools. They were also using these tools as tutoring aids in the University reading clinic.

The next assignment was a chapter presentation glogster. In small cooperative groups the students work to synthesize what they learned from the chapter of choice in the course text. Utilizing Blooms taxonomy, they were to create a glogster reflective of the chapter's objectives and how they understood them. Students produced eleven high quality content/topic specific glogsters to demonstrate the way in which they processed the chapter-topic and they were able to demonstrate their understanding through the redelivery and sharing of the glogster with peers. This tool was also an authentic assessment for the instructor to determine on what levels within Bloom's Taxonomy the students were working. The choice of this particular evidentiary source reflects the essential activity of the use and exploration of emerging technologies that improve opportunities for student learning. A Glogster is described as an instructional tool that was borrowed from social media and reformatted for the educational environment. According to its developers, "Glogster is a social network that allows users to create free interactive posters, or glogs. A glog, short for graphical blog, is an interactive multimedia image. It looks like a poster, but readers can interact with the content. The other members of the class had public access to the Glogster and they use them in several ways. They were used for learning studying reviewing and clarification about concepts and audiences as well as delivery methods (Glogster; Jensen & Tunon, 2012).

The visual thinking representation blog-within the course-learning management system was used to house facilitate and organize the-learning process for the course design. One of the tools in the-learning management system was a student blog feature. Visual thinking is the common phenomenon of thinking through visual processing using the part of the brain that is emotional and creative to organize information in an intuitive and simultaneous way (Song & Turner, 2010). The process of translating visual thinking onto paper (or electronic document) is visual mapping. A visual mapper combines words and images to create a visual record of the spoken and written words – plainly revealing the "big picture." Construction of mind maps forces students to sort through information and make meaning of information through organization and connection of concepts. Advances in classroom technology now offer various advanced mind mapping and visual tools, which are slowly becoming essential components of a student-centered classroom environment (Nesbit & Adesope, 2006).

Visual mapping was used in the course to facilitate metacognition and get teacher education students an opportunity to measure and categorize their understandings using Bloom's taxonomy. Students were allowed and encouraged to use tablets smart phones and laptops to take pictures of other groups cognitive maps also known as graphic organizers. After five exposures to a particular concept, small cooperative groups of students show the graphic organizer to illustrate the understanding of the concept for objective. Once the map with constructed by the students they posted them in the classroom and using the gallery walk protocol, they could take pictures of the graphic organizers for study guide. The instructor posted pictures of all of the graphic organizers and posted them for the class blog. From there the students comments on other students processing.

They could also ask three levels of questions: literal inferential and evaluative. Literal, inferential, and evaluative questions help learners read and think in different ways. The answers to literal questions can be found in the text. They are directly stated. This information is *on the surface*. The answers to inferential questions can be found in the text too, but they are implied, not directly stated. We often say the information is "*in between the lines* or *under the surface.*" The answers to evaluative questions require information outside of the text. We sometimes say the information is "*in the head* or *somewhere else*" (Alonzo, Basaraba, Tindal, & Carriveau, 2009). The three levels of questions allow the instructor to clarify any misconstrued information and analyze how these graphic organizer maps responded to questions about their map hence reteaching or peer teaching. This is a true vision of how well the instructor structure or is set up the course to reflect a process not just an outcome.

The Case of Technology in the Creative Arts

In this graduate methods course on the creative arts the instructor conceptualized course to be a change agent for diversity using technology as a method of delivery. Social media has provided a lens through which the journey can be viewed, examined and critiqued. In this particular course, the change agent tool is voice. Voice is defined in this sense as the author's style, the quality that makes his or her writing unique, and which conveys the author's attitude, personality, and character.

Voice is one of the most critical tools and narrative storytelling. Digital Storytelling is the practice of using computer-based tools to tell stories. As with traditional storytelling, most digital stories focus on a specific topic and contain a particular point of view. However, as the name implies, digital stories usually contain some mixture of computer-based images, text, recorded audio narration, video clips and/or music (Wang & Zhan, 2010). Digital stories can vary in length, but most of the stories used in education typically last between two and ten minutes.

The topics that are used in Digital Storytelling range from personal tales to the recounting of historical events, from exploring life in one's own community to the search for life in other corners of the universe, and literally, everything in between (Hartley, Rennie, Russo & Watkins, 2005; Heo, 2009). Coaching and guiding students through critical reflection is an integral part of the process and furthers adventures into the limits of social media and digital storytelling. In order the integrate to the instructional design of the artifacts and the digital demands of its delivery, the instructor relied on the following learning theories; Rosenblatt's Reader Response and Bloom's Taxonomy of Cognitive-learning.

In the literature of that diversity and multiculturalism is the authentic tool available to reflect differences of experiences perception and perspective. The instructor designed the course to utilize developmentally and culturally appropriate practices as well as state-mandated curriculum performance standards. This graduate-level course included more demands on not only performance but transparency from the student as a part of the process of understanding themselves and others; cultural awareness and appreciation of differences. There was a signature web-based assignment to document the mastery of the course, the creative arts video lesson. The activity worked at the highest level of Bloom's taxonomy as well as the incorporation of Rosenblatt's reader response theory. The teacher's creative arts drama lesson required the graduate students to do the following:

- The lesson includes and addresses at least one Georgia Performance Standard in language arts, social studies, science, or math.
- The lesson includes and addresses at least one Georgia Performance Standard in Theatre Arts.
- The lesson should include two or more creative drama techniques from class and the texts.
- It is suggested that you use a social studies or science topic as a "lens" for the lesson… and consider global themes.

This artifact was designed to meet a number of objectives. First, it was designed to develop and explore materials, resources, and current research in the area of creative dramatics and then recognize creative drama as an educational tool. They also had to learn skills, which will enable them to integrate drama with content areas, gain knowledge of current resources in the field of creative drama and communication; and finally plan and implement a research project in creative dramatics. It was the intent of the instructor to deepen the level of understanding not only reflected in the graduate student's analysis but how their construction of the lesson impact student learning and achievement.

The Pedagogical Changes in Teaching Techniques

Student feedback items were analyzed through open coding and axial coding. Phenomena, or the central ideas (themes) represented in the data, were identified in order to create concepts for categories. The central themes or ideas were represented by each question. A basic code list was generated in order to analyze the open-ended survey data line by line. The data from the interviews were coded line by line in order to identify what basic codes group themselves into categories (Strauss & Corbin, 1998). From here, categories and clusters create distinct responses and caveats for each central theme.

Undergraduate Reading Methods Course Feedback

The instructor analyzes the student feedback specifically using qualitative coding she look for codes related to technology-based assignments. The descriptive data revealed clusters sub clusters themes and descriptors related to those clusters of sub clusters. In the case of the reading methods courses the grand things of the data included complexity impact on K-12 student learning and views of themselves as future teachers. The first grand thing the students spoke to was complexity. The students reported that the complexity of the assignment reflected a high level of involvement. Involvement in the preplanning and construction was evident. The complexity is also apparent in the required reflection and animalization of the mapping unpacking and crosschecking of other class members thoughts and ideas on the visual mapping blogs.

The next grand theme was the impact on K-12 student learning. Impact on student learning is described as, "A positive impact on student learning means that a teacher through instruction and assessment has been able to document students' increased knowledge and/or demonstration of

a skill or skills related to the state goals and/or essential academic learning requirements." Teachers must use these descriptions of practice to demonstrate they have had a positive impact on student learning. Some, but not all of those descriptions, are:

- Students use a variety of assessment tools, and know how those tools measure their performance of the-learning targets.
- Students regularly use their work to examine and reflect on their achievement of learning targets. Students set individual goals and outline the steps required to reach those goals.
- Students can articulate the required learning targets.
- Students know what is needed to move to the next level of performance.
- Students can articulate how the new learning builds on their prior knowledge and individual needs. Students understand the importance of their learning and why it is useful to them.
- Students reflect on their thinking strategies, communicate what strategies worked well and what strategies did not, and adjust as compulsory.

The teacher education students communicated that the assignment would help them with addressing diversity in their future classrooms or the learners they would encounter during practicum. On the diversity spectrum this statements reflect their engagement level at cultural awareness the initial and lowest level on the scale of cultural fluency development (Thomas, 2010).

The last grand theme identified the student feedback data was their view of themselves as future teachers. The students reported that the technology infused assignments influence the effectiveness knowledge and views of classroom management. Students view themselves as more capable in the aforementioned sub clusters.

Teacher education students reported that they could be more effective in making instructional decisions about technology and lesson planning. Teacher education students also view themselves as more capable in getting a handle on classroom management because of the exposure to technology. Classroom management is usually the area in which preservice teachers struggled the most during educator preparation programs and their first two years of teaching. Overall views of themselves as future teachers are positive and optimistic based on the feedback provided.

Graduate Creative Arts Methods Course Feedback

When examining the graduate in service teacher's feedback about the creative arts video lesson the instructor identify three grand things complexity impact on student learning and views of themselves as change agents. When investigating the theme of complexity it was communicated through factors and levels of difficulty and degrees of involvement. Students reported that the difficulty of the web-based assignment was multilayered. It required macro and micro processes during its construction and implementation phases. It was sequential in nature and required backtracking the system or application within the project did not operate as they intended. They found that the intensity of the project construction was more laborious but worth the effort according to their feedback.

This led to the cluster of responses revealing a pattern of involvement. The students reported that the involvement was initially expected to be in and students had a preconceived notion of how much time to spend even after looking at the recommended course organizer within the syllabus, which was more than what they anticipated initially. They also found that they involve each other as they constructed the artifact. They reported that they communicated with each other from a moderate to consistent level on the build-

ing of the web-based assignment. They involve each other in the technical aspects as well as the aesthetic aspects of their creative arts video lessons. This included coaching on construction and demo student trial runs as a student user of the web-based artifact.

The next grand theme that student's comments clustered around was impact on student learning. This was especially important to the inservice teachers in the course because the states new teacher evaluation system, which was, tied the common core Georgia performance standards required impact on student learning data as part of the annual report to the principal and the school districts. The impact on student learning report required a targeted reporting section on meeting the needs of diverse learners and English-language learners.

The last theme that surfaced in the student feedback data was their view of themselves as change agents. A change agent is defined as someone who knows and understands the dynamics that facilitate or hinder change. Change Agents define, research, plan, build support, and partner with others to create change. They have the courage and the willingness to do what is best for the community. Since they were experienced teachers, they view themselves as a part of an education system; a part of a larger entity not isolated in the classroom (Marchel, Shields & Winter, 2011). A number of the graduate students identified themselves as teacher leaders within the grade levels of school buildings. The operationally defined definition of teacher leader is normally applied to teachers who have taken on leadership roles and extra professional responsibilities. The teacher-leader concept is closely related to perception and shared governance, or the division of leadership roles and decision-making tasks beyond the administrative team. A number of research studies have acknowledged the distinctiveness of teacher leaders, together with the following:

- Alliance with peers, parents, and communities that engages them in discussions of open inquiry.
- Risk taking and contribution in school decision making.
- Established expertise in instruction and the willingness to allocate that knowledge with other professionals, connect in uninterrupted action research, and consistently take part in a professional learning curve.
- Social consciousness and political activity (Wynne, 2001).
- Recurrent reflection on their work and staying on the cutting edge of what is considered best practices for learners.

They reported that using technology was a form of advocacy for students were generally to include female students English-language learners and students from working-class families. They also convey that access to the arts is a form of equity for these marginalize students. They expressed that at title I schools the administration was quick to cut the arts program when there was a budget shortfall. This is also a national trend. The students recognize that they are not only general education teachers but creative arts teachers as well. They all stated that if they did not at least expose their students to the creative arts they would not get the chance to be exposed outside of school due to limited opportunities in their communities. Once again, they were back at the profile of the advocate.

The graduate students finally stated that they depended on the use of technology to assist down and unpacking common core standards. They report in the course evaluation and class discussions that they were intimidated by the common core standards not because they were not capable teachers but because they did not feel that they had adequate training from the school district and the state department of education. A number of students reported they were somewhat panicking actually.*Instructor Decisions upon Feedback*

The instructor monitor the student feedback paralleled with her teaching style based on the framework of Grasha's five teaching styles. Anthony Grasha (2001) identified the following five teaching styles as depictions of dominant aspects of instructor/trainer in the classroom.

Expert. Possesses knowledge and expertise that students need. They strive to retain status as an expert among students by displaying comprehensive knowledge and by challenging students to increase their competence. They are interested with conveying information and insuring that students are well prepared. The information, knowledge, and skills such individuals possess. If worn-out, the show of knowledge can be intimidating to less experienced students. They may not always show the fundamental processes that produced answers.

Formal Authority. Possesses status among students because of knowledge and role as a faculty member. They are concerned with giving positive and negative feedback, establishing learning goals, expectations, and rules of conduct for students. Interested with the correct, suitable, and orthodox ways to do things and with providing students with the organization they need to learn. They focus on transparent expectations and acceptable ways of doing things. A strong investment in this style can lead to strict, standardized, and less adaptable ways of addressing students and their trepidations.

Personal Model. Believes in "teaching by personal example" and institutes an example for how to think and act. They supervise, lead, and direct by illustrating how to do things, and persuade students to observe and then to imitate the instructor's approach. They underscore direct study and following a role model. Some teachers may suppose their method is the best way leading some students to feel ineffective if they cannot live up to such potential and standards.

Facilitator. Emphasizes the personal nature of teacher-student interactions. Guides and directs students by asking questions, exploring choices, offering alternatives, and persuading them to develop criterion to make educated choices. Their total goal is to develop in students the capability for autonomous action, resourcefulness, and responsibility. They work with students on projects in a consultative fashion and tries to provide as much support and encouragement as possible. Their personal flexibility, the focus on students' needs and objective, and the motivation to explore options and alternative courses of action is a hallmark. Their method is often time consuming and is sometimes employed in a positive and encouraging style.

Delegator. They are concerned with developing students' competence to operate in an autonomous fashion. Students work autonomously on projects or as part of self-governing teams. The teacher is accessible at the demand of students as a resource person. They help students to distinguish themselves as independent learners. They may misinterpret student's inclination for self-sufficient work. Some students may become apprehensive when given independence.

The instructor identified her teaching style as cluster three. The instructor review the teaching behaviors associated with cluster three under which she fell. She extrapolated specific behaviors that directly correlated with the prescribed theoretical frameworks of the cases and strategically implemented technology strategies within the course design. The instructor found that the instructional activities reflect the personal facilitator expert traits of cluster three.

NRP booklet-The expert style. When comparing the instructor behaviors throughout the feedback for this assignment it reflected the knowledge and expertise of the scientific-based reading research. She strived to maintain her status as an expert among her students by displaying her detailed knowledge through web based lessons she taught to young learners in a classroom setting. The instructor showed her concern with transmit-

ting information and ensuring that students were well prepared for the reading pedagogy teaching certification test for the state.

Glogster. The Glogster store web based assignment reflected Grasha's personal model. The Glogster assignment reflected the idea of teaching about personal example by creating a collaborative glogster with the students during a class to observe and analyze the construction of a Glogster. This was based on a literature unit created by the instructor. This established a prototype for the student's construction of his or her own Glogster. The personal example allowed students to see the skill and thoughtfulness required to construct a standards-based Glogster. She used think aloud during her construction of the collaborative glogster to model her process. She allowed students to provide feedback and she constructed the Glogster and allowed them to question why she chose Pacific applications within the Glogster to profile specific standards or student learning objectives.

Discussion Boards. Does the discussion boards allow the instructor to act as a facilitator because it highlighted her ability to nurture students and teacher interactions. Because the instructor planted got a questions as the root of her discussions she was able to probe and elicit more questions to stimulate students thinking.

Video Lessons. Instructor feedback also elicited facilitator model characteristics for the video lessons. The video lesson construction was an overall consultative phenomenon. The instructor had the opportunity to provide options and alternatives as the students participated in their own think aloud during the construction of the highly individualized video-based lessons. She could refer students back to the rubric to refine the criteria required for the lesson as well. She could also guide students in using their informed choices and clarifying the criteria to further tailor the lessons to the unpacked standards for diverse city content and technology. That would also reflect relevance to instruction. The role of facilitator allows students to gauge their own capacity for independence expression and level of responsibility to reflect the effectiveness of their project and the integrity of its delivery. This created some dissonance and disequilibrium for small number of the students.

SOLUTIONS AND RECOMMENDATIONS

Some overall considerations must be considered as a recommendation for the field of education. It is imperative that the field of education at work with all students in an effective and equitable fashion as well as an ethic of caring. This is an appropriate way to respond and respect adversity as it relates to ethnicity, race, gender, and the exceptional needs of each learner served. We must also be active and engage learners who are constantly seeking assessing applying a communicating instructional technology and pedagogy. We must exercise the characteristics of reflective practitioners throughout our careers.

It is critical that we develop and apply knowledge of curriculum instruction of the principles learning theories, evaluation, and assessment in order to effectively improve-learning for all. Instructional technology and its employ is that vehicle. The field of education and each teacher and it must be vigilant in initiating collaborating valuing and exercising partnerships with students, colleagues, families, the community at large and other social agencies. The field of education and each teacher should also find ways to appreciate and practice principles of learning ethical and legal behavior that reflects the responsibility of the teaching profession. The field of education overall as a whole should develop a philosophy of teaching that is personally and professionally informed by the organizations it serves, the community, society and the global concerns of education.

There also recommendations and solutions for preservice and inservice teachers specifically. This would include a change agent framework under which they should operate. This can be achieved through building bridges and developing trust as well as respecting one another and their ideas and opinions. Preservice and inservice teachers can also work to the framework of change agent by valuing diversity in honing in on individual skills necessary to manage change and affect any environment. Finally, in service and preservice teachers can continue to forage change agent behaviors through collectively addressing mutual interest concerns and issues within their schools and communities.

Teacher educators can also operate as change agents but they must take initiative. This can happen on several levels through major reform. Not only certification but also educator preparation along with field experience partnerships with neighboring school districts can participate in reform. When we look at the power of teacher educators within a change agent framework, there are several best practices that must be reflected. Teacher educators must display behaviors that reflect production of teachers who are themselves change agents and strive for improvement is society. They must commit to constant improvement through program innovation and evaluation.

This is also to specifically include instructional technology. It is also critical that they practice in value exemplary teaching and engage in a consistent form of inquiry in their teaching. Teacher educators must also be considered and respected as an integral part of university and educator preparation programs. Teacher educators must also be visible in value on a national front and show how their contributions add to educational communities locally and globally. Teacher educators must work collaboratively to build local regional national and international networks within their discipline if they facilitate how instructional technology is part of their discipline discourse.

Finally, there is a call to all in terms of being a change agent and what questions one must ask in order to develop the behaviors of a change agent. Integral questions that must be asked to elicit entered inner change agent. Do you see opportunities for changes that are positive in your school that others may not recognize? The most efficient change agents do not do additional work they actually do their assigned work differently that is how they refine education within their school and embrace an idea of collaborative culture. Do you have a direct place in which you look for new ideas? Ideas that many say are mundane in one situation can actually be rather innovative in another situation; especially when challenges are presented challenges that have come to define school culture.

The next questions for developing change agent is, are you getting the most effective contributions from the people around you? In addition, are you committed to being consistent in your effort to make appropriate changes in your educational environment? If you want to act as a change agent in be a teacher leader and you want to make permanent and lasting changes then your practices goals and objectives have to stay consistent even when the mission seems as if it is going awry or not moving as fast as you would like. The final question you must pose to yourself as a change agent is, how fast are you learning and is your learning keeping up with your constantly changing environment?

Models

The distributed collaborative research model is anticipated as a way to build up a collaborative inquiry procedure for conducting research across various teacher education institutions permitting researchers to gain access to larger populations by taking advantage of known contacts in a professional technology in the teacher education population (Pierson, Shepard & Leneway, 2009). Swain (2008) specifically address the second research

purpose of exploring the meaning of the phase integrating technology into a teacher education program and the successive production of foundational work for an innovation design regarding the combination of technology into the teacher education program. Another aspect of integrating technology into teacher education programs is to grant a teacher educator with realistic and relevant examples of how technology meshes with social justice disposition adopted by many teacher educators.

Crafting an innovation configuration map for implementing technology into teacher education programs at every institution will not make certain that there is a genuine integration of technology into teacher education programs. It will however provide a universal language and starting point for conversation on weather changes need to take place how change my look and what sort of uses of technology are considered important by faculty. As a final point developing in Innovation configuration map regarding the innovation of technology into our teacher education programs will also allow teacher educators who use technology in their teaching an opportunity to show how technology can be effortlessly entwined with other vital concepts of teacher education this includes culturally responsive teaching classroom management and effectual instructional strategies.

Dawson (2012) looked at using action research projects to explore teacher technology integration practices. This study observed technology integration practices using a car project from teachers participating in statewide technology integration initiative. The thematic analysis produced five themes. Data within the first theme content showed their teachers that elementary, middle and high school levels partake equally and that the majority of these teachers focused on using technology to help their student's master content objectives.

Anthony (2012) examined activity theory as a framework for considering district classroom system interactions and their impact on technology integration. This study conceptualizes technology implementation as a network of planning and integration activities conducted by technology specialist teachers and administrators. The researchers conducted a case study of the school district laptop program to examine how a district and classroom systems and directed to influence technology use. Finding suggests that continuous improvement efforts aimed at aligning intersystem linkages can support technology integration. These aforementioned models serve as spring boards for innovative models and starting points for integrating diversity, technology and educator preparation.

FUTURE RESEARCH DIRECTIONS

These case studies warrant more direct research. It is imperative that we research technology access and self efficacy in urban learners as well as rural learners. We must also research technology implementation and its relationship with English language learners. Future research should examine the impact of teachers who are technologically adept influence on student learning in the early childhood classrooms as this trend is now a consistent mainstay in early childhood education curricula in the latest literature. Finally future research should analyze technology access influencing from a programmatic standpoint especially as this is an essential component in the language of accreditation bodies for educator preparation and specialty program accreditations.

CONCLUSION

Diversity and technology are issues that dovetail. In order to close the achievement gap equity and access must be addressed in terms of opportunities to engage in technology. This is more important to marginalize students than any other popula-

tion of learners. As we examine access points for status of diverse backgrounds research shows that those opportunities are fewer than their dominant culture counterparts. Research also reveals that the opportunities are more infrequent. This gap or delay in access impacts learners throughout their educational careers preschool through graduate school. The gap gets wider as learners age. Rectifying this issue must be intentional explicit and consistent. This means understanding and implementing technological practices as an approach not just a set of tools or strategies. It must also be linked to the idea and the theory that intelligence is modifiable and technology is a pathway to enacting that theory as a form of advocacy for diverse learners.

REFERENCES

Akmal, T., Oaks, M. M., & Barker, R. (2002, September 06). The Status of Technology Education: A National Report on the State of the Profession. *Journal of Industrial Teacher Education*, *39*(4), 6–25.

Alonzo, J., Basaraba, D., Tindal, G., & Carriveau, R. S. (2009, January 01). They Read, but How Well Do They Understand? An Empirical Look at the Nuances of Measuring Reading Comprehension. *Assessment for Effective Intervention*, *35*(1), 34–44. doi:10.1177/1534508408330082

Anthony, A. B. (2012, September 06). Activity Theory as a Framework for Investigating District-Classroom System Interactions and Their Influences on Technology Integration. *Journal of Research on Technology in Education*, *44*(4), 335–356. doi:10.1080/15391523.2012.10782594

Arnseth, H. C. (2008, October 01). Activity theory and situated learning theory: Contrasting views of educational practice. *Pedagogy, Culture & Society*, *16*(3), 289–302. doi:10.1080/14681360802346663

Bjekic, D., Krneta, R., & Milosevic, D. (2010, January 01). Teacher Education from E-Learner to E-Teacher: Master Curriculum. *Turkish Online Journal of Educational Technology*, *9*(1), 202–212.

Bloom, B. S. (1956). *Taxonomy of educational objectives: The classification of educational goals.* New York: Longmans, Green.

Broad, K., & Labercane, G. (2001, January 01). Reader response pedagogy in the information age. *Technology and Teacher Education Annual*, *3*, 2187–2192.

Cardon, P. L. (2001, March 08). At-Risk Students and Technology Education: A Qualitative Study. *Journal of Technology Studies*, *26*(1), 49–57.

Conkling, S. (2007, January 01). The Possibilities of Situated Learning for Teacher Preparation: The Professional Development Partnership. *Music Educators Journal*, *93*(3), 44–48. doi:10.1177/002743210709300319

Crowe, A. R. (2004, September 06). Teaching by Example: Integrating Technology into Social Studies Education Courses. *Journal of Computing in Teacher Education*, *20*(4), 159–165.

Dawson, K. (2012, March 01). Using Action Research Projects to Examine Teacher Technology Integration Practices. *Journal of Digital Learning in Teacher Education*, *28*(3), 117–123. doi:10.10 80/21532974.2012.10784689

Donovan, L., & Green, T. (2010, September 06). One-to-One Computing in Teacher Education: Faculty Concerns and Implications for Teacher Educators. *Journal of Digital Learning in Teacher Education*, *26*(4), 140–148.

Duran, M., Runvand, S., & Fossum, P. R. (2009, October 01). Preparing Science Teachers to Teach with Technology: Exploring a K-16 Networked Learning Community Approach. *Turkish Online Journal of Educational Technology*, *8*(4), 21–42.

Ernst, J. V., & Moyc, J. J. (2013, June 06). Social Adjustment of At-Risk Technology Education Students. *Journal of Technology Education*, *24*(2), 2–13.

Gaudelli, W. (2007, March 08). Convergence of Technology and Diversity: Experiences of Two Beginning Teachers in Web-Based Distance-learning for Global/Multicultural Education. *Teacher Education Quarterly*, *33*(1), 97–116.

Glogster. (n.d.). *Glogster.com*. Retrieved from http://edu.glogster.com/?ref=com

Goodson-Espy, T., Lynch-Davis, K., Schram, P., & Quickenton, A. (2010, September 06). Using 3D Computer Graphics Multimedia to Motivate Preservice Teachers' Learning of Geometry and Pedagogy. *Srate Journal*, *19*(2), 23–35.

Grasha, A. F., & Yangarber-Hicks, N. (2001, March 08). Integrating Teaching Styles and Learning Styles with Instructional Technology. *College Teaching*, *48*(1), 2–10. doi:10.1080/87567550009596080

Greenhow, C., Dexter, S., & Hughes, J. E. (2008, March 01). Teacher Knowledge about Technology Integration: An Examination of Inservice and Preservice Teachers' Instructional Decision-Making. *Science Education International*, *19*(1), 9–25.

Habre, S., & Grundmeier, T. A. (May 01, 2006). Prospective Mathematics Teachers' Views on the Role of Technology in Mathematics Education. *Issues in the Undergraduate Mathematics Preparation of School Teachers, 3*.

Hairston, K. R., & Strickland, M. J. (2011, January 01). Contrapuntal Orchestration: An Exploration of an Interaction between Researchers' and Teachers' Stories around the Concept of Culture. *Race, Ethnicity and Education*, *14*(5), 631–653. doi:10 .1080/13613324.2010.493358

Hartley, J., Rennie, E., Russo, A., & Watkins, J. (2005, January 01). Digital Storytelling. *International Journal of Cultural Studies*, *8*(4), 4. doi:10.1177/1367877905061532

Heafner, T. L., Petty, T. M., & Hartshorne, R. (2011, January 01). Evaluating Modes of Teacher Preparation: A Comparison of Face-to-Face and Remote Observations of Graduate Interns. *Journal of Digital Learning in Teacher Education*, *27*(4), 153–164. doi:10.1080/21532974.2011.10784672

Heo, M. (2009, October 01). Digital Storytelling: An Empirical Study of the Impact of Digital Storytelling on Preservice Teachers' Self-Efficacy and Dispositions towards Educational Technology. *Journal of Educational Multimedia and Hypermedia*, *18*(4), 405–428.

Herron, J. (2010, March 08). Implementation of Technology in an Elementary Mathematics Lesson: The Experiences of Preservice Teachers at One University. *Srate Journal*, *19*(1), 22–29.

Horzum, M. B., & Canan, G. O. (2012, July 01). A model for beliefs, tool acceptance levels and web pedagogical content knowledge of science and technology preservice teachers towards web based instruction. *Turkish Online Journal of Distance Education*, *13*(3), 50–69.

Huang, K., Lubin, I. A., & Ge, X. (2011, November 01). Situated learning in an educational technology course for preservice teachers. *Teaching and Teacher Education*, *27*(8), 1200–1212. doi:10.1016/j.tate.2011.06.006

Jensen, J., & Tunon, J. (2012, January 01). Free and Easy to Use Web Based Presentation and Classroom Tools. *Journal of Library & Information Services in Distance Learning*, *6*(3-4), 323–334. doi:10.1080/1533290X.2012.705157

Johnson, C., & Brescia, W. J. (2006, August 01). Connecting, Making Meaning, and Learning in the Electronic Classroom: Reflections on Facilitating Learning at a Distance. *Journal of Scholarship of Teaching and Learning*, *6*(1), 56–74.

Kajder, S. B. (2005, December 07). "Not Quite Teaching for Real:" Preservice Secondary English Teachers' Use of Technology in the Field Following the Completion of an Instructional Technology Methods Course. *Journal of Computing in Teacher Education*, *22*(1), 15–21.

Kalemoglu, V. Y. (2014, April 01). The Relationship between attitudes of prospective physical education teachers towards education technologies and computer self-efficacy beliefs. *Turkish Online Journal of Educational Technology*, *13*(2), 157–167.

Keeler, C. G. (2008, December 07). When Curriculum and Technology Meet: Technology Integration in Methods Courses. *Journal of Computing in Teacher Education*, *25*(1), 23–30.

Lautenbach, G. (2008, July 01). Stories of Engagement with E-Learning: Revisiting the Taxonomy of Learning. *International Journal of Information and Communication Technology Education*, *4*(3), 11–19. doi:10.4018/jicte.2008070102

Marchel, C. A., Shields, C., & Winter, L. (2011, December 07). Preservice Teachers as Change Agents: Going the Extra Mile in Service-Learning Experiences. *Teaching Educational Psychology*, *7*(2), 3–16.

Matthew, K., Felvegi, E., & Callaway, R. (2009, January 01). *Collaborative-learning Using a Wiki*.

Meagher, M., Ozgun-Koca, A., & Edwards, M. T. (2011, September 01). Preservice Teachers' Experiences with Advanced Digital Technologies: The Interplay between Technology in a Preservice Classroom and in Field Placements. *Contemporary Issues in Technology & Teacher Education*, *11*(3), 243–270.

Mulrine, C. F. (2007, June 06). Creating a Virtual Learning Environment for Gifted and Talented Learners. *Gifted Child Today*, 30(2), 37–40.

National Council for Accreditation of Teacher Education. (2010). *Transforming teacher education through clinical practice: A national strategy to prepare effective teachers*. Washington, DC: Author.

Nesbit, J. C., & Adesope, O. O. (2006, January 01). Learning With Concept and Knowledge Maps: A Meta-Analysis. *Review of Educational Research*, 76(3), 413–448. doi:10.3102/00346543076003413

Pierson, M., Shepard, M. F., & Leneway, R. (2009, September 06). Distributed Collaborative Research Model: Meaningful and Responsive Inquiry in Technology and Teacher Education. *Journal of Computing in Teacher Education*, 25(4), 127–133.

Potts, A., & Schlichting, K. (2011, January 01). Developing Professional Forums that Support Thoughtful Discussion, Reflection, and Social Action: One Faculty's Commitment to Social Justice and Culturally Responsive Practice. *International Journal of Teaching and Learning in Higher Education*, 23(1), 11–19.

Skouge, J. R., & Rao, K. (2009, January 01). Digital Storytelling in Teacher Education: Creating Transformations through Narrative. *Educational Perspectives*, 42, 54–60.

Smith, L. K., Draper, R. J., & Sabey, B. L. (2005, September 06). The Promise of Technology to Confront Dilemmas in Teacher Education: The Use of WebQuests in Problem-Based Methods Courses. *Journal of Computing in Teacher Education*, 21(4), 99–108.

Song, K. H., & Turner, G. Y. (January 01, 2010). *Visual Literacy and Its Impact on Teaching and Learning*.

Starcic, A. I. (2010, July 01). Educational Technology for the Inclusive Classroom. *Turkish Online Journal of Educational Technology*, 9(3), 26–37.

Steinke, L. J., & Putnam, A. R. (2008, January 01). Influencing Technology Education Teachers to Accept Teaching Positions. *Journal of Industrial Teacher Education*, 45(2), 71–90.

Stevens, E. Y., & Brown, R. (2011, January 01). Lessons Learned from the Holocaust: Blogging to Teach Critical Multicultural Literacy. *Journal of Research on Technology in Education*, 44(1), 31–51. doi:10.1080/15391523.2011.10782578

Strauss, A. L., & Corbin, J. M. (1998). *Basics of qualitative research: Techniques and procedures for developing grounded theory*. Thousand Oaks: Sage Publications.

Swain, C. (2008, September 06). Are We There Yet? The Power of Creating an Innovation Configuration Map on the Integration of Technology into Your Teacher Education Program. *Journal of Computing in Teacher Education*, 24(4), 143–147.

Thomas, U. (2010). *Culture or chaos in the village: The journey to cultural fluency*. Lanham, MD: Rowman & Littlefield Education.

Wang, S., & Zhan, H. (2010, April 01). Enhancing Teaching and Learning with Digital Storytelling. *International Journal of Information and Communication Technology Education*, 6(2), 76–87. doi:10.4018/jicte.2010040107

Wright, V. H., & Wilson, E. K. (2011, September 06). Teachers' Use of Technology: Lessons Learned from the Teacher Education Program to the Classroom. *State Journal*, 20(2), 48–60.

Wynne, J. (2001). *Teachers as Leaders in Education Reform. ERIC Digest*. Washington, DC: American Association of Colleges for Teacher Education.

KEY TERMS AND DEFINITIONS

Assessment: An evaluated activity or task used by a program or unit to determine the extent to which specific learning proficiencies, outcomes, or standards have been mastered by candidates. Assessments usually include an instrument that details the task or activity and a scoring guide used to evaluate the task or activity.

Best Practices: Techniques or methodologies that, through experience and research, have proven to lead reliably to a desired result.

Content: The subject matter or discipline that teachers are being prepared to teach at the elementary, middle, and/or secondary levels. Content also refers to the professional field of study (e.g., special education, early childhood education, school psychology, reading, or school administration).

Cultural Background: The context of one's life experience as shaped by membership in groups based on ethnicity, race, socioeconomic status, gender, exceptionalities, language, religion, sexual orientation, and geographical area.

Distance-Learning.: A formal educational process in which instruction occurs when the learner and the instructor are not in the same place at the same time. Distance-learning can occur through virtually any media including asynchronous or synchronous, electronic or printed communications.

Diversity: Differences among groups of people and individuals based on ethnicity, race, socioeconomic status, gender, exceptionalities, language, religion, sexual orientation, and geographical area. The types of diversity compulsory for addressing the elements on candidate interactions with diverse faculty, candidates, and P–12 students are stated in the rubrics for those elements.

Exceptionalities: Physical, mental, or emotional conditions, including gifted/talented abilities, which require individualized instruction and/or other educational support or services.

Information Technology: Computer hardware and software; voice, data, network, satellite and other telecommunications technologies; and multimedia and application development tools. These technologies are used for the input, storage, processing, and communication of information.

Professional Knowledge: The historical, economic, sociological, philosophical, and psychological understandings of schooling and education. It also includes knowledge about learning, diversity, technology, professional ethics, legal and policy issues, pedagogy, and the roles and responsibilities of the profession of teaching.

Technology Education: The study of technology, which provides an opportunity for students to learn about the processes and knowledge related to technology that are needed to solve problems and extend human capabilities (NCATE, 2010).

Chapter 14
Towards a Theory of Formative Assessment in Online Higher Education

Joyce W. Gikandi
Mount Kenya University, Kenya

ABSTRACT

The affordances of online learning have coincided with increasing demand for higher education across disciplines. The need to provide appropriate learning support while fostering self-regulation in online higher education calls for formative assessment to facilitate meaningful learning. This chapter attempts to conceptually generalize the findings of a recent collective case study and develop a relevant theoretical framework for online formative assessment. The theoretical framework is intended to inform successful implementation of formative assessment in online learning contexts. The collective case study purposefully conceptualized formative assessment from a holistic pedagogical approach. Investigating application of formative assessment in the recent study explored multifaceted elements including provision of a variety of embedded authentic assessment activities. The theoretical framework advanced through this chapter is therefore an attempt to coherently unify the diverse elements and techniques from the collective case study, and explicate how this creates an effective pedagogical design to promote meaningful learning.

INTRODUCTION

In an attempt to conceptually generalize the findings a recent collective case (broader) study (Gikandi, 2012), two congruent theories have been identified to provide basis to advance a relevant theoretical framework in the context of online higher education. The individual case studies have already been published in a series of journal papers (Gikandi, 2013; Gikandi & Mackey, 2013;

Gikandi, & Morrow, in press). The theoretical framework developed and presented in this chapter therefore aims to uncover the broader and deeper conceptual meanings of the findings, and link the key outcomes of the recent study to the existing knowledge.

The chapter starts with a brief review of the identified theories. Secondly, review of the key findings of the recent study is presented. The discussion that follows seeks to elucidate a theoretical

DOI: 10.4018/978-1-4666-8363-1.ch014

framework that can guide assessment of situated and authentic learning with a particular focus on online formative assessment. Lastly, conclusions are offered.

As identified in Gikandi, Morrow and Davis (2011), previous studies did not explicate all relevant aspects of formative assessment which amplifies the purpose of this chapter. The collective case study (Gikandi, 2012) conceptualized online formative assessment from a more holistic pedagogical strategy purposefully incorporating diverse elements. Investigating application of formative assessment in Gikandi (2012) focused on exploring multifaceted elements including provision of a variety of authentic assessment activities which were embedded within the learning processes to engage the students within the online discourse and real-life contexts.

Developing a theoretical framework through this chapter is an attempt to coherently unify the diverse elements and techniques evidenced in the recent collective case study from the perspective of authentic learning. More importantly, the recent findings by Gikandi (2012) reveal some relationships with the identified previous empirical studies in ways that indicate that the findings confirm previous research. Notably, these relationships also reinforce the theoretical framework presented in this chapter.

BACKGROUND

Assessment of Situated and Authentic Learning

Over the years, situated and authentic learning have been recognized as viable perspectives for promoting meaningful learning in (online) higher education through fostering higher-order learning and the development of metacognitive skills (Gikandi, 2012). The theoretical understandings being advanced here are mainly underpinned on the theory of situated cognition (Brown, Collins,

& Duguid, 1989) which suggests that meaningful and transferable learning occurs when learning and knowledge is situated within social and authentic contexts where meanings are negotiated and validated. Brown et al. (1989) among others situativists (e.g. Barab, Squire,& Dueber, 2000; Lave & Wenger, 1991) have argued that perceiving and acting (perception-action process) are fundamental components of meaningful and transferable learning, and knowledge is embedded in the authentic activity, context and culture in which it is constructed and used. The situated cognition theorists (Brown et al., 1989; Collins, Brown, & Newman, 1989; Collins, Brown, & Holum, 1991) also emphasize that it is necessary to go beyond the physical skills in formal learning (craft or standard apprenticeship) to focus on the development of metacognitive skills (or cognitive apprenticeship) in order to promote construction of robust knowledge and its transferability to new situations.

Drawing from the aforementioned theorists, Young (1993) suggests that learning is situated and an ongoing perceptual change as learners increase their ability to detect information and navigate through a problem solving situation. Learning goes further to figuring out appropriate strategies that can enable one to solve a complex and realistic problem situation that constitute an authentic activity. Problem solving in this context refers to "an interaction between the problem solving skills of the learner and the activities and manipulations that a particular problem affords" (Young, 1995, p. 90). As Young (1995) emphasized, problem solving is not linear in nature, but a complex and dynamic evolving process within which sub-dilemmas are discovered with the initial strategies for achieving solutions being revised. This may also lead to reconstruction of the initial goals.

Accordingly, previous research indicates that situated learning necessitates congruent assessment approaches (Herrington & Oliver, 2000; McLellan, 1993; The Cognition and Technology

Group at Vanderbilt (CTGV), 1996; Young, 1995). In the same vein, assessment of situated and authentic learning can be enhanced through embedding of ongoing authentic assessment activities to enable measurement of complex and non-linear processes and products that characterize authentic learning activities and contexts (Young, 1995). In explaining the basis for embedded authentic assessment activities, Young (1995) asserted that:

Accepting situated learning means accepting that assessment must be validated by its real-world usefulness…instruction and measurement must be constructed and implemented as one. Assessment must not only be integrated with instruction, but also focus on problem-solving process along with problem solutions… [there is] need for assessments that externalize the perceptions of each problem solver that are only implicitly available from verbal protocols… [a viable] approach is to acquire as much information about the context and actions of the problem solver while engaging in the problem solving process. (Young, 1995b, p. 91)

As Young (1995) noted, embedded assessment (which entails assessment situated within the same context and based on the similar authentic learning activities) is valuable in recognition of the cumulative and interrelated nature of learning. Moreover, in order to adequately account for situated learning, it is essential to assess the dynamics of context in which the goals and strategies are constantly reconstructed throughout the process of accomplishing an authentic activity (Young, Kulikowich, & Barab, 1997). This provides a means for gathering of information about students' understandings of learning goals and expected outcomes, and ongoing monitoring of their progress with the aim to offer desirable formative feedback, which supports learners to revise their learning strategies for improved outcomes (Young, 1995; Young, Kulikowich, & Barab, 1997).

Various benefits may emerge from the aforementioned process-oriented assessment approach such as offering individual learners the opportunities for adequate interactions with the problem space (the authentic activity at hand and its constituent constraints). This in turn enables a productive process of discovering relevant information (resources) and the activity sub-components (Gikandi, 2012). It is within these processes that the learner is stimulated to interactively collaborate with peers and the teacher, and engage in meaningful reflections about the use value of the activities they are engaged in (Gikandi, 2013). Similarly, the complexity that characterize authentic activities necessitate prolonged period of engagement which provide opportunities to collect adequate information about the evolving goals and perceptions as students identify and actualize the best strategies to accomplish the tasks at hand. Such assessment information is valuable to both the teacher and the students in informing (both external and internal) feedback processes, and self-regulation in the light of that feedback. Moreover, as Young (1995) and Young et al. (1997) noted, effective assessment of situated and authentic learning is not obvious but potentially challenging due to its complex and non-linear nature, and it is therefore important for educators to apply innovative strategies that will enable assessment of both processes and products.

In the same vein, the levels of capabilities being developed have implications for assessment strategies whether in online or face-to-face settings (Oosterhof, Conrad, & Ely, 2008). In articulating how to assess the three core types of desirable capabilities (declarative, procedural, and problem solving) in formal learning settings, Oosterhof et al. (2008) noted that problem-solving capabilities (higher-order and metacognitive skills) may be assessed adequately using authentic formative assessment activities. As such, fformative assessment can be conceptualized from the perspective of embedded assessment of situated and authentic learning to enable process-oriented interactions among the learner, authentic assessment activity and the members of the learning community (particularly the teacher and peers) (Young et al., 1997).

Drawing upon Young et al. (1997), these interactive processes within formative assessment are aimed at obtaining information about the evidence of learning to inform desirable formative feedback. In turn, this supports the learner move to higher levels of competence manifested by their ability to accomplish more complex tasks and development of self-regulation dispositions. Therefore, the assessment of situated and authentic learning is dynamic with the intention of achieving expected performances and having the information focused on interactions that provide opportunities for ongoing formative feedback. This also implies that, assessment within situativity perspectives necessitates going beyond assessment of current ability (the already learned content) to assess the learning potential with an aim to support the learners to become self-regulated and independent users of the knowledge they develop, thus promoting a developmental perception-action process that stimulate life-long learning.

As discussed in the following section, it is also apparent that assessment of situated and authentic learning is interrelated and overlaps with the Vygotsky's (1978) developmental theory of the Zone of proximal development (ZPD) and its integral notion of scaffolding. As Brown et al. (1989) acknowledged, the theory of situated cognition draws on Vygotsky's (1978) view of learning as a perception-action process within a social context. Engagement in complex problem solving (authentic activity) is a key feature in both situated cognition and ZPD theories. Other overlaps relate to embedded authentic assessment activities, emphasis on assessment of processes and products, focus on both current and potential capabilities, and the collaboration between the teacher and learners as well as among the learners.

Such collaborations allow for shared meanings and dialogic feedback as a means of scaffolding to support individual learners exploit their cognitive development potential.

The ZPD and Formative Assessment

Vygotsky's (1978) perspectives on learning and development draws attention to ongoing assessment of both the competences that have already been developed and those that are in the process of formation (or development) in order to inform the desirable formative feedback. In emphasizing the role of interactions with knowledgeable others as a means of scaffolding learning and supporting cognitive development, Vygotsky defined the ZPD as 'the distance between the actual developmental level as determined by independent problem solving and the level of potential development as determined under adult guidance or in collaboration with more capable peers' (1978, p. 86). Although the Vygostsky's ZPD was initially applied in the context of a knowledgeable adult working with a child, this notion of socially mediated learning have also been applied in higher education contexts (Yorke, 2003), and is conceivably a fundamental conception that underpin formative assessment (Allal, 2000; Ash & Levitt, 2003; Clark, 2010; Yorke, 2003).

Scaffolding is an integral concept of the ZPD that encompasses social interactions and collaborations at the centrality of learning and assessment processes. Purposeful interactions with knowledgeable others is integral to the concept of formative assessment in order to provide opportunities for scaffolding, a process which support the learner to accomplish a complex activity or achieve a goal which would otherwise be beyond his or her initial capability without support of others. The concept of scaffolding in this context therefore implies an interactive and developmental process that allows the learners to exploit their current capabilities to accomplish an appropriately complex task within a supportive social context, which assist them (individually and/or collectively) to go beyond their initial capabilities and accomplish more complex levels of the task (Wood, Bruner, & Ross, 1976).

The processes underlying Vygotsky's ZPD closely align with formative assessment as it emphasizes interactive and process-oriented assessment. It also aligns well with the core purpose of formative assessment in that it involves establishing both what the learners can do on their own and what they can potentially achieve with support of others, through an ongoing scaffolding process within which formative feedback is offered to support learners to close their performance gaps. Moreover, the ZPD relates to engagement with complex learning and assessment activities within social contexts to foster development of higher-order problem-solving and metacognitive skills that permits self-regulation desirable for independent thinking, transferable and life-long learning. These aspects are fundamental in higher education and professional learning.

As identified in Gikandi (2012), formative assessment can also be conceptualized as assessment *within* the ZPD (which is assessment *for* learning) (as opposed to assessment *of* ZPD or assessment *of* learning that denote summative assessment). Other authors (Allal, 2000; Ash & Levitt, 2003; Clark, 2010) have attempted to conceptualize formative assessment from the perspective of assessment within the ZPD. Allal (2000) further emphasized that formative assessment necessitate opportunities for ongoing interactions because the ZPD is created by social interaction. Allal also clarified that it is the current level of learner's capability that determines the type of interactions in which the learner get involved in and from which they can benefit. This implies that, assessment *within* the ZPD (formative assessment) is a developmental process that requires the learner to willingly take responsibility to self-regulate and use feedback to engage at more complex levels which in turn creates opportunities for further scaffolding.

Formative assessment offers a strategy to operationalize on-going expansion of the ZPD through offering opportunities for iterative establishment of the differences between the teacher and the learner's understanding of the learning goals and expected outcomes within an ongoing collaborative process in which meanings are negotiated (Ash & Levitt, 2003). Formative assessment also enables ongoing monitoring, assessment and interpretation of the distance between the learner's current and potential level of intellectual development within the ZPD to inform desirable formative feedback which expands the learner ZPD implying that "the student will [potentially] be able to operate autonomously in the original ZPD (thus making it no longer a ZPD, and creating a new ZPD further up the developmental gradient" (Yorke, 2003, p. 492). Accordingly, more effective formative assessment requires explicitly defined learning goals and expected outcomes, and feedback that is formative (Ash & Levitt, 2003; Clark, 2010; Yorke, 2003). Feedback is formatively effective if it supports the students to close their current performance gaps and create opportunities for further development. As Clark puts it " feedback becomes formative when students are provided with scaffolded instruction or thoughtful questioning that serve as a prompt for further inquiry, which then closes the gap between their current level of understanding, and the desired learning goal" (2010, p. 344).

Similarly, Yorke (2003) suggested that expected performance is best guided by and measured against clear assessment criteria, and it is necessary to foster shared understanding of the criteria through opportunities for dialogue between the teacher and learners. Yorke also noted that formative feedback is a key determinant of effectiveness of formative assessment and is more productive when it is dialogic in order to create opportunities for better understanding of that feedback. The core purpose of formative assessment is thus to support the student to engage in an authentic activity developmentally through opportunities for dialogic formative feedback, within which the pre-existing ZPD is increasingly expanded to support further cognitive development.

Revealing the centrality of social interactivity and collaborations in formative assessment, Clark (2010) further conceptualized formative assessment as 'assessment within the collaborative ZPD' which he defined as a "process based on high-quality interactions between teacher/student and crucially between peers" (p. 343). High-quality interactions entail equality (shared expertise), honesty, collaboration, and reciprocity as a community that is bound by common goals in accomplishing an authentic activity in a particular domain (Clark, 2010). Such interactions leads to processes that stimulate learners to make their thinking visible to others, apply and share their existing knowledge and experiences, provide peers' with critical feedback, and mutually learn from peers' ideas and work.

Consistent with the theoretical perspectives articulated thus far, the importance of embedded assessment in online higher education has also been well documented in the recent reviews of related literature (Gikandi et al., 2011; Young & Kim, 2010). However, the theoretical literature reviewed above did not reveal substantial guidelines to inform operationalization of embedded assessment in online learning settings. This reveals a gap in theory of embedded assessment in online learning. Speck (2002) in reviewing related literature previously identified this gap in explaining that,

Insufficient attention to pedagogical questions and concerns arising from the practice of online teaching quite naturally and logically raises questions about assessment of learners in on-line classrooms...In considering assessment, I take the position that if it is to be effective, assessment must be part and parcel of the entire learning enterprise and therefore is not a distinct stage of pedagogical theory. Assessment must be integrated into a holistic view of pedagogy. This means that

any theory of assessment presumes and informs a theory of learning. Unfortunately, professors often assess students under the authority of an inchoate theory of learning (Speck, 2002, pp. 5-6).

As speck noted, a suitable theory on embedded assessment informed by relevant empirical evidence is desirable in order to provide online educators with a framework that can support them to make informed choices about effective formative assessment in online courses. Following critical analysis of related literature it appears that there is only a few empirical studies (e.g. Mackey, 2009; Mackey & Evans, 2011; Russell, Elton, Swinglehurst, & Greenhalgh, 2006; Sorensen & Takle, 2005; Vonderwell, Liang, & Alderman, 2007) have focused on embedded assessment in online settings in ways that conform to the concept of formative assessment as conceptualized in the recent collective case study by Gikandi (2012. This is particularly with respect to ongoing authentic assessment activities and interactive formative feedback as a means of facilitating meaningful learning. While the aforementioned related empirical studies reveal some commonality with the findings of the recent collective case study, it is important to note that development of a theory for effective online formative assessment has to be more diverse and deeper than what each of the prior studies reveal separately. As such these previous studies did not exhaust all relevant aspects of formative assessment which amplifies the purpose of this chapter informed by the recent collective case study.

As presented in the following section, the findings' of the recent collective case study (Gikandi, 2012) are first re-examined relative to the related empirical studies, and then synthesized to inform the theoretical framework.

REVIEW OF THE COLLECTIVE CASE STUDY FINDINGS AND LINK TO RELATED STUDIES

The recent collective case study by Gikandi (2012) conceptualized online formative assessment from a holistic pedagogical approach purposefully incorporating diverse elements. This collective case study (also referred in this chapter as the recent study) entailed a multiple-case design that constituted embedded individual cases of online courses. The collective case study was therefore the broader study in which the findings of studied cases were aggregated to gain collective understanding of the phenomenon under investigation. Investigating application of formative assessment in this research focused on exploring multifaceted elements including provision of a variety of embedded authentic assessment activities which were interrelated and structured to engage the students within the online discourse and real-life contexts. Other elements included shared understanding of learning goals and expected outcomes; ongoing monitoring and assessment; and opportunities for ongoing and dialogic formative feedback. Developing a theoretical framework as presented through this chapter is therefore an attempt to coherently unify the diverse elements and techniques from the perspective of authentic learning, and explicate how these can create an effective pedagogical design to promote meaningful learning and ongoing assessment.

This section therefore reviews the key findings of the recent collective case study relative to previous empirical research. The related empirical studies examined here reveal a focus on embedded assessment in online higher education which is consistent with conceptualization of formative assessment in the recent study. The recent study findings showed that engaging students with authentic assessment activities can promote meaningful learning. This is consistent with recent studies (Mackey, 2009, 2011; Mackey & Evans, 2011) within the context of continuing online education

at postgraduate level which reported that engaging students with authentic learning and assessment activities promoted meaningful and transferable learning. Mackey's findings demonstrated that embedding authentic assessment that are situated within social and real-life professional contexts can promote meaningful learning that is transferable to own professional practice and contexts.

The findings of the recent study, as well as those by Mackey and others (Mackey, 2009, 2011; Mackey & Evans, 2011) showed that provision of authentic assessment activities that were appropriately complex stimulated on-going on-task interactions as the students engaged with their peers within the online discourse. The emergent peer-peer engagement was characterized by sharing of diverse perspectives, contextualized and reflective dialogue as the students connected the online discourse to their assessment work (authentic projects) that was situated within their professional practice environments. The interactivity within the asynchronous online discourse offered the students valuable opportunities to engage in critical dialogue and reflection about their understanding of content while making connections to their own professional practice. Russell et al. (2006) within the context of health science online education at postgraduate level also demonstrated the importance of engaging students with embedded authentic assessment as a means of promoting meaningful and transferable learning. Russell et al.'s study also highlighted the necessity to offer students with the opportunities to mutually engage with peers, and offer constructive peer-peer feedback in the process of accomplishing the authentic assessment activities.

Similar to what Mackey's studies showed, findings of the recent study by Gikandi (2012) confirmed that the open-endedness and learner autonomy that characterized the authentic activities prompted the students to go beyond the assessment requirements to self-regulate in pursuit of their own learning goals that aligned with their professional needs and interests. Through such opportunities, the students were able to develop and confidently demonstrate their capabilities in ICT (information communication technology) as the subject domain, and transform their identity as professional experts in regard applying ICT in their own professional practice. The findings of the recent study further demonstrated that mutual engagement within the constraints afforded by authentic task resonates with culture of real practices which engage learners in complex problem solving, and in turn support them to develop skills that are relevant and transferable to real-world professional settings. These findings are also consistent with Mackey's related studies (Mackey, 2009, 2011; Mackey & Evans, 2011).

It is important to point out that Mackey's studies were in a similar context with the recent study in that both studies were situated within the same university's postgraduate programme in related online courses within the context of ICT-related professional development for teachers; however, these studies differed in their specific focus. The recent case study mainly focused on researching classroom contexts with particular interest on how application of online formative assessment can enhance meaningful learning and its assessment. The Mackey's related studies were mainly focused on how students were transferring their developed competences and skills to their real-life professional settings particularly in regard to how their experiences in online learning communities and communities of practices interconnected. As illustrated in the recent study, the broader study illuminated rich evidence about the online classroom interactions and formative assessment processes that supported meaningful learning experiences as a manifestation of transferable learning.

Through opportunities to investigate operationalization of embedded assessment within online classroom settings, the recent case study explored in-depth the learning and assessment activities and processes within their naturalistic contexts which provided rich evidence about how on-going

authentic assessment activities coupled with the learner autonomy and adequate opportunities for negotiating meanings of learning goals and expected outcomes promoted meaningful learning and opportunities for effective formative feedback. Through observations and analysis of the archived course discourse, the recent case study went further to uncover the nature of learning and formative assessment processes within the online discourse that supported the students to productively engage with authentic assessment that were situated in real-life contexts. The recent study findings illustrated that the authentic assessment activities and learner autonomy were not mutually exclusively, instead, they were tightly interlinked resulting to a synergy that fostered shared authenticity. The findings further indicate that shared authenticity that emerged from opportunities for negotiated meanings within the online course discourse promoted shared ownership, expertise and responsibility among the students and the teacher. These in turn promoted interactivity, contextualization and reflectivity within learning and assessment processes, which is a manifestation of deep and transferable learning. For instance, this emerged strongly in both courses as students engaged with the authentic projects that were situated in real-life contexts while having opportunities to engage in meaningful dialogue with others online.

Through the in-depth analysis of learning and assessment processes within online classroom settings, the recent study findings also revealed how authentic assessment activities stimulated the students to apply their existing knowledge and experiences as knowledgeable professionals, thus fostering contextual learning and opportunities to engage in meaningful online dialogue in ways that prompted critical thinking and rich peer formative feedback, as well as stimulating students to connect and apply their learning to own professional practice and other real-life contexts. This study also showed that productive engagement with authentic activities necessitates opportunities for on-going monitoring, and interactive formative feedback in order to foster shared understanding of learning goals, and provide desirable learning scaffold to ensure that the inherent complexity that often characterize authentic activities do not result to learning barriers.

The recent study findings further showed that it is important for online educators to recognize diversity among learners in relation to their previous experiences and learning needs including their capabilities to active and productively engage with others online, and thus the necessity to provide learning support that recognizes and responds to their diverse needs. Teachers in the recent study recognized that their students had varying background, capabilities and needs, and this prompted these teachers to offer some individualized support. This is consistent with the findings of Russell et al. (2006). However, the recent collective case study went beyond Russell et al.'s study to reveal the need for teachers to maintain an optimal blend between private interactions (for instance, through emails) and public interactions (within open online discussion forums) between the teacher and the students in order to provide adequate opportunities for students to voice their learning needs and elicit formative feedback.

Russell et al. (2006) conceptualized on-going assessment of higher-order learning as part of effective teaching and learning. Their study was underpinned on constructivist theoretical perspectives in which they emphasized that assessment in online settings necessitates a focus on both processes and products of learning, and active learners' involvement in learning and on-going assessment processes as a way to promote active knowledge construction. Consistent with the recent case study, Russell et al. showed that the assessment activities require to be accompanied by clear assessment criteria in order to promote shared understanding of learning gals and expected outcomes. Their study was similar to the recent study in identifying that formative feedback is more effective when it is dialogic and a shared responsibility among the students and the teacher.

However, Russell et al.'s (2006) study present their findings as a narrative case study in which they shared their experiences in two online courses as course teachers but the scope of their study did not include an exhaustive account to illustrate the nature of the online classroom interactions, and on-going formative assessment processes that occurred among the course participants. While Russell et al.'s study is substantially informative; it may not be obvious to draw all the relevant insights on the nature of interactions and collaborations that characterized effective on-task interactions and on-going formative feedback processes.

The collective study illustrated use of asynchronous online discussion as a technique for facilitating formative assessment which concurs with a study by Vonderwell et al. (2007) who studied five online educational courses at postgraduate level. Consitent with the recent case study findings, Vonderwell et al. (2007) emphasized collaborative learning and process-oriented assessment in which learners were prompted as active participants in their learning and its on-going assessment. Vonderwell et al. (2007) investigated students' learning experiences within the asynchronous online discussions and demonstrated use of asynchronous online settings as a technique for facilitating ongoing formative peer and self assessment. Similar to the findings of the recent study, their findings showed that indicated that online environments provided enhanced opportunities for students to self assess and offer constructive peer-peer feedback. The recent study findings also confirm Vonderwell et al. (2007) in showing that the asynchronous threaded discussions promoted reflective learning and self-assessment by allowing students to have adequate time to review peers' thinking, compose and reflect about their own understanding of content before they shared their thinking with other online participants. In these ways, collaborative learning and assessment promoted reflective inquiry and enabled opportunities for dynamic and meaningful interactions, multiple perspectives, and shared understanding of content as a learning community with common goals. Findings from both Vonderwell et al. (2007) and the recent study also demonstrated that permitting learner autonomy within the online discussion stimulate learners to actively participate within collaborative online discourse in productive ways.

The findings of the recent study were also similar to Sorensen and Takle's (2005) study which was framed within collaborative learning to supports learner centred focus and process-oriented assessment in which students were actively engaged as co-facilitators and participants. Sorensen and Takle's study included two online courses, one in physical science education at undergraduate level and the other one in social science at postgraduate level. Similar to the findings of the recent study as well as those of Vonderwell et al. (2007), and Sorensen and Takle's study also demonstrated use of asynchronous online discussions as a technique that supported on-going assessment for both processes and products of learning. Confirming previous findings, the recent study also showed that effective integration of formative assessment in online learning environments has the potential to offer an appropriate structure for sustained meaningful interactions among learners and the teacher, and foster development of interactive and collaborative learning communities to in ways that promote self and peer-peer formative assessment.

Consistent with the recent study, research by Vonderwell et al. (2007), and Sorensen and Takle (2005) emphasize that assessment in online higher learning should be on-going and encompass both processes and products in order to enable assessment to inform teaching and contribute to learning. These studies also demonstrated that active interactive collaboration among the students and the teacher in learning and on-going assessment as a means to stimulate students to perceive themselves as capable learners and assume primary responsibility for their learning.

The findings of the recent study also conforms to those of Sorensen and Takle (2005), and Vonderwell et al. (2007) in showing that it is necessary to go beyond individual involvement to consider collaborative engagement in development and negotiation of meanings within social contexts. It is important to note that although findings from the recent study were relatively similar to those from Sorensen and Takle (2005), and Vonderwell et al. (2007), the evidence from the recent study was considered richer compared to the two studies as they did not go further to illuminate the nature of learning and assessment activities on which the interactions they exemplified were based on. Unlike the recent study that illustrated engagement with variety of authentic assessment including authentic projects that were situated in real-life contexts, the nature of interactions revealed by Sorensen and Takle (2005), and Vonderwell et al. (2007) only illuminated learners' engagement with content and assessment of their understanding within the collaborative online discussion forums.

The recent study findings further showed that online environments can provide dynamic opportunities for sustained interactions among learners in way that enable them to productively share their on-going assessment work, views and experiences. The recent findings illustrated that through opportunities for sustained interactions with others, both the teacher and learners alike were involved actively as knowledge resources through shared responsibilities in facilitating collaborative learning and on-going assessment within which online discussion forums were utilized innovatively to support various formative assessment techniques. Integrating of formative assessment within online courses fostered a sense of an interactive and collaborative online learning community, which provided learners with diverse opportunities for dynamic and meaningful interactions with others (particularly the teacher and peers) (Gikandi, 2012). For instance, such opportunities offered a means of facilitate collaborative formative assessment of both processes and products of learning within both courses. Through these formative processes, student participation, motivation and ownership of learning were enhanced.

The recent study went further to provide explicit evidence on the nature of the interactivity within collaborative feedback processes as illustrated by Gikandi (2012) which reveals how situating learning and assessment within social contexts expanded opportunities for enriched formative feedback in terms of interactivity, immediacy and adequacy. These forms of interactions provided opportunities for on-going monitoring and formative feedback as learners engaged in various authentic learning and assessment activities.

The recent collective case study also illustrated that online settings can offer enhanced opportunities to provide more detailed and clearly written feedback that is integrated within student assessment work. This was previously identified by Wolsey (2008) whose study focused on analyzing the efficacy of teacher's formative feedback on students' submitted work on specific assessment activities within postgraduate online courses for teachers. Like Wolsey (2008), the recent study identified these aspects as critical in online settings in stimulating meaningful dialogue between the teacher and the learner. The recent case study as well as Wolsey (2008) also demonstrated that interactive formative feedback is essential in order for feedback to serve as a means of scaffolding learning to support learners to improve their subsequent learning strategies and close their performance gaps. The recent study also confirm Wolsey illustrating that formative feedback is effective when characterized by immediacy (timeliness), which relates to feedback that is given at or close to the time the learning occurs, as well as providing opportunities for the students to repeat and/or revise their work.

While Wolsey (2008) specifically focused on efficacy of teacher's feedback on submitted assessment work his study did not go further to illuminate the nature of assessment activities involved. The recent study went beyond to demonstrate that applying variety of techniques in online formative assessment can foster opportunities for effective feedback. These additional techniques relates to:

students' engagement within collaborative online discussions as they engaged with various interrelated authentic assessment activities including authentic projects that were related to real-life applications, on-going sharing and documentation of learning and assessment processes, and shared responsibility among the students and the teacher in on-going monitoring, assessment and provision of formative feedback. The recent study illustrated productivity that emerged by incorporating such different techniques, and in particular increased quality of formative feedback in relation to its immediacy, interactivity and adequacy. Shared responsibility in on-going formative feedback processes as one of the applied techniques in the recent study was also vital in stimulating students' active participation and ownership of their learning and its assessment in ways that promoted self-regulation and metacognitive skills.

Another finding in the recent study that is consistent with Wolsey (2008) is that, clear, timely, on-going and adequately detailed formative feedback is important in online environments due to physical interaction barriers among online participants, which may discourage or limit some learners to seek clarity. Similar to the recent study findings, Wolsey (2008) also illustrated that indirect feedback, such as offering references and hints, as well as asking leading questions, facilitates student's development and achievement by encouraging the student to self-correct and to engage in reflective inquiry. These aspects manifest effective formative feedback that promotes student's motivation towards self-regulatory processes and confidence to demonstrate their capabilities.

The recent study as well as that by Wolsey (2008) indicated that it is essential for the teacher to share rubrics with the learners, provide exemplars where applicable and to ensure openness and transparency of rubrics as part of formative feedback processes. Consistent with the findings of Wolsey (2008), the recent study illustrated that online environments offered flexible opportunities to share and review rubrics thus promoting rubrics' openness and flexibility. However unlike the recent study, Wolsey (2008) did not illustrate how sharing of meaning of rubrics and exemplars was achieved. The recent study explicitly demonstrated processes of how sharing of goals and expected outcomes were achieved through use of analytical rubrics and exemplars, including opportunities for sharing their meanings. Another notable finding in the recent study is that the openness of students' work in progress to peers served as valuable exemplars. This openness was enabled through opportunities for on-going documentation, and sharing of learning and assessment processes and products that also included publicity of learning needs and received feedback which enhanced effectiveness and efficiency of feedback as well as clarity of the expected outcomes.

Consistent with the evidence obtained in the recent study, Wolsey (2008) identified that "feedback is tied to specific criteria and an indication of how to close the gap between the current and expected performance" (2008, p. 313). The recent study findings demonstrated that formative feedback is effective when it is timely and supported by a well-designed rubrics coupled with opportunities for interactions about that feedback in order to support the student better understand the feedback. This is also consistent with the findings of Gaytan and McEwen (2007). Unlike the other prior studies referenced here, the recent study by Gaytan and McEwen's (2007) was designed as a survey while the other studies applied case study design with a bias in varying qualitative methodological techniques such as obsrevations, analysis of online course discourse, and interviews. Gaytan and McEwen's (2007) study entailed an online survey that included 85 online educators and 1,963 students enrolled in different online courses (and programmes including education, business, arts, sciences, at both undergraduate and postgraduate level) offered in two different universities. Albeit the identified differences in methodological approach, the recent study findings confirm the findings of Gaytan and McEwen (2007) in identifying

that effectiveness of feedback is closely linked to offering opportunities for frequent and meaningful interactions to enable shared purpose and meaning of learning goals and expected outcomes. It is through such processes that formative feedback can be effective in supporting and scaffolding learning towards achievement of targeted goals. Similar to the recent study, Gaytan and McEwen's findings also indicate that on-going formative feedback as a vital element in online assessment. Agreeing with the findings of Gaytan and McEwen, the recent case study demonstrated that interactivity among online participants influence the effectiveness and efficiency of formative feedback.

The recent study also found that effective online assessment necessiates provision of various ongoing activities that encompass different techniques such engaging students with authentic projects, self assessment tasks and asynchronous collaborations within online discusions forums. The findings of Gaytan and McEwen (2007) are consistent with the recent case study in regard to this aspect. Like Gaytan and McEwen, the recent study findings showed that provision of variety of on-going assessment activities can facilitate multidimensional approaches. In the recent study, the findings showed that such approaches fostered learner autonomy and meaningful engagement through enabling diverse opportunities for learners to apply varying approaches and learning strategies in the development of expected artefacts as a means to demonstrate their capabilities and enhance their competences. As Gaytan and McEwen identified, the recent case study findings also illustrated that provision of variety of on-going assessment activities coupled with clearly shared goals and expected outcomes, and opportunities for dynamic interactions can foster opportunities for self and peer formative assessment that leads to meaningful engagement and timely interactive formative feedback.

Although the findings by Gaytan and McEwen (2007) are agreeably consistent with the recent findings, the nature of their study based on the survey design did not provide suffient information to illustrate how such elements may be operationalized effectively in online classroom settings. The elements identified by Gaytan and McEwen were well illustrated in depth in the recent study through illuminating learning and assessment activities and related formative processes. These elements included provision of a variety of authentic assessment activities was illustrated as a key component in embedded assessment, coupled with clarity of learning goals and expected outcomes, and opportunties for ongoing monitoring, assessment and interactive formative feedback in which development of an interactive learning community with active learners' involvement was at the centrality.

As key contributions of the recent collective case study, a number of new strategies and techniques were identified. As summarized in Table 1, these new strategies and/or techniques included an interweave between formative and summative assessment, on-going sharing and documentation of learning and assessment processes and products including individual students' assessment work in progress, and the emergent synergies that resulted from active and collaborative engagement among teacher, self and peer a with shared responsibility in formative assessment processes. One of the emergent synergy was the development of a robust, interactive and supportive learning community with shared goals, ownership and responsibility which reciprocally enriched formative processes as the students became mutually responsible for their own learning and assessment as well as that of their peers. The evidence obtained from the recent study, as reported earlier, showed that the students recognized their peers as source of valuable feedback.

Another important synergy resulting from strategies and techniques indicated in Table 1 relates to how opportunities for interaction with others within individual reflective processes, dialogic feedback and meaning making resulted to a constructive link between internal and external feedback. This in turn supported the student to better understand and internalize the external feedback, and use it to self regulate for productive improvements. For instance, the analysis of the content from the archived online discourse in the recent study illustrated that opportunities for self-assessment through reflective articulation of individual's developing understandings of content and expected outcomes, and their learning experiences as online learners provided both the teacher and peers with enriched information to better understand the strengths and needs of individual students which in turn informed desirable formative feedback. In this way, self-reflections (internal feedback) prompted tailored external formative feedback which enhanced opportunities for dialogue about that feedback. The analysis of the online discourse and participants' interview transcripts in in the recent study further showed that opportunities for dialogue supported student to better understand and construct their own meanings out of the feedback they received which inevitably increased its uptake and productivity in supporting them to revise their learning strategies and improve their performance. Such a synergy between self and peer formative assessment emerged more richly in students' reflective journals (Gikandi, 2013). The use of the open reflective journals in that online course provided students with opportunities to directly elicit external feedback from others (both the teacher and/or peers) as they self assessed and shared their progress and achievements. As identified by Gikandi (2013), the aspect of reflective journals being open implied that the individual student's journal was public to both the teacher and peers in ways that allowed the course participants to interact with and provide external feedback on self reflections. Such opportunities stimulated meaningful reflectivity and interactivity within formative feedback processes. In these ways, the recent study demonstrated that applying a holistic approach that incorporates multifaceted techniques in operationalization of embedded assessment

Table 1. The strategies of online formative assessment as part of embedded assessment that facilitated meaningful learning

Strategy in Studied Cases		Techniques (Facilitating Tools and Opportunities) Presented Based on their First Instance of Occurrence Includes Overlap	Manifestation in the Categories Emerging from the Gathered Data (Illustrative Sample Categories Selected from Coded Themes that were Common across the Cases)
1	Teacher engagement with formative assessment	• Offering to the students the formative assessment activities coupled with learner autonomy and explicit expected outcomes • Offering opportunities for collaboration and shared meanings through use of asynchronous topical discussion forums and open forums • Ongoing guidance and fostering the collaborative discourse and shared role with students in ongoing monitoring, assessing and providing formative feedback to students • Direct engagement in ongoing monitoring, assessing and provision of formative feedback • Enabling ongoing documentation and publicity of artefact enriched opportunities for ongoing monitoring of evidence of learning and formative feedback	• Teacher formative feedback - responses to students question and/or teacher feedback prompted by her monitoring the student's progress and achievement • Teacher guidance, scaffolding, modelling and fostering shared purpose and role • Teacher as a co-participant in the discussion forums • Reference to previous contributions (by self or others) within the discussion forums • Teacher recognition of peer-peer feedback
2	The overlap and interweave between formative and summative assessment	• The formative and summative assessment activities were ongoing, that is, they were offered at the outset of the course, and were distributed throughout the course • They mapped onto each other (such that they interweaved to inform the next.) • Opportunities for students to receive and use the formative feedback they received to revise their work, and improve their understanding of content and achievement over time for both formative and summative purposes • Ongoing documentation and publicity of artefacts by enhancing the opportunities for ongoing monitoring, assessment, and feedback	• Students recognizing the building of a bigger picture from a variety of assessment activities- students able to connect how the assessment activities maps onto each other • Students' awareness and identifying connections across a variety of assessment activities, and applying ideas from one assessment to inform another assessment activity • Teacher fostering and supporting students to achieve meaningful artefact (products and processes) and helping them to see connection among assessment tasks - how one assessment can inform or build into another assessment task
3	Self formative assessment	• Topical online discussion forums as the individual students compared their thinking with that of others and reflected upon the responses (feedback) from others • Ongoing documentation and publicity of artefact – this provided the students an opportunity to review previous contribution (by self and/or others, rethink and reflect upon their contributions before posting online) • Analytical rubrics as applied by self to assess own work • Open forums as the student reflected upon and sought to validate their own understanding of expected outcomes • Peer-peer review and formative feedback on completed artefacts as each student discerned what was meaningful in their own contexts from peers' work	• Awareness and debriefing of individual's progress or current way of thinking in relation to understandings of content, accomplishment of expected outcomes • Self awareness of individual's perceptions and recognition of changing perceptions and developing abilities • Self awareness of individual's learning needs and style as an online learner • Debriefing or articulating of own learning experiences within the course • Connecting ideas/experiences to own work (professional) contexts, experiences and practices • Connecting ideas to broader real-life contexts, issues and practices • Reference to previous contributions (by self or others) within the discussions
4	Peer formative assessment	• Topical online discussion forums as students interacted with peers' contributions and offered feedback on this • Ongoing documentation and publicity of artefact, which allowed self review and reflection upon peers' thinking and reflections before offering their feedback • Analytical rubrics as applied by individual to formatively assess (or review) peer's work • Open forums as students responded to peers' thoughts • Peer-peer review and feedback on completed artefacts as students interacted with peer's work, reviewed it against the rubrics and offered constructive feedback	• Peer formative feedback - constructive responses from peers upon one's idea/work or question • Recognition of feedback or support from peers • Recognition of self as a source of learning support or feedback • Sharing individual views and understanding of content - initiating or extending a discussion thread within the class forum - learners as thread starters or extenders • Identifying and connecting with common ideas and interests among peers • Connecting ideas to own professional contexts, experiences and practices • Connecting ideas to broader real-life contexts, issues and practices • Reference to previous contributions (by self or others) within the discussions

continued on following page.

Table 1. continued.

Strategy in Studied Cases		Techniques (Facilitating Tools and Opportunities) Presented Based on their First Instance of Occurrence Includes Overlap	Manifestation in the Categories Emerging from the Gathered Data (Illustrative Sample Categories Selected from Coded Themes that were Common across the Cases)
5	Development of a robust and supportive learning community	• Dynamic interactions and collaboration within the topical and open online discussion forums • Learner autonomy through stimulating dynamic interactivity and meaningful dialogue • Shared professional identity (as teachers) which stimulated meaningful dialogue and sharing of lived experiences • Ongoing documentation and publicity of artefact which enhanced interactivity	• Recognition of the class as a learning community (manifested in various ways, such as: use of collective terms, sense of reciprocity or mutuality, identifying and connecting with common ideas and interests among peers) • Directly asking peer a question or prompting for feedback from others (peers/teacher) • Teacher recognition and fostering the view of the class as a supportive learning community - seeing learners as a learning support for peers in their class • Connecting ideas to own professional contexts, experiences and practices • Connecting ideas to broader real-life contexts, issues and practices

can facilitate meaningful learning and its ongoing assessment.

To that end the recent case study reveals some relationships with the identified previous empirical studies in ways that confirm previous research. These relationships reinforce the advanced theoretical framework as presented in the following section.

THE THEORETICAL FRAMEWORK FOR ONLINE FORMATIVE ASSESSMENT AS PROCESS-ORIENTED ASSESSMENT WITHIN THE ZPD

The theories of situated cognition and ZPD as articulated so far offer a unified theoretical basis to develop a theoretical framework from the findings of the studies reviewed above. These theories are applied to develop a theoretical framework that explicates how effective integration of formative assessment as illustrated in the recent study facilitated meaningful learning and its ongoing assessment through creating a synergy between the components of cognitive engagement and social interactions within the constraints imposed by a variety of ongoing authentic assessment activities.

In the recent collective case study, a systematic process-oriented assessment of situated and authentic learning was operationalized through online formative assessment. The ongoing assessment was achieved through embedding authentic assessment activities coupled with opportunities for learner autonomy, negotiated meanings, and ongoing documentation and sharing of learning and assessment processes and products including student-created artefacts. These opportunities in turn facilitated opportunities for ongoing formative feedback processes which provided the students with opportunities to improve their achievement over time as they self-regulated and use the feedback to achieve deep understandings (of learning goals and content), as well as develop competences that were transferable to their own professional contexts. Online formative assessment was therefore part of the embedded assessment of situated and authentic learning that facilitated process-oriented interactions among the learner, authentic assessment activity and the other participants (teacher and peers) within the ZPD. This in turn enabled collaborations in ongoing monitoring, assessment and formative feedback. As reported in Gikandi (2012), the embedded authentic assessment activities, and related formative assessment processes were purposefully designed by the teachers in the studied online courses with the aim to facilitate ongoing assessment of situated and authentic learning within a social context.

The recent study findings showed that teachers designed for situated and authentic learning within which they explicitly shared the purpose of the ongoing authentic assessment activities from the outset of their respective course. This fostered collaborative engagement as individual students interacted with others within the processes of accomplishing the assessment activities while receiving formative feedback that supported them to self-regulate and close their performance gaps.

As shown in Table 2, the advanced theoretical framework comprises four fundamental conceptual elements of assessment of situated and authentic learning; namely: embedded authentic assessment activities, shared goals and ownership, emphasis on both processes and products, and collaboration in developmental scaffolding. The related guiding sub-elements are also identified. As well, the development of this framework is also focused on re-examining and synthesizing how these elements and sub-elements were operationalized in the collective case study, with a particular focus on online formative assessment. The framework also highlights the evident strategies and benefits with respect to promoting meaningful learning and development.

Discussion: Operationalization of the Framework in Online Learning Contexts

It is now apparent that assessment of situated and authentic learning is more effective when deeply embedded as an integral part of teaching and learning which is fundamentally aimed at promoting meaningful and transferable learning. This implies that effectively embedded assessment is a hallmark of effective teaching and meaningful learning in higher education. In the same vein, ongoing assessment within the ZPD closely aligns with the concept of online formative assessment

as it emphasizes interactive and process-oriented assessment, which as Oosterhof et al. (2008) suggests is particularly crucial in online learning settings for sustaining productive engagement

The findings from the collective case study as reviewed above and the advanced framework as summarized in Table 2 indicate that provision of a variety of ongoing and authentic assessment activities enabled operationalization of the four fundamental conceptual elements (and related sub-elements) of assessment of situated and authentic learning. The learner autonomy that was inherent within the assessment activities provided students with opportunities to choose relevant activities that also aligned well with their own goals, and needs. Notably, the students in the recent study were continuing professionals which offered them enriched opportunities to capitalize on learner autonomy and engage with activities that were situated within their own professional practices and contexts. The assessment activities also required the students to apply various abilities and skills which provided them with opportunities to draw on their prior knowledge and experiences. The evident authenticity stimulated valuable processes as the students engaged in constructive dialogue with others (within and/or beyond their online learning community) as they exchanged ideas/resources, sought and/or provided feedback to peers in the process of accomplishing the assessment activities. This in turn, prompted contextualized dialogue characterized by diverse perspectives emerging from students as they shared their lived experiences as continuing professionals. This further stimulated reflectivity as individuals attempted to compare and evaluate these against their peers' perspectives. Indeed, such processes inherently embodied ongoing process-oriented assessment.

The overlap and interweave between formative and summative assessment stimulated active and interactive collaborations amongst the individual student, teacher and peers as a learning community with shared goals and responsibility. These opportunities fostered shared authenticity and

Table 2. Online formative assessment as process-oriented assessment of situated and authentic learning within the ZPD

	Conceptual Elements for Assessment of Situated and Authentic Learning	Guiding Sub-Elements for Design and Implementation in Online Courses	Operationalization as Manifested in the Collective Case Study	The Underlying Strategies for Online Formative Assessment (as described in Table 1)	Emergent Meaningful Learning Experiences
1	Embedded authentic assessment activities (Allal, 2000; Barab et al., 2000; Oosterhof et al., 2008; Yorke, 2003; Young, 1995; Young et al., 1997)	Variety of ongoing and interrelated authentic assessment activities that are integrated within teaching and learning processes	• Provision of assessment activities that are open-ended and involves real-life applications • Activities that are complex to engage learners in multiple roles and sustain their cognitive engagement over prolonged period • Intentional overlap and interweave between formative and summative assessment activities • Activities that require and stimulate learners to apply their existing knowledge and experiences	• Teacher engagement with formative assessment • The overlap and interweave between formative and summative assessment	• Active cognitive engagement • Contextual • Reflective • Self regulation
		Activities that require and stimulate learner cognitive engagement both individually and collaboratively	• Variety of activities that are ongoing to provide multiple sources of evidence and provide opportunities for learners to demonstrate varying capabilities • Activities that require student to create own artefacts and demonstrate their capabilities individually • Collaborative activities that offered sustainable opportunities for collaborative learning and contextualization through emergence of multiple and diverse perspectives situated within (individual and/or broader) real-life experiences and contexts	• Teacher engagement with formative assessment • The overlap and interweave between formative and summative assessment • Development of an interactive and supportive learning community (in each online course) with shared goals and responsibilities	• Interactive • Collaborative • Contextual • Reflective
2	Shared goals and ownership (Ash & Levitt, 2003; Clark, 2010; Oosterhof et al., 2008; Yorke, 2003)	Learner autonomy	• Opportunities for choice of relevant activities to allow for multidimensional perspectives and contextualized learning • Flexibility within assessment guidelines and rubrics based on shared understanding of expected outcomes and emerging needs	• Teacher engagement with formative assessment • Development of a learning community	• Self regulation • Contextual • Active cognitive engagement • Multidimensional • Reflective
		Clarity of learning goals and expected outcomes from the outset of the course	• Clear assessment guidelines and analytical rubrics • Ongoing teacher's guidance, and modelling through offering illustrations and/or exemplars • Opportunities for negotiated meanings of the rubrics within the open discussion forums	• Teacher engagement with Formative assessment • Peer formative assessment • Development of a learning community	• Interactive • Collaborative • Reflective

Continued on following page.

Table 2. continued.

Conceptual Elements for Assessment of Situated and Authentic Learning		Guiding Sub-Elements for Design and Implementation in Online Courses	Operationalization as Manifested in the Collective Case Study	The Underlying Strategies for Online Formative Assessment (as described in Table 1)	Emergent Meaningful Learning Experiences
3	Emphasis on both processes and products (Allal, 2000; Clark, 2010; Oosterhof et al., 2008; Young, 1995; Young et al., 1997)	Process-oriented focus that emphasizes ongoing assessment of both processes and products	• Opportunities for dynamic and sustained interactions among the course participants (individual learner, teacher and peers) within the topical and open discussion forums that fostered with shared understanding of goals and the development of an interactive learning community • Opportunities for ongoing documentation and sharing (publicity or openness) of learning and assessment processes and resulting artefacts including work in progress that fostered shared responsibility	• Teacher engagement with formative assessment • Development of a learning community	• Interactive • Collaborative • Reflective
		Interactive collaborations in ongoing monitoring and assessment of evidence of learning by self and others (teacher and peers)	Shared responsibility within an interactive and supportive learning community in ongoing monitoring and assessment of progress and achievements for purposes of informing desirable feedback and further learning	• Teacher engagement with formative assessment • The overlap and interweave between formative and summative assessment • Self formative assessment • Peer formative assessment • Development of a learning community	• Interactive • Collaborative • Reflective
4	Collaboration in developmental scaffolding (Allal, 2000; Ash & Levitt, 2003; Clark, 2010; Yorke, 2003)	Ongoing formative feedback processes as means of scaffolding within ZPD - Shared responsibility in iterative and dialogic formative feedback processes in which the teacher and peers are sources of external feedback, and self assessment (self reflections) as source of internal feedback	• Teacher engagement in offering formative feedback to the students • Peer formative assessment - peer-peer review and formative feedback • Self assessment - opportunities for self monitoring and reflections • The strong sense of interactive online learning community with shared goals and responsibility facilitated synergy between external and internal feedback. This supported achievement of: (a) performance goals (what I am I expected to do and can I demonstrate the expected capabilities?), and (b) learning goals (what I am I capable of doing and how can I improve my competence?), thus revealing how effective online formative assessment promoted both learning and development characterized by ongoing expansion of ZPD as students developmentally engaged with the various ongoing authentic assessment activities.	• Teacher engagement with formative assessment • The overlap and interweave between formative and summative assessment • Self formative assessment • Peer formative assessment • Development of a learning community	• Interactive • Collaborative • Reflective • Contextual • Self regulation • Active cognitive engagement

meaningful learning experiences that were emergent from learners' engagement with authentic learning and embedded assessment activities with opportunities for socially negotiated meanings and ongoing scaffolding. The evident productivity resulting from collaborative engagement in learning and ongoing assessment demonstrates assessment of situated and authentic learning environments as a collaborative endeavour that is enhanced through shared authenticity. That is, shared authenticity emerges through engagement in an authentic activity within a social context that allow participants to actively collaborate as they construct, share, negotiate, evaluate and validate meanings, from which the individuals reconstruct interpretations in ways that is meaningful within their own conceptual knowledge structures. This implies *designing for shared authenticity* is more productive as compared to attempting to *pre-authenticate* the learning environment because it promotes meaningful learning experiences and learner's development that are emergent from the social interactions-on-authentic activity.

The on-going authentic assessment activities and the inherent formative processes in this study promoted and sustained students' engagement with meaningful processes and learning experiences both individually and collectively. It is through engagement with these activities that the meaningful learning experiences emerged (as depicted in Table 2), which included: active cognitive engagement, contextual, interactive collaborative, multidimensional perspectives, reflective and self regulation. As identified earlier, these experiences are critical in higher education particularly in teacher education because teachers need to engage meaningfully in ways that support them to develop both content knowledge and other relevant professional skills (Correia & Davis, 2008; Mackey, 2011) in the light of transferable and life-long learning that is desirable in the rapidly changing knowledge societies (Gillard et al., 2008).

As indicated in the framework presented in Table 2, various strategies supported the emergence of the illustrated meaningful learning experiences. These strategies comprise various techniques, such as the analytical rubrics that supported the sharing of goals and expected outcomes, and assessment towards their achievement. Other techniques included the topical and open discussion forums, and the enabled on-going documentation and sharing of processes and student-created artefacts which were useful in facilitating ongoing monitoring and assessment of both process and products. These in turn, fostered collaborations in ongoing formative feedback as a means of scaffolding learning that was characterized immediacy, and opportunities for ongoing interactions making feedback an iterative and dialogic process that triggered self-reflections and scaffolded further inquiry. This prompted self-regulatory strategies in pursuit of solutions to the newly identified focus for further inquiry, thus ongoing expansion of the ZPD.

The immediacy, interactivity and adequacy of formative feedback manifested the effectiveness of formative assessment in the recent study. On-going documentation and openness of evidence of learning was a key aspect that contributed to this effectiveness. It offered the teacher enriched opportunities to engage with and reflect upon students' evidence of learning and in turn offer adequate and tailored formative feedback. In addition, ongoing documentation and openness increased opportunities for self and peer formative assessment, through facilitating internal feedback (self-reflections) as students had sufficient opportunities to review and reflect upon the feedback that they received from the teacher and peers, while at the same time giving them sufficient time to review and rethink upon previous contributions before providing feedback to peers. This resulted in feedback that was deeply thought and constructive, which in turn fostered meaningful dialogue.

The on-going documentation and openness of learning and assessment processes and products also increased the uptake of peer-peer feedback as it enabled the students to make their thinking visible to others through articulating their learning strengths and needs. This elicited formative feedback that was tailored to individual's needs, thus prompting students to initiate dialogue about that feedback which influenced the eventual acceptance and/or reconstruction of the feedback. Moreover, this offered students the opportunities to interact with peers' feedback in ways that prompted them to compare their thinking and/or work with that of peers, which in turn stimulated them to revise their learning strategies in order to achieve desired performances. These aspects reveal the importance of ongoing documentation and publicity of processes and student-created artefacts (including work in progress) in enhancing formative feedback in ways that promote meaningful dialogue, reflectivity and self-regulation, which are particularly critical for effective online learning.

It was evident that opportunities for self, peer-peer and teacher formative assessment facilitated a valuable link between internal and external feedback, which supported the students to better internalize external feedback (from the peers and teacher) through constructing their own meaning of the feedback and intentionally use it for productive improvements. The opportunities for ongoing formative feedback while accomplishing the ongoing authentic assessment activities supported students to develop self-regulation and metacognitive dispositions by productively engaging in ways that stimulated further inquiry. This manifested expanding ZPD, which increasingly enabled students to go beyond achievement of performance goals (what they were expected to do as part of summative assessment requirements) to pursuing learning goals (keenness on how to improve own competences for use in their professional practice). This also reveals mastery learning, which suggests that contextualization of assessment activities inevitably reduced the gap between learning for transfer, and performing to demonstrate knowledge for both formative and summative assessment. Self-regulated learning dispositions supported learners to take primary responsibility for their own learning and develop new (or improve) their competences, as well as increasingly transform their identity both individually and as a group. It was evident that the emergent learning experiences supported meaningful learning as manifested by how the students critically reflected on what and how they were learning, and made contextualized connections. This manifests enhanced ability to transfer learning to own professional practice and development of life-long learning dispositions.

The recent study showed that effective online formative assessment promoted meaningful reflectivity that was often characterized by three processes in which students were able to return to experiences, attend to feelings and re-evaluate their experiences. Various researchers have articulated these three sub-processes (returning to the experience, attending to feelings, and re-evaluating the experience) in conceptualization of a meaningful reflective process within the context of professional learning (Boud, 2006; Boud, Keogh, & Walker, 1985; Boud & Walker, 1998). According to Boud (2006), these processes manifest meaningful reflectivity that goes beyond reflecting upon one's learning to reveal reflexivity (reflection in the context of practice) which may support professional teachers as learners to apply their learning in their professional practices, and become reflective practitioners and life-long learners. As reviewed above, the findings of the recent study revealed such reflective processes as students constantly returned to the experience through publicly debriefing their progress in accomplishing the formative assessment activities as well as articulating their developing understandings of content and abilities. Students were also able to accommodate the positive and negative feelings about their learning experiences within the course by inherently narrating their lived experiences as both learners and professionals. The findings further reveal that the students were also able to re-evaluate self and/or peers' learning experiences and integrate new knowledge into their conceptual framework. This was manifested through their constant articulations of how varying learning experiences amongst the course participants had exposed them to multiple and diverse perspectives that shifted their thinking and perceptions. This in turn stimulated students to consider alternative perspectives and motivated them to explore and/or try out new possibilities. In these ways, providing learners (particularly as professional teachers) with opportunities for sharing their existing knowledge and lived experiences supported them to learn more meaningfully as they articulated and reflected upon issues affecting their daily practice within a supportive online learning community, and discerned what they could transfer to their own professional practice.

The opportunities for dynamic and sustained interactivity were vital in sustaining productive learners' engagement with the authentic assessment activities in both online courses. The sustained meaningful interactions and collaborative processes among the self, peers, and the teacher as a supportive online learning community enhanced the opportunities for shared understanding of learning goals and expected outcomes, and ongoing and interactive formative feedback in both courses. The development of an effective learning community with shared goals and responsibility increasingly stimulated the students to become mutually responsible for their own and peers' learning and assessment. The emergent learning community fostered meaningful dialogue that immensely enriched the discourse with divergent perspectives and expanded opportunities for immediate and critical formative feedback. Within these processes, learners were able to build new interpretive frameworks through adopting per-

spectives that were meaningful and relevant to their own contexts.

In summary, the theoretical framework advanced through this chapter and synthesized in Table 2 conforms to situativists' perspectives in that, "authentic activity…is important for learners, because it is the only way they gain access to the standpoint that enables practitioners to act meaningfully and purposefully…activity also provides experience, which is plainly important for subsequent action" (Brown et al., 1989, p. 36). Similarly, the theoretical framework is consistent with the notion of 'assessment within the collaborative ZPD' which emphasize "sustained dialogue [that] is characterized by on-task interaction through which students may consider the perspectives of others, resolve conflicts, and mediate learning during collaborative problem solving"(Clark 2010, p. 346). It is thus agreeable to affirm that, the integration of ongoing authentic assessment activities situated within social and realistic contexts facilitated a dialogical scaffolding structure in studied cases from which valuable learning experiences emerged including the development of an interactive and supportive community within which both the teacher and learners were stimulated to actively collaborate in ongoing formative assessment. Sustained interactive collaborations and ongoing scaffolding were evidently critical in sustaining productive engagement in the studied online learning settings.

Moreover, the theoretical framework advanced from the collective case study reveals appropriate alignment between formative assessment (assessment within the ZPD) and summative assessment (assessment of ZPD) through explicating how they interweaved in beneficial ways to enable the ongoing assessment of situated and authentic learning. Online formative assessment as *assessment within the collaborative ZDP* involved process-oriented assessment of the learners' developmental progress in relation to the learning goals and expected outcomes through shared responsibility in ongoing monitoring, assessment and provision of desirable formative feedback. This in turn supported students to increasingly enhance their achievement in summative assessment which involved the *assessment of ZPD* for the individual students in each of the various ongoing and interweaved authentic assessment activities, which were eventually aggregated into their overall grade in their respective course. Thus, effective online formative assessment is as a function of a developmental process within the collaborative ZPD in which ongoing authentic assessment activities, shared learning goals, ongoing monitoring and interactive formative feedback are at the centrality.

CONCLUSION AND RECOMMENDATION FOR FUTURE RESEARCH

The theoretical framework advanced through this chapter indicates that effective online formative assessment necessiates being undrepinned on situated and authentic learning perspectives. This in turn provides learners with diverse opportunities to develop and demonstrate their knowledge. The theoretical framework as articulated above encompassed overlapping elements and techniques that were utilized in operationalization of embedded assessment of situated and authentic learning.

The framework further illustrates the importance of integrating a variety of on-going assessment activities that encompassed different techniques such engaging students with authentic activities, self assessment tasks and asynchronous collaborations within online discusions forums. One of the key emergent synergy from these variety of techniques and authentic activities is the development of a robust, interactive and supportive learning community with shared goals, ownership and responsibility which in turn enable students to engage meaningfully and became mutually responsible for their own learning.

Acknowledging that this chapter is mainly informed by a limited number of studies, there is need to conduct further empirical studies in order to test application of this framework in varying online contexts. This will contribute further towards its refinement and build further knowledge in the field of online formative assessment in higher education.

REFERENCES

Allal, L., & Pelgrims Ducrey, G. (2000). Assessment of—or in—the zone of proximal development. *Learning and Instruction, 10*(2), 137–152. doi:10.1016/S0959-4752(99)00025-0

Ash, D., & Levitt, K. (2003). Working within the zone of proximal development: Formative assessment as professional development. *Journal of Science Teacher Education, 14*(1), 23–48. doi:10.1023/A:1022999406564

Barab, S. A., Squire, K. D., & Dueber, W. (2000). A co-evolutionary model for supporting the emergence of authenticity. *Educational Technology Research and Development, 48*(2), 37–62. doi:10.1007/BF02313400

Boud, D. (2006). Relocating reflection in the context of practice: rehabilitation or rejection? Proceedings of the Professional Lifelong Learning. Leeds: Beyond Reflective Practice, Trinity and All Saints College; Retrieved from http://www.bretton.ac.uk/medicine/meu/lifelong06/P_DavidBoud.pdf

Boud, D., Keogh, R., & Walker, D. (1985). Promoting reflection in learning: A model. In D. Bould, R. Keogh, & D. Walker (Eds.), *Reflection: Turning experience into learning* (pp. 18–40). London: Kogan Page.

Boud, D., & Walker, D. (1998). Promoting reflection in professional courses: The challenge of context. *Studies in Higher Education, 23*(2), 191–207. doi:10.1080/03075079812331380384

Brown, J. S., Collins, A., & Duguid, P. (1989). Situated cognition and the culture of learning. *Educational Researcher, 18*(1), 32–42. doi:10.3102/0013189X018001032

Clark, I. (2010). Formative assessment: 'There is nothing so practical as a good theory. *Australian Journal of Education, 54*(3), 341–362. doi:10.1177/000494411005400308

Collins, A., Brown, J. S., & Holum, A. (1991). Cognitive apprenticeship: Making thinking visible. *American Educator, 15*(3), 6–11, 38–46.

Collins, A., Brown, J. S., & Newman, S. E. (1989). Cognitive apprenticeship: Teaching the crafts of reading, writing, and mathematics. In L. B. Resnick (Ed.), *Knowing, learning and instruction: Essays in honour of Robert Glaser* (pp. 453–494). Hillsdale, NJ: Erlbaum.

Correia, A. P., & Davis, N. (2008). Intersecting communities of practice in distance education: The program team and the online course community. *Distance Education, 29*(3), 289–306. doi:10.1080/01587910802395813

Gaytan, J., & McEwen, B. C. (2007). Effective online instructional and assessment strategies. *American Journal of Distance Education, 21*(3), 117–132. doi:10.1080/08923640701341653

Gikandi, J. W., Morrow, D., & Davis, N. E. (2011). Online formative assessment in higher education: A review of the literature. *Computers & Education, 57*(4), 2333–2351. doi:10.1016/j.compedu.2011.06.004

Gikandi, J. W. (2012). *Online formative assessment in higher education: Enhancing E-Learning in continuing teacher education.* Unpublished doctoral thesis, University of Canterbury, New Zealand.

Gikandi, J. W., & Mackey, J. (2013). Synergy between authentic assessment activities and learner autonomy: How does this promote shared authenticity in online higher education? *International Journal on E-Learning, 12*(4), 273–301.

Gikandi, J. W. (2013). How can open reflective journals enhance online learning in teacher education? *Journal of Technology and Teacher Education, 21*(1), 5–26.

Gikandi, J. W., & Morrow, D. (in press). Designing and implementing peer formative feedback within online learning environments. *Journal of Technology. Pedagogy and Education.*

Gillard, S., Bailey, D., & Nolan, E. (2008). Ten reasons for IT educators to be early adopters of IT innovations. *Journal of Information Technology Education, 7*, 21–33.

Herrington, J., & Oliver, R. (2000). An instructional design framework for authentic learning environments. *Educational Technology Research and Development, 48*(3), 23–48. doi:10.1007/BF02319856

Lave, J., & Wenger, E. (1991). *Situated Learning: Legitimate Peripheral Participation.* Cambridge: Cambridge University Press. doi:10.1017/CBO9780511815355

Mackey, J. (2009). Virtual learning and real communities: Online professional development for teachers. In E. Stacey & P. Gerbic (Eds.), *Effective Blended Learning Practices: Evidence-Based Perspectives in ICT-Facilitated Education* (pp. 163–181). Hershey: Information Science Reference. doi:10.4018/978-1-60566-296-1.ch009

Mackey, J. (2011). *New Zealand teachers' online professional development and communities of practice.* Unpublished doctoral thesis, Deakin University.

Mackey, J., & Evans, T. (2011). Interconnecting networks of practice for professional learning. *International Review of Research in Open and Distance Learning, 12*(3), 1–18.

McLellan, H. (1993). Evaluation in a situated learning environment. *Educational Technology, 33*(3), 39–45.

Oosterhof, A., Conrad, R. M., & Ely, D. P. (2008). *Assessing Learners Online*. New Jersey: Pearson.

Russell, J., Elton, L., Swinglehurst, D., & Greenhalgh, T. (2006). Using the online environment assessment for learning: A case study of a web-based course in primary care. *Assessment & Evaluation in Higher Education, 31*(4), 465–478. doi:10.1080/02602930600679209

Sorensen, E. K., & Takle, E. S. (2005, April). Investigating knowledge building dialogues in networked communities of practice: A collaborative learning endeavor across cultures. *Interactive Educational Multimedia,* (10), 50-60.

Speck, B. W. (2002). New Learning-teaching-assessment paradigms and the online classroom. *Directions for Teaching and Learning, 91*(91), 5–18. doi:10.1002/tl.61

The Cognition and Technology Group at Vanderbilt (CTGV). (1996). Anchored instruction and situated cognition revisited. In H. McLellan (Ed.), *Situated Learning Perspectives* (pp. 123–154). Englewood Cliffs, NJ: Educational Technology Publications.

Vonderwell, S., Liang, X., & Alderman, K. (2007). Asynchronous discussions and assessment in online learning. *Journal of Research on Technology in Education, 39*(3), 309–328. doi:10.1080/1539 1523.2007.10782485

Vygotsky, L. S. (Ed.). (1978). *Mind in Society: The Development of Higher Psychological Processes*. Cambridge, MA: Harvard University Press.

Wolsey, T. (2008). Efficacy of instructor feedback on written work in an online program. *International Journal on E-Learning, 7*(2), 311–329.

Wood, D., Bruner, J. S., & Ross, G. (1976). The role of tutoring in problem-solving. *Journal of Child Psychology and Psychiatry, and Allied Disciplines, 17*(2), 89–100. doi:10.1111/j.1469-7610.1976. tb00381.x PMID:932126

Yorke, M. (2003). Formative assessmnet in Higher education: Move towards theory and the enhancement of pedagogical practice. *Higher Education, 45*(4), 477–501. doi:10.1023/A:1023967026413

Young, M. F. (1993). Instructional design for situated learning. *Educational Technology Research and Development, 41*(1), 43–58. doi:10.1007/BF02297091

Young, M. F. (1995). Assessment of situated learning using computer environments. *Journal of Science Education and Technology, 4*(1), 89–96. doi:10.1007/BF02211586

Young, M. F., Kulikowich, J. M., & Barab, S. A. (1997). The unit of analysis for situated assessment. *Instructional Science, 25*(2), 33–150. doi:10.1023/A:1002971532689

Young, V., & Kim, D. H. (2010). Using assessment for instuctional improvement: A literature review. *Education Policy Analysis Archives, 18*(19), 1–37. PMID:21841903

KEY TERMS AND DEFINITIONS

Authentic Assessment Activities: Embedded assessment activities that have real-world relevance in ways that provide appropriate level of complexity within a supportive learning community (the individual student, teacher and peers).

Formative Assessment: Also known as 'assessment for learning'. It's a holistic iterative process of establishing what, how much and how well students are learning in relation to the learning goals and expected outcomes in order to inform tailored formative feedback and support further learning.

Formative Feedback: Is type of feedback that supports students to identify their strengths and weaknesses, revise their work, and continuously refine their understanding, which in turn supports them towards engaged and self-regulated learning.

Meaningful Learning: Learning that is robust and transferable to real-life professional practices and contexts; in online learning contexts, it is manifested as active, collaborative and reflective discourse in ways that foster self-regulation.

Online Learning: A form of distance education (or e-learning) primarily conducted through web-based ICT to support the teaching and learning process, and does not require the teacher and the learner to be available at the same time and place.

Self-Regulation: It refers to an active constructive process which stimulates the learners to assume primary responsibility for their learning by going beyond achievement of the expected learning outcomes to engage with tasks and processes that match their own learning goals, interests and contextual needs.

Chapter 15
Challenges and Opportunities for E–Learning in Education:
A Case Study

Ayoub C Kafyulilo
Dar Es Salaam University College of Education, Tanzania

ABSTRACT

This chapter presents a review of literature on the existing opportunities and challenges of adopting e-learning in education in Tanzania and the possible measures to overcome some challenges. The study also assessed the primary factors contributing to the slow and limited use and integration of technology tools by teachers and students despite the availability of technology in their schools. Based on the findings from literature review and government documents (policies and reports), it is evident that one of the determinants of a sustainable e-learning program in education in Tanzania is the availability of reliable and sound infrastructure. In the presence of appropriate technological tools and uninterrupted electricity, better access to Internet, and availability of a good model for technology use, both teachers and students might be willing to implement e-learning programs in their learning institutions.

INTRODUCTION

Technology integration in education to enhance teaching and learning can take place in different forms. Teachers can integrate technology as a presentation tool; by using PowerPoint, animations, video, simulations etc. Technology can also be integrated as a learning platform using Moodle, Blackboard, Rcampus and other virtual learning environments. There are also opportunities to integrate technology as a tool for facilitating distance learning through the use of emails, video conferencing, teleconferencing, Skyping and other synchronous and asynchronous communications. In recent development of educational technology, most of the technology uses in education are moving beyond the normal classroom teaching and learning to virtual learning (Kafyulilo, 2014). Technology is becoming an important tool to facilitate learning from "anywhere anytime" (cf. Collis & Moonen, 2001; Collis & Van der Wende, 2002; de Boer & Collis, 2005). Use of learning platforms and communication tools becomes an important instrument towards an effective implementation of

DOI: 10.4018/978-1-4666-8363-1.ch015

learning flexibility among students and teachers. In facilitating the "anywhere anytime" learning opportunities for students, educational institutions need to develop strong and reliable e-learning systems. Nihuka (2011) citing several authors argues that, e-learning technologies support the following flexibilities: interactions and collaboration between instructor and students; location and time barriers between instructors and students, and delivery of instructional contents. With the use of e-learning systems, teachers can use technology as a presentation tool, learning platform and also a communication tool.

According to Nihuka (2011) e-learning technologies such as e-mail have made web-enhanced teaching and learning possible to complement with the traditional course delivery processes in distance education in developing countries. Nihuka adds that, e-learning technologies such as computer and internet can enhance flexibility in searching and accessing resources from webs, thus, contributing to greater students achievements.

While there are multitudes of approaches to integrate technology in education, Tanzania has invested mostly on the use of technology as a presentation tool through the use of PowerPoint, animations, videos and simulations. A number of ongoing projects to integrate technology in education in Tanzania are focused on developing teachers' knowledge and skills of using technology to demonstrate some concepts or present some learning materials to students (Kafyulilo, 2014). Technology is integrated as a tool to help teachers to present a subject matter to students rather than a tool for mutual interaction between students and a teacher. Most of the technology integration efforts have paid little focus on the development of online learning systems at both low and high level of education so as to facilitate interactive learning. The Ministry of Education and Vocational Training of Tanzania is investing a significant amount of resources on the installation of computers in schools and training of teachers on how to use those computers for simplifying the

presentation of materials (cf. Hooker et al., 2011). Little is done to install facilities that facilitate e-learning in Tanzania; also there are limited efforts to develop teachers' and students' knowledge of using ICT tools for e-learning.

BACKGROUND TO ICT DEVELOPMENT EDUCATION IN TANZANIA

ICT Policies in Tanzania

The first national ICT policy in Tanzania was developed in 2003. This policy had two main objectives: (1) to provide a national framework to enable ICT to contribute towards achieving national development goals; and (2) to transform Tanzania into a knowledge-based society through the application of ICT (URT, 2003). The 2003 ICT policy did not specifically focus on the ICT development in education, and had no relationship with the earlier initiatives to integrate technology in education. It rather focused on guiding the overall use of ICT in the country, including mobile phones, computer, internet and other related ICT tools, be it in schools, in offices or at the market. According to Tilya (2008) the 2003 policy can be described as an emerging policy in education, where ICT is just in the process of getting introduced in schools.

In 2007 the "ICT policy for basic education" was formulated which aimed to promote the acquisition and appropriate use of literary, social, scientific, vocational, technological, professional and other forms of knowledge, skills and understanding for the development and improvement of man and society (URT, 2007). This policy incorporates the integration of ICT in pre-primary, primary, secondary and teacher education, as well as non-formal and adult education (Hare, 2007; URT, 2007). This policy considers issues of ICT infrastructure, curriculum and content, training and capacity development, planning, procurement and administration. It also pays attention to the management, support and sustainability, and monitoring and evaluation (Hare, 2007; URT, 2007). Such a policy, according to Tilya (2008) could be described as an applying policy, which refers to teachers' use of ICT for both administration and instruction purposes.

ICT Policy Implementation in Schools and Teacher Education in Tanzania

The ICT (2003 and 2007) policies are implemented in collaboration with other education development policies governing the education sector in Tanzania. These are; the Education and Training Policy of 1995, the Primary Education and Development Plan (PEDP) 2002-2006, and the Secondary Education Development Plan (SEDP) 2004-2009 (URT, 2009). All three documents emphasize the need for access to and improved quality of education for all despite the increasing number of enrolments. PEDP and SEDP prioritize ICT-based information management at all levels and an introduction of computer courses into primary and secondary education (Hare, 2007; URT, 2009).

Although there is evidence that pre-service teachers are prepared to use technology in their teaching, studies (Hare, 2007; Vesisenaho, 2007) report poor technology integration in schools. Teachers are not using technology as a pedagogical tool to enhance teaching and learning in their subjects despite the fact that they learn from colleges on how to integrate technology in teaching. Studies (Hare, 2007; Ottevanger et al, 2007; Vesisenaho, 2007) report that ICT use in schools in Tanzania is mostly confined to management and administration purposes. According to Hare (2007) in most of the schools ICT is used for keeping students' records and typing office documents such as letters. In 2009, the government of Tanzania developed the Information and Communication Technology for Teacher Professional Development (ICT-TPD)

as an implementation of the ICT for basic education policy and the Education Sectoral Plans and programmes. The framework aimed at developing teachers' capacity of integrating technology in Science, Mathematics and English subjects in Tanzania secondary schools (URT, 2009).

E-Learning Development in Education in Tanzania

The learning approach, which does not necessarily require the students to be at the learning institution, was first introduced in Tanzania in 1979 when the Anglo-Tanzanian study to explore the distance education mode of delivery particularly for university education was commissioned (Cutting, 1989). The recommendations by the Anglo-Tanzanian study, lead to the establishment of the Open University of Tanzania (OUT), which was the first Tanzanian institution to offer distance education in the country. According to Nihuka (2011), the Open University of Tanzania saves two important functions; first it offers learning opportunities for those who could not be given places in conventional universities for reasons of their inflexible schedules. Second, the university provides methods of learning not limited in time, pace and place. The "anywhere anytime" learning opportunity is the most important learning aspect that learners miss from conventional universities.

At the beginning, distance learning was offered through printed documents, which were exchanged between the learner and the teacher through posting. According to Nihuka (2011) this learning approach posed some challenges to both students and teachers. Example there were delays in the delivery of study materials, course outlines and learning resources, lack of regular interaction between instructors and students, lack of immediate feedback on student learning, and feelings of isolation among students. In order to overcome these challenges the Open University of Tanzania introduced the e-learning system in which students started first to learn through the use of emails and later-on through learning management systems such as Moodle. As from late 2005 most higher learning institutions in the country were using different learning management system for course registration, and display of examination results. For example the University of Dar es salaam started to use ZALONGWA program and later-on ARIS. In recent years, use of e-learning programs, including learning management systems has been observed in private secondary schools and some colleges. However, the e-learning application in lower levels of education in Tanzania is still low.

E-LEARNING PROGRAMS IN TANZANIA: CHALLENGES

While there are significant efforts by the government and non-governmental organization to integrate technology in teaching at all levels of education in Tanzania, findings from several studies conducted in Tanzania (Kafyulilo, Mafumiko and Mkonongwa, 2012; Mwalongo, 2011) reveal a number of factors contributing to low uptake of technology in education. According to Kafyulilo et al. (2012) some of these factors include; limited teachers' knowledge and confidence of using technology to facilitate e-learning programs; limited access to technology and low level of technology use (practical use) in the courses they attend in teacher training colleges. The limited opportunity for pre-service teachers to practice the use of ICT for teaching limits their ability to use various ICT tools to support teaching and learning when they get employed (LeBaron, McDonough& Robinson, 2009). According to LeBaron et al. (2009) and Kirschner, Wubbels and Brekelmans (2008) teachers' incompetency in technology integration poses some challenges on how teachers are trained to integrate technology with pedagogy and content. The limited technological knowledge and limited opportunity to practice the use of technology while at the teacher training college, contribute to lack of teachers' motivation and self-confidence (Cox,

Preston & Cox, 1999; Pelgrrum, 2001), which is caused by the fear that ICT is complicated and difficult to use (Snoeyink & Ertmer, 2001). According to Kafyulilo et al. (2012) the first thing that is supposed to be addressed in the effort to integrate technology in education in Tanzania, is the development of teachers' competencies of using technology in their own learning. Teachers need to experience e-learning approach in their own learning programs so as to be able to implement it in their own teaching. Thus, emphasis should be put on how teachers learn through the use of technology. This will enable them to use technology in the same was as they learned, when they engage in the actual teaching.

Most of the sophisticated technological tools require the use of electricity. In Tanzania, power rationing is a major problem and is causing a serious setback to the integration of ICT in teaching. In a study by Kafyulilo et al. (2012), majority of the pre-service teachers reported that, their efforts to prepare technology-based lessons are overturned by the uncertainty resulting from unreliable electricity supply. In addition, less than 10% of Tanzania's population is using electricity, thus more than 90% of the country's population is without electricity (Msyani, 2013), as well, more than 90% of schools are not connected to electricity. This makes it very difficult for a teacher to think of ICT when planning a lesson, and therefore limited use of ICT to facilitate e-learning programs.

Findings on ICT in education in Tanzania (Swarts and Wachira, 2010) also revealed that majority of schools do not have technological tools. Absence of technological tools has an impact on the teachers' motivation and development of their technology integration knowledge and skills. Teachers who learned to use technology from colleges do not have an opportunity to practice the use technology in schools because of lack of technology in schools. This causes some teachers to lose their ICT knowledge and skills and sometimes become disinterested in technology and lose their technology integration competencies they acquired from teacher training colleges. According to Knezek and Christensen (2008), successful integration of technology in teaching, requires; teachers' "technological skills", teachers' "willingness to use technology" and "availability of technological tool" which makes up the Will Skill Tool (WST) model. Thus, lack of technological tools and limited teachers' technological skills in most schools in Tanzania, makes the WST model incomplete and leads to ineffective development of e-learning programs in Tanzania.

While e-learning would offer an opportunity for students to interact with the technology, the subject and the teachers, at anytime anywhere, schools in Tanzania are banning the use of some technological tools which can easily facilitate e-learning; example mobile phones and internet (Kafyulilo, 2014). According to Kafyulilo (2014) the government of Tanzania is banning the use of mobile phones in schools, which is a potential e-learning tool. Moreover, some teachers admitted to have negative attitude towards the new technologies. For example there are teachers who believe that when students are exposed to Internet, they can surf materials other than those related to learning. According to Kafyulilo (2014) "teachers have some anticipated negative outcomes of technology use in schools, some of which is the likelihood of the students to use technology for flirting, which is not allowed to students, and also the likelihood of students to engage in immoral acts such as watching pornographic videos" (p.13). This belief has also influenced the banning of the use of social networks among students. Students in schools are not allowed to use Facebook, hi5, twitter, blogs etc., for fear that they may engage in appropriate behaviour learned on the Internet.

Practically, mobile phones are the defacto most important networked knowledge exchange technology and the most powerful universally-accessible computing device in the hands of Tanzanians and Africans (Ford and Batchelor 2007). Mobile phones are believed to have the capacity of saving best the purpose of e-learning

in education, yet it is the most unaccepted learning tool by both the government and teachers in Tanzania. Ban of the use of some technology among children is also evidence among parents who prevent their children from accessing internet from internet café or at home with the fear that they may be subjected to unacceptable behaviours. The existing fear of the parents, teachers and the government of Tanzania over the use of some technologies in teaching and learning, present a serious barrier to the development of e-learning programs in the country.

Until now, it is only the Open University of Tanzania, which embraces the use of e-learning programs to support students' learning. All other learning institutions (particularly lower education) do not have any e-learning programs, not even the online learning platforms. In recent developments, most of the Tanzanian higher education institutions have developed an online system for course registration and display of examination results. For example the University of Dar es Salaam, which is the oldest university in the country, had once used Zalongwa as a platform for displaying students' results, and currently they are using ARIS for the same purpose. There are no efforts so far made to have a well-established platform for offering an e-learning program for students.

Al-adwan and Smedle (2012) citing Macpherson et al. (2006) argue that any organization striving to obtain a successful e-learning strategy must be prepared culturally as well as technologically. They further argue that, cultural factors have tremendous impact on how people learn, including the style of interaction and communication, constituting the core foundation of e-learning. According to Al-adwan and Smedle (2012) cultural factors affect system development and design as well as system usability and acceptance. This is true in Tanzania, where the development of e-learning systems has been delayed on the fear of the negative consequences resulting from the adoption of the approaches. This has made the design and deployment of e-learning systems in the country to become difficult and unreliable. Some efforts need to be taken by the government and stakeholders in education in Tanzania to develop an understanding of the importance of technology in students' learning and strategies to ensure safe use of technology in education. Al-adwan and Smedle (2012) argue that in order to design and promote a successful system in an e-learning environment, cultural orientation must be considered.

Schools also face challenges due to power cuts and limited access to computers and the Internet (Nihuka & Voogt, 2011). However, although the challenge of power cut is persisting in the country, the access to computers and Internet is improving compared to the situation reported in Nihuka (2008). Currently the challenge remains the poor Internet speeds due to narrow bandwidth that most of the educational institutions are allowed to buy from the Internet supplying companies such as Simba net. In the recent study by Nzilano and Kafyulilo (2014) at Dar es salaam University College of Education, it was revealed that the whole college was buying a total of 2 GB internet bandwidth per month. This amount of bundle was reported to be insufficient for normal internet access, hindering the opportunity to read emails and download some learning materials.

E-LEARNING PROGRAMS IN EDUCATION IN TANZANIA: OPPORTUNITIES

Despite the challenges that the government, schools and teachers encounter in integrating technology in education, there are opportunities to enhance ICT integration in teaching in the country. Some of these opportunities include the high level of teachers and students' motivation to use ICT in teaching and learning. According to Cox et al (1999) and Pelgrum (2001), teachers' motivation towards technology use has a significant impact on their decision to integrate ICT in their teaching.

Given that there is an environment that supports technology integration in teaching and learning. Motivated teachers and students are more likely to integrate technology in their teaching and learning respectively, than teachers and students who are not motivated to use ICT.

Although some teachers reportedly had negative attitudes towards the use of technology in teaching and learning (particularly internet and mobile phones), there are majority of them who were positive and motivated to use technology in teaching. However, the reported negative attitude of some of the teachers should not be neglected since it retards the efforts to have e-learning developed in education in Tanzania. Evidence from studies (Cox et al, 1999; Snoeyink & Ertmer, 2001) shows that teachers' attitude towards technology is related to their competency on the use of ICT in teaching. Teachers, who have ability to use technology without problems in teaching, are the ones, who will embrace the use of technology in the classroom, and teachers who are incompetent in technology will cite reasons for not using technology. However, the government of Tanzania is currently investing significant amount of resources in the development of technology in schools. Several projects are currently being conducted to develop teachers' knowledge and skills of integrating technology in teaching. For example in the meanwhile an ICT for science mathematics and English subjects (ICT-SMEs) project is being conducted in the country under the consultancy of Global e-School and Community Initiatives (GeSCI). The project is being implemented throughout the country to develop in-service teachers' knowledge and skills of integrating technology in science, mathematics and English teaching.

Additionally, negative attitude towards ICT use, is related to the presumed high costs of technological tools.

Some schools leaders tend to discourage ICTs in order to avoid the costs of buying computers, television, video set, CD ROM and other technological tools for their schools. Currently there are a numerous funding organizations, which are providing computers to schools as a grant or selling at the lowest possible prices. For example in the recent development VIAFRICA is being involved in the development of teachers' knowledge and skills of using online learning materials to enhance students' learning in science subjects. On the other hand, the Swedish International Development Agency (SIDA) and the International Institute of Community Development (IICD) have helped Tanzania to install computers in all secondary schools that are connected to electricity. The ICT development in education in Tanzania is currently focusing on the installation of Internet, which can easily facilitate the learning from "anywhere at any time".

The other opportunity for teachers to integrate technology in education is the availability of ICT Policy for Basic Education, which was formulated in 2007. According to Hare (2007) and Mambo (2001) delay in the implementation of ICT in education in Tanzania was partly caused by the absence of a policy that guides the integration of technology in education. The presence of ICT policy for basic education can guide the government, schools, and teachers' plans to integrate technology in education in the country (cf. Tilya, 2008). However, for a policy to have an impact on the effective integration of technology in teaching particularly e-learning there is a need for commitment from the government officials and school leaders.

The coming up of Technological Pedagogical Content Knowledge (TPACK) which is considered to be an effective framework for technology integration in education (Koehler & Mishra, 2009; Niess et al., 2009) can best serve the development of technology in education in Tanzania. Koehler and Mishra (2009) and Niess et al. (2009) see the low uptake of ICT by teachers as being associated with the poor knowledge of the content, instructional strategies and representations of a particular science or mathematical topics sup-

ported by digital technologies to demonstration, verification, and drill and practice (cf. Webb, 2008). Thus, understanding of TPACK will provide a better guide for effective development of e-learning in education in Tanzania.

In addition, the growing concept of teachers' collaboration in teams and professional learning communities provide a new hope towards enhanced confidence and competencies of integrating ICT in teaching among teachers. Recent researches in Tanzania have proposed teachers learning in teams as an effective approach for developing technology integration knowledge and skills. Through working collaboratively, teachers can get an opportunity to share knowledge, skills, ideas and concepts between and among each other (Handelzalts, 2009). This can help teachers to develop knowledge of various technology integration approaches and enhance their motivation towards ICT use to support various learning processes. In the meantime, Tanzania is planning to build a large internet supply program through the national fibre optic cable. This is expected to offer a better supply of internet for educational institutions and for individuals. In turn this will open up a door for students in all level of education to engage in the learning wherever they are and at a time, which is convenient to them.

IMPLEMENTING E-LEARNING IN EDUCATION IN TANZANIA

Hare (2007) and Resta & Laferriere (2008), present several factors promoting and or hindering the implementation of e-learning in education in Tanzania (see Table 1).

CONCLUSION

One of the major factors determining the development and implementation of e-learning in education is the presence of reliable infrastructure for

Table 1. Enabling and constraining factors for e-learning implementation in schools

Factors	Promoting Features	Hindering Features
Policy framework and implementation	The new policy (ICT in basic Education of 2007), is expected to help in guiding the development of ICT in education including the use of e-learning and therefore make the ministry assume leadership	The policy puts emphasis on the installation of hardware in schools with less attention on the benefits teachers and students can get from ICT. While the policy mentions e-learning, no strategic plans are addressed in the policy on how e-learning will be implemented in schools (Hare, 2007).
Infrastructure and cost of Bandwidth	More hardware and software are being installed in colleges and secondary schools. However, the building up of the national fibre optic cable would serve the best internet provision in the country, thus, better e-learning programs.	Despite the liberalization of the telecommunications sector, the cost of bandwidth is still out of reach of many schools especially in rural areas, making it difficult to implement e-learning programs.
Language of the Internet	Currently there are online content in Kiswahili and some applications come with Kiswahili dictionaries. The advent of open source software can help to localize ICTs and the Internet and thus increased access to e-learning content.	Language is one of the major inhibitors of ICT use in Tanzania. Many people are comfortable in Kiswahili and only learn English in later years of primary school or early secondary school. This poses a challenge to both teachers and students on the use of e-learning programs because most of the electronic devices are operated in English.
Electricity	There are plans at hand to have a reliable supply of electricity in the country.	The national electricity grid is still limited to commercially viable areas missing out most of the schools, which are in the rural areas. This has increased the cost of owning ICT infrastructure and implementing e-learning programs in rural areas.
Tutor technicians		ICT in education is still a new concept. The teacher training colleges are now training teachers in ICT. A lot more effort is required to give in-service training to teachers on ICT.
New technologies	There is proliferation of new technologies that are promising to drastically lower the cost of entry and ownership of ICT in schools. These include open source software and wireless connectivity which have a wider coverage in the country. This would enhance the "anywhere anytime" learning opportunities for students.	Majority of teachers and student are not competent in using most of the new technological tools thus a need for training so as to be able to use those ICT tools (cf. Resta & Laferriere, 2008).

e-learning programs. Once there are sufficient technological tools, sufficient supply of electricity, accessibility to internet, availability of a good model for technology use, both teachers and students will implement e-learning programs in their learning institutions. Given the opportunities that Tanzania is currently having, for the integration of ICT in education, there is more likelihood that the future of e-learning in the country is promising. However, some efforts should be made to train teachers on the implementation of e-learning programs instead of the focus on the training of teachers on the use of ICT to present or demonstrate some concepts in the classroom by using data projector and a projection screen. Training program should go beyond, lesson presentation in the classroom to a more flexible learning opportunities for students. Teacher training programs should prepare teachers to design lessons by using some learning platforms such as teletop, blackboard, Moodle etc. Teacher training programs should not only focus on the preparation of teachers to use a computer based software such as PowerPoint, it should also focus on the preparation of teachers to use the wide range of technologies such as mobile phones, iPads, TV, Radios, digital cameras, videos etc. to facilitate learning within and away from school.

With the emerging demand for learning flexibility, there is no way will Tanzania continue to avoid the use of mobile phones for education purposes including e-learning programs. Mobile phone is the only networked technology that is on the hands of most of the Tanzanians. At least 60% of the students in Tanzania are reported to have access to mobile phones and that majority of them have the knowledge of operating mobile phones (Kafyulilo, 2014). Mobile phones can save the costs of buying technology for the school, instead there will only be a cost for the training of teachers and students on how to use mobile phones to access online materials and enhance their learning through the use of various learning management systems.

Overall, the author of this chapter is having a view that an effective implementation of ICT in education in Tanzania will only be meaningful when technology is able to offer learning flexibility to students and teachers. There should be efforts to enhance e-learning programs in both schools and other learning institutions (particularly higher learning institutions) in the country. Bringing technology particularly desktop computers in schools will not help to overcome the current challenges of students' learning in science and mathematics subjects in the country. The impact of technology will be significant when students are exposed to learning at any time and at any place, and when students can access the learning materials from wherever they are.

REFERENCES

Al-adwan, A., & Smedle, J. (2012). Implementing E-Learning in the Jordanian Higher Education System: Factors Affecting Impact. *International Journal of Education and Development using Information and Communication Technology, 8*(1), 121-135.

Collis, B., & Moonen, J. (2001). *Flexible learning in a digital world: Experiences and expectations.* London, UK: Routledge.

Collis, B., & Van der Wende, M. C. (Eds.). (2002). *Models of technology and change in higher education: An international comparative survey on the current and future use of ICT in Higher Education.* Enschede: PrintPartners Ipskamp.

Cox, M., Preston, C., & Cox, K. (1999, September). What motivates teachers to use ICT? *Paper presented at the British Educational Research Association Annual Conference.* University of Sussex, Brighton.

Cutting, A. K. (1989). *The role of media technology within the proposed Open University of Tanzania.* Dar es Salaam: The Open University of Tanzania.

De Boer, W., & Collis, B. (2005). Becoming more systematic about flexible learning: Beyond time and distance. *Research in Learning Technology, 13*(1), 33–48. doi:10.1080/0968776042000339781

Ford, M., & Batchelor, J. (2007). From zero to hero: Is the mobile phone a viable learning tool for Africa? *3rd International Conference on Social and Organizational Informatics and Cybernetics: SOIC.* 12-15 July 2007, Orlando, USA.

Handelzalts, A. (2009). *Collaborative curriculum development in teacher design teams*. Enschede: PrintPartners Ipskamp.

Hare, H. (2007). Survey of ICT in Education in Tanzania. In G. Farrell, S. Isaacs & M. Trucano, (eds). Survey of ICT and education in Africa (volume 2): 53 country reports. Washington, DC: infoDev /World Bank.

Hooker, M., Mwiyeria, E., & Verma, A. (2011). *ICT Competency Framework for Teachers in Tanzania: Teacher Development for the 21ˢᵗ Century (TDev21) pilot*. Dar Es Salaam: Ministry of Education and Vocational Training.

Kafyulilo, A. C. (2014). Access, use and perceptions of teachers and students towards mobile phones as a tool for teaching and learning in Tanzania. *Education and Information Technologies*, *19*(1), 115–127. doi:10.1007/s10639-012-9207-y

Kafyulilo, C. A., Mafumiko, F. M. S., & Mkonongwa, L. (2012). Challenges and opportunities of integrating technology in education in Tanzania. *Journal of Adult Education*, *19*, 18–33.

Kirscher, P., Wubbrls, T., & Brekelmans, M. (2008). Benchmarks for teacher education programs in the pedagogical use of ICT. In J. Voogt & G. Knezek (Eds.), *International handbook of information and technology in primary and secondary education* (pp. 435–447). New York, NY: Springer. doi:10.1007/978-0-387-73315-9_26

Knezek, G., Christensen, R., & Fluke, R. (2003, April). *Testing a Will, Skill, Tool Model of Technology Integration*. Paper Presented at the Annual Meeting of the American Educational Research Association. Chicago, IL.

Koehler, M., & Mishra, P. (2009). What is technological pedagogical content knowledge? *Contemporary Issues in Technology & Teacher Education*, *9*(1), 60–70.

LeBaron, J., McDonough, E., & Robinson, J. M. (2009). *Research Report for GeSCI Meta-Review of ICT in Education*. Retrieved from http://gesci.org/assets/files/Research/meta-research-phase2.pdf

Mambo, H. L. (2001). Tanzania: An overview of information communications technology (ICT) development in libraries and information services. *The International Information & Library Review*, *33*(1), 89–96. doi:10.1006/iilr.2000.0161

Msyani, C. M. (2013). *Current status of energy sector in Tanzania: executive exchange on developing an ancillary service market*. Washington, DC: USEA.

Mwalongo, A. (2011). Teachers' perceptions about ICT for teaching, professional development, administration and personal use. *International Journal of Education and Development using Information and Communication Technology*, *7*(3), 36-49.

Niess, M. L., Ronau, R. N., Shafer, K. G., Driskell, S. O., Harper, S. R., Johnston, C., & Kersaint, G. (2009). Mathematics teacher TPACK standards and development model. *Contemporary Issues in Technology & Teacher Education*, *9*(1), 4–24.

Nihuka, K. A. (2008). *The feasibility of e-learning integration in course delivery at the Open University of Tanzania*. Unpublished, Master Dissertation, University of Twente, Enschede.

Nihuka, K. A. (2011). *Collaborative course design to support implementation of e-learning by instructors*. Enschede: PrintPartners Ipskamp. doi:10.3990/1.9789036532358

Nihuka, K. A., & Voogt, J. (2011). Instructors and students competences, perception and access to e-learning technologies: Implications for e-learning technologies at the Open University of Tanzania. *International Journal on E-Learning*, *10*(1), 63–85.

Nzilano, J., & Kafyulilo, A. C. (2012). Development of Information and Communication Technology in Education in Tanzania: How is DUCE playing its role? *Journal of Education, Humanities and Sciences*, *1*(2), 64–78.

Ottevanger, W., van den Akker, J., & de Feiter, L. (2007). Developing science, mathematics, and ICT education in Sub-Saharan Africa: Patterns and promising practices. (World Bank Working Paper No.101). Washington, DC: The World Bank. doi:10.1596/978-0-8213-7070-4

Pelgrum, W. (2001). Obstacles to the integration of ICT in education: Results from a worldwide educational assessment. *Computers & Education*, *37*(2), 163–178. doi:10.1016/S0360-1315(01)00045-8

Resta, P., & Laferriere, T. (2008). Issues and challenges related to digital equity. In J. Voogt & G. Knezek (Eds.), *International handbook of information technology in primary and secondary education* (pp. 765–778). New York, NY: Springer. doi:10.1007/978-0-387-73315-9_44

Snoeyink, R., & Ertmer, P. (2001). Thrust into technology: How veteran teachers respond. *Journal of Educational Technology Systems*, *30*(1), 85–111. doi:10.2190/YDL7-XH09-RLJ6-MTP1

Swarts, P., & Wachira, E. M. (2010). Tanzania: ICT in education situational analysis. Dar Es Salaam: Global e-Schools and Communities Initiatives (geSCI).

Tilya, F. (2008). IT and educational policy in the sub-Saharan African region. In J. Voogt & G. Knezek (Eds.), *International handbook of information technology in primary and secondary education* (pp. 1145–1159). New York, NY: Springer. doi:10.1007/978-0-387-73315-9_73

United Republic of Tanzania. (2003). *National Information and Communication Technology policy*. Dar es Salaam: Ministry of Communication and Transport.

URT. (2007). *Information and Communication Technology policy for basic education*. Dar es salaam: Tanzania Printing House.

URT. (2009). *A framework for ICT use in teacher professional development in Tanzania*. Dar es Salaam: Tanzania Printing House.

Vesisenaho, M. (2007). *Developing university-level introductory ICT education in Tanzania: A contextualized approach*. (Unpublished, PhD Dissertation). University of Joensuu, Joensuu.

Webb, M. (2008). Impact of IT on science education. In J. Voogt & G. Knezek (Eds.), *International handbook of information technology in primary and secondary education* (pp. 133–148). New York, NY: Springer. doi:10.1007/978-0-387-73315-9_8

KEY TERMS AND DEFINITIONS

E-Learning: E-learning refers to the kind of learning conducted via electronic media and devices such as computers, mobile phones, iPads etc., to deliver part, or the whole course through in-school or full distance learning.

ICT: The terms ICT and technologies are used interchangeably to refer to any digital tool that can support teaching and learning.

Learning Flexibility: Refers to the learning opportunities that are offered by technology, where a learner can learn from any place and at any time, provided that she has a digital device that can be connected to the Internet, such as mobile phone, laptop, or iPad.

Learning Platforms: Refers to digital learning environment that facilitate students learning from anywhere at any time. Examples of such learning platforms include Moodle and blackboard.

PEDP: Is a short term for Primary Education and Development Plan. The plan was developed between 2002 and 2006 to address the problem of low enrolment rates of pupils in primary school and quality of education in Tanzania.

SEDP: Is a short term for Secondary Education Development Plan. The plan was developed between 2004 and 2009 to address the problem of low enrolment rates of students in secondary schools and quality of secondary education in Tanzania.

Technology Integration: Refers to the use of various digital and hardware tools to facilitate the process of teaching and learning in and outside the classroom.

TPACK: Is a short term for Technological Pedagogical Content Knowledge – a model to describe the knowledge requirements for teachers to integrate technology in teaching.

Chapter 16
Opportunities and Challenges in Implementing Distance Learning and e-Learning:
A Case Study

Jennifer Kasanda Sesabo
Mzumbe University, Tanzania

Rashid Mfaume
Mzumbe University, Tanzania

Dominik T. Msabila
Mzumbe University, Tanzania

ABSTRACT

In Tanzania, the growing demand for education due to massive enrolment in universities calls for adoption of Distance Learning (DL) and e-learning. Other factors for adoption include limited space and pace of learning, pedagogical weaknesses, and shortage of teaching staff. Mzumbe University also experiences the same as it operates satellite teaching centres of Morogoro town, Mbeya, Dar es Salaam, Tanga and Mwanza. This has made the university consider shifting from conventional delivery modes to alternative pedagogical strategies using Information and Communications Technology (ICT). The aim is to ensure effective delivery of quality education. There are opportunities and challenges. The challenges include absence of national and institutional quality assurance system framework on e-learning and distance education, and shortage of teaching staff and ICT facilities. Thus, universities need appropriate budget and resource investment to support capacity building for teaching staff and students, and formulating policies, guidelines and operational framework on distance learning and e-learning.

DOI: 10.4018/978-1-4666-8363-1.ch016

INTRODUCTION

In the recent years significant changes have been taking place in higher education institutions that have led to significant transformations of their policies and practices. Irrespective of its delivering protocols including e-learning, and home studies in Tanzania, Distance Learning (DL) has been advocated as a means of increasing access and addressing constrained infrastructures in conventional higher education centres. These changes have been necessitated by a need to meet a growing demand for higher education. This demand has placed education institutions in a situation where they are needed to respond creatively and innovatively to the needs of the students, within the constraints of limited funding and inadequate infrastructures. Flexible learning is seen as a means by which institutions can address this challenge. E-learning has been hailed as a cheaper and flexible alternative tool for raising the number of students who have access to higher education, especially marginalized groups in rural areas (Dhanarajan, 2001; Patton, 2000; Potashnik & Capper, 1998). Consequently, many universities today offer more flexible learning, including technology-based mode of delivery of e-learning, and open - distance education, the use and demand of which has been growing steadily over recent years. However, e-learning can thus improve teaching and learning practices in the higher education, if pedagogical and quality assurance issues are properly considered.

Like in many other countries in sub Saharan Africa, the absence of national and institutional quality operational framework of education offered through distance and e-learning portfolio has generated skepticism and intense debates about quality of delivery and hence degree outcomes. In Tanzania, and Mzumbe University in particular, this challenge is apparent. Likewise literature indicates that the successful implementation of DL and e-learning in developing countries is hindered by many factors which include wrong perception of internal stakeholders who are the main users; inadequate technical capacity; inadequate infrastructure to support distance learning and e-learning; absence of Learning Management Systems (LMS); and organizations culture. For example, Anderson and Grönlund (2009) showed that individuals characteristics, course content, support services, context (organization and culture) as well as technology availability play an important role in e-learning utilization. In DL, course content development is an important input which influences the quality of education (Douidi, Djoudi and Khentount, 2006). All these factors provide both opportunities and challenges that are likely to enhance or compromise the quality of instituting DL and e-learning as a teaching and learning tools in higher education institutions such as Mzumbe University.

There is a widespread belief that Education Technology or e-learning, can enhance teaching and learning practices (Higgins, 2003), and create an "ideal" learning environment (Newborne, 2002, Marshall, 2002, Honey & McMillan, 2005). Therefore, its adoption and use have become an integral part of both the teaching and learning process in many universities today. Educational Technology can have the greatest impact on improving student learning and achieving measurable educational objectives (Nutball, 2000; Hawkins, Panush, & Spielvogel, 1996). In addition, it can empower teachers and learners, transforming teaching and learning processes from being highly teacher-dominated to student-centred (Higgins, 2003; Trucano, 2005). This transformation can improve the quality of learning. Moreover, Educational Technology may provide students with valuable skills that are sought by the job market.. Thus, such technology creates opportunities for learners to develop their creativity as well as cognitive skills, critical thinking skills, information reasoning skills, communication skills and other higher order thinking skills (Trucano, 2005; Means, Penuel & Padilla, (2001). 1994; Chigona & Chigona, 2010).

This chapter is organized into five main parts. The first part, the introduction, unpacks the general concepts and essence of Distance Education (DE) and e-learning. In the second part, we present theoretical framework for e-learning and distance education. The purpose is to set grounds for reflections and discussion on opportunities and challenges of instituting and implementing DL and e-learning. In the third part we present the perspective of Mzumbe University, and show different efforts undertaken to institute DL and e-learning. In the fourth part we present opportunities and challenges of e-learning and DL at Mzumbe University. The last part covers conclusion and recommendations on how Mzumbe University and the like institutions can effectively institute and implement DL and e-learning.

Theoretical and Conceptual Perspective

Distance Learning and E-Learning

Over the past seven years, the e-learning community in Africa has grown in leaps and bounds (E-Learning Africa Report 2012). According to UNESCO E-learning has started to make way into developing countries and is believed to have huge potential for governments struggling to meet a growing demand for education while facing an escalating shortage of teachers (UNESCO, 2006). E-learning is seen as a tool for raising the number of students in having access to higher education, especially marginalized groups in rural areas, by being a cheaper and more flexible alternative (Dhanarajan, 2001; Patton, 2000; Potashnik and Capper, 1998)

According to Naidu (2006), e-learning is commonly referred to the intentional use of networked information and communications technology in teaching and learning. Other common and interchangeably used terminologies are online learning, virtual learning, distributed learning, network and web-based learning. Fundamentally,

they all refer to educational processes that utilize information and communications technology to mediate asynchronous as well as synchronous learning and teaching activities.

E-learning (or eLearning) is the use of electronic media and information and communication technologies (ICT) in education. E-learning is broadly inclusive of all forms of educational technology in learning and teaching. E-learning is inclusive of, and is broadly synonymous with multimedia learning, technology-enhanced learning (TEL), computer-based instruction (CBI), computer managed instruction, computer-based training (CBT), computer-assisted instruction or computer-aided instruction (CAI), internet-based training (IBT), web-based training (WBT), online education, virtual education, virtual learning environments (VLE) (which are also called learning platforms), mobile-learning, and digital educational collaboration (Naidu, 2006).

E-learning content can include: text, images, animation, audio, and video. The ways of delivering e-learning content include: Internet, Intranet, CD, DVD and USB. Ways of accessing e-learning content include: Personal computer, tablet computer, mobile phone or device, television, DVD, and player CD player. "E-Learning is the use of new multimedia technologies and the Internet to improve the quality of learning by facilitating access to resources and services as well as remote exchanges and collaboration" (Naidu, 2006). E-learning is not intended to replace conventional methods of training such as classroom teaching. Its aim is to create an augmented learning environment where technology is used to deliver a combined range of teaching techniques aimed at maximizing the individual's participation in the learning process (JISC, 2004).

E-learning platform provides a flexible and versatile learning system that enables organizations and learners alike to tailor their training to fit with their own specific circumstances. Furthermore, when e-learning is coupled with instructor-led training, it can bring additional dimensions and enhance the learning process overall. More and more learners and organizations are choosing to learn online using e-learning technology (Thomas, 2010).

The Benefits of E-Learning

Adoption and use of e-learning has been confirmed to provide number of benefits to both learners and teachers, such as: lower costs, faster delivery, more effective learning, and lower environmental impact. For example, a study by Ruiz, Mintzer & Leipzig (2006) revealed that e-learning can result in significant cost savings while a study by Adanu, Adu-Sarkodie, Opare-Sem, Nkyekyer, Donkor, Lawson & Engleberg (2010) indicated that students in Ghana perceived that e-learning programmes were more effective compared to other methods of learning.

Distance Learning (DL)

Distance Learning, often synonymous with distance education, can be defined as learning that takes place with the instructor and learner(s) in physically separate locations. It can be either synchronous ('live', meaning interaction between instructor and learners takes place simultaneously, as with videoconferencing) or asynchronous ('not live', meaning interaction takes place at different times, as with posting on an internet discussion board or e-mail) (Nartker, Shumays, Stevens, Potter, Kalowela, Kisimbo, Kinemo, & Egan, 2009).

Distance Learning uses both print media and a variety of technologies, including computers, mobile phones, and personal digital assistants (PDAs). It can also encompass e-learning (Nartker et al., 2009). Like in other developing countries, distance education is reasonably prevalent in Tanzania. Use of educational technologies other than print is, however, very minimal in those institutions reviewed below. The main technologies used other than prints are radio and audio, with no use made of either television or computers to support teaching and learning directly. There has though been an increase in access to the Internet and to computers over the past few years, and this is reflected in growing use of e-mail as a communication tool. Furthermore, there is still minimal use of information and communication technologies to support management and administration of distance education in Tanzania. Possibly the best example of this is continued reliance on manual stock-taking and materials dispatch systems at organizations like the Open University of Tanzania and the Institute of Adult Education.

Quality Assurance

Quality assurance has been defined as "systematic management and assessment procedures adopted by higher education institutions and systems in order to monitor performance against objectives, and to ensure achievement of quality outputs and quality improvements" (Harman, 2000: 1). Quality assurance facilitates recognition of the standards of awards, serves public accountability purposes, helps inform student choice, contributes to improved teaching learning and administrative processes, and helps disseminate best practices with the goal of leading to overall improvement of higher education systems. Setting common standards and evaluation criteria, however, must take into account diversity and plurality of higher education within national, as well as regional systems (Manghani, 2011).

Higher education institutions are challenged to develop new visions and, new forms of collaboration across institutions and nations (Harman, 2000). Brennan and Shah (2000) use the term 'quality assessment,' whose common methods and elements include 1) a national coordinating body; 2) institutional self-evaluation; 3) external evaluation by academic peers; and 4) published reports. They further identify four main types of "quality values" they determine to underpin different approaches to quality assurance: academic, managerial, pedagogic, and employment focus.

In general, the term QA refers to a process of defining and fulfilling a set of quality standards consistently and continuously with the goal of satisfying all consumers, producers, and the other stakeholders (Belawati, 2007).

While the call is advocated on institutionalization of e-learning and distance education in most institutions of education, there has been a parallel concern about quality of e-learning and distance education delivery. Most concerns related to the context in which the DL is offered as well as the extent to which learners can take self-responsibility and accountability of their education. For example Garrison (1993) is skeptical on quality of DL when he laments that; quality has always been an issue in DL (DL) and E-learning. Since DL inception and subsequent widespread diffusion, DL has been increasing access to education, a reality that has compelled many countries to adopt DE as part of their educational system. Further, this paradigm of 'access to education' is in line with the belief of student autonomy and independence, as students studying at a distance often do so alone (Moore, 1993). Quality of DL and e-learning can be unveiled on several fronts such as:

Resource Constraints

The most common problem mentioned by Nartker et al. (2009) was lack of funding. Many projects, such as those of the Southern African Extension Unit and the Institute of Adult Education, have relied on donor funding for their existence, and this creates problems of sustainability (Nartker et al., 2009). According to the South African Institute for Distance Education (SAIDE) (1999) there are at least four challenges facing implementation of distance education. They include:

Infrastructural Limitations

While this links to the above point, there are a few points specifically worth making. First, a common complaint was about the difficulties of relying on the postal service in Tanzania. This is a fundamental problem for any distance education, and creates serious problems for implementing distance education programmes in the country.

Professional Development: For educational and administrative staff members are sporadic and limited, resulting in insufficient skills amongst personnel to sustain distance education systems.

Administrative Systems

The administrative systems either do not exist or are highly underdeveloped.

Physical Communication Network: National communication systems (roads, telecommunications, and postal systems) are not sufficiently reliable or pervasive to meet the requirements of distance education provision. Taking into consideration the above discussion, it is evident that quality of DL and elearning reflects the attributes of any effective teaching as in a the traditional classroom mode. Academic staff members in any higher education institution need to know their subject and how to teach them. They must also have an idea of the profile of their students, stay up to date in their subject areas, and manage as well as monitor their students' academic progress to ensure success. This indicate that quality in DL and elearning is very important for ensuring the quality of input, process, output and outcome in teaching and learning process

Mzumbe University and Institutionalization of DL and E-Learning

Mzumbe University (MU) is one of the eleven public universities in Tanzania and is under Ministry of Education and Vocational Training (MOEVT). The university started as a Local Government Training Centre in the 1950s. After independence, in the early 1970s, it was elevated to a higher learning institution focusing on management training. After 29 years of successful functioning as an

Institute of Development Management, in 2001 it was, promoted to university status. Its mission is to provide opportunities for the acquisition, development, preservation and dissemination of knowledge and skills through training, research, technical and/or professional services.

The vision of MU is to be recognized as a leading institution in Africa for demand-driven knowledge generation, application, preservation and dissemination for socio-economic development by 2025. MU operates at three campuses: the main campus at Morogoro, MU Dar es Salaam Campus College, and MU Mbeya Campus College. The University consists of the following academic organs; Three (3) faculties (Faculty of Social Sciences, Faculty of Law and Faculty of Science and Technology); Two (2) schools (School of Business, and School of Public Administration and Management); One (1) Institute (Institute of Development Studies); Three (3) Directorates (Directorate of Research, Publication and Post-graduate Studies, Directorate of External Linkage and Community Engagement, and Directorate of Library and Technical Services).

Mzumbe University offers over 200 courses delivered through over 42 Study Programmes. By 2014, the university had a total number of 5032 enrolled undergraduate students of which 47% are female and 53% are male students. The total postgraduate students enrolment is 2161 of which 38% are female and 62% are male. Students' number is increasing annually, for example, in 2007 the students' number was 3,474 and in 2011 this number increased to 6,165. The number is projected to reach 9,000 by June 2017. Regarding the number of academic staff, the university has a total of 299 of which 23% are female. The total number of support staff is 271 of which female staff members represent 43% of the total number of staff (MU Annual Report, 2013).

The university has a modest ICT infrastructure covering all academic buildings with fibre cable. The infrastructure supports the teaching and learning process as well as welfare services. In addition,

the MU has in place a Corporate Strategic Plan (2012-2017), and policies for areas such as gender, quality assurance, staff employment, student admission, student examination, and financial and procurement regulations.

Adoption and operationalization of e-learning at Mzumbe University started in 2009 to a great extent with inspiration from Agder University of Norway. Since then, Mzumbe University has institutionalized e-learning by formulating number of strategic and pragmatic approaches. The University has defined and incorporated in its five years strategic corporate plan number of strategies, targets and expected outcome results to Strengthen *digital environment for teaching and learning.* Some of the targets and milestones developed to be met by year 2017 includes: increased standard students to computer and students to access points ratios supporting access to digital knowledge environment, strengthening requisite computer network infrastructure (Ethernet, wireless) for intranet, internet and virtual private networks rehabilitated and installed, and having availability of digital collaboration environment. It also includes platforms and supporting application software, ensuring that teaching and learning related documents for all courses of Mzumbe University are available on virtual and online learning, and improving Mzumbe University network infrastructure connected to national backbone (fiber optic cable) by June 2016.

On the investment on human capital, infrastructures and software, Mzumbe has made some concerted effort. Adoption and customization of *Moodle* platform and some apt basic capacity building to teaching members of staff were made. However, the training on the use of e-learning was done for few staff members. On DL, the attempt to institutionalize was stalled at very initial stages. The first attempt to run formal DL at MU was made in 2008 under support of NPT project funded through Dutch government. Under that project Faculty of Public Administration and Management (FPAM) wanted to prepare a curriculum for staff working in local government authorities. The aim was to bridge and address the shortage of competent staff working in LGAs particularly at lower level governments by providing flexible attainment of certificate, diploma and degree programme of local government management while they continue to serve at their working stations. A team of local staff with support from Dutch education staff visited Mzumbe University, Uganda Martyrs University and conducted survey to LGAs, and Open University of Tanzania for the purpose of learning on how best the faculty can prepare and run DL programme.

On the attitude and readiness to enrol for DL, most leaders and staff of LGAs indicated their readiness. Leaders of Council were ready to commit and sponsor staff working in LGAs particularly village executive officers (VEOs) and ward executive officers (WEOs) to register in the DL programme if Mzumbe starts. Staff, WEOs and VEOs interviewed showed interest and their readiness, but worried about cost of studying in the programme.

Therefore, despite the window of opportunity created by the availability of staff knowledgeable and competent in teaching local government management issues and university leadership to support the programme, the endeavour to implement the ambition was challenged and thus stalled due to three main challenges:

- Huge cost implications required to invest in learning infrastructures such as ICT, preparations of learning materials to support students and communication
- Technical competence of teaching staff – teaching staff were revealed to have no requisite competence to prepare curriculum, and run the DL portfolio.
- Teaching staff seemed to worry about availability of extra motivation and incentives of running such demanding programme portfolio.

Since then, there have been no further attempts to reinvigorate the endeavour to establish systematic offering of DL for Mzumbe programmes. However, the university is currently operating three campuses (the Main campus Morogoro, Dar es Salaam Campus College, and Mbeya campus college) and two distant teaching centres in Mwanza and Tanga. Academic Staff members from the main campus run from one place to another to teach at two teaching centres. Apart from three campuses, the quality of education offered in its two teaching centres remains at stake.

Quality Assurance represents a key element of higher education and includes the establishment, implementation, enhancement and monitoring of standards and guidelines. It contributes to the credibility and to the scientific as well as professional value of higher education providers and aims at ensuring delivery of high quality study programmes and research activities. As part of improving quality in higher education, most universities in East Africa and Tanzania in particular have embarked on reforms in higher education with the aims of enhancing the relevance, strengthening the quality and increasing the contribution of the tertiary education sector to country's poverty reduction strategies and overall sustainable and accelerated national development. The Tanzania government educational reform has resulted in significant increase in overall student population. The rapid expansion of higher education sector has taken place despite the shortage of teaching and learning infrastructures, lack of qualified personnel, and overburdened administration processes. In order to assure qualities of different services offered by the university, deliberate decision was taken to establish and capacitate the new Directorate of Quality Assurance (DQA) in 2010. Important roles of the directorate include assuring quality of teaching delivery and student learning. The directorate has additional responsibility of developing quality standards and supports departments on activities relating to the quality assurance system.

INSTITUTIONALIZING AND IMPLEMENTING OF DL AND E-LEARNING AT MZUMBE UNIVERSITY: CHALLENGES AND OPPORTUNITIES

With MU strategic plan (2012-2017) providing clear and articulate vision, strategies and target of institutionalizing and embracing e-learning in its quest to improve teaching and learning environment (MU SP, 2012); with internal academic secular requiring adoption and use of e-learning into about 75% of courses taught by 2015; on the one hand, the existing situation presents an opportunity in achieving the stated target. On the other hand, realities unveil number of challenges that are likely to beset realization of such ambition. A rapid diagnostic survey conducted by the Directorate of Information Technology (DICT) and the DQA to establish level of adoption, use and quality of e-learning delivery revealed number of opportunities, and also challenges that stand on way to beset the realization of the stated objectives and target. The results are similar to findings from research reported by Andersson and Grönlund in 2009. There are general challenges related to *characteristics of the individual* (student and teacher); *technology*; and *context* (organizational, cultural and societal challenges).

Opportunities and Challenges Related to Individuals

The characteristics of the individual lecturer and student including perception and attitude, awareness, knowledge and competence and readiness are key factors for successful implementation of DL and E-learning. Student *motivation* is a factor that is frequently discussed in surveys on what affects students' satisfaction and capacity. The use of ICTs enhances learning and increase motivation of students to learn (Kulik, 1994; Kosakowski, 1998; Andersson and Grönlund, 2009).

There are a number of opportunities to adopt and use e-learning portfolio at Mzumbe University. The most important opportunity is the incorporation of e-learning adoption in the Mzumbe Strategic Corporate Plan. This of course, assures top management commitment, availability of financial resources and programming at the university level. Another important opportunity is availability of teaching staff which is eager and enthusiastic to adopt and use e-learning, availability of computers and fairly internet connectivity. Another opportunity is availability of institutional collaboration with universities abroad which are competent in the use of e-technology – here experts in VLIR UOS programme are committed to support Mzumbe in both technologies and resources.

Despite such opportunities, there are a number of challenges in the adoption and use of e-learning as revealed in the rapid survey study and observable realities. The study conducted in 2013 on extent of awareness of academic staff on e-learning system and adoption revealed a number of challenges related to the three domains (individual, technological and contextual) essential for adoption and successful implementation of e-learning. The main focus of the study was to determine and analyse the state of e-learning systems adoption and utilization at Mzumbe University. The followings were key findings revealed by the survey.

Low Awareness Among Teaching Staff

The survey findings revealed that there is low awareness and that very few features within e-learning system are utilized. Most of the lecturers using the system do use it for uploading learning materials only. The reason revealed includes the lack of knowledge on the use of other features. On the level of adoption and use, six faculties (Faculty of Social Sciences (FSS), Science and Technology (FST), School of Business (SoB), School of Public Administration and Management (SOPAM), Faculty of Law (FoL) and institute of

Figure 1. Utilization of e-learning system by different schools, faculties and institutes.

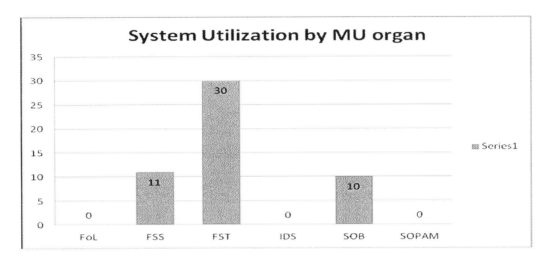

Development Studies (IDS) offering academic programmes were analysed on the extent of utilization of e-learning system. As can it be seen in Figure 1, the adoption and utilization is just low. In order to identify lecturers' system adoption and utilization, number of subjects populated with content was used.

Level of Adoption and Use

On the adoption and use of blended learning/ teaching method, analyses of available report presents a very gloomy situation. There is seriously low level of ICT adoption in teaching with only overall total of 0.8% of staff using university adopted e-learning software "Moodle". The frequency and use of this e-learning platform is quite uneven with lecturers with ICT knowledge application using more frequently than others. In other words, there is little use of blended learning approaches. Analysis done against the e-learning access logs to identify the number of MU staff and courses using the system for the academic delivery depict the utilization of the system by internal staff confirms that the level of adoption is extremely low.

Availability of Courses in the E-learning System

Both students and academic staff were asked regarding their perception concerning the importance of some of the course requirements to be available on e-learning system and platform. The results are shown in Figure 2. The results in Figure 2 reveal that many courses are not available in the e-learning system suggesting that many teaching staff are not uploading them in the system. Only 20 courses out of over 100 courses taught at the university are uploaded in the system. The range from department on using e-learning with those not using it completely is just too high (Procurement and Logistics Management 46% and Information Technology 41% while departments in the faculty of law, IDS and SOPAM are almost not using the platform at all.

Regarding the students perception, the survey conducted revealed that students are ready to use e-learning, but the process has to be initiated by lecturers. A good number of students stated that they tried to access materials in the e-learning system but failed to come across with any learning materials. In essence this suggests that on the one hand students are ready to use the system; the

Table 1. Utilization of e-learning system by different schools, faculties and institutes departments' summary (ranked)

Faculty	Department's Name	E-Learning Usage
SOB	Procurement and Logistics Management	46%
FST	Information and Communications Technology	41%
FST	Quantitative Methods	32%
SOB	Business Administration	30%
SOB	Accountancy and Finance	29%
FSS	Economics	28%
FSS	Languages and Communication Skills	25%
IDS	Centre for Environment, Poverty and Sustainable Development	17%
FSS	Educational Foundations and Teaching Management	13%
FST	Production and Operations Management	6%
SOPAM	Public Services and Human Resource Management	2%
FOL	Criminal Law	0%
FOL	Economic Law	0%
FOL	Constitutional and Administrative Law	0%
FOL	International Law	0%
SOPAM	Health Systems and Management	0%
SOPAM	Local Government Management	0%
FSS	Population Studies	0%
IDS	Development Policy	0%
IDS	Centre for Gender Development	0%
IDS	Centre for Rural Development	0%

Source: DICT. E-learning utilization report for the semester II 2011/12

only obstacle is that no material contents were uploaded in the system by course lecturers.

The analysis revealed that a significant number of students attempted to access a number of subjects. A total of 6578 user hits were recorded during the study period of which some of them were directed to subjects (109) that had no content. (see Figure 2) As for the utilization, FST, FSS, and SOB attracted a number of activities. (see Table 1) Although it is understood that number of hits can easily be influenced by the number of students in such organ, the general implication is that very few users were logging in the e-learning system. Students as most important stakeholders indicated that they are ready to adopt and use e-learning

with fair request to university to address existing and potential problems and barriers.

Perception Concerning the Barriers for Implementing E-Learning

Regarding the perception of students and academic staff concerning the barriers for adopting and using e-learning, the findings show that students believe that the major barriers for adopting and using e-learning in their learning activities include the following: insufficient computing facilities (45%); difficulty of getting internet connectivity (78%); lack of assistance when facing technical problems (45%); low competence in using e-learning port-

Figure 2. Top twenty hit subjects
Source: DICT. E-learning utilization report for the semester II 2011/1Students' Attitude, Awareness, Adoption and Use of E-learning

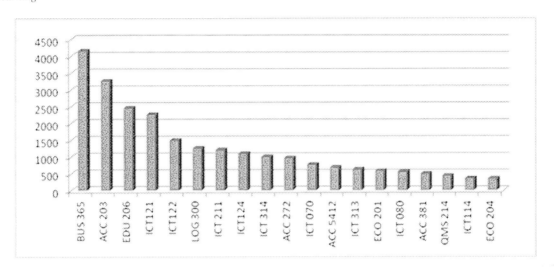

Figure 3. Perception and readiness of students on the use e-learning
Source: Random Survey, 2013

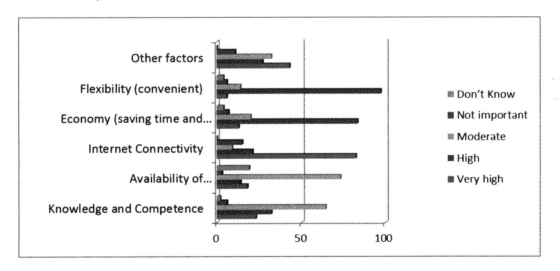

folio (79%) and practices and experiences (18%). (see Figure 3) On the part of academic staff, the findings do not have significant differences with students' observations as shown in Table 2.

Technological Opportunities and Challenges

Technology including computers, mobile and internet bandwidth connectivity is very key in the successful implementation of DL and e-Learning. This category concerns the "e" in e-learning and refers to technological requirements. Issues discussed are choices of technologies – radio, computers, audio cassettes, different Learning Management Systems (LMS) and so forth; the costs of using the technologies, how they are accessed and in what language they are available. One commonly discussed factor is access. The use of ICT for distance education evidently makes access to the technology an enabling or disabling factor and in developing countries the issue of access is often discussed in terms of availability of so called telecentres and Internet cafés. Access refers not only to whether one has physical access to a computer and an internet connection, but also to the reliability of the connection and the

bandwidth – basically everything that is needed to access the full range of the content needed. A second factor is the cost of these technologies.

Opportunities in Technology includes, availability of computer laboratories with fairly good internet connection, availability of mobile smart phone, competent staff knowledgeable in ICT and e-learning and again presence of institutional collaborations with other universities abroad.

Despite these opportunities, there are challenges likely to beset the adoption and successful use of e-learning at Mzumbe University. From quick survey and on site observations reveals the following challenges:

- Internet connectivity as MU experiences intermittent and un reliable internet and intranet connectivity;
- Limited availability of online learning management systems (LMSs) such as software tools that enable the management and facilitation of a range of learning and teaching activities and services such as Blackboard, WebCT, FirstClass, Moodle and Lotus Learning Space.
- Complementary to LMS is lack of learning content management system (LCMS), which is a set of software tools that enables the storage, use and reuse of the subject matter content.

Contextual Opportunities and Challenges: Organizational, Cultural and Society

For DL and E-Learning to be successful and effective context and management support is very crucial. There is a need to have high commitment on the part of leadership and management of the institution as policy and institutional frameworks, resource availability and motivation and incentives need to be present. The context of e-learning includes the context of the delivering organisation (typically a university setting) as well as the context

Table 2. Barriers in Adoption and use of E-Learning

Barrier	Staff %	Students %
Insufficient computing facilities (labs, etc.)	56%	45%
Lack of assistance when facing technical problems	49%	45%
Difficulty of gaining internet connectivity	73%	(78%)
Low competence in using e-learning portfolio	86%	(79%)
Practices and experiences	34%	(18%)
Not interested in using technology	24%	16%

Source: Random Survey, 2013

of the society in which the e-learning takes place, including culture, traditions, rules and regulations. A common issue here is that of the organisation's knowledge management or knowledge building. There is a need to put emphasis in terms of the need for a knowledge repository built on research and evaluations. Some researchers (cf: Andersson and Grönlund, 2009) have discussed the importance of sharing experiences among e-learning institutions and to establish e-learning units. E-learning programmes also need economy and funding for their activities (both in terms of human resource development and for the technology). Another institutional issue is to make provision for the required training of teachers and staff, an often neglected factor. Here also comes the issue of culture and traditions for members of teaching staff and students.

One opportunity exists at institutional level that Mzumbe University has consistent and clear goals, targets and strategies and commitments to institutionalize E-learning portfolio. Complementary to this there are also some policies on various academic, administration and management frontiers including Quality Assurance Policy and Operational Guidelines (2010); Mzumbe University Examinations and Student Assessment Criteria By-Laws (2012) as well as Research and Publication Policy and Guidelines (2009). The most highly placed opportunity and strength is the availability of the university wide five-year strategic plan (2012-2017).

While the availability of these instruments and management portfolio would be an opportunity for adopting DL and e-learning, culture and long lived tradition of staff and students could behest the potential opportunities. Most staff have been using chalk and talk method and at best the power point in the delivery of courses in classrooms. There are also challenges of offering alternative incentives and motivations to staff as momentum building strategy to inculcate changes from long lived 'talk and chalk' style to a new e-based teaching and learning. More serious is the challenge

of designing home grown and contextualized QA mechanism to oversee that the setting of DL centres that comply with quality framework and prescribed standards. There is also a challenge of designing and delivering courses and all learning portfolio that are up to standard and ensuring that there are no changes and possibility of compromising with QA framework.

CONCLUSION AND RECOMMENDATIONS

In the quest to improve teaching and learning at Mzumbe University, the Strategic Corporate Plan (2012-2017) has identified and put e-Learning as a means and strategy. This paper has attempted to review, albeit, in brief, empirical realities and theoretical evidence on adoption and institutionalization of DL and e-learning at Mzumbe University. With the emerging trend of mass students' enrolment, opening of more remote campuses and teaching centres, adherence to QA framework and guidelines issue remains at stake. The empirical evidence and realities unveiled in the preceding sections of this paper suggest that even if DL and e-learning are adopted and used accordingly, the university still has a long way to go before the whole ambition of institutionalization is implemented. Despite the huge opportunities available including strong desire as evidenced in the university strategic plan, top management commitment as indicated earlier in this paper, still many challenges stand to disrupt the opportunities. There are challenges related to individual characteristics, technology as well as contextual, organizational and management issues. There are dire needs to mobilize financial, human as well as technological resources. The remaining questions seems to be: How can the university assure quality of the electronic delivery process, learning management system (LMS) and learning content management system (LCMS)? Does the university possess requisite competence in terms of staff and technology to monitor and manage DL and E-learning portfolio?

Evidences and realities unveiled in this paper have provided sufficient grounds and lessons for providing recommendations. The findings provide us with adequate evidence to concede with argument that the adoption and use of e-learning will improve teaching and learning processes as proved by several studies (Kulik, 1994; Fletcher et al, 1990; Kosakowski, 1998). At the theoretical level, we feel strongly urged to recommend to all individual stakeholders, students and teaching staff in particular to conceptualize and understand the cues of DL and e-learning and find ways of assuring quality of their operationalization. At the functional and reality level, we also strongly recommended that in order to be successful in the institutionalization of DL and E-learning endeavor, capacity building on use of e-learning platform to both teaching staff and students has to be a continuous process. There is also a dire need to build capacity in the area of application of ICT–based quality assurance systems to support e-learning and DL at Mzumbe University and the like institutions in Tanzania. There is also a strong need for Mzumbe to collaborate with other stakeholders in acquiring and improving infrastructures and process of institutionalizing and implementing e-learning and DL.

REFERENCES

Adanu, R., Adu-Sarkodie, Y., Opare-Sem, O., Nkyekyer, K., Donkor, P., Lawson, A., & Engleberg, N. C. (2010). Electronic learning and open educational resources in the health sciences in Ghana. *Ghana Medical Journal, 44*(4), 159–162. PMID:21416051

Al-Ammary, J. (2013). Educational technology: A way to enhance student achievement at the University of Bahrain. *The Online Journal of New Horizons in Education, 7*(3), 54–65.

Anderson, A., & Grönlund, Å. (2009). A conceptual framework for e-learning in developing countries: A critical review of research challenges. *The Electronic Journal on Information Systems in Developing Countries, 38*(8), 1–16.

Belawati, T. (2007). The practice of a quality assurance system in open and DL. A case study of Universitas Terbuka Indonesia. *The International Review of Research in Open and DL, 8*(1), 1–15.

Brennan, J., & Shah, T. (Eds.). (2000). *Managing quality in higher education*. Milton Keynes: OECD, SRHE & Open University Press.

Cassidy, M. F. (1982). Toward integration: Education, instructional technology, and semiotics. *Educational Communications and Technology Journal, 20*(2), 75–89.

Chigona, A., & Chigona, W. (2010). An investigation of factors affecting the use of ICT for teaching in Western Cape Town. In *Proceedings of the 18th European Conference on Information System-ECIS 2010* (Paper 6).

Dhanarajan, G. (2001). Distance Education: Promise, Performance and Potential. *Open Learning, 16*(1), 61–68. doi:10.1080/02680510124465

Faculty of Public Administration and Management (2008).*Report on Possibility of establishing DL programmes.*

Fletcher, J., & Tobias, S. (2000) (Eds.). Training and Retraining; A handbook for Business, Industry, Government, and the Military. New York: Macmillan

Fletcher, J. D., Hawley, D. E., & Piele, P. K. (1990). Costs, Effects and Utility of Microcomputer Assisted Instruction in the Classroom. *American Educational Research Journal, 27*(4), 783–806. doi:10.3102/00028312027004783

Garrison, D. R. (1993). Quality and access in distance education: Theoretical considerations. In D. Keegan (Ed.), *Theoretical principles of distance education* (pp. 9–21). New York: Routledge.

Harman, G. (2000). *Quality assurance in higher education*. Bangkok: Ministry of University Affairs & UNESCO PROAP.

Hawkins, J., Panush, E., & Spielvogel, R. (1996). *National study tour of district technology integration (summary report)*. New York: Center for Children and Technology, Education Development Center.

Higgins, S. (2003). Partez-Vous Mathematics? In *Enhancing Primary Mathematics Teaching and Learning, Thompson, I.* Buckingham: Open University press.

Honey, M & McMillan, K. (2005). *Critical issues: using technology to improve student achievement*. New York: North Central regional educational laboratory.

Isaacs, S., & Hollow, D. (Eds.). (2012). *The eLearning Africa 2012 Report*. Germany: ICWE.

JISC. (2004). *Effective practice with e-learning: A good practice guide in designing for learning*. Bristol: HEFCE.

Kosakowski, J. (1998). *The benefits of information technology*. Syracuse, NY: Clearinghouse on Information and Technology.

Kulik, J. A. (1994). Meta-analytic studies of findings on computer-based instruction. In E. L. Baker & H. F. O'Neil Jr., (Eds.), *Technology Assessment in Education and Training*. Hillsdale, NJ: Lawrence Erlbaum.

Manghani, K. (2011). Quality assurance: Importance of systems and standard operating procedures. *Perspectives in Clinical Research, 2*(1), 34–37.

Marshall, D. (2002). *Learning with Technology: Evidence that technology can and does support learning*. San Diego CA: Cable in classroom.

Means, B., Penuel, W., & Padilla, C. (2001). *The connected school: Technology and learning in high school*. San Francisco, CA: Jossey-Bass.

Moore, M. G. (1993). Theory of transactional distance. In D. Keegan (Ed.), *Theoretical principles of distance education* (pp. 22–38). New York, NY: Routledge.

Mumtaz, S. (2000). Factors affecting teachers' use of information and communications technology: A review of the literature. *Journal of Information Technology for Teacher, 9*(3), 319–324.

Mzumbe University (2010). *Quality assurance Policy and Operational Guidelines 2010*

Mzumbe University (2012). *Third Strategic Corporate Plan (2012-2017)*

Mzumbe University (2013). *Adoption and Utilization of E-Learning at Mzumbe University. Survey Report*

Naidu, S. (2006). *E-Learning: A Guidebook of Principles, Procedures and Practices. Commonwealth Educational Media Center for Asia.* CEMCA.

Nartker, A., Shumays, A., Stevens, L., Potter, K., Kalowela, M., Kisimbo, D., & Egan, J. (2009). *Distance Learning assessment.* Washington, DC: I-Tech.

Newborne, A. (2002). Challenges in instituting E-learning in universities. *Journal of Informetrics, 10*(3), 117–138.

Nutball, K. (2000). *Strategies for improving Academic Achievement and teaching effectiveness: education development center,* NEIRTEC, www.neirtec.org

Patton, J. W. (2000). Protecting privacy in public? Surveillance technologies and the value of public places. *Ethics and Information Technology, 2*(3), 181–187. doi:10.1023/A:1010057606781

Potashiki, M., & Capper, J. (1998). Distance education: Growth and diversity. *Finance & Development,* (March): 1998.

Ruiz, J. G., Mintzer, M. J., & Leipzig, R. M. (2006). The impact of e-learning in medical education. *Academic Medicine, 81*(3), 207–212. doi:10.1097/00001888-200603000-00002 PMID:16501260

SAIDE. (1999). *Distance education in Tanzania.* Retrieved September 3, 2014, from http://colfinder.net/materials/supporting-distance education.htm

Tait, A. (Ed.). (1993). *Quality assurance in open and Distance Learning: European and international perspectives.* Cambridge: Open University.

Thomas, P. Y. (2010). *Towards developing web-based blended learning environment at the University of Botswana.* Retrieved September 3, 2014, from http://uir.unisa.ac.za/handle/1050/4245

Trucano, M. (2005). *Knowledge maps: ICTs in educations.* Washington, DC: InfoDev/WorldBank.

UNESCO. (2006). *Teachers and Educational Quality: Monitoring Global Needs for 2015.* Retrieved September 6, 2014, from http://www.uis.unesco.org/TEMPLATE/pdf/Teachers2006/TeachersReport.pdf'

Willett, J. B., Yamashita, J. J., & Anderson, R. D. (1983). A Meta-Analysis of Instructional Systems Applied in Science Teaching. *Journal of Research in Science Teaching, 20*(5), 405–417. doi:10.1002/tea.3660200505

Zuhairi, A., Purwanto, A., & Isman, S. (2002). Implementing quality assurance system in open and DL: the experience of Indonesia's Universitas Terbuka. Paper presented to 16th Annual Conference of Asian Association of Open Universities (AAOU), Seoul, Korea, 5-7 November 2002.

KEY TERMS AND DEFINITIONS

Distance Learning: A method of studying in which lectures are broadcast or lessons are conducted by correspondence or via internet without the student needing to attend a school or college.

E-Learning: Learning conducted via electronic media, typically on the Internet. It entails the use of electronic media, education technology, as well as information technology communications.

Quality Assurance: The maintenance of a desired level of quality in a service or product, especially by means of attention to every stage of the process of delivery or production.

Quality Control: A system of maintaining standards in manufactured products by testing a sample of the output against the specification. Or is a procedure or set of procedures intended to ensure that a manufactured product or performed service adheres to a defined set of quality criteria or meets the requirements of the client or customer.

Quality Culture: An attitude and set of values employed by a company or organisation to improve the levels of quality in service. It can also be defined as a set or group of values that guide how improvements are made to everyday working practices and consequent outputs.

Chapter 17
Active Learning with Technology Tools in the Blended/Hybrid Classes

Catherine Gakii Murungi
Kenyatta University, Kenya

Rhoda K. Gitonga
Kenyatta University, Kenya

ABSTRACT

Blended/hybrid classrooms technological tools and resources in this paper refers to: Personal and public computers, Projectors (LCD), E-learning management system, E-journals, Interactive CD or DVD, Video cameras, search engines and video conferencing. Universities in Kenya are buying computers, for departments, lecturers' offices and equipping computer labs for the students while increasing bandwidth and internet connectivity. But is the investment in technology translating to faculty and student use in blended classrooms? This chapter seeks to find out the answer to this critical question. A sample of 231 students and 219 lecturers from universities within Nairobi metropolitan was selected. Data was analyzed using descriptive statistics. The findings reveal that the universities made available blended/hybrid education and its technological tools and resources to students and lecturers for interaction in the teaching/learning process but they were less aware of the online technical resources and tools that can be used in the blended classrooms.

INTRODUCTION

The need for effective functioning in the knowledge society and coping with continuous change has led to the demand for higher levels of competencies (Kozma, 2005). There are new learning approaches such as active learning, resource-based, problem-based, project-based and competency-based learning that demand a high degree of information literacy. These new learning approaches demand a paradigm shift from dominant teaching methods involving pre-packaging information for the students, to facilitating learning in authentic and information rich contexts. There are different ways in which teaching and learning can be made more efficient

DOI: 10.4018/978-1-4666-8363-1.ch017

especially in program delivery through the use of technology. The justification for use of technology in and learning is that it highly motivates students as well as having unique instructional capabilities such as helping students visualize data/problems, or tracking learning progress. It also provides support for innovative instructional approaches such as collaborative learning and problem-based learning and increased teacher productivity and student knowledge construction (Roblyer, Edwards, & Havriluk 2004; Moallem, 2003; Wilson & Lowry, 2000). Computer-based learning and teaching has made learning more efficient and more interesting for the learners. Use of technology is likely to bring about learner-centred approaches to teaching and learning. These approaches are supported by Freire's liberation theory of 1970's that stressed on the importance of dialogical approach to education. One of the learner-centred approach to teaching and learning is the active learning approach.

Several studies have revealed that introducing active learning at the beginning of a class as opposed to the teacher giving readings ends up in bringing about intense learning, understanding, and transfer of knowledge from one student to another (Schwartz, 1998; Kapur, & Bielaczyc, 2011; Kapur, 2010; Kapur, 2012; Kapur & Bielaczyc 2012)

Learners in an active learning environment are engaged in different learning experiences that enable them to have meaning-making inquiry, enable them to act on issues learnt in class, imagine, invent, interact, hypothesize and have a personal reflection Cranton (2012). For example in a class discussion which is held online, students can explore different perspectives, increase intellectual agility as well as develop the habits of collaborative knowledge building. Students also develop skills of synthesis and integration (Brookfield 2005). Another example of active learning is when students engage in reacting to videos. The learner

can replay the video several times and this helps the student to understand what they are learning at the time in an alternative presentation mode (McKinney, 2010).

Numerous studies have shown evidence to support active learning (Hake 1998; Hoellwarth & Moelter 2011; Prince 2004; Michael 2006). From the studies, active learning increases learner's retention and improve the performance.

When interacting with technology, it is important to stick to the tools and resources that one knows and is familiar with especially in the blended/hybrid classrooms (Cholin, 2005). Interacting with technology is known to bring about a number of efficiencies in teaching; whether face to face, e-learning only as well as for the blended/hybrid learning. But the big question that remains unanswered is this: are the lecturers and students interacting with the provided technology to achieve the expected blended teaching/learning outcome? To establish this, the researchers decided to find out what lecturers and students know about learning and teaching with technology that is commonly available in our universities that are used in the blended/hybrid classrooms such as; Personal and public computers, Projectors (LCD), E-learning management system, E-journals, Interactive CD or DVD, Video cameras among other technological tools. This means that it is important to focus on tools and resources available in the Kenyan universities such as: personal and public computers in the laboratories, LCD projectors, e-learning management system, E-journals, interactive CDs and DVDs, video cameras, search engines to subscribed journals as well as video conferencing facilities. This paper highlights what lecturers and students know about the above mentioned teaching and learning technological tools as well as their interaction with them.

The knowledge of and interaction with technology will specifically touch on; availability and use of the listed tools used in blended/hybrid teaching and learning in our Kenyan Universities. What Collin 2005, argues is very true especially since both lecturers and students have to access video clips taken in classroom demonstrations and presentations with the current class or a different class, readings as well as do practice with the assignments and projects posted online both for face to face and online students. This necessitated the current study to establish whether both lecturers and students are interacting with the technological tools and resources availed by their universities in teaching and learning in the blended/hybrid classes. The technological tools and resources are important in the teaching and learning process since they allow the lecturers to share teaching and learning materials such as slides and videos, practice quizzes for students through the e-learning platforms or portals like moodle or blackboard.

Ani, 2010 & Badu, 2005 argue that computers with internet connection are important technological tools and resources that can provide a platform for active learning as student and lectures both interact with technology, in posting and doing assignments. This is very true especially when students are given assignments to do, by researching through the internet search engines like goggle scholar, or subscribed journals by universities. At the same time lecturers are able to expose the students to variety e-library resources in the universities. This in turn enables the students to be aware of the available resources as well as to know how to use and interact with such technology with ease. Mutula, 2007 also asserts that interacting with technological tools and resources in blended classrooms may work better with some lecturers and students but not all/ everybody, even where such tools and resources are available. This therefore emphasized on the need to establish whether lectures and students are aware of these tools and resources and at the same time find out if they are using them.

Videos are an important resource that lectures need to incorporate in their learning, (Chandra, 2007). In support of this Lee, 2007 also asserts that video conferencing is beneficial to the learners whereby the lectures in charge of a class can connect their classes to lecturers or expert speakers from another country to communicate with their classes. This is very true and can be possible through Skype conferencing between lecturers and students, also when students use video cameras to capture demonstrations in class and sharing them with the rest of the class for further discussions on the same online. This paper highlights the student and lecturers awareness of video resource for use in teaching and learning.

Research work by Yalcan, 2011 shows that students attitude to technological tools and resources determines the successful online instruction and student learning satisfaction. This is very true especially since when lecturers provide ways for students to ask questions and give feedback to each other then the individual student decides on whether to participate actively on such forums or not. Technological tools and resources are meant to enhance the student learning in the face to face or the blended /hybrid classes. This is so because the students are supposed to engage with the materials posted by the lecturer, student to student discussion on the same online, think critically as well as learn in the way that is most effective for them. And now for the face to face learners they are able to use the valuable class time to solve problems that would otherwise left unsolved in the normal class time hours. There is therefore a need to establish whether students are using the technological resources such as e-journals, search engines, interactive CDs/DVDs cameras and video conferencing in the learning process.

Students have changed over the years perhaps due to technology rich upbringing. They appear to have different needs, goals, and learning preferences than students in the past (Oblinger and Oblinger,

2005). Therefore, there is need to understand them and cater for their needs. The kind of students today are interested in self-directed learning opportunities, interactive environments, multiple forms of feedback, and assignment choices that use different resources to create personally meaningful learning experiences. They want assignments and class activities that have more hands-on, inquiry-based approaches to learning (Glenn, 2000). Hay (2000) argues that these students want more of hands-on, inquiry-based approaches to learning and are less willing simply to absorb what is put before them. According to Carlson (2005), these students demand independence and autonomy in their learning styles, which is impacting on a broad range of educational choices and behaviors, from "what kind of education they buy " *to* "what, where, and how they learn" hence the need to accommodate these students through the use of ICT. There is need to explore various ways to accommodate these students.

METHODOLOGY

Research Design

The research design was descriptive survey. Descriptive survey design lays a greater emphasis on sample selection because the major concerns is to obtain a broad picture of the social problem prevailing in the defined universe and make recommendations to bring about the desired change (Majumdar, 2005). It was ideal because surveys are suitable for sampling a relatively large population. Ndirangu (2000) argues that surveys are very good vehicles for collecting original data for the purpose of studying attitudes and orientations of a very large population.

Location of the Study

The study was carried out in the Nairobi metropolitan. According to the Ministry of Nairobi Metropolitan (2008), Nairobi metropolitan is that region that extends some 32,000 square kilometers from Nairobi city centre. This covers 15 No. local authority areas – City Council of Nairobi (684 km2); County Councils of Kiambu, Olkejuado, Masaku and Thika; Municipal Councils of Ruiru, Thika, Kiambu, Limuru, Mavoko, and Machakos; and Town Councils of Karuri, Kikuyu, Kajiado, and Kangundo. This region includes areas in which the institutions of the study are located. This region significantly depends on the city for employment and social facilities. This region has the highest number of both public and private universities.

Target Population

The target population comprised of all individuals and objects that the researcher could reasonably generalize findings to (Cooper & Schindler, 2006; Mugenda, 2008). The target population for this study was all the students and lecturers, in all the public and private universities in Nairobi Metropolitan totaling to 74739 students and 3987 lecturers.

There were some key characteristics of the population that were of interest in this study. Nairobi metropolitan area has experienced a decline in the cost per megabyte in KES of data transmitted. ICT services are closer to the people than any other region in Kenya (Kenya National Bureau of Statistics, 2010). This area has highest proportion of the population in Kenya using computers and the Internet. The region leads in the ownership of all basic household ICT equipment and Internet connectivity in the country. This implies that the population in this region is likely to be exposed to higher experiences in using Web 2.0 technologies and has a generally good ICT infrastructure.

Sampling Procedures and Sample Size

Purposive sampling was used to select the universities from which the sample was drawn. The main objective in this type of sampling was to pick cases that were typical of the population being studied. The researcher's judgment was used to select the respondents who best met the purposes of the study. Three public universities were selected because they were the only public universities with their main campuses within Nairobi metropolitan. The three private universities were selected because they were among the first established among all the private universities. Stratified random sampling was then used to select the respondents namely the students and the lecturers from the target population.

The sample size was determined using Mugenda and Mugenda (1999), formulae. According to Mugenda and Mugenda (1999), the minimum sample size can be determined using the following formula: Where: n= the minimum sample size if the target population is greater than 10,000 Z= the standard normal deviate at the required confidence level. p = the proportion in the target population estimated to have characteristics being measured. Use 0.5 if unknown. q = 1-p d= the margin of error.

If the target population is less than 10,000 then the minimum sample size is obtained using the formula: Where: ns= the minimum sample if the target sample size is less than 10,000 n = the minimum sample size if the target population is greater than 10,000 N = the estimate of the population size.

Using the Mugenda and Mugenda formulae, the relationship between sample size and total population was that as the population increases the sample size increases at a diminishing rate and remains relatively constant at slightly more than 380 cases. A sample size of 386 students and 344 lecturers was obtained. Once the required sample size was determined, proportional allocation was used to obtain the number of students and lecturers that were included in the sample from each of the selected universities. To select individual student respondents, the researcher visited the university students 'common halls where the questionnaires were given to the individual students who had identifications. The respondents of interest in this case were the university students and hence, there

was no need to identify the respondents through their departments or faculties. For the lecturers, the researcher visited their offices and gave individual respondents the questionnaire to fill. The researcher administered the questionnaires in person to the lecturers in order to increase the response rates. The lecturers were given two weeks to fill them in and thereafter the researcher collected them for analysis.

Response Rate

Two hundred and thirty one (231) students' questionnaires and 219 lecturers questionnaires were filled, and returned. This gave a response rate of 60% for students and 64% for lecturers. This response rate was favorable according to Mugenda and Mugenda (2003) in which they assert that a 50% response rate is adequate, 60% good and above 70% rated very well. Saunders, Lewis and Thornhill (2007) suggest that an average response rate of 30% to 40% is reasonable for deliver and collect survey method. Hager, Wilson, Pollack and Rooney (2003) recommend 50% while Sekaran (2003) recommends 30% as an adequate response rate for descriptive surveys. Based on these assertions, this implied that the response rate for this study was adequate.

RESEARCH RESULTS AND DISCUSSIONS

The main objective of the study was to find out the knowledge of and interaction of lecturers and students with blended/Hybrid education and its technologies in the teaching and learning process. This was measured by establishing what students and lecturers knew in relation to blended/hybrid education technological tools and resources, its availability and use by both students and lecturers in each university was therefore surveyed and the findings presented in twofold. First we explored student knowledge and use of technological tools and resources and secondly lecturers knowledge

Table 1. Students Knowledge of technological tools and resources used in teaching/learning

Technological Tools and Resources	N	Student Awareness (%)	
		Yes	No
Personal computers	231	89.2	10.8
Projectors (LCD)	230	82.6	17.4
E-learning management system	231	65.4	34.6
E-journals	228	55.7	44.3
Interactive CD or DVD	226	62.8	37.2
Video cameras	227	57.3	42.7
Search engines	221	61.5	38.5
Video conferencing	225	39.1	60.9

and use of technological tools and resources. The findings were as indicated below.

Students' Knowledge of Technological Tools and Resources Used in Teaching and Learning

Students were asked whether they were aware of the availability of technological tools and resources used for instruction in their universities. Their responses are indicated in Table 1.

Responses on table 1 above shows that, majority of the universities sampled had computers and projectors used for teaching and learning, judging by the high percentage of students' responses on their awareness of the existence of personal computers (89.2%) and projectors (82.6%) in their learning. At the same time, it was apparent that according to the findings on table 1, that, the computers were connected to the internet based on the high percentage rate of awareness of e-learning management systems (65.4%) and search engines (61.5%). Comparing the findings on table 1 above to those of Karshoda in 2008 on the e-readiness survey report of East African universities, which was carried out in 2009, about 50% of the universities had an e-learning management system. This

appears to be so in table 1 above whereby, there was a high number of students who were aware of the existence of the e-learning management system in the Metropolitan universities, but also noted that, very few students and lecturers are using it. However despite the provisions done by universities in providing the relevant blended / hybrid education and its technological resources and tools used in instruction, table 1 above also shows that, many students were not aware of Video conferencing (61%) as a tool /resource for use in the blended classroom meaning that the lecturers did not use this resource to enhance their teaching. In the following section students' were asked whether they used the specific technological resources and tools used in the blended /hybrid education in their learning.

Use of Technological Tools and Resources by the Students

Students were asked whether they interacted with technology in their learning process whether face to face, blended or e-learning. Their responses are shown in Table 2.

Table 2 shows that not all the blended /hybrid education technological resources and tools that

Table 2. Students interaction with the identified technological tools and resources

Technological Tools and Resources	N	Student Interaction (%)		
		Agree	Neutral	Disagree
Personal computers	230	70.8	11.8	17.4
Projectors (LCD)	226	61.5	16.8	21.7
E-learning management system	229	48.5	16.1	35.4
E-journals	228	37.8	21.8	40.4
Interactive CD or DVD	230	40.0	20.4	39.6
Video cameras	229	28.4	16.6	55.0
Search engines	229	56.3	14.0	29.7
Video conferencing	228	21.4	20.2	58.4

were available in the universities were being utilized by the students. For example, 55.7% of students were aware of the availability of e-journals but only 37.8% used them to help them in their learning and research. Sixty five point four percent (65.4%) of the students were aware of the e-learning management systems but only 48.5% were using them. This observation was earlier reported by Badu and Markwei (2005), in a study to explore the awareness and use of the internet and its resources by students at the University of Ghana. It was found that most students were aware of the resources in the internet but used them relatively infrequently. It seems from Table 2 that students were using Personal computers (70.8%), Projection systems (61.5%) and Search engines (56.3%) in their learning and this could also mean that these are the technologies that teachers preferred to use in their teaching. This explains why students became more familiar with them especially from the lecture rooms as compared to other E-learning management system, E-journals, Interactive CD or DVD, Video cameras and Video conferencing. The following topic focuses on lecturer's knowledge of the blended / hybrid and its technological resources and tools.

Lecturers' Knowledge of Technological Tools and Resources Used in Teaching and Learning

Lecturers' were asked whether they were aware of the availability of blended /hybrid education and its technological resources and tools identified for use in teaching and learning in their universities. Their responses are presented in Table 3.

From table 3, it is clear that the universities had made available technological tools and resources for use by their teaching staff, judging by the fact that the majority were aware of the existence of personal computers (96.1%), LCD projection systems (93.7%), e-learning management systems (86.3%) and e-journals (80.5%). It would also appear from table 3 that individual

Table 3. Lecturers' knowledge technological tools and resources used in teaching and learning

Technological Tools and Resources	Knowledge of Availability (%)		
	N	Yes	No
Personal computers	207	96.1	3.9
Projectors (LCD)	206	93.7	6.3
E-learning management system	183	86.3	13.7
E-journals	174	80.5	19.5
Interactive CD or DVD	168	79.8	20.2
Video cameras	154	51.3	48.7
Search engines	147	60.5	39.5
Video conferencing	148	37.8	62.2

universities in the Nairobi metropolitan area were investing substantially in technological tools and resources and in particular making available the internet. This is because lecturers were aware of the availability of technological tools and resources services such as e-learning management systems (86.3%), e-journals (80.5%), Face-book/twitter (64.7%), search engines (60.5%) and online experts (51.3%) that become available with internet connectivity. Kenyan universities have continued to invest in increasing bandwidth through the KENET Consortium of Kenyan Higher Education Institutions while the government on the other hand is improving the regulatory environment to ensure the growth of the technological tools and resources sector (Kashorda & Waema, 2008). The following section contains a report of lecturers' perception of technological tools and resources use in instruction.

Lecturers' Responses on Use of Technological Tools and Resources in Teaching

Lecturers were asked whether they were using the technological tools and resources in teaching. Their responses were as shown in Table 4:

Table 4. Technological tools and resources in use by lecturers

Technological Tools and Resources	Lecturers' Use (%)			
	N	Agree	Neutral	Disagree
Personal computers	187	91.5	1.6	6.9
Projectors (LCD)	195	87.7	5.1	7.2
E-learning management system	174	67.2	15.0	17.8
E-journals	161	59.6	23.7	16.7
Interactive CD or DVD	157	59.8	16.0	24.2
Video cameras	142	40.2	21.1	38.7
Search engines	141	57.5	9.2	33.3
Video conferencing	139	25.9	1.6	51.8

Source: Field data

Table 4 reveals that the lecturers were using personal computers (91.5%), projection systems (87.7%), e-learning management systems (67.2%), e-journals (59.6%) and search engines (57.5%). Not every technological tools and resources available to the lecturers was being fully utilized in instruction. For example, 86.3% of lecturers were aware of e-learning management systems but only 67.2% were using them in teaching, while 80.5% of the lecturers knew of the availability of the e-journals but only 59.6% were using them. This probably could be as a result of ignorance on their use, negative attitude, lack of appropriate skills on internet use and/or technophobia.

This observation is also supported by Otieno (2008) who pointed out that the expertise levels of lecturers in IT skills were very low. He observed that attitude towards new technologies was a factor responsible for low usage of technological tools and resources in colleges. Similarly, Peansupap and Walker (2005) found out that technological tools and resources user's motivation was also related to their attitude toward technology such as perceived clear advantage of use, ease of use, relevance to their jobs, and professional credibility. Likewise, Igbaria, Parasuraman and Baroudi (1996) observed that usefulness and ease of use

motivated professionals and managers to use computers. In technology acceptance model that explains the use, intention to use and acceptance of new technology, the two Technological tools and resources of information technology usage are perceived usefulness and ease of use (Lancaster et al., 2007). Users were more likely to use and adopt computer technology if they thought that it was useful in improving their productivity and performance and if it required less effort to learn how to it. Sawant (2012) further argues that effective use of technology is dependent on academics' familiarity and interaction with technology tools, the opportunities they have for exposure and their level of skills. The universities have a role to play in helping lecturers and students to use technological tools and resources facilities by facilitating institution based technological tools and resources professional development through technological tools and resources seminars or conferences. Cao and Hong (2011) argue that the more ready the faculty members feel they are, the more likely they will utilize web 2.0 technologies such as blogs, wikis and podcasts for instruction.

CONCLUSION

The study found that the universities had made available technological tools and resources to students and lecturers for use in teaching and learning. The technological tools and resources identified as made available for teaching and learning by the universities, were for example, personal computers, LCD projection systems, E-learning management systems and internet connectivity. However, students and lecturers were less aware of online resources for teaching and learning such as video-conferencing.

There were major differences in percentages between technological tools and resources availability and their use. Students and lecturers were aware of the availability of technological tools and resources but their usage was quite low and particularly the usage of online technological tools and resources. It would be of interest to investigate further why this was so.

RECOMMENDATION

With regard to the use of technological tools and resources in blended/hybrid learning, universities should set aside resources for training of students and lecturers on the use of technological tools and resources and especially online resources in instruction. The universities should evaluate their curricula to integrate the use of technological tools and resources in teaching and learning while at the same time develop policies that promote, recognize and award those who integrate these tools in their teaching and learning.

REFERENCES

Ani, E. O. (2010). Internet access and use: A study of undergraduate students in three Nigerian universities. *The Electronic Library, 28*(4), 555–567. doi:10.1108/02640471011065373

Badu, E. E., & Markwei, E. D. (2005). Internet awareness and use: The University of Ghana. *Information Development, 21*(4), 260–268. doi:10.1177/0266666905060069

Brookfield, S. D. (2005). *Discussion as the way of teaching: Tools and techniques for democratic classrooms* (2nd ed.). San Francisco: Jossey-Bass.

Cao, Y., & Hong, P. (2011). Antecedents and consequences of social media utilization in college teaching: A proposed model with mixed-methods investigation. *On the Horizon, 19*(4), 297–306. doi:10.1108/10748121111179420

Carlson, S. (2005). The Net Generation goes to college. *The Chronicle of Higher Education*, Section: Information Technology, *52*(7), A34. Retrieved from http://www.msmc.la.edu/include/learning_resources/todays_learner/The_Net_Generation.pdf

Cholin, V. S. (2005). Study of the application of information technology for effective access to resources in Indian university libraries. *The International Information & Library Review, 37*(3), 189–197. doi:10.1016/j.iilr.2005.07.002

Cooper, D. R., & Schindler, P. S. (2006). *Business research methods* (9th ed.). Boston: McGraw-Hill Irwin.

Cranton, P. (2012). *Planning instruction for adult learners* (3rd ed.). Toronto: Wall & Emerson, Inc.

Glenn, J. M. (2000). Teaching the Net Generation. *Business Education Forum, 54*(3), 6–14.

Hager, M. A., Wilson, S., Pollak, T. H., & Rooney, P. M. (2003). Response Rates for Mail Surveys of Nonprofit Organisations: A Review and Empirical Test. *Nonprofit and Voluntary Sector Quarterly, 32*(2), 252–267. doi:10.1177/0899764003032002005

Hake, R. R. (1998). Interactive-engagement versus traditional methods: A six-thousand-student survey of mechanics test data for introductory physics courses. *American Journal of Physics, 66*(1), 64. doi:10.1119/1.18809

Hay, L. E. (2000). Educating the Net Generation. *School Administrator, 57*(54), 6–10.

Hoellwarth, C., & Moelter, M. J. (2011). The implications of a robust curriculum in introductory mechanics. *American Journal of Physics, 79*(5), 540. doi:10.1119/1.3557069

Igbaria, M., Parasuraman, S., & Baroudi, J. J. (1996). A Motivational Model of Microcomputer Usage. *Journal of Management Information Systems, 13*(1), 127–143.

Kapur, M. (2010). Productive failure in mathematical problem solving. *Instructional Science*, *38*(6), 523–550. doi:10.1007/s11251-009-9093-x

Kapur, M. (2012). Productive failure in learning the concept of variance. *Instructional Science*, *40*(4), 651–672. doi:10.1007/s11251-012-9209-6

Kapur, M., & Bielaczyc, K. (2011). Classroom-based experiments in productive failure. In *Proceedings of the 33rd annual conference of the cognitive science society* (pp. 2812-2817).

Kapur, M., & Bielaczyc, K. (2012). Designing for productive failure. *Journal of the Learning Sciences*, *21*(1), 45–83. doi:10.1080/10508406.2011.591717

Kashorda, M., & Waema, T. (2008) *E-readiness survey of East African Universities*. Retrieved from http://kenet.or.ke/eready/staging/Ereadiness%20Survey%20of%20East%20African%20Universities%20Report%202009.pdf

Kenya National Bureau of Statistics (2010). *Kenya - National Information and Communication Technology Survey 2010*. KNE-KNBS-NICTS-2010-v01

Kozma, R. (2005). *ICT, education reform, and economic growth*. Chandler, AZ: Intel Corporation. Retrieved September 17, 2009, from Http://download.intel.com/education/wsis/ICT_Education_Reform_Economic_Growth.pdf/

Lancaster, S., David, C. Y., Albert, H. H., & Shin-Yuan, H. (2007). The selection of instant messaging or e-mail: College students' perspective for computer communication. *Information Management & Computer Security*, *15*(1), 5–22. doi:10.1108/09685220710738750

Lee, M. M., & Hutton, D. S. (2007). Using Interactive Videoconferencing Technology for International Education: The Case of ISIS. *International Journal of Instructional Technology and Distance Learning*, *4*(8).

Majumdar, P. K. (2005). *Research Methods in Social Science*. New Delhi, India: Viva Books Private Limited.

McKinney, K. (2010). *Active Learning. Illinois State University*. Center for Teaching, Learning & Technology.

Michael, J. (2006). Where's the evidence that active learning works? *Advances in Physiology Education*, *30*(4), 159–167. doi:10.1152/advan.00053.2006 PMID:17108243

Ministry of Nairobi Metropolitan Development. (2008). *Nairobi Metro 2030 A World Class African Metropolis. Government of the Republic of Kenya*. Retrieved from http://www.tatucity.com/DynamicData/Downloads/NM_Vision_2030.pdf

Moallem, M. (2003). An interactive online course: A collaborative design model. *Educational Technology Research and Development*, *51*(4), 85–103. doi:10.1007/BF02504545

Mugenda, A. G. (2008). Social science research: Theory and principles: Nairobi: Applied research and training services, Kenya.

Mugenda, M. O., & Mugenda, G. A. (1999). *Research methods: Quantitative and qualitative approaches*. Nairobi: ACTS press.

Mugenda, M. O., & Mugenda, G. A. (2003). *Research Methods Quantitative and Qualitative Approaches*. Nairobi: ACTS press.

Mutula, S. M., & Musakali, O. D. (2007). Internet adoption in Kenyan university libraries. *Emerald Publishing Limited, 56*(6), 464–475.

Ndirangu, M. (2000). *A study of the perceptions of students, teachers and their influence of teaching projects on the teaching of science in selected secondary schools in Kenya*. Unpublished PHD Thesis, Egerton University, Kenya.

Oblinger, D. G., & Oblinger, J. L. (2005*). Educating the Net Generation*. In D. Oblinger & J. Oblinger (Eds), *Educating the Net generation* (pp. 2.1–2.20). Boulder, CO: EDUCAUSE. Retrieved August 14, 2013 from http://net.educause.edu/ir/library/pdf/pub7101m.pdf

Otieno, O. J. (2008) *A frame work for evaluating technological tools and resources use in teacher education: A case study of the primary teacher training colleges in Kenya*. Unpublished MEd Thesis, Strathmore university, Kenya.

Peansupap, V., & Walker, D. H. T. (2005). Factors enabling information and communication technology diffusion and actual implementation in construction organizations. *ITcon, 10*, 193–218.

Prince, M. (2004). Does active learning work? A review of the research. *The Journal of Engineering Education, 93*(3), 223–231. doi:10.1002/j.2168-9830.2004.tb00809.x

Roblyer, M. D., Edwards, J., & Havriluk, M. A. (2004). *Integrating educational technology into teaching* (4th ed.). Upper Saddle River, NJ: Prentice Hall.

Saunders, M., Lewis, P., & Thornhill, A. (2007). *Research Methods for Business Students* (4th ed.). Harlow: FT Prentice Hall.

Sawant, S. (2012). The study of the use of Web 2.0 tools in LIS education in India. *Library Hi Tech News, 29*(2), 11–15. doi:10.1108/07419051211236549

Schwartz, D. L., & Bransford, J. D. (1998). A time for telling. *Cognition and Instruction, 16*(4), 475–5223. doi:10.1207/s1532690xci1604_4

Sekaran, U. (2003). *Research method of business: A skill Building Approach* (4th ed.). New York, NY: John Willey & Sons, Inc.

Wilson, B., & Lowry, M. (2000). Constructivist learning on the web. New directions for adults and continuing education, 88, 79-88.

Yalçan, F. (2011). An international dimension of the student's attitudes towards the use of English in Web 2.0 technology. *The Turkish Online Journal of Educational Technology, 10*(3), 63–68.

KEY TERMS AND DEFINITIONS

Blended/Hybrid Classes: Blended/hybrid classrooms refer to classrooms where technological tools and resources such as Personal and public computers, Projectors (LCD), E-learning management system, E-journals, Interactive CD or DVD, Video cameras, search engines and video conferencing are being used together with the traditional tools and resources.

Learning: Learning is the process of acquiring new, or modifying and reinforcing, existing knowledge, behaviors, skills, values, or preferences and may involve synthesizing different types of information presented to the learner.

Lecturer: According to Cambridge Advanced Learner's Dictionary a lecturer is someone who teaches at a university or college. For the purpose of this study, a Lecturer included personnel whose primary assignment is instruction, research, or public service. This included staff personnel who hold an academic rank with titles such as professor, associate professor, assistant professor, instructor, lecturer, or the equivalent of any of these academic ranks. The category did not include personnel with other titles, (e.g. dean, director, associate dean, assistant dean, chair or head of department), even if their principal activity is instruction or research.

Students: According to Cambridge Advanced Learner's Dictionary, a student is a person who is learning at a college or university, or sometimes at a school. For the purpose of this study, a university student was a person enrolled in a degree program in one of Kenya's Public or private universities.

Teaching: Teaching is an instruction or delivering a particular skill or subject or something that someone tells you to do. For Teaching in this case may refer to showing or explaining to a student how to do something.

Technology Tools and Resources: These are a collection of resources used for creating, storing, managing and communicating information. These technologies can be used to support teaching, learning, research activities, collaboration learning and inquiry.

University: A university is an institution of higher education and research, which grants academic degrees in a variety of subjects. A university provides both undergraduate education 13 and postgraduate education. For the purpose of this research, a Public University was one which is established by Act of Parliament and largely supported from public funds while a Private University was one which is established in accordance with the Universities Act 1985 (cap 210B) and the Establishment of Universities rules .

Chapter 18
Appraisal Theory:
Opportunities for Social Networking Sites' Complementation of Writing Centres

Patient Rambe
Central University of Technology, South Africa

ABSTRACT

While Writing Centres provide dialogic spaces for student articulation of voice, they insufficiently deal with asymmetrical power relations built into expert-novice conversations, which potentially disrupt novices' democratic expression of their voices. Yet the conversational nature of Facebook presents opportunities for ESL students to express their voices. This chapter: 1) Employs draft essays of first-year ESL students submitted to a Writing Centre to unravel their challenges with asserting their voice, 2) Uses reflective narratives of Writing consultants and ESL students to understand how their English language acquisition is impacted by their appropriation of Facebook and 3) Unravels how Facebook complements the mandate of Writing Centres of developing the academic voice of students. Findings suggest that students lacked confidence in asserting their authorial presence and familiarisation with academic conventions. Students and consultants' essays demonstrated a balanced appropriation of attitudinal and judgement categories and engagement resources, with implications for the potential of Facebook to mediate student expression of their voice.

INTRODUCTION

One of the most complex academic endeavours is to initiate first year students into the writing practices and academic discourses of their disciplines at university. Literature on language literacy in South Africa higher education (SAHE) underscores academically underprepared students' (especially English as Second Language (ESL)) problems with academic writing in general (McKenna,

2004; Archer, 2010). More so, the same body of literature also acknowledges students' inadequate knowledge of how to assert their academic authority due to a lack of familiarisation with academic conventions (Hodges, 1997; Lea & Street, 1998; Read, Francis, & Robson, 2001). Conventions of academic writing in mainstream academia are ambiguous, assumed and often confusing to students (Ballard & Clanchy, 1988; Lea & Street, 1998). As such, novices often struggle to develop,

DOI: 10.4018/978-1-4666-8363-1.ch018

extend and challenge the ideas and arguments of established authors in ways that enact and assert their voice in writing. Hodges (1997) postulates that when novices first encounter theory, they often rely on parrot-speech in their endeavour to ventriloquise the academic voices of the established authors in their fields.

In recognition of this perennial challenge of scholarly writing, the need to increase consciousness of academic conventions and enactment individual voices, South African higher educational institutions (HEIs) have instituted structural interventions such as Writing Centres under the broader ambit of Academic Development Programmes (ADP) to tackle head on these literacy challenges. Among the various mandates of Writing Centres are training and socialising students into their disciplinary discourses (i.e. ways of conceptualising ideas and logical argumentation) and engaging in scholarly discourses through the enactment and development of student voices in writing. The challenge however, is that these Language and ADP created to assist students with their English language skills are often offered as support services situated out of the main teaching curricula within the disciplines (Wingate, 2006; Arkoudis & Tran, 2010). This 'quick fix' model contributed to the conception of Writing Centres as "mostly 'add on' measures where the weaker students were siphoned off from the mainstream" and "remediation centres to rectify language 'deficiencies' in individual students" (Archer, 2010, p. 496). This 'deficiency-based' approach seems inconsistent with the highly discipline-specific nature of the discourses that unfold within departments at university. Furthermore, the fact that Writing Centres are physically located as separate entities on the main campuses (and not in different disciplines) presents additional challenges for the delivery of academic support for part time students, students on distributed campuses, distance learners, disabled students who enroll at South African universities. More so, the philosophy of Writing Centres such as their assumptions

that scholarly discourses can be articulated and that student voices can be enacted and developed through academic training presupposes students' clear understanding of the conventions of academic engagement and argumentation of their disciplines. Yet the conventions of academic writing can be seen metaphorically as a type of 'code' to be 'cracked,' a form of knowledge that students must uncover for themselves (Read, Francis, & Robson, 2001, p. 388). Therefore, academic writing is considered rewarding for students who have identified, internalised and become effective in verbalising this code in academic writing.

Mindful of the heavy presence of South African young adults on social networking sites (SNSs)(e.g. Facebook, Twitter, wikis and blogs), the inherently text-based nature of social media communication coupled with its capacity to support reflective writing and commentary, it is self evident that SNSs such as Facebook present potentially productive tools for training students in foreign language literacy, improving communicative competence and accessing academic conventions of their disciplines (Chen, 2013; Chen & Yang, 2014). Despite this emerging body of research, there still exists a concomitant recognition that the potential of SNSs to shape student [language] literacy practices and enact learner voices remains underexplored in mainstream literature (Pavlenko & Norton, 2007; Chen, 2013). Yet Internet based tools like SNSs have challenged traditional notions of language literacy and literacy as acquiring linguistic elements that are fixed, rule-governed, monomodal, and static through their redefinition of literacy as social practices that are fluid, sociocultural, multimodal, and dynamic (Chen, 2013). Similarly, SNSs such as weblogs provide a safe and structured online discussion environment for the articulation and discussion of personal stories by students across the world in their preferred digital form (Chen & Yang, 2014). Mindful of the aforementioned linguistic challenges of South African university entrants and the capacity of SNSs to transform academic literacy practices, this study considers Facebook as a social technology with immerse potential to complement academic writing in Writing Centres.

This study, therefore: 1) Employs selected draft essays of first-year ESL students submitted to a Writing Centre to unravel their challenges in articulating their voice in academic writing, 2). Draws on the reflective narratives of these students and their Writing consultants to understand how their appropriation of Facebook shapes their English language acquisition and development respectively and 3). Investigates the potential of Facebook to complement the functions of Writing Centres of nurturing the voice and agency of novices in scholarly writing.

LITERATURE REVIEW

Concept of Voice

Voice is a heavily contested term in literature and dissensus persists on whether it is personally generated or socially constructed (Elbow, 1994; Ramanathan & Atkinson, 1999; Sherlock, 2008). In university writing, the term describes the discursive tone and academic personality employed by college level writers, which are often stepped in relative objectivity, precision and conservative language (Sherlock, 2008, p. 1). Voice in its strict sense, therefore, subtly delineates an author's stance and modes of reasoning from those of peers she engages and draws reference to in her textual constructions (i.e. the author's positionality). Ramanathan and Atkinson (1999, p. 48-50, 60) contend that voice describes [discoursal practices of] an assertive individual who displays originality and skepticism, emphasises self-ownership of texts, and individual discovery of ideas through reflection and revision. Voice, emphasises the stamping of one's academic authority in textual constructions through commitment to objectivity, relational consciousness and open critique of contexts, ideas and arguments.

Student Challenges with Voice

One of the enormous challenges of academic writing at university is articulation of student voice (Bailey & Pieterick, 2008; Correa, 2010; Hewings, 2012). Bailey and Pieterick (2008) contend that students often consider academic essay writing at university to be a daunting and overwhelming task owing to the complexities of developing a clear focus and presenting a well reasoned argument in a logical and formal way. For ESL learners, a double tragedy manifests not only in their grappling with articulating themselves in a foreign language but understanding and interpreting the conventions of the language in which the tasks are conveyed. Correa (2010) highlights how international students struggled to attribute voice, paraphrase when expressing their own thoughts and draw on conventions of writing expository essays. She further documents the complexities of giving access to privileged linguistic genres to students while acknowledging the variability of student writing styles in class. Even online learning environments such as discussion forums, which are often conceived as empowering spaces for self-presentation and articulation of authorial voice can constitute an "interaction of the unwilling where real engagement with issues and other students is not clearly observable" (Hewings, 2012, p. 3). Student unwillingness to participate in online learning environments, [which negatively impacts on their voice] is attributable to the permanence of their digital footprint and the availability of their comments for public scrunity (Hewings, 2012).

Appropriateness of Social Media Technologies (STMs) for Academic Writing

The dependence of SMTs on narrative communication, their highly social nature enabled by diverse interactions and their fostering of large information flows make them ideal environments for foreign language acquisition (Guiterrez, Morales, & Martinez, 2009; Hamilton-Hart, 2010; Rosen, 2010; Mills, 2011). Self-narratives like those inherent in Facebook communication are conceived as the heartbeat of socialisation into foreign languages (Pavlenko, 2001; Mills, 2011). Cortazzi, Jin, Wall and Cavendish (2001) argue that when student tell stories of their learning experiences [e.g. via social media platforms], the process of recounting them enables self-reflection, consolidation of the content learnt as well as validation of learning by peers, tutors and senior academics. The narrative-based communication and dialogic conversations inherent in SMTs like Facebook perfectly make them best candidates for enabling the enactment and development of student voice.

From a functional linguistics perspective, Facebook therefore, enables language learning through "fostering students' awareness about the connections between contextual features (activity, identity, relations as well as the role performed by text in the situation) and their respective linguistic realizations (expression of content, instantiation of relationships between interlocutors and organization of text)" (Motta-Roth, 2009, p. 317). As such, the informal talk embodied in Facebook not only externalises student personal experiences with writing, but also instantiates the processes of acquiring one's positionality and assimilation of new knowledge through self-articulation. Similarly, the New Literacy Studies that adopt a cultural-historical perspective to literacy development, connect literacy development and fostering of voice to their context of production. Street (2003) conceives literacy as embedded in social practices and the acquisition and advancement of literacy as deeply implicated in their immediate context of development. On Facebook, students write their identities into being and develop their own "scripts" and "counter scripts" of voices through self-representation, exhibition, critical questioning, peer commenting and collaborative knowledge building.

RESEARCH METHOD

Case Study

Since the rationale for this study was to explore student challenges with articulating their voice as a precursor to investigating how these agents' (i.e. students and writing consultants) reflective narratives of using Facebook demonstrate its (i.e. Facebook) capacity to enable the enactment and development of student voice, a case study approach best suited this investigation. A case study is ideal when the study intention is to focus on individual actors or groups with a view to understand their perceptions of events and to provide a rich, vivid description of events relevant to the case (Hitchcock & Hughes, 1995, p. 317). For this study, a case of student challenges with voice including theirs and writing consultants' reflective narratives of Facebook use for language acquisition is discussed to provide some rich descriptions of how Facebook could complement Writing Centre practices.

To examine students' challenges with articulating voice and how these agents articulate their voice, this study draws on Appraisal Theory, which comprises three systems namely, *engagement, attitude* and *graduation* (Hyland, 2005; Martin & White, 2005; Swain, 2007, 2010). Martin and White (2005, p. 35) suggest that *attitude* comprises linguistic resources concerned with "our feelings, including emotional reactions, judgements of behaviour and evaluations of things". Graduation resource involves grading phenomena whereby feelings are amplified and categories blurred, while engagement comprises those resources concerned with sourcing attitudes and the play of voices around opinions in discourse (Ibid). These resources include different kinds of reporting verbs, modal verbs, frequency adverbs, negatives, contrastive discourse markers and comment adjuncts (Swain, 2010). Swain (2010) further suggests that attitude can either be inscribed or invoked and includes affect, judgement and appreciation. Therefore, varying proportions of inscribed and evoked judgement (e.g. social sanction and esteem), appreciation (e.g. social valuation) and engagement resources are necessary to develop a good essay. To unravel student challenges with voice, the first stage involved an examination of the introductions of 5 ESL students to unpack their extent or proportions of using engagement resources, appreciation and judgement. Of these students two students were from the Science faculty, one from Humanities faculty, one from Arts faculty and one from the Commerce faculty. Three consultants were from the Linguistics departments while one was from the humanities faculty.

Since the other objective of the study was to establish the potential of Facebook to complement Writing Centres, an ideal intervention was to examine the use of Facebook by students with language problems and judge whether their appropriation of various linguistic resources was comparatively better than when they did not use Facebook. However, given that Writing Centres are walk-in academic support services accessed by students based on individual needs, it was difficult to access these students' work over a long duration. Similarly, introducing the Facebook intervention required ADP management's direct involvement and support. Consequently, a reasonable proxy to understanding student voice was to request both the 5 ESL students and their 4 writing consultants to write short reflective narratives on how their use of Facebook impacted on their language acquisition and development respectively.

The study findings are therefore, grouped into two components namely: 1). 5 ESL students' unedited drafts essays submitted to the Writing Centres for the researcher to analyse (with the permission of these respective students), 2). The reflective narrative essays of these ESL students and those of writing consultants on their use of Facebook for acquiring and improving English

Table 1. Analysis of extracts of student essays using Appraisal analysis

Attribute	Acknowledge	Excerpts of Introduction *Many scholars criticized* the lack of absolute power to impose its power on states […]
	Distance	It is *claimed* that [...]
Entertain		With effective communication, there *will be* more integration, interconnectedness [...]

Engagement: dialogic expansion (adapted from White, 2003)

language proficiency respectively. The reflective essays were voluntarily written by them at the request of the researcher.

Data Analysis

The research data was analysed using Appraisal Analysis as shown in Table 1.

Appraisal analysis was applied to all the draft essay introductions and reflective narratives from the five ESL learners and the four Writing Centre consultants on their use of Facebook for improving English language acquisition and development. Given this essay's preoccupation with exploring students' challenges with academic voice, it was necessary to substantiate student problems with academic writing as a precursor to exploring the support Facebook could give to students. Since the purpose of this work was not necessarily to distinguish between high scoring and lower scoring essays (as all drafts submitted to the Writing Centre were classified as problematic), a comparative approach between them was deemed less informative. The interest in demonstrating instances of student expression of voice in their (problematic) writing enticed the researcher to examine their application of engagement and attitude resources in their draft introductions. While all introductions were examined using appraisal analysis (Martin & White, 2005; Swain, 2010) for both attitude (inscribed and evoked judgement and appreciation) and engagement (entertain and attribute: acknowledge and distance; disclaim and proclaim), they were not calculated as proportions of the total instances of attitude and engagement for each essay. This is because this paper was interested in the discursive and attitudinal expressions in the introduction and not the whole essay. All numerical values and tokens of attitude and instances of engagement were annotated and counted.

With regard to academic discourse, Hyland (2005) seems to value engagement resources more than attitude resources although the evaluative component in attitude resources tends to offer writers far more freedom to position themselves interpersonally than academic genres. This freedom can be fully exploited in a Facebook consultative environment given its quasi-formal nature and capacity to project personal, sentimental expressions in textual constructions. In addition, its technology-mediated nature potentially filters out (for novices) the conceivably 'intimidating' identity-based descriptors (e.g. tone of voice, facial expressions, gaze, body posture) often immanent in face-to-face consultations.

Engagement resources are grouped under the subsystems *entertain* (for example, may, perhaps, must) and *proclaim*: concur (for instance, certainly, of course, obviously) in additional to other resources like evidentiality, boosters and hedges. The capacity of the writer to recognise and engage with other voices in the field emerges as a critical component of engagement resources. The academic discourse exploits attitudinally neutral reporting verbs from the attribute: acknowledge category (like said, stated, maintained, observed, noted and argued) (Jordan, 1989, as cited in Swain, 2010). Mindful of the insufficient use of engagement resources, communicative repertoires and academic vocabulary by novices and their difficulty with engaging with scholarly texts, the study envisaged their problematic writing to employ more of judgemental resources than these reporting verbs. Engagement resources include both dialogic expansion and contraction and these are reflected in Tables 2.

Table 2. Analysis of extracts of students essay drafts

Disclaim	Deny	It is *no surprise* to think that NEPAD will succeed to achieve neither economic development and political democratization […].
	Counter	*However,* a global subsidy mechanism is contemplated in order to make ACTs accessible and affordable.
Proclaim	Concur	*Of course,* we have to understand that […]
	Pronounce	It is *really important* therefore, for medical practitioners to be cogniscent of the fact that effective communication […].
	Endorse	Research *has shown* that […]

Engagement: dialogic contraction (adapted from Swain, 2010)

Vignettes of Student Challenges with Voice

The following introduction extract came from a first year student from a department in the Faculty of Engineering and Built Environment at a Southern African university. Students were asked to review a science related book of their choice and to articulate thought provoking scientific ideas conveyed in that academic text. The aim was not only to examine students' grasp of scientific concepts and descriptions, but their effective use of scientific (academic) language in their writing: The extract below is the student's unedited introduction (NB. All these original extracts from students were reproduced in this work with their permission) which a Writing consultant was tasked to work on and give feedback to the student (NB. Words in capitals constitute the application of Appraisal analysis to the student's work). The student's introduction is a component of his review of Richard. P. Feynman's book entitled "Surely you're joking Mr Feynman."

Excerpt 1:

There are some science books that don't *[DIS-CLAIM: DENY]* look interesting *[APPRECIA-*

TION: -SOCIAL VALUATION] no *[DISCLAIM: deny] matter which section of the library you find them in.* Thankfully *[+APPRECIATION: SOCIAL VALUATION] for Richard Feynman's* "Surely you're joking Mr Feynman" *[ATTRIBUTE: ACKNOWLEDGE], science is* purely illustrated *[PROCLAIM: ENDORSE] in a* funny way *[APPRECIATION: + SOCIAL VALUATION].* Though *[DISCLAIM: COUNTER] i usually find it* annoying *[APPRECIATION:-REACTION] to read science-related books, this book* has changed my pespection *(perspective)* on science novels *[APPRECIATION: + SOCIAL VALUATION].* *"Surely you're joking Mr Feynman," a book written by Richard. P. Feynman [ATTRIBUTE: ACKNOWLEDGE] is a collection of stories about a* very *[GRADUATION]* curious character *[AP-PRECIATION: + SOCIAL VALUATION] Feyn-man. It is a story that has to do with [ATTRIBUTE: EVIDENTIALS] physics and research,* much more like *[ENTERTAIN: EVIDENTIALS] the work of a chemical engineer. This book contains* outrageous, shocking, *[-APPRECIATION:-REACTION],* but interesting *[APPRECIATION: + SOCIAL VALU-ATION] stories, gathered through* Feynman's life *[ATTRIBUTE: ACKNOWLEDGE].*

In this excerpt, there are:

- 2 values of explicit, unattributed attitude: appreciation
- 6 values of explicit, attributed attitude: appreciation
- 1 value of graduation
- 7 values of engagement, of which 4 are expanding (1 entertain; 1 attribute: 2 acknowledge) and
- 3 contracting (3 disclaim: 1 counter; deny 1, 1 proclaim: endorse).

A majority of the *attitude* category items are from the system APPRECIATION, and most of them are attributed. Although there is a balance between expanding and contracting resources

(4:3), the high presence of emotive language seems to undermine the academic worth of this academic piece. The student struggles to articulate his voice as evidenced by the use of contractions *[don't]*, improper use of verbs *[look* instead of appear or seem], the unusual use of superlatives (the adjective *purely, very*), and negative reactions (*annoying, outrageous and shocking*). The experimentation with an authorial voice embodied in the DISCLAIM *"don't* look interesting" and *"no* matter" shows that the writer anticipates and pre-empts a counter position from a prospective critical reader that the books in question could be interesting. The use of a superlative "*purely*" conjures a deliberate intention to conspire the reader into agreement and forecloses any counter claims about the representation of science. Emotive language like '*annoying*' can be replaced by disappointing or unfortunate, and the perceivably colloquial expression of approval '*thankfully*' can be changed to 'Richard Feynman deserves credit for.'

The following is a student introduction responding to the research question "Afro-pessimists depict NEPAD as dead." Is this an accurate characterisation?

Excerpt 2:

It is no [DISCLAIM: DENY] surprise [ATTITUDE] to think that NEPAD will succeed [APPRECIA-TION: + SOCIAL VALUATION] to achieve neither *[-JUDGEMENT: SOCIAL ESTEEM: CAPACITY] economic development and political democrati-zation in the African continent. There have been* many *[GRADUATION: FORCE] precedent proj-ects which have* failed *[JUDGEMENT: SOCIAL ESTEEM: CAPACITY] to meet their objectives such as the* Lagos Plan of Action (adopted in 1980) *[ATTRIBUTE: ACKNOWLEDGE], and the* Africa's Priority Programme for Economic Re-covery *(APPER, adopted in 1985) [ATTRIBUTE: ACKNOWLEDGE] adopted by the Organisation of African Unity.* Many *[GRADUATION FORCE]* scholars *[ATTRIBUTE: ACKNOWLEDGE]* criticized *[ATTRIBUTE: -ACKNOWLEDGE] the* lack *[JUDGEMENT: SOCIAL ESTEEM: CA-PACITY] of* absolute power *[APPRECIATION:-SOCIAL VALUATION] to* impose its power *[APPRECIATION:-SOCIAL VALUATION] on states, the* lack of funds *[JUDGEMENT: SOCIAL ESTEEM: CAPACITY] for policy implementation, unstable [APPRECIATION: -SOCIAL VALUA-TION] political environment and conflict, and* more importantly *[PROCLAIM: PRONOUNCE], the* lack *[JUDGEMENT: SOCIAL ESTEEM: CA-PACITY] of political will of member states. Wheth-er all member states recognise [ATTRIBUTE: ACKNOWLEDGE] the defects [JUDGEMENT: SOCIAL ESTEEM: CAPACITY] of the previous examples or not, African leaders adopted the* New Partnership for Africa's Development (NEPAD) *[ATTRIBUTE: ACKNOWLEDGE] to create an* investment friendly climate *[APPRECIATION: + SOCIAL VALUATION], to* rid *[APPRECIA-TION: + SOCIAL VALUATION] the continent of conflicts, to stick to good governance, and to* strengthen *[APPRECIATION: + SOCIAL VALU-ATION] regional integration in 2001 during the OAU summit.*

From the excerpt above, there are:

- 8 values of explicit, attributed attitude: appreciation,
- 6 token of judgements,
- 2 value of graduation,
- 6 values of engagement, of which 5 are expanding (attribute: 5 acknowledge) and
- 1 is contracting (disclaim: 1 deny).

Although the student attributes the barriers to the effective implementation of NEPAD to several authors, he makes no effort to cite them or engage with their ideas. Developing, critiquing and extending these views could help the student articulate his voice. The prevalence of judgement (6 values) suggests that novice learners rely more on unsubstantiated evaluations that may not be empirically justified. Although attempts are made to draw on engagement resources, there is a huge asymmetry between expanding and contracting resources (5:1). Similarly, while the student provides multiple reasons that explain Africa's pariah status in global affairs, these are not sufficiently linked to the overall argument about NEPAD's predestined failure enunciated in the preceding sentences. The student's voice is immanent in the reasons for the establishment of NEPAD but these reasons are unproblematically stated and are not sufficiently engaged with to provide a holistic, nuanced analysis.

The student's work lacks evaluative coherence. It presents a simplistic view that NEPAD will not achieve its intended developmental goals by merely examining prior interventions that failed. The DISCLAIM "*no surprising*" comes across as this writer's lack of anticipation of an objection from a critical reader to his assertion. The judge-ment inherent in the phrase "Its *no surprise* to think that NEPAD *will succeed to achieve neither* […]" further conflates the meaning intended. Al-though the student employs ATTRIBUTE system: ACKNOWLEDGE, that is the past failures of the then OAU as predictors of NEPAD's failure, he fails to acknowledge the different circumstances under which NEPAD evolved that potentially warrant qualitatively different judgements.

In excerpt 3, which is an introduction of a Health Science proposal, the Masters student ar-ticulates Artemisinin-based combination therapies (ACTs) for treating Malaria in West Africa.

Excerpt 3:

Malaria is a major *[GRADUATION: FORCE]* cause of morbidity and mortality *[ATTRIBUTE: ACKNOWLEDGE], especially among children and pregnant women in Africa (Citation provided) [ATTRIBUTE; EVIDENTIALITY]. In Nigeria, at least 300 000 children die of malaria annually (Citation provided) [ATTRIBUTE; EVIDENTIAL-ITY]. According to statistics [ATTRIBUTE: AC-KNOWLEDGE] malaria is responsible for 60% of* outpatients' visits *[ATTRIBUTE; EVIDENTIAL-ITY]*, 30% of childhood mortality *[ATTRIBUTE; EVIDENTIALITY]* (Citation provided). Nigeria accounts for a quarter of all malaria cases in the African region *[ATTRIBUTE: AKNOWLEDGE]* World Health Organisation (WHO) *[ATTRIBUTE: ACKNOWLEDGE]* and there is no *[DISCLAIM: DENY]* evidence *[ATTRIBUTE: EVIDENTIAL-ITY]* of any systematic decline *[APPRECIATION:-SOCIAL VALUATION]* in the burden despite *[DISCLAIM: COUNTER]* a progressive increase *[APPRECIATION: +SOCIAL VALUATION]* in funding to control it (Citation provided) *[AT-TRIBUTE: ACKNOWLEDGE]*.

Evidence have (has) shown *[ATTRIBUTE: EVIDENTIALITY]* that the affordable and widely available anti-malaria chloroquine (CQ) *[APPRE-CIATION: +SOCIAL VALUATION]-which was the* major *[GRADUATION: FORCE] first line drug has* lost its efficacy *[JUDGEMENT: SOCIAL ESTEEM: CAPACITY] due to the emergence of CQ-resistent (resistant) strains of Plasmodium falciparum (Citation provided [ATTRIBUTE: AC-KNOWLEDGE]. Artemisinin-based combination therapies (ACTs)* have been found *[ATTRIBUTE: ACKNOWLEDGE] to be* highly effective *[APPRE-CIATION: +SOCIAL VALUATION] at treating P. Falciparum in* most places *[GRADUATION: FORCE] where* they have been studied *[ATTRIBU-TION-ACKNOWLDGE]. In April 2001*, the WHO *[ATTRIBUTE: ACKNOWLEDGE] recommended the use of ACTs in countries where P. Falciparum is resistant to CQ, sulphurdoxine-pyrimethamine (SP) and amodiaquine (Citation provided) [AT-TRIBUTE: ACKNOWLEDGE]. ACTs* even though *[DISCLAIM: COUNTER]* far more expensive *[APPRECIATION:- SOCIAL VALUATION] than CQ and SP, are currently* the WHO recommended first line drugs *[APPRECIATION:+SOCIAL VALUATION] for treating uncomplicated malaria in areas of resistance to CQ and SP (Citation provided) [ATTRIBUTE: ACKNOWLEDGE].* However *[DISCLAIM: COUNTER], a global

subsidy mechanism is contemplated* in order to make ACTs accessible and affordable *[APPRE-CIATION: +SOCIAL VALUATION].*

- 3 values of explicit, unattributed attitude: appreciation
- 4 values of explicit, attributed attitude: appreciation
- 2 value of graduation
- 2 value of evidentiality
- 17 values of engagement, of which are 13 are expanding (attribute: 13 acknowledge) and
- 4 are contracting (disclaim: 1 deny, 3 counter).

In the two extracts above, there are 3 values of unattributed attitude (appreciation) and 4 values of attributed attitude and an imbalance between expanding and contracting resources (13:4). As Swan (2010) suggests, high scoring essays were found to have a balance between contracting and expanding resources and the asymmetry between these resources possibly point to the limitation of this essay. The bulk of this introduction comprises citations that have been insufficiently engaged with, and this serves to undermine the student' voice and assertion of authority in her work. AC-KNOWLEDGE and APPRECIATION dominate both excerpts and the student fails to adequately balance the different values of appreciation, judgement and engagement to effectively assert their agency and stamp their authority.

Although a lack of a systematic decline in malaria cases and increase in funding for malaria control are cited, no attempt is made to provide evidence (EVIDENTIALITY) in terms of statistics from other African countries to back up these claims. Although the use of DISTANTIATION embodied in phrases like *It is estimated... evidence have (has) shown* and "*have been found to be,* constitutes useful engagement resources for the projection of an impersonal academic voice, such use is not sufficiently supported by other engagement (especially contracting), evidentiality and graduation resources to render some convincing arguments on the interventions to combat malaria in Africa. Overally, therefore, this distantiation ultimately comes across as parroting of established authorial views than a critical reflection and evaluation of divergent and complementary positions.

In excerpt 4, an introduction of another science-related proposal, the Masters student explores the use of communicative skills by medical practitioners to assist patients and their families to cope with patients' transition from curative to palliative care:

Excerpt 4:

This study explores how medical practitioners use communication skills especially during the phase of disclosing to the patient and family that curative measures have been exhausted *[APPRECIATION:-SOCIAL VALUATION] and the patient's* illness is incurable *[APPRECIATION:-SOCIAL VALUATION] or* may *[ENTERTAIN]* not *[DISCLAIM: DENY] be cured. Frank [ATTRIBUTE: ACKNOWLEDGE] states that communication is* pivotal *[APPRECIATION: +SOCIAL VALUATION] to the medical profession as patients and their families have a right to access any information doctors have [APPRECIATION: +SOCIAL EVALUATION], so that they may [ENTERTAIN] be empowered [APPRECIATION: +SOCIAL EVALUATION] to take an active part in decision making [APPRECIATION: + SOCIAL VALUATION]. Thus medical practitioners have a* moral, ethical and legal duty to inform *[APPRECIATION: + SOCIAL VALUATION] patients of the* disease prognosis and available treatment options *[APPRECIATION: + SOCIAL VALUATION].*

It is really *important [PROCLAIM: PRONOUNCE] therefore, for medical practitioners to be* cogniscent of the fact *[ATTRIBUTE: ACKNOWLEDGE] that effective communica-*

tion within the interdisciplinary team, including patients and family members, needs to be their focus from early stages of illness *[APPRECIATION:+ SOCIAL VALUATION]. Such focus* will *[ENTERTAIN] ensure that the holistic approach and continuum in palliative care is realised as health professionals draw on each* other's strengths and expertise, together with experiences unique to them *[APPRECIATION: + SOCIAL VALUATION].*

In Excerpt 4, there are:

- 6 values of explicit, unattributed attitude: appreciation
- 3 values of explicit, attributed attitude: appreciation
- 7 values of engagement, of which are 5 are expanding (3 entertain, attribute: 2 acknowledge) and 2 contracting (disclaim: 1 deny, 1 proclaim)

There is a dominance of APPRECIATION: SOCIAL EVALUATION much of which is unattributed and an overemphasis on expanding resources: ENTERTAIN at the expense of contracting resources DISCLAIM (5:2). Although the introduction provides a citation to demonstrate the importance of communication, overall, it is argumentatively weak to the extent that its fails to balance the argument by providing conditions under which the patient and her relatives' rights to information might be infringed and disclosure might not be plausible. For example, if patients are diagnosed with life-threatening sickness that might cause undue emotional stress and psycho-social problems that could exacerbate their sickness. Under these circumstances, although doctors are legally required to disclose this information, ethically this can exacerbate the patient's anxiety and stress levels.

The claim that doctors have a moral, ethical and legal duty to inform the patient about the course and outcome of their disease and the different medical interventions possible needs to be sufficiently argued for. The citation given is just stated in passing without unravelling the conditions under which this prognosis is conceivably justifiable. If positioning embodies one's stance in relation to the content conveyed and in relation to a body of scholarship, and if voice is about the distinctness of one's authorial signature, then the citation of one source is insufficient to make one's voice discernible, their presence felt and their positioning conceived. The essence of an inter-disciplinary team in palliative care and a holistic approach to the transition from curative to palliative care are not sufficiently engaged with and this undermines the evaluative coherence and persuasive power of the argument.

The fifth excerpt was a student proposal on the evaluation of funding for paediatric HIV intensified care. The student's introduction commences as follows:

Excerpt 5:

For many *[GRADUATION: FORCE] years, Tanzania has* not [DISCLAIM: DENY] *managed to establish (a) database to show (the)* burden *[APPRECIATION: -SOCIAL VALUATION] of HIV diseases among children below 14 years of age.* This fact *[EVIDENTIALITY] has led to* limited capacity *[APPRECIATION: -SOCIAL VALUATION] to forecast paediatrics medication requirements hence* expiration *[APPRECIATION:-SOCIAL VALUATION] of paediatrics medication (ARVs)* which have to be destroyed *[APPRECIATION:-SOCIAL VALUATION]*. As stated *in* the Tanzania health sector strategic health plan (2008-2012) *[ATTRIBUTE: ACKNOWLEDGE] that,* 20% of HIV patients *[ENTERTAIN: EVIDENTIALS] who are on ARV should [ENTERTAIN] be children. In 2009, only 8% of people [ENTERTAIN: EVIDENTIALS] initiated on ARV were children below 14 years of age. HIV has* caused devastation *[GRADUATION: TENOR] in many families here in Tanzania and sub Sahara Africa. HIV positive*

children who fall under this disadvantaged group [APPRECIATION: -SOCIAL VALUATION] *face* huge *[GRADUATION: FORCE]* limitations [APPRECIATION: -SOCIAL VALUATION] *of accessing medical care.* Study done by Mbando *[ATTRIBUTE: ACKNOWLEDGE] reported social determinants of health for infants and children with one or more parents* dying or dead from HIV [APPRECIATION:-SOCIAL VALUATION] *include,* pervasive *[GRADUATION: TENOR] poverty,* weak *[JUDGEMENT: SOCIAL ESTEEM: CAPACITY] community social support systems,* lack *[APPRECIATION: -SOCIAL VALUATION] of policy commitments by government or foreign donors,* lack *[APPRECIATION: -SOCIAL VALUATION] of access to anti-retroviral drugs,* limited *[APPRECIATION: -SOCIAL VALUATION] access to schools and gender. The current approaches of identifying HIV positive children (VCT and PICT) are* not *[DISCLAIM: DENY] sensitive enough to identify HIV children in the community with* destroyed family unit *[APPRECIATION: -SOCIAL VALUATION].*

In this excerpt there are

- 7 values of explicit, unattributed attitude: appreciation
- 4 values of explicit, attributed attitude: appreciation
- 1 evidential
- 3 values of graduation
- 6 values of engagement, of which are 4 expanding (2 entertain, attribute: 2 acknowledge) and 2 contracting (disclaim: 2 deny).

In the excerpt, there is an imbalance between expanding and contracting resources and there are several unattributed attribute values (7). There seems to be an overreliance on attitude and judgements (graduation) at the expense of engagement. Although the social determinants of health for infants are highlighted, they are insufficiently engaged with to sufficiently inform the understanding of the problem under investigation.

Reflective Accounts of Using Facebook for Language Acquisition

Student and consultants' reflective narratives of their Facebook behavior suggested its use for three purposes namely: *sharing linguistic resources*, the *enactment of academic agency* and its deployment for the *conduct of academic research*. The enactment of student voice could only be inferred from these diverse uses demonstrated in the following sections.

Sharing Linguistic Resources

Given the concerns about violations of student privacy often reported in mainstream literature, the researcher could not use individual students' Facebook postings. Rather he requested the same ESL students and their writing consultants to provide brief reflective narratives of their Facebook use for language acquisition and language improvement/development respectively. The narratives revealed these agents' use of Facebook for the appropriation and sharing of linguistic resources with their peers:

Adele (consultant):

I specialize in applied language and literacy. On my Facebook profile page are many *[GRADUATION: FORCE] conversations that I have with friends and comments that they make on my profile. If I read an e-book or* interesting *[APPRECIATION: +SOCIAL VALUATION] article on linguistics issues then I* just *[EVIDENTIAL: EMPHATIC] provide the link on Facebook for my peers to access.*

- 1 unattributed attitude: appreciation
- 1 value of judgement
- 1 value of graduation
- 1 value of evidential

Facebook is projected as a productive space for English language acquisition through the sharing of language-based conversations and linguistic resources like books, articles and URLs. The use of emphatics, linguistic signs of assertion and emphasis, such as *just* (Vázquez & Giner, 2009) suggests the writer's commitment to her claims. Evidentials, like boosters, help to anchor the author's illocutionary position in relation to her interlocutors and to convince them of the authenticity and sincerity of her utterances. Reference to conversations, social affinities (friendships), linguistic resources and practices (providing links) is indicative of author's attempt to create a dialogical space with the reader both inter-textually and socially, for the grasping of her thoughts. Hyland (2005) observes that in claiming a right to be heard, writers must display a competence as disciplinary insiders through a writer–reader dialogue, which situates both their research and themselves, establishing relationships between people, and between people and ideas.

Another student openly acknowledged eavesdropping into peers' Facebook conversations to access their ways of expression and argumentation. If language literacy is conceived as a social practice situated in context, then, visiting, reading and reflecting on peers' Facebook spaces created an ambient milieu for appropriating English language vocabulary, assimilating lexico-grammatical expressions and understanding conventions of the language:

MaKhumalo (student):

Sometimes *[ENTERTAIN] I use Facebook to see how other people are communicating culturally, I sneak into other people's pages and I get to know how they use their English language and express themselves. This is because we [READER PRONOUN] have different [APPRECIATION: -SOCIAL VALUATION] cultures that prey [APPRECIATION: -SOCIAL VALUATION] on each other's communicative practices [...] So I get to know how they express themselves and how that is* different *[APPRECIATION: -SOCIAL VALUATION] from the way I do it.* Basically [EVIDENTIAL], *I want to* prove [ATTITUDE] *that language is* related to *[APPRECIATION: +SOCIAL VALUATION] culture.*

- 4values of explicit, unattributed attitude: appreciation,
- 1 value of self-attributed attitude,
- 1value of engagement, which is expanding (1 entertain) and
- 1 evidential and 1 reader pronoun

The frequency adverb "sometimes" suggests a degree of epistemic probability of use of Facebook by the student. The collective pronoun "we" and attitude verb "prove" are deliberately harnessed to develop "an assumption of shared attitudes, […] express a position and pull readers into a conspiracy of agreement so that it can be difficult to dispute these judgements (Hyland, 2005, p. 180). As such, the system of engagement encompasses the linguistic resources for aligning the listener/ reader with the value positions of the speaker/ writer (Derewianka, 2009, p. 144). The claims about language being related to culture and the borrowing from the communicative practices of other cultures are constitutive of engagement and display the author's positionality in relation to the universe of readers in her discipline.

Linguistic resources were also exchanged through student provision of excerpts of their readings and articles to peers on Facebook. Students also appropriated Facebook to foster communities of language practice through sustained notifications of language-related social events and activities:

Darrell (student):

I am a student in the Dept of Linguistics. I frequently [ENTERTAIN: FREQUENCY ADVERBS] use Facebook and Mxit to communicate with friends. On Facebook I put snippets of language-based

readings and articles that I really [PROCLAIM: PRONOUNCE] like [APPRECIATION: +SOCIAL VALUATION] to share with my Facebook group. I also receive notification and updates from friends on language learning events and exhibition activities.

- 1 value of explicit, unattributed attitude: appreciation
- 1 value of engagement, which is expanding (1 entertain) and
- 1 value of engagement, contracting (proclaim: 1 pronounce)

In Darrell's short reflective narrative, the relative proportionality of appreciation and engagement values suggests logical academic writing. Swain (2007) compared and contrasted two undergraduate essays, one high scoring and the other low scoring, in terms of their deployment of attitude and engagement resources. Her findings were that the high-scoring essay appropriated a wider range of resources from the different subsystems of engagement, and also showed a more even balance between expanding and contracting resources. On the contrary, the low scoring essay relied heavily on the contracting resource disclaim: deny, and was lacking in the expanding resources of attribute. That said, a caveat on classifications of text by attitude markers, attributions and emphatics is that, notwithstanding the plausibility of classification and easiness of application, one area of difficulty is the possibility of some particular instances / items falling into more than one group and the subjective boundaries between adjectives (Hewings & Hewings, 2002, p. 369).

Enactment of Academic Agency

The enactment of academic agency was another benefit of using Facebook for foreign language acquisition and development. Adele, a consultant who was investigating the relationship between academic identities and scholarly writing in her project appropriated Facebook and blogs as alternative learning environments for student reflective writing. In her narrative on student linguistic practices on Facebook, Adele highlighted that:

Adele, a consultant:

I found *[ATTRIBUTE: ACKNOWLEDGE]* that students do felt *[ATTRIBUTE: ACKNOWLEDGE]* that there is a strong relationship *[GRADUA-TION: FORCE]* between academic identity and scholarly writing. On Facebook and blogs, they *[ENGAGEMENT: DISTANCE]* felt *[ATTRIBUTE: ACKNOWLEDGE]* that they could freely *[AP-PRECIATION: + SOCIAL VALUATION]* express their writing something that they cannot *[DIS-CLAIM: DENY]* necessarily do in conventional academic writing. In academic writing students often *[GRADUATION: FORCE]* were not sure *[APPRECIATION: - SOCIAL VALUATION]* of what they were expected of *[APPRECIATION: - SOCIAL VALUATION]* by educators so they were limited *[GRADUATION: FORCE]* expressions of their self-identities as would *[ENGAGEMENT: ENTERTAIN]* be the case in blogs and on Facebook. For in an essay, they would not *[DISCLAIM: DENY]* use "I" but would *[ENGAGEMENT: ENTERTAIN]* use the third person or the passive voice as a way to hide their agency.*

- 3 values unattributed attitude: appreciation,
- 3 values of graduation,
- 8 values of engagement, of which 6 are expanding (2 entertain, 1 attribute, 3 acknowledge) and 2 are contracting (disclaim: 2 deny).

Academic agency was exhibited in student claims about the democratic expression of personal identities and perspectives on social media environments more than they would normally do in conventional academic writing. The use of the first person pronoun in their blog reflec-

tions and Facebook commentaries constituted an articulation of embodied agency. In the narrative above, there is a relative balance between values of appreciation and graduation but an imbalance between contracting and expanding resources. Although proportions of these values and tokens could vary depending on whether the narrative is responding to an explorative, expository or explanatory question, the narrative was premised on the expository question on the different ways in which students and consultants used Facebook for language learning and development respectively. Expository questions, do not assume a specific answer, and in the engagement framework are grouped under the entertain system (Swain, 2010).

Claims about sincere conversations online were also immanent in other students' reflective narratives about the fecundity of Facebook with regard to language learning. Perhaps, the asynchronous nature of Facebook conversations coupled with the opportunities to reflect on peer' comments without breaking the conversation flow potentially made Facebook conversations more sincere and vibrant than offline conversations:

Murphy, a student:

I [SELF MENTION] have many [GRADUATION: FORCE] friends that are part of my virtual life whom I chat with quite [GRADUATION: FORCE] honestly [JUDGEMENT: TENOR] [APPRECIA-TION: + SOCIAL VALUATION] [ATTITUDE] on line about language matters but [DISCLAIM: COUNTER] in the physical world I don't see [DIS-CLAIM: COUNTER] that quite often [GRADU-ATION: FORCE].

- 1 value of unattributed attitude: appreciation,
- 1 token on judgement,
- 3 values of graduation,
- 3 values of engagement, of which 1 is expanding (1 attribute) and 2 are contracting (disclaim: 2 counter).

Since productive academic writing targets discerning the degrees of dialogic engagement represented in essays—i.e., the degrees to which the essays are negotiating with others' voices by denying, countering, concurring, endorsing, or entertaining those voices (Lancaster, 2012), the few dialogic resources in text above could be conceived as evidence of low profile academic writing. However, since this writing was a self-reflective report in which the researcher did not necessarily expect students to draw on mainstream literature, the incidences of drawing on dialogic resources were therefore, optional and not mandatory.

Conduct of Academic Research

While Facebook was conceived as instrumental for language learning, its application for research on language acquisition yielded qualitatively different results. One student's research into student use of Facebook and blogs for language learning revealed that these constituted ineffective tools for acquiring English language literacy:

Talent, a consultant:

On my blog, I research on how students reflexively think *[APPRECIATION: + SOCIAL VALUA-TION] about academic writing. Here students can share thoughts about an excerpt of an article. I* would *[ENTERTAIN]* be called upon *[APPRECIA-TION: - SOCIAL VALUATION] to respond and a conversation* would *[PROCLAIM: CONCUR] start. We* complement *[APPRECIATION: + SOCIAL VALUATION] blog social commentary with Facebook interactions,* critique [ACKNOW-LEGDE] *and writing workshops. Students* did not *[DISCLAIM: DENY] find them (Facebook and blog commentaries) useful [APPRECIATION: - SOCIAL VALUATION] because they were* not tightly linked *[DISCLAIM: DENY] to the curricu-lum but I wanted their interactions to be informal so that they* could [ENTERTAIN] *write about their linguistic experiences and* reflect on *[APPRE-CIATION: + SOCIAL VALUATION] them when*

they felt *[ATTRIBUTE: ACKNOWLEDGE] they* should *[ENTERTAIN] and* not feel *[DISCLAIM: DENY]* coerced *[APPRECIATION: - SOCIAL VALUATION] to do that. The hunch is,* unless *[DISCLAIM: COUNTER] you* explicitly tell *[EN-TERTAIN] students what they* will *[ENTERTAIN] use these social networking technologies for, they* will not *[DISCLAIM: DENY] find them* useful *[APPRECIATION: + SOCIAL VALUATION].*

- 7 values of explicit, attributed attitude: appreciation,
- 13 values of engagement, of which are 8 are expanding (5 entertain, 2 acknowledge, 1 concur) and 5 are contracting (disclaim: 4 deny, 1 counter).

Talent's account displays a relative balance between expansive and contractive engagement resources. In good scholarly writing, writers should strive to vary and ultimately balance their stock of engagement resources- expanding and contracting. As Swain (2010) aptly suggests, the quantitative analysis for attitude and engagement suggests that effective discussion writing entails an ability to exploit the full range of available engagement resources and use effective combina-tions of these resources. As such the process of writing on text constitutes "social engagement", in which there is active involvement of the reader and the imagined reader in the construction of text (Hyland & Tse, 2004, p. 156).

DISCUSSION

Asymmetrical Balance between Appraisal System Resources

In students' introductions, imbalances persisted between appreciation, judgement and engagement resources with a strong inclination towards ap-preciation resources. Mindful of Swain's (2010) argument that a coherently argued essay should strike a balance between inscribed and evoked judgement (social sanction and esteem), appreciation (social valuation) and engagement resources, the dominance of appreciation resources in students' introductions is indicative of limited appropriation of their voice. On average, appreciation resources (unattributed and attributed) combined tended to be fairly higher than engagement values (expanding and contracting) suggesting that students were less assertive in articulating their stance (positioning) and voice. The dominance of unattributed appreciation demonstrates that they were less confident with or inexperienced in engaging with other authors (inter-personally) and with text (inter-textually), an affirmation of claims about some undergraduates' incapacity to affirm their authority in writing. As Read, Francis and Robson (2001) suggest, in their essay writing, undergraduate students are not only conceptually challenged by engaging with a particular domain of knowledge, but with successfully utilising the language necessary in order to communicate this engagement. This is predicated on the shared view that despite their meeting of the minimal standards for admission at university, many students often possess insufficient engagement and linguistic resources to effectively articulate their worldviews and ideas. Such shortcomings demonstrate the need for complementary ideological spaces which provide cognitive and linguistic scaffolding for students.

Limited Use of Engagement Resources

In terms of the balance between engagement resources, there was an asymmetry between expanding and contracting resources. Students tended to rely more on mere acknowledgement and attribution of ideas to established authorities than asserting their presence (voice) in their academic writing. The affirmation of their voice could be realised through heightening their con-

tracting (i.e. counter, deny) resources and keeping judgement resources in balance with engagement resources. The under-representation of engagement resources alludes to student inadequate induction and mastery of academic discourses because the mastery of disciplinary discourses often empowers them to appropriate such resources to sufficiently engage with authoritative sources. As Hyland (2005) reminds us, engagement resources are more important than attitude resources, although the evaluative component in attitude resources gives students more latitude to position themselves interpersonally than textually. Therefore, the suboptimal articulation of engagement resources, which reflect the capacity of the writer to recognise and engage with other voices in the field, weakened the academic merit of their arguments. The overrepresentation of judgement resources in some students' introductions lends itself to their reliance on undeveloped linguistic resources, which complicated reflexive and dialogic reasoning in argument building. Derewianka (2007, p. 162) highlights the challenge of dialogic writing as the shift from a relatively undialogised writer position, which fails to problematise the subtleties of the field to a reflexive writer position, which accommodates other voices and recognises the need to negotiate these voices. Student reliance on judgement resources seem to cohere with this inability to transit undialogised writer position.

Flouting of Grammatical Rules

One vivid expression of student challenges with articulation of voice was their use of negative reactions, contractions, inappropriate verbs and superlatives. This is notwithstanding the academic convention in scholarly writing which stipulates the use of impartial and impersonal language. This convention emphasises that academic texts should foreground the object of discussion and distances the subject from their actions. Active voice, engagement subsystems (entertain, proclaim), distantiation, boosters and hedges

Table 3. How Facebook complements Writing Centre (WC) practices of developing student voice

Descriptor	WC Context	How Facebook Complements WC	Implications for Voice
Location **Location-dependent strategies**	Writing Centres are academic development interventions that usually offer campus-based support to students. Students on remote campuses are often underserved because of commuting demands, travel costs, and time to access WC services. Writing consultants' strategies for articulating voice include eliciting methods like expecting students to "read aloud" their work to make apparent the implications of expressions, probing questions that seek clarification and semantic and explanation-seeking questions. These strategies are often availed to students who physically visit the Writing Centres. The strategies are constrained by time (usually 45 minutes per session) and strict booking schedules	A Facebook tutorial group with dedicated writing consultants can be established to support regular students (in successive consultations) and students on remote campus that cannot access WCs at designated times. Students do not need to travel to campus to access WC resources. Facebook tutorial consultations can employ complementary strategies like-role play, simulations, digital storytelling, video-based learning of language and group engagements. The consultations can be more extended unconstrained by location-based/ appointment-dependent booking times. Support provided can be customized to meet individual reflection (using Facebook as a reflective blog), cluster or group based needs (using Facebook discussion board as a virtual class). Facebook affordances for attaching MS Word documents allow consultants and students to work collaboratively on documents and to give comments (using a closed Facebook page)	Facebook applications offer diverse customized interactions –private chat (for consultant-novice interactions) and Wall post features (for group interactions) on language based issues. This flexibility provides a safe, realistic context for novice voice, opinions and self-reflections. "Facebook simplifies the process of managing a large network of connections. Users are presented with multiple communication channels, including private messages, public "Wall" postings, status updates, instant messaging, groups, and applications" (Lampe, Wohn, Vitak, Ellison, & Wash, 2011) Facebook's voyeuristic character, student-controlled nature and affective presence afford students on remote campus the opportunity to reflexively engage with and critique remote online consultants in a learner-regulated environment.
Interdisciplinarity	Although academic voice development necessitates consultant understanding of the disciplinary conventions and the subject matter content, consultants with knowledge of particular disciplines are not always available. This is not withstanding the contentious nature of the content and language debate. "The debate between integration of language and content is ongoing and the degree of integration varies across departments, faculties, as well as institutions" (Archer, 2010, p. 496-497). Although WC appointments tend to reflect inter-disciplinarity by appointing candidates from diverse discipline, discipline-based consultants may not always be available when students need them as consultants are postgraduates employed on a part-time basis and have other competing academic commitments.	WCs can assign to students on Facebook consultants from specific disciplines or with inter-disciplinary knowledge to inculcate discipline-specific conventions and entrench academic authority in writing. These consultants can access students anywhere, anytime. Provision of 'ground rules' and netiquette for online communication would formalise student socialisation and induction into disciplinary conventions, which are critical to developing their voice.	Students are better able to assert their voice when they engage with consultants who are more informed about their disciplinary conventions, ways of positioning, and assertion of voice in particular disciplines. Recruitment of experts with interdisciplinary knowledge would complement WC where discipline-based support is emphasised

Continued on following page.

Table 3. Continued

Descriptor	WC Context	How Facebook Complements WC	Implications for Voice
Sustainability	Consultants' devotion to developing novice voice is constrained by duration of consultations (usually 45 minutes per session) per novice and number of novices supported per day. While consultants are committed to optimising time during their consultations, there is loss of discursive memory, continuity and momentum as students are not guaranteed the same consultants in successive consultations.	Assigning Facebook consultants who continue with conversations on voice development enunciated in WC would ensure sustainability of such conversations. Using Facebook as a reflective blog also allows critical self-reflection, group collaborative engagement, critical commenting on peers' ideas and provision of URLs to web resources unconstrained by time	The complementation of WC consultations with Facebook consultations lies in continuity of conversations on voice enunciated in WC context.
Group Dynamics	While WCs allow individual and group conversations, group interactions are often not optimally used because of the resource constraints, challenges of managing group dynamics, and limited consultant training in handling group consultations. The walk-in centres often function with a very small budget often coming from outside the institution (Archer, 2010). Assertion of personal voice is often complicated by peer dominance in group interactions and shyness of some novices when they are exposed to group interactions.	Consultant training in Facebook group moderation and in asserting novice through open, sincere articulation of arguments/perspectives would complement the individual and cluster consultation in WCs.	Students develop their voice in academic writing when face-to-face individual consultations are complemented by group consultations via Facebook wall or discussion board.
Power relations	Although WCs are meant to be democratic and dialogic learning spaces, novices often reinforce hierarchy and asymmetrical power when they perceive consultants as "experts" in language and voice development. Depending on the novice's personality and academic maturity, what ideally should be dialogic interaction that ultimately shifts power from the consultant to the student might become an authoritative practice, when consultants inadvertently fail to render a sense of ownership to novices.	Facebook is a student-controlled, self-organising space available to them. Consultants use of this non-traditional, "affinity space" (Gee, 2004) potentially neutralizes power relations if they support an ambient environment for self expression and articulation of novice intentions/voice. Salavuo (2008) project that social networking sites are ideal for constructivist pedagogies because 1). Students are in control of the environment, 2). Information contained in personal profiles may highlight an individual's expertise and identify common interests, thus building a sense of community and co-operative learning (cited in Ryan, Magro, and Sharp, 2011)	Developing multiple spaces for improving writing would give students more leverage and ownership of their voice.

help shift the focus of the debate from the agent towards the object under investigation. The assertive and expressive articulation of voice was thus constrained by some students' appeal to emotive language. As Ramanathan and Atkinson (1999)

cogitate, the most common use of metaphorical notion of voice appears to involve linguistic (or near-linguistic) communication inclined towards a particular ideology or worldview of such communication-one in which the individual is foregrounded and valorised. "Voice" in this sense, is seen to represent linguistic behaviour, which is clear, *overt, expressive,* and even *assertive* and *demonstrative* (Ramanathan & Atkinson, 1999).

How Facebook Complements Writing Centres' (WCs) Developmental Functions

The different ways in which Facebook complements WCs are provided (see Table 3). The table documents the WC context, the academic value that Facebook brings when used in conjunction with WCs and the implication of this union for developing student voice.

CONCLUSION

The essay demonstrated that students struggled to articulate their voice and assert their agency in their academic work. The use of emotive language, contractions, superlatives and unsubstantiated statements suggests student challenges in stamping authorial presence in their work. While their reliance on value judgments constitutes a genuine attempt at asserting their voice and agency, such assessments were not always backed by sufficient evidence. These challenges mirror the need for lecturers to educate students on the conventions of academic writing and to make explicit those practices that are academically rewarding. Reflective narratives of students and consultants demonstrated Facebook's multimedia affordances, its capacity to engender student-generated linguistic resources and foster the articulation of academic agency, which is critical to the development of student voice.

Consistent with Swain's (2010) analysis, students' essays often demonstrated some symmetry between expanding and contracting resources and privileged affect and social valuation at the expense of engagement resources. Students who consulted with the WC portrayed lack of familiarisation with academic conventions and incapacity to deploy them in academically useful ways. While WC present dialogic spaces for the development of scholarly writing in an iterative, recursive and progressive manner, time constraints and the inadequate collaborative production of knowledge in groups make additional spaces necessary. Facebook ideally complements Writing Centres through its support for peer-based critique and group-based reflexive engagements. It constitutes a collective hybrid space (Bhabha, 1994) through which formal knowledge structures and informal, community and peer-based forms of knowing could interact to bring student epistemic shifts and transformative learning.

REFERENCES

Archer, A. (2010). Challenges and potentials for Writing Centres in South African tertiary institutions. *South African Journal of Higher Education, 24*(4), 495–510.

Arkoudis, S., & Tran, L. (2010). Writing blah, blah, blah: Lecturers' approaches and challenges in supporting international students. *International Journal of Teaching and Learning in Higher Education, 22*(2), 169–178.

Bailey, C., & Pieterick, J. (2008). Finding a new voice: Challenges facing international (and home!) students writing university assignments in the UK. *Third Annual European First Year Experience Conference,* University of Wolverhampton.

Ballard, B., & Clanchy, J. (1988). Literacy in the university: An "anthropological" approach. In G. Taylor, B. Ballard, V. Beasley, H. K. Bock, J. Clanchy, & P. Nightingale (Eds.), *Literacy by Degrees* (pp. 7–23). Milton Keynes: Society for Research into Higher Education/Open University Press.

Bhabha, H. (1994). *The location of culture.* New York: Routledge.

Chen, H. I. (2013). Identity practices of multilingual writers in social networking spaces. *Language Learning & Technology*, *17*(2), 143–170.

Chen, J. J., & Yang, S. C. (2014). Fostering foreign language learning through technology-enhanced intercultural projects. *Language Learning & Technology*, *18*(1), 57–75.

Correa, D. (2010). Developing academic literacy and voice: Challenges faced by a mature ESL student and her instructors. *Profile*, *12*(1), 79–94.

Cortazzi, M., Jin, L., Wall, D., & Cavendish, S. (2001). Sharing Learning through Narrative Communication. *International Journal of Language & Communication Disorders*, *36*(s1), 252–257. doi:10.3109/13682820109177893 PMID:11340792

Derewianka, B. (2007). Using appraisal theory to track interpersonal development in adolescent academic writing. In A. McCabe, M. O'Donnell, & R. Whittaker (Eds.), *In Advances in Language and Education* (pp. 142–165). London: Continuum.

Elbow, P. (1994). What do we mean when we talk about voice in texts. In K. Yancey (Ed.), *Voices on Voice: Perspectives, Definitions, Inquiry* (pp. 1–35). Urbana, IL: National Council of Teachers of English.

Gee, J. P. (2004). *Situated language and learning: A critique of traditional schooling*. New York: Routledge.

Guiterrez, K., Morales, P. Z., & Martinez, D. (2009). Re-mediating Literacy: Culture, Difference, and Learning for Students from Non-dominant Communities. *Review of Research in Education*, *33*, 213–245.

Hamilton-Hart, J. (2010). *Using Facebook for language learning. Innovation in Language Teaching and Learning*. Retrieved from: http://iltl.wordpress.com/2010/11/11/using-facebook-for-language-learning/

Hewings, A. (2012). Stance and voice in academic discourse across channels. In K. Hyland & C. Sancho (Eds.), *Stance and voice in written academic genres* (pp. 187–201). Basingstoke: Palgrave Macmillan. doi:10.1057/9781137030825.0021

Hewings, M., & Hewings, A. (2002). It is interesting to note that...a comparative study of anticipatory "it" in student and published writing. *English for Specific Purposes*, *21*(4), 367–383. doi:10.1016/S0889-4906(01)00016-3

Hitchcock, G., & Hughes, D. (1995). *Research and the teacher* (2nd ed.). London: Routledge.

Hodges, D. C. (1997). Re: Academic Voice. Retrieved October 5, 2014, from http://lchc.ucsd.edu/MCA/Mail/xmcamail.1997_10.dir/0366.html

Hyland, K. (2005). Stance and engagement: A model of interaction in academic discourse. *Discourse Studies*, *7*(2), 173–192. doi:10.1177/1461445605050365

Hyland, K., & Tse, P. (2004). Metadiscourse in academic writing: A reappraisal. *Applied Linguistics*, *25*(2), 156–177. doi:10.1093/applin/25.2.156

Lampe, C., Wohn, D. Y., Vitak, J., Ellison, N. B., & Wash, R. (2011). Student use of Facebook for organizing collaborative classroom activities. *International Journal of Computer-Supported Collaborative Learning*. 1-27. Retrieved from: http://www.springerlink.com/content/h9m4233168200637/ (Date accessed 15/06/2014)

Lancaster, C. (2012). *Stance and Reader Positioning in Upper-Level Student Writing in Political Theory and Economics*. PhD Thesis, University of Michigan.

Lea, M. R., & Street, B. (1998). Student writing in higher education: An academic literacies approach. *Studies in Higher Education*, *23*(2), 157–172. doi:10.1080/03075079812331380364

Martin, J. R., & White, P. R. (2005). *The Language of evaluation: Appraisal in English*. Basingstoke: Palgrave Macmillan.

McKenna, S. (2004). *A critical investigation into discourses that construct academic literacy at the Durban Institute of Technology*. PhD Thesis, Rhodes University, South Africa.

Mills, N. (2011). Situated learning through social networking communities: The development of joint enterprise, mutual engagement, and a shared repertoire. *CALICO Journal*, *28*(2), 345–368. doi:10.11139/cj.28.2.345-368

Motta-Roth, D. (2009). The Role of context in academic text production and writing pedagogy. In C. Bazerman, A. Bonini, & D. Figueiredo. (Eds.), Genre in a changing world (pp. 317-336). The WAC Clearinghouse and Parlor Press.

Pavlenko, A. (2001). *Multilingualism, second language learning, and gender*. New York: Walter De Gruyter. doi:10.1515/9783110889406

Pavlenko, A., & Norton, B. (2007). Imagined communities, identity, and English language learning. In J. Cummins & C. Davison (Eds.), *International handbook of English language teaching* (pp. 669–680). Dordrecht, Netherlands: Springer. doi:10.1007/978-0-387-46301-8_43

Ramanathan, V., & Atkinson, D. (1999). Individualism, academic writing, and ESL Writers. *Journal of Second Language Writing*, *8*(1), 45–75. doi:10.1016/S1060-3743(99)80112-X

Read, B., Francis, B., & Robson, J. (2001). Playing Safe: Undergraduate essay writing and the presentation of the student voice. *British Journal of Sociology of Education*, *22*(3), 387–399. doi:10.1080/01425690124289

Rosen, L. D. (2010). *Rewired: Understanding the iGeneration and the way they learn*. New York: Palgrave Macmillan.

Ryan, S. D., Magro, M. J., & Sharp, J. H. (2011). Exploring Educational and Cultural Adaptation through Social Networking Sites. *Journal of Information Technology Education*, *10*, 1–16.

Salavuo, M. (2008). Social media as an opportunity for pedagogical change in music education. *Journal of Music. Technology and Education*, *1*(2/3), 121–136.

Schalkwyk, S. C. (2008). Acquiring academic literacy: A case of first year extended degree programme students at Stellenbosch University. Stellenbosch University.

Sherlock, K. (2008). *Advice on academic tone*. Retrieved September 27, 2014, from www.grossmont.edu/karl.sherlock/English098/.../Academic_Tone.pdf

Street, B. V. (2003). What's new in New Literacy Studies? Critical approaches to literacy in theory and practice. *Current issues in comparative education*, *5*(2), 1-14.

Swain, E. (2007). Constructing an effective voice in academic discussion writing: An appraisal theory perspective. In A. McCabe, M. O'Donnell, & R. Whittaker (Eds.), *Advances in Language and Education* (pp. 166–184). London: Continuum.

Swain, E. (2010). Getting engaged: dialogistic positioning in novice academic discussion writing. In E. Swain (Ed.), *Thresholds and potentialities of systemic functional linguistics: multilingual, multimodal and other specialised discourses* (pp. 291–317). Trieste: EUT Edizioni Università di Trieste.

Vázquez, I., & Giner, D. (2009). Writing with Conviction: The use of boosters in modelling persuasion in academic discourses. *Revista Alicantina de Estudios Ingleses*, *22*, 219–237.

White, P. R. R. (2003). Beyond modality and hedging: A dialogic view of the language of intersubjective stance. *Text*, *23*(2), 259–284. doi:10.1515/text.2003.011

Wingate, U. (2006). Doing away with 'study skills'. *Teaching in Higher Education*, *11*(4), 457–469. doi:10.1080/13562510600874268

KEY TERMS AND DEFINITIONS

Academic Conventions: Rules and principles of academic engagement of a discipline that are generally acceptable among scholars of that discipline.

Academic Development Programmes: Institutional, faculty-wide and departmental interventions to develop students academically, cognitively, emotionally and socially through the advancement of literary and numeracy practices including the provision of academic support.

Attitudinal Resources: Linguistic resources concerned with agents' perceptions, emotional dispositions, judgements and reactions to various behavior.

Authorial Presence: The author's positionality and objective articulation in text in relation to other authors and textual resources.

Engagement Resources: Deal with attitudes and voices of agents in discourses.

English As Second Language Learner: students whose mother tongue is not English.

Facebook: A social networking site developed by Mark Zackerburg, a Harvard University, and his peers in 2004 as an online directory for students contact and social engagement.

Social Networking Technologies: Conversational Web based sites that allow users to develop profiles of self, upload personal resources and connect with multiple networks via the Internet.

Voice: Assertion of authorial presence and positioning by a writer in textual expressions.

Chapter 19
Perceptions of Competencies Developed in an Active Learning Course Featuring the Design of Web–Based Instruction on Mathematics

Hatice Sancar Tokmak
Mersin University, Turkey

Lutfi Incikabi
Kastamonu University, Turkey

ABSTRACT

This chapter presents a research study on mathematics education pre-service teachers' perceptions of competencies developed in an active learning course. During the course, the pre-service teachers designed web-based instruction (WBI) to teach mathematics to a targeted group of children. Data were collected through a demographic questionnaire, unstructured focus group interviews, open-ended questionnaires, and WBI design documents. WBI documents were analyzed according to Khan's (1997) identified components. The results of the study showed that, according to the mathematics education pre-service teachers, their internet search skills, content knowledge about distance education, web interface design skills, and technological knowledge increased or improved due to the WBI project. Moreover, participants observed how the constructivist philosophy did not apply to their designs. In addition, their designs were created from the perspectives of users rather than producers, as many components of WBI were not taken into account during or after the project.

INTRODUCTION

Web-based instruction has been described as the new center of educational policies because, as Moe and Blodget (2000) have stated, by 2025, about 40 million people will have participated in an online course. Sancar Tokmak (2013) has identified reasons for this increase in use as de-

DOI: 10.4018/978-1-4666-8363-1.ch019

mand for higher education and lifelong learning as well as advancements in technology, making WBI attractive for people all over the world. Khan (1997) described WBI:

Web-based instruction (WBI) is a hypermedia-based instructional program which utilizes the attributes and resources of the World Wide Web to create a meaningful learning environment where learning is fostered and supported. (p. 6)

Khan (1997) has categorized the components of WBI as content development, multimedia components, internet tools, computers and storage devices, connections and service providers, authoring programs, servers, browsers, and other applications. Hedberg, Brown, and Arrighi (1997) have emphasized that while the roles of teachers and students cannot be equated during traditional learning, roles can change in WBI. They distinguish the modes of teaching in this environment as user or producer. As users, teaching includes the use of interactive multimedia (IMM) and WBI tools; as producers, teaching includes IMM and Web page construction (Hedberg, Brown, & Arrighi, 1997).

However, the success of instruction offered online depends on the instructional design, not the medium. Ozonur (2013) compared two groups of learners who attended courses offered by Adobe Connect Pro and Secondlife Environment, where the applied instructional design was stable for both. According to the results, there was no significant difference between the two groups of learners' success rates. Bostock (1997) has stated that active learning can be an alternative that allows learners to construct their knowledge and that only placing content on a page cannot support active learning. The literature has showed that educators who offer online courses should enhance their design competencies by considering characteristics of online education and active learning. Accordingly, the main research question of the study was, what are mathematics education pre-service teachers'

perceptions of competencies developed in a WBI design activity structured for active learning?

ACTIVE LEARNING AND MATHEMATICS TEACHING

Generally defined as the implementation of any instructional method that engages students in the learning process, active learning requires students to conduct meaningful learning activities and think about what they are doing. Recently, national mathematics teaching programs and respected, internationally recognized mathematics teacher organizations such as National Council of Teachers of Mathematics (NCTM) have promoted the value of active learning in their processes.

The mathematics teaching program in Turkey has defined the general objectives and goals of mathematics education (MoNE, 2005) as seeking to provide students with

- An understanding of mathematical concepts and systems, their interrelationships, and the ability to apply these concepts and systems to daily life and in other academic subjects;
- Mathematics knowledge and skills for higher education;
- The ability to use deductive and inductive reasoning;
- The ability to use mathematical reasoning to solve problems;
- The ability to use correct terminology to explain mathematical processes;
- The ability to make efficient use of prediction and mental computation;
- The ability to develop problem solving strategies and apply them to real life situations;
- The ability to construct mathematical models;
- High self-esteem and positive attitudes toward mathematics;

- Belief in the power of and the interconnected structure of mathematics;
- Comprehension of the historical development of mathematics, the role of mathematics in the improvement of human thinking, and uses of mathematics in other disciplines;
- Scientific, attentive, patient and responsible attitudes; and
- The ability to relate mathematics to the arts. (p. 9)

The Turkish mathematics program places a heavy emphasis on promoting teaching and learning environments in which students can actively share their ideas and participate.

Applying a constructivist approach, the learning principles of the NCTM (2000) make students responsible for their own learning: "Students must learn mathematics with understanding, actively building new knowledge from experience and previous knowledge" (p. 2). The mathematics program in Turkey also emphasizes students' active participation in their learning process by underlining the improvement of such skills as problem solving, creative and critical thinking, decision making, communication, reasoning, and linking new knowledge to existing knowledge. Problem solving skills, an inseparable part of the Turkish program, aim to evaluate the entire process, rather than simply the final product. The NCTM also promotes problem solving, communication, reasoning, and proof standards, which are categorized under strategies that promote active learning. The NCTM (2000) requires students' active participation in the problem solving process by providing

...frequent opportunities to formulate, grapple with, and solve complex problems that involve a significant amount of effort. They are to be encouraged to reflect on their thinking during the problem solving process so that they can apply and adapt the strategies they develop to other problems and in other contexts (p. 4).

The way mathematics learning is defined changes the way it should be taught. In order to create an active learning environment, teachers must become providers of guidance in students' learning. The mathematics teaching program in Turkey stresses concrete experiences, meaningful learning, communication using mathematical knowledge, teaching organized based on appropriate phases (introduction, investigation, explanation, advancement, and assessment), linking new knowledge to existing knowledge, student motivation, efficient uses of technology, and learning based on collaboration. Similarly, NCTM asks mathematics teachers to create a classroom environment in which students are challenged to communicate the results of their thinking to others orally or in writing, which allows students to discuss mathematical ideas from multiple perspectives to sharpen their thinking and make connections.

The constructivist nature of mathematics teaching programs affects the assessment of students' learning. Teachers consider whether students can apply mathematics to daily life; improvements to problem solving, reasoning, association and communication skills; student attitudes towards mathematics; and student confidence engaging with mathematics. The program emphasizes that previous knowledge affects future gains, and a deficiency or inaccuracy impedes growth. In order to prevent such obstacles, in-class examinations, discussions, presentations, experiments, projects, observations, portfolios, self-evaluation, and peer evaluation are recommended to evaluate pupils' progress. Rubrics, checklists, and diaries are additional tools for evaluating students' work. Moreover, in line with the principles of active learning, students are also required to evaluate and assess their own and their peers' progress.

The mathematics teaching program in Turkey encourages students to be mentally and physically ready for active participation. Students are expected to be responsible for their learning, to negotiate ideas, to ask questions, to listen, to establish and solve problems, to think, to debate, and to study in groups. On the other hand, teachers are responsible for guiding and motivating students, listening to them and allowing them to ask questions.

METHOD

The current research was a qualitative case study aiming to investigate mathematics education pre-service teachers' perceptions about competencies developed in an active learning course requiring WBI design. The study documented the pre-service teachers' perceptions on developed competencies and the reasons behind their opinions, asking what and why questions as well as how to gain a whole picture from their point of view. According to Yin (2003), a case study provides the opportunity to investigate a single aspect of a problem in depth while answering the "why" and "how" questions. Moreover, Yin (2003) stated that case studies may contain one or multiple cases; this study was a single case that collected data from one setting, consistent with Bogdan and Biklen's (1998) description of "a detailed examination of one setting, or a single subject, a single depository of documents, or a particular event" (p. 59).

SAMPLING

The convenience sampling strategy was applied in the study. The participants were therefore both readily accessible and volunteers, as defined by Teddlie and Yu (2007). All participants were Primary Mathematics Teacher Education Programme pre-service teachers enrolled in an Instructional Technology and Material Design course. Out of 24 students in the class, 21 agreed to participate in the study. Although the other three pre-service teachers completed all requirements of the course, they did not want their data used for research purposes. Eight participants were female, and 13

were male. All of them were in their second year in the Primary Mathematics program at Mersin University. The mean age of participants was 21, ranging from 19 to 22. The participants had been using computers for about 6 years, and most of them stated that they were aware of websites or products offering math education online. However, all but seven pre-service teachers pointed out that they had investigated these sites and products and found them lacking. Moreover, 20 participants explicitly stated that math cannot be taught through distance education. According to them, math can only be taught face-to-face, preferably through private lessons. However, the participants hadn't heard or participated in any discussion about how math courses should be designed through the web before.

INSTRUMENTS

Data were collected through a demographic questionnaire, unstructured focus group interviews, open-ended questionnaires, evaluations of WBI designs according to Khan's (1997) components, and guided materials provided to assist pre-service teachers in preparing their WBI documents (APPENDIX A). The unstructured interview format, open-ended questionnaires, and WBI preparation guidelines were prepared by the researchers and checked by two experts before administration.

- **Demographic Questionnaire:** This questionnaire included questions about gender, age, program and grade year, computer use, and previous WBI evaluations, if any. The questionnaire also had one open-ended question about perceptions on teaching mathematics through WBI.
- **Unstructured Interviews:** Two primary questions were asked: "Could you describe your experience using WBI to teach the math content you selected?" and "Which

skills did you use during the activity?" According to the answers, more detailed questions were asked to determine the competencies developed.

- **The Open Ended Questionnaire:** The questionnaire included four questions:
    ◦ What did you take into account while designing your WBI?
    ◦ What difficulties did you face while designing your WBI?
    ◦ What were the strengths and weaknesses of your WBI?
    ◦ What sources did you use while designing your WBI?
- **WBI Design Evaluation:** The documents presented by the mathematics education pre-service teachers were evaluated according to WBI components suggested by Khan (1997). Khan's (1997) WBI components are shown in Table 1.

COURSE DESIGN AND ACTIVE LEARNING

A course design proposed for technological, pedagogical, and content knowledge (TPACK) development in a WBI design course by Sancar Tokmak (2013) was applied to the present study. This course design is consistent with the features of active learning acknowledged by Grabinger and Dunlap (1996 as cited in Bostock, 1997). Moreover, according to Power and Guan (2000), WBI design should consider multiple factors, such as computing capacity and ability of students, active learning environments, and equity of students' access to the course. The applied WBI design course did not neglect these factors and took several steps to ensure active learning features (modified from Sancar Tokmak, 2013).

- **Analysis of Pre-Knowledge:** The knowledge of mathematics education pre-service teachers on content presented in the WBI, technologies used, and instructional design strategies applied were analyzed through questionnaires, brainstorming techniques, and concept maps. The instructor helped pre-service teachers identify incomplete skills or misconceptions and then developed appropriate instructional strategies.

Instructional Strategies

- **Content Knowledge:** During this step, the mathematics education pre-service teachers examined the national math program in terms of topics, aims, learning philosophy, teachers' and students' roles in activities, materials, and instructional strategies. The mathematics education pre-service teachers designed a WBI to teach to a selected grade level (5-8).
- **Pedagogical Knowledge:** The WBI design activity required pre-service teachers to know which instructional strategies to use according to their target population. They searched for WBI examples online, paying attention to strategies and preparing a report about which ones they would use. During this step, the mathematics education pre-service teachers also considered the target group's interests, pre-knowledge, preferences, required preparation, and computing competencies.
- **Technological Knowledge:** This step aimed to equip mathematics education pre-service teachers with technologies they may use in their WBI. They were encouraged to choose technologies that had the capabilities to support their chosen instructional strategies, particularly with regard to

Table 1. WBI Components proposed by Khan (1997)

Main Components	Sub Components	
1. Content Developments	1.a. Learning and instructional theories	
	1.b. Instructional design	
	1.c. Curriculum development	
2. Multimedia Component	2.a. Text and graphics	
	2.b. Audio Streaming (e.g. Real Audio)	
	2.c. Video Streaming (e.g. Quick Time)	
	2.d. Graphical user interface	
	2.e. Compression technology (e.g Shock Wave)	
3. Internet Tools	3.a. Communication Tools	
		3.a.i. Asynchronous
		3.aii. Synchronous
	3.b. Remote Access Tools	
		3bi. Telnet, ftp etc.
	3c. Internet Navigation Tools (Access to database and Web documents)	
		3ci. Gopher, Lynx etc.
	3d. Search and Other Tools	
		3di. Search engines
		3dii.Counter Tool
4. Computers and Storage Devices	4a. Computer platforms running unix, dos, windows, mac operating systems	
	4b. Servers, hard drives, CD ROMs etc	
5. Connections and Service Providers	5.a. Modems	
	5.b. Dial-in	
	5.c. Gateaway provider, Internet Service Provider	
6. Authoring Programs	6.a. Programming Languages	
	6.b. Authoring Tools	
	6.c. HTML converters and Editors, etc.	
7. Servers	7.a. HTTP servers, HTTPD software, Web site, URL	
	7.b. Common Gateway interface	
8. Browsers and Other Applications	8.a. Text based browsser, graphical browser, VRML browser etc.	
	8.b. Links (e.g. Hypertext links, hypermedia links, 3-D links, image maps etc.	
	8.c. Applications that can be added to Web browsers such as plug ins.	

the computing capacity and ability of students and equity of students' access.

- **Defining Roles:** During a WBI design activity, instructors should guide pre-service teachers to think about alternatives during design decisions, ensuring that the pre-service teachers remain active participants in the learning process. Pre-service teachers searched for information, built upon their knowledge, shared and discussed ideas, and reflected on their potential WBI designs. They were coached to pay attention to the following items while searching for examples:

  ○ The presentation of topics (subtopics, interfaces, format, names of links and buttons, background colors, colors and fonts of text, etc.)

- Instructor-learner, learner-learner, and learner-content interaction
- Incorporated technologies
- Instructional strategies
- Activities
- Out-of-class activities and required technologies
- Evaluation and assessment methods

Participants were also coached to pay attention to the above items while designing their WBIs. The mathematics education pre-service teachers were assessed according to their performances during the WBI design process. Their reports on the national math program and WBI examples as well as their own WBI designs contributed to their grades.

DATA ANALYSIS

Descriptive statistics were used to analyze the demographic questionnaire by determining the mean age range of participants and their computer backgrounds. Moreover, the frequency of participants offering opinions about WBI math courses was also collected. The unstructured interviews and open-ended questionnaire were analyzed through open coding. As Patton (1990) suggested, the interviews and open-ended questionnaire were transcribed first and then coded into common themes and patterns; finally, generalizations were outlined. During coding, categories were formed according to themes created by significant statements, as advised by Ayres, Kavanaugh, and Knalf (2003).

VALIDITY AND RELIABILITY

While conducting and analyzing research, the appropriate validity and reliability procedures for qualitative studies were followed. Among verifi-

cation procedures suggested by Creswell (1998), the following methods were applied to this study:

- **Triangulation:** The data were collected through unstructured focus group interviews, an open-ended questionnaire, and the mathematics education pre-service teachers' WBI design evaluations.
- **Peer Review or Debriefing:** In every step of the study, from planning and conducting research to analyzing and writing results, colleague opinions were sought out.
- **Member Checks:** The unstructured focus group interviews, open-ended questionnaire, and WBI design documents were analyzed by two researchers. Inter-coder reliability for all methods was calculated by applying Miles and Huberman's (1994) formula. The inter-coder reliability was 0.78 for focus group interviews, 0.81 for open-ended questionnaire, and 0.77 for the WBI design documents.
- **Rich, Thick Description:** The context and procedures of the study were described in detail.
- **External Audits**: All procedures and instruments were checked by two external experts in math and instructional technology.

RESULTS

Focus Group Interview and Open-Ended Questionnaire Results

The mathematics education pre-service teachers described their experiences as rich, creative, difficult, and amateurish. They stated that the WBI design activity required them to combine multiple knowledge bases; for that reason, it was described as rich. Moreover, they emphasized that this activity required creativity, which posed distinct challenges:

We are a group that is very open to share each others' works. But this causes us to design very similar WBIs. The WBI design activity required us to be creative, and actually, we have not done such homework before. Maybe the reason is that we do not have pre-knowledge about WBI.

Pre-service teachers also felt that the activity was difficult because they had to consider too many aspects of instruction all at once. Open-ended questionnaire results supported focus group interview comments about difficulty deciding topics, technologies, and how to present through the web. One pre-service teacher said:

Explain the aims, how the interface would be, how to present the questions, what the name of web address would be: there are too many things to consider. To prepare a video is very difficult. [Deciding] which program I would use for video conferencing, for example, is very difficult. You have to also think as a user. Which action would be easy for them? Too many things.

In the first open-ended questionnaire, participants pointed out how they must take into account content, grade level, technology, usability issues, and design of the WBI. However, the pre-service teachers omitted the additional considerations of the aims of national programs, instructional design, and communication tools. The mathematics education pre-service teachers described their designs as amateurish since they had not designed WBIs before. Moreover, they stated that although they found their interfaces easy to use and suitable for the design principles, they had difficulty with the technology and instructional components of the assignment. Similarly, in the open-ended questionnaire, the pre-service teachers identified interface design as a strength of their WBIs, while technology represented a weakness.

During focus group interviews, the pre-service teachers stated that they struggled to understand and establish their learning philosophies. One pre-service teacher stated:

For me, I do not have a learning philosophy yet. My instruction is not a constructivist WBI. According to me, we could not yet understand the learning philosophies. Actually, I feel myself close to constructivism, but my WBI is a bit behaviorist.

Six categories emerged as a result of the analysis of developed competencies: Internet search skills, learning about distance education, awareness of institutions offering distance education, changes in ideas about teaching math online, technologies used in WBI, and web design skills. The pre-service teachers stated that they searched the web specifically for WBI information and examples. They discovered that many institutions, including their university, offered WBI. Moreover, they started to change their perspectives:

I had said that math could not be taught through distance education. But after searching, I saw the good examples and started to think, "Why not?" Math also can be taught in this way.

The mathematics education pre-service teachers mentioned that they learned about distance education, WBI, and technologies. They expressed that they suffered from limited technological knowledge but were pleased to gain new experiences with technology. One pre-service teacher explained, "Video conferencing, for example. I searched and learned about Adobe Connect Pro. Then I learned from forums that there are languages such as Asp, C, and so on." Statements made in interviews about searching and sharing were supported by the open-ended questionnaire, which identified the internet, friends, and instructors as sources of information.

WBI Design Documents Evaluation

The documents prepared by the mathematics education pre-service teachers were evaluated by two researchers in line with Khan's (1997) WBI components. For content development, results showed that all participants followed a teacher-centered behaviorist approach. They presented their documents, sources, examples, exercises, and content presentations through videos, and both asynchronous and synchronous communication tools. Activities were determined and led by the instructor, and students were expected to read or watch provided content and answer questions. Moreover, no pre-service teachers completely applied an instructional design model. For example, only two mathematics education pre-service teachers took into account the analysis step by testing students' pre-knowledge about content. Similarly, only four participants implemented evaluation in their designs by applying student ideas. Most pre-service teachers performed the design, development, and implementation steps but did not conduct analysis or evaluation.

As for Khan's (1997) curriculum development component of WBI, only six mathematics education pre-service teachers addressed the goals of the national math program in their designs. Eight pre-service teachers prepared their WBIs for eighth grade subjects, eight for seventh grade subjects, three for sixth grade subjects, and two for fourth to eighth grade subjects. When investigating accuracy under curriculum development, except three pre-service teachers, all presented correct knowledge. However, all the mathematics education pre-service teachers' WBI designs were not appropriate to activities suggested by the national math program.

With regard to multimedia, ten of the mathematics education pre-service teachers used both graphics and text while presenting content. Nine of them used graphics sufficiently related to content and in suitable places. Ten others used only text, and one used a small font size that was very difficult

to read. A total of 20 mathematics education pre-service teachers used headings, bold/italic/color options, and similar elements. One pre-service teacher only used videos for content presentation and incorporated no graphics or text. Three participants used audio tracks recorded for their WBIs. None of the mathematics education pre-service teachers specifically named the video streaming programs they would incorporate in their designs. However, 19 of them did integrate videos: nine indicated that they would use synchronous lesson presentations through web cameras in addition to previously recorded course videos, while ten said they would only use previously recorded videos. Three pre-service teachers did not use videos at all. Most (n = 18) of the mathematics education pre-service teachers' WBI designs included user-friendly graphical interfaces where headings and subheadings were presented logically. Users were regularly informed about their actions. No significant problems were identified in terms of understandability of buttons, directions, or text in the designs, and most text, buttons, and headings were consistent in terms of color, naming, size, and placement. Only three pre-service teachers did not pay attention to color, size, or placement consistency in their designs. One in three pre-service teachers did not carefully review grammar or understandability of text. For example, in this pre-service teacher's WBI, there were significant spelling errors. No compression technology was used in the WBI designs.

For internet tools, all except one of the mathematics education pre-service teachers (n = 20) used asynchronous communication tools in their designs, and 15 of them used more than one. The most used tools were e-mail (n = 14), social media such as Facebook, blogs, and Twitter (n = 14), and forums (n = 9). For synchronous communication tools, three mathematics education pre-service teachers used only chats, and nine used video conferencing. Two of them used Skype, and two used MSN; the other five did not list a tool. Nine mathematics education pre-service teachers did not use synchronous communication tools. Four of them used Adobe Connect, and another two used Lotus Live. Three other pre-service teachers did not mention the tools they used for video conferencing. One participant used FTP as a remote access tool.

Table 2 shows the most frequently referenced components by pre-service math teachers in line with Khan's (1997) WBI components. The pre-service teachers failed to address computers and storage devices; connections and service providers; authoring programs, servers, and browsers; and other applications.

In summary, the results showed that the mathematics education pre-service teachers considered the WBI design a rich experience since it required the use of many skills regarding technology, content knowledge about distance education, and application of WBI. Since they had no prior experience with WBI, they faced difficulties during the process. The competencies they developed included internet searching and distance education concepts. However, during interviews, they stated that they were not pleased with their final products because they could not manage the instruction part well. The WBI design evaluation supported that the mathematics education pre-service teachers only used behaviorist approaches and did not successfully apply instructional design as a whole.

DISCUSSION

This chapter outlined the results of a research study on mathematics education pre-service teachers' perceptions about competencies developed in an active learning course featuring WBI design. During the study, the course design proposed by Sancar Tokmak (2013) was applied by addressing WBI factors identified by Powers and Guan. The course design included three main steps: (a) Pre-knowledge of the Mathematic Education Pre-service Teachers, (b) Instructional Strategies to Complete Required Skills and Correct Misconceptions, and (c) Defining the Role of Instructor and Mathematic Education Pre-service Teachers. These steps included active learning features designed to shift the responsibility of learning to the pre-service teachers, to define the instructors' roles as coaches or guides, and to prompt pre-service teachers to cooperate in an authentic context with a goal-driven approach. All these features were consistent with active learning as described by Grabinger, Dunlap, and Duffield (1997), focusing on student responsibility, dynamic generative learning, authentic context, collaboration, and reflection.

The data were collected through a demographic questionnaire, unstructured focus group interviews, open-ended questionnaires, and the mathematics education pre-service teachers' WBI documents. Except for the WBI components proposed by Khan (1997), all instruments were prepared by the researchers. Descriptive statistics were used to analyze the demographic questionnaire results, while open coding analyses were used by two researchers to interpret the results of the unstructured focus group interviews and open-ended questionnaires. WBI design documents were analyzed in line with the elements defined by Khan (1997).

The results showed that the mathematics education pre-service teachers had a rich experience during the WBI design activity. However, the activity was reported as being difficult, and participants felt their products were amateurish. Despite the step-by-step approach implemented during the course, they could not completely imagine how to proceed since they had no previous experience with teaching via distance education. They acknowledged that they lacked pre-knowledge about WBI. Mayer (2009) has stated the importance of new knowledge being integrated with the prior knowledge of students. Similarly, Şimşek (2013) indicated that analysis of the learners is a main component of many instructional design models. The instructional design of this course was based on defining the pre-knowledge of the mathemat-

Table 2. The most frequently used components by the mathematics education pre-service teachers in line with Khan (1997) WBI

Main Components	Sub Components	Summary of Results
1. Content Developments	1a. Learning and instructional theories	1a. Behaviorism
	1b. Instructional Design	1b. Application of ID Partly
	1c. Curriculum Development	1c. 7th and 8th grade contents Correct knowledge presentation No Curriculum aims
2. Multimedia Component	2a. Text and graphics	2a. Both text and graphics Only texts
	2b. Audio Streaming (e.g. Real Audio)	2b. No audio
	2c. Video Streaming (e.g. Quick Time)	2c. Previously recorded course Videos
	2d. Graphical user interface	2d. User friendly
	2e. Compression technology	2e. No defined
3. Internet tools	3a. Communication tools	
	3ai. Asynchronous	3ai. E-mail Social media (facebook, Twitter, blog)
	3b. Remote Access Tools	
	3bi. Telnet, ftp etc.	
	3c. Internet Navigation Tools	
	3ci. Gopher, Lynx, etc	
	3d. Search and Other Tools	
	3di. Search enginges	
	3dii. Counter tool	
4. Computers and Storage Devices	4a. computer platforms running unix, dos, windows, mac operating systems	
	4b. Servers, hard drives, CD ROMs, etc	
5. Connections and Services Providers	5.a. Modems	
	5b. Dial-in	
	5c. Gateaway providers, Internet Service Provider	
6. Authoring Programs	6a. Programming languages	
	6b. Authoring tools	
	6c. HTML converters and Editors, etc.	
7. Servers	7a. HTTP servers, HTTPD software, Website, URL	
	7b. Common Gateaway interface	
8. Browers and other Applications	8a. Text based browser, graphical browser, VRML browser, etc	
	8b. Links (e.g. Hypertext links, hypermedia links, 3-D links, image maps, etc)	
	8c. Applications that can be added to web browsers such as plug ins.	

Note: The mathematics education pre-service teachers did not pointed out anything after the item 3bi according to Khan (1997).

ics education pre-service teachers about WBI and providing them with the required knowledge and skills before the activity. The mathematics education pre-service teachers also stated that the activity required creativity. They did not find themselves to be very creative, which also affected peer designs. Sancar Tokmak, Surmeli, and Ozgelen (2014) found similar results in their research study on the TPACK development of pre-service science teachers after the creation of digital stories. In their study, participants stated that because the activity required creativity, they struggled.

Although the national curriculum for all grades is rooted in creating projects, problem-based learning, and active learning drawn from the constructivist philosophy, students mostly focus on national exams, which generally determine student selection and placement. Thus, students have only the standard skills of industrial age labor requirements, as described by Reigeluth (1999). To provide future children with the skills required of the information age, educators must continue to design engaging and relevant activities.

The pre-service math teachers stated that they could not design their WBI in line with the constructivist philosophy, despite their efforts. They emphasized how their designs were still based on the behaviorist philosophy. The WBI design evaluation supported this result. However, the mathematics education pre-service teachers stated that their searching skills, knowledge about distance education, and understanding of the technologies used during the WBI design did improve. According to the results, they were also satisfied with the interface designs of their WBIs. The WBI evaluations were consistent with these results; interface designs were user-friendly and appropriate for the design principles. However, participants did not consider other components proposed by Khan (1997), such as computers and storage devices; connections and service provid-

ers; authoring programs, servers, and browsers; and other applications. The mathematics education pre-service teachers' pre-knowledge was increased through activities such as searching for WBI examples online. It could be said that the pre-service math teachers took on not the role of the designer (producer) but of the user while designing their WBIs. According to Hedberg, Brown, and Arrighi (1997), the producer role requires interactive multi media (IMM) and webpage design and construction, rather than simply the use of them. The mathematics education pre-service teachers placed components in their WBI designs to the degree they recognized they were necessary while searching the Internet as users. Yet, a deep understanding is required to progress to the role of designer. Activities such as interviewing a designer may provide pre-service teachers a valuable look from another perspective.

REFERENCES

Ayres, L., Kavanaugh, K., & Knafl, K. A. (2003). Within-case and across-case approaches to qualitative data analysis. *Qualitative Health Research*, *13*(6), 871–883. doi:10.1177/1049732303013006008 PMID:12891720

Bogdan, R. C., & Biklen, S. K. (1998). *Qualitative Research for Education: An Introduction to Theory and Methods*. Boston, MA: Allyn and Bacon.

Bostock, S. J. (1997). Designing Web-based instruction for active learning. In B. H. Khan (Ed.), *Web-based Instruction* (pp. 225–230). Englewood Cliffs, New Jersey: Educational Technology Publications.

Creswell, J. W. (1998). *Qualitative inquiry and research design: Choosing among five traditions*. Thousand Oaks, CA: Sage Publications.

Grabinger, S., Dunlap, J. C., & Duffield, J. A. (1997). Rich environments for active learning in action: Problem-based learning. *Research in Learning Technology, 5*(2), 5–17. doi:10.1080/0968776970050202

Hedberg, J., Brown, C., & Arrighi, M. (1997). Interactive multimedia and Web-based learning: Similarities and differences. In B. H. Khan (Ed.), *Web-based Instruction* (pp. 47–58). Englewood Cliffs, New Jersey: Educational Technology Publications.

Khan, B. H. (1997). Web-based instruction: What is it and why is it? In B. H. Khan (Ed.), *Web-based Instruction* (pp. 1–18). Englewood Cliffs, New Jersey: Educational Technology Publications.

Mayer, R. E. (2009). *Multi-media learning* (2nd ed.). New York: Cambridge University Press. doi:10.1017/CBO9780511811678

Miles, M. B., & Huberman, A. M. (1994). *Qualitative data analysis: An expanded sourcebook* (2nd ed.). Thousand Oaks, CA: Sage.

Moe, M. T., & Blodget, H. (2000). *The knowledge web: Part 1. People power: Fuel for the new economy.* New York: Merrill Lynch.

MoNE. (2005). Ilkogretim matematik dersi (6-8 siniflar) ogretim programi [Elementary school mathematics teaching program (grades 6-8)]. Ankara, Turkey.

NCTM (National Council of Teachers of Mathematics). (2000). *Principles and Standards for School Mathematics.* Reston, VA: Commission on Standards for School Mathematics.

Ozonur, M. (2013). *Sanal gerçeklik ortamı olarak ikincil yaşam (second life) uygulamalarının tasarlanması ve bu uygulamaların internet tabanlı uzaktan eğitim öğrencilerinin öğrenmeleri üzerindeki etkilerinin farklı değişkenler açısından incelenmesi* [The design of second life applications as virtual world and examining the effects of these applications on the learning of the students attending internet-based distance education in terms of different variables]. Phd thesis: Mersin University.

Patton, M. Q. (1990). *Qualitative research and evaluation methods* (2nd ed.). Newbury Park, CA: Sage.

Powers, S., & Guan, S. (2000). Examining the range of student needs in the design and development of a web-based course. In B. Abbey (Ed.), *Instructional and cognitive impacts of Web-based education* (pp. 200–216). Hershey, PA: Idea Group Publishing. doi:10.4018/978-1-878289-59-9.ch013

Reigeluth, C. M. (1999). What is instructional-design theory and how is it changing? In C. M. Reigeluth (Ed.), *Instructional-design theories and models: A new paradigm of instructional theory* (Vol. II, pp. 5–29). Mahwah, NJ: Lawrence Erlbaum Associates.

Sancar Tokmak, H. (2013). TPAB - temelli öğretim teknolojileri ve materyal tasarımı dersi: matematik öğretimi için web-tabanlı uzaktan eğitim ortamı tasarlama. [TPACK-based instructional technology and material design course: Designing web-based instruction for mathematic teaching] In T. Yanpar Yelken, H. Sancar Tokmak, S. Ozgelen, & L. Incikabi (Eds.), *Fen ve matematik eğitiminde TPAB temelli öğretim tasarımları* [TPACK-based course designs in Science and Math education]. (pp. 239–260). Ankara: Ani Publication.

Sancar-Tokmak, H., Surmeli, H., & Ozgelen, S. (2014). Pre-service science teachers' perceptions of their TPACK development after creating digital stories. *International Journal of Environmental and Science Education, 9*(3), 247–264.

Şimşek. (2013). Öğretim tasarımı ve modelleri. [Instructional design and models] In K. Cagıltay & Y. Goktas (Eds.), *Öğretim teknolojilerinin temelleri: Teoriler, araştırmalar, eğitimler* [Foundations of instructional technology: Theories, researches, and trends]. Ankara: Pegem Publishing.

Teddlie, C., & Yu, F. (2007). Mixed methods sampling: A typology with examples. *Journal of Mixed Methods Research, 1*(1), 77–100. doi:10.1177/2345678906292430

Yin, R. K. (2003). *Case study research: Design and methods* (3rd ed.). Thousand Oaks, CA: Sage.

KEY TERMS AND DEFINITIONS

Active Learning: Active Learning is an instructional method that engages students in the learning process, and requires students to conduct meaningful learning activities and think about what they are doing.

Distance Education: Distance education is institution based, formal education where the learner group separated and where interactive communications systems are used to connect learners, resources, and instructors (Simonson, 2003 as cited in Schlossers and Simonson, 2010, p.1).

Ministry of National Education (MoNE): The name of the National Ministry of Education in Turkey.

National Council of Teachers of Mathematics (NCTM): NCTM is an association in the United States for the purpose of serving math teachers, math educators, and administrators by providing math resources and professional development opportunities (retrieved from from www.nctm.org).

Technological Pedagogical Content Knowledge – TPACK: Sulman (1986) proposed a framework as Pedagogical Content Knowledge (PCK). TPACK is a framework proposed as an extension of Sulman (1986)'s PCK by Mishra and Kohler (2006). It focuses on teachers' technology integration and is based on the understanding that content, pedagogy, and technology can interact with one another to produce effective discipline-based teaching (Mishra & Kohler, 2006).

WBI Components: The components of WBI proposed by Khan (1997). It includes mainly content developments; multimedia components; internet tools; computers and storage devices; connections and service providers; authoring programs; servers, and browsers; and other applications.

Web-Based INSTRUCTION (WBI): Web-based instruction (WBI) is a hypermedia-based instructional program which utilizes the attributes and resources of the World Wide Web to create a meaningful learning environment where learning is fostered and supported (Khan, 1997, p. 6).

APPENDIX

WBI Preparation Guidance

The guidelines included four parts: purpose, requirements, deadline, and assessment.

Purpose. This technology-dominated century has affected the functions, missions, and visions of schools, since society now demands members who are creative, have critical thinking skills, and know how to find information and use technology. In addition, the information explosion has forced people to maintain and update their professional knowledge constantly. Lifelong learning concepts and WBI are very popular as a result. However, research indicates that it is not the technology but the method, or how the technology is integrated into the instruction, that affects learning. As a teacher candidate, you have to know how to integrate technology effectively. Designing courses with these technologies can help improve your skills.

Requirements. You will prepare a detailed report including the following items:

- **Topic:** The WBI you design should be on topics from the national mathematics curriculum.
- **Technology:** The technologies you use should be listed in your report. Moreover, screenshots of your WBI interface should be in the report.
- **Design:** Design principles you pay attention to during interface design of the WBI should be in the report.
- **Integration:** Technology integration strategies and models you used should be in the report.

Deadline. The report and all products should be finalized and sent to the instructor before the day of the final exam.

Assessment. The report and products will be 40% of your semester course grade.

NOTE: You can contact me when you are stuck during the WBI activity through e-mail or face-to-face (during office times).

Chapter 20

Deployment and Adoption Strategy of Cloud Computing for Blended Learning in Higher Education Institutions in Sub–Saharan Africa

Joel S. Mtebe
University of Dar es Salaam, Tanzania

Mussa M. Kissaka
University of Dar es Salaam, Tanzania

ABSTRACT

Many higher education institutions in sub-Saharan Africa have been blending traditional face-to-face delivery with various Information and Communication Technologies (ICT) to meet the strong demand for higher education as well as to improve the quality of traditional campus programs. Despite the increased adoption of various forms of blended learning in the region, the cost of acquiring and managing ICT infrastructure remained to be the biggest challenge. While cloud computing can provide powerful computing at a fraction of the cost of traditional ICT infrastructure, its potential to enhance blended learning in higher education in sub-Saharan Africa is unexplored. This chapter proposes deployment and adoption strategy of cloud computing to enhance blended learning services in the region. This work contributes towards helping higher education in sub-Saharan Africa to understand cloud services and to make plans for successful migration of computing services into cloud.

INTRODUCTION

Over the past few years there has been a dramatic increase in the use of various Information and Communication Technologies (ICT) in higher education institutions in sub-Saharan Africa. Many institutions are integrating ICT into education as a way to meet the strong demand for higher education – a demand they simply cannot meet with traditional campus programs (Adkins,

DOI: 10.4018/978-1-4666-8363-1.ch020

2013). Institutions have also been viewing ICT as a solution to cost reduction as well as improving the quality of teaching and learning in the region (Selim, 2007). The cost reduction is described in terms of the costs of classrooms and facilities, training, travel, printed materials, and labor (Bhuasiri, Xaymoungkhoun, Zo, Rho, & Ciganek, 2012).

In light of these benefits, it is not surprising that institutions and international agencies have been spending many thousands of dollars to pilot and implement various eLearning solutions in the region (Farrell & Isaacs, 2007). For example, the African Development Bank Group (AfDB) provided a grant of $15.6 million to African Virtual University (AVU) to build eLearning centers and train content developers at 31 partner institutions in the region (Adkins, 2013). Similarly, the Partnership of Higher Education Africa (PHEA) has given funding to seven institutions in Africa to implement various eLearning solutions (Hoosen & Butcher, 2012).

With these initiatives and many others, the integration of ICT with traditional face-to-face classroom has been increasing significantly in the past few years. According to Adkins (2013), the blended learning in the region has been growing at the rate of 15% per annum between 2011 and 2016. This is also evident from the number of Learning Management Systems (LMS) which have continued to be implemented in higher education in the region. For instance, 80% of higher education institutions in Tanzania were found to have installed various LMS with Moodle being the most popular (Munguatosha, Muyinda, & Lubega, 2011). Similarly, five institutions surveyed by Ssekakubo et al. (2011), six by Lwoga (2012), and seven institutions that participated in PHEA project were found to have installed various LMS (Hoosen & Butcher, 2012).

Similarly, 74 per cent of 447 respondents across 41 African countries said they were using various ICT to support teaching and learning; with 48 per cent using mobile phones, 36 per cent Shared Resource Computing, and 29 per cent

desktop virtualization (Isaacs & Hollow, 2012). Additionally, a recent eLearning Africa conference 2013 report indicates that 83 per cent (out of 413 respondents) from 42 African countries were using laptops, 71 per cent mobile phones, and 67 per cent stand-alone computers to support teaching and learning (Isaacs, Hollow, Akoh, & Harper-Merrett, 2013). The majority of these institutions have been combining various ICT with traditional face-to-face delivery to create the so called "blended learning".

Despite the adoption and penetration blended learning in higher education institutions in the region, several challenges exist. The majority of the challenges faced by these institutions are unique from developed countries (Bhuasiri et al., 2012). For instance, one of the main challenge is the cost of acquiring and maintaining ICT infrastructure to facilitate blended learning delivery (Lwoga, 2012; Ssekakubo et al., 2011; Tedre, Ngumbuke, & Kemppainen, 2010; Unwin et al., 2010). The cost of hardware, software and Internet in the region is still high and unaffordable to the majority of institutions. For example, one institution surveyed by Lwoga (2012) was paying 104 million TShs per year for Internet connection, while another institution surveyed by Tedre et al. (2010) was paying 4 million TShs (2140€ = 3100$) per month for a dedicated 704kb/128kb satellite connection for 300 computers.

In addition to the cost of the Internet connection, the ICT infrastructure is not reliable due to frequent power cuts and shortage of technical staff to provide maintenance to on-campus ICT infrastructure. According to Selim (2007), the success of blended learning depends on the availability of rich and reliable ICT infrastructure capable of providing the courses with the necessary tools to make the delivery process as smooth as possible.

In recognizing these challenges, several initiatives have been underway to overcome these challenges especially improving the Internet connectivity and increasing Internet bandwidth. The most recent initiatives are the three broadband submarine fiber-optic cables (SEACOM, EASSy, WACS). These broadband submarine fiber-optic cables promises to bring increased connectivity, leading to a spurt of broadband penetration to the region (Laverty, 2011). Despite these initiatives and many others, the potential of cloud computing is unexplored. Cloud computing can provide powerful computing solutions at a fraction of the cost of traditional ICT infrastructure required to implement blended learning (Laverty, 2011).

Cloud computing involves hosting ICT infrastructure, software applications, and other computing services into cloud servers and being accessed via the Internet. Institutions can only pay for services based on usage the same way as utility services, such as water, electricity, gas, and telephony (Buyya, Yeo, Venugopal, Broberg, & Brandic, 2009; Carroll, Merwe, & Kotzé, 2011). As a result, institutions will no longer be required to procure and host ICT infrastructure in their premises and therefore, reduce the cost associated with hardware purchase, software licensing and updating, electric power, cooling, and salaries for IT support staff (Carroll et al., 2011; Koch, Assuncao, & Netto, 2012; Mircea & Andreescu, 2011; Mokhtar, Ali, Al-Sharafi, & Aborujilah, 2013; Sultan, 2010).

Therefore, the appropriate adoption and implementation of cloud computing in higher education in the region will contribute significantly towards reducing ICT investment required to deliver blended learning. This chapter proposes deployment and adoption strategy of cloud computing to enhance blended learning services in the region. This work contributes towards helping higher education in sub-Saharan Africa to understand cloud services and to make plans for successful migration of computing services into cloud.

BLENDED LEARNING IN HIGHER EDUCATION

The adoption of blended learning in higher education institutions is becoming common as many institutions have continued to combine various ICT with face-to-face delivery (Porter, Graham, Spring, & Welch, 2014). The ICT environment involves the use of video conferencing, learning management systems, the Internet, and other related technologies (Kumar, 2012). Kumar (2012) added that, the majority of these institutions have chosen blended learning in order to take the best of both face-to-face delivery and eLearning based delivery. The ICT environment provides opportunities for students to learn and express themselves in the written form while face-to-face discussions enables them to have enthusiasm that are spontaneous and contagious (Garrison & Kanuka, 2004).

The adoption of blended learning also enables instructors to use variety of instructional techniques with available ICT to achieve effective learning outcome. More importantly, the blended learning can potentially enable institutions in the region to widen access to their courses through distance courses. With blended distance courses, learners have greater flexibility of studying anywhere, and anytime regardless of work commitments, or distance limitations (Kumar, 2012). As a result, even those learners described as "hard-to-reach" learners such as those located in rural areas can easily benefit from courses offered in these institutions without being required to attend physically at a given institution.

For instance, the University of Dar es Salaam in Tanzania has introduced three blended courses namely the Postgraduate Diploma in Education, the Postgraduate Diploma in Engineering Management, and Master degree in Engineering Management (Mtebe & Raphael, 2013). These courses are offered via regional centers located in Mwanza, Arusha, and Dar es Salaam. Several institutions in sub-Saharan Africa have also adopted the same mode of delivery.

Regardless of these benefits, the success of blended depends on many factors. Selim, (2007) identified four critical factors for successful implementation of blended learning in a given institution. These factors are ICT infrastructure, university support, learner characteristics, and instructor characteristics. Similarly, Bhuasiri et al. (2012) described learners' characteristics, instructors' characteristics, institution and service quality, infrastructure and system quality, course and information quality as the critical factors for implementing blended learning.

Another study conducted in higher education institutions in South Africa higher education revealed that the technological infrastructure, high cost of technology, instructional efforts, graduate competencies, and technology satisfaction as the factors that affect institutions from continuing to use the eLearning technologies in their institutions (Venter, Rensburg, & Davis, 2012). The findings from this study corroborate with the findings obtained by Lwoga (2014) in higher education institutions in Tanzania. Lwoga (2014) found infrastructure and system quality as the main determinants of blended learning implementation as they had direct impact on perceived usefulness and user satisfaction.

Combing the findings from these studies, and many others in the literature, it is clear that the reliability of ICT infrastructure as well as the costs required to implement it are the key determinants to the success of blended learning in higher education institutions in sub-Saharan Africa. However, the majority of institutions in the region are affected by regular power outrage. Due to the frequent power cuts, many servers have been unavailable especially those hosted on-premises. Nonetheless, migrating the ICT infrastructure into the cloud will enable these services to be available 24/7 as cloud hosted servers are not affected by any power cuts.

Another main challenge that is well described in the literature is the lack of skilled technical staff to support to maintain various ICT infrastructure hosting blended learning services. These technical staff members do not have skills to perform various services such as the upgrading of software, virus protection, and performance maintenance of computer servers and associated accessories. According to Selim (2007), if the technical support is lacking, the blended learning will not succeed. Studies have shown that migrating blended learning services into the cloud will increase the reliability of blended services, but also, will reduce the costs for hiring in-house technical staff. The burden of hiring staff, and management of hardware with its accessories will be moved to cloud service provider.

In conclusion, the appropriate adoption and application of cloud computing in blended learning has the potential to reduce the costs of hardware and software that institutions must spend to run blended learning programs. It should be noted that early investigations into the cloud readiness of countries in the region has shown that there is the potential for growth of at least one form of the cloud technology in the future (Laverty, 2011).

CLOUD COMPUTING

The National Institute for Standards and Technology (NIST) defines cloud computing as "a model for enabling convenient, on-demand network access to a shared pool of configurable computing resources (e.g., networks, servers, storage, applications, and services) that can be rapidly provisioned and released with minimal management effort or service provider interaction" (Mell & Grance,

2011, p.2). The idea behind cloud computing is to enable clients (e.g., users, or institutions) to access computing resources via the Internet and pay per use as utilities; the same way users normally pay water, electricity and related services.

CLOUD COMPUTING SERVICE MODELS

The cloud computing is divided into three service models namely Software as a Service (SaaS), Platform as a Service (PaaS), and Infrastructure as a Service (IaaS). SaaS means the software or applications run on cloud provider's servers and users interact with it via the Internet (Mathew, 2012; Mokhtar et al., 2013). Google Apps such as Gmail and YouTube are typical examples of SaaS (Babar & Chauhan, 2011). For example, institutions can use Gmail for students and staff instead of institutional email system.

The PaaS enables users to access development platform and tools through APIs which support a specific set of programming languages (Babar & Chauhan, 2011). PaaS basically aims to help developers who want to create, test, and deploy software applications on provider's servers via the Internet without installing them locally (Hosam, Tayeb, Alghatani, & El-seoud, 2013; Mokhtar et al., 2013). Google Application Engine, and Microsoft Azure are good examples of such platforms.

The third cloud computing service model is IaaS that enables users to manage processing, computing services, storage, networks, and are able to configure the cloud servers similar to the physical servers (Mell & Grance, 2011). This model enables users to get rid of problems of purchasing the latest technology, maintenance, upgrading of software and software licenses (Mokhtar et al., 2013).

CLOUD COMPUTING DEPLOYMENT MODELS

The cloud computing can be deployed in four different ways: private cloud, public cloud, community cloud, and hybrid cloud. A public cloud is where cloud infrastructure is made available to several clients and this infrastructure is owned by a cloud service provider (Carroll et al., 2011; Mokhtar et al., 2013). Companies such as Google, Amazon, Microsoft provides several public cloud services. The private cloud is where cloud infrastructure is operated solely for particular organization with services made available for internal users (Babar & Chauhan, 2011; Bansal, Singh, & Kumar, 2012). Normally, the private cloud is managed by an ICT department within an organization or commissioned to a service provider or a third party organization but all services are dedicated to that organization.

The community cloud deployment model enables organizations with shared interests to control and share cloud infrastructure (Carroll et al., 2011; Mokhtar et al., 2013). One amongst participating organizations may manage the infrastructure or it may be managed by a third party organization. The last type of cloud computing deployment is called hybrid cloud. This is a mix of two or more cloud models (Mokhtar et al., 2013). Normally, organizations that adopt private deployment model aims to expand its services by outsourcing services with less security and legal requirements to public cloud providers to create a hybrid cloud. For example, organization might use public cloud basic business applications such as email and their private cloud for storing sensitive data such as financial data (Bansal et al., 2012).

CLOUD COMPUTING IN HIGHER EDUCATION

The adoptions of cloud computing to embrace education is growing fast as many institutions have been are migrating computing services into the cloud. This is further facilitated by existence of cloud service providers that provide cloud services for free or at a discount to educational institutions (Alshuwaier, Alshwaier, & Areshey, 2012; Bansal et al., 2012; Mokhtar et al., 2013). Typical examples of such cloud service providers are: Microsoft, Google, IBM, and Amazon. They have established special packages to provide institutions with access to ICT infrastructure, software, platforms, and other educational services hosted in their clouds.

For example, Google educational package consists of collection of web-based messaging (e.g., Gmail, Google Talk, and Google Calendar), productivity and collaboration tools (Google Docs: text files, spreadsheet, presentation, and form creation and sharing), Google Video, and Google sites. This package is offered at zero cost to unlimited number of users (Chandra & Malaya, 2012). The Microsoft package for education (called Live@edu) is also available at no cost (Chandra & Borah, 2012). The package consists of Microsoft Office, Windows Live SkyDrive, Windows Live Spaces, Microsoft SharedView Beta, Microsoft Outlook Live, Windows Live Messenger, and Windows Live Alerts.

The support and involvement of these companies in educational field has attracted dozens of institutions all over the world to adopt and use cloud services to enhance education. There are already several successfully deployments of cloud services in institutions such as in countries like United States, United Kingdom, Asia, and Africa. Some few examples of such institutions include North Carolina State University (Mokhtar et al., 2013), Colorado State University (Herrick, 2009), University of California in the United States (Sultan, 2010). Other institutions include Leeds Metropolitan University, the University of Glamorgan, the University of Aberdeen, and the University of Westminster in the United Kingdom.

Cloud services have also found its way in African institutions. Over 30 institutions across Africa partnered with Google to use Google cloud services (Obi, 2012). The partnership includes grants, technical, consulting, and training. These institutions include University of Pretoria, University of Ibadan, University of Mauritius, and University of Ghana. Some East African institutions that have partnered with Google are: National University of Rwanda, Kigali Institute for Education, Kigali Institute for Science and Technology, and the University of Nairobi (Wanjiku, 2009).

ADVANTAGES OF CLOUD COMPUTING IN EDUCATION

One of the biggest advantages of migrating eLearning services into the cloud is the reduction of cost associated with acquiring, managing, and maintaining ICT infrastructure. This cost reduction will be realized in three ways. First, institution will no longer incur expenses to procure computer servers needed to run blended learning. All computing services will be hosted in the cloud servers. The cost reduction has been demonstrated by Florida Atlantic University which reduced IT costs by at least U.S. $600,000 by migrating Blackboard LMS into the cloud (Chandra & Borah, 2012). Likewise, the Wake Community College reduced by nearly 50 percent of Total Cost of Ownership (TCO) through migrating traditional ICT infrastructure into the cloud (Rindos et al., 2009).

Second, the cost reduction can be realized as a result of reducing the number of IT support staff often employed to maintain ICT infrastructure in the campuses. The burden of hiring staff and management of hardware with its accessories will be moved to the cloud service provider. Similar benefits was demonstrated by the North Carolina State University which reduced the number of IT staff from 15 to 3 employees with full working schedule by migrating its computing services into the cloud (Chandra & Borah, 2012).

Finally, the cost reduction can be realized due to pay-per-use cost structure offered by cloud computing providers. In the current situation, institutions are charged flat rates even if the computing services are not used. However, the majority of institutions require intensive computing services in a short period due to the structure of teaching semesters (Truong, Pham, Thoai, & Dustdar, 2012). When students are on vacation, computing services are normally not used. The pay-per-use payment mechanism will help institution to make significant savings due to the fact that institutions will pay for only services they have used similar ways as already done for other utilities such water, electricity, and other related services (Buyya et al., 2009).

Another biggest advantage of cloud computing is the provision of high computing facilities for research and teaching especially for science and mathematics. These facilities are expensive to procure, and therefore, the majority of institutions cannot afford them. According to Truong et al. (2012), due to financial constraints, investment for research facilities is normally prioritized after teaching facilities. Institutions can use already existing facilities such as Virtual Computing Lab (VCL) offered by cloud providers to support high performance computational facilities. For instance, University of Pretoria uses VCL from IBM to enable students access and use the next-generation medical research to test the development of drugs, which are expected to cure serious illnesses unique to Africa (Kshetri, 2010).

CLOUD COMPUTING ADOPTION STRATEGY

The capabilities and practices that can help in the adoption of the cloud computing into higher education are not yet defined (Nasir & Niazi,

2011). It should be noted that cloud computing adoption has an impact on accounting, security, compliance, project management, system support, work of end users, authority of the ICT department, ICT governance, ICT provisioning, ICT procurement, and ICT policies (Khajeh-hosseini, Greenwood, & Sommerville, 2010). Therefore, it is important for institutions to develop a strategy that will provide a smooth migration of blended learning services into the cloud. We have adopted and proposed a strategy suggested by Mircea and Andreescu (2011) which consists of five stages. The description of each stage is explained next.

1. **Developing the Knowledge Base about Cloud Computing:** The first step is to ensure that all people involved in the implementation of cloud computing are well informed about the benefits and risks, policies and the best usage practices of the technology. The knowledge about cloud computing can be gained through attending seminars, workshops as well as conducting discussions with the suppliers and consulting the most recent researches in the field.
2. **Institutional ICT Assessment:** The cloud computing strategy should take into account the institutional needs and the overall institutional strategy. Therefore, it is important to evaluate the needs, structure and usage of various IT services. This will help the institution to understand which data, services, processes and applications that may be migrated or need to be maintained within the institution.
3. **Experimenting the Cloud Computing Solutions:** The third stage is to experiment selected cloud computing solutions. This can be done gradually as pilot test projects, and thereafter scaling it to all users within the institution.
4. **Choosing the Cloud Computing Solution:** At this stage, institutions are required to conduct thorough evaluation to compare cloud

service providers' capabilities, licensing mechanisms, and pricing models in order to make sustainable choices. The choice will also depend on cloud deployment options presented in section 6.

5. **Implementation and Management:** This stage involved the migration of computing services and data into the selected cloud solution. Mircea and Andreescu (2011) suggested that data migration should be performed while keeping balance between the data accuracy, migration speed, nonfunctioning time and minimum costs.

The cloud adoption strategy is shown in Figure 1.

CLOUD COMPUTING DEPLOYMENT OPTIONS

After selecting a suitable adoption strategy, the next step is to select deployment option. The selection of deployment option will vary from institution to institution depending on a number of factors such as the cost constraints, security and privacy requirements, number of users, competence of internal IT staff, and institutional policies.

Regardless of the deployment option, Mtebe and Raisamo (2014) proposed the following computing requirements for blended delivery:

- **Learning Management System (LMS):** This is the main system used to deliver course content and facilitate interaction between students and instructors and between students and course content.
- **Multimedia Software:** These are software used to develop multimedia enabled blended courses.
- **Student Laboratories:** These are labs to provide Internet access to blended learning students.
- **Course Content:** Learning resources integrated with audio, video, animation, and text to foster student learning.
- **Digital Libraries:** Repositories of journals, books, and other learning resources.

Figure 1. Cloud strategy in Higher Education. Adapted from (Mircea & Andreescu, 2011)

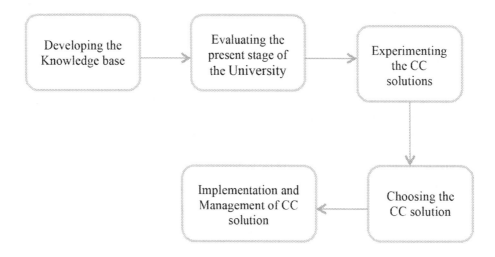

- **Computer Server:** A computer server and a computer backup server with associated accessories.
- **Other Services:** The ICT unit is also responsible for providing students and staff with software (e.g., email accounts, operating systems, productivity applications, malware detectors, and cleaners, and hardware (e.g., PCs, Servers, etc.).

These requirements can be deployed in various cloud models. In next sub section, we propose two deployment options that can be adapted to enhance blended learning in higher education in sub-Saharan Africa.

PUBLIC CLOUD OPTION

This is an option that can be adopted by small or new institutions that have limited budgets to procure computing infrastructures to run blended learning courses. This option enables institutions to host all necessary computing requirements into the cloud providers. As shown in Figure 2,

mail servers, LMS servers, digital library, course content development tools, multimedia tools, and other tools will be accessed directly from cloud provider's servers via Internet.

There are numerous companies that provide public cloud services. These companies include Microsoft, Google, IBM, Amazon, Salesforce. com, and HP Cloud Computing.

The main challenge of public computing option is security and privacy concerns on confidential and valuable data such as research results, students' and employees' records, and financial data (Mircea & Andreescu, 2011; Mokhtar et al., 2013). It is advisable that institutions migrate low risk computing services such as learning resources, timetable, emails and other learning activities into the cloud until they have developed enough capacity to deal with security issues.

HYBRID CLOUD OPTION

The hybrid deployment option is proposed for institutions that have already invested their own ICT infrastructure over the years and have enough

Figure 2. Proposed public cloud option for blended delivery

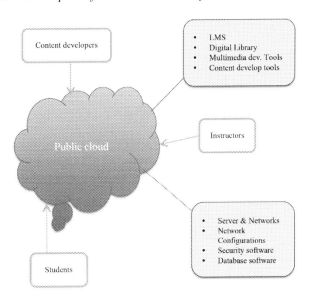

technical staff to manage such infrastructure. In the hybrid cloud, institutions will use the private cloud to host and control high sensitive data such as students' academic records, financial systems, faculty records, and medical records. On the other hand, low risk data can be hosted in the public cloud. These include course notes, student projects, websites for faculty, and news and announcements. Figure 3 shows hybrid cloud option that can be adopted for higher education institutions in sub Saharan Africa.

CONCLUSION AND RECOMMENDATIONS

Cloud computing technology is not a new concept in higher educational institutions in sub-Saharan Africa. Faculty members as well as students are already using various cloud services for personal purposes. For example, majority of social networking applications such as Facebook, Twitter, YouTube, and Flickr are based on cloud platforms

(Babar & Chauhan, 2011). Services from Google cloud services such as Gmail, GoogleDrive, YouTube are widely used by students and faculty members. Therefore, migrating existing blended services into the cloud will not be something new to institution community. In fact, students and staff expect to gain the same benefits in academic activities through these cloud services as they do in their day-to-day activities. In order to benefit from these technologies, the following are recommended:

First, institutions should develop and/or update policies that increase ICT infrastructure and increase availability of cloud computing tools (Laverty, 2011). The majority of these polices are those related to regulatory compliance and payments mechanisms. These policies were developed when technologies such as cloud computing was not in place.

Second, institutions should improve the reliability and speed of the Internet. Cloud computing is an Internet based service, obviously, if the bandwidth is insufficient it will be very difficult

Figure 3. Proposed Hybrid cloud option for blended delivery

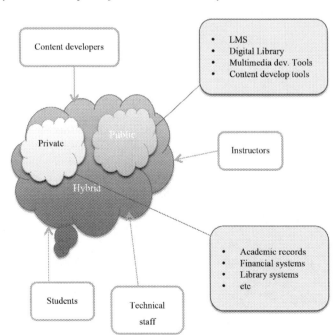

to deliver educational services (Laisheng & Zhengxia, 2011). The majority of higher education institutions in sub Saharan Africa are faced with low Internet speed. For example, in a study conducted by Mtebe and Raisamo (2014b) in Tanzania found that 82% of 11 surveyed institutions had Internet speed between 7Mbps and 20Mbps. Similar situation can be observed in many institutions in the region. Some eLearning solutions such as cloud services, video based learning resources will not benefit many users in the region, as they require good Internet speed.

Third, many institutions in the region do not have cloud computing experts for both technology and regulatory compliance (laws, data compliance, tax & payment, etc.). These institutions should equip their staff members with skills and competence with various aspects of cloud computing adoption and implementation.

REFERENCES

Adkins, S. S. (2013). *The Africa Market for Self-paced eLearning Products and Services : 2011-2016 Forecast and Analysis* (pp. 2011–2016). Retrieved from http://www.ambientinsight.com/Resources/Documents/AmbientInsight-2011-2016-Africa-SelfPaced-eLearning-Market-Abstract.pdf

Alshuwaier, F. A., Alshwaier, A. A., & Areshey, A. M. (2012). Applications of cloud computing in education. In *8th International Conference on Computing and Networking Technology (ICCNT)* (pp. 26–33).

Babar, M. A., & Chauhan, M. A. (2011). A tale of migration to cloud computing for sharing experiences and observations. In *Proceeding of the 2nd international workshop on Software engineering for cloud computing - SECLOUD '11* (p. 50). New York, New York, USA: ACM Press. doi:10.1145/1985500.1985509

Bansal, S., Singh, S., & Kumar, A. (2012). Use of cloud computing in academic institutions. *International Journal of Clothing Science and Technology, 3*(1), 427–429. Retrieved from http://www.ijcst.com/vol31/3/amit.pdf

Bhuasiri, W., Xaymoungkhoun, O., Zo, H., Rho, J. J., & Ciganek, A. P. (2012). Critical success factors for e-learning in developing countries: A comparative analysis between ICT experts and faculty. *Computers & Education, 58*(2), 843–855. doi:10.1016/j.compedu.2011.10.010

Buyya, R., Yeo, C. S., Venugopal, S., Broberg, J., & Brandic, I. (2009). Cloud computing and emerging IT platforms: Vision, hype, and reality for delivering computing as the 5th utility. *Future Generation Computer Systems, 25*(6), 599–616. doi:10.1016/j.future.2008.12.001

Carroll, M., Van Der Merwe, A., & Kotzé, P. (2011). Secure cloud computing benefits, risks and controls. In *Information Security South Africa* (pp. 1–9). Johannesburg: ISSA; doi:10.1109/ISSA.2011.6027519

Chandra, D. G., & Borah, M. D. (2012). Cost benefit analysis of cloud computing in education. In *2012 International Conference on Computing, Communication and Applications (ICCCA)* (pp. 1–6). doi:10.1109/ICCCA.2012.6179142

Chandra, D. G., & Malaya, D. B. (2012). Role of cloud computing in education. In *2012 International Conference on Computing, Electronics and Electrical Technologies (ICCEET)* (pp. 832–836). Ieee. doi:10.1109/ICCEET.2012.6203884

Farrell, G., & Isaacs, S. (2007). *Survey of ICT and Education in Africa: A Summary Report, Based on 53 Country Surveys* (pp. 0–74). Washington, DC. United States. Retrieved from http://www.infodev.org/en/Publication.353.html

Garrison, D. R., & Kanuka, H. (2004). Blended learning: Uncovering its transformative potential in higher education. *The Internet and Higher Education, 7*(2), 95–105. doi:10.1016/j.iheduc.2004.02.001

Herrick, D. R. (2009). Google this! Using Google apps for collaboration and productivity. In *Proceedings of the ACM SIGUCCS fall conference on User services conference - SIGUCCS '09* (p. 55). New York, New York, USA: ACM Press. doi:10.1145/1629501.1629513

Hoosen, S., & Butcher, N. (2012). ICT Development at African Universities: The Experience of the PHEA Educational Technology Initiative. In e/merge 2012.

Hosam, F., Tayeb, A. Al, Alghatani, K., & Elseoud, S. A. (2013). The impact of cloud computing technologies in E-learning. *iJET, 8*(1), 37–44.

Isaacs, S., & Hollow, D. (2012). *The eLearning Africa 2012 Report. ICWE: Germany.* Germany. Retrieved from http://www.elearning-africa.com/pdf/report/ela_report_2012.pdf

Isaacs, S., Hollow, D., Akoh, B., & Harper-Merrett, T. (2013). Findings from the eLearning Africa Survey 2013. Germany.

Khajeh-hosseini, A., Greenwood, D., & Sommerville, I. (2010). Cloud migration : A case study of migrating an enterprise IT system to IaaS. In *3rd International Conference on Cloud Computing (CLOUD).* IEEE. doi:10.1109/CLOUD.2010.37

Koch, F., Assuncao, M. D., & Netto, M. A. S. (2012). A cost analysis of cloud computing for education. *Lecture Notes in Computer Science, 7714*, 182–196. Retrieved from http://www.marconetto.me/Publications_files/gecon2012.pdf

Kshetri, N. (2010). Cloud computing in developing economies: Drivers, effects, and policy measures. In *Proceedings of PTC* (pp. 1–22).

Kumar, A. (2012). Blended learning in Higher Education: A comprehensive study. In *International Conference on Business Management & Information Systems*. Retrieved from http://ojs.ijacp.org/index.php/ICBMIS/article/view/82

Laisheng, X., & Zhengxia, W. (2011). Cloud computing: A new business paradigm for e-learning. In *2011 Third International Conference on Measuring Technology and Mechatronics Automation* (pp. 716–719). Ieee. doi:10.1109/ICMTMA.2011.181

Laverty, A. (2011). The Cloud and Africa – Indicators for Growth of Cloud Computing. *The African File.* Retrieved September 08, 2014, from http://theafricanfile.com/ict/the-cloud-and-africa-indicators-for-growth-of-cloud-computing/

Lwoga, E. (2012). Making learning and Web 2.0 technologies work for higher learning institutions in Africa. *Campus-Wide Information Systems, 29*(2), 90–107. doi:10.1108/10650741211212359

Lwoga, E. (2014). Critical success factors for adoption of web-based learning management systems in Tanzania. [IJEDICT]. *International Journal of Education and Development Using Information and Communication Technology, 10*(1), 4–21.

Mathew, S. (2012). Implementation of cloud computing in education - A revolution. *International Journal of Computer Theory and Engineering, 4*(3), 473–475. doi:10.7763/IJCTE.2012.V4.511

Mell, P., & Grance, T. (2011). *The NIST Definition of Cloud Computing.* USA. Retrieved from http://csrc.nist.gov/publications/nistpubs/800-145/SP800-145.pdf

Mircea, M., & Andreescu, A. (2011). Using cloud computing in Higher Education: A strategy to improve agility in the current financial crisis. *Communications of the IBIMA, 2011*, 1–15. doi:10.5171/2011.875547

Mokhtar, S. A., Ali, S. H. S., Al-Sharafi, A., & Aborujilah, A. (2013). Cloud computing in academic institutions. In *Proceedings of the 7th International Conference on Ubiquitous Information Management and Communication - ICUIMC '13* (pp. 1–7). New York, New York, USA: ACM Press. doi:10.1145/2448556.2448558

Mtebe, J. S., & Raisamo, R. (2014a). eLearning cost analysis of on-premise versus cloud-hosted implementation in Sub-Saharan Countries. *The African Journal of Information Systems*, *6*(2), 48–64. Retrieved from http://digitalcommons.kennesaw.edu/cgi/viewcontent.cgi?article=1216&context=ajis

Mtebe, J. S., & Raisamo, R. (2014b). Investigating Perceived Barriers to the Use of Open Educational Resources in Higher Education in Tanzania. *International Review of Research in Open and Distance Learning*, *15*(2), 43–65.

Mtebe, J. S., & Raphael, C. (2013). Students' experiences and challenges of blended learning at the University of Dar es Salaam, Tanzania. [IJEDICT]. *International Journal of Education and Development Using Information and Communication Technology*, *9*(3), 124–136.

Munguatosha, G. M., Muyinda, P. B., & Lubega, J. T. (2011). A social networked learning adoption model for higher education institutions in developing countries. *On the Horizon*, *19*(4), 307–320. doi:10.1108/10748121111179439

Nasir, U., & Niazi, M. (2011). Cloud computing adoption assessment model (CAAM). In Profes '11 (Vol. 44, pp. 34–37). TORRE CANNE (BR), Italy: ACM.

Obi, E. (2012). Helping to bring African universities online. *Google Africa Blog*. Retrieved July 18, 2013, from http://google-africa.blogspot.com/2012/09/helping-to-bring-african-universities.html

Porter, W. W., Graham, C. R., Spring, K., & Welch, K. R. (2014). Blended learning in higher education: Institutional adoption and implementation. *Computers & Education*, *75*, 185–195. doi:10.1016/j.compedu.2014.02.011

Rindos, A., Vouk, M., Vandenberg, A., Pitt, S., Harris, R., Gendron, D., & Danford, T. (2009). The Transformation of Education through State Education Clouds (pp. 1–12). Retrieved from http://www.ibm.com/ibm/files/N734393J24929X18/EBW03002-USEN-00.pdf

Selim, H. M. (2007). Critical success factors for e-learning acceptance: Confirmatory factor models. *Computers & Education*, *49*(2), 396–413. doi:10.1016/j.compedu.2005.09.004

Ssekakubo, G., Suleman, H., & Marsden, G. (2011). Issues of adoption : Have e-Learning Management Systems fulfilled their potential in developing countries? In *Proceedings of the South African Institute of Computer Scientists and Information Technologists Conference on Knowledge, Innovation and Leadership in a Diverse, Multidisciplinary Environment* (pp. 231–238). Cape Town, South Africa.: ACM New York, NY, USA. doi:0.1145/2072221.2072248

Sultan, N. (2010). Cloud computing for education: A new dawn? *International Journal of Information Management*, *30*(2), 109–116. doi:10.1016/j.ijinfomgt.2009.09.004

Tedre, M., Ngumbuke, F., & Kemppainen, J. (2010). Infrastructure, human capacity, and high hopes : A decade of development of e-Learning in a Tanzanian HEI. *Redefining the Digital Divide in Higher Education*, *7*(1).

Truong, H., Pham, T.-V., Thoai, N., & Dustdar, S. (2012). Cloud computing for education and research in developing countries. In Cloud Computing for Education and Research (pp. 78–94). doi:10.4018/978-1-4666-0957-0.ch005

Unwin, T., Kleessen, B., Hollow, D., Williams, J., Oloo, L. M., Alwala, J., & Muianga, X. et al. (2010). Digital learning management systems in Africa: Myths and realities. *Open Learning. The Journal of Open and Distance Learning*, *25*(1), 5–23. doi:10.1080/02680510903482033

Venter, P., Van Rensburg, M. J., & Davis, A. (2012). Drivers of learning management system use in a South African open and distance learning institution. *Australasian Journal of Educational Technology*, *28*(2), 183–198.

Wanjiku, R. (2009, June 12). East Africa universities take advantage of Google cloud. *Computerworld*. Retrieved from http://news.idg.no/cw/art.cfm?id=D3ED873F-1A64-6A71-CE3B759E5A305061

KEY TERMS AND DEFINITIONS

Blended Learning: A combination of face-to-face delivery with a certain eLearning technology. The combination can be face-to-face delivery with the learning management system where students' access learning resources via the system with some selected face-to-face teaching. The similar combination can be between face-to-face teaching with video conferencing technologies.

Cloud Service Provider: This is a company that offers customers with computing services such as storage or software services available via the Internet. Typical examples of such companies include the Amazon, HP, and Google.

Elearning Technologies: Any technology that can facilitate students learning such as video conferencing, Internet, web based systems and the likes.

Higher Education Institutions: These are institutions that offer post secondary courses including universities and non-universities.

ICT Infrastructure: Include computer hardware (servers and related workstations), network connectivity with accessories, and all necessary equipment.

Learning Management System: A web based system used by institutions to provide students with access to learning resources and other learning resources. The systems have communication tools such as discussion forums, chat and whiteboards.

Sub-Saharan Africa: This is an area that lies south of the Sahara Desert of the African continent. All countries that are located in this region are termed as sub-Saharan African countries.

Compilation of References

AACTE. (2008). *Handbook of technological pedagogical content knowledge for educators (TPCK)*. New York, NY: Routledge.

Ackerman, E. (2013). Google Acquires Seven Robot Companies, Wants Big Role in Robotics. *IEEE Spectrum*. Retrieved December 15, 2013, from http://spectrum.ieee.org/automaton/robotics/industrial-robots/google-acquisition-seven-robotics-companies

Ackermann, E. K. (2001). *Piaget's constructivism, Papert's constructionism: What's the difference?* Retrieved from http://learning.media.mit.edu/content/publications/EA.Piaget%20_%20Papert.pdf

Ackermann, E. K. (1996). Perspective-taking and object construction: Two keys to learning. In Y. Kafai & M. Resnick (Eds.), *Constructionism in Practice: Designing, Thinking, and Learning in a Digital World* (pp. 25–37). Mahwah, New Jersey: Lawrence Erlbaum Associates.

Ackermann, E. K. (2004). Constructing Knowledge and Transforming the World. In M. Tokoro & L. Steels (Eds.), *A Learning Zone of One's Own: Sharing Representations and Flow in Collaborative Learning Environments* (pp. 15–37). Washington, DC: IOS Press.

Adanu, R., Adu-Sarkodie, Y., Opare-Sem, O., Nkyekyer, K., Donkor, P., Lawson, A., & Engleberg, N. C. (2010). Electronic learning and open educational resources in the health sciences in Ghana. *Ghana Medical Journal, 44*(4), 159–162. PMID:21416051

Adkins, S. S. (2013). *The Africa Market for Self-paced eLearning Products and Services : 2011-2016 Forecast and Analysis* (pp. 2011–2016). Retrieved from http://www.ambientinsight.com/Resources/Documents/AmbientInsight-2011-2016-Africa-SelfPaced-eLearning-Market-Abstract.pdf

Agbetsiafa, D. (2010). Evaluating effective teaching in college level Economics using student ratings of instruction: A factor analytic approach. *Journal of College Teaching & Learning, 7*(5), 57–66.

Aguti, B., Walters, R., & Wills, G. (2013). A framework for evaluating the effectiveness of blended e-learning within universities. In R. McBride & M. Searson (Eds.), *Proceedings of Society for Information Technology & Teacher Education International Conference 2013* (pp. 1982-1987). Chesapeake, VA: AACE.

Akmal, T., Oaks, M. M., & Barker, R. (2002, September06). The Status of Technology Education: A National Report on the State of the Profession. *Journal of Industrial Teacher Education, 39*(4), 6–25.

Akyol, Z., Garrison, D., & Ozden, M. Y. (2009). Online and Blended Communities of Inquiry: Exploring the developmental and perceptional differences. *International Review of Research in Open and Distance Learning, 10*(6), 65–83.

Al-adwan, A., & Smedle, J. (2012). Implementing E-Learning in the Jordanian Higher Education System: Factors Affecting Impact. *International Journal of Education and Development using Information and Communication Technology, 8*(1), 121-135.

Al-Ammary, J. (2013). Educational technology: A way to enhance student achievement at the University of Bahrain. *The Online Journal of New Horizons in Education, 7*(3), 54–65.

Aldrich, J. (2002). Early childhood teacher candidates evaluate computer software for young children. *Information Technology in Childhood Education Annual, (1):* 295–300.

Al-Huneidi, A., & Schreurs, J. (2013). Constructivist based blended learning in higher education. *CCIS*, 581-591, Springer-Verlag, Berlin and Heidelberg.

Alimisis, D., & Kynigos, C. (2009). Constructionism and Robotics in Education. In D. Alimisis (Ed.), *Teacher Education on Robotics-Enhanced Constructivist Pedagogical Methods*. Athens, Greece: School of Pedagogical and Technological Education.

Ali, W. (2012). Factors affecting nursing students' satisfaction with e-learning experience in King Khalid University, Saudi Arabia. *International Journal of Learning and Development*, *2*(2), 201–215. doi:10.5296/ijld.v2i2.1666

Allal, L., & Pelgrims Ducrey, G. (2000). Assessment of—or in—the zone of proximal development. *Learning and Instruction*, *10*(2), 137–152. doi:10.1016/S0959-4752(99)00025-0

Allen, E., & Seaman, J. (2006). *Making the grade: Online education in the United States, 2006*. US: Sloan Consortium. Available at: http://sloanconsortium.org/publications/survey/making_the_grade_southern06

Allen, E., & Seaman, J. (2013). Changing course: Ten years of tracking online in the United States. Babson Park, MA: Babson Survey Research Group and Quahog Research Group; Retrieved from http://faculty.washington.edu/rvanderp/DLData/AllenSeaman2013.pdf

Allen, E. (2005). *Growing by degrees: online education in the United States, 2005*. The Sloan Consortium.

Alonzo, J., Basaraba, D., Tindal, G., & Carriveau, R. S. (2009, January01). They Read, but How Well Do They Understand? An Empirical Look at the Nuances of Measuring Reading Comprehension. *Assessment for Effective Intervention*, *35*(1), 34–44. doi:10.1177/1534508408330082

Alshuwaier, F. A., Alshwaier, A. A., & Areshey, A. M. (2012). Applications of cloud computing in education. In *8th International Conference on Computing and Networking Technology (ICCNT)* (pp. 26–33).

Alyahya, S., & Gall, J. E. (2012). *iPads in education: A qualitative study of students' attitudes and experiences*. Paper presented at the World Conference on Educational Multimedia, Hypermedia and Telecommunications.

Amazon.com Inc. (2014). *Amazon Prime Air*. Retrieved July 30, 2014, from http://www.amazon.com/b?node=8037720011

American College Personnel Association (ACPA) & Nation Association of Student Personnel Administrators (NASPA). (1997). Principles of good practice for student affairs. Washington DC: Author.

Amiel, T., & Reeves, T. C. (2008). Design-based research and educational technology: Rethinking technology and the research agenda. *Journal of Educational Technology & Society*, *11*(4), 29–40.

Amo, E. ve Jareño, F. (2011). Self, peer and teacher assessment as active learning methods. *Research Journal of International Studies*, *18*, 41–47.

Anastasiadou, S. D. (2011). Reliability and validity testing of a new scale for measuring attitudes toward learning statistics with technology. *Acta Didactica Napocensia*, *4*(1), 1–10.

Anderson, J., Brown, G., & Spaeth, S. (2006). Online student evaluations and response rates reconsidered. *Innovate: Journal of Online Education*, *2*(6). Retrieved from https://rugby.ou.edu/content/dam/provost/documents/evaluations/evaluate–Online–Student–Evaluations–and–Response–Rates.pdf

Anderson, A., & Grönlund, Å. (2009). A conceptual framework for e-learning in developing countries: A critical review of research challenges. *The Electronic Journal on Information Systems in Developing Countries*, *38*(8), 1–16.

Anderson, J. B., & Erickson, J. A. (1999). Service learning in pre-service teacher education. *Academic Exchange Quarterly*, *7*(2), 111–115.

Anderson, J. B., & Pickeral, T. (1999). *Challenges and strategies for success with service learning in pre-service teacher education*. Washington, DC: Corporation for National Service.

Ani, E. O. (2010). Internet access and use: A study of undergraduate students in three Nigerian universities. *The Electronic Library*, *28*(4), 555–567. doi:10.1108/02640471011065373

Anthony, A. B. (2012, September06). Activity Theory as a Framework for Investigating District-Classroom System Interactions and Their Influences on Technology Integration. *Journal of Research on Technology in Education, 44*(4), 335–356. doi:10.1080/15391523.2012.10782594

Archer, A. (2010). Challenges and potentials for Writing Centres in South African tertiary institutions. *South African Journal of Higher Education, 24*(4), 495–510.

Arditi, A. (2013). *Designing for People with Partial Sight.*

Arkoudis, S., & Tran, L. (2010). Writing blah, blah, blah: Lecturers' approaches and challenges in supporting international students. *International Journal of Teaching and Learning in Higher Education, 22*(2), 169–178.

Arnseth, H. C. (2008, October01). Activity theory and situated learning theory: Contrasting views of educational practice. *Pedagogy, Culture & Society, 16*(3), 289–302. doi:10.1080/14681360802346663

Aronson, N., & Arfstrom, K. M. (2013). *Flipped learning in higher education.* Boston, MA: Pearson.

Ash, D., & Kluger-Bell, B. (2000). Identifying Inquiry in the K-5 Classroom. In Division of Elementary Secondary and Informal Education (Ed.), Foundations, Volume 2: Inquiry: Thoughts, Views, and Strategies for the K-5 Classroom (pp. 79-86). Arlington, VA: National Science Foundation.

Ash, D., & Levitt, K. (2003). Working within the zone of proximal development: Formative assessment as professional development. *Journal of Science Teacher Education, 14*(1), 23–48. doi:10.1023/A:1022999406564

Aslanian, C. (2001). *Adult students today.* New York: The College Board.

Association of American Colleges and Universities (AACU). (2002). *Greater expectations: A new vision for learning as a nation goes to college.* Retrieved April 13th from http://www.greaterexpectations.org/

Association of American Colleges and Universities (AACU). (2007). *College learning for the New global century.* Retrieved January 26th from http://www.aacu.org/advocacy/leap/documents/GlobalCentury_final.pdf

Astin, A. W. (1984). Student Involvement: A developmental theory for higher education. *Journal of College Student Personnel, 25,* 297–308.

Astin, A. W. (1985). *Achieving education excellence: A critical assessment of priorities and practices in higher education.* San Francisco, CA: Jossey Bass.

Astin, A. W. (1993). *What matters in college? Four critical years revisited.* San Francisco, CA: Jossey Bass.

Atmatzidou, S., & Demetriadis, S. (2012). *Evaluating the role of collaboration scripts as group guiding tools in activities of eduational robotics.* Paper presented at the 2012 12th IEEE International Conference on Advanced Learning Technologies, Rome, Italy.

Atmatzidou, S., Markelis, I., & Demitridis, S. (2008). *The Use of LEGO Mindstorms in Elementary and Secondary Education: Game as a way of triggering learning.* Paper presented at the International Conference of Simulation, Modeling and Programming for Autonomous Robots (SIMPAR), Venice, Italy.

Ayres, L., Kavanaugh, K., & Knafl, K. A. (2003). Within-case and across-case approaches to qualitative data analysis. *Qualitative Health Research, 13*(6), 871–883. doi:10.1177/1049732303013006008 PMID:12891720

Azevedo, R. (2005). Using hypermedia as a metacognitive tool for enhancing student learning? The role of self-regulated learning. *Educational Psychologist, 40*(4), 199–209. doi:10.1207/s15326985ep4004_2

Babar, M. A., & Chauhan, M. A. (2011). A tale of migration to cloud computing for sharing experiences and observations. In *Proceeding of the 2nd international workshop on Software engineering for cloud computing - SECLOUD '11* (p. 50). New York, New York, USA: ACM Press. doi:10.1145/1985500.1985509

Badu, E. E., & Markwei, E. D. (2005). Internet awareness and use: The University of Ghana. *Information Development, 21*(4), 260–268. doi:10.1177/0266666905060069

Bailey, C., & Pieterick, J. (2008). Finding a new voice: Challenges facing international (and home!) students writing university assignments in the UK.*Third Annual European First Year Experience Conference*, University of Wolverhampton.

Baker, R. (2010). *Examples of scaffolding and chunking in online and blended learning environments.* Available at http://ssrn.com/abstract=1608133 or10.2139/ssrn.1608133

Baki, A. (2008). *Kuramdan uygulamay matematik eğitimi* [Mathematics education from theory to practice]. Ankara, Turkey: Harf Education Publishing.

Balacheff, N., Ludvigsen, S., De Jong, T., Lazonder, A., Barnes, S., & Montandon, L. (2009). *Technology-Enhanced Learning.* Berlin, Germany: Springer. doi:10.1007/978-1-4020-9827-7

Ballard, B., & Clanchy, J. (1988). Literacy in the university: An "anthropological" approach. In G. Taylor, B. Ballard, V. Beasley, H. K. Bock, J. Clanchy, & P. Nightingale (Eds.), *Literacy by Degrees* (pp. 7–23). Milton Keynes: Society for Research into Higher Education/Open University Press.

Ball, D. L., & Cohen, D. K. (1999). Developing practice, developing practitioners: Toward a practice-based theory of professional education. In G. Sykes & L. Darling-Hammond (Eds.), *Teaching as the learning profession: Handbook of policy and practice* (pp. 3–32). San Francisco, CA: Jossey Bass.

Bandura, A. (1977). Self-efficacy: Toward a unifying theory of behaviors change. *Psychological Review*, *84*(2), 191–215. doi:10.1037/0033-295X.84.2.191 PMID:847061

Bandura, A. (1986). *Social foundations of thought and action: A social cognition theory.* Englewood Cliffs, NJ: Prentice-Hall.

Bansal, S., Singh, S., & Kumar, A. (2012). Use of cloud computing in academic institutions. *International Journal of Clothing Science and Technology*, *3*(1), 427–429. Retrieved from http://www.ijcst.com/vol31/3/amit.pdf

Barab, S. A., Squire, K. D., & Dueber, W. (2000). A co-evolutionary model for supporting the emergence of authenticity. *Educational Technology Research and Development*, *48*(2), 37–62. doi:10.1007/BF02313400

Barr, A., Nicas, J., & Bensinger, G. (2014). Google Drones Lift Industry Hopes: Internet Giant's Entry Brings Financial and Lobbying Clout to Fledging Field. *The Wall Street Journal.* http://online.wsj.com/articles/google-drones-lift-industry-hopes-1409353944

Barr, D., Harrison, J., & Conery, L. (2011). Computational Thinking: A Digital Age Skill for Everyone. *Learning and Leading with Technology*, (March/April): 20–23.

Barron, B., & Darling-Hammond, L. (2008). *Teaching for meaningful learning: A review of research on inquiry-based and cooperative learning in Powerful learning: What we know about teaching for understanding.* San Francisco, CA: Jossey-Bass.

Barrows, H. S. (1988). *The tutorial process.* Springfield, IL: Southern Illinois University School of Medicine.

Barrows, H. S. (2000). *Problem-based learning applied to medical education.* Springfield, IL: Southern Illinois University School of Medicine.

Barrows, H. S., & Wee, K. N. L. (2007). *Principles and practice of a PBL.* Singapore: Pearson Prentice Hall.

Barry, R. A. (2010). Teaching effectiveness and why it matters. *Marylhurst University and the Chalkboard Project*, Retrieved from http://chalkboardproject.org/wp– content/uploads/2010/12/teacher–effectiveness–and–why–it–matters.pdf

Baylor, A. L., & Ritchie, D. (2002). What factors facilitate teacher skill, teacher morale, and perceived student learning in technology-using classrooms? *Computers & Education*, *29*(4), 395–414. doi:10.1016/S0360-1315(02)00075-1

Beacham, B. (1994). Making connections: Transforming ivory towers and little red school houses. In J. Willis, B. Robin, & D. A. Willis (Eds.), *Technology and teacher education annual 1994* (pp. 742–744). Charlottesville, VA: Association for Advancement of Computing in Education.

Bednarz, S. W., & Schee, J. V. D. (2006). Europe and the United States: The implementation of geographic information systems in secondary education in two contexts. *Technology, Pedagogy and Education*, *15*(2), 191–205. doi:10.1080/14759390600769573

Beetham, H., & Sharpe, R. (Eds.). (2013). *Rethinking pedagogy for a digital age: Designing for 21st century learning.* New York, NY: Routledge.

Belawati, T. (2007). The practice of a quality assurance system in open and DL. A case study of Universitas Terbuka Indonesia. *The International Review of Research in Open and DL, 8*(1), 1–15.

Benitti, F. B. V. (2012). Exploring the educational potential of robotics in schools: A systematic review. *Computers & Education, 58*(3), 978–988. doi:10.1016/j.compedu.2011.10.006

Beran, T., & Rokosh, J. (2009). Instructors' perspectives on the utility of student ratings of instruction. *Instructional Science, 37*(2), 171–184. doi:10.1007/s11251-007-9045-2

Beran, T., Violato, C., & Kline, D. (2007). What's the "Use" of student ratings of instruction for administrators? One university's experience. *Canadian Journal of Higher Education, 37*(1), 27–43.

Beran, T., Violato, C., Kline, D., & Frideres, J. (2009). What do students consider useful about student ratings? *Assessment & Evaluation in Higher Education, 34*(5), 519–527. doi:10.1080/02602930802082228

Bereiter, C., & Scardamalia, M. (Eds.). (1989). *Intentional learning as a goald of instruction.* Hilsdale, NJ: Lawrence Erlbaum.

Berk, R. A. (2005). Survey of 12 strategies to measure teaching effectiveness. *International Journal of Teaching and Learning in Higher Education, 17*(1), 48–62.

Berns, K., Braun, T., Hillenbrand, C., & Luksch, T. (2005). *Developing Climbing Robots for Education.* Paper presented at the Climbing and Walking Robots: Proceedings of the 8th International Conference on Climbing and Walking Robots and the Support Technologies for Mobile Machines (CLAWAR 2005).

Berrett, D. (2012, February 19). How 'flipping' the classroom can improve the traditional lecture. *The Chronicle of Higher Education.* Retrieved from http://chronicle.com/article/How-Flipping-the-Classroom/130857/

Berry, D. C., Miller, M. G., & Berry, L. M. (2004). Effects of clinical field-experience setting on athletic training students' perceived percentage of time spent on active learning. *Journal of Athletic Training, 39*(2), 176–184. PMID:15173870

Bers, M. U. (2008). *Blocks to Robots: Learning with Technology in the Early Childhood Classroom.* New York, NY: Teachers College Press.

Beyer, K. B. (1988). *Developing a thinking skills program.* Boston, MA: Allyson & Bacon.

Bhabha, H. (1994). *The location of culture.* New York: Routledge.

Bhuasiri, W., Xaymoungkhoun, O., Zo, H., Rho, J. J., & Ciganek, A. P. (2012). Critical success factors for e-learning in developing countries: A comparative analysis between ICT experts and faculty. *Computers & Education, 58*(2), 843–855. doi:10.1016/j.compedu.2011.10.010

Bickmore, K. (2005). Teacher Development for Conflict Participation: Facilitating Learning for 'Difficult Citizenship.'. *Education International Journal of Citizenship and Teacher Education, 1*(2), 2–16.

Bingimlas, K. A. (2009). Barriers to successful integration of ICT in Teaching and learning environments: A review of the literature. *Eurasia Journal of Mathematics. Science & Technology Education, 5*(3), 235–245.

Bjekic, D., Krneta, R., & Milosevic, D. (2010, January01). Teacher Education from E-Learner to E-Teacher: Master Curriculum. *Turkish Online Journal of Educational Technology, 9*(1), 202–212.

Bjork, E., Ottosson, S., & Thorsteinsdottir, S. (2008). e-Learning for All. In A. R. Lipshitz and S. P. Parsons (Eds.), E-Learning: 21st Century Issues and Challenges. Nova Science Publishers, Inc.

Bland, J., & Altman, D. G. (1997). Cronbach's Alpha. BMJ: British Medical Journal (International Edition), 314(7080), 572.

Bloom, B. S. (1956). *Taxonomy of educational objectives: The classification of educational goals.* New York: Longmans, Green.

Bloom, B. S., Engelhart, M. D., Furst, F. J., Hill, W. H., & Krathwohl, D. R. (1956). *Taxonomy of educational objectives: Cognitive domain.* New York: McKay.

Bloom, B. S., & Krathwohl, D. R. (1956). *Taxonomy of educational objectives: The classification of educational goals, by a committee of college and university examiners. Handbook 1: Cognitive domain.* London: Longmans.

413

Bogdan, R. C., & Biklen, S. K. (1998). *Qualitative Research for Education: An Introduction to Theory and Methods*. Boston, MA: Allyn and Bacon.

Bohlin, R. (2002). *Avoiding computer avoidance*. Retrieved from http://it.coe.uga.edu/itforum/paper35/paper35.html

Bolick, C., Berson, M., Coutts, C., & Heinecke, W. (2003). Technology applications in social studies teacher education: A survey of social studies methods faculty. *Contemporary Issues in Technology & Teacher Education*, *3*(3), 300–309. Retrieved July 27, 2014 from http://www.citejournal.org/vol3/iss3/socialstudies/article1.cfm

Bolliger, D., & Inan, F. (2012). Development and validation of the online student connectedness survey (OSCS). *International Review of Research in Open and Distance Learning*, *13*(3), 41–65.

Bonwell, C. C., Eison, J. A., & Association for the Study of Higher Education. (1991). Active learning: Creating excitement in the classroom. *1991 ASHE-ERIC Higher Education Reports* (pp. 121): ERIC Clearinghouse on Higher Education, Washington, DC.

Bonwell, C. C., & Eison, J. A. (1991). ASHEERIC Higher Education Report: Vol. 1. *Active learning: Creating excitement in the classroom*. Washington, DC: George Washington University.

Booker, E. (2013). *Why Moodle Matters To Teachers*. Retrieved from http://www.informationweek.com/education/instructional-it/why-moodle-matters-to-teachers/240145508

Bosch, K. A. (1993). Is there a computer crisis in the classroom? *Schools in the Middle*, *2*(4), 7–9.

Bostock, S. J. (1997). Designing Web-based instruction for active learning. In B. H. Khan (Ed.), *Web-based Instruction* (pp. 225–230). Englewood Cliffs, New Jersey: Educational Technology Publications.

Boud, D. (2006). Relocating reflection in the context of practice: rehabilitation or rejection? Proceedings of the Professional Lifelong Learning. Leeds: Beyond Reflective Practice, Trinity and All Saints College; Retrieved from http://www.bretton.ac.uk/medicine/meu/lifelong06/P_DavidBoud.pdf

Boud, D., Keogh, R., & Walker, D. (1985). Promoting reflection in learning: A model. In D. Bould, R. Keogh, & D. Walker (Eds.), *Reflection: Turning experience into learning* (pp. 18–40). London: Kogan Page.

Boud, D., & Walker, D. (1998). Promoting reflection in professional courses: The challenge of context. *Studies in Higher Education*, *23*(2), 191–207. doi:10.1080/03075079812331380384

Bowen, J. A. (2012). *Teaching naked: How moving technology out of your college classroom will improve student learning*. John Wiley & Sons.

Bower, B. L. (2001). Distance education: Facing the faculty challenge. *Online Journal of Distance Learning Administration*, *4*(2), 1–6. Available at http://www.westga.edu/~distance/ojdla/summer42/bower42.html

Bo, Z., Johnston, L., & Kilic, G. (2008). Assessing the reliability of self– and peer rating in student group work. *Assessment & Evaluation in Higher Education*, *33*(3), 329–340. doi:10.1080/02602930701293181

Bransford, J. D., Brown, A. L., & Cocking, R. R. (1999). *How people learn: Brain, mind, experience, and school*. Washington, DC: National Academy Press.

Brennan, J., & Shah, T. (Eds.). (2000). *Managing quality in higher education*. Milton Keynes: OECD, SRHE & Open University Press.

British Educational Communications and Technology Agency (BECTA). (2003) Primary Schools-ICT and Standards. Retrieved from http://www.becta.org.uk

Broad, K., & Labercane, G. (2001, January01). Reader response pedagogy in the information age. *Technology and Teacher Education Annual*, *3*, 2187–2192.

Brocade. (2011). *Enterprise and mobility: What e-living is teaching about e-learning?* San Jose, CA: Brocade Communication System. Available at: http://www.brocade.com/downloads/documents/technical_briefs/mobility-e-living-teaching-e-learning-tb.pdf

Brookfield, S. D. (1987). *Developing critical thinkers: Challenging adults to explore alternative ways of thinking and acting*. San Francisco, CA: Jossey-Bass.

Brookfield, S. D. (2005). *Discussion as the way of teaching: Tools and techniques for democratic classrooms* (2nd ed.). San Francisco: Jossey-Bass.

Brown, J. S., Collins, A., & Duguid, P. (1989). Situated cognition and the culture of learning. *Educational Researcher, 18*(1), 32–42. doi:10.3102/0013189X018001032

Bruce, B. C., & Levin, J. A. (1997). Educational technology: Media for inquiry, communication, construction, and expression. *Journal of Educational Computing Research, 17*(1), 79–102. doi:10.2190/7HPQ-4F3X-8M8Y-TVCA

Bruner, J. (1990). *Acts of meaning*. Cambridge, MA: Harvard University Press.

Brunner, J. (1973). *The relevance of education*. New York: W.W. Norton & Company.

Bryce, J., & Wither, G. (2003). Engaging secondary school students in lifelong learning. *Australian Council for Educational Research*. Retrieved November 23, 2008 from http://www.acer.edu.au/documents/LifeLongLearning_Engaging.pdf

Bryce, J., Frigo, T., McKenzie, P., & Withers, G. (2002). *The era of lifelong learning: Implications for secondary schools*. Australian Council for Education Research. Retrieved November. 15th 2008 from http://www.acer.edu.au/documents/LifelongLearning.pdf

Bucci, T. T., Copenhaver, L. J., Lehman, B., & O'Brien, T. (2003). Technology integration: Connections to educational theories. *Contemporary Issues in Technology & Teacher Education, 3*(1), 26–42.

Buckleitner, W. (2006). The relationship between software design and children's engagement. *Early Education and Development, 17*(3), 489–505. doi:10.1207/s15566935eed1703_8

Bullen, M., Morgan, T., & Qayyum, A. (2011). Digital learners in higher education: Generation is not the issue. *Canadian Journal of Learning and Technology/La revue canadienne de l'apprentissage et de la technogie, 37*(1). Retrieved from http://www.cjlt.ca/index.php/cjlt/issue/view/71

Bullen, M., Morgan, T., Belfer, K., & Qayyum, A. (2008, October). *The digital learner at BCIT and implications for an e-strategy*. Paper presented to the EDEN Research Workshop, Paris.

Bull, G., & Kajder, S. (2004). Digital storytelling in the language arts classroom. *Learning and Leading with Technology, 32*(4), 46–49.

Burge, E., Campbell Gibson, C., & Gibson, T. (2011). *Flexible pedagogy, flexible practice: Notes from the trenches of distance education*. Athabasca, AB: AU Press.

Burgstahler, S. (2012). *Working Together: People with Disabilities and Computer Technology*. Retrieved from https://www.washington.edu/doit/Brochures/PDF/wtcomp.pdf

Buyya, R., Yeo, C. S., Venugopal, S., Broberg, J., & Brandic, I. (2009). Cloud computing and emerging IT platforms: Vision, hype, and reality for delivering computing as the 5th utility. *Future Generation Computer Systems, 25*(6), 599–616. doi:10.1016/j.future.2008.12.001

Buzducea, D. (2010). Social work in the new millennium: A global perspective. *Social Work Research, 1*, 31–42.

Callahan, P. (2003, March 28-30). *UCEA 88th Annual conference*. Chicago, Illinois.

Campbell, G. (2009). A Personal Cyberinfrastructure. *EDUCAUSE Review, 44*(5), 58–59.

Cao, Y., & Hong, P. (2011). Antecedents and consequences of social media utilization in college teaching: A proposed model with mixed-methods investigation. *On the Horizon, 19*(4), 297–306. doi:10.1108/10748121111179420

Carbonaro, M., Rex, M., & Chambers, J. (2004). Using LEGO Robotics in a Project-Based Learning Environment. *Interactive Multimedia Electronic Journal of Computer Enhanced Learning, 6*(1).

Cardon, P. L. (2001, March08). At-Risk Students and Technology Education: A Qualitative Study. *Journal of Technology Studies, 26*(1), 49–57.

Cardullo, V., Zygouris-Coe, V., & Wilson, N. S. (2014). The benefits and challenges of mobile learning and ubiquitous technologies. In S. J. Keengwe (Ed.), *Promoting Active Learning through the Integration of Mobile and Ubiquitous Technologies* (pp. 185–196).

Carlson, S. (2005). The Net Generation goes to college. *The Chronicle of Higher Education*, Section: Information Technology, *52*(7), A34. Retrieved from http://www.msmc.la.edu/include/learning_resources/todays_learner/The_Net_Generation.pdf

Carroll, M., Van Der Merwe, A., & Kotzé, P. (2011). Secure cloud computing benefits, risks and controls. In *Information Security South Africa* (pp. 1–9). Johannesburg: ISSA; doi:10.1109/ISSA.2011.6027519

Carter, L., Graham, R., & Nowrouzi, B. (2013). The coming down of fences: What Continuing educators are doing and saying about online and other forms of technology-supported learning. *Canadian Network for Innovation in Education Conference*. Ottawa, ON.

Carter, L., Nowrouzi, B., & Fitzgerald, S. *What undergraduate business students have to say about the iPad as a teaching and learning tool.* (in review)

Carter, L. M., & Brockerhoff-Macdonald, B. (2011). The continuing education of faculty as teachers at a mid-sized Ontario university. *The Canadian Journal for the Scholarship of Teaching and Learning*, *2*(1). http://ir.lib.uwo.ca/cjsotl_rcacea/vol2/iss1/4 doi:10.5206/cjsotl-rcacea.2011.1.4

Carter, L. M., Salyers, V., Myers, S., Hipfner, C., Hoffart, C., MacLean, C., & Barrett, P. et al. (2014). Qualitative insights from a Canadian multi-institutional research study: In search of meaningful e-learning. *Canadian Journal of Scholarship of Teaching and Learning*, *5*(1), 1–17. doi:10.5206/cjsotl-rcacea.2014.1.10

Carter, L., & Graham, R. (2012). The evolution of online education at a small northern university: Theory and practice. *Journal of Distance Education*, *26*(2).

Carter, L., & Rukholm, E. (2008). A study of critical thinking, teacher-student interaction, and discipline-specific writing in an online educational setting for registered nurses. *Journal of Continuing Education in Nursing*, *39*(3), 133–138. doi:10.3928/00220124-20080301-03 PMID:18386701

Carter, L., & Salyers, V. (2013). E-learning as educational innovation in Canada: Two case studies. In L. Shavinina (Ed.), *International handbook of innovation education*. New York: Taylor & Francis/Routledge.

Carter, L., Salyers, V., Page, A., Williams, L., Hofsink, C., & Albl, L. (2012). Highly relevant mentoring (HRM) as a faculty development model for web-based instruction. *Canadian Journal of Learning Technology*, *38*(1).

Casey, B. (2004). Mathematics problem-solving adventures: A Language-arts-based supplementary series for early childhood that focuses on spatial sense. In D. H. Clements, J. Sarama, & A. M. DiBiase (Eds.), *Engaging young children in mathematics: Standards for early childhood mathematics education* (pp. 377–389). Mahwah, NJ: Erlbaum.

Casey, B., Erkut, S., Ceder, I., & Young, J. M. (2008). Use of a Storytelling Context to Improve Girls' and Boys' Geometry Skills in Kindergarten. *Journal of Applied Developmental Psychology*, *29*(1), 29–48. doi:10.1016/j.appdev.2007.10.005

Casey, B., Kersh, J. E., & Young, J. M. (2004). Storytelling Sagas: An effective medium for teaching early childhood mathematics. *Early Childhood Research Quarterly*, *19*(1), 167–172. doi:10.1016/j.ecresq.2004.01.011

Cassidy, M. F. (1982). Toward integration: Education, instructional technology, and semiotics. *Educational Communications and Technology Journal*, *20*(2), 75–89.

CAST. (2008). *Universal design for learning guidelines version 1.0*. Wakefield, MA: Author.

Center for Assistive Technology and Environmental Access. (2006). *Individuals who are Blind or have Low Vision*. Retrieved from http://www.accesselearning.net/mod1/1_04.php

Center for Research on Learning and Teaching. (2014). *Active learning*. Retrieved from, http://www.crlt.umich.edu/tstrategies/tsal

Chan, A., & Lee, M. J. W. (2007). We want to be teachers, not programmers: In pursuit of relevance and authenticity for initial teacher education students studying an information technology subject at an Australian University. *Electronic Journal for the Integration of Technology*, Retrieved from http://ejite.isu.edu

Chandler, T., & An, H. (2007) Using Digital Mapping Programs to Augment Student Learning in Social Studies http://innovateonline.info/pdf/vol4_issue1/Using_Digital_Mapping_Programs_to_Augment_Student_Learning_in_Social_Studies.pdf

Chandra, D. G., & Borah, M. D. (2012). Cost benefit analysis of cloud computing in education. In *2012 International Conference on Computing, Communication and Applications (ICCCA)* (pp. 1– 6). doi:10.1109/ICCCA.2012.6179142

Chandra, D. G., & Malaya, D. B. (2012). Role of cloud computing in education. In *2012 International Conference on Computing, Electronics and Electrical Technologies (ICCEET)* (pp. 832–836). Ieee. doi:10.1109/ICCEET.2012.6203884

Changing Minds. (2013). *Active learning.* Retrieved from http://changingminds.org/explanations/learning/active_learning.htm

Chen, G., & Watkins, D. (2010). Stability and correlates of student evaluations of teaching at a Chinese university. *Assessment & Evaluation in Higher Education, 35*(6), 675–685. doi:10.1080/02602930902977715

Chen, H. I. (2013). Identity practices of multilingual writers in social networking spaces. *Language Learning & Technology, 17*(2), 143–170.

Chen, J. J., & Yang, S. C. (2014). Fostering foreign language learning through technology-enhanced intercultural projects. *Language Learning & Technology, 18*(1), 57–75.

Chen, L.-L. (2004). Pedagogical strategies to increase pre-service teachers' confidence in computer learning. *Journal of Educational Technology & Society, 7*(3), 50–60.

Chickering, A. W., & Ehrmann, S. C. (1996). Implementing the seven principles: Technology as lever. *AAHE Bulletin, 49*(2), 3–6.

Chickering, A., & Gamson, Z. (1987). Seven principles for good practice in undergraduate education. *AAHE Bulletin, 39*(7), 3–6.

Chigona, A., & Chigona, W. (2010). An investigation of factors affecting the use of ICT for teaching in Western Cape Town. In *Proceedings of the 18th European Conference on Information System-ECIS 2010* (Paper 6).

Childs, S., Blenkinsopp, E., Hall, A., & Walton, G. (2005). Effective e-learning for health professionals and students: Barriers and their solutions. A systematic review of the literature: Findings from the HeXL project. *Health Information and Libraries Journal, 22*(2), 20–32. doi:10.1111/j.1470-3327.2005.00614.x PMID:16279973

Chi, M. T. H., Bassok, M., Lewis, M. W., Reimann, P., & Glaser, R. (1989). Self-explanations: How students study and use examples in learning to solve problems. *Cognitive Science, 13*(2), 145–182. doi:10.1207/s15516709cog1302_1

Cholin, V. S. (2005). Study of the application of information technology for effective access to resources in Indian university libraries. *The International Information & Library Review, 37*(3), 189–197. doi:10.1016/j.iilr.2005.07.002

Christenson, T. K. (2008). The role of theory in instructional design: Some views of an ID practitioner. *Performance Improvement, 47*(4), 25–32. doi:10.1002/pfi.199

Christmann, E. P., & Badgett, J. L. (2003). A meta-analytic comparison of the effects of computer-assisted instruction on elementary students' academic achievement. *Information Technology in Childhood Education Annual*, 91–104.

Chuang, S., & Tsai, C. (2005). Preferences toward the constructivist internet-based learning environments among high school students in Taiwan. *Computers in Human Behavior, 21*(2), 255–272. doi:10.1016/j.chb.2004.02.015

Chu, J. (2001). Class size effects on the adult student learning social environment. *Asia Pacific Adult Education, 1*, 161–210.

Chung, S. K. (2007). Art education technology: Digital storytelling. *Art Education, 60*(2), 17–22.

Churches, A. (2007). *Bloom's Digital Taxonomy.* Retrieved from http://edorigami.wikispaces.com/file/view/bloom%27s+Digital+taxonomy+v3.01.pdf

Churches, A. (2008). *Bloom's Digital Taxonomy v2.12.* Retrieved from http://www.scribd.com/doc/8000050/Blooms-Digital-Taxonomy-v212

Clarke, J., Dete, C., & Dieterle, E. (2008). Emerging technologies for collaborative, mediated, immersive learning. In International Handbook of Information Technology in Primary and Secondary Education. (Vol. 20, pp. 901-909). Springer.

Clark, I. (2010). Formative assessment: 'There is nothing so practical as a good theory. *Australian Journal of Education, 54*(3), 341–362. doi:10.1177/000494411005400308

Clayson, D. E. (2009). Student evaluations of teaching: Are they related to what students learn? *Journal of Marketing Education*, *31*(1), 16–30. doi:10.1177/0273475308324086

Clements, D., & Battista, M. (1990). Constructivist learning and teaching. *The Arithmetic Teacher*, *38*(1), 34–35.

Cleveland-Innes, M., Garrison, R., & Kinsel, E. (2008). The role of learner in an online community of inquiry: Responding to the challenges of first-time online learners. In N. Karacapilidis (Ed.), *Solutions and innovations in web-based technologies for augmented learning: Improved platforms, tools and applications*. Hersey, Penn.: IGI Global Publishing.

Cobb, S. C. (2011). Social presence, satisfaction, and perceived learning of RN-to-BSN students in web-based nursing courses. *Nursing Education Perspectives*, *32*(2), 115–119. doi:10.5480/1536-5026-32.2.115 PMID:21667794

Code.org. (2013). *Anybody can learn*. Retrieved January 13, 2014, from http://codeorg.tumblr.com/post/70175643054/stats

Coffman, T. (2006). Using simulations to enhance teaching and learning: Encouraging the creative process. *The VSTE Journal*, *21*(2), 1–7.

Cohen, D. (1987). Educational technology, policy, and practice. *Educational Evaluation and Policy Analysis*, *9*(2), 153–170. doi:10.3102/01623737009002153

Cohen, L., Manion, L., & Morrrison, K. (2007). *Research Methods in Education* (6th ed.). New York, NY: Routledge.

Collins, A., Brown, J. S., & Holum, A. (1991). Cognitive apprenticeship: Making thinking visible. *American Educator*, *15*(3), 6–11, 38–46.

Collins, A., Brown, J. S., & Newman, S. E. (1989). Cognitive apprenticeship: Teaching the crafts of reading, writing, and mathematics. In L. B. Resnick (Ed.), *Knowing, learning and instruction: Essays in honour of Robert Glaser* (pp. 453–494). Hillsdale, NJ: Erlbaum.

Collis, B., & Moonen, J. (2001). *Flexible learning in a digital world: Experiences and expectations*. London, UK: Routledge.

Collis, B., & Van der Wende, M. C. (Eds.). (2002). *Models of technology and change in higher education: An international comparative survey on the current and future use of ICT in Higher Education*. Enschede: Print-Partners Ipskamp.

Combs, M., & Beach, J. D. (1994). Stories and storytelling: Personalizing the social studies. *The Reading Teacher*, *47*(6), 464–471.

Commission on Instructional Technology. (1970). *To improve learning: A report to the President and the Congress of the United States*. Washington, DC: Commission on Instructional Technology.

Conkling, S. (2007, January01). The Possibilities of Situated Learning for Teacher Preparation: The Professional Development Partnership. *Music Educators Journal*, *93*(3), 44–48. doi:10.1177/002743210709300319

Conole, G., Dyke, M., Oliver, M., & Seale, J. (2004). Mapping pedagogy and tools for effective learning design. *Computers & Education*, *43*(1), 17–33. doi:10.1016/j.compedu.2003.12.018

Conrad, R. M., & Donaldson, A. (2004). *Engaging the online learner: Activities and resources for creative instruction*. San Francisco: Jossey-Bass.

Contact North. (2012). *Online Learning in Canada: At the Tipping Point. A Cross-Country Check-up*. Retrieved from http://contactnorth.ca/online-learning-canada

Cook, D. A., Levinson, A. J., & Garside, S. (2010). Time and learning efficiency in Internet-based learning: A systematic review and meta-analysis. *Advances in Health Sciences Education: Theory and Practice*, *15*(5), 755–770. doi:10.1007/s10459-010-9231-x PMID:20467807

Cook, R. G., Ley, K., Crawford, C., & Warner, A. (2009). Motivators and inhibitors for university faculty in distance and e-learning. *British Journal of Educational Technology*, *1*(1), 149–163. doi:10.1111/j.1467-8535.2008.00845.x

Cooper, D. R., & Schindler, P. S. (2006). *Business research methods* (9th ed.). Boston: McGraw-Hill Irwin.

Cooper, J. M., & Bull, G. (1997). Technology and teacher education: Past practice and recommended directions. *Action in Teacher Education*, *19*(2), 97–106. doi:10.1080/01626620.1997.10462871

Cooper, R. (2010). *Those who can teach*. Boston, MA: Wadsworth Cengage Learning.

Copley, J., & Ziviani, J. (2004). Barriers to the use of assistive technology for children with multiple disabilities. *Occupational Therapy International*, *11*(4), 229–243. doi:10.1002/oti.213 PMID:15771212

Correa, D. (2010). Developing academic literacy and voice: Challenges faced by a mature ESL student and her instructors. *Profile*, *12*(1), 79–94.

Correia, A. P., & Davis, N. (2008). Intersecting communities of practice in distance education: The program team and the online course community. *Distance Education*, *29*(3), 289–306. doi:10.1080/01587910802395813

Cortazzi, M., Jin, L., Wall, D., & Cavendish, S. (2001). Sharing Learning through Narrative Communication. *International Journal of Language & Communication Disorders*, *36*(s1), 252–257. doi:10.3109/13682820109177893 PMID:11340792

Coskun, H. (2011). The effects of group size, memory instruction, and session length on the creative performance in electronic brainstorming groups. *Educational Sciences: Theory and Practice*, *11*(1), 91–95.

Cox, C. (2014). *Virtual field trips*. Retrieved from, http://www.readingrockets.org/article/42383

Cox, M., Preston, C., & Cox, K. (1999, September). What motivates teachers to use ICT? *Paper presented at theBritish Educational Research Association Annual Conference*. University of Sussex, Brighton.

Coyle, D. (2009). *The talent code*. New York, NY: Random House.

Cradler, J., McNabb, M., Freeman, M., & Burchett, R. (2002). How does technology influence student learning? *Learning and Leading*, *29*(8), 46–49.

Cramer, K. M., Collins, K. R., Snider, D., & Fawcett, G. (2007). The virtual lecture hall: Utilization, effectiveness and student perceptions. *British Journal of Educational Technology*, *38*(1), 106–115. doi:10.1111/j.1467-8535.2006.00598.x

Cranton, P. (2012). *Planning instruction for adult learners* (3rd ed.). Toronto: Wall & Emerson, Inc.

Crawford, G., & Rudy, J.EDUCAUSE Current Issues Committee. (2003)... *Fourth Annual EDUCAUSE Survey*, *38*(11), 12–26.

Creswell, J. W. (1998). *Qualitative inquiry and research design: Choosing among five traditions*. Thousand Oaks, CA: Sage Publications.

Creswell, J. W. (2009). *Research design: Qualitative, quantitative, and mixed methods approaches*. Los Angeles, CA: Sage.

Creswell, J. W., & Plano Clark, V. L. (2007). *Designing and conducting mixed methods research*. Thousand Oaks, CA: Sage.

Creswell, J. W., Plano Clark, V. L., Gutmann, M., & Hanson, W. (2003). Advanced mixed methods research designs. In A. Tashakkori & C. Teddlie (Eds.), *Handbook of mixed methods in social and behavioral research* (pp. 209–240). Thousand Oaks, CA: Sage.

Cronbach, L. J. (1951). Coefficient alpha and the internal structure of tests. *Psychometrika*, *16*(3), 297–334. doi:10.1007/BF02310555

Cropley, J. A. (1981). Lifelong learning: A rationale for teacher training. *Journal of Education for Teaching*, *7*(1), 57–69. doi:10.1080/0260747810070107

Crowe, A. R. (2004, September06). Teaching by Example: Integrating Technology into Social Studies Education Courses. *Journal of Computing in Teacher Education*, *20*(4), 159–165.

Cruickshank, L., Tsekleves, E., Whitham, R., Hill, A., & Kondo, K. (2007). Making interactive TV easier to use: Interface design for a second screen approach. *The Design Journal*, *10*(3), 41–53. doi:10.2752/146069207789271920

Cruz-Martin, A., Fernandez-Madrigal, J. A., Galindo, C., Gonzalez-Jimenez, J., Stockmans-Daou, C., & Blanco-Claraco, J. L. (2012). A LEGO Mindstorms NXT approach for teaching at Data Acquisition, Control Systems Engineering and Real-Time Systems undergraduate courses. *Computers & Education*, *59*(3), 974–988. doi:10.1016/j.compedu.2012.03.026

Csikszentmihalyi, M. (1990). *Flow: The psychology of optimal experience*. New York, NY: Harper and Row.

Cuban, L. (1986). *Teachers and machines: The classroom use of technology since 1920*. New York, NY: Teachers College Press.

Cuban, L. (1993). *How teachers taught: Constancy and change in American classrooms, 1880–1990* (2nd ed.). New York, NY: Teachers College Press.

Curtis, M., Luchini, K., Bobrowsky, B., Quintana, C., & Soloway, E. (2002). Handheld Use in K-12: a descriptive account.*Proceedings of the IEEE International Workshop on Wireless and Mobile Technologies in Education*, Los Alamitos, CA: IEEE Computer Society. doi:10.1109/WMTE.2002.1039217

Cuseo, J. (1992). Collaborative & cooperative learning in higher education: A proposed taxonomy. *Cooperative Learning and College Teaching, 2*(2), 2–4.

Cutting, A. K. (1989). *The role of media technology within the proposed Open University of Tanzania*. Dar es Salaam: The Open University of Tanzania.

Czerniewicz, L., & Brown, C. (2005). Information and Communication Technology (ICT) use in teaching and learning practices in Western Cape higher education institutions. In L. Czerniewicz, & C. Hodgkinson-Williams (Eds.), (In press). Education in South Africa: what have Information and Communication Technologies (ICTs) got to do with it? Special Issue of Perspectives in Education.

Dahlstrom, E., Walker, J., & Dziuban, C. (2013). ECAR study of undergraduate students and information technology, 2013 (Research Report). Louisville, CO: EDU-CAUSE Center for Analysis and Research; Available at http://www.educause.edu/ecar

Darling-Hammond, L. (2006). *Powerful teacher education: Lessons from exemplary programs*. San Francisco: John Wiley & Sons.

Davidoff, F. (2011). Music lessons: What musicians can teach doctors (and other health professionals). *Annals of Internal Medicine, 154*(6), 426–429. doi:10.7326/0003-4819-154-6-201103150-00009 PMID:21403078

Dawson, K. (2012, March01). Using Action Research Projects to Examine Teacher Technology Integration Practices. *Journal of Digital Learning in Teacher Education, 28*(3), 117–123. doi:10.1080/21532974.2012.10784689

De Boer, W., & Collis, B. (2005). Becoming more systematic about flexible learning: Beyond time and distance. *Research in Learning Technology, 13*(1), 33–48. doi:10.1080/0968776042000339781

Deed, C., & Edwards, A. (2011). Unrestricted student blogging: Implications for active learning in a virtual text-based environment. *Active Learning in Higher Education, 12*(1), 11–21. doi:10.1177/1469787410387725

Derewianka, B. (2007). Using appraisal theory to track interpersonal development in adolescent academic writing. In A. McCabe, M. O'Donnell, & R. Whittaker (Eds.), *In Advances in Language and Education* (pp. 142–165). London: Continuum.

Derrick, G. M. (2003). Creating environments conducive for lifelong learning. *New Directions for Adult and Continuing Education, 100*(100), 5–18. doi:10.1002/ace.115

Deslauriers, L., Schelew, E., & Wieman, C. (2011, May13). Improved learning in a large enrollment Physics class. *Science, 332*(6031), 862–864. doi:10.1126/science.1201783 PMID:21566198

Dettori, G., & Paiva, A. (2009). Narrative learning in technology-enhanced environments. In N. Balacheff, S. Ludvigsen, T. De Jong, A. Lazonder, S. Barnes, & L. Montandon (Eds.), *Technology-Enhanced Learning* (pp. 55–69). Berlin: Springer. doi:10.1007/978-1-4020-9827-7_4

Dewey, J. (1938). *Experience and education*. New York: Touchstone.

Dexter, S. (2002). eTips – educational technology integration and implementation principles: Why a set of principles to guide teachers about integrating and implementing educational technology into the K12 classroom? Hershey, PA: IGI Global.

Dhanarajan, G. (2001). Distance Education: Promise, Performance and Potential. *Open Learning, 16*(1), 61–68. doi:10.1080/02680510124465

Dias, L. B. (1999). Integration technology: Some things you should know. *Learning and Leading with Technology, 27*(3), 10–13.

Dick, W. E. (2012). Typometric Rx: New for Low Vision Readers. *CSUN Conference on Technology and People with Disabilities.*

Dick, W., Carey, L., & Carey, O. (2000). *The systematic design of instruction.* Glenview, IL: Addison Wesley.

Digenti, D. (1998). Toward an understanding of the learning community. *Organization Development Journal, 16*(2), 91–96.

Dimitrova, M., Mimirinis, M., & Murphy, A. (2004, Aug/Sept.). Evaluating the flexibility of a pedagogical framework for e-learning. *Proceedings of the IEEE International Conference on Advance Learning Technologies, Joensuu, Finland.* doi:10.1109/ICALT.2004.1357422

Dockstader, J. (1999). Teachers of the 21st Century Know the What, Why, and How of Technology Integration. Technological Horizons in Education, 26(6).

Dogan, B., & Robin, B. (2008). Implementation of digital storytelling in the classroom by teachers trained in a digital storytelling workshop. In *Society for Information Technology & Teacher Education International Conference.* Las Vegas, NV: USA.

Donaldson, J. (2003). *Continuing education organizational models.* Unpublished email correspondence.

Donnon, T., Delver, H., & Beran, T. (2010). Student and teaching characteristics related to ratings of instruction in medical sciences graduate programs. *Medical Teacher, 32*(4), 327–332. doi:10.3109/01421590903480097 PMID:20353330

Donovan, L., & Green, T. (2010, September06). One-to-One Computing in Teacher Education: Faculty Concerns and Implications for Teacher Educators. *Journal of Digital Learning in Teacher Education, 26*(4), 140–148.

Dori, Y. J., & Belcher, J. (2005). How does technology-enabled active learning affect undergraduate students' understanding of electromagnetism concepts? *Journal of the Learning Sciences, 14*(2), 243–279. doi:10.1207/s15327809jls1402_3

Dornan, T., Brown, M., Powley, D., & Hopkins, M. (2004). A technology using feedback to manage experience based learning. *Medical Teacher, 26*(8), 736–738. doi:10.1080/01421590400016340 PMID:15763881

Dorner, R., Grimm, P., & Abawi, D. F. (2002). Synergies between interactive training simulations and digital storytelling: A component-based framework. *Computers & Graphics, 26*(1), 45–55. doi:10.1016/S0097-8493(01)00177-7

Dorrian, J., & Wache, D. (2009). Introduction of an online approach to flexible learning for on-campus and distance education students: Lessons learned and ways forward. *Nurse Education Today, 29*(2), 157-167. doi:10/jnedt.2008.08.010

Downes, S. (2008). *The Future of Online Learning: Ten Years On.* Retrieved August, 2014: http://halfanhour.blogspot.com/2008/11/future-of-online-learning-ten-years-on_16.html

Downes, S. (2012, February 11). *Half an hour: E-learning generations.* Retrieved from: http://halfanhour.blogspot.ca/2012/02/e-learning-generations.html

Drexler, W. (2008). *Finally! A video that explains what I'm aiming for as a teacher.* Dougbelshaw.com Retrieved August 2014: http://dougbelshaw.com/blog/2008/11/28/finally-a-video-that-explains-what-im-aiming-for-as-a-teacher/

Driver, R., & Bell, E. (1986). Students' thinking and the learning of science: A constructivist view. *The School Science Review, 67*, 443–456.

Duckworth, E. (2005). Critical Exploration in the Classroom. *New Educator, 1*(4), 257–272. doi:10.1080/15476880500276728

Duffield, J. A. (1997). Trials, tribulations, and minor successes: Integrating technology into a preservice preparation program. *TechTrends, 42*(4), 22–26. doi:10.1007/BF02818596

Dunn, S. (2000). The futurist. *Virtual World,* Mar/Apr, 34-38.

Duran, M., Runvand, S., & Fossum, P. R. (2009, October01). Preparing Science Teachers to Teach with Technology: Exploring a K-16 Networked Learning Community Approach. *Turkish Online Journal of Educational Technology, 8*(4), 21–42.

Earle, R. S. (2002). The integration of instructional technology into public education: Promises and challenges. *Educational Technology, 42*(1), 5–13.

Eguchi, A. (2007a). *Educational Robotics for Elementary School Classroom*. Paper presented at the Society for Information Technology and Education (SITE), San Antonio, TX.

Eguchi, A. (2007b). *Educational Robotics for Undergraduate Freshmen*. Paper presented at the Proceedings of World Conference on Educational Multimedia, Hypermedia and Telecommunications, Vancouver, Canada.

Eguchi, A. (2014). *Learning Experience Through RoboCupJunior: Promoting STEM Education and 21st Century Skills with Robotics Competition*. Paper presented at the Society for Information Technology and Education (SITE), Jacksonville, FL.

Eguchi, A., Hughes, N., Stocker, M., Shen, J., & Chikuma, N. (2012). RoboCupJunior: A decade later. In T. Röfer, N. M. Mayer, J. Savage & U. Saranlı (Eds.), RoboCup 2011: Robot Soccer World Cup XV: Springer.

Eison, J. (2010). *Using active learning instructional strategies to create excitement and enhance learning*. Retrieved from, http://www.cte.cornell.edu/documents

Ekwall, E. E., & Shanker, J. L. (1998). *Diagnosis and remediation of the disabled reader*. Needham Heights, USA: Allyn and Bacon.

El Hassan, K. (2009). Investigating substantive and consequential validity of student ratings of instruction. *Higher Education Research & Development*, 28(3), 319–333. doi:10.1080/07294360902839917

Elbow, P. (1994). What do we mean when we talk about voice in texts. In K. Yancey (Ed.), *Voices on Voice: Perspectives, Definitions, Inquiry* (pp. 1–35). Urbana, IL: National Council of Teachers of English.

Elkind, D. (2008). Forward. In M. U. Bers (Ed.), *Block to Robots* (pp. xi–xiv). New York, NY: Teachers College Press.

Elliott, A. (2011). Increasing higher education access and pathways through normalization of flexible pedagogies and course structures. *Proceedings of the 2011 Barcelona European Academic Conference, Barcelona, Spain*. Retrieved from: http://conferences.cluteonline.com/index.php/IAC/2011SP/paper/viewFile/538/55

Ely, D. P. (1995). *Technology is the answer! But what was the question?* Capstone College of Education Society, University of Alabama (ERIC Document Reproduction Service No. ED 381 152).

Ericsson, K. A. (2004). Deliberate practice and the acquisition and maintenance of expert performance in medicine and related domains. *Academic Medicine*, 79(10Supplement), S70–S81. doi:10.1097/00001888-200410001-00022 PMID:15383395

Ernst, J. V., & Moye, J. J. (2013, June06). Social Adjustment of At-Risk Technology Education Students. *Journal of Technology Education*, 24(2), 2–13.

Ertmer, P., & Ottebbreit-Leftwich, A. (2009). Teacher technology change: How knowledge, beliefs, and culture intersect. AERA. Retrieved from, http://www.edci.purdue.edu/ertmer/docs/aera09_ertmer_leftwich.pdf

Ertmer, P. (1999). Addressing first- and second-order barriers to change: Strategies for technology implementation. *Educational Technology Research and Development*, 47(4), 47–61. doi:10.1007/BF02299597

Ertmer, P. (1999). Addressing first-and second-order barriers to change: Strategies for technology integration. *Educational Technology Research and Development*, 47(4), 47–61.

Ertmer, P. A. (2005). Teacher pedagogical beliefs: The final frontier in our quest for technology integration? *Educational Technology Research and Development*, 53(4), 25–39.

Faculty of Public Administration and Management (2008). *Report on Possibility of establishing DL programmes*.

Farell, J. B. (2009). *Active learning: theories and research*. Retrieved from, http://www.lookstein.org/online_journal.php?id=260

Farrell, G., & Isaacs, S. (2007). *Survey of ICT and Education in Africa: A Summary Report, Based on 53 Country Surveys* (pp. 0–74). Washington, DC. United States. Retrieved from http://www.infodev.org/en/Publication.353.html

Farrow, M., & Sims, R. (1987). Computer-assisted learning in occupational therapy. *Australian Occupational Therapy Journal, 34*(2), 53–58. doi:10.1111/j.1440-1630.1987.tb01569.x

Fauvel, J., Maanen, J., & van Maanen, J. A. (Eds.). (2000). *History in mathematics education: An ICMI study* (Vol. 6). Springer Science & Business Media.

Fauvel, J., & Van Maanen, J. (1997). The role of the history of mathematics in the teaching and learning of mathematics: Discussion document for an ICMI study (1997-2000). *Educational Studies in Mathematics, 34*(3), 255–259. doi:10.1023/A:1003038421040

Fehr, J. J., Honkanen, A., & Murray, D. J. (2012). Simulation in pediatric anesthesiology. *Paediatric Anaesthesia, 22*(10), 988–994. doi:10.1111/pan.12001 PMID:22967157

Fernandez, A. (2009). The role of new technologies in the learning process: Moodle as a teaching tool in Physics. *Computers & Education, 52*(10), 35–44.

Ferreira-Meyers, K., & Nkosi, J. (2010). *Incorporating the Enquiry-Based Approach into Moodle? Academic Literacy Development*. Swaziland: University of Swaziland.

Field, A. (2009). *Discovering statistics using spss* (3rd ed.). Thousand Oaks, CA: SAGE Publications Inc.

Fisher, R. (2009). Should we be allowing technology to remove the "distance" from "distance education"? *New Zealand Annual Review of Education, 18*, 31–46.

Fitzgerald, S., Beattie, B., Carter, L., & Caswell, W. (2014). Responsive BScN programming at Nipissing University: The continuing education of Ontario nurses. *Canadian Journal of University Continuing Education, 40*(1).

Fleming, L., Motomedi, V., & May, L. (2007). Predicting preservice teacher competence in computer technology: Modeling and application in training environments. *Journal of Technology and Teacher Education, 15*(2), 207–231.

Fletcher, J., & Tobias, S. (2000) (Eds.). Training and Retraining; A handbook for Business, Industry, Government, and the Military. New York: Macmillan

Fletcher, J. D., Hawley, D. E., & Piele, P. K. (1990). Costs, Effects and Utility of Microcomputer Assisted Instruction in the Classroom. *American Educational Research Journal, 27*(4), 783–806. doi:10.3102/00028312027004783

Flood, J. (2002). Read all about it: Online learning facing 80% attrition rates. *TOJDE 3*(2).

Flores, K. (2003). *Special needs, "Mainstream" classroom Inclusive education isn't easy, but it benefits kids with-and without-disabilities.*

Fok, A., & Watkins, D. (2007). Does a critical constructivist learning environment encourage a deeper approach to learning? *Asia-Pacific Education Researcher, 12*(1), 1–10.

Ford, M., & Batchelor, J. (2007). From zero to hero: Is the mobile phone a viable learning tool for Africa? *3rd International Conference on Social and Organizational Informatics and Cybernetics:* SOIC. 12-15 July 2007, Orlando, USA.

Freire, P. (1970). *Pedagogy of the oppressed*. New York: Herder and Herder.

Freire, P. (1994). *Pedagogy of the Oppressed* (30th ed.). New York, NY: Bloomsbury Academic.

Frick, T., Chadha, R., Watson, C., Wang, Y., & Green, P. (2009). College student perceptions of teaching and learning quality. *Educational Technology Research and Development, 57*(5), 705–720. doi:10.1007/s11423-007-9079-9

Friedman, A., & Kajder, S. (2006). Perceptions of beginning teacher education students regarding educational technology. *Journal of Computing in Teacher Education, 22*(4), 147–151.

Friedman, T. L. (2005). *The World is Flat: A Brief History of the Twenty-First Century*. New York, NY: Farrar, Straus & Giroux.

Gagné, R. M., Briggs, L. J., & Wager, W. W. (1992). *Principles of instructional design* (4th ed.). Fort Worth, TX: Harcourt Brace Jovanovich.

Gallupe, R. B., Dennis, A. R., Cooper, W. H., Valacich, J. S., Bastianutti, L., & Nunamaker, J. F. (1992). Electronic brainstorming and group size. *Academy of Management Journal, 35*(2), 350–369. doi:10.2307/256377

Gardner, J. E., Wissick, C. A., Schweder, W., & Canter, L. S. (2003). Enhancing interdisciplinary instruction in general and special education: Thematic units and technology. *Remedial and Special Education*, 24(3), 161–172. doi:10.1177/07419325030240030501

Garrison, D. R. (1993). Quality and access in distance education: Theoretical considerations. In D. Keegan (Ed.), *Theoretical principles of distance education* (pp. 9–21). New York: Routledge.

Garrison, D. R. (2009). Communities of inquiry in online learning: Social, teaching and cognitive presence. In C. Howard, ... (Eds.), *Encyclopedia of distance and online learning* (2nd ed., pp. 352–355). Hershey, PA: IGI Global.

Garrison, D. R., Anderson, T., & Archer, W. (2001). Critical thinking and computer conferencing: A model and tool to assess cognitive presence. *American Journal of Distance Education*, 15(1), 7–23. doi:10.1080/08923640109527071

Garrison, D. R., & Kanuka, H. (2004). Blended learning: Uncovering its transformative potential in higher education. *The Internet and Higher Education*, 7(2), 95–105. doi:10.1016/j.iheduc.2004.02.001

Garrison, D., Anderson, T., & Archer, W. (2000). Critical inquiry in a text-based environment: Computer conferencing in higher education. *The Internet and Higher Education*, 2(2-3), 87–105. doi:10.1016/S1096-7516(00)00016-6

Garrison, D., & Cleveland-Innes, M. (2005). Facilitating cognitive presence in online learning: Interaction is not enough. *American Journal of Distance Education*, 19(3), 133–148. doi:10.1207/s15389286ajde1903_2

Gaudelli, W. (2007, March08). Convergence of Technology and Diversity: Experiences of Two Beginning Teachers in Web-Based Distance-learning for Global/Multicultural Education. *Teacher Education Quarterly*, 33(1), 97–116.

Gaytan, J., & McEwen, B. C. (2007). Effective online instructional and assessment strategies. *American Journal of Distance Education*, 21(3), 117–132. doi:10.1080/08923640701341653

Gee, J. P. (2004). *Situated language and learning: A critique of traditional schooling*. New York: Routledge.

Geertz, C. (1973). Thick description: Towards an interpretive theory of culture. In C. Geertz (Ed.), *The Interpretation of cultures*. New York, NY: Basic Books.

Gentry, C. G. (1995). Educational technology: A question of meaning. In G. Anglin (Ed.), *Instructional technology: Past, present, and future*. Englewood, CO: Libraries Unlimited.

Georgina, D. A., & Olson, M. R. (2008). Integration of technology in higher education: A review of faculty self-perceptions. *The Internet and Higher Education*, 11(1), 1–8. doi:10.1016/j.iheduc.2007.11.002

Gerlach, J. (2012). STEM: Defying a Simple Definition. *NSTA WebNews Digest - NSTA Reports*. Retrieved February 10, 2014, from http://www.nsta.org/publications/news/story.aspx?id=59305

Gibson, C. C. (2000). When disruptive approaches meet disruptive technologies: Learning at a distance. *The Journal of Continuing Education in the Health Professions*, 20(2), 69–75. doi:10.1002/chp.1340200202 PMID:11232222

Gikandi, J. W. (2012). *Online formative assessment in higher education: Enhancing E-Learning in continuing teacher education*. Unpublished doctoral thesis, University of Canterbury, New Zealand.

Gikandi, J. W. (2013). How can open reflective journals enhance online learning in teacher education? *Journal of Technology and Teacher Education*, 21(1), 5–26.

Gikandi, J. W., & Mackey, J. (2013). Synergy between authentic assessment activities and learner autonomy: How does this promote shared authenticity in online higher education? *International Journal on E-Learning*, 12(4), 273–301.

Gikandi, J. W., & Morrow, D. (in press). Designing and implementing peer formative feedback within online learning environments. *Journal of Technology. Pedagogy and Education*.

Gikandi, J. W., Morrow, D., & Davis, N. E. (2011). Online formative assessment in higher education: A review of the literature. *Computers & Education*, 57(4), 2333–2351. doi:10.1016/j.compedu.2011.06.004

Gillard, S., Bailey, D., & Nolan, E. (2008). Ten reasons for IT educators to be early adopters of IT innovations. *Journal of Information Technology Education, 7*, 21–33.

Gillmore, G. M., Kane, M. T., & Naccarato, R. W. (1978). The generalizability of student ratings of Instruction: Estimation of the teacher and course components. *Journal of Educational Measurement, 15*(1), 1–13. doi:10.1111/j.1745-3984.1978.tb00051.x

Gill, P., Kitney, L., Kozan, D., & Lewis, M. (2010). Online learning in paediatrics: A student-led web-based learning modality. *The Clinical Teacher, 7*(1), 53–57. doi:10.1111/j.1743-498X.2009.00337.x PMID:21134144

Ginat, D. (2009). Interleaved pattern composition and scaffolded learning. *Proceedings of the Annual Conference on Innovation and Technology in Computer Science Education (ITiCSE)*. Paris, France.

Glenn, J. M. (2000). Teaching the Net Generation. *Business Education Forum, 54*(3), 6–14.

Glogster. (n.d.). *Glogster.com*. Retrieved from http://edu.glogster.com/?ref=com

Goddard, M. (2002). What do we do with these computers? Reflections on technology in the classroom. *Journal of Research on Technology in Education, 35*(1), 19–26. doi:10.1080/15391523.2002.10782367

Goe, L., Bell, C., & Little, O. (2008). Approaches to evaluating teacher effectiveness: A research synthesis. *National Comprehensive Center for Teacher Quality*, Retrieved from http://www.tqsource.org/publications/EvaluatingTeachEffectiveness.pdf

Gold, M., & Lowe, C. (2010). The Integration of Assistive Technology into Standard Classroom Practices: Practical Recommendations for K-12 General Educators. *The Journal of Multiculturalism in Education, 6*(1), 1–16.

Goldman, S. R., Lawless, K., Pellegrino, J. W., & Plants, R. (2005). Technology for teaching and learning with understanding. In J. M. Cooper (Ed.), *Classroom Teaching Skills* (8th ed., pp. 185–234). Boston: Houghton Mifflin.

Goodman, L. A., & Kruskal, W. H. (1954). Measures of association for Part I. *Journal of the American Statistical Association, 49*, 732–764.

Goodnough, K. (2005). Fostering teacher learning through collaborative inquiry. *The Clearing House: A Journal of Educational Strategies, Issues and Ideas, 79*(2), 88–92. doi:10.3200/TCHS.79.2.88-93

Goodson-Espy, T., Lynch-Davis, K., Schram, P., & Quickenton, A. (2010, September06). Using 3D Computer Graphics Multimedia to Motivate Preservice Teachers' Learning of Geometry and Pedagogy. *Srate Journal, 19*(2), 23–35.

Goodyear, P., & Retalis, S. (2010). *Technology-enhanced learning*. Rotterdam: Sense Publishers.

Government of Kenya. (2013). *Kenyan Constitution, 2013*.

Grabinger, R. S. (1996). Rich environments for active learning. In D. H. Jonassen (Ed.), *Handbook of Research for Educational Communications and Technology*. New York: Simon Schuster McMillan.

Grabinger, S., & Dunlap, J. C. (1995). Rich environments for active learning: A definition. *Research in Learning Technology, 3*(2), 5–34.

Grabinger, S., Dunlap, J. C., & Duffield, J. A. (1997). Rich environment for active learing, in action: Problem-based learning. *Research in Learning Technology, 5*(2), 5–17. doi:10.1080/0968776970050202

Graffam, B. (2007). Active learning in medical education: Strategies for beginning implementation. *Medical Teacher, 29*(1), 38–42. doi:10.1080/01421590601176398 PMID:17538832

Grasha, A. F., & Yangarber-Hicks, N. (2001, March08). Integrating Teaching Styles and Learning Styles with Instructional Technology. *College Teaching, 48*(1), 2–10. doi:10.1080/87567550009596080

Gravestock, P., & Gregor–Greenleaf, E. (2008). Student course evaluations: Research, models and trends. Toronto, ON: Higher Education Quality Council of Ontario; Retrieved from http://www.heqco.ca/SiteCollectionDocuments/Student%20Course%20Evaluations.pdf

Gravetter, F. J., & Wallnau, L. B. (2007). *Statistics for the behavioral sciences* (7th ed.). Belmont, CA: Thomson Wadsworth.

Greenhow, C., Dexter, S., & Hughes, J. E. (2008, March01). Teacher Knowledge about Technology Integration: An Examination of Inservice and Preservice Teachers' Instructional Decision-Making. *Science Education International, 19*(1), 9–25.

Green, K. (2002). *Campus Computing 2002: The 13th National Survey of Computing and Information Technology in American Higher Education.* Encino, CA: Campus Computing.

Groff, J., & Mouza, C. (2008). A framework for addressing challenges to classroom technology use. *Association for the Advancement of Computing In Education Journal, 16*(1), 21–46.

Grover, S. (2011). *Robotics and Engineering for Middle and High School Students to Develop Computational Thinking.* Paper presented at the Annual Meeting of the American Educational Research Association, New Orleans.

Guiterrez, K., Morales, P. Z., & Martinez, D. (2009). Re-mediating Literacy: Culture, Difference, and Learning for Students from Non-dominant Communities. *Review of Research in Education, 33*, 213–245.

Guri-Rosenblit, S. (2005). 'Distance education' and 'e-learning': Not the same thing. *Higher Education, 49*(4), 467–493. doi:10.1007/s10734-004-0040-0

Guzman, A., & Nussbaum, M. (2009). Teaching competencies for technology integration in the classroom. *Journal of Computer Assisted Learning, 25*(5), 453–469. doi:10.1111/j.1365-2729.2009.00322.x

Habre, S., & Grundmeier, T. A. (May 01, 2006). Prospective Mathematics Teachers' Views on the Role of Technology in Mathematics Education. *Issues in the Undergraduate Mathematics Preparation of School Teachers, 3.*

Hager, M. A., Wilson, S., Pollak, T. H., & Rooney, P. M. (2003). Response Rates for Mail Surveys of Nonprofit Organisations: A Review and Empirical Test. *Nonprofit and Voluntary Sector Quarterly, 32*(2), 252–267. doi:10.1177/0899764003032002005

Hairston, K. R., & Strickland, M. J. (2011, January01). Contrapuntal Orchestration: An Exploration of an Interaction between Researchers' and Teachers' Stories around the Concept of Culture. *Race, Ethnicity and Education, 14*(5), 631–653. doi:10.1080/13613324.2010.493358

Hake, R. R. (1998). Interactive-engagement versus traditional methods: A six-thousand-student survey of mechanics test data for introductory physics courses. *American Journal of Physics, 66*(1), 64. doi:10.1119/1.18809

Hamilton-Hart, J. (2010). *Using Facebook for language learning. Innovation in Language Teaching and Learning.* Retrieved from: http://iltl.wordpress.com/2010/11/11/using-facebook-for-language-learning/

Hammersley, A., Tallantyre, F., & Le Cornu, A. (2013). Flexible learning: A practical guide for academic staff. York: Higher Education Academy; Retrieved from http://www.heacademy.ac.uk/resources/detail/flexible- learning/fl_guides/staff_guide

Hancock, V., & Betts, J. (1994). From the lagging to the leading edge. *Educational Leadership, 51*(7), 24–29.

Handelzalts, A. (2009). *Collaborative curriculum development in teacher design teams.* Enschede: PrintPartners Ipskamp.

Han, H., Resch, D. S., & Kovach, R. A. (2013). Educational technology in medical education. *Teaching and Learning in Medicine, 25*(sup1), S39–S43. doi:10.1080/10401334.2013.842914 PMID:24246105

Han, H., Roberts, N., & Korte, R. (in press). Learning in the real place: Medical students' learning and socialization in clerkships. *Academic Medicine.* PMID:25354072

Hanover Research. (2011). *Trends in global distance learning.* Washington, DC. Retrieved from: http://www.hanoverresearch.com/wp-content/uploads/2011/12/Trends-in- Global-Distance-Learning-Membership.pdf

Hans, A., & Akhter, S. (2013). Emerging trends in teacher's education. *The Macrotheme Review, 2*(2), 23-31. Retrieved from http://macrotheme.com/

Han, S., & Bhattacharya, K. (2001). Constructionism, Learning by Design, and Project Based Learning. In M. Orey (Ed.), *Emerging Perspectives on Learning.* Teaching and Technology.

Hardy, D., & Boaz, M. (1997). Learner development: Beyond the technology. *New Directions for Teaching and Learning, 71*(71), 41–48. doi:10.1002/tl.7106

Hare, H. (2007). Survey of ICT in Education in Tanzania. In G. Farrell, S. Isaacs & M. Trucano, (eds). Survey of ICT and education in Africa (volume 2): 53 country reports. Washington, DC: infoDev /World Bank.

Harman, G. (2000). *Quality assurance in higher education.* Bangkok: Ministry of University Affairs & UNESCO PROAP.

Hartley, S. S. (1977). *Meta-analysis of the effects of individually paced instruction in Mathematics.* Unpublished Doctoral dissertation, University of Colorado at Boulder.

Hartley, J., Rennie, E., Russo, A., & Watkins, J. (2005, January01). Digital Storytelling. *International Journal of Cultural Studies, 8*(4), 4. doi:10.1177/1367877905061532

Hassel, B. C. (2009). How should state define teacher effectiveness? *Center for American Progress,* Retrieved from http://publicimpact.com/publications/PublicImpact–How_Should_States_Define_Teacher_Effectiveness.pdf

Hawkins, J., Spielvogel, B., & Panush, E. M. (1996). *National study tour of district technology integration* (Summary report). Retrieved from http://cct.edc.org/admin/publications/report/natstudy_dti96.pdf

Hawkins, J., Panush, E., & Spielvogel, R. (1996). *National study tour of district technology integration (summary report).* New York: Center for Children and Technology, Education Development Center.

Hay, L. E. (2000). Educating the Net Generation. *School Administrator, 57*(54), 6–10.

Heafner, T. L., Petty, T. M., & Hartshorne, R. (2011, January01). Evaluating Modes of Teacher Preparation: A Comparison of Face-to-Face and Remote Observations of Graduate Interns. *Journal of Digital Learning in Teacher Education, 27*(4), 153–164. doi:10.1080/21532974.2011.10784672

Hedberg, J., Brown, C., & Arrighi, M. (1997). Interactive multimedia and Web-based learning: Similarities and differences. In B. H. Khan (Ed.), *Web-based Instruction* (pp. 47–58). Englewood Cliffs, New Jersey: Educational Technology Publications.

Héfer, B. (2009). Teaching effectiveness, course evaluation, and academic performance: The role of academic delay of gratification. *Journal of Advanced Academics, 20*(2), 326–355. doi:10.1177/1932202X0902000206

Heinrichs, K. I. (2002). Problem-based learning in entry-level athletic training professional-education programs: A model for developing critical-thinking and decision-making skills. *Journal of Athletic Training, 37*(4suppl.), S-189–S-198. PMID:12937544

Heo, M. (2009, October01). Digital Storytelling: An Empirical Study of the Impact of Digital Storytelling on Preservice Teachers' Self-Efficacy and Dispositions towards Educational Technology. *Journal of Educational Multimedia and Hypermedia, 18*(4), 405–428.

Herrick, D. R. (2009). Google this! Using Google apps for collaboration and productivity. In *Proceedings of the ACM SIGUCCS fall conference on User services conference - SIGUCCS '09* (p. 55). New York, New York, USA: ACM Press. doi:10.1145/1629501.1629513

Herrington, J., & Oliver, R. (2000). An instructional design framework for authentic learning environments. *Educational Technology Research and Development, 48*(3), 23–48. doi:10.1007/BF02319856

Herrington, J., Reeves, T. C., & Oliver, R. (2010). *A guide to authentic e-learning.* New York: Routledge.

Herron, J. (2010, March08). Implementation of Technology in an Elementary Mathematics Lesson: The Experiences of Preservice Teachers at One University. *Srate Journal, 19*(1), 22–29.

Hewings, A. (2012). Stance and voice in academic discourse across channels. In K. Hyland & C. Sancho (Eds.), *Stance and voice in written academic genres* (pp. 187–201). Basingstoke: Palgrave Macmillan. doi:10.1057/9781137030825.0021

Hewings, M., & Hewings, A. (2002). It is interesting to note that…a comparative study of anticipatory "it" in student and published writing. *English for Specific Purposes, 21*(4), 367–383. doi:10.1016/S0889-4906(01)00016-3

Hew, K. F., & Brush, T. (2007). Integrating technology into K-12 teaching and learning: Current knowledge gaps and recommendations for future research. *Educational Technology Research and Development, 55*(3), 223–252. doi:10.1007/s11423-006-9022-5

Hickman, C. (2003). Results of survey regarding distance education offerings. University Continuing Education Association (UCEA). *Distance Learning Community of Practice, Research Committee Report.*

Higgins, S. (2003). Partez-Vous Mathematics? In *Enhancing Primary Mathematics Teaching and Learning, Thompson, I.* Buckingham: Open University press.

Higher Education Academy. (2013). *Flexible pedagogies: Technology-enhanced learning.* Retrieved from: http://www.heacademy.ac.uk/assets/documents/flexible-learning/Flexiblepedagogi es/tech _enhanced_learning/TEL_report.pdf

Hinkle, D. E., Wiersma, W., & Jurs, S. G. (2003). *Applied statistics for the behavioral sciences* (5th ed.). Boston, MA: Haughton Mifflin.

Hirst, A. W. & Bailey, D. G. (1983). *A study to identify effective classroom teaching competencies for community college faculty.* ED227890.

Hitchcock, G., & Hughes, D. (1995). *Research and the teacher* (2nd ed.). London: Routledge.

Hmelo-Silver, C., Duncan, R. G., & Chinn, C. A.Hmelo-Silver. (2007). Scaffolding and Achievement in Problem-Based and Inquiry Learning: A Response to Kirschner, Sweller, and Clark. *Educational Psychologist, 42*(2), 99–107. doi:10.1080/00461520701263368

Hoberman, S., & Mailick, S. (1994). Frame of reference. In S. Hoberman & S. Mailick (Eds.), *Professional education in the United States* (pp. 3–37). Westport, CT: Praeger.

Hodges, D. C. (1997). Re: Academic Voice. Retrieved October 5, 2014, from http://lchc.ucsd.edu/MCA/Mail/xmcamail.1997_10.dir/0366.html

Hoellwarth, C., & Moelter, M. J. (2011). The implications of a robust curriculum in introductory mechanics. *American Journal of Physics, 79*(5), 540. doi:10.1119/1.3557069

Hoffman, B., & Ritchie, D. C. (1998). Teaching and learning online: Tools, templates, and training. In WillisJ. WillisD.PriceJ. (Eds.), *Technology and Teacher Education Annual Conference,*1998. Charlottesville, VA: Association for Advancement of Computing in Education.

Hogan, T. P. (1973). Similarity of student ratings across instructors, courses, and time. *Research in Higher Education, 1*(2), 149–154. doi:10.1007/BF00991336

Hollingsworth, P., & Lewis, G. (2006). *Active learning: Increasing flow in the classroom.* Norwalk, CT: Crown House.

Holzer, S. M. (1994). From constructivism to active learning.*The Innovator, 2.* Retrieved from http://www.succeednow.org/innovators/innovator_2/innovator002.html

Honey, M & McMillan, K. (2005). *Critical issues: using technology to improve student achievement.* New York: North Central regional educational laboratory.

Honey, M., & Kanter, D. E. (2013). Design, Make, Play: Growing the Next Generation of Science Innocators. In M. Honey & D. E. Kanter (Eds.), *Design, Make, Play: Growing the Next Generation of STEM Innovators* (pp. 1–6). New York, NY: Routledge.

Hooker, M., Mwiyeria, E., & Verma, A. (2011). *ICT Competency Framework for Teachers in Tanzania: Teacher Development for the 21st Century (TDev21) pilot.* Dar Es Salaam: Ministry of Education and Vocational Training.

Hoosen, S., & Butcher, N. (2012). ICT Development at African Universities: The Experience of the PHEA Educational Technology Initiative. In e/merge 2012.

Hope, W. C. (1997). Why technology has not realized its potential in schools. *American Secondary Education, 25*(4), 2–9.

Horzum, M. B., & Canan, G. O. (2012, July01). A model for beliefs, tool acceptance levels and web pedagogical content knowledge of science and technology preservice teachers towards web based instruction. *Turkish Online Journal of Distance Education, 13*(3), 50–69.

Hosam, F., Tayeb, A. Al, Alghatani, K., & El-seoud, S. A. (2013). The impact of cloud computing technologies in E-learning. *iJET, 8*(1), 37–44.

Huang, H. (2002). Toward constructivism for adult learners in online learning environments. *British Journal of Educational Technology, 33*(1), 27–37. doi:10.1111/1467-8535.00236

Huang, K., Lubin, I. A., & Ge, X. (2011, November01). Situated learning in an educational technology course for preservice teachers. *Teaching and Teacher Education, 27*(8), 1200–1212. doi:10.1016/j.tate.2011.06.006

Huber, M. T., & Hutchings, P. (2005). *The advancement of learning: Building the teaching commons.* San Francisco, CA: Jossey-Bass.

Hudson, J. N. (2004). Computer-aided learning in the real world of medical education: Does the quality of interaction with the computer affect student learning? *Medical Education, 38*(8), 887–895. doi:10.1111/j.1365-2929.2004.01892.x PMID:15271050

Hull, G. A., & Katz, M. L. (2006). Crafting an agentive self: Case studies of digital storytelling. *Research in the Teaching of English, 41*(1), 43–81.

Hung, D., Chee, T. S., & Seng, K. T. (2006). Engaged learning: making learning an authentic experience. In D. Hung & M. S. Khine (Eds.), *Engaged learning with emerging technologies* (pp. 29–48). Dordrecht, The Netherlands: Springer. doi:10.1007/1-4020-3669-8_2

Hunsaker, S. L., Nielsen, A., & Bartlett, B. (2010). Correlates of teacher practices influencing student outcomes in reading instruction for advanced readers. *Gifted Child Quarterly, 54*(4), 273–282. doi:10.1177/0016986210374506

Hyland, K. (2005). Stance and engagement: A model of interaction in academic discourse. *Discourse Studies, 7*(2), 173–192. doi:10.1177/1461445605050365

Hyland, K., & Tse, P. (2004). Metadiscourse in academic writing: A reappraisal. *Applied Linguistics, 25*(2), 156–177. doi:10.1093/applin/25.2.156

Ibrahim, A. (2011). Using generalizability theory to estimate the relative effect of class size and number of items on the dependability of student ratings of instruction. *Psychological Reports, 109*(1), 252–258. doi:10.2466/03.07.11.PR0.109.4.252-258 PMID:22049666

Igbaria, M., Parasuraman, S., & Baroudi, J. J. (1996). A Motivational Model of Microcomputer Usage. *Journal of Management Information Systems, 13*(1), 127–143.

ILO-International Labour Organization. (2009). Inclusion of people with Disabilities in Kenya.

Incikabi, L., & Kildan, A. O. (2013). An analysis of early childhood teacher candidates' digital stories for mathematics teaching. *International Journal of Academic Research Part B, 5*(2), 77–81. doi:10.7813/2075-4124.2013/5-2/B.10

Inoue, Y. (2007). *Online education for lifelong learning.* Hershey, PA: Information Science Publication. doi:10.4018/978-1-59904-319-7.ch001

Inquiry-Based Learning. (n.d.). Retrieved from http://teorije-ucenja.zesoi.fer.hr/doku.php?id=instructional_design:inquiry-based_learning

International Society for Technology in Education (ISTE), & Computer Science Teachers Association (CSTA). (2012). *Operational Definition of Computational Thinking for K-12 Education.* Retrieved February 15, 2014, from http://www.iste.org/docs/ct-documents/computational-thinking-operational-definition-flyer.pdf?sfvrsn=2

International Society for Technology in Education. (2000). *National education technology standards for teachers.* Eugene, OR: Author.

Irby, D. M., Cooke, M., & O'Brien, B. C. (2010). Calls for reform of medical education by the Carnegie Foundation for the Advancement of Teaching: 1910 and 2010. *Academic Medicine, 85*(2), 220–227. doi:10.1097/ACM.0b013e3181c88449 PMID:20107346

Irby, D. M., & Wilkerson, L. (2003). Educational innovations in academic medicine and environmental trends. *Journal of General Internal Medicine, 18*(5), 370–376. doi:10.1046/j.1525-1497.2003.21049.x PMID:12795736

Isaacs, S., & Hollow, D. (2012). *The eLearning Africa 2012 Report. ICWE: Germany.* Germany. Retrieved from http://www.elearning-africa.com/pdf/report/ela_report_2012.pdf

Isaacs, S., Hollow, D., Akoh, B., & Harper-Merrett, T. (2013). Findings from the eLearning Africa Survey 2013. Germany.

Isaacs, S., & Hollow, D. (Eds.). (2012). *The eLearning Africa 2012 Report*. Germany: ICWE.

Issenberg, S. B., McGaghie, W. C., Hart, I. R., Mayer, J. W., Felner, J. M., Petrusa, E. R., & Ewy, G. A. (1999). Simulation technology for health care professional skills training and assessment. *Journal of the American Medical Association*, 282(9), 861–866. doi:10.1001/jama.282.9.861 PMID:10478693

Issenberg, S. B., McGaghie, W. C., Petrusa, E. R., Gordon, D. L., & Scalese, R. J. (2005). Features and uses of high-fidelity medical simulations that lead to effective learning: A BEME systematic review. *Medical Teacher*, 27(1), 10–28. doi:10.1080/01421590500046924 PMID:16147767

ITS Training Services at Penn State. (2013). *ANGEL: Using teams and peer reviews for collaborative learning*. Retrieved from, http://ittraining.psu.edu/wp-content/uploads/sites/7689/2013/12/ANGEL_Using-Teams-and-Peer-Reviews-for-Collaborative-Learning_HO_02142014.pdf

Jablin, F. M. (1981). Cultivating imagination: Factors that enhance and inhibit creativity in brainstorming groups. *Human Communication Research*, 7(3), 245–258. doi:10.1111/j.1468-2958.1981.tb00572.x

James, J., & Iverson, S. (2009). Striving for Critical Citizenship in a Teacher Education Program: Problems and Possibilities. *Michigan Journal of Community Service Learning*, 33–46.

Jarmon, L., Traphagan, T., Mayrath, M., & Trevidi, A. (2009). Virtual world teaching, experiential learning, and assessment: An interdisciplinary communication course in Second Life. *Computers & Education*, 53(1), 169–182. doi:10.1016/j.compedu.2009.01.010

Jenkins, M., & Lonsdale, J. (2007). Evaluating the effectiveness of digital storytelling for student reflection. In *ICT: Providing choices for learners and learning. Proceedings ASCILITE*. Singapore.

Jenkinson, J. (2009). Measuring the effectiveness of educational technology: What are we attempting to measure? *Electronic Journal of e-Learning*, 7 (3), 273-280.

Jensen, J., & Tunon, J. (2012, January01). Free and Easy to Use Web Based Presentation and Classroom Tools. *Journal of Library & Information Services in Distance Learning*, 6(3-4), 323–334. doi:10.1080/1533290X.2012.705157

JISC. (2004). *Effective practice with e-learning: A good practice guide in designing for learning*. Bristol: HEFCE.

Johnson, D., & Johnson, R. (2004). Cooperation and the use of technology. In D. H. Johanssen Handbook of research on educational communications and technology (2nd ed.) (pp. 785-811). Mahwah, NJ: Lawrence Erlbaum Associates.

Johnson, L., Adams-Becker, S., Cummins, M., Estrada, V., Freeman, A., & Ludgate, H. (2013). NMC Horizon Report: 2013 Higher Education Edition. Austin, TX: The New Medium Consortium; Retrieved from http://www.nmc.org/pdf/2013-horizon-report-HE.pdf

Johnson, L., Smith, R., Willis, H., Levine, A., & Haywood, K. (2011). The 2011 Horizon Report. Austin, TX: The New Media Consortium; Retrieved from http://wp.nmc.org/horizon2011/

Johnson, C., & Brescia, W. J. (2006, August01). Connecting, Making Meaning, and Learning in the Electronic Classroom: Reflections on Facilitating Learning at a Distance. *Journal of Scholarship of Teaching and Learning*, 6(1), 56–74.

Johnson, D., & Johnson, R. (1989). *Cooperation and competition: Theory and research*. Edina, MN: Interaction Book Company.

Johnson, D., Johnson, R., & Smith, K. (1991). *Active learning: Cooperation in the college classroom*. Edina, MN: Interaction Book Company.

Johnston, S. (2002). Student learning as academic currency. *ACE Center for Policy Analysis*. Retrieved January 2006:http://www.acenet.edu/bookstore/pdf/distributed-learning/distributed-learning-04.pdf

Jonassen, D. H. (2003). Designing research-based instruction for story problems. *Educational Psychology Review*, 15(3), 267–296. doi:10.1023/A:1024648217919

Jonassen, D. H. (2008). Instructional design as a design problem solving: An iterative process. *Educational Technology, 48*(3), 21–26.

Jonassen, D. H., & Hernandez-Serrano, J. (2002). Case-based reasoning and instructional design using stories to support problem solving. *Educational Technology Research and Development, 50*(2), 65–77. doi:10.1007/BF02504994

Jonassen, D. H., Howland, J. L., Moore, J., & Marra, R. M. (Eds.). (2003). *Learning to solve problems with technology: A constructivist perspective*. Pearson Education.

Jones, B. (2010). An examination of motivation model components in face–to–face and online instruction. *Electronic Journal of Research in Educational Psychology, 8*(3), 915–944.

Jones, D. P., & Wolf, D. M. (2010). Shaping the future of nursing education today using distant education and technology. *The Association of Black Nursing Faculty Journal, 21*(2), 44–47. PMID:20533754

Jones, L. (2007). *The student-centered classroom*. New York, NY: Cambridge University Press.

K-12 Teachers Alliance. (2014). Online collaboration tools for 21st century learning. Retrieved from, http://www.teachhub.com/online-collaboration-tools-21st-century-learning

Kafyulilo, A. C. (2014). Access, use and perceptions of teachers and students towards mobile phones as a tool for teaching and learning in Tanzania. *Education and Information Technologies, 19*(1), 115–127. doi:10.1007/s10639-012-9207-y

Kafyulilo, C. A., Mafumiko, F. M. S., & Mkonongwa, L. (2012). Challenges and opportunities of integrating technology in education in Tanzania. *Journal of Adult Education, 19*, 18–33.

Kagima, L. K., & Hausafus, C. O. (2000). Integration of electronic communication in higher education: Contributions of faculty computer self-efficacy. *The Internet and Higher Education, 2*(4), 221–235. doi:10.1016/S1096-7516(00)00027-0

Kajder, S. B. (2005, December07). "Not Quite Teaching for Real:" Preservice Secondary English Teachers' Use of Technology in the Field Following the Completion of an Instructional Technology Methods Course. *Journal of Computing in Teacher Education, 22*(1), 15–21.

Kalemoglu, V. Y. (2014, April01). The Relationship between attitudes of prospective physical education teachers towards education technologies and computer self-efficacy beliefs. *Turkish Online Journal of Educational Technology, 13*(2), 157–167.

Kalil, T., & Miller, J. (2014, February 3). *Announcing the First White House Maker Faire*. Retrieved September 8, 2014, from http://www.whitehouse.gov/blog/2014/02/03/announcing-first-white-house-maker-faire

Kanuka, M. (2006, Sept.). Instructional design and e-learning: A discussion of pedagogical content knowledge as a missing construct. *e-Journal of Instructional Science and Technology, 9*(2). Retrieved from: http://www.ascilite.org.au/ajet/ejist/docs/vol9_no2/papers/full_papers/kanuka.htm

Kapur, M. (2010). Productive failure in mathematical problem solving. *Instructional Science, 38*(6), 523–550. doi:10.1007/s11251-009-9093-x

Kapur, M. (2012). Productive failure in learning the concept of variance. *Instructional Science, 40*(4), 651–672. doi:10.1007/s11251-012-9209-6

Kapur, M., & Bielaczyc, K. (2011). Classroom-based experiments in productive failure. In *Proceedings of the 33rd annual conference of the cognitive science society* (pp. 2812-2817).

Kapur, M., & Bielaczyc, K. (2012). Designing for productive failure. *Journal of the Learning Sciences, 21*(1), 45–83. doi:10.1080/10508406.2011.591717

Kashorda, M., & Waema, T. (2008) *E-readiness survey of East African Universities*. Retrieved from http://kenet.or.ke/eready/staging/Ereadiness%20Survey%20of%20East%20African%20Universities%20Report%202009.pdf

Katehi, L., Pearson, G., & Feder, M. Committee on K 12 Engineering Education, & National Academy of Engineering and National Research Council. (2009). Engineering in K–12 Education: Understanding the status and improving the prospects. Washington, DC: The National Academies Press.

Kearney, M., Schuck, S., Burden, K., & Aubusson, P. (2012). Viewing mobile learning from a pedagogical perspective. *Research in Learning Technology, 20*(1).

Keeler, C. G. (2008, December07). When Curriculum and Technology Meet: Technology Integration in Methods Courses. *Journal of Computing in Teacher Education, 25*(1), 23–30.

Keeley, J., Furr, R., & Buskist, W. (2010). Differentiating psychology students' perceptions of teachers using the teacher behavior checklist. *Teaching of Psychology, 37*(1), 16–20. doi:10.1080/00986280903426282

Kennedy, G., Jones, D., Chambers, C., & Peacock, J. (2011, Dec.). Understanding the reasons academics use–and don`t use–endorsed and unendorsed learning technologies. *Proceedings of the Ascilite 2011 Changing Demands, Changing Directions Conference*. Hobart Tasmania, Australia. Available at: http://www.ascilite.org.au/conferences/hobart11/downloads/papers/Kennedy- full.pdf

Kenya National Bureau of Statistics (2010). *Kenya - National Information and Communication Technology Survey 2010*. KNE-KNBS-NICTS-2010-v01

Kerns, A., McDonongh, J. P., Groom, J. A., Kalynych, N. M., & Hogan, G. T. (2006).. . *American Association of Nurse Anesthetists, 74*(1), 19–21.

Kervin, L., & Mantei, J. (2010). Supporting educators with the inclusion of technology within literacy classrooms: A framework for "action". *Journal of Technology Integration in the Classroom, 2*(3), 43–54.

Khajeh-hosseini, A., Greenwood, D., & Sommerville, I. (2010). Cloud migration : A case study of migrating an enterprise IT system to IaaS. In *3rd International Conference on Cloud Computing (CLOUD)*. IEEE. doi:10.1109/CLOUD.2010.37

Khan, B. H. (1997). Web-based instruction: What is it and why is it? In B. H. Khan (Ed.), *Web-based Instruction* (pp. 1–18). Englewood Cliffs, New Jersey: Educational Technology Publications.

Khoiny, F. E. (1995). Factors that contribute to computer-assisted instruction effectiveness. *Computers in Nursing, 13*, 165–168. PMID:7641135

Kiili, K. (2005). Digital game-based learning: Towards an experiential gaming model. *The Internet and Higher Education, 8*(1), 13–24. doi:10.1016/j.iheduc.2004.12.001

Kildan, A. O., & Incikabi, L. (2013). Effects on the technological pedagogical content knowledge of early childhood teacher candidates using digital storytelling to teach mathematics. *Education 3-13: International Journal of Primary. Elementary and Early Years Education, 41*(3). doi:10.1080/03004279.2013.804852

Killam, L., & Carter, L. (2010). The challenge of the student nurse on clinical placement in the rural setting: A review of the literature. *Rural and Remote Health, 10*(1523). Retrieved from http://www.rrh.org.au PMID:20715883

Killam, L., Carter, L., & Graham, R. (2013). Facebook and issues of professionalism in undergraduate nursing education: Risky business or risk worth taking? *Journal of Distance Education, 13*(2).

Kim, K. J., & Kee, C. (2013). Evaluation of an e-PBL model to promote individual reasoning. *Medical Teacher, 35*(3), E978–E983. doi:10.3109/0142159X.2012.717185 PMID:22938685

Kim, M., & Hannafin, M. (2011). Scaffolding problem solving in technology-enhanced learning environments (TELEs): Bridging research and theory with practice. *Computers & Education, 56*(2), 403–417. doi:10.1016/j.compedu.2010.08.024

King-Sears, M., & Evmenova, A. S. (2007). Premises, principles, and processes for integrating technology into instruction. *Teaching Exceptional Children, 40*, 6–14.

Kirchner, P. A., Sweller, J., & Clark, R. E. (2006). Why minimal guidance during instruction does not work: An analysis of the failure of constructivist, discover, problem-based experiential, and inquiry-based teaching. *Educational Psychologist, 41*(2), 75–86. doi:10.1207/s15326985ep4102_1

Kirscher, P., Wubbrls, T., & Brekelmans, M. (2008). Benchmarks for teacher education programs in the pedagogical use of ICT. In J. Voogt & G. Knezek (Eds.), *International handbook of information and technology in primary and secondary education* (pp. 435–447). New York, NY: Springer. doi:10.1007/978-0-387-73315-9_26

Klopfer, E., Osterweil, S., Groff, J., & Haas, J. (2009). *Using the technology of today, in the classroom today.* Retrieved from http://education.mit.edu/papers/Games-SimsSocNets_EdArcade.pdf

Knapper, K. C., & Cropley, A. (2000). *Lifelong learning in higher education.* London: Kogan Page.

Knee, R. (1995). Factors limiting technology integration in education: The leadership gap. In *Society for Information Technology & Teacher Education International Conference* (pp. 556-560). Charlottesville, VA: Association for Advancement of Computing in Education.

Kneipp, L. B., Kelly, K. E., Biscoe, J. D., & Richard, B. (2010). The impact of instructor's personality characteristics on quality of instruction. *College Student Journal, 44*(4), 901–905.

Knezek, G., Christensen, R., & Fluke, R. (2003, April). *Testing a Will, Skill, Tool Model of Technology Integration.* Paper Presented at the Annual Meeting of the American Educational Research Association. Chicago, IL.

Knowles, M. S. (1978). *The adult learner: The neglected species* (2nd ed.). Houston: Club Publication Company.

Knox, E. W., Lindsay, P., & Kolb, N. M. (1993). *Does college make a difference? Long-term changes in activities and attitudes.* Westport, CT: Greenwood Press.

Koch, F., Assuncao, M. D., & Netto, M. A. S. (2012). A cost analysis of cloud computing for education. *Lecture Notes in Computer Science, 7714,* 182–196. Retrieved from http://www.marconetto.me/Publications_files/gecon2012.pdf

Koehler, M. J., & Mishra, P. (2005). What happens when teachers design educational technology? The development of technological pedagogical content knowledge. *Journal of Educational Computing Research, 32*(2), 131–152. doi:10.2190/0EW7-01WB-BKHL-QDYV

Koehler, M., & Mishra, P. (2009). What is technological pedagogical content knowledge? *Contemporary Issues in Technology & Teacher Education, 9*(1), 60–70.

Kolb, A. D. (1984). *Experiential learning: Experience as the source of learning and development.* Upper Saddle River, NJ: Prentice Hall.

Kolberg, E., & Orlev, N. (2001). *Robotics Learning as a Tool for Integrating Science-Technology Curriculum in K-12 Schools.* Paper presented at the 31st ASEE/IEEE Frontiers in Education Conference, Reno, NV. Maker Education Initiative. (n.a.). Maker Education Initiative - Mission. Retrieved January 13, 2014, from http://www.makered.org/about/

Kosakowski, J. (1998). *The benefits of information technology.* Syracuse, NY: Clearinghouse on Information and Technology.

Kotrlik, J. W., Harrison, B. C., & Redmann, D. H. (2000). A comparison of information technology training sources, value, knowledge, and skills for Louisiana's secondary vocational teachers. *Journal of Vocational Education Research, 35*(4), 396–444. doi:10.5328/JVER25.4.396

Kozma, R. (2005). *ICT, education reform, and economic growth.* Chandler, AZ: Intel Corporation. Retrieved September 17, 2009, from Http://download.intel.com/education/wsis/ICT_Education_Reform_Economic_Growth.pdf/

Kozub, R. M. (2010). Relationship of course, instructor, and student characteristics to dimensions of student ratings of teaching effectiveness in business schools. *American Journal of Business Education, 3*(1), 33–40.

Krauss, J. (2012). Infographics: More than words can say. *Learning and Leading with Technology, 39*(5), 10–14.

Kshetri, N. (2010). Cloud computing in developing economies: Drivers, effects, and policy measures. In *Proceedings of PTC* (pp. 1–22).

Kuh, G. D. (2003). *The National Survey of Student Engagement: Conceptual framework and overview of psychometric properties.* Indiana University Center for Postsecondary Research & Planning. Retrieved June 10th 2009 from http://nsse.iub.edu/pdf/conceptual_framework_2003.pdf

Kuh, G. D., Kinzie, J., Buckley, A. J., Bridges, K. B., & Hayek, C. J. (2007). Piecing together the student success puzzle: Research, propositions, and recommendations. *ASHE Higher Education Report*, *32*(5).

Kulik, J. A. (1994). Meta-analytic studies of findings on computer-based instruction. In E. L. Baker & H. F. O'Neil Jr., (Eds.), *Technology Assessment in Education and Training*. Hillsdale, NJ: Lawrence Erlbaum.

Kumar, A. (2012). Blended learning in Higher Education: A comprehensive study. In *International Conference on Business Management & Information Systems*. Retrieved from http://ojs.ijacp.org/index.php/ICBMIS/article/view/82

Laisheng, X., & Zhengxia, W. (2011). Cloud computing: A new business paradigm for e-learning. In *2011 Third International Conference on Measuring Technology and Mechatronics Automation* (pp. 716–719). Ieee. doi:10.1109/ICMTMA.2011.181

Lam, P., Au Yeung, M., Cheung, E., & McNaught, C. (2009). Using the development of elearning material as challenging and authentic learning experiences for students. In same places, different spaces. In *Proceedings Ascilite Auckland 2009*. Retrieved from: http://www.ascilite.org.au/conferences/auckland09/procs/lam.pdf

Lambert, J. (2003). *Digital storytelling cookbook and traveling companion*. Berkeley, CA: Digital Diner Retrieved May 10, 2010, from http://www.storycenter.org/cookbook.pdf

Lamont, A. (2011). The beat goes on: Music education, identity and lifelong learning. *Music Education Research*, *13*(4), 369–388. doi:10.1080/14613808.2011.638505

Lampe, C., Wohn, D. Y., Vitak, J., Ellison, N. B., & Wash, R. (2011). Student use of Facebook for organizing collaborative classroom activities. *International Journal of Computer-Supported Collaborative Learning*. 1-27. Retrieved from: http://www.springerlink.com/content/h9m4233168200637/ (Date accessed 15/06/2014)

Lancaster, C. (2012). *Stance and Reader Positioning in Upper-Level Student Writing in Political Theory and Economics*. PhD Thesis, University of Michigan.

Lancaster, S., David, C. Y., Albert, H. H., & Shin-Yuan, H. (2007). The selection of instant messaging or e-mail: College students' perspective for computer communication. *Information Management & Computer Security*, *15*(1), 5–22. doi:10.1108/09685220710738750

Lan, J. (2000). Leading teacher educators to a new paradigm: Observations on technology integration. *AACTE Briefs*, *21*(10), 4–6.

Laurent, T., & Weidner, T. G. (2001). Clinical instructors' and student athletic trainers' perceptions of helpful clinical instructor characteristics. *Journal of Athletic Training*, *36*(1), 58–61. PMID:12937516

Laurillard, D. (2002). *Rethinking university teaching: A conversational framework for the effective use of learning technologies* (2nd ed.). London: Routledge/Falmer. doi:10.4324/9780203304846

Lautenbach, G. (2008, July01). Stories of Engagement with E-Learning: Revisiting the Taxonomy of Learning. *International Journal of Information and Communication Technology Education*, *4*(3), 11–19. doi:10.4018/jicte.2008070102

Lave, J., & Wenger, E. (1991). *Situated learning: Legitimate peripheral participation*. Cambridge, United Kingdom: Cambridge University Press. doi:10.1017/CBO9780511815355

Laverty, A. (2011). The Cloud and Africa – Indicators for Growth of Cloud Computing. *The African File*. Retrieved September 08, 2014, from http://theafricanfile.com/ict/the-cloud-and-africa-indicators-for-growth-of-cloud-computing/

Lawless, K. A., & Pellegrino, J. W. (2007). Professional development in integrating technology into teaching and learning: Knowns, unknowns, and ways to pursue better questions and answers. *Review of Educational Research*, *77*(4), 575–614. Retrieved June 6 2014 from http://www.jstor.org/stable/4624911. doi:10.3102/0034654307309921

Lea, M. R., & Street, B. (1998). Student writing in higher education: An academic literacies approach. *Studies in Higher Education*, *23*(2), 157–172. doi:10.1080/03075079812331380364

LeBaron, J., McDonough, E., & Robinson, J. M. (2009). *Research Report for GeSCI Meta-Review of ICT in Education*. Retrieved from http://gesci.org/assets/files/Research/meta-research-phase2.pdf

Leech, N. A., Barrett, K. C., & Morgan, G. A. (2011). *IBM: SPSS for intermediate statistics use and interpretation* (4th ed.). New York, NY: Taylor & Francis Group.

Lee, M. M., & Hutton, D. S. (2007). Using Interactive Videoconferencing Technology for International Education: The Case of ISIS. *International Journal of Instructional Technology and Distance Learning, 4*(8).

Lee, M., & Tsai, C. (2005). Exploring high school students' and teachers' preferences toward the constructivist internet-based learning environments in Taiwan. *Educational Studies, 31*(2), 149–167. doi:10.1080/03055690500095522

Lee, W. C. (1990). *The effectiveness of computer assisted instruction and computer programming in elementary and secondary mathematics: A meta-analysis*. Amherst: University of Massachusetts-Amherst.

Leggett, W. P., & Persichitte, K. A. (1998). Blood, sweat, and TEARS: 50 years of technology implementation obstacles. *TechTrends, 43*(3), 33–36. doi:10.1007/BF02824053

Lemke, C., & Lesley, B. (2009). Advance 21st century innovation in schools through smart, informed state policy. In E. Coughlin & S. Kajder (Eds.), *The Impact of Online Collaborative Learning on Educators and Classroom Practices*. The Metiri Group in Collaboration with Cisco.

Lessen, E., & Sorensen, C. (2006). Integrating technology in schools, colleges, and departments of education: A primer for deans. *Change, 38*(2), 44–49. doi:10.3200/CHNG.38.2.44-49

Levin, A. R., Pargas, R. P., & Austin, J. (2005). Appreciating music: An active approach. *New Directions for Teaching and Learning, 2005*(101), 27–35. doi:10.1002/tl.183

Lipponen, L., Rahikainen, M., Lallimo, J., & Hakkarainen, K. (2003). Patterns of participation and discourse in elementary students' computer-supported collaborative learning. *Learning and Instruction, 13*(5), 487–509. doi:10.1016/S0959-4752(02)00042-7

Lipscomb, L., Swanson, J., & West, A. (2004). Scaffolding. In M. Orey (Ed.), *Emerging perspectives on learning, teaching, and technology*. Retrieved from: http://projects.coe.uga.edu/epltt/

Li, Q., & Ma, X. (2010). A meta-analysis of the effects of computer technology on school students' mathematics learning. *Educational Psychology Review, 22*(3), 215–243. doi:10.1007/s10648-010-9125-8

Liu, C. C., Chen, H. S., Shih, J. L., Huang, G. T., & Liu, B. J. (2011). An enhanced concept map approach to improving children's storytelling ability. *Computers & Education, 56*(3), 873–884. doi:10.1016/j.compedu.2010.10.029

Lombardi, M. M. (2007). Authentic learning for the 21st century: An overview. *EDUCAUSE*. Retrieved from, http://net.educause.edu/ir/library/pdf/ELI3009.pdf

Lüdtke, O., Trautwein, U., Kunter, M., & Baumert, J. (2006). Reliability and agreement of student ratings of the classroom environment: A reanalysis of TIMSS data. *Learning Environments Research, 9*(3), 215–230. doi:10.1007/s10984-006-9014-8

Lumley, D., & Bailey, G. D. (1993). *Planning for technology: A guidebook for school administrators*. New York, NY: Scholastic.

Lwoga, E. (2012). Making learning and Web 2.0 technologies work for higher learning institutions in Africa. *Campus-Wide Information Systems, 29*(2), 90–107. doi:10.1108/10650741211212359

Lwoga, E. (2014). Critical success factors for adoption of web-based learning management systems in Tanzania.[IJEDICT]. *International Journal of Education and Development Using Information and Communication Technology, 10*(1), 4–21.

Mackey, J. (2011). *New Zealand teachers' online professional development and communities of practice*. Unpublished doctoral thesis, Deakin University.

Mackey, J. (2009). Virtual learning and real communities: Online professional development for teachers. In E. Stacey & P. Gerbic (Eds.), *Effective Blended Learning Practices: Evidence-Based Perspectives in ICT-Facilitated Education* (pp. 163–181). Hershey: Information Science Reference. doi:10.4018/978-1-60566-296-1.ch009

Mackey, J., & Evans, T. (2011). Interconnecting networks of practice for professional learning. *International Review of Research in Open and Distance Learning, 12*(3), 1–18.

Madden, T. J., Dillon, W. R., & Leak, R. L. (2010). Students' evaluation of teaching: Concerns of item diagnosticity. *Journal of Marketing Education, 32*(3), 264–274. doi:10.1177/0273475310377759

Majumdar, P. K. (2005). *Research Methods in Social Science.* New Delhi, India: Viva Books Private Limited.

Mambo, H. L. (2001). Tanzania: An overview of information communications technology (ICT) development in libraries and information services. *The International Information & Library Review, 33*(1), 89–96. doi:10.1006/iilr.2000.0161

Manghani, K. (2011). Quality assurance: Importance of systems and standard operating procedures. *Perspectives in Clinical Research, 2*(1), 34–37.

Mangione, S., Nieman, L. Z., & Gracely, E. J. (1992). Comparison of computer-based learning and seminar teaching of pulmonary auscultation to first-year medical-students. *Academic Medicine, 67*(10), S63–S65. doi:10.1097/00001888-199210000-00041 PMID:1382428

Marchel, C. A., Shields, C., & Winter, L. (2011, December07). Preservice Teachers as Change Agents: Going the Extra Mile in Service-Learning Experiences. *Teaching Educational Psychology, 7*(2), 3–16.

Margaryan, A., Littlejohn, A., & Vojt, G. (2011). Are digital natives a myth or reality? University students' use of digital technologies. *Computers & Education, 56*(2), 429–440. doi:10.1016/j.compedu.2010.09.004

Markel, M. (1999). Distance education and the myth of the new pedagogy. *Journal of Business and Technical Communication, 13*(2), 208–223. doi:10.1177/1050651999013002005

Marshall, D. (2002). *Learning with Technology: Evidence that technology can and does support learning.* San Diego CA: Cable in classroom.

Marsh, H. W. (1982). The use of path analysis to estimate teacher and course effects in student rating's of instructional effectiveness. *Applied Psychological Measurement, 6*(1), 47–59. doi:10.1177/014662168200600106

Marsh, H. W. (2007). Students' evaluations of university teaching: Dimensionality, reliability, validity, potential biases, and usefulness. In R. Perry & J. C. Smart (Eds.), *The scholarship of teaching and learning in higher education: An evidence–based perspective* (pp. 319–383). Netherlands: Springer. doi:10.1007/1-4020-5742-3_9

Marsh, H. W., Ginns, P., Morin, A. S., Nagengast, B., & Martin, A. J. (2011). Use of student ratings to benchmark universities: Multilevel modeling of responses to the Australian Course Experience Questionnaire (CEQ). *Journal of Educational Psychology, 103*(3), 733–748. doi:10.1037/a0024221

Martin, F., Kim, H. J., Silka, L., & Yanco, H. (2007). *Artbotics: Challenges and Opportunities for Multi-Disciplinary, Community-Based Learning in Computer Science, Robotics, and Art.* Paper presented at the Workshop on Research in Robotics for Education at the Robotics Science and Systems Conference, Atlanta, GA.

Martinez, M. (2003). High attrition rates in e-learning: Challenges, predictors and solutions. *The e-learning Developers' Journal,* Retrieved August 2014: http://www.elearningguild.com/pdf/2/071403MGT-L.pdf

Martin, F., Mikhak, B., Resnick, M., Silverman, B., & Berg, R. (2000). To Mindstorms and Beyong: Evolution of a Construction Kit for Magical Machines. In A. Druin & J. Hendler (Eds.), *Robots for Kids: Exploring New Technologies for Learning* (pp. 9–33). San Diego, CA: Academic Press.

Martin, J. R., & White, P. R. (2005). *The Language of evaluation: Appraisal in English.* Basingstoke: Palgrave Macmillan.

Massa, N. M. (2008). Problem based learning (PBL). *New England Journal of Higher Education, 22*(4), 19–20.

Mataric, M. J. (2004). *Robotics Education for All Ages.* Paper presented at the American Association for Artificial Intelligence Spring Symposium on Accessible, Hands-on AI and Robotics Education. http://robotics.usc.edu/~maja/publications/aaaissymp04-edu.pdf

Mathew, S. (2012). Implementation of cloud computing in education - A revolution. *International Journal of Computer Theory and Engineering, 4*(3), 473–475. doi:10.7763/IJCTE.2012.V4.511

Matthew, K., Felvegi, E., & Callaway, R. (2009, January 01). *Collaborative-learning Using a Wiki.*

Mayer, R. E. (2009). *Multi-media learning* (2nd ed.). New York: Cambridge University Press. doi:10.1017/CBO9780511811678

Mazzolini, M., & Maddison, S. (2003). Sage, guide or ghost? The effect of instructor intervention on student participation in online discussion forums. *Computers & Education, 40*(3), 237–253. doi:10.1016/S0360-1315(02)00129-X

McCannon, M., & Crews, T. (2000). Assessing the technology training needs of elementary school teachers. *Journal of Technology and Teacher Education, 8*(2), 111–121.

McCombs, B. L. (2004). The learner-centered psychological principles: A framework for balancing a focus on academic achievement with a focus on social and emotional learning needs. In J. E. Zins, R. P. Weissberg, M. C. Wang, & H. J. Walberg (Eds.), *Building academic success on social and emotional learning: What does the research say?* New York: Teachers College Press.

McCord, L., & McCord, W. (2010). Online learning: Getting comfortable in cyber class. *Teaching and Learning in Nursing, 5*(1), 27–32. doi:10.1016/j.teln.2009.05.003

McDonald, C., & Loch, B. (2008). Adjusting the community of inquiry approach to a synchronous mathematical context (pp. 603-606). In *ASCILITE 2008: 25th Annual Conference of the Australasian Society for Computers in Learning in Tertiary Education: Hello! Where Are You in the Landscape of Educational Technology?* 30 Nov - 03 Dec 2008, Melbourne, Australia.

McEwan, H., & Egan, K. (Eds.). (1995). *Narrative in teaching, learning, and research.* New York: Teachers College Press.

McGaghie, W. C., Issenberg, S. B., Cohen, E. R., Barsuk, J. H., & Wayne, D. B. (2011). Does simulation-based medical education with deliberate practice yield better results than traditional clinical education? A meta-analytic comparative review of the evidence. *Academic Medicine, 86*(6), 706–711. doi:10.1097/ACM.0b013e318217e119 PMID:21512370

McGaghie, W. C., Issenberg, S. B., Petrusa, E. R., & Scalese, R. J. (2010). A critical review of simulation-based medical education research: 2003-2009. *Medical Education, 44*(1), 50–63. doi:10.1111/j.1365-2923.2009.03547.x PMID:20078756

McGlynn, A. P. (2005). Teaching millennials, our newest cultural cohort. *Education Digest*, 12–16.

McGrath, E., Lowes, S., Sayres, J., & Lin, P. (2008). *Underwater LEGO Robotics as the Vehicle to Engage Students in STEM: The BUILD IT Project's First Year of Classroom Implementation.* Paper presented at the American Society for Engineering Education Mid-Atlantic, Hoboken, NJ.

McGrath, E., Lowes, S., Sayres, J., & Lin, P. (2009). *Analysis of Middle- And High-School Students' Learning Of Science, Mathematics, And Engineering Concepts Through A Lego Underwater Robotics Design Challenge.* Paper presented at the American Society for Engineering Education Annual Conference, Austin, TX.

McKeachie, W. J. (2007). Good teaching makes a difference—And we know what it is. In R. Perry & J. C. Smart (Eds.), *The scholarship of teaching and learning in higher education: An evidence–based perspective* (pp. 457–474). Netherlands: Springer. doi:10.1007/1-4020-5742-3_11

McKenna, S. (2004). *A critical investigation into discourses that construct academic literacy at the Durban Institute of Technology.* PhD Thesis, Rhodes University, South Africa.

McKenzie, J. (2003). Pedagogy does matter. *The Educational Technology Journal, 13*(1).

McKenzie, B. K., Mims, N., Bennett, E., & Waugh, M. W. (2000). Needs, concerns and practices of online instructors. *Online Journal of Distance Learning Administration, 3*(3), 1–9. Available at http://www.westga.edu/~distance/ojdla/summer42/bower42.html

437

McKinney, K. (2010). *Active Learning. Illinois State University.* Center for Teaching, Learning & Technology.

McKnight, M. (2000). *Distance education: Expressing emotions in video-based classes.* Paper presented at the Annual meeting of the Conference on College Composition and Communication, Minneapolis, Minnesota. (Eric Document Reproduction Service No. ED 441 270).

McLaughlin, J. E., Roth, M. T., Glatt, D. M., Gharkholonarehe, N., Davidson, C. A., Griffin, L. M., & Mumper, R. J. (2014). The flipped classroom: A course redesign to foster learning and engagement in a health professions school. *Academic Medicine, 89*(2), 236–243. doi:10.1097/ACM.0000000000000086 PMID:24270916

McLean, S., & Carter, L. (2013). University continuing education for adult learners: History and key trends. In T. Nesbit, S. M. Brigham, N. Taber, & T. Gibb (Eds.), *Building on critical traditions. Adult education and learning in Canada.* Toronto: Thompson Educational Publishing.

McLellan, H. (1993). Evaluation in a situated learning environment. *Educational Technology, 33*(3), 39–45.

McLeod, P. L. (2011). Effects of anonymity and social comparison of rewards on computer-mediated group brainstorming. *Small Group Research, 42*(4), 475–503. doi:10.1177/1046496410397381

McLinden, M. (2013). Flexible pedagogies: Part-time learners and learning in higher education. York, UK: The Higher Education Academy, University of Birmingham; Retrieved from http://www.heacademy.ac.uk/assets/documents/flexiblelearning/Flexiblepedagogi es/ptlearners/fp_ptl_report.pdf

McMillan, J. H., & Hearn, J. (2008). *Student self-assessment: The key to stronger student motivation and higher achievement.* Retrieved from, http://files.eric.ed.gov/fulltext/EJ815370.pdf

Meagher, M., Ozgun-Koca, A., & Edwards, M. T. (2011, September01). Preservice Teachers' Experiences with Advanced Digital Technologies: The Interplay between Technology in a Preservice Classroom and in Field Placements. *Contemporary Issues in Technology & Teacher Education, 11*(3), 243–270.

Means, B., Toyama, Y., Murphy, R., Bakia, M., & Jones, K. (2009). *Evaluation of evidence-based online learning: A meta-analysis and review of online learning studies.* U.S. Department of Education Report, Office of Planning Evaluation and Policy Development, Policy and Program Studies Service, 1-66. Retrieved from: http://www2.ed.gov/rschstat/eval/tech/evidence-based- practices/finalreport.pdf

Means, B., Penuel, W., & Padilla, C. (2001). *The connected school: Technology and learning in high school.* San Francisco, CA: Jossey-Bass.

Meichenbaum, D. (1985). *Stress inoculation training.* New York: Pergamon Press.

Mell, P., & Grance, T. (2011). *The NIST Definition of Cloud Computing.* USA. Retrieved from http://csrc.nist.gov/publications/nistpubs/800-145/SP800-145.pdf

Mentkowski, M. et al.. (2000). *Learning that last.* San Francisco, CA: Jossey Bass.

Merrill, M. D. (2002). First principles of instruction. *Educational Technology Research and Development, 50*(3), 43–59. doi:10.1007/BF02505024

Michael, J. (2006). Where's the evidence that active learning works? *Advances in Physiology Education, 30*(4), 159–167. doi:10.1152/advan.00053.2006 PMID:17108243

Michael, J. A., & Modell, H. I. (2003). *Active learning in secondary and college science classrooms: A working model for helping the learner to learn.* Mahwah, NJ: Erlbaum.

Michel, N., Cater, J. J. III, & Varela, O. (2009). Active versus passive teaching styles: An empirical study of student outcomes. *Human Resource Development Quarterly, 20*(4), 397–418. doi:10.1002/hrdq.20025

Midwestern University. (2012). *Uncorrected vision issues misdiagnosed as learning disabilities in children.* Retrieved from, https://www.midwestern.edu/news-and-events/university-news/uncorrected-vision-issues-misdiagnosed-as-learning-disabilities-in-children.html

Miles, M. B., & Huberman, A. M. (1994). *Qualitative data analysis: An expanded sourcebook.* London: Sage.

Miller, D. P., Nourbakhsh, I. R., & Sigwart, R. (2008). Robots for Education. In B. Siciliano & O. Khatib (Eds.), *Springer Handbook of Rootics* (pp. 1283–1301). New York, NY: Springer-Verlag New York, LLC. doi:10.1007/978-3-540-30301-5_56

Miller, G. (2001). General education and distance education: Two channels in the new mainstream. *The Journal of General Education, 50*(4), 314–322. doi:10.1353/jge.2001.0028

Miller, M. (2009). *Teaching for a new world: Preparing high school educators to deliver college- and career-ready instruction. Policy Brief, Washington*. D.C.: Alliance for Excellent Education.

Miller, S. M., & Miller, K. L. (2000). Theoretical and practical considerations in the design of Web-based instruction. In B. Abbey (Ed.), *Instructional and cognitive impacts of Web-based instruction* (pp. 156–177). Hershey, PA: IGI Global. doi:10.4018/978-1-878289-59-9.ch010

Mills, N. (2011). Situated learning through social networking communities: The development of joint enterprise, mutual engagement, and a shared repertoire. *CALICO Journal, 28*(2), 345–368. doi:10.11139/cj.28.2.345-368

Milman, N. B., Kortecamp, K., & Peters, M. (2007). Assessing teacher candidates' perceptions and attributions of their technology competencies. *International Journal of Technology in Teaching and Learning, 3*(3), 15–35.

Ministry of Nairobi Metropolitan Development. (2008). *Nairobi Metro 2030 A World Class African Metropolis. Government of the Republic of Kenya*. Retrieved from http://www.tatucity.com/DynamicData/Downloads/NM_Vision_2030.pdf

Mircea, M., & Andreescu, A. (2011). Using cloud computing in Higher Education: A strategy to improve agility in the current financial crisis. *Communications of the IBIMA, 2011*, 1–15. doi:10.5171/2011.875547

Mishra, P., & Koehler, M. J. (2006). Technological Pedagogical Content Knowledge: A new framework for teacher knowledge. *Teachers College Record, 108*(6), 1017–1054. doi:10.1111/j.1467-9620.2006.00684.x

Mithaug, E. D., Mithaug, K. D., Agran, M., Martin, E. J., & Wehmeyer, L. M. (Eds.). (2003). *Self-determined learning theory: Construction, verification, and Evaluation*. Mahwah, NJ: Lawrence Erlbaum.

Moallem, M. (2003). An interactive online course: A collaborative design model. *Educational Technology Research and Development, 51*(4), 85–103. doi:10.1007/BF02504545

Moe, M. T., & Blodget, H. (2000). *The knowledge web: Part 1. People power: Fuel for the new economy*. New York: Merrill Lynch.

Mokhtar, S. A., Ali, S. H. S., Al-Sharafi, A., & Aborujilah, A. (2013). Cloud computing in academic institutions. In *Proceedings of the 7th International Conference on Ubiquitous Information Management and Communication - ICUIMC '13* (pp. 1–7). New York, New York, USA: ACM Press. doi:10.1145/2448556.2448558

MoNE. (2005). Ilkogretim matematik dersi (6-8 siniflar) ogretim programi [Elementary school mathematics teaching program (grades 6-8)]. Ankara, Turkey.

Monk, M., & Osborne, J. (1997). Placing the history and philosophy of science on the curriculum: A model for the development of pedagogy. *Science education, 81*(4), 405–424. doi:10.1002/(SICI)1098-237X(199707)81:4<405::AID-SCE3>3.0.CO;2-G

Moodle. (2012). *Installation Quickstart*. Retrieved from http://docs.moodle.org/23/en/Installation_Quickstart

Moore, J., Dickson-Deane, C., & Galyen, K. (2011). E-learning, online learning and distance learning environments: Are they the same? *The Internet and Higher Education, 14*(2), 129–135. doi:10.1016/j.iheduc.2010.10.001

Moore, M. G. (1993). Theory of transactional distance. In D. Keegan (Ed.), *Theoretical principles of distance education* (pp. 22–38). New York, NY: Routledge.

Moran, C., & Young, C. A. (2014). Active learning in the flipped English language arts classroom. *Promoting Active Learning Through the Flipped Classroom Model*, 163.

Mott, J. (2010). *Envisioning the Post-LMS Era: The Open Learning Network*. Educational Review online. Retrieved from http://www.educause.edu/ero/article/envisioning-post-lms-era-open-learning-network

Motta-Roth, D. (2009). The Role of context in academic text production and writing pedagogy. In C. Bazerman, A. Bonini, & D. Figueiredo. (Eds.), Genre in a changing world (pp. 317-336). The WAC Clearinghouse and Parlor Press.

Msyani, C. M. (2013). *Current status of energy sector in Tanzania: executive exchange on developing an ancillary service market.* Washington, DC: USEA.

Mtebe, J. S., & Raisamo, R. (2014a). eLearning cost analysis of on-premise versus cloud-hosted implementation in Sub-Saharan Countries. *The African Journal of Information Systems*, 6(2), 48–64. Retrieved from http://digitalcommons.kennesaw.edu/cgi/viewcontent.cgi?article=1216&context=ajis

Mtebe, J. S., & Raisamo, R. (2014b). Investigating Perceived Barriers to the Use of Open Educational Resources in Higher Education in Tanzania. *International Review of Research in Open and Distance Learning*, 15(2), 43–65.

Mtebe, J. S., & Raphael, C. (2013). Students' experiences and challenges of blended learning at the University of Dar es Salaam, Tanzania.[IJEDICT]. *International Journal of Education and Development Using Information and Communication Technology*, 9(3), 124–136.

Mugenda, A. G. (2008). Social science research: Theory and principles: Nairobi: Applied research and training services, Kenya.

Mugenda, M. O., & Mugenda, G. A. (1999). *Research methods: Quantitative and qualitative approaches.* Nairobi: ACTS press.

Mugenda, M. O., & Mugenda, G. A. (2003). *Research Methods Quantitative and Qualitative Approaches.* Nairobi: ACTS press.

Muirhead, R. J. (2007). E-Learning: Is this teaching at students or teaching with students? *Nursing Forum*, 42(4), 178–185. doi:10.1111/j.1744-6198.2007.00085.x PMID:17944698

Mulrine, C. F. (2007, June06). Creating a Virtual Learning Environment for Gifted and Talented Learners. *Gifted Child Today*, 30(2), 37–40.

Mumtaz, S. (2000). Factors affecting teachers' use of information and communications technology: A review of the literature. *Journal of Information Technology for Teacher*, 9(3), 319–324.

Munar, A. (2010). Digital Exhibitionism: The Age of Exposure. *Culture Unbound*, 2, 401–422. http://www.cultureunbound.ep.liu.se

Munguatosha, G. M., Muyinda, P. B., & Lubega, J. T. (2011). A social networked learning adoption model for higher education institutions in developing countries. *On the Horizon*, 19(4), 307–320. doi:10.1108/10748121111179439

Murgatroyd, S. (2012, November). *Online learning: MOOC's, iPads and other things that can support or get in the way of engaged learning.* Presentation to Nipissing University Board of Directors. Huntsville, ON.

Murphy, K. L., Richards, J., Lewis, C., & Carman, E. (2005). Strengthening educational technology in K-8 urban schools and in preservice education: A practioner-faculty collaborative process. *Journal of Technology and Teacher Education*, 13(1), 125–139.

Murphy, P. K., & Alexander, P. A. (2001). A motivated exploration of motivation terminology. *Contemporary Educational Psychology*, 25(1), 3–53. doi:10.1006/ceps.1999.1019 PMID:10620380

Murray, T. (2006). Collaborative knowledge building and integral theory: On perspectives, uncertainty, and mutual regard. *Integral Review*, 2, 210–268.

Murtagh, L., & Webster, M. (2010). Scaffolding teaching, learning and assessment. *Teacher Education Advancement Network*, 1(2). Retrieved from http://bit.ly/tyfJ5M

Mutula, S. M., & Musakali, O. D. (2007). Internet adoption in Kenyan university libraries. *Emerald Publishing Limited*, 56(6), 464–475.

Mwalongo, A. (2011). Teachers' perceptions about ICT for teaching, professional development, administration and personal use. *International Journal of Education and Development using Information and Communication Technology*, 7(3), 36-49.

Myers, C., & Brandt, W. C. (2010). *A summary of external program evaluation findings for the e-MINTS (enhancing Missouri's Instructional Networked Teaching Strategies) program from 1999-2009*. Naperville, ILL. Learning Points Associates, Retrieved July 30, 2014 from http://www.emints.org/wp-content/uploads/2013/09/summary_emints_research.pdf

Mzumbe University (2010). *Quality assurance Policy and Operational Guidelines 2010*

Mzumbe University (2012). *Third Strategic Corporate Plan (2012-2017)*

Mzumbe University (2013). *Adoption and Utilization of E-Learning at Mzumbe University. Survey Report*

Naidu, S. (2004). Trends in faculty use and perceptions of e-learning. *Asian Journal of Distance Education, 2*(2). Retrieved from http://www.asianjde.org/2004v2.2.Naidu.Abstract.htm

Naidu, S. (2006). Pedagogical designs for e-learning. In S. Naidu (Ed.), E-learning: A Guidebook of Principles, Procedures and Practices (pp. 11-28). Commonwealth Educational Media Center for Asia (CEMCA) University of Melbourne, Australia.

Naidu, S. (2009). Pedagogical affordances of technology. In S. Mishra (Ed), E-learning (STRIDE Handbook 8). New Delhi, IGNOU.

Naidu, S. (2006). *E-Learning: A Guidebook of Principles, Procedures and Practices. Commonwealth Educational Media Center for Asia*. CEMCA.

Nartker, A., Shumays, A., Stevens, L., Potter, K., Kalowela, M., Kisimbo, D., & Egan, J. (2009). *Distance Learning assessment*. Washington, DC: I-Tech.

Nasir, U., & Niazi, M. (2011). Cloud computing adoption assessment model (CAAM). In Profes '11 (Vol. 44, pp. 34–37). TORRE CANNE (BR), Italy: ACM.

National Center for Education Statistics. (2000). *Teachers' tools for the 21st century: A report on teacher's use of technology* (Report No. NCES 2000-102). Washington, DC: U.S. Department of Education. Retrieved June 15, 2015, from http://nces.ed.gov/pubsearch/pubsinfo.asp?pubid=2000102

National Center for Education Statistics. (2010). *Teacher' use of educational technology in U.S. public schools: 2009*. Washington, DC: U.S. Department of Education.

National Council for Accreditation of Teacher Education. (2010). *Transforming teacher education through clinical practice: A national strategy to prepare effective teachers*. Washington, DC: Author.

National Council for the Accreditation of Teacher Education. (2008). Professional standards for the accreditation of schools, colleges, and departments of education: NCATE Glossary. Washington, DC: Author. Retrieved July 31, 2014, from http://ncate.org/Standards/NCATEUnitStandards/NCATEGlossary/tabid/477/Default.aspx

National Governors Association Center for Best Practices, Council of Chief State School Officers. (2010). Common Core State Standards. National Governors Association Center for Best Practices, Council of Chief State School Officers, Washington D.C.

National Survey of Student Engagement (NSSE). (2009). *About the National Survey of Student Engagement*. Retrieved July 27th 2009 from http://nsse.iub.edu/html/about.cfm

NCTM (National Council of Teachers of Mathematics). (2000). *Principles and Standards for School Mathematics*. Reston, VA: Commission on Standards for School Mathematics.

Ndirangu, M. (2000). *A study of the perceptions of students, teachers and their influence of teaching projects on the teaching of science in selected secondary schools in Kenya*. Unpublished PHD Thesis, Egerton University, Kenya.

Nerland, M. (2007). One-to-one teaching as cultural practice: Two case studies from an academy of music. *Music Education Research, 9*(3), 399–416. doi:10.1080/14613800701587761

Nesbit, J. C., & Adesope, O. O. (2006, January01). Learning With Concept and Knowledge Maps: A Meta-Analysis. *Review of Educational Research, 76*(3), 413–448. doi:10.3102/00346543076003413

Newborne, A. (2002). Challenges in instituting E-learning in universities. *Journal of Informetrics, 10*(3), 117–138.

Newton, R. (2003). Staff attitudes to the development and delivery of e-learning. *New Library World, 104*(10), 412–425. doi:10.1108/03074800310504357

Ng'ambi, D., & Johnston, K. (2006). An ICT-mediated constructivist approach for increasing academic support and teaching critical thinking skills. *Journal of Educational Technology & Society, 9*, 244–253.

Nguyen, A. (2011). *Negotiations and challenges: An investigation into the experience of creating a digital story.* Doctoral Dissertation, University of Houston, TX, USA.

Niemi, H. (2012). Relationships of teachers' professional competencies, active learning and research studies in teacher education in Finland. *Reflecting Education, 8*(2), 23-44. Retrieved from http://www.reflectingeducation.net/

Niess, M. L., Ronau, R. N., Shafer, K. G., Driskell, S. O., Harper, S. R., Johnston, C., & Kersaint, G. (2009). Mathematics teacher TPACK standards and development model. *Contemporary Issues in Technology & Teacher Education, 9*(1), 4–24.

Niess, N. L. (1991). Computer-using teachers in a new decade. *Education and Computing, 7*(3), 151–156. doi:10.1016/S0167-9287(09)90002-4

Nihuka, K. A. (2008). *The feasibility of e-learning integration in course delivery at the Open University of Tanzania.* Unpublished, Master Dissertation, University of Twente, Enschede.

Nihuka, K. A. (2011). *Collaborative course design to support implementation of e-learning by instructors.* Enschede: PrintPartners Ipskamp. doi:10.3990/1.9789036532358

Nihuka, K. A., & Voogt, J. (2011). Instructors and students competences, perception and access to e-learning technologies: Implications for e-learning technologies at the Open University of Tanzania. *International Journal on E-Learning, 10*(1), 63–85.

Nourbakhsh, I. R., Hamner, E., Crowley, K., & Wilkinson, K. (2004). *Formal Measures of Learning in a Secondary School Mobile Robotics Course.* Paper presented at the 2004 IEEE International Conference on Robotics & Automation, New Orleans, LA. doi:10.1109/ROBOT.2004.1308090

November, A. (2008). *Web literacy for educators.* Thousand Oaks, CA: Corwin Press.

Ntuli, E. (2010). *A study of K-3 inservice teachers' understanding, selection, and use of developmentally appropriate technology.* (Doctoral Dissertation). Illinois State University, ProQuest Dissertation & Thesis A& I. 3485926.

Ntuli, E., & Kyei-Blannkson, L. (2010). Teachers' understanding and use of developmentally appropriate computer technology in early childhood education. *Journal of Technology Integration in the Classroom, 2*(3), 23–35.

Nutball, K. (2000). *Strategies for improving Academic Achievement and teaching effectiveness: education development center,* NEIRTEC, www.neirtec.org

Nzilano, J., & Kafyulilo, A. C. (2012). Development of Information and Communication Technology in Education in Tanzania: How is DUCE playing its role? *Journal of Education, Humanities and Sciences, 1*(2), 64–78.

O'Shea, A. (2004). Teaching 'critical citizenship' in an age of hedonistic vocationalism. *Learning and Teaching in the Social Sciences, 1*(2). doi:10.1386/ltss.1.2.95/0

Obi, E. (2012). Helping to bring African universities online. *Google Africa Blog.* Retrieved July 18, 2013, from http://google-africa.blogspot.com/2012/09/helping-to-bring-african-universities.html

Oblinger, D. G., & Oblinger, J. L. (2005*). Educating the Net Generation.* In D. Oblinger & J. Oblinger (Eds), *Educating the Net generation* (pp. 2.1– 2.20). Boulder, CO: EDUCAUSE. Retrieved August 14, 2013 from http://net.educause.edu/ir/library/pdf/pub7101m.pdf

Office of Postsecondary Education, Office of Policy, Planning and Innovation. (2005). Third report to congress on the distance education demonstration program. *U.S. Department of Education.* Washington, DC, Retrieved January 2006: http://www.ed.gov/programs/disted

Office of Social and Economic Data Analysis. (2001). *Final results from the e-MINTS teacher survey.* Columbia, MO: Author.

Office of Technology Assessment. (1995). *Teachers and technology: Making the connection.* Washington, DC: U.S. Government Printing Office.

Office of the Chief Information Officer. (2012). *Section 508 Reference Guide Appendix B: Tips for Creating Accessible Products*. The United States Patent and Trademark Office. Retrieved from http://www.uspto.gov/about/offices/cio/section508/11b.jsp

Ohler, J. (2008). *Digital storytelling in the classroom: New media pathways to literacy, learning, and creativity*. Thousand Oaks, CA: Corwin Press.

Oigara, J. N., & Wallace, N. (2012). Modeling, training, and mentoring teacher candidates to use SMART Board technology. *Issues in Informing Science and Information Technology*, *9*, 297–315.

Oosterhof, A., Conrad, R. M., & Ely, D. P. (2008). *Assessing Learners Online*. New Jersey: Pearson.

Oppliger, D. (2002). *Using FIRST LEGO League to Enhance Engineering Education and to Increase the Pool of Future Engineering Students (Work in Progress)*. Paper presented at the 32nd ASEE/IEEE Frontiers in Education Conference, Boston, MA. doi:10.1109/FIE.2002.1158731

Orlando, A. (2005). *The Integration of Learning Technologies in the Elementary Classroom: Identifying Teacher Pedagogy and Classroom Culture*. PhD Thesis, Drexel University.

Osler, J. E. (2012). Trichotomy–Squared – A novel mixed methods test and research procedure designed to analyze, transform, and compare qualitative and quantitative data for education scientists who are administrators, practitioners, teachers, and technologists. iManager's Journal on Mathematics, 1(3).

Osler, J. E. (2013a). The Psychometrics of Educational Science: Designing Trichotomous Inventive Investigative Instruments for Qualitative and Quantitative for Inquiry. December 2012 – February 2013 *iManager's. Journal of Educational Psychology*, 8(3).

Osler, J. E. (2013b). The Psychological Efficacy of Education as a Science through Personal, Professional, and Contextual Inquiry of the Affective Learning Domain. February – April *iManager's. Journal of Educational Psychology*, 6(4).

Otieno, O. J. (2008) *A frame work for evaluating technological tools and resources use in teacher education: A case study of the primary teacher training colleges in Kenya*. Unpublished MEd Thesis, Strathmore university, Kenya.

Ottevanger, W., van den Akker, J., & de Feiter, L. (2007). Developing science, mathematics, and ICT education in Sub-Saharan Africa: Patterns and promising practices. (World Bank Working Paper No.101). Washington, DC: The World Bank. doi:10.1596/978-0-8213-7070-4

Ouyang, R. (1993). *A meta-analysis: Effectiveness of computer-assisted instruction at the level of elementary education*. Unpublished Dissertation, Indiana University of Pennsylvania, Indiana.

Oye, N. D., Salleh, M., & Iahad, N. A. (2011). Challenges of e-learning in Nigerian university education based on the experience of developed countries. *International Journal of Managing Information Technology*, *3*(2), 39–48. doi:10.5121/ijmit.2011.3204

Ozonur, M. (2013). *Sanal gerçeklik ortamı olarak ikincil yaşam (second life) uygulamalarının tasarlanması ve bu uygulamaların internet tabanlı uzaktan eğitim öğrencilerinin öğrenmeleri üzerindeki etkilerinin farklı değişkenler açısından incelenmesi* [The design of second life applications as virtual world and examining the effects of these applications on the learning of the students attending internet-based distance education in terms of different variables]. Phd thesis: Mersin University.

Palfrey, J., Gasser, U., Simun, M., & Barnes, R. F. (2009). Youth, creativity and copyright in the digital age. *International Journal of Learning and Media*, *1*(2), 79–97. doi:10.1162/ijlm.2009.0022

Palloff, R., & Pratt, K. (2000). "Making the transition: Helping teachers to teach online". Paper presented at *EDUCAUSE: Thinking it through*. Nashville, Tennessee. (ERIC Document Reproduction Service No. ED 452 806).

Palloff, R. M., & Pratt, K. (2007). *Building online learning communities*. San Franciso, CA: Jossey-Bass.

Pamuk, S. (2012). Understanding preservice teacher's technology use through TPACK framework. *Journal of Computer Assisted Learning*, *28*(5), 425–439. doi:10.1111/j.1365-2729.2011.00447.x

Panasuk, R. M., & Horton, L. B. (2013). Integrating History of Mathematics into the Classroom: Was Aristotle Wrong? *Journal of Curriculum & Teaching*, *2*(2), 37–46. doi:10.5430/jct.v2n2p37

Panda, S., & Mishra, S. (2007). E-learning in Mega Open University: Faculty attitudes, barriers and motivators. *Educational Media International*, *44*(4), 328–338. http://cohortresearch.wiki.westga.edu/file/view/faculty+attitude+barriers+and+mo tivators.pdf doi:10.1080/09523980701680854

Panel on Educational Technology. (1997). *Report to the President on the use of technology to strengthen K-12 education in the United States*. Washington, DC: President's Committee of Advisors on Science and Technology.

Papert, S. (1993). *Mindstorms - Children, Computers, and Powreful Ideas* (2nd ed.). New York, NY: Basic Books.

Papert, S., & Harel, I. (1991). *Constructionism*. New York, NY: Ablex Publishing Corporation.

Park, E. L., & Choi, B. K. (2014). Transformation of classroom spaces: Traditional versus active learning classroom in colleges. *Higher Education*, 1–23.

Parker, J., Maor, D., & Herrington, J. (2013). Authentic online learning: Aligning learner needs, pedagogy and technology. *Issues in Educational Research*, *23*(2), 227–241. Retrieved from http://www.iier.org.au/iier23/parker.html

Park, S. Y. (2009). An analysis of the technology acceptance model in understanding university students' behavioral intention to use e-learning. *Journal of Educational Technology & Society*, *12*(3).

Pascarella, T. E., & Terenzini, T. P. (2005). *How college affects students: A third decade of research*. San Francisco, CA: Jossey Bass.

Patton, J. W. (2000). Protecting privacy in public? Surveillance technologies and the value of public places. *Ethics and Information Technology*, *2*(3), 181–187. doi:10.1023/A:1010057606781

Patton, M. Q. (1990). *Qualitative research and evaluation methods* (2nd ed.). Newbury Park, CA: Sage.

Paula, S. (2006). *What is inquiry-based learning?* Retrieved from http://www.inquirylearn.com/Inquirydef.htm

Paulson, K. (2002). Reconfiguring faculty roles for virtual settings. *The Journal of Higher Education*, *73*(1), 123–140. doi:10.1353/jhe.2002.0010

Pavlenko, A. (2001). *Multilingualism, second language learning, and gender*. New York: Walter De Gruyter. doi:10.1515/9783110889406

Pavlenko, A., & Norton, B. (2007). Imagined communities, identity, and English language learning. In J. Cummins & C. Davison (Eds.), *International handbook of English language teaching* (pp. 669–680). Dordrecht, Netherlands: Springer. doi:10.1007/978-0-387-46301-8_43

Peansupap, V., & Walker, D. H. T. (2005). Factors enabling information and communication technology diffusion and actual implementation in construction organizations. *ITcon*, *10*, 193–218.

Peck, A. C., Ali, R. S., Matchock, R. L., & Levine, M. E. (2006). Introductory psychology topics and student performance: Where's the challenge? *Teaching of Psychology*, *33*(3), 167–170. doi:10.1207/s15328023top3303_2

Pelgrum, W. (2001). Obstacles to the integration of ICT in education: Results from a worldwide educational assessment. *Computers & Education*, *37*(2), 163–178. doi:10.1016/S0360-1315(01)00045-8

Penland, J., & Rice, D. (2005).Emerging changes under the education canopy. *Teaching in Higher Education Forum*. April 17-19, 2005. Louisiana State University, Baton Rouge.

Perry, B., & Edwards, M. (2010). Creating a culture of community in the online classroom using artistic pedagogical technologies. In G. Veletsianos (Ed.), Using emerging technologies in distance education. Edmonton, AB: AU Press; Retrieved from http://www.veletsianos.com/2010/11/14/data-on-our-open- access-book/

Perry, R., & Smart, J. C. (2007). *The scholarship of teaching and learning in higher education: An evidence–based perspective*. Netherlands: Springer. doi:10.1007/1-4020-5742-3

Philippou, G. N., & Christou, C. (1998). The effects of a preparatory mathematics program in changing prospective teachers' attitudes towards mathematics. *Educational Studies in Mathematics*, *35*(1), 189–206. doi:10.1023/A:1003030211453

Piaget, J. (1929). *The Child's Conception of the World.* New York: Harcourt, Brace and Company.

Piaget, J. (1936). *Origins of intelligence in the child.* London: Routledge & Kegan Paul.

Piaget, J. (1954). *The Construction of Reality in the Child.* New York: Basic Books. doi:10.1037/11168-000

Piaget, J. (1977). *The development of thought: Equilibration of cognitive structures.* New York: The Viking Press.

Pierson, M., Shepard, M. F., & Leneway, R. (2009, September06). Distributed Collaborative Research Model: Meaningful and Responsive Inquiry in Technology and Teacher Education. *Journal of Computing in Teacher Education, 25*(4), 127–133.

Pinsonneault, A., Barki, H., Gallupe, R. B., & Hoppen, N. (1999).Electronic brainstorming. Retrieved from http://pubsonline.informs.org/doi/pdf/10.1287/isre.10.2.110

Pond, W. (2003). *Lifelong learning: The changing face of higher education. E-Learning Summit, 2003.* California: La Quinta Resort.

Ponnusawmy, H., & Santally, M. (2008). Promoting (quality) participation in online forums: A study of the use of forums in two online modules at the University of Mauritius http://www.itdl.org/Journal/Apr_08/article04.htm

Ponza, M. V. (1998). A Role for the History of Mathematics in the Teaching and Learning of Mathematics: An Argentinian Experience. *Mathematics in school, 27*(4), 10-13.

Porter, A. (2013). *The problem with technology in schools.* Retrieved from, http://www.washingtonpost.com

Porter, W. W., Graham, C. R., Spring, K., & Welch, K. R. (2014). Blended learning in higher education: Institutional adoption and implementation. *Computers & Education, 75,* 185–195. doi:10.1016/j.compedu.2014.02.011

Potashiki, M., & Capper, J. (1998). Distance education: Growth and diversity. *Finance & Development,* (March): 1998.

Potts, A., & Schlichting, K. (2011, January01). Developing Professional Forums that Support Thoughtful Discussion, Reflection, and Social Action: One Faculty's Commitment to Social Justice and Culturally Responsive Practice. *International Journal of Teaching and Learning in Higher Education, 23*(1), 11–19.

Pounder, J. (2007). Is student evaluation of teaching worthwhile? An analytical framework for answering the question. *Quality Assurance in Education, 18*(1), 47–63.

Powell, N. W., Cleveland, R., Thompson, S., & Forde, T. (2012). Using multi-instructional teaching and technology-supported active learning strategies to enhance student engagement. *Journal of Technological Integration in the Classroom, 4*(2), 41–50.

Powers, S., & Guan, S. (2000). Examining the range of student needs in the design and development of a web-based course. In B. Abbey (Ed.), *Instructional and cognitive impacts of Web-based education* (pp. 200–216). Hershey, PA: Idea Group Publishing. doi:10.4018/978-1-878289-59-9.ch013

Prensky, M. (2001). Digital natives, digital immigrants. On the Horizon (MCB University Press, Vol. 9 No. 5, October 2001).

Prince, M. (2004). Does active learning work? A review of the research. *The Journal of Engineering Education, 93*(3), 223–231. doi:10.1002/j.2168-9830.2004.tb00809.x

Prober, C. G., & Khan, S. (2013). Medical education reimagined: A call to action. *Academic Medicine, 88*(10), 1407–1410. doi:10.1097/ACM.0b013e3182a368bd PMID:23969367

Puentedura, R. (2006). *Transformatiom, technology, and education.* Presentation given August 18, 2006 as part of the Strengthening Your District Through Technology workshops, Maine, US. Retrieved from http://hippasus.com/resources/tte/part1.html

Pugsley, L., & McCrorie, P. (2007). Improving medical education: Improving patient care. *Teaching and Teacher Education, 23*(3), 314–322. doi:10.1016/j.tate.2006.12.023

Radford, A. (2011). Learning at a distance: Undergraduate enrollment in distance education courses and degree programs. *U.S. Department of Education, National Center for Education Statistics,* Retrieved July 2014: http://nces.ed.gov/pubsearch/pubsinfo.asp?pubid=2012154

Radford, L. (1997). On psychology, historical epistemology and the teaching of mathematics: Towards a socio-cultural history of mathematics. *For the Learning of Mathematics, 17,* 26–33.

Rakes, C. R., Valentine, J. C., McGatha, M. B., & Ronau, R. N. (2010). Methods of instructional improvement in Algebra: A systematic review and meta-analysis. *Review of Educational Research, 80*(3), 372–400. doi:10.3102/0034654310374880

Rakes, G. C., Flowers, B. F., Casey, H. C., & Santana, R. (2006). Analysis of instructional technology use and constructivist behaviors in K-12 teachers. *International Journal of Educational Technology, 1*(12).

Ramanathan, V., & Atkinson, D. (1999). Individualism, academic writing, and ESL Writers. *Journal of Second Language Writing, 8*(l), 45–75. doi:10.1016/S1060-3743(99)80112-X

Rambe, P. (2010). Using Contradictions to Ravel Teaching and Learning Challenges in a Blended IS Course in an African University. *Journal of Information, Information Technology, and Organizations, 5,* 101–124.

Ramos, T. (2003). *Top Challenges Teachers Face in Special Needs Inclusive Classrooms.*

Rea, D. (2003). Optimal motivation for creative intelligence. In D. Ambrose, L. M. Cohen, & A. Tannenbaum (Eds.), *Creative intelligence: Toward theoretic integration* (pp. 211–225). Cresskill, NJ: Hampton Press.

Read, B., Francis, B., & Robson, J. (2001). Playing Safe: Undergraduate essay writing and the presentation of the student voice. *British Journal of Sociology of Education, 22*(3), 387–399. doi:10.1080/01425690124289

Redmann, D., Kotrlik, J., & Douglas, B. (2003). Factors related to technology integration in instruction by marketing education teachers. *Journal of Career and Technical Education, 19*(2), 29–46.

Reeves, P. M., & Reeves, T. C. (2008). Design considerations for online learning in health and social work. *Learning in Health and Social Care, 7*(1), 46–58. doi:10.1111/j.1473-6861.2008.00170.x

Reigeluth, C. M. (1999). What is instructional-design theory and how is it changing? In C. M. Reigeluth (Ed.), *Instructional-design theories and models: A new paradigm of instructional theory* (Vol. II, pp. 5–29). Mahwah, NJ: Lawrence Erlbaum Associates.

Reiser, R. A., & Dempsey, J. V. (2012). *Trends and issues in Instructional Design and Technology* (3rd ed.). Saddle River, NJ: Pearson Education.

Rennie, F., & Morrison, T. (2013). *E-learning and social networking handbook: Resources for higher education.* New York: Taylor & Francis.

Report, C. (1998). *Education for Citizenship and the teaching of Democracy in Schools.* http://www.qca.org.uk/downloads/6123_crick_report_1998.pdf

Resta, P., & Laferriere, T. (2008). Issues and challenges related to digital equity. In J. Voogt & G. Knezek (Eds.), *International handbook of information technology in primary and secondary education* (pp. 765–778). New York, NY: Springer. doi:10.1007/978-0-387-73315-9_44

Richardson, J., & Swan, K. (2003). Examining social presence in online courses in relation to students' perceived learning and satisfaction. *Journal of Asynchronous Learning Networks, 7,* 78–82.

Richardson, W. (2010). *Blogs, wikis, podcasts, and other powerful web tools for classrooms.* Thousand Oaks, CA: Corwin.

Rinaldi, C. (2001). Making Learning Visible: Children as Individual and Group Learners. In Project Zero & Reggio Children (Ed.), Making Learning Visible: Children as Individual and Group Learners (pp. 78-89). Bloomfield, MI: Olive Press.

Rindos, A., Vouk, M., Vandenberg, A., Pitt, S., Harris, R., Gendron, D., & Danford, T. (2009). The Transformation of Education through State Education Clouds (pp. 1–12). Retrieved from http://www.ibm.com/ibm/files/N734393J24929X18/EBW03002-USEN-00.pdf

Robey, E. (Ed.). (1992). *Opening the doors: Using technology to improve education for students with disabilities.* Silver Spring, MD: Macro International Inc.

Robin, B. (2008). *Handbook of research on teaching literacy through the communicative and visual arts* (Vol. 2). New York: Lawrence Erlbaum Associates.

Robin, B. R. (2008). Digital storytelling: A powerful technology tool for the 21st century classroom. *Theory into Practice, 47*(3), 220–228. doi:10.1080/00405840802153916

Robinson, K. (2010). *Changing education paradigms.* Retrieved from http://www.ted.com/talks/ken_robinson_changing_education_paradigms.html

Robler, M. D. (2003). *Integrating educational technology into teaching* (3rd ed.). Upper Saddle River, NJ: Merrill Prentice Hall.

Roche, L. A., & Marsh, H. W. (2000). Multiple dimensions of university teacher self concept. *Instructional Science, 28*(5), 439–468. doi:10.1023/A:1026576404113

Rogers, C. (2008). A Well-Kept Secret: Classroom Management with Robotics. In M. U. Bers (Ed.), *Blocks to Robots* (pp. 46–52). New York, NY: Teachers College Press.

Rogers, C., & Portsmore, M. (2004). Bringing Engineering to Elementary School. *Journal of STEM Education, 5*(3&4), 17–28.

Roschelle, J., & Teasley, S. (1995). The construction of shared knowledge in collaborative problem-solving in computer communication and cognition Vygotskian perspectives, 67-197. Cambridge: Cambridge University Press.

Rosenberg, M. J. (2005). *Beyond e-learning: Approaches and technologies to enhance organizational knowledge, learning, and performance.* San Francisco, CA: Wiley.

Rosen, K. R., McBride, J. M., & Drake, R. L. (2009). The use of simulation in medical education to enhance students' understanding of basic sciences. *Medical Teacher, 31*(9), 842–846. doi:10.1080/01421590903049822 PMID:19811190

Rosen, L. D. (2010). *Rewired: Understanding the iGeneration and the way they learn.* New York: Palgrave Macmillan.

Rouse, D. P. (2000). The effectiveness of computer-assisted instruction in teaching nursing students about congenital heart disease. *Computers in Nursing, 18,* 282–287. PMID:11105402

Royal National Institute for the Blind. (2004). *Communicating with blind and partially sighted people.* Peterborough, England.

Rudnesky, F. (2003). From vision to classroom. *Principal Leadership, 3*(6), 44–47.

Ruiz, J. G., Mintzer, M. J., & Leipzig, R. M. (2006). The impact of e-learning in medical education. *Academic Medicine, 81*(3), 207–212. doi:10.1097/00001888-200603000-00002 PMID:16501260

Rumble, G. (2001). Re-inventing distance education, 1971-2001. *International Journal of Lifelong Education, 20*(1/2), 31–43.

Russell, J., Elton, L., Swinglehurst, D., & Greenhalgh, T. (2006). Using the online environment assessment for learning: A case study of a web-based course in primary care. *Assessment & Evaluation in Higher Education, 31*(4), 465–478. doi:10.1080/02602930600679209

Ryan, S. D., Magro, M. J., & Sharp, J. H. (2011). Exploring Educational and Cultural Adaptation through Social Networking Sites. *Journal of Information Technology Education, 10,* 1–16.

Sabry, K., & Baldwin, L. (2003). Web-based learning interaction and learning styles. *British Journal of Educational Technology, 34*(4), 443–454. doi:10.1111/1467-8535.00341

Sadik, A. (2008). Digital storytelling: A meaningful technology-integrated approach for engaged student learning. *Educational Technology Research and Development, 56*(4), 487–506. doi:10.1007/s11423-008-9091-8

Safavi, S., Bakar, K., Tarmizi, R., & Alwi, N. (2012). The role of student ratings of instruction from perspectives of the higher education administrators. *International Journal of Business and Social Science, 3*(9), 233–239.

Sage, K. (1999). Science activities using the World Wide Web: Grade 4–6+. Monterey, CA: Evan-Moor Educational Publishers.

SAIDE. (1999). *Distance education in Tanzania*. Retrieved September 3, 2014, from http://colfinder.net/materials/supporting-distance education.htm

Salavuo, M. (2008). Social media as an opportunity for pedagogical change in music education. *Journal of Music. Technology and Education, 1*(2/3), 121–136.

Salmivalli, C., Sainio, M., & Hodges, E. V. E. (2013). Electronic victimization: Correlates, antecedents, consequences among elementary and middle school students. *Journal of Clinical Child and Adolescent Psychology, 42*(4), 442–453. doi:10.1080/15374416.2012.759228 PMID:23384048

Salyers, V., Carter, L., & Barrett, P. (2010a). *Evaluating student and faculty satisfaction with a pedagogical framework*. Presentation at the Centennial Symposium on Scholarship of Teaching and Learning Conference. Banff, AB.

Salyers, V., Carter, L., Barrett, P., & Williams, L. (2010b). Evaluating student and faculty satisfaction with a pedagogical framework. *Journal of Distance Education/Revue de l'Éducation à Distance, 24*(3). Available at: http://www.jofde.ca/index.php/jde/article/view/695/1145

Salyers, V. (2005). Web-enhanced and face-to-face classroom instructional methods: Effects on course outcomes and student satisfaction. *International Journal of Nursing Education Scholarship, 2*(1). Article, 29, 1–13.

Salyers, V., Carter, L., Cairns, S., & Durrer, L. (2014). Strategies in online courses for working nurses: Implications for adult and online education. *Canadian Journal of University Continuing Education, 40*(1).

Salyers, V., Carter, L., Carter, A., Myers, S., & Barrett, P. (2014). The search for meaningful e-learning at Canadian universities: A multi-institutional research study. *International Review of Research in Open and Distributed Learning, 15*(6), 313–337. Available at http://www.irrodl.org/index.php/irrodl/article/view/1713

Sancar Tokmak, H. (2013). TPAB - temelli öğretim teknolojileri ve materyal tasarımı dersi: matematik öğretimi için web-tabanlı uzaktan eğitim ortamı tasarlama. [TPACK-based instructional technology and material design course: Designing web-based instruction for mathematic teaching] In T. Yanpar Yelken, H. Sancar Tokmak, S. Ozgelen, & L. Incikabi (Eds.), *Fen ve matematik eğitiminde TPAB temelli öğretim tasarımları* [TPACK-based course designs in Science and Math education]. (pp. 239–260). Ankara: Ani Publication.

Sancar-Tokmak, H., Surmeli, H., & Ozgelen, S. (2014). Pre-service science teachers' perceptions of their TPACK development after creating digital stories. *International Journal of Environmental and Science Education, 9*(3), 247–264.

Santer, D. M., Michaelsen, V. E., Erkonen, W. E., Winter, R. J., Woodhead, J. C., Gilmer, J. S., & Galvin, J. R. (1995). A comparison of educational interventions: Multimedia textbook, standard lecture, and printed textbook. *Archives of Pediatrics & Adolescent Medicine, 149*(3), 297–302. doi:10.1001/archpedi.1995.02170150077014 PMID:7532074

Saunders, M., Lewis, P., & Thornhill, A. (2007). *Research Methods for Business Students* (4th ed.). Harlow: FT Prentice Hall.

Sawant, S. (2012). The study of the use of Web 2.0 tools in LIS education in India. *Library Hi Tech News, 29*(2), 11–15. doi:10.1108/07419051211236549

Scalese, R. J., Obeso, V. T., & Issenberg, S. B. (2008). Simulation technology for skills training and competency assessment in medical education. *Journal of General Internal Medicine, 23*(S1), 46–49. doi:10.1007/s11606-007-0283-4 PMID:18095044

Schalkwyk, S. C. (2008). Acquiring academic literacy: A case of first year extended degree programme students at Stellenbosch University. Stellenbosch University.

Schank, R. C. (2002). *Designing world class e-learning: How IBM, GE, Harvard Business School, and Columbia University are succeeding at e-learning*. New York: McGraw-Hill.

Schiro, M. (2004). *Oral storytelling and teaching mathematics*. Thousand Oaks, CA: SAGE Publications.

Schmidt, H. G., Loyens, S. M. M., van Gog, T., & Paas, F. (2007). Problem-based learning is compatible with human cognitive architecture: Commentary on Kirschner, Sweller, and Clark (2006). *Educational Psychologist, 42*(2), 91–97. doi:10.1080/00461520701263350

Schram, P., Wilcox, S. K., Lapan, G., & Lanier, P. (1988). Changing preservice teachers' beliefs about mathematics education. In C. A. Mahers, G. A. Goldin, & R. B. Davis (Eds.), *Proceedings of PME-NA 11* (Vol. 1, pp. 296-302). New Brunswick, NJ: Rutgers University.

Schrodt, P., Witt, P. L., Myers, S. A., Turman, P. D., Barton, M. H., & Jernberg, K. A. (2008). Learner Empowerment and Teacher Evaluations as Functions of Teacher Power Use in the College Classroom. *Communication Education, 57*(2), 180–200. doi:10.1080/03634520701840303

Schrum, L. (1995, April). *Telecommunications for personal and professional uses: A case study*. Paper presented at the annual meeting of the American Educational Research: Association, San Francisco.

Schrum, L., & Levin, B. B. (2013). Preparing future teacher leaders: Lessons from exemplary school systems. *Journal of Digital Learning in Teacher Education, 29*(3), 97–103. doi:10.1080/21532974.2013.10784711

Schrum, L., Thompson, A., Maddux, C., Sprague, D., Bull, G., & Bell, L. (2007). Editorial: Research on the effectiveness of technology in schools: The roles of pedagogy and content. *Contemporary Issues in Technology & Teacher Education, 7*(1), 456–460.

Schultz, B. (2003). Collaborative learning in an online environment: Will it work for teacher training? In *Proceedings of the 14th annual Society for Information Technology and Teacher Education International Conference* (pp. 503-504). Charlottesville, VA: Association for the Advancement of Computers in Education.

Schunk, D. (2008). *Learning theories: An educational perspective* (5th ed.). Upper Saddle River, NJ: Pearson.

Schwartz, D. L., & Bransford, J. D. (1998). A time for telling. *Cognition and Instruction, 16*(4), 475–5223. doi:10.1207/s1532690xci1604_4

Secretary's Commission on Achieving Necessary Skills (SCANS). (1991). *What work requires of schools: A SCANS report for America 2000*. Washington, DC: U.S. Department of Labor. Retrieved January 28th 2009 from http://wdr.doleta.gov/SCANS/whatwork/whatwork.pdf

Sekaran, U. (2003). *Research method of business: A skill Building Approach* (4th ed.). New York, NY: John Willey & Sons, Inc.

Selim, H. M. (2007). Critical success factors for e-learning acceptance: Confirmatory factor models. *Computers & Education, 49*(2), 396–413. doi:10.1016/j.compedu.2005.09.004

Selwyn, N. (2009). The digital native: Myth and reality. *Aslib Proceedings: New Information Perspectives, 61*(4), 364–379. doi:10.1108/00012530910973776

Settles, B. (2010). Active learning literature survey. University of Wisconsin, Madison, 52, 55-66.

Shaffer, D., & Resnick, M. (1999). "Thick" authenticity: New media and authentic learning. *Journal of Interactive Learning Research, 10*(2), 195–215.

Sharples, M. (2005). *Re-thinking learning for the mobile age*. Retrieved from: http://www.noe-kaleidoscope.org/pub/lastnews/last-0-read159-display

Sharples, M. (2000). The design of personal mobile technologies for lifelong learning. *Computers & Education, 34*(3-4), 177–193. doi:10.1016/S0360-1315(99)00044-5

Sheingold, K., & Hadley, M. (1990). *Accomplished teachers: Integrating computers into classroom practice*. New York: Bank Street College of Education, Center for Technology in Education.

Shelton, M., & Jones, M. (1996). Staff development that works! A tale of four T's. *NAASP Bulletin, 80*(582), 99–105. doi:10.1177/019263659608058214

Sherlock, K. (2008). *Advice on academic tone*. Retrieved September 27, 2014, from www.grossmont.edu/karl.sherlock/English098/.../Academic_Tone.pdf

Shiengold, K., & Hadley, M. (1990). *Accomplished teachers: integrating computers into classroom practice*. New York: Centre for Technology in Education, Bank Street College of Education.

Siemens, G. (2010). *Connectivism*. Retrieved from: http://connectivism.ca/?p=220

Siemens, G., & Matheos, K. (2010). Systemic changes in higher education. *Education: Technology & Social Media, 16*(1). Retrieved June 20, 2014, from http://www.ineducation.ca/

Siemens, G., & Conole, G. (2011). Connectivism: Design and delivery of social networked learning. *International Review of Research in Open and Distance Learning, 12*(3), i–iv.

SIIA. (2009). *Best practices for using games & simulations in the classroom: Guidelines for K–12 Educators,* Retrieved from, http://siia.net/index.php?option=com_docman&task=doc_view&gid=610&tmpl=component&format=raw&Itemid=59

Sikora, A. (2000). A profile of participation in distance education: 1999-2000. *U.S. Department of Education, National Center for Education Statistics,* Retrieved July 2014: http://www.nces.ed.gov/pubs2006/2006187.pdf

Silberman, M. (1996). *Active learning: 101 strategies to teach any subject.* Boston, MA: Allyn and Bacon.

Şimşek. (2013). Öğretim tasarımı ve modelleri. [Instructional design and models] In K. Cagıltay & Y. Goktas (Eds.), *Öğretim teknolojilerinin temelleri: Teoriler, araştırmalar, eğitimler* [Foundations of instructional technology: Theories, researches, and trends]. Ankara: Pegem Publishing.

Sirinterlikci, A., Zane, L., & Sirinterlikci, A. L. (2009). Active learning through toy design and development. *Journal of Technology Studies, 35*(2), 14–22.

Sirkin, M. R. (2006). *Statistics for the social sciences* (3rd ed.). Thousand Oaks, CA: Sage.

Siu, M.-K. (2004). No, I do not use history of mathematics in my class. Why? In S. Kaijser (Ed.), *History and pedagogy of mathematics: Proceedings of HPM 2004* (pp. 375-376). Uppsala, Sweden: HPM.

Sklar, E., Eguchi, A., & Johnson, J. (2002). *Examining the Team Robotics through RoboCupJunior.* Paper presented at the the Annual Conference of Japan Society for Educational Technology, Nagaoka, Japan.

Sklar, E., & Eguchi, A. (2004). RoboCupJunior - Four Years Later. *Proceedings of RoboCup-2004: Robot Soccer World Cup VIII.*

Sklar, E., Eguchi, A., & Johnson, J. (2003). Scientific Challenge Award: RoboCupJunior - Learning with Educational Robotics. *AI Magazine, 24*(2), 43–46.

Skouge, J. R., & Rao, K. (2009, January01). Digital Storytelling in Teacher Education: Creating Transformations through Narrative. *Educational Perspectives, 42*, 54–60.

Skowronek, J., Friesen, B., & Masonjones, H. (2011). Developing a statistically valid and practically useful student evaluation instrument. *International Journal for the Scholarship of Teaching and Learning, 5*(1), 1–19.

Slavin, R. E., & Lake, C. (2008). Effective programs in elementary mathematics: A best evidence synthesis. *Review of Educational Research, 78*(3), 427–455. doi:10.3102/0034654308317473

Slavin, R. E., Lake, C., & Groff, C. (2009). Effective programs in middle and high school mathematics: A best evidence synthesis. *Review of Educational Research, 79*(2), 839–911. doi:10.3102/0034654308330968

Smestad, B. (2009). *Teachers' conceptions of history of mathematics.* Retrieved from http://home.hio.no/~bjorsme/HPM2008paper.pdf

Smith, G., Ottewill, R., Jubb, E., Sperling, E., & Wyman, M. (2007). Teaching citizenship in higher education, PSA 2007. Retrieved from www.psa.ac.uk/2007/pps/Smith2.pdf

Smith, J. A., & Osborn, M. (2008). Interpretative phenomenological analysis. In J. A. Smith (Ed.), *Qualitative Psychology* (2nd ed., pp. 53–80). London: Sage.

Smith, L. K., Draper, R. J., & Sabey, B. L. (2005, September06). The Promise of Technology to Confront Dilemmas in Teacher Education: The Use of WebQuests in Problem-Based Methods Courses. *Journal of Computing in Teacher Education, 21*(4), 99–108.

Smith, S. J., & Okolo, C. (2010). Response to intervention and evidence-based practices: Where does technology fit? *Learning Disability Quarterly, 33*(4), 252–272. http://www.jstor.org/stable/23053229 Retrieved June 6, 2014

Snoeyink, R., & Ertmer, P. (2001). Thrust into technology: How veteran teachers respond. *Journal of Educational Technology Systems, 30*(1), 85–111. doi:10.2190/YDL7-XH09-RLJ6-MTP1

Soares, F., Leão, C. P., Santos, S., Ribeiro, F., & Lopes, G. (2011). An Early Start in Robotics - K-12 Case-Study. [iJEP]. *International Journal of Engineering Pedagogy, 1*(1), 50–56.

SoftBank Mobile Corp., & Aldebaran Robotics SAS. (2014). *SoftBank Mobile and Aldebaran Unveil "Pepper" – the World's First Personal Robot That Reads Emotions.* Retrieved June 8, 2014, from http://www.softbank.jp/en/corp/group/sbm/news/press/2014/20140605_01/

Somekh, B. (1998). Supporting information and communication technology innovations in higher education. *Journal of Information Technology for Teacher Education, 7*(1), 11–32. doi:10.1080/14759399800200028

Song, K. H., & Turner, G. Y. (January 01, 2010). *Visual Literacy and Its Impact on Teaching and Learning.*

Sorensen, E. K., & Takle, E. S. (2005, April). Investigating knowledge building dialogues in networked communities of practice: A collaborative learning endeavor across cultures. *Interactive Educational Multimedia,* (10), 50-60.

Speck, B. W. (2002). New Learning-teaching-assessment paradigms and the online classroom. *Directions for Teaching and Learning, 91*(91), 5–18. doi:10.1002/tl.61

Spooren, P. P., Mortelmans, D. D., & Denekens, J. J. (2007). Student evaluation of teaching quality in higher education: Development of an instrument based on 10 Likert–scales. *Assessment & Evaluation in Higher Education, 32*(6), 667–679. doi:10.1080/02602930601117191

Springer, L., Stanne, M. E., & Donovan, S. S. (1999). Effects of small-group learning on undergraduates in science, mathematics, engineering, and technology: A meta-analysis. *Review of Educational Research, 69*(1), 21–51. doi:10.3102/00346543069001021

Sprinkle, J. E. (2008). Student perceptions of effectiveness: An examination of the influence of student biases. *College Student Journal, 42*(2), 276–293.

Ssekakubo, G., Suleman, H., & Marsden, G. (2011). Issues of adoption : Have e-Learning Management Systems fulfilled their potential in developing countries? In *Proceedings of the South African Institute of Computer Scientists and Information Technologists Conference on Knowledge, Innovation and Leadership in a Diverse, Multidisciplinary Environment* (pp. 231–238). Cape Town, South Africa.: ACM New York, NY, USA. doi:0.1145/2072221.2072248

Stander, D. (1989). The use of the history of mathematics in teaching. In P. Ernest (Ed.), *Mathematics teaching: The state of the art* (pp. 241–246). Philadelphia, PA: The Falmer Press.

Starcic, A. I. (2010, July01). Educational Technology for the Inclusive Classroom. *Turkish Online Journal of Educational Technology, 9*(3), 26–37.

Steimbert, Y., Ram, J., Nachmia, R., & Eshel, A. (2006). An online discussion for supporting students in preparation for a test. *Journal of Asynchronous Learning Networks, 10*(4). Retrieved June 20, 2014http://www.soan-c.org/publications/jaln/index.asp Retrieved June 20, 2014

Steinke, L. J., & Putnam, A. R. (2008, January01). Influencing Technology Education Teachers to Accept Teaching Positions. *Journal of Industrial Teacher Education, 45*(2), 71–90.

Steinkuehler, C. A. (2006). Massively multiplayer online video gaming as participation in a discourse. *Mind, Culture, and Activity, 13*(1), 38–52. doi:10.1207/s15327884mca1301_4

Stepien, B. (n.d.). Tutorial on problem-based learning: Taxonomy of Socratic questioning. In C. A. Toledo "Does your dog bite?" creating good questions for online discussions. *International Journal of Teaching and Learning in Higher Education, 18*(2). Retrieved from: http://www.isetl.org/ijtlhe/pdf/IJTLHE85.pdf

Stevens, E. Y., & Brown, R. (2011, January01). Lessons Learned from the Holocaust: Blogging to Teach Critical Multicultural Literacy. *Journal of Research on Technology in Education, 44*(1), 31–51. doi:10.1080/15391523.2011.10782578

Stoddard, J. (2009). Toward a virtual field trip model for the social studies. *Contemporary Issues in Technology & Teacher Education, 9*(4). Retrieved from http://www.citejournal.org/vol9/iss4/socialstudies/article1.cfm

Stowell, J. R., Addison, W. E., & Smith, J. L. (2012). Comparison of online and classroom– based student evaluations of instruction. *Assessment & Evaluation in Higher Education, 37*(4), 465–473. doi:10.1080/02602 938.2010.545869

Strauss, A., & Corbin, J. (1998). *Basics of qualitative research: Techniques and procedures for developing grounded theory.* Thousand Oaks, CA: SAGE Publications.

Street, B. V. (2003). What's new in New Literacy Studies? Critical approaches to literacy in theory and practice. *Current issues in comparative education, 5*(2), 1-14.

Suler, J. (2004). The online disinhibition effect. *Cyberpsychology & Behavior, 7*(3), 321–326. doi:10.1089/1094931041291295 PMID:15257832

Sultan, N. (2010). Cloud computing for education: A new dawn? *International Journal of Information Management, 30*(2), 109–116. doi:10.1016/j.ijinfomgt.2009.09.004

Sutton, S. R. (2011). The preservice technology training experiences of preservice teachers. *Journal of Digital Learning in Teacher Education., 28*(1), 39–47. doi:10.1 080/21532974.2011.10784678

Swain, C. (2008, September06). Are We There Yet? The Power of Creating an Innovation Configuration Map on the Integration of Technology into Your Teacher Education Program. *Journal of Computing in Teacher Education, 24*(4), 143–147.

Swain, E. (2007). Constructing an effective voice in academic discussion writing: An appraisal theory perspective. In A. McCabe, M. O'Donnell, & R. Whittaker (Eds.), *Advances in Language and Education* (pp. 166–184). London: Continuum.

Swain, E. (2010). Getting engaged: dialogistic positioning in novice academic discussion writing. In E. Swain (Ed.), *Thresholds and potentialities of systemic functional linguistics: multilingual, multimodal and other specialised discourses* (pp. 291–317). Trieste: EUT Edizioni Università di Trieste.

Swan, K. (2007). Research on online learning. *Journal of Asynchronous Learning Networks, 11*(1). http://www.sloan-c.org/publications/jaln/index.asp Retrieved May 15, 2014

Swarts, P., & Wachira, E. M. (2010). Tanzania: ICT in education situational analysis. Dar Es Salaam: Global e-Schools and Communities Initiatives (geSCI).

Swetz, F. J. (1994). *Learning activities from the history of mathematics.* Portland, ME: J. Weston Walch.

Swetz, F., Fauvel, J., Bekken, O., Johansson, B., & Katz, V. (Eds.). (1995). *Learn from the masters.* Washington, DC: The Mathematical Association of America.

Szulewski, A., & Davidson, L. K. (2008). Enriching the clerkship curriculum with blended e-learning. *Medical Education, 42*(11), 1114. doi:10.1111/j.1365-2923.2008.03184.x PMID:18826396

Tait, A. (Ed.). (1993). *Quality assurance in open and Distance Learning: European and international perspectives.* Cambridge: Open University.

Tapscott, D. (2008). *Grown up digital: How the net generation is changing your world.* McGraw-Hill.

Tate, M. L. (2014). *Brainstorming and discussion.* Retrieved from, http://www.corwin.com/upm-data/58810_Tate_RLA_Worksheets_Don%27t_Grow_Dendrites_ch_1.pdf

Teclehaimanot, B., Mentzer, G., & Hickman, T. (2011). A mixed methods comparison of teacher education faculty perceptions of the integration of technology into their courses and student feedback of technology proficiency. *Journal of Technology and Teacher Education, 19*(1), 5–21.

Teddlie, C., & Yu, F. (2007). Mixed methods sampling: A typology with examples. *Journal of Mixed Methods Research, 1*(1), 77–100. doi:10.1177/2345678906292430

Tedre, M., Ngumbuke, F., & Kemppainen, J. (2010). Infrastructure, human capacity, and high hopes : A decade of development of e-Learning in a Tanzanian HEI. *Redefining the Digital Divide in Higher Education, 7*(1).

Tenebaum, G., Naidu, S., Jegede, O., & Austin, J. (2001). Constructivist pedagogy in conventional on-campus and distance learning practice: An exploratory investigation. *Learning and Instruction, 11*(2), 87–111. doi:10.1016/S0959-4752(00)00017-7

Tennyson, R. D. (2010). Historical reflection on learning theories and instructional design. *Contemporary Educational Technology, 1*(1), 1–16.

The Cognition and Technology Group at Vanderbilt (CTGV). (1996). Anchored instruction and situated cognition revisited. In H. McLellan (Ed.), *Situated Learning Perspectives* (pp. 123–154). Englewood Cliffs, NJ: Educational Technology Publications.

The Glossary of Education Reform. (2013). Retrieved from http://edglossary.org/carnegie-unit/

The Royal Society - Education Section. (2012). Shut down or restart? The way foeard for computing in UK schools - Executive summary. London, UK.

The United Kingdom Department of Education. (2013). *The national curriculm in England - Framework document.* United Kingdom: Crown Retrieved from https://http://www.gov.uk/government/uploads/system/uploads/attachment_data/file/210969/NC_framework_document_-_FINAL.pdf

Theall, M. (2010). Evaluating teaching: From reliability to accountability. *New Directions for Teaching and Learning, 2010*(123), 85–95. doi:10.1002/tl.412

Thomas, P. Y. (2010). *Towards developing web-based blended learning environment at the University of Botswana.* Retrieved September 3, 2014, from http://uir.unisa.ac.za/handle/1050/4245

Thomas, U. (2010). *Culture or chaos in the village: The journey to cultural fluency.* Lanham, MD: Rowman & Littlefield Education.

Tilya, F. (2008). IT and educational policy in the sub-Saharan African region. In J. Voogt & G. Knezek (Eds.), *International handbook of information technology in primary and secondary education* (pp. 1145–1159). New York, NY: Springer. doi:10.1007/978-0-387-73315-9_73

Titus, J. (2008). Student ratings in a consumerist academy: Leveraging pedagogical control and authority. *Sociological Perspectives, 51*(2), 397–422. doi:10.1525/sop.2008.51.2.397

Toledo, C. A. (2006). "Does your dog bite?" Creating good questions for online discussions. *International Journal of Teaching and Learning in Higher Education, 18*(2), 150–154.

Torp, L., & Sage, S. (1998). *Problems as possibilities: Problem-based learning for K-12 education.* Alexandria, VA: Association for Supervision and Curriculum Development.

Torres, J. L., Trapero, J., Martos, F., Vazquez, G., & Soluziona, A. F. (2002). *Voice for Information Society Universal Access and Learning* (VISUAL). Retrieved from http://www.afb.org

Toth-Cohen, S. (1995). Computer-assisted-instruction as a learning-resource for applied anatomy and kinesiology in the occupational-therapy curriculum. *The American Journal of Occupational Therapy, 49*(8), 821–827. doi:10.5014/ajot.49.8.821 PMID:8526228

Trinder, K., Guiller, J., Margaryan, A., Littlejohn, A., & Nicol, D. (2008). *Learning from digital natives: bridging formal and informal learning.* The Higher Education Academy.

Trotter, A. (1997). Taking technology's measure. *Education Week, 17*(11), 6–11.

Trucano, M. (2005). *Knowledge maps: ICTs in educations.* Washington, DC: InfoDev/WorldBank.

Truong, H., Pham, T.-V., Thoai, N., & Dustdar, S. (2012). Cloud computing for education and research in developing countries. In Cloud Computing for Education and Research (pp. 78–94). doi:10.4018/978-1-4666-0957-0.ch005

Tsou, W., Wang, W., & Tzeng, Y. (2006). Applying a multimedia storytelling website in foreign language learning. *Computers & Education, 47*(1), 17–28. doi:10.1016/j.compedu.2004.08.013

U.S. Department of Education. (2008). *HBCUs: A National Resource.* White House Initiative on Historically Black Colleges and Universities.

U.S. Department of Education. (2008). *National educational technology trends study: Local-level data summary.* Washington, DC: Office of Planning, Evaluation and Policy Development, Policy and Program Studies Service.

UNESCO. (2006). *Teachers and Educational Quality: Monitoring Global Needs for 2015.* Retrieved September 6, 2014, from http://www.uis.unesco.org/TEMPLATE/pdf/Teachers2006/TeachersReport.pdf"

United Health Care. (2012). *Did you know that 80% of what kids learn in school is learned visually?* Retrieved from, http://www.indstate.edu/humres/staff-benefits/docs/100-10982%20VI%20Children%20Eye%20Health.pdf

United Republic of Tanzania. (2003). *National Information and Communication Technology policy.* Dar es Salaam: Ministry of Communication and Transport.

University Assessment Office (UAO). (2009). *NSSE 2007 data collection procedures.* Midwestern State University.

Unwin, T., Kleessen, B., Hollow, D., Williams, J., Oloo, L. M., Alwala, J., & Muianga, X. et al. (2010). Digital learning management systems in Africa: Myths and realities. *Open Learning. The Journal of Open and Distance Learning, 25*(1), 5–23. doi:10.1080/02680510903482033

URT. (2007). *Information and Communication Technology policy for basic education.* Dar es salaam: Tanzania Printing House.

URT. (2009). *A framework for ICT use in teacher professional development in Tanzania.* Dar es Salaam: Tanzania Printing House.

Valentine, D. (2002). Distance learning: Promises, problems, possibilities, Retrieved August 2014: http://www.westga.edu/~distance/ojdla/fall53/valentine53.html

van Hattum-Janssen, N., & Lourenço, J. M. (2008). Peer and self-assessment for first-year students as a tool to improve learning. *Journal of Professional Issues in Engineering Education and Practice, 134*(4), 346–352. doi:10.1061/(ASCE)1052-3928(2008)134:4(346)

van Merriënboer, J. J. G., Clark, R. E., & de Croock, M. B. M. (2002). Blueprints for complex learning: The 4C/ID-model. *Educational Technology Research and Development, 50*(2), 39–64. doi:10.1007/BF02504993

van Puijenbroek, T., Poell, R. F., Kroon, B., & Timmerman, V. (2014). The effect of social media use on work-related learning. *Journal of Computer Assisted Learning, 30*(2), 159–172. doi:10.1111/jcal.12037

Vázquez, I., & Giner, D. (2009). Writing with Conviction: The use of boosters in modelling persuasion in academic discourses. *Revista Alicantina de Estudios Ingleses, 22*, 219–237.

Veletsianos, G. (2010b). *Emerging technologies in distance education. Theory and practice.* Edmonton: AU Press. Retrieved from http://www.aupress.ca/books/120177/ebook/99Z_Veletsianos_2010-Emerging_Technologies_in_Distance_Education.pdf

Veletsianos, G. (2010a). A definition of emerging technologies for education. In G. Veletsianos (Ed.), *Emerging technologies in distance education* (pp. 3–22). Edmonton, AB: Athabasca University Press.

Veletsianos, G., & Kimmons, R. (2012). Scholars and faculty members' lived experiences in online social networks. *The Internet and Higher Education, xxx-xxx.* doi:10.1016/j.iheduc.2012.01.004

Venter, P., Van Rensburg, M. J., & Davis, A. (2012). Drivers of learning management system use in a South African open and distance learning institution. *Australasian Journal of Educational Technology, 28*(2), 183–198.

Verenikina, I. (2008). Scaffolding and learning: Its role in nurturing new learners. In Kell, P., Vialle, W., Konza, D., & Vogl, G. (Eds.), Learning and the learner: Exploring learning for new times (pp. 161-80). Wollogong, AU: University of Wollongong.

Vernon, D. T. A., & Blake, R. L. (1993). Does problem-based learning work? A meta-analysis of evaluative research. *Academic Medicine, 68*(7), 550–563. doi:10.1097/00001888-199307000-00015 PMID:8323649

Vesisenaho, M. (2007). *Developing university-level introductory ICT education in Tanzania: A contextualized approach.* (Unpublished, PhD Dissertation). University of Joensuu, Joensuu.

Vichitvejpaisal, P., Sitthikongsak, S., Preechakoon, B., Kraiprasit, K., Parakkamodom, S., Manon, C., & Petcharatana, S. (2001). Does computer-assisted instruction really help to improve the learning process? *Medical Education, 35*(10), 983–989. doi:10.1046/j.1365-2923.2001.01020.x PMID:11564203

Vogt, W. (1984). Developing a teacher evaluation system. *Spectrum (Lexington, Ky.), 2*(1), 41–46.

Vogt, W. P. (2007). *Quantitative Research Methods for Professionals.* Boston, MA: Allyn & Bacon.

Vonderwell, S., Liang, X., & Alderman, K. (2007). Asynchronous discussions and assessment in online learning. *Journal of Research on Technology in Education*, *39*(3), 309–328. doi:10.1080/15391523.2007.10782485

Vrasidas, C., & Kyriakou, E. (2008). Integrating Technology in the classroom. *Pliroforiki*, 18-20. www.pliroforiki.org/joomla/index.php?option=com...gid

Vygotsky, L. (1978). *Mind in society: the development of higher psychological processes*. Cambridge, MA: Harvard University Press.

Vygotsky, L. S. (Ed.). (1978). *Mind in Society: The Development of Higher Psychological Processes*. Cambridge, MA: Harvard University Press.

W3Schools. (2013). *CSS Font*. Retrieved from http://www.w3schools.com/css/css_font.asp

Wadsworth, B. J. (2004). *Piaget's theory of cognitive and affective development: Foundations of constructivism*. Longman Publishing.

Wager, W. (1992). Educational technology: A broader vision. *Education and Urban Society*, *24*(4), 454–465. doi:10.1177/0013124592024004003

Wang, F., & Reeves, T. C. (2003). Why do teachers need to use technology in their classroom? Issues, problems, and solutions. *Computers in the Schools*, *20*(4), 49–65. doi:10.1300/J025v20n04_05

Wang, L., Ertner, P. A., & Newby, T. J. (2004). Increasing preservice teacher's self-efficacy beliefs for technology integration. *Journal of Research in Education*, *3*(3), 231–250.

Wang, S., & Zhan, H. (2010, April01). Enhancing Teaching and Learning with Digital Storytelling. *International Journal of Information and Communication Technology Education*, *6*(2), 76–87. doi:10.4018/jicte.2010040107

Wanjiku, R. (2009, June 12). East Africa universities take advantage of Google cloud. *Computerworld*. Retrieved from http://news.idg.no/cw/art.cfm?id=D3ED873F-1A64-6A71-CE3B759E5A305061

Ward, M., Peters, G., & Shelley, K. (2010). Student and faculty perceptions of the quality of online learning experiences. *International Review of Research in Open and Distance Learning*, *11*(3), 57–77.

Ware, P. D. (2006). From sharing time to showtime! Valuing diverse venues for storytelling in technology-rich classrooms. *Language Arts*, *84*(1), 45–54.

Weathersbee, J. (2008). Impact of Technology Integration in Public Schools on Academic Performance of Texas School Children. Masters Thesis, Texas State University, Spring 2008.

Webb, L. (2011). Supporting technology integration: The school administrator's role. *National Forum of Educational administration & Supervison Journal*, *28*(4), 1-6.

Webb, M. (2008). Impact of IT on science education. In J. Voogt & G. Knezek (Eds.), *International handbook of information technology in primary and secondary education* (pp. 133–148). New York, NY: Springer. doi:10.1007/978-0-387-73315-9_8

Weber, J. (1996). "The compressed video experience". Paper presented at *Summer Conference of the Association of Small Computer Users*. North Myrtle Beach, South Carolina. (ERIC Document Reproduction Service No. ED 405 838).

Weimer, M. (2002). *Learner-centered teaching: Five key changes to practice*. San Francisco, CA: Jossey-Bass.

Welch, G. F., Howard, D. M., Himonides, E., & Brereton, J. (2005). Real-time feedback in the singing studio: An innovatory action-research project using new voice technology. *Music Education Research*, *7*(2), 225–249. doi:10.1080/14613800500169779

Weng Kin, H. (2008). Using history of mathematics in the teaching and learning of mathematics in Singapore. In *Proceedings of 1st RICE*, Singapore.

Wenger, E. (2004). Communities of practice: A brief introduction. Retrieved from: http://onlinelibrary.wiley.com/store/10.1002/9781405198431/asset/homepages/7_Online_Communities_of_Practice.pdf?v=1&s=cfd3645273384e59ea802c0d8cb2a b87e98054c4

Wenger, E., McDermott, R., & Snyder, W. M. (2002). *Cultivating communities of practice*. Boston, MA: Harvard Business School Press.

Wenglinsky, H. (2005). *Using technology wisely: The keys to success in schools*. New York, NY: Teachers College Press.

West, D. (2012). *Digital schools: How technology can transform education.* Brookings Institution Press.

West, G. (1994). Teaching and learning adaptations in the use of interactive compressed video. *T.H.E. Journal, 21*(9), 71–74.

White, C., Bradley, E., Martindale, J., Roy, P., Patel, K., Yoon, M., & Worden, M. K. (2014). Why are medical students 'checking out' of active learning in a new curriculum? *Medical Education, 48*(3), 315–324. doi:10.1111/medu.12356 PMID:24528466

White, L. (2003). Deconstructing the public-private dichotomy in higher education. *Change, 35*(3), 48–54. doi:10.1080/00091380309604102

White, P. R. R. (2003). Beyond modality and hedging: A dialogic view of the language of intersubjective stance. *Text, 23*(2), 259–284. doi:10.1515/text.2003.011

Whitworth, A., & Benson, A. (2010). Learning, design, and emergence: Two cases of Moodle in distance education. *Emerging technologies in distance education* (pp. 195-213).

Willett, J. B., Yamashita, J. J., & Anderson, R. D. (1983). A Meta-Analysis of Instructional Systems Applied in Science Teaching. *Journal of Research in Science Teaching, 20*(5), 405–417. doi:10.1002/tea.3660200505

Williamon, A., Aufegger, L., & Eiholzer, H. (2014). Simulating and stimulating performance: Introducing distributed simulation to enhance musical learning and performance. *Frontiers in Psychology, 5.* doi:10.3389/fpsyg.2014.00025 PMID:24550856

Wilson, B., & Lowry, M. (2000). Constructivist learning on the web. New directions for adults and continuing education, 88, 79-88.

Wilson, N., Zygouris-Coe, V., Cardullo, V., & Fong, J. (2013). Pedagogical frameworks of e-reader technologies in education. In S. Keengwe (Ed.), *Pedagogical applications and social effects of mobile technology integration.* doi:10.4018/978-1-4666-2985-1.ch001

Windschitl, M., & Sahl, K. (2002). Tracing teachers' use of technology in a laptop computer school: The interplay of teacher beliefs, social dynamics, and institutional culture. *American Educational Research Journal, 39*(1), 165–205. doi:10.3102/00028312039001165

Wingate, U. (2006). Doing away with 'study skills'. *Teaching in Higher Education, 11*(4), 457–469. doi:10.1080/13562510600874268

Winter, J., Cotton, D., Gavin, J., & Yorke, J. (2010). Effective e-learning? Multitasking, distractions and boundary management by graduate students in an online environment. *Research in Learning Technology, 18*(1), 71–83. doi:10.1080/09687761003657598

Wolsey, T. (2008). Efficacy of instructor feedback on written work in an online program. *International Journal on E-Learning, 7*(2), 311–329.

Wood, D., Bruner, J. S., & Ross, G. (1976). The role of tutoring in problem-solving. *Journal of Child Psychology and Psychiatry, and Allied Disciplines, 17*(2), 89–100. doi:10.1111/j.1469-7610.1976.tb00381.x PMID:932126

Wood, E., Specht, J., Willoughby, T., & Mueller, J. (2008). Integrating computer technology in early childhood education environments: Issues raised by early childhood educators. *The Alberta Journal of Educational Research, 54*(2), 210–226.

World Health Organization (2010). *International Statistical Classification of Diseases and Related Health Problems.*

World Health Organization Media Centre. (2012). *Visual impairment and blindness.* Retrieved from http://www.who.int/mediacentre/factsheets/fs282/en/

Wright, V. H., & Wilson, E. K. (2011, September06). Teachers' Use of Technology: Lessons Learned from the Teacher Education Program to the Classroom. *State Journal, 20*(2), 48–60.

Wynne, J. (2001). *Teachers as Leaders in Education Reform. ERIC Digest.* Washington, DC: American Association of Colleges for Teacher Education.

Xie, K., Durrington, V., & Yen, L. (2011). Relationship between Students' Motivation and their Participation in Asynchronous Online Discussions. *MERLOT Journal of Online Learning and Teaching*, *7*(1), 17–29.

Yalçan, F. (2011). An international dimension of the student's attitudes towards the use of English in Web 2.0 technology. *The Turkish Online Journal of Educational Technology*, *10*(3), 63–68.

Yanco, H. A., Kim, H. J., & Martin, F. G., & Silka, Linda. (2006). *Artbotics: Combining art and robotics to broaden participation in computing*. Paper presented at the AAAI Spring Symposium on Robots and Robot Venues: Resources for AI Education.

Yang, Y. T. C., & Wu, W. C. I. (2012). Digital storytelling for enhancing student academic achievement, critical thinking, and learning motivation: A year-long experimental study. *Computers & Education*, *59*(2), 339–352. doi:10.1016/j.compedu.2011.12.012

Yin, R. K. (2003). *Case study research: Design and methods* (3rd ed.). Thousand Oaks, CA: Sage.

Yoon, S. W. (2008). Technologies for learning and performance. In A. Rozanski, K. P. Kuchinke, & E. Boyar (Eds.), *Human resource development theory and practice* (pp. 245–262). Lublin, Poland: Lublin Technical University.

Yorke, M. (2003). Formative assessmnet in Higher education: Move towards theory and the enhancement of pedagogical practice. *Higher Education*, *45*(4), 477–501. doi:10.1023/A:1023967026413

Young, S., & Shaw, D. G. (1999). Profiles of effective college and university teachers. *Journal of Higher Education*, *70*(6), 670–686.

Young, M. F. (1993). Instructional design for situated learning. *Educational Technology Research and Development*, *41*(1), 43–58. doi:10.1007/BF02297091

Young, M. F. (1995). Assessment of situated learning using computer environments. *Journal of Science Education and Technology*, *4*(1), 89–96. doi:10.1007/BF02211586

Young, M. F., Kulikowich, J. M., & Barab, S. A. (1997). The unit of analysis for situated assessment. *Instructional Science*, *25*(2), 33–150. doi:10.1023/A:1002971532689

Young, V., & Kim, D. H. (2010). Using assessment for instuctional improvement: A literature review. *Education Policy Analysis Archives*, *18*(19), 1–37. PMID:21841903

Youniss, J. (2006). Situating ourselves and our inquiry: A first-person account. In C. Conrad & R. Serlin (Eds.), *The SAGE handbook for research in education: Engaging ideas and enriching inquiry* (pp. 303–314). Thousand Oaks, CA: SAGE. doi:10.4135/9781412976039.n17

Yukawa, T., Kawano, K., Suzuki, Y., Suriyon, T., & Fukumura, Y. (2008). Implementing a sense of connectedness in e-learning. In LucaJ.WeipplE. (Eds.), *Proceedings of World Conference on Educational Multimedia, Hypermedia and Telecommunications 2008* (pp. 1198-1207). Chesapeake, VA: AAC.

Yuksel Arslan, P. (2013). Eğitim amaçlı dijital öykünün hazırlanması ve kullanılması: TPAB temelli örnek bir Fen Bilgisi eğitimi uygulaması. In Tuğba Yanpar Yelken, Hatice Sancar Tokmak, Sinan Özgelen ve Lutfi İncikabı (eds.), Fen ve matematik eğitiminde teknolojik, pedagojik alan bilgisi (TPAB) temelli öğretim tasarımları (pp.106-128). Ankara: Anı Publishing.

Yuksel, P. (2011). *Using digital storytelling in early childhood education: A phenomenological study of teachers' experiences* (Upublished doctoral dissertation), Middle East Technical University, Ankara.

Yuksel, P., Robin, B., & McNeil, S. (2010). Educational uses of digital storytelling around the world. In *Proceedings of Society for Information Technology & Teacher Education International Conference* (pp. 1264-1271). Chesapeake, VA: AACE. 2011.

Zbiek, R. M., Heid, M. K., Blume, G. W., & Dick, T. P. (2007). Research on technology in mathematics education: A perspective of constructs. In F. Lester (Ed.), *Second handbook of research on mathematics teaching and learning* (pp. 1169–1208). Reston, VA: National Council of Teachers on Mathematics.

Zbiek, R. M., & Hollebrands, K. (2008). A research-informed view of the process of incorporating mathematics technology into classroom practice by inservice and prospective teachers. In M. K. Heid & G. W. Blume (Eds.), *Research on technology and the teaching and learning of mathematics* (Vol. 1, pp. 287–344). Charlotte, NC: Information Age.

Zerbini, T., & Abbad, G. (2009). Reação aos procedimentos instrucionais de um curso via internet: Validação de uma escala. *Estudos de Psicologia, 26*(3), 363–371. doi:10.1590/S0103-166X2009000300009

Zhao, J., & Gallant, D. J. (2012). Student evaluation of instruction in higher education: Exploring issues of validity and reliability. *Assessment & Evaluation in Higher Education, 37*(2), 227–235. doi:10.1080/02602938.2010.523819

Zhao, Y. (2007). Social studies teachers' perspectives of technology integration. *Journal of Technology and Teacher Education, 15*(3), 311–333.

Zualkernan, I. (2006). A framework and a methodology for developing authentic constructivist e-learning environments. *Journal of Educational Technology & Society, 9*, 198–212.

Zuberi, R. W., Bordage, G., & Norman, G. R. (2007). Validation of the SETOC instrument – student evaluation of teaching in outpatient clinics. *Advances in Health Sciences Education: Theory and Practice, 12*(1), 55–69. doi:10.1007/s10459-005-2328-y PMID:17160501

Zuhairi, A., Purwanto, A., & Isman, S. (2002). Implementing quality assurance system in open and DL: the experience of Indonesia's Universitas Terbuka. Paper presented to 16th Annual Conference of Asian Association of Open Universities (AAOU), Seoul, Korea, 5-7 November 2002.

About the Contributors

Sagini "Jared" Keengwe is a Professor of Teaching and Learning at the College of Education and Human Development, University of North Dakota (UND), USA. Keengwe is the editor-in-chief of two IGI Global Book Series: "*Advances in Higher Education and Professional Development*" (AHEPD) and "*Advances in Early Childhood and K-12 Education*" (AECKE). Keengwe has published over 85 journal articles, book chapters, and books with a focus on active learning pedagogies and mobile learning technologies in education. Keengwe's work was honored with the 2011 UND McDermott Faculty Award for Excellence in Academic Advising. He was also a recipient of the 2010 North Dakota Spirit Faculty Achievement Award, and the 13th Annual Martin Luther King Jr. Award in recognition of significant contribution in scholarship and service respectively. At the national level, Keengwe was one of the 10 recipients selected to receive the 2010 American Educational Research Association (AERA) Teacher Education Travel Award.

***

Edem Agbobli is a lecturer in the Faculty of Management Sciences at the Central University of Technology, Free State, South Africa. In addition to coordinating Project Management Programme in the Faculty, he also lectures various subjects including Entrepreneurship, Strategic Management, Project Quality and Risk Management in the Business Support Studies Department. His research interests lie in Entrepreneurship and Innovation; and social development. He also researches the area of application of emerging technologies for enhancing teaching-learning encounter between educators and learners. His current research focuses on emerging technology-driven pedagogical designs.

Victoria M. Cardullo is an assistant professor of Reading in the College of Education and the Department of Curriculum and Teaching at Auburn University. She is actively involved in publications and presentations related to her research in digital literacies, specifically New Literacies. Her work has been published in *School-University Partnerships: The Journal of the National Association for Professional Development Schools, Journal of Reading Education,* and *American Reading Forum Annual Yearbook.* She is particularly interested in exploring how to support adolescent readers' reading and comprehension skills to prepare them for 21st century learning. She serves in several editorial roles, including associate editor of *Florida Educational Leadership Journal,* associate editor for *American Reading Forum* as well as a reviewer for *NAPDS National Association of Professional Development Schools, NAPDS Award Committee* and an invited reviewer for *ALER Association of Literacy Educators and Researchers.*

Lorraine Carter Effective July 1, 2015, Dr. Lorraine Carter is the Director of the Centre for Continuing Education at McMaster University in Hamilton, Ontario, Canada. Prior to this appointment, Dr. Carter worked for Nipissing University in North Bay, Ontario where she was a Full Professor and former Director of the School of Nursing. Prior to this, Dr. Carter was the Director of the Centre for Flexible Teaching and Learning. Dr. Carter holds a PhD in Educational Studies from the University of Windsor, a Master of English from University of Western Ontario, and a Bachelor of Education from the University of Toronto. Dr. Carter is an accomplished educator and researcher most recognized for her work in e-learning and adult and continuing education. She has also served as the President of the Canadian Network for Innovation in Education and the Canadian Association for University Continuing Education.

Caroline Chemosit is a lecturer and head of department Educational Administration Planning and Management at the University of Kabianga. Prior to this, she was an Adjunct Professor of Research Methods at Lincoln College, Normal, Illinois. Her research and scholarship interest is in lifelong learning, learning strategies and student achievement. She has published and co-authored several articles both in refereed journals such as the *Journal of Personnel Evaluation in Education, and Educational Research Quarterly,* and in other professional sources and presented papers at various annual meetings of regional (SERA, MSERA, MWERA, IERC) and national professional organizations (AERA, NAAAS).

Amy Eguchi is an Associate Professor of Education at Bloomfield College in New Jersey, USA. She holds her M.A. in Child Development from Pacific Oaks College, Ed.M. in Education from Harvard Graduate School of Education, and Ph.D. in Education from the University of Cambridge and has an extensive experience using educational robotics as a learning tool both with students and teachers in K-12 setting. She also teaches educational robotics to undergraduates. In addition, she runs a competitive robotics after school team at The School at Columbia University. She has been involved in RoboCupJunior, an educational robotics competition, since 2000, as the technical committee and organizing committee members, as well as the co-chair and general chair, in international, national, and local levels. In addition, she is a Vice President of RoboCup Federation representing RoboCupJunior and a member of the RoboCup Federation Board of Trustees. In addition, she has been involved in several international collaboration with educational robotics projects including the CoSpace educational robotics projects with the Advanced Robotics and Intelligent Control Centre (ARICC) at Singapore Polytechnic, Singapore.

Judi Simmons Estes is an Assistant Professor and Chair of the Department of Elementary and Secondary Teacher Preparation at Park University, USA. Dr. Estes is seminar faculty for candidates during their directed teaching semester; she has an interest in candidates' self-efficacy in use of technology and integration of technology with instruction to increase high quality P-12 lesson planning, authentic student learning, and critical thinking. Results of several semesters of administering a student technology self-efficacy survey have demonstrated a need for beginning a process of integration of technology activities and experiences throughout teacher preparation coursework, modeling strategies for candidates to use with their future students. Dr. Estes conducts trainings and writes about the process of modeling technology-powered instruction.

Joyce Gikandi is an ICT and E-Learning specialist. She has a PhD in ICT in Education & E-Learning and MSc in Computer-Based Information Systems. Dr Joyce is currently a lecturer and Postgraduate coordinator at Mt. Kenya University, mainly teaching Information Technology (IT)/Computing related courses. Her current interests include research and development of effective strategies for ICT application in various fields especially in Education. Another area of interest is promoting innovative development, adaptation and use of open source educational content and software. Joyce is also interested in development and adaptation of computer-based management/decision support systems. She is also interested in collaborating with individuals/organisations who share similar research focus.

Rhoda Karimi Gitonga completed her undergraduate work at Kenyatta University and received her Bachelor of Education (Science). She received her Master of Science Degree in Information Management and completed her PHD degree in Curriculum and Instruction in 2013 from Egerton University. Her specific interest is in ICT integration and E-learning. She has worked in the university as a teaching staff member for 6 years. She has published two papers in 2013, *The Perceived extent of ICT Integration in Intra-University Communication among Kenyan Universities:* doi: 10.11648/j.com.20130102.11. and *The Perception of the Influence of ICT Integration on Quality of Student's Records Management in Kenyan Universities:* ISSN: 2278-0211 (Online). Two other publications are in press: *Web 2.0 Technologies Use by Students in Higher Education: A Case of Kenyan Universities* and *Students Experiences of Using Wiki Spaces to Support Collaborative Learning in a Blended Classroom; A Case of Kenyatta and KCA Universities in Kenya.*

Heeyoung Han is an assistant professor in the Department of Medical Education at Southern Illinois University School of Medicine. Her primary research interest focuses on active learning and performance improvement in technology-rich environments. She serves as a deputy editor of Teaching and Learning in Medicine.

Seung-Hyun (Caleb) Han is a Ph.D. student in the Human Resource Development division at the University of Illinois, USA. He taught Work Analysis and Learning Technology at the University of Illinois and Human Resource Management at Yanbian University, China. His research interests lie in integration of learning technology and knowledge management to enhance organization performance. He holds master degree in Human Resource and Industrial Relations and bachelor degrees in Business and Laws. Prior to his academic career, he worked at Samsung Economic Research Institute and Korea Labor Central Institute in Korea.

Lutfi Incikabi is an associate professor of Mathematics Education at Kastamonu University. He received the Bachelor of Science degree in Mathematics in 1984 from Ataturk University, Erzurum, Turkey. He held the doctor of education degree in mathematics education from Teachers College, Columbia University in 2011. He lectured at Elementary Mathematics Education Department at Mersin University until 2012 in which he joined the Department of Elementary Mathematics Education at Kastamonu University, Kastamonu, Turkey. He is the author of numerous papers in refereed journals, book chapters, and conference proceedings. His research interests are teacher education, elementary mathematics education, comparative education, educational technology.

Ayoub C Kafyulilo is a lecturer in educational curriculum and educational technology at the Dar Es Salaam University College of Education. He received his PhD from the University of Twente in the Netherlands. Kafyulilo has two master degrees: A Master of Science (Educational Science and Technology) whereby he studied the practical use of ICT in teaching and learning in Tanzania and a Master of Arts (Education) whereby he studied the prevalence of overweight and obesity among primary school children in Dar Es Salaam and Njombe. Dr. Kafyulilo has published more than ten articles in both international and local journals. Dr. Kafyulilo is currently conducting a research on community-based initiatives to enhance the education of the most vulnerable children in Lindi, Tanzania. The project is funded by the Center for Advanced Study of International Development, in Michigan, USA under the Tanzania Partnership Program.

Mussa M. Kissaka received B.Sc. degree in Electrical Engineering from the University of Dar es Salaam (UDSM), Dar es Salaam, Tanzania in 1989 and Ph.D. degree in Telecommunications Engineering from the University of Manchester, United Kingdom in 1994. Currently he is a Senior Lecturer in the Department of Electronics and Telecommunications Engineering, College of Information and Communication Technologies (CoICT), University of Dar es Salaam. He is also the Director, Centre for Virtual Learning (CVL) at the University of Dar es Salaam.

Doo Hun Lim is an Associate Professor of Workforce Learning and Development at the University of Oklahoma. His research interests have been in the areas of performance improvement systems and technology, neuro-science approaches for learning design, and cross-cultural research on organizational development and workplace issues.

Mahmud Mansaray is the Research Analyst in the Department of Research, Evaluation and Planning at the North Carolina Central University. Prior to this, he was, for five years, the Assessment Specialist at the University of North Carolina General Administration (UNCGA). At UNCGA, Mahmud was in charge of all student surveys received from the 16 campuses within the system. He was also involved in research activities relating to education policy analyses. Mahmud is a graduate of Fourah Bay College, the University of Sierra Leone and holds a Bachelor of Art degree with Honors in Geography. He also holds a Master's degree in Applied Economics and Policy Analysis from North Carolina State University. He is also a doctoral candidate in policy analysis, statistics and research designs.

Dominik T. Msabila is a lecturer in Education Management; Research Methods, and Communication Skills. He holds Master of Arts with Education and Bachelor of Education attained at the University of Dar es Salaam in Tanzania. Apart from being a lecturer he is also a prolific writer who has published various books in Geography, Literature, Soil Science and Legal Communication Skills. He has also published various papers both in local and international journals, as well as chapters in books. More-over, the author has a rich and profound experience in research as he has participated in various research projects some of which are international and has attended different international conferences on research in Nairobi, Kenya; Hiroshima and Tokyo in Japan; Penang in Malaysia, and Alberta in Canada. He is currently involved in a collaborative research project undertaken by Mzumbe University of Tanzania and Universities of Alberta and Brock of Canada.

Joel S. Mtebe is a Lecturer in Computer Science and eLearning at University of Dar es Salaam in the Department of Computer Science and Engineering. He received B.Sc. Computer Science and Statistics from the University of Dar es Salaam (UDSM), Dar es Salaam, Tanzania in 2002 and Master of Online Education from the University of Southern Queensland, Australia in 2004. He recently completed his doctoral degree in Interactive Technology/Human Computer Interaction at University of Tampere, Finland. Dr. Mtebe has published more than 10 publications in refereed journals and conference proceedings. His research areas include OER, MOOCs, Cloud computing in education, usability of eLearning systems, Learning management systems, Mobile learning, and eLearning system success.

Catherine Gakii Murungi is a Lecturer at Kenyatta University in the Department of Early Childhood Studies. She holds a PhD in Education, M.Ed and a Bachelors degree in Early Childhood Studies all from Kenyatta University. She is currently an editorial board member and peer reviewer to many international journals. Catherine is a mentor, academic advisor, e-learning trainer and facilitator, as well as a supervisor to several undergraduate and graduate students in the university. She is a passionate researcher in the field of developmental psychology and she is published widely. She has a keen interest on community education and development and in particular basic education. Besides being an academician, she is married and a proud mother of two adorable children, Ethan and Valerie.

Viviline Ngeno is a lecturer of Planning and Economics of Education at the University of Kabianga. Prior to this she worked as a high school teacher of Business Studies and Economics. For the last 10 years she has participated as a panelist in the development and adaptation of Business Studies syllabus for the blind students at the Kenya Institute of Education (KIE). Viviline has participated in local, regional and national research and education conferences. Her research work include: Impact of the Free Secondary Education Policy on Equity, Quality and Education wastage in Kericho County, Kenya; Cost Effectiveness Analysis of Educating Girls in Day and Boarding Secondary Schools; Effects of Communication on CDF projects in Ainamoi Constituency Primary School; and The relationship between students' riots, drug abuse and Head Teacher transfers in Kericho County. Viviline has authored and co-authored several papers and journal articles. Currently, Viviline is pursuing her Doctorate studies.

Esther Ntuli is an Assistant Professor in the Department of Teaching and Educational Studies at Idaho State University. Her expertise and training is in curriculum and instruction, instructional technology, early childhood education, children's literature and writing. Dr. Ntuli teaches undergraduate instructional technology courses, foundational undergraduate and graduate courses at ISU. Her research focuses on technology use and practice in the classroom, teacher education, and assessment. She co-edited a book: *"Practical Applications and Experiences in K-20 Blended Learning Environments"* (2014).

Robert O. Oboko specializes in Educational Technology research. His specific areas of research include learning support for online learning with complex problem solving using adaptive e-learning features and metacognitive control scaffolds. He also has research interests in other supportive technologies, such as adaptive user interfaces using Machine Learning, concept maps, advance organizers, modeling and coaching, early grade learning including literacy, games for learning, learning support for learners with disabilities, among others. He researches in both e-Learning and M-Learning for both higher education institutions and co-orporate organizations. Robert is also interested in the evaluation of e-learning and m-learning systems for formal, non-formal and informal learning.

James E. Osler II, Program Coordinator of the Online Graduate Program in Educational Technology, and Associate Professor of Education, Department of Curriculum Instruction, North Carolina Central University, Durham North Carolina, and an Adjunct Professor in the Department of Leadership Studies, School of Education, Ed. D. in Technology Education, with a concentration on Instructional Design, Instructional Technology, Statistics and Research 1996 (North Carolina State University), M.A. in Educational Technology, with a concentration on Instructional Design and Instructional Development North Carolina Central University, 1991, and a B.A. in Studio Art with a concentration on Illustration, Painting, and Design North Carolina Central University, 1990. Licenses and Certifications: Art Educator (NCDPI), Instructional Technology Specialist (NCDPI), Technology Endorsement (NCDPI), Human Subjects Research (CITI), Human Subjects Research – IRB (NIH - OEMR), Test Proctor (UNC-General Administration/Online), Digital Literacy (MS). Expertise: Instructional Design, Instructional Development, Instructional Technology, Teaching K-24, Publishing & E-Publishing, Instructional Media, Illustration, Graphic Design, Statistics, Research, Technology, and Training and Professional Development. Serves on the Editorial Board of several National and International Journals as well as the Boards of many organizations.

Jenny Penland is currently the Director of Experiential Learning at Sul Ross State University, Alpine, Texas. She holds an Ed.D. in Educational Leadership from Lamar University with an Emphasis on Multicultural Studies. She has previously worked with Shepherd University, Western Wyoming Community College, Dickinson State University, Texas A & M University -C/ Navarro College, Lamar University and Region V Education Service Center in Texas. Dr. Penland's research has been published in such journals as *The Qualitative Report, the Journal of Mentoring & Tutoring, the National Forum of Educational Administration* and *Supervision, E-Learn 2005,* the *Peace Studies Journal,* the *Fourth World Journal, SAGE Multicultural Reference Encyclopedia, Intercontinental Cry Magazine, XanEdu Publishing* and a forthcoming article in the *Journal of Teaching* and *Teacher Education* with the University of Bahrain. Dr. Penland continues to work on projects, which involve her doctoral thesis on cultural resiliency and persistence in higher education, and has been appointed as a Tribal scholar and educational consultant with the AAIWV.

Patient Rambe is a Senior Researcher in the Faculty of Management Sciences at the Central University of Technology, Free State, South Africa. He coordinates and leads research in the Faculty in the area of emerging technology, entrepreneurship and emerging businesses. His research focuses on the appropriation of emerging technologies such as social media and mobile technologies to leverage performance of emerging small scale businesses and support the teaching and learning of previously disadvantaged groups. Dr Rambe has published over 45 publications in peer reviewed international journals, book chapters and international conferences. His co-authored book is entitled: "Leveraging quality in African higher educational systems: A practitioners' perspective" (2013).

John Rugutt is an Associate Professor of educational research, applied statistics and educational technology in the Department of Educational Administration and Foundations at Illinois State University. His research and scholarship focus on teaching and learning environments with special emphasis on multilevel techniques to understand the contribution of individual and institutional factors on learning. John engagement in scholarly activities has enabled him to publish and co-author several articles both in refereed journals such as the *Journal of Personnel Evaluation in Education, Planning and Chang-*

ing, Educational Research Quarterly, Journal of Educational Research and Policy Studies and in other professional sources. He has also presented papers at various annual meetings of regional, national and international professional organizations and has also written *research monographs, research grants, book chapters* and *project reports* pertaining to student dropout and youth risk behavior, and on correlates and predictors of Intent to Remain Employed in Family and Children Services.

Vince Salyers is the Interim Associate Vice President, Research at Mount Royal University in Calgary, Alberta, Canada. The integration of technology and e-learning strategies into program curricula is a personal passion for Vince. He has conducted research in Ethiopia, Dominican Republic, Mexico, and Peru as part of his commitment to vulnerable populations. He sustains a research program that strives to make a difference for students, faculty, and recipients of care. Results from his research hold implications for nursing faculty, instructional designers, and administrators in university settings where e-learning is part of the institutional mandate. Vince has an impressive list of publications and presentations in national and international settings. In 2014, he was the recipient of the American Nurses Association—California JoAnne Powell Research Award and was inducted as a Fellow into the National League of Nursing's Academy of Nursing Education. He is currently editor of the *International Journal of E-Learning and Distance Education (IJEDE)*.

Jennifer Kasanda Sesabo is a lecturer in Department of Economics at Mzumbe University. She holds a PhD in Economics, Master of Science in Sustainable Natural Resource Management: Specialization in Development and Resource Economics and an Advanced Diploma in Economic Planning. Jennifer is an academic advisor, quality assurance trainer and facilitator in the university and East African Region. She is a researcher in the field of economics and she has publications in economics related issues. Jennifer has interest on issues related to quality assurance in higher education and in particular the use of ICT as a teaching methodology as well as a quality of Open and distance learning. Jennifer has attended number of scholarly local and international conferences. She is currently a member in two collaborative research projects undertaken by Mzumbe University of Tanzania and Universities of Belgium as well as University of Copenhagen.

Dorothy Soi is a lecturer of Education Administration at the University of Kabianga. Prior to this she worked as a high school teacher of mathematics and a part-time tutor at Kenya Highlands Evangelical University. Her particular research interest centers on gender and mathematics learning, and school leadership. During the last six years, she has authored and co-authored research and development projects, conference and journal research papers and has participated in local, regional and national research and professional conferences. She was part of a team that conducted research funded by Daystar University on "combating sexual harassment in Kenyan Universities to enhance academic performance and career development". Dorothy has participated as a subject panelist in the adaptation of the Mathematics syllabus for the blind at The Kenya Institute of Education. She is currently pursuing her doctorate studies which centers on female school leadership. Her abiding interest remains in gendered school leadership.

Rashid Mfaume Taka is a Senior lecturer, Researcher and Consultant at Mzumbe University in Tanzania. He holds Masters of Public Administration and Organization Theory from University of Bergen-Norway. Before attaining graduate degrees he studied Diploma in Agricultural Education, and undergraduate degree in Public Administration at the then Institute of Development Management (IDM)

Mzumbe Tanzania. He also attained Diploma in Agricultural Education. He also holds a number of certificates of awards and achievement by participating and attending various short courses training from within and outside Tanzania. His main professional interest is in the areas of Public Administration; Political Sciences, Organizational Theory/Design; Governance, Supervisory Management Skills; Course design methodology; Strategic planning, Policy Analysis, HIV/AIDS work place programme design and policy, Management of capacity building programme. Mr. Mfaume has attended good number of practitioners and scholarly local and international conferences. He has authored and published a number of policy papers, book chapters and scholarly papers in local and international journals.

Ursula Thomas, Ed.D currently serves as the Director of Field Experience and Assessment at Georgia Perimeter College. Her extensive research with teacher knowledge gives her the insight needed to help teachers adopt age appropriate strategies that are culturally relevant. She has presented and consulted on program evaluation and assessment at national conferences such as the National Association for the Education of Young Children, and the National Association of Early Childhood Teacher Educators. Dr. Thomas has carved out a professional development niche as well. She has more than 20 publications in the fields of early childhood teacher education, social justice, and cultural mediation.

Hatice Sancar Tokmak, is the faculty in the Department of Computer Education and Instructional Technology at Mersin University. She received PHD degree at Middle East Technical University, the Department of Computer Education and Instructional Technology in 2010. Sancar-Tokmak has lectured at the the Department of Computer Education and Instructional Technology since 2011. She teaches and conducts research in the areas of technology integration, especially, TPACK (technological-pedagogical-content knowledge) based course designs for improvement in teacher candidates' self efficacy, confidence, and teaching practices about technology integration. Moreover, her research interests include Evaluation / Design of Online Courses, Educational Simulations / Simulators,and Educational Games.

Ruth Nthenya Wambua is a Chief Information Communication and Technology (ICT) Officer at the ICT Centre, of the University of Nairobi, Kenya. She is a qualified consultant in Management Information Systems (MIS), and in Web Development. Ms. Wambua has professionally specialized in the area of Computing and Informatics. She successfully completed a Master of Science Degree in Computer Science, and is working on registering for a PhD in a Computer Science related discipline. Ms. Wambua's current focus areas are in ICT for Development, with a keen eye on eLearning for All, and Information Systems. Moreover, she is an individual of pleasant attitude and with good natured personality.

Nance S. Wilson is an Associate Professor of literacy education at SUNY Cortland. Her research focuses in professional development, new literacies, comprehension, and adolescent literacy. Dr. Wilson's work has been published in *Middle School Journal, Journal of Adolescent and Adult Literacy, Reading Horizons, Literacy, Metacognition and Learning, California Reader, Florida Educational Leadership Journal*, and *Florida Association of Teacher Educators* among others. She serves in several editorial roles, including *Reading and Writing Quarterly: Overcoming Reading Difficulties* and *Reading in the Middle*. She has served in leadership positions in the American Reading Forum and the Middle School Reading Special Interest Group of the International Reading Association.

Seung Won Yoon is a professor of instructional technology/workplace learning and performance in the Department of Instructional Design and Technology at Western Illinois University. His research focuses on improving workplace performance through connecting leadership, learning, technology, and organizational behavior.

Vassiliki Zygouris-Coe is a Professor of Education at the University of Central Florida, College of Education. Her research focuses in literacy in the content areas, online learning, and professional development. Dr. Zygouris-Coe has impacted reading instruction in the state of Florida through the Florida Online Reading Professional Development project—Florida's first online large-scale project for preK-12 educators. Her work has been published in *The Reading Teacher, Reading & Writing Quarterly, Reading Horizons, Childhood Education, Early Childhood Education Journal, The International Journal of Qualitative Studies in Education, Focus in the Middle, Journal of Technology and Teacher Education, The International Journal of E-Learning, Florida Educational Leadership Journal,* and *Florida Reading Quarterly* among others. She serves in several editorial roles, including Co-Editor of the *Literacy Research and Instruction* journal, Associate Editor of *Florida Educational Leadership Journal,* and former Associate Editor of the *Florida Association of Teacher Educators Journal.*

Index

Printed in the United States
By Bookmasters